APOLLONIA-ARSUF
FINAL REPORT OF THE EXCAVATIONS, VOLUME II

Excavations Outside the Medieval Town Walls

TEL AVIV UNIVERSITY
SONIA AND MARCO NADLER INSTITUTE OF ARCHAEOLOGY

MONOGRAPH SERIES
NUMBER 38

APOLLONIA-ARSUF FINAL REPORT OF THE EXCAVATIONS, VOLUME II

Excavations Outside the Medieval Town Walls

OREN TAL

With contributions by
Issa Baidoun, Gabriela Bijovsky, Itai Elad, Ian C. Freestone, Alexander Glick, Tamar Harpak, Mark Iserlis, Ruth E. Jackson-Tal, Rafael Y. Lewis, Henk K. Mienis, Yossi Nagar, Miriam Pines, Oz Rittner, Lidar Sapir-Hen, Itamar Taxel, Marcio Teixeira Bastos and Hagi Yohanan

EISENBRAUNS
University Park, Pennsylvania

EMERY AND CLAIRE YASS
PUBLICATIONS IN ARCHAEOLOGY OF
THE INSTITUTE OF ARCHAEOLOGY
Tel Aviv University

Monograph Series under the auspices of the
Friends of the Institute of Archaeology of Tel Aviv University

Library of Congress Cataloging-in-Publication Data

Names: Tal, Oren, Author.

Title: Apollonia-Arsuf : final report of the excavations, Volume II / [by] Oren Tal ; with contributions by Issa Baidoun [and sixteen others].

Description: University Park, Pennsylvania : Eisenbrauns, [2020] | Series: Tel Aviv University Sonia and Marco Nadler Institute of Archaeology Monograph series ; volume 38 | Includes bibliographical references and index.

Summary: "Reports findings from the 1996, 2002, 2006, 2012, 2013, and 2017 excavation seasons at the Apollonia-Arsuf archaeological site, located on a fossilized sandstone dune ridge on the Mediterranean coast of Israel."—Provided by publisher.

Identifiers: LCCN 00292080 | ISBN 9781575067476 (hardback)

Subjects: LCSH: Excavations (Archaeology)—Arsuf (Extinct city) | Arsuf (Extinct city) | Israel—Antiquities.

Classification: DS110.A73 A66 1999

LC record available at https://lccn.loc.gov/00292080

Eisenbrauns is an imprint of The Pennsylvania State University Press.
The Pennsylvania State University Press is a member of the Association of University Presses.

It is the policy of The Pennsylvania State University Press to use acid-free paper. Publications on uncoated stock satisfy the minimum requirements of American National Standard for Information Sciences—Permanence of Paper for Printed Library Material, ANSI Z39.48–1992.

Dedicated to the late Prof. Israel Roll (1937–2010)
A friend, educator and above all *mensch*

CONTENTS

SECTION ONE: STRATIGRAPHY AND ARCHITECTURE

SECTION TWO: THE FINDS

SECTION THREE: FAUNA

SECTION FOUR: REGIONAL STUDIES

SECTION FIVE: SUMMARY AND CONCLUSIONS

PREFACE

Oren Tal

This publication forms a final report of the excavations carried out in areas outside the walled medieval town and within the site's immediate hinterland to its east (see Figs. 1.1–1.2). First, it deals with areas excavated to the east of Apollonia National Park during the 1996 season (Area T8), within the environs of the then-active Israel Military Industries Ltd. (hereafter IMI) plant, by the late Professor I. Roll on behalf of the Institute of Archaeology of Tel Aviv University (hereafter TAU). Following these, the report covers the 2012 and 2013 season excavations (Areas AA, CC and DD, and their derivatives) which took place outside the plant area in the fields between its fences and the coastal highway (Road No. 2) by Eli Hadad in 2012 and Moshe Ajami and Oren Tal in 2013, on behalf of the Israel Antiquities Authority (hereafter IAA) and the Institute of Archaeology of TAU. These excavations were trial and salvage-oriented in nature due to planned development works in the area.

The report also deals with areas excavated during 2002 (Area N), 2006 (Area M), 2009 (Areas M and O) and 2017 (Area N1) within the perimeter of the Apollonia National Park (Areas N1 and O) or just outside it (Areas N and M), but still outside the walled medieval town. These excavations were academic in nature due to research questions raised in the framework of the Apollonia-Arsuf Excavation Project. It may be added that most of the archaeological remains and finds dealt with in this report belong to the occupation of the site during the Byzantine period.

The 1996 season (License No. G-36/1996; the site's 11th season of excavations) was previously summarized in some detail (Roll 1999: 43–46). A contract excavation initiated by the legal owner of the site, The Israel Land Administration, was carried out on behalf of the Institute of Archaeology of TAU within the area of the IMI plant. The aim was to determine the maximum extension of the ancient site and to define its eastern limits in order to plan future development works. Excavations were carried out using two different methods, trial trenches (1 m wide and up to 25 m long) by means of mechanical tools, as well as manually-excavated squares in Area J (the Crusader town gate), Area K (the site of the Byzantine church) and in Trench T8 (Late Roman and/or Early Byzantine cist tombs). The budget of the dig was administrated by Ramot (TAU's Authority for Applied Research and Industrial Development Ltd.).

The 2002 season (License No. G-28/2002; the site's 15th season of excavations) was carried out on behalf of the Institute of Archaeology of TAU and financed by the Municipality of Herzliyya and the Israel Nature and Parks Authority (hereafter INPA). The season was divided into two parts. The first took place in February in the gate complex of the Crusader castle (Area F) and the premises of the archaeological site gate area (Area N) in the context of the opening of the Apollonia National Park. The second half of the season took place during July–August in Areas E and G and in Area N, as a study dig for students in archaeology of the Department of Classics of TAU, with the help of students and scholars of the Universidade Federal do Rio Grande do Sul of Porto Alegre, Brazil (headed by F. Marshall). Excavations were directed by I. Roll and the senior staff included H. Yohanan (deputy director), T. Harpak (registration) and B. Arubas (surveying and drawing). The budget of the dig was administrated by Ramot.

The 2006 season (License No. G-59/2006; the site's 18th season of excavations) was carried out by the Institute of Archaeology of TAU, in conjunction with the Joukowsky Institute for Archaeology and the Ancient World of Brown University (headed by K. Galor). This season was a transition, during which the directorship and responsibility over future excavations at Apollonia-Arsuf was transferred from I. Roll to O. Tal. The work was concentrated in two areas, M and P. This season was a study dig for students in archaeology of two academic institutions: The Department of Archaeology and Ancient Near Eastern Cultures of TAU and the Joukowsky Institute for Archaeology and the Ancient World of Brown University. Excavations were directed by I. Roll and O. Tal and the senior staff included M. Fischer (deputy director), H. Yohanan (deputy director) and T. Harpak (registration), as well as I. Shachar (volunteer coordinator), G. Gardner, M. Edrey, G. Lerner, D. Walshe (area supervisors), U. Birman (administration), B. Arubas (surveying and drawing) and P. Shrago (photography). The season lasted four weeks, from August 7 through September 1, 2006, with an average of 35 participants per day. The budget of the dig was administrated by the Faculty of Humanities of TAU and the Israeli Institute of Archaeology; financial contribution of the volunteers was spent on their own lodging, food and insurance.

The 2009 season (License No. G-56/2009; the site's 19th season of excavations) was the fruit of collaboration between the Institute of Archaeology of TAU and the Division of Engineering of Brown University (headed by David B. Cooper with B. Kimia, G. Taubin and K. Galor). The Brown University researchers were responsible for computer vision research (digital archaeology), documentation of the site's excavated remains and finds in order to promote archaeological research in Israel and beyond. The work was concentrated in five areas: F, L, M, O and R. The season was also a study dig for students of the Department of Archaeology and Ancient Near Eastern Cultures of TAU. Excavations were directed by O. Tal and the senior staff included H. Yohanan (deputy director) and T. Harpak (registration), as well as I. Shachar (volunteer coordinator), G. Lerner and N. Reshef (Israeli student coordinator and Israeli co-coordinator of the Brown University digital archaeology project), M. Edrey and N. Lect (area supervisors), D. Shachar (administration), D. Porotsky and S. Pirsky (surveying and drawing) and P. Shrago (photography). The season lasted five weeks, from July 5 through August 7, 2009, with an average of 45 participants per day. The budget of the dig was provided by the Faculty of Humanities of TAU, Brown University (via sub-award of the National Science Foundation grant, titled III-CXT-Core Large: Computer Vision Research: Promoting Paradigm Shifts in Archaeology; Grant #0808718), the INPA and the German-Israeli Foundation for Scientific Research and Development. Financial contributions of the volunteers was spent on their own lodging, food and insurance. The budget of the dig was administrated by the Faculty of Humanities and the research authority of TAU, as well as the Israeli Institute of Archaeology.

The 2012 season (License No. G-74/2012; the site's 21st season of excavations) lasted intermittently from June to December, whereas the 2013 season (License No. G-46/2013; the site's 22nd season of excavations) lasted from late July to August. Both of these seasons, as part of the ongoing Apollonia-Arsuf Excavation Project carried out by the Institute of Archaeology of TAU, were largely concentrated in areas within the medieval town wall. Excavations on the premises of the Apollonia National Park either formed part of our Deutsche Forschungsgemeinschaft funded-project: Die kreuzfahrerzeitliche Stadt Apollonia/ Arsur in Israel: Struktur - Kulturadaption - Stadt-Umland-Beziehungen (co-headed by B. Scholkmann of the University of Tübingen), as excavated in Areas T, U and W, or concentrated on development works (accessibility for the disabled), as excavated in Areas P1, P2, and X. In both of these seasons excavations were also focused on the Crusader castle western façade (Area F), as well as on various remains in Area R. From July to October 2012, a trial excavation (Permit No. A-6549; map ref. 182256–3052/677516–8371) was conducted in the fields between the fences of the evacuated IMI plant and the coastal highway (Road No. 2), where an evacuated compound of Bezeq (Telecommunications company) exists. In previous publications this area was referred to as Apollonia (East), which also formed an eastern appendage of the Nof Yam neighborhood in Herzliyya (Haddad *et al.* 2015). The trial excavation of 2012 was followed by a salvage excavation in June–August 2013 (Permit No. A-6825). Both excavations, undertaken on behalf of the IAA and TAU and financed by the Israel Lands Authority through the Yahel Engineers Project Initiation Company, Ltd., were directed by E. Haddad (trial excavation) and M. Ajami and O. Tal (salvage excavation), with the participation of T. Harpak (deputy director and registration), D. Golan, T. Greenwald, M. Molokandov and A. Buchennino (preliminary inspections), I. Meir, A. Yaron, I. Elad, M. Pines, E. Jakoel, A. Buchennino, R. Lewis, M. Edrey and H. Venda (area supervisions), Y. Amrani and E. Bachar (administration), and the assistance of H. Yohanan (the then manager of the Apollonia National Park on behalf of the INPA), V. Essman, Y. Shmidov, M. Kahan, R. Mishayev, A. Hajian, and M. Kunin (surveying and drawing), H. Ben-Ari and A. Dagot (GPS), M. Johananoff (metal detecting), A. Peretz and P. Shrago (area photography), Sky View Company (aerial photography), A. Keinan and A. Moshe (safety), M. Avrahami and A. Ronkin (conservation), I. Taxel (pottery), R. Jackson-Tal (glass), Y. Nagar (anthropology), M. Pines (archaeozoology), H. Mienes and O. Rittner (molluscs), R. Pelta (pottery restoration), Y. Kupershmidt (metallurgical laboratory), C. Amit and P. Shrago (studio photography) and workers and students from the Department of Archaeology and Ancient Near Eastern Cultures of TAU field archaeologist's training track. Volunteers from Israel and abroad and pupils from schools participating in the Educational Archaeological Center of the IAA formed an additional part of the labor force, with an average of 100 participants per day.

The 2017 season (Permit No. A-7911/2017; the site's 26th season of excavations) was a salvage excavation at the request of the INPA, after trial trenches were mechanically dug in July 2016 with the assistance of inspectors from the IAA. Work was carried out to improve the sewage line and install a sewer pipe in the national park. It was co-directed by M. Ajami (IAA), H. Yohanan (INPA) and O. Tal (TAU), with the assistance of T. Harpak (registration and photography), S. Pirsky (surveying and drawing), R.E. Jackson-Tal (find analysis), Y. Avivi, I. Elad, J. Stern (IAA), Y. Betababo, G. Haviv, Y. Farhi and T. Tsuk (INPA). The season lasted around three weeks, from January 30 through February 27, 2017; approximately ten high school students instructed by the Educational Archaeological Center of the IAA participated in the excavation. The budget of the dig was provided by the INPA and administrated by the IAA.

I wish to express my thanks to all the above-mentioned people and institutions, who were involved in the Apollonia-Arsuf Excavation Project over the years. I am grateful to S. Holzman for improving the language of the manuscript and proofreading the text. I am indebted to members of the graphics studio of the Institute of Archaeology of Tel Aviv University, I. Ben-Ezra, Y. Gottlieb and N. Earon who skillfully designed the figures of the finds to their current form, and the Publications Department, N. Evron who elegantly formatted the text and to M. Pollak who oversaw its publication. I am also indebted to members of the editorial board, especially O. Lipschits and I. Finkelstein, for prioritizing its publication. Last, but certainly not least, my thanks go to the scholars who contributed of their knowledge to this volume, in the form of know-how and written contributions; the senior team members of the Apollonia-Arsuf Excavation Project: T. Harpak, R.E. Jackson-Tal and H. Yohanan; as well as I. Baidoun, G. Bijovsky, I. Elad, I. Freestone, A. Glick, M. Iserlis, R.Y. Lewis, H.K. Mienis, Y. Nagar, M. Pines, O. Ritner, L. Sapir-Hen, I. Taxel and M. Teixeira Bastos.

The Apollonia-Arsuf Excavation Project is an ongoing research project and the current report forms a portion of the work carried out over the last four decades. Excavations at Apollonia-Arsuf have continued in order to gain better understanding of the site's economic basis and political affinity, as well as its cultural and economic interactions with other Mediterranean centers during its periods of successive occupation. In the tables below, 1 and 2, we have summarized our excavation seasons and areas of excavation, as well as periods/centuries of occupation (based on architectural remains).

REFERENCES

Haddad, E., Tal, O., Ajami, M. and Harpak, T. 2015. Apollonia (East). Ḥadashot Arkheologiyot—Excavations and Surveys in Israel 127. http://www.hadashot-esi.org.il/report_detail_eng.aspx?id=15728&mag_id=122

Roll, I. 1999. Introduction: History of the Site, Its Research and Excavations. In: Roll, I. and Tal, O. *Apollonia-Arsuf: Final Report of the Excavations, Volume 1: The Persian and Hellenistic Periods (with Appendices on the Chalcolithic and Iron Age II Remains)* (Tel Aviv University, Monograph Series of the Institute of Archaeology 16). Tel Aviv: 1–62.

Table 1: Apollonia-Arsuf Excavation Project: Seasons and Areas of Excavations*

Season	*Permit/License No./Year*	*A*	*B*	*C*	*D*	*E (S)*	*E (N)*	*F*	*G*	*H*	*J*	*K*	*TT8*	*L*	*M*	*N*	*N1*	*O*	*P*	*P1*	*P2*	*P3*	*Q*	*Q1*	*R*	*S*	*T*	*U*	*W*	*X*	*Nof-Yam (AA, BB, CC, DD)*	*Underwater*
I	A-667/1976 [= 1977]	+	+	+	+																											
II	A-1007/1980					+																										
III	A-1059/1981					+		+																								
IV	A-1116/1982					+		+?		+																						
V	A-1194/1983 G-30/1983							+?		+																						
VI	G-1/1984								+	+																						
VII	G-71/1990						+																									
VIII	G-38/1991						+			+																						
IX	G-116/1992					+																										
X	G-93/1993					+																										
XI	G-36/1996										+	+	+																			
XII	G-94/1998					+		+																								
XIII	G-94/1999					+		+						+																		
XIV	G-6/2000					+	+	+																								
XV	G-28/2002						+	+								+																
XVI	G-45/2003																		+													
XVII	G-67/2004																		+													
XVIII	G-59/2006														+			+	+													
XIX	G-56/2009							+						+	+			+							+							
XX	G-55/2010							+																	+	+						
-	S-291/2011																															+
XXI	G-46/2012							+												+	+		+		+		+	+	+	+		
-	S-363/2012																															+
	A-6549/2012 [E. Hadad]																														+	
XXII	G-74/2013																			+							+	+				
	A-6825/2013 [O. Tal/M. Ajami]																														+	

* Excavations directed by I. Roll (1976–2006) and O. Tal (2006–2018), unless stated otherwise, Areas of Excavations include trial trenches (TT) and underwater probing (water jetting)

Season	*Permit/License No./Year*	*A*	*B*	*C*	*D*	*E (S)*	*E (N)*	*F*	*G*	*H*	*J*	*K*	*TT8*	*L*	*M*	*N*	*N1*	*O*	*P*	*P1*	*P2*	*P3*	*Q*	*Q1*	*R*	*S*	*T*	*U*	*W*	*X*	*Nof-Yam (AA, BB, CC, DD)*	*Underwater*
-	S-83/2013																															+
XXIII	G-57/2014																			+							+					
XXIV	G-40/2015					+														+				+			+					
XXV	G-78/2016																										+					
XXVI	A-7911/2017 [O. Tal/M. Ajami/H. Yohanan]																+															
XXVII	G-32/2018							+														+										

Table 2: Apollonia-Arsuf Excavation Project: Areas of Excavations and Periods/Centuries of Occupation (Based on Architectural Remains)

Period	*Centuries*	*A*	*B*	*C*	*D*	*E (S)*	*E (N)*	*F*	*G*	*H*	*J*	*K*	*TT8*	*L*	*M*	*N*	*N1*	*O*	*P*	*P1*	*P2*	*Q*	*R*	*S*	*T*	*U*	*W*	*X*	*Nof-Yam (AA, BB, CC, DD)*
	BCE																												
Persian	5th									+																			
	4th									+																			
Hellenistic	3rd									+																			+
	2nd									+																			+
Hellenistic/ Roman	1st																												
	CE																												
	1st					+																							+
	2nd					+																							
	3rd																												+
Roman/ Byzantine	4th												+																+
	5th											+	+					+		+?									+
	6th					+			+			+			+	+	+	+		+			+	+			+?	+?	+
Byzantine/ Early Islamic	7th					+			+			+			+	+	+	+		+			+	+			+?	+?	+
	8th		+	+			+							+					+?	+?			+?	+					
	9th		+	+			+							+					+?	+?			+?	+?					
	10th		+	+			+							+					+?	+?			+?	+?					
	11th		+	+			+							+					+?	+?			+?	+?					
Crusader	12th		+	+			+			+	+			+						+?				+?	+	+			
	13th		+	+			+	+		+	+			+					+	+	+		+	+?	+	+	+?		

CHAPTER 1

INTRODUCTION

Oren Tal

Apollonia-Arsuf is located in the northwestern part of the modern city of Herzliyya on a *kurkar* (fossilized dune sandstone) ridge overlooking the Mediterranean. The site lies 17 km north of Joppa and 34 km south of Caesarea (Fig. 1.1). The ground of the eastern part of the site rises 35 m above sea level and from there gently slopes down to the west, to about 20 m above sea level.

The site's history of excavations until 1999 was thoroughly summarized by Roll in the first final report (Roll and Tal 1999). Below is an abridged history of the excavations until the last, 27th season, which took place in July and October-November 2018. The Preface above provides a more thorough history of excavations for the seasons whose finds are discussed in this report.

The first systematic excavations at Apollonia-Arsuf were carried out in 1950, north of the medieval town wall on behalf of the Israel Department of Antiquities, first by I. Ben-Dor and then by P. Kahane. These salvage excavations were carried out owing to the establishment of the Israel Military Industries Ltd. (hereafter IMI) plant that occupied the greater part of the site, leaving its western portion relatively unharmed. These excavations, whose exact locations remain largely unknown, unearthed architectural remains of Late Roman tombs, Early Byzantine oil presses and Late Byzantine/Early Islamic raw glass furnaces. In 1962 and 1976, following development works at the IMI plant area, a polychrome mosaic floor and several column bases located along an east-west axis were uncovered (Area K), all belonging to a Byzantine church. The first large-scale excavations at Apollonia-Arsuf were carried out in 1977 by I. Roll, who directed 17 seasons of excavations at the site until 2004. The 1977 season was a salvage excavation on behalf of the Israel Department of Antiquities and Museums (in areas within the IMI plant), and only in 1982 the project became an academic excavation on behalf of the Institute of Archaeology of Tel Aviv University (in localities outside the IMI plant area). The 1996 season was a contract excavation initiated by the legal owner of the site, The Israel Land Administration, and carried out on behalf of the Institute of Archaeology of TAU (see Preface, above). From 1996 through the present all excavation seasons were carried out in localities outside the IMI plant area. The 1998, 1999 and 2000 season excavations were organized in part as a joint venture of the Tel Aviv University Institute of Archaeology and the Universidade Federal do Rio Grande do Sul of Porto Alegre, Brazil with the financial backing of the Municipality of Herzliyya and the Israel Nature and Parks Authority (INPA). The 2001, 2002 and 2004 season excavations were organized as a sole venture of the Tel Aviv University Institute of Archaeology.

In 2001, the site of Apollonia-Arsuf became a national park. In 2004, the site was formally recognized as one of the 100 most endangered world monuments by the World Monuments Fund. In 2006, it was included in the tentative list of world heritage Crusader castles by UNESCO. In the same year (2006), the 18th season of excavations was carried out in conjunction with the Artemis and Martha Sharp Joukowsky Institute for Archaeology and the Ancient World of Brown University. This season was a transition during which the directorship and responsibility over future excavations at Apollonia-Arsuf were transferred from I. Roll to O. Tal.

The 19th and 20th seasons, carried out in 2009 and 2010 respectively, continued in conjunction with Brown University (for the 2009 season see Preface). Excavations in 2010 focused on areas within the national park (Areas F, R and S). In Area F (the Crusader castle), excavations that began in 2009 (after a hiatus from 2000) were confined to the castle's western façade. In Area R (located in the center of the medieval walled town), excavations that also began in 2009 continued to uncover a large Crusader dwelling (mid-13th century CE) and industrial installations of the Byzantine/Early Islamic periods used in medieval times. In Area S (located in the far western end of the walled site next to the western medieval town wall), the existence of a doorway in the western medieval town wall has been investigated because of the area topography.

From 2012 to 2016 (the 21st through 25th seasons), excavations on the premises of the Apollonia National Park formed part of the Deutsche Forschungsgemeinschaft funded project: Die kreuzfahrerzeitliche Stadt Apollonia/Arsur in Israel: Struktur - Kulturadaption - Stadt-Umland-Beziehungen (co-headed by B. Scholkmann of the University of Tübingen), and also concentrated on development works (accessibility for the disabled) in Areas Pl, P2, and X (in 2012) or alternatively formed part of the ongoing Apollonia-Arsuf Excavation Project as a sole venture of Tel Aviv University Institute of Archaeology.

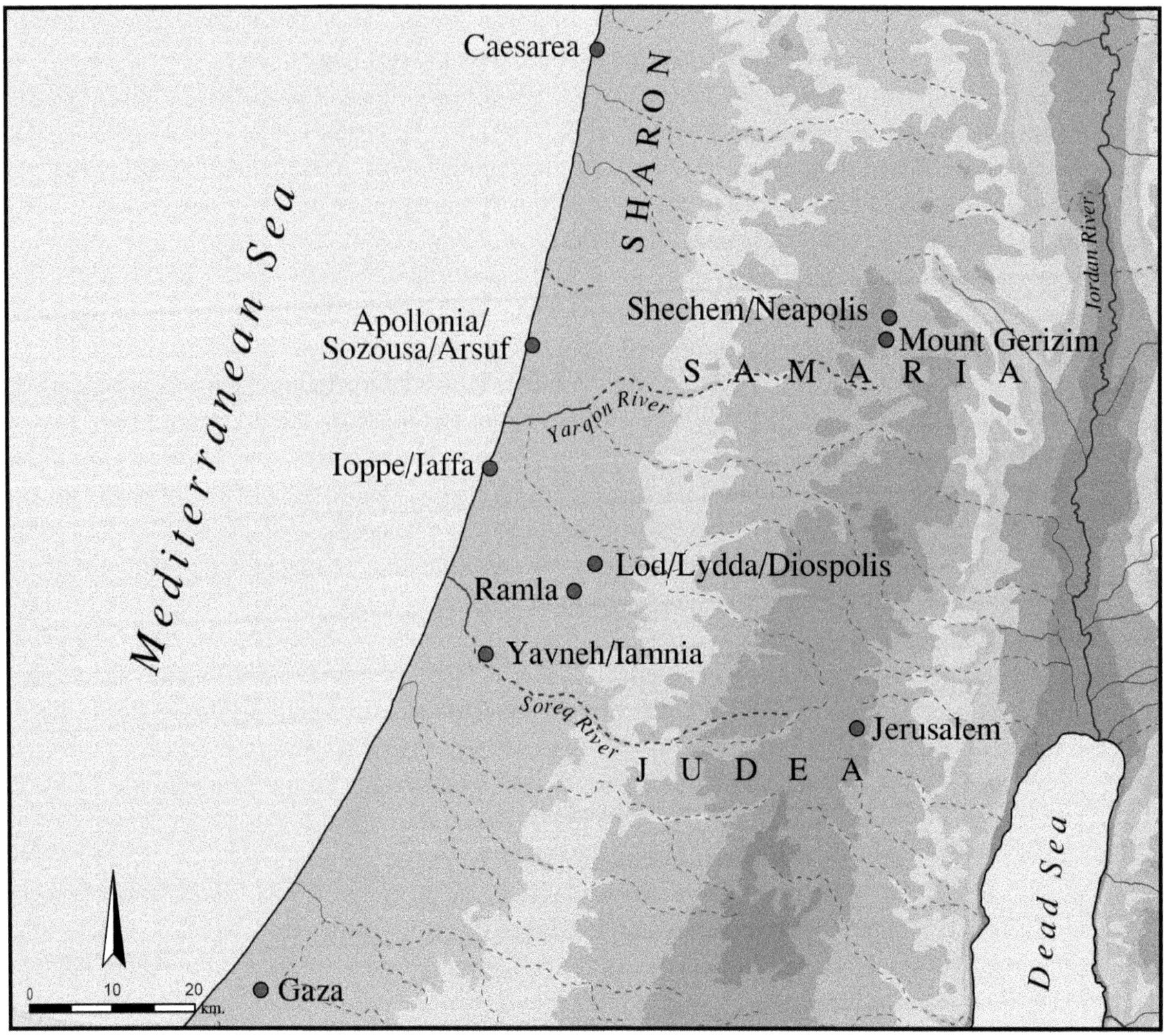

Fig. 1.1: General location map.

The aim of the joint University of Tübingen and Tel Aviv University expedition was to explore the structure, cultural adaptations and urban-rural relations of the Crusader town of Apollonia/Arsur. The project sought to better understand the European and local cultural influences that dictated the structure and organization of the town and its hinterland. The town's abandonment, which followed its destruction by the Mamluks, provides a unique archaeological setting in which the Crusader layers were left largely undisturbed by later settlement activities and thus are suitable for intense research. These layers were the object of extensive light detection and ranging (LIDAR) analysis as well as geo-magnetic surveys, which detected the layout of structures still hidden below the ground, allowing the reconstruction of the original topography and the design of the entire medieval town. The expedition chose to open three excavation areas (Areas T, U and W) where the results of the geo-magnetic surveys showed walls forming small structures and units. Areas T and U were opened in the southwestern part of the site, and Area W was opened in the western part of the site—the center of the walled medieval town. The finds from these areas complete the research by allowing insight into the material culture and daily activities of the town's inhabitants. Other excavation areas (and collaborations) which were opened in 2012 and 2013 are mentioned in the Preface. The 23rd and 24th seasons carried out in 2014 and 2015, respectively, were confined to the medieval period dwellings of Area T (of the joint University of Tübingen and Tel Aviv University expedition) and the Byzantine-Medieval period remains of Area P1 (an extension of Area P whose excavations ended in 2006). The 2016 excavations focused on the completion of the work in Area T (Zeischka-Kenzler *et al.* 2018).

While excavations in 2017 (see Preface) form part of this report, the 27th (July and October-November) season carried out in 2018, which was concentrated in Area F (Crusader castle), was carried out in the framework of an Israel Science Foundation (ISF) Personal Research Grant, entitled "Contextualizing the Architectural Language of the Military Orders: Reconstructing the Frankish Castle of Arsur in Light of its Recently Discovered Chapel." The project aims at identifying and locating, for the first time, the two religious institutions of Arsur: the castle chapel and the town church. In order to reinforce the archaeological evidence of the assumption regarding the location of the Hospitaller chapel, an excavation has been launched along the full length of the castle's western façade halls, which are located below the castle courtyard level. The goal is to uncover the architectural and sculptural elements buried close to the floor level and to expedite the preservation and conservation of the castle's western façade, which will likewise include means to slow down the erosion of the sea cliff. Retrieving these elements will significantly contribute to the reconstruction of the original layout of the donjon in its later stage under the Hospitallers. It will also facilitate the distinction between the different phases of construction. Most importantly, it will enable, for the first time, the proposal of a reconstruction of the castle chapel based on the analysis of the architectural decorative items of Crusader date found thus far.

Over the years, and especially during the last 26 seasons of excavations, numerous areas have been excavated throughout the site (Fig. 1.2): Area O revealed dismantled raw glass furnaces on top of a winepress, both from the Byzantine period; Area F revealed a castle from the Crusader period; Area R revealed Early Islamic and Byzantine remains below a residential building from the Crusader period; Area X revealed a water cistern from the Byzantine period; Area S revealed Early Islamic fortifications and casemates from the Crusader period; Areas P, P1 and P2 revealed a Samaritan synagogue from the Byzantine period, fortifications from the Early Islamic and Crusader periods and Early Islamic industrial facilities; Area M revealed a refuse pit from the Byzantine period; Area L revealed a town wall from the Early Islamic period and a corner tower of the Crusader fortifications; and Areas N and N1 revealed raw glass furnaces from the Byzantine period. Additional areas excavated in the 1970s–1990s (A–E, G, H, J and K) yielded remains from the Persian through the Crusader periods. These included a Roman *villa littorale* (Area E south), a Byzantine Church (Area K) and the Crusader town gate (Area J). Areas Q and Q1 were excavated in 2012, revealing no significant remains, while Areas AA–DD (and their derivatives), excavated in 2012–2103, revealed tombs, industrial installations and refuse as discussed at some length in the following chapters.

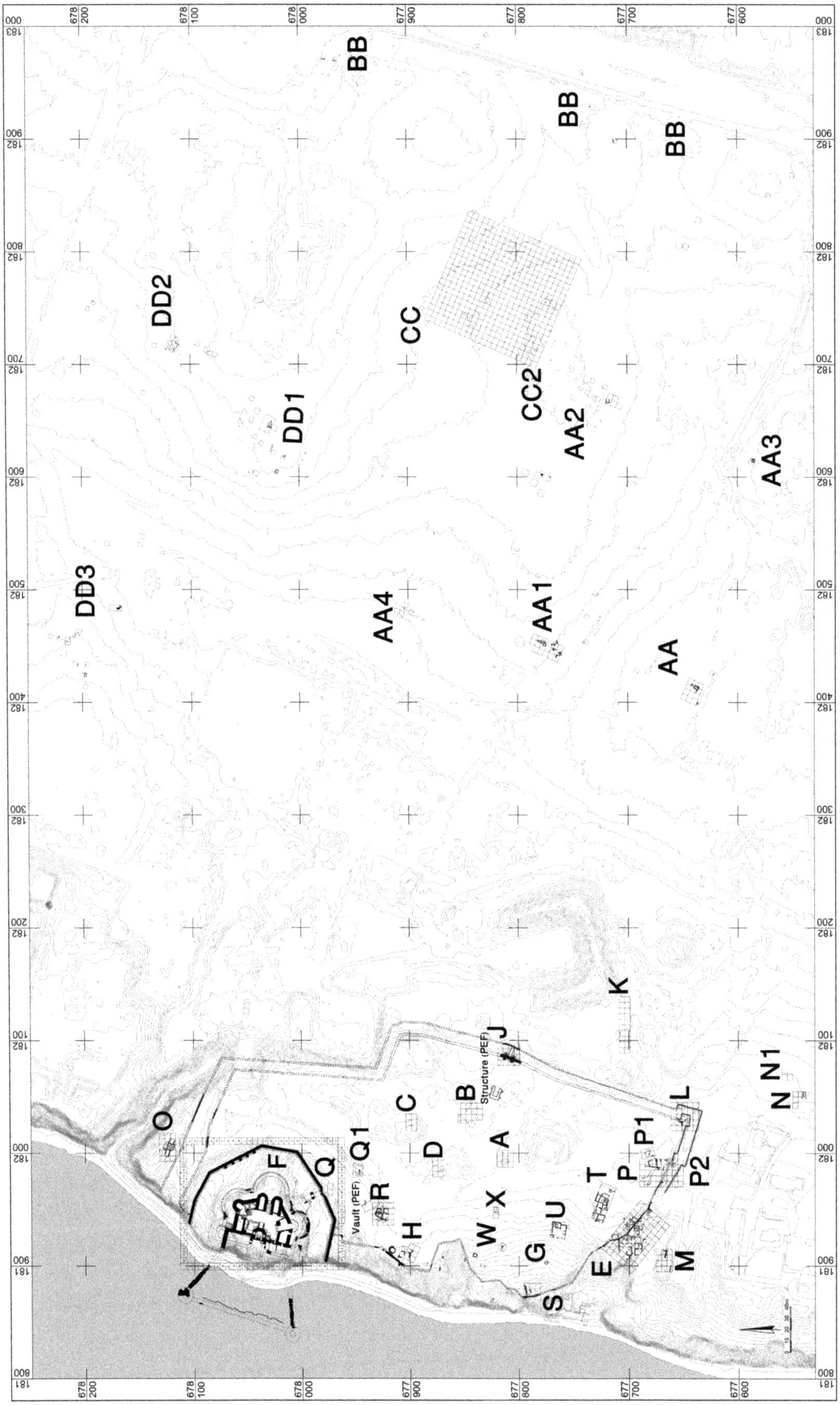

Fig. 1.2: Apollonia-Arsuf, general site plan, marking excavation areas.

All the above seasons of excavations, together with the analysis of the available historical sources, suggest that the site of Apollonia-Arsuf was inhabited continuously from the late 6th century BCE until the Crusader period. Several wall segments, refuse pits and a few tombs were revealed from the Persian and Hellenistic periods (Roll and Tal 1999). The foremost architectural structure from Roman Apollonia is a villa-type structure facing the sea; it includes a peristyle courtyard bounded by a peripheral corridor with rooms arranged along it (Roll and Tal 2008). Recently it was identified as a *mansio* (Tal and Roll 2018). During the Byzantine period, the town, called Sozousa, extended over an unfortified area of ca. 280 dunams. It included a church (Birnbaum and Ovadiah 1990), a Samaritan synagogue (Tal 2015) and industrial quarters with wine and oil presses (Tal 2009b), and plastered pools and furnaces used to produce raw glass (Tal, Jackson-Tal and Freestone 2004; Freestone, Jackson-Tal and Tal 2008). During the reign of the Umayyad caliph ʿAbd al-Malik (685–705 CE), the town, called Arsuf, contracted to an area of ca. 77 dunams and was enclosed within a wall. It was during the Early Islamic period that a *ribat* (stronghold) was constructed in the town (Khalilieh 2008; see also Roll and Ayalon 1987), becoming the home of Muslim religious scholars. In 1101 CE, the site fell to the Crusaders, and its name was changed to Arsur. Toward the middle of the 12th century CE, the site was given to one of the noble families of the Crusader state and became the center of a feudal estate (*seigniory*). After the Ayyubid overtook the site in 1187 CE (Ayalon, Tal and Yehuda 2013), it remained largely deserted for several decades. In 1241 CE, work began on the construction of a castle in the northern part of the town. In 1261 CE, the control of the castle, town and *seigniory* of Arsur were turned over to the Knights Hospitaller. In 1265 CE, following a Mamluk siege, the fortified town and castle were destroyed (Amitai 2005; Tal 2011), and the site has remained uninhabited since then.

The Apollonia-Arsuf Excavation Project focuses on the analysis and publication of all finds and periods recovered during excavations undertaken at the site since 1977, which include the inhabited town, the Crusader castle, the hinterland and the sea coast (cf. Mirkin, Cvikel and Tal 2016).

REFERENCES[1]

Amitai, R. 2005. The Conquest of Arsuf by Baybars: Political and Military Aspects. *Mamluk Studies Review* 9: 61–83.

Amitai-Preiss, N. and Tal, O. 2015. A Lead Bulla from Apollonia-Arsūf with the Place Name Arsūf Ashkenazi, D. and Tal, O. Appendix: Archaeometallurgical Characteristics of the Bulla. Appendix by Dana Ashkenazi and Oren Tal: Archaeometallurgical Characteristics of the Bulla. *Israel Numismatic Research* 10: 191–206.

Ashkenazi, D., Golan, O. and Tal, O. 2013. An Archaeometallurgical Study of 13th-Century Arrowheads and Bolts from the Crusader Castle of Arsuf/Arsur. *Archaeometry* 55: 235–257.

Ayalon, E., Tal, O. and Yehuda, E. 2013. A Twelfth Century Oil Press Complex at the Crusader Town of Arsur (Apollonia) and the Olive Oil Industry in the Latin Kingdom of Jerusalem. *Journal of Eastern Mediterranean Archaeology and Heritage Studies* 1: 259–291.

Birnbaum, R. and Ovadiah, A. 1990. A Greek Inscription from the Early Byzantine Church at Apollonia. *Israel Exploration Journal* 40: 182–191.

Fischer, M. and Tal, O. 2003. A Fourth-Century BCE Attic Marble *Totenmahlrelief* at Apollonia-Arsuf. *Israel Exploration Journal* 53: 49–60.

Freestone, I.C., Jackson-Tal, R.E. and Tal, O. 2008. Raw Glass and the Production of Glass Vessels at Late Byzantine Apollonia-Arsuf, Israel. *Journal of Glass Studies* 50: 67–80.

Galili, E., Dahari, U. and Sharvit, J. 1991. Underwater Survey along the Coast of Israel. *Excavations and Surveys in Israel* 10: 160–166.

1 Cited- and site-oriented works.

Galili, E., Dahari, U. and Sharvit, J. 1993. Underwater Surveys and Rescue Excavations along the Israeli Coast. *International Journal of Nautical Archaeology* 22: 61–77.

Galor, K., Roll, I. and Tal, O. 2009. Apollonia-Arsuf: Between Past and Future. *Near Eastern Archaeology* 72: 4–27.

Gophna, R. and Ayalon, E. 1998. *Archaeological Survey of Israel: Map of Herzliyya (69)*. Jerusalem.

Grossmann, E. 2001. *Maritime Tel Michal and Apollonia: Results of the Underwater Survey 1989–1996* (BAR International Series 915). Oxford.

Haddad, E., Tal, O., Ajami, M. and Harpak, T. 2015. Apollonia (East). *Ḥadashot Arkheologiyot—Excavations and Surveys in Israel* 127. http://www.hadashot-esi.org.il/report_detail_eng.aspx?id=15728&mag_id=122

Heidemann, S., Zeischka-Kenzler, A. and Tal, O. 2018. A Magical Rock Crystal Gem from Apollonia-Arsūf, Israel; Ashkenazi, D., Dvir, O. and Tal, O. Appendix: Mineralogical Characterization of the Magical Rock Crystal Gem from Apollonia-Arsūf. *Journal of Islamic Archaeology* 5/2: 225–239.

Jackson-Tal, R.E. and Tal, O. 2013. Crusader Glass in Context: The Destruction of Arsur (Apollonia-Arsuf, Israel), April 1265. *Journal of Glass Studies* 55: 85–100.

Kahane, P. 1951. Rishpon (Apollonia); B. *Bulletin of the Department of Antiquities of the State of Israel* 3: 42–43 (Hebrew, with English summary in Perkins 1951).

Kaplan, E.H. and Kaplan, B. 1975. The Diversity of Late-Byzantine Oil Lamps at Apollonia (=Arsuf). *Levant* 7: 150–156.

Kenzler, H. 2016. Medieval Town Structure of Arsur on the Basis of Non-Invasive Methods: Results of German-Israeli Project Collaboration. *Zeitschrift des Deutschen Palästina-Vereins* 132: 151–174.

Kenzler, H. Scholkmann, B. and Zeischka-Kenzler, A. 2014. Arsur – Stadt der Kreuzfahrer. *Archäologie in Deutschland* 4: 12–17.

Kenzler, H. and Zeischka-Kenzler, A. 2015. Reports: German-Israeli Research on the Crusader Town of Arsur and Its Former Lordship. *The European Archaeologist* 43: 72–79.

Khalilieh, S.H. 1999. The *Ribât* System and its Role in Coastal Navigation. *Journal of the Economic and Social History of the Orient* 42: 212–225.

Khalilieh, S.H. 2008. The *Ribāt* of Arsūf and the Coastal Defence System in Early Islamic Palestine. *Journal of Islamic Studies* 19: 159–177.

Kool, R. and Tal, O. 2015. 'Underground' Money in an *Outremer* Estate: Token Molds and Lead Tokens from Crusader Arsur. *Israel Numismatic Research* 10: 215–228.

Mirkin, D. 2018. *Sailing to the Holy Land: Crusader Ships, Seamanship, Logistics and Landing Operations* (BAR International Series 2904). Oxford.

Mirkin, D., Cvikel, D. and Tal, O. 2016. Arsur Castle Maritime Installation (1241–1265 CE). *Palestine Exploration Quarterly* 148: 294–312.

Perkins, A. 1951. Archaeological News: The Near East. *American Journal of Archaeology* 55: 81–100.

Pines, M., Sapir-Hen, L. and Tal, O. 2017. Crusader Diet in Times of War and Peace: Arsur (Israel) as a Case Study. *Oxford Journal of Archaeology* 36: 307–328.

Pines, M., Sapir-Hen, L. and Tal, O. 2017. Consumption and Disposal Practices in the Southern Levant in Late Antiquity: Animal Bones from 'Απολλωνία/Σώζουσα's Hinterland as a Case Study. *Zeitschrift des Deutschen Palästina-Vereins* 133: 186–204.

Raphael, K. and Tepper, Y. 2005. The Archaeological Evidence from the Mamluk Siege of Arsuf. *Mamluk Studies Review* 9: 85–100.

Roll, I. 1996. Medieval Apollonia-Arsuf: A Fortified Coastal Town in the Levant of the Early Muslim and Crusader Periods. In: Balard, M., ed. *Autour de la première Croisade. Actes du Colloque de la Society for the Study of the Crusades and the Latin East (Clermont-Ferrand, 22–25 juin 1995)*. Paris: 595–606.

Roll, I. 2006. Apollonia-Arsuf: A Coastal Town of the Eastern Mediterranean Shore in Early Christian and Byzantine Times. In: Harreither, R. *et al. Akten des XIV Internationalen Kongresses für Christlische Archäologie*. Vienna: 681–685.

Roll, I. 2008. Der frühislamische Basar und die Kreuzfahrerburg in Apollonia-Arsuf. In: Piana, M., ed. *Burgen und Städte der Kreuzzugszeit*. Petersberg: 252–262.

Roll, I. and Arubas, B. 2006. Le château d'Arsur: Forteresse côtière pentagonale du type concentrique du milieu du XIIIe siècle. *Bulletin Monumental* 164: 67–81.

Roll, I. and Ayalon, E. 1987. The Market Street at Apollonia-Arsuf. *Bulletin of the American Schools of Oriental Research* 267: 61–76.

Roll, I. and Ayalon, E. 1989. *Apollonia and Southern Sharon: Model of a Coastal City and its Hinterland.* Tel Aviv (Hebrew).

Roll, I., Yohanan, H., Tepper, Y. and Harpak, T. 2000. Apollonia-Arsuf during the Crusader Period in Light of New Discoveries. *Qadmoniot* 119: 18–31 (Hebrew).

Roll, I. and Tal, O. 1999. *Apollonia-Arsuf: Final Report of the Excavations, Volume I: The Persian and Hellenistic Periods (with Appendices on the Chalcolithic and Iron Age II Remains)* (Monograph Series of the Institute of Archaeology of Tel Aviv University 16). Tel Aviv.

Roll, I. and Tal, O. 2008. A Villa of the Early Roman Period at Apollonia-Arsuf. *Israel Exploration Journal* 58: 132–149.

Roll, I. and Tal, O. 2009. A New Greek Inscription from Byzantine Apollonia-Arsuf/Sozousa: A Reassessment of the "Eis Theos Monos" Inscriptions of Palestine. *Scripta Classica Israelica* 28: 139–148.

Roll, I., Tal, O. and Winter, M., eds. 2007. *The Encounter of Crusaders and Muslims in Palestine: as Reflected in Arsuf, Sayyiduna 'Ali and Other Coastal Sites*. Tel Aviv (Hebrew).

Sapir-Hen, L., Pines, M. and Tal, O. 2014. Animal Economy and Social Diversity in Byzantine Apollonia/Sozousa. *Levant* 46: 371–381.

Shachar, I. 2000. Greek Colonization and the Eponymous Apollo. *Mediterranean Historical Review* 15: 1–26.

Sussman, V. 1983. The Samaritan Oil Lamps from Apollonia-Arsuf. *Tel Aviv* 10: 71–96.

Tal, O. 1995. Roman–Byzantine Cemeteries and Tombs around Apollonia. *Tel Aviv* 22: 107–120.

Tal, O. 2000. Some Notes on the Settlement Patterns of the Persian Period Southern Sharon Plain in Light of Recent Excavations at Apollonia-Arsuf. *Transeuphratène* 19: 115–125.

Tal, O. 2009a. A Portable Sundial from Byzantine Apollonia-Arsuf/Sozousa? *Semitica et Classica* 2: 91–96.

Tal, O. 2009b. A Winepress at Apollonia-Arsuf: More Evidence on the Samaritan Presence in Roman–Byzantine Southern Sharon. *Liber Annuus* 59: 319–342.

Tal, O. 2010. Apollonia-Arsuf 2006, 2009. *Israel Exploration Journal* 60: 107–114.

Tal, O., ed. 2011. *The Last Supper at Apollonia: The Final Days of the Crusader Castle in Herzliya.* Tel Aviv (Bilingual Hebrew/English).

Tal, O. 2012. A Portable Sundial from Apollonia-Arsuf Revisited. *Semitica et Classica* 5: 245–248.

Tal, O. 2015. A Bilingual Greek-Samaritan Inscription from Apollonia-Arsuf/Sozousa: Yet More Evidence of the Use of εἷς θεὸς μόνος Formula Inscriptions among the Samaritans. *Zeitschrift für Papyrologie und Epigraphik* 194: 169–175.

Tal, O. and Baidoun, I. 2010. A Hoard of Mamlūk, Ottoman and Venetian Coins (Fifteenth to Sixteenth Centuries) from Apollonia-Arsuf, Israel. *The Numismatic Chronicle* 170: 484–493.

Tal, O. and Bijovsky, G. 2017. A Hoard of Fourth–Fifth Century CE Copper Coins from Sozousa. *Israel Numismatic Research* 12: 147–158.

Tal, O., Jackson-Tal, R.E. and Freestone, I.C. 2004. New Evidence of the Production of Raw Glass at Late Byzantine Apollonia-Arsuf, Israel. *Journal of Glass Studies* 46: 51–66.

Tal, O., Kool, R. and Baidoun, I. 2013. A Hoard Twice Buried? Fatimid Gold from Thirteenth Century Crusader Arsur (Apollonia-Arsuf). *The Numismatic Chronicle* 173: 261–292.

Tal, O. and Roll, I. 2018. The Roman Villa at Apollonia (Israel). In: Marzano, A. and Métraux, G.P.R., eds. *The Roman Villa in the Mediterranean Basin: Late Republic to Late Antiquity*. Cambridge: 308–315.

Tal, O. and Taxel, I. 2012. Socio-Political and Economic Aspects of Refuse Disposal in Late Byzantine and Early Islamic Palestine. In: Matthews, R. and Curtis, J., eds. *Proceedings of the 7th International Congress on the Archaeology of the Ancient Near East, 12–16 April 2010, the British Museum and UCL, London 1: Mega-cities and Mega-sites: The Archaeology of Consumption and Disposal, Landscape, Transport and Communication.* Wiesbaden: 497–518.

Tal, O. and Taxel, I. 2017. More Than Trash – Cultic Use of Pottery Lamps Found in Late Antique Dumps: Apollonia (Sozousa) as a Test Case. In: Tal, O. and Weiss, Z., eds. *Expressions of Cult in the Southern Levant in the Greco-Roman Period: Manifestations in Text and Material Culture* (Contextualizing the Sacred 6). Turnhout: 181–193.

Tal, O., Taxel, I. and Zeischka-Kenzler, A. 2018. A *Basmala*-Inscribed Jug from Arsur's Mamluk Destruction of AD 1265: The Religious Manifestation of a Christian-Used Table Vessel? *Journal of Near Eastern Studies* 77: 91–98.

Tal, O. and Teixeira Bastos, M. 2013. Intentionally Broken Discus Lamps from Roman Apollonia: A New Interpretation. *Tel Aviv* 39: 104–114.

Tal, O. and Teixeira Bastos, M. 2015. More on the Intentionally Broken Discus Lamps from Roman Palestine: Mutilation and Its Symbolic Meaning. In: Blömer, M., Lichtenberger, A. and Raja, R., eds. *Religious Identities in the Levant from Alexander to Muhammed: Continuity and Change* (Contextualizing the Sacred 4). Turnhout: 345–368.

Tal, O., Yohanan, H., Ajami, M. and Jackson-Tal, R.E. Apollonia. 2017. *Ḥadashot Arkheologiyot—Excavations and Surveys in Israel* 129. http://www.hadashot-esi.org.il/Report_Detail_Eng.aspx?id=25296&mag_id=125

Taragan, H. 2004. The Tomb of Sayyidnā ʿAlī in Arsūf: The Story of a Holy Place. *Journal of the Royal Asiatic Society* 14: 83–102.

Wexler, L. and Gilboa, G. 1994. A Signet Ring from the Apollonia-Arsuf Excavations. *Tel Aviv* 21: 288–291.

Wexler, L. and Gilboa, G. 1996. Oil Lamps of the Roman Period from Apollonia-Arsuf. *Tel Aviv* 23: 115–131.

Zeischka-Kenzler, A., Yohanan, H., Kenzler, H., Harpak, T., Scholkmann, B. and Tal, O. Apollonia. 2018. *Ḥadashot Arkheologiyot—Excavations and Surveys in Israel* 130. http://www.hadashot-esi.org.il/Report_Detail_Eng.aspx?id=25454&mag_id=126

SECTION ONE

STRATIGRAPHY AND ARCHITECTURE

CHAPTER 2

AREA AA (2012–2013)

Tamar Harpak and Oren Tal

Area AA is located in the southern part of the immediate hinterland area, also known as Apollonia [East]), excavated in 2012–2013 [Fig. 1.2]). It includes nine squares which were dug during the 2012 season and an additional 11 squares which were dug during the 2013 season.

Excavation revealed a structure built from fieldstones combined in part with roughly hewn stones. It was identified as a field tower (at least in its later use; approximately 2.30 × 3.70 m external dimensions) that exhibited two architectural stages, probably dated to the Byzantine and Early Islamic periods, respectively. A misalignment of the stones was apparent in the cross-section of the walls of the structure, which is characteristic of structures built on shifting sand dunes. In addition, another (partially surviving) installation was unearthed, with a threshold and two connecting walls. There are also parts of a paved surface made of a layer of gravel, and next to it a small refuse pit. The finds (primarily pottery) recovered in the area were, for the most part, eroded (Fig. 2.1).

FIELD TOWER (INSTALLATION 10091)

The structure shows two stages; the earlier stage included four walls: Wall 10082 to the north, Wall 10074 to the west, Wall 10086 to the south, and Wall 10088 to the east. The later stage included an additional four walls: Wall 139 to the west, Wall 10041 to the south, Wall 10072 to the east and Wall 123 (connecting to Wall 139) to the west (Fig. 2.3).

Walls 10086 and 10088 from the earlier stage are connected to Wall 10074. All are built of fieldstones. Walls 10086 and 10088 are connected, with one course of stones preserved and partially hidden under later walls. On the other hand, Wall 10074 is measurable to its full extent: 0.90 m long, 0.50 m thick, with one course of stones preserved as well. Locus 10085 represents a robber trench (Installation 11091) of Wall 10086.

Wall 139 is from the later stage and is built of fieldstones and four courses of stones are preserved. It is 4.40 m long and 0.40 m thick. Wall 10074 is directly below Wall 139. In the northeastern part of Wall 139, solid ground with mortar remains was uncovered. Wall 139 is connected to Wall 10041 and forms a corner, and is built from large roughly hewn stones. Wall 10041 is 2.30 m long and 0.60 m thick. Three courses of stones are preserved. Wall 123 is an appended wall from the later stage located outside on the southwestern corner of the field tower in an east–west orientation. In the northeast corner, at the connecting point of Walls 123 and 139, landslide (Locus 125) was unearthed. Wall 10072 from the later stage on the east is parallel to Wall 139; it is 3.70 m long and 0.55 m thick. Five courses of roughly hewn stones (and fieldstones) are preserved. Wall 10082 is connected to Wall 10071. Wall 10082 is oriented east–west and built from fieldstones and is 1.90 m long and 0.50 m thick.

The few sherds found may attest to two stages of use for the field tower, one in the Byzantine period and the other in the Early Islamic period, although no secured (well-stratified) locus was recovered and dating is hypothetical.

INSTALLATION 10089

An installation built on the sand was also unearthed in the area. Three walls were preserved from the installation—the western, northern and eastern (Fig. 2.4). Wall 148 on the east aligned north–south was built from fieldstones with no mortar remains. It is 0.95 m. long, 0.25 m. thick, preserved to approximately 0.30 m. high. The wall is connected to Wall 149 on the north aligned east–west, was built from roughly hewn stones, with both corners made of ashlar stones. Walls 148 and 155 were connected to Wall 149. It seems that the two threshold stones were of secondary use. The western wall of the installation, Wall 155 aligned north–south, was also built of small fieldstones with no mortar remains. It is 1 m long and 0.50

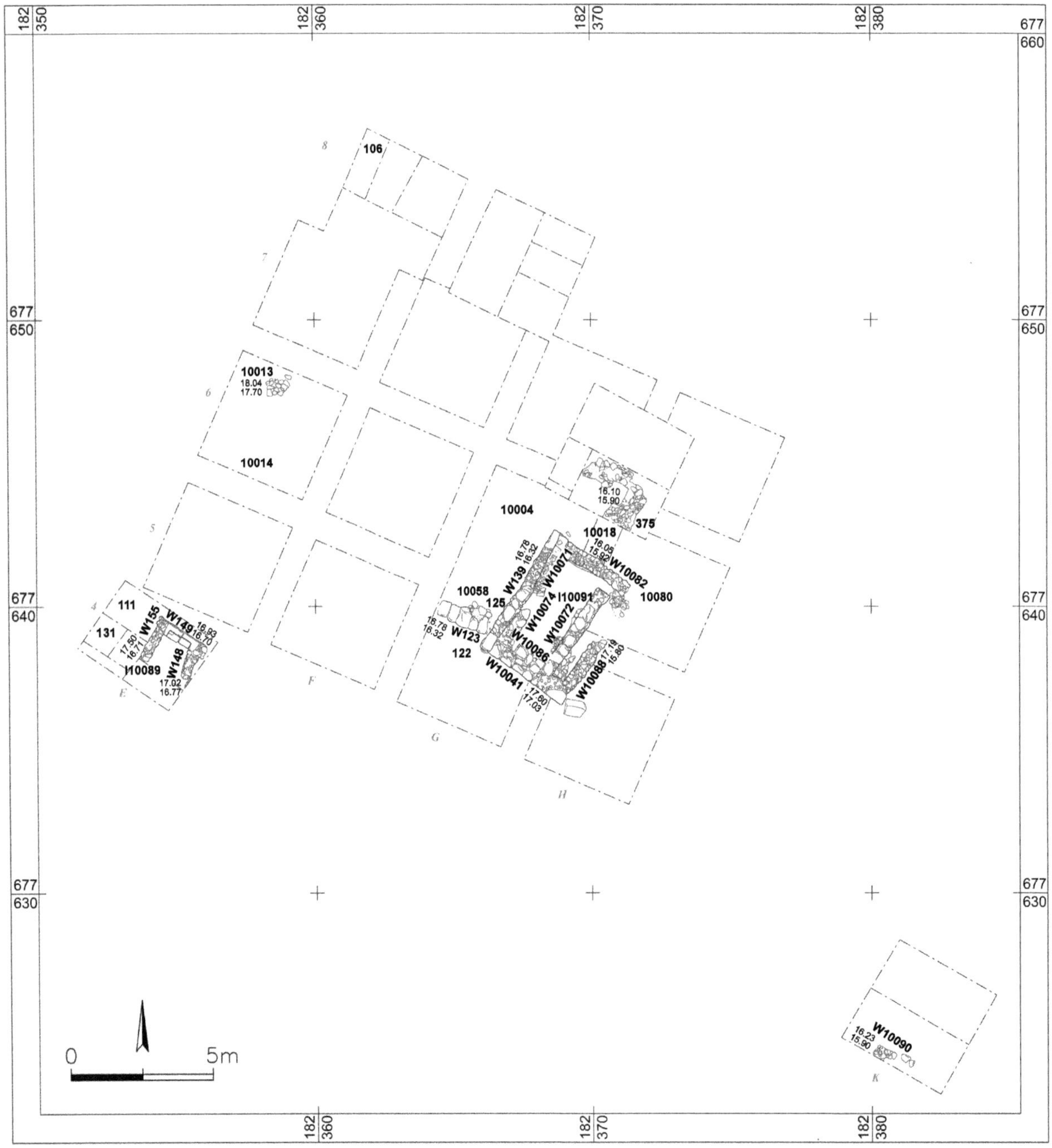

Fig. 2.1: Plan of Area AA.

m thick. It is connected to Wall 149 with a slight deviation, probably caused by shifting sand dunes. All walls were built without any foundation and with one course of stones preserved. A few sherds recovered within the installation suggest a date in the Byzantine period.

Loci 10013 and 10014 represent a small section of a paved surface that was characterized by a layer of gravel, where no finds were recovered. Further north in the area an hourglass-shaped krater fashioned as a deep conical bowl with a solid conical base was found when the area was opened (Chapter 15: Fig. 15.1: 1).

Wall 10090, which is built of fieldstones, was unearthed as an isolated element from which no finds were recovered (Fig. 2.2, top right).

Fig. 2.2: Area AA, aerial view.

Fig. 2.3: Area AA, field tower (I10091); (a) looking east; (b) looking west.

Fig. 2.4:Area AA, threshold (I10089), looking west.

CHAPTER 3

AREA AA1 (2012–2013)

Itai Elad, Tamar Harpak and Oren Tal

This area is located in the southern part of the immediate hinterland excavated in 2012–2013 (Fig. 1.2). During the 2012 excavation, seven squares were dug. An additional 11 squares were dug during the 2013 season.

In the area, several plastered facilities were revealed, among them round and square collecting/settling (and fermentation) vats paved with mosaics. The vats were part of a winepress where two construction phases from the Byzantine period were discerned. In the early phase the press included two small, round collecting vats; in the later phase it was expanded to three large vats, one rounded and the other two square. The walls of the winepress were built of medium-sized kurkar stones bonded with grayish-white mortar. The winepress had a treading floor close to surface level which was apparently destroyed by later activity. In the southern part of the area, several sections of a working surface built of medium-sized fieldstones, probably dating from the Byzantine or Early Islamic period, were exposed. A single pit grave excavated in the center of the area was aligned in an east–west direction (Tomb 11064) and is identified as a later Islamic tomb (Chapter 11) (Fig. 3.1).

WINEPRESS COMPLEXES

In this area, the remains of several features of an agricultural product processing/industrial nature were unearthed, spread over an area of some 420 sq m. The main feature is a large complex of a winepress found in the northern part of the area (Fig. 3.2). Two phases of use were identified. An earlier phase is characterized by two small circular collecting vats adjoining each other in a south–north axis. Both of the vats were built of medium-sized *kurkar* stones coated on their interior and exterior walls with a dense, hydraulic, white-grayish plaster (Fig. 3.3). The vats were paved with medium-sized white-*tesserae* (of some 1.50 × 1.50 cm) arranged in a circular pattern. The outline of the northern vat (Installation 11022) was preserved in full, with an internal diameter of 1.20 m, but its walls were partially preserved to a height of approximately 0.40 m. A deep conical sedimentation basin (measuring 0.30 m deep, 0.40 m in diameter on its top and 0.22 m on its bottom) was found on the vat's floor, positioned slightly off-center, which allowed easier access to a single beach-rock plaster-covered ("maintenance") stair inserted in the western wall. The outline of the southern vat (Installation 11021) was partially preserved since it was cut by the large circular vat built in the later phase. The space between the earlier and later vats (Locus 11026) was filled with brown soil mixed with medium-sized stones which were intentionally placed to support the outer facet of the new wall. Among those stones, a segment of mosaic floor was uncovered, probably dismantled from the floor of the earlier vat when it went out of use. A coin, dated between 403–408 CE found in Locus 11026, gives the construction of the later phase vats a *terminus post quem* (see Chapter 18: No. 187).

In the later phase, the two small collecting vats were partially demolished and three new larger ones were built which significantly increased the capacity of the winepress complex. These vats were also built of medium-sized *kurkar* stones. The interior sides of their walls were covered with several

Fig. 3.1: Plan of Area AA1.

Fig. 3.2: Area AA1, aerial view.

layers of white-grayish plaster, possibly indicating protracted repairs and use. The upper layer of plaster included fragments of ribbed storage jars, which seems to be a typical coating technique for vats of the Byzantine period. All three vats were paved with medium-sized, white *tesserae*. The northern vat is circular (Installation 214; 2 m in diameter and 1.05 m deep) with two levels: an upper cylindrical-shaped level, approximately 0.55 m deep, and a lower conical-shaped level (measuring 0.50 m deep, 0.85 m in diameter on its top and 0.62 m on its bottom). The total volume of this vat is about 2,565 liters. On its western wall two beach-rock plaster-covered stairs were inserted, which allowed easier access. A marble slab set into the northern part of the mosaic surface between the two levels indicates the direction from which the must would have flowed into the vat. As the treading floor of the winepress did not survive due to its proximity to the surface level, it is logical to assume that the marble slab was placed immediately under the outlet of a pipe (or a channel) which lead the must from the treading floor to prevent erosion on the vat's floor. The same phenomenon can be seen in other winepresses with circular collecting vats, for example at Ramat Gan (ʿAd 2011: Fig. 11) and Rishon Le-Zion (Shavit 2009: Fig. 42.2). This supports the idea that the treading floor was located to the north of the large circular vat, perhaps even directly above the smaller partially preserved vats of the earlier phase. In this manner, the large quantity of white *tesserae* found in the fills inside the three vats of the later phase most probably originated in the treading floor.

From the circular vat the must would have continued to flow; once the vat was filled, it passed into two additional (secondary) collecting vats, located to its south, first to the eastern one and then to the western one. The connection between the circular vat and the eastern vat was made through a small and relatively shallow intermediary (filtration) vat that was partially preserved (Installation 247; about 0.80 × 0.66 m). The eastern collecting vat is rectangular in shape (Installation 222; 2.10 × 1.40 m and 1.15 m deep, with a capacity of some 3,381 liters) with two beach-rock plaster-covered stairs inserted in its southwestern corner walls (Fig. 3.4). A tunnel in the northern part of the joint wall of the two additional vats led the must to the western vat. This one is larger and square-shaped (Installation 215; 2.10 × 2.10

Fig. 3.3: Area AA1, circular collecting vats (I11022 and I11021 on left of the earlier phase, and I214 on right of the later phase), looking east.

m and 1.15 m deep, with a capacity of approximately 5,071 liters), with two beach-rock plaster-covered stairs inserted in its northwestern corner walls. In the center of the mosaic floors of both the additional vats, a shallow circular sump was set.

All three collecting vats of the later phase of the winepress complex contained large amounts of pottery dated to the Byzantine and Early Islamic periods (see Chapter 13), as well as large amounts of medium-sized white *tesserae*. This indicates that the vats became refuse pits once the winepress ceased to function.

The remains of three additional smaller vats were discovered to the south of the winepress complex. Installations 224 and 11066 are both square in shape. Vat I224 is larger (0.82 × 0.60 m) and better preserved. Its corners were strengthened by a diagonal thickening typical to vats of the Roman and Byzantine periods (e.g., Ayalon and Levy 2011: 23*, Fig. 6). Its inner sides and floor were covered with a layer of grayish-white hydraulic plaster (Figs. 3.1, 3.5, 3.7). Vat I11066 was poorly preserved but was apparently very small (0.55 × 0.33 m). Both vats were built of medium-sized *kurkar* stones bound with gray mortar. Vat I234 is roughly circular and was found in a poorly preserved state. It has a diameter of 0.80 m and is preserved to a maximum height of about 0.45 m. A few *in situ* white *tesserae* in the base indicate it had a mosaic floor. Based on the building technique and orientation of these three smaller vats, it seems that they were related to the winepress. Large winepress complexes, such as the one discussed here, are often accompanied by small vats used for multiple purposes (Fig. 3.2).

The winepress complex in Area AA1 suggests a strong connection, both by shape and building technique, to the winepress uncovered at Apollonia-Arsuf's/Sozousa Area O during the 2009 season of excavation (Chapter 10). Circular-shaped collecting vats were apparently frequently used in the southern Sharon, although the most common plan for winepresses in this area remains that of the "four-

Fig. 3.4: Area AA1, collecting vats of the later phase, from right to left, I215, I222 and I214, looking west.

Fig. 3.5: Area AA1, collecting vats (I224 and I11066), looking east.

rectangular" (Frankel 1999: 149–150). Calculating the capacities of the three collecting vats of the winepress complex second phase gives an estimated total of 11017 liters. Judging by this sheer volume, it is obvious that the winepress produced wine on an industrial scale. Its location, approximately some 450 m to the east of the town and within the narrow plain between the first and second *kurkar* ridges, seems ideal for this purpose. As much of the wine was destined for export purposes (Dan 1984: 291–292), its production took place in and around the town; though situated in an area where grapevines were probably cultivated extensively, still it was located in close proximity to the commercial center. This meant easier transportation of the product to the place where many potential buyers were, being either the local populations or international traders.

WORKING SURFACE (FLOOR 11038)

Segments of what seems to be a rather large working surface (Floor 11038) were found in the center and the southern parts of the excavated area. The surface seems to be of an industrial nature and is generally built of small- to medium-sized *kurkar* stones with some clay bricks, with glass production debris and pottery sherds integrated among them (Figs. 3.2, 3.6). One segment of the mosaic floor that seems to originate from the winepress complex was also found integrated among the stones of the working surface. Several coins were found adjacent to the different segments of the working surface and are dated between the end of the 4th century to the beginning of the 5th century CE. These include a 4th century CE coin that was extracted from beneath one of the working surface stones (see Chapter 18: No. 159). This indicates that the construction of the working surface should probably be

Fig. 3.6: Area AA1, working surface (F11038), looking north.

dated to the same period of time as the winepress complex second phase, the end of the 4th or the beginning of the 5th century CE.

INSTALLATION (FLOOR 209)

Remains of a partially preserved installation of an enigmatic nature were revealed in the southeastern part of the excavated area. It includes a 1.30 × 1.20 m segment of elevated stone flooring (Floor 209) which was encircled on its southern and western sides by a wall preserved to a height of one course (Wall 228) (Figs. 3.1, 3.7). Adjacent to the western side of the installation, a scattering of collapsed stones was found (Locus 11032), probably originating from its walls. Among the collapsed stones, a few coins dated to the Mamluk period were found (see Chapter 18: Nos. 375–378). This late date is also supported by the level of the installation, about 0.50 m above the level of the Byzantine period working surface, which could be explained by the continuous migration of sand which caused the surface level to rise over time.

PIT GRAVE (TOMB 11064)

In the center of the excavated area, a single pit grave (Tomb 11064) was revealed and based on its features it is suggested that it can be assigned to a later (later Islamic/modern) period activity (Chapter 11).A single skeleton was found in articulation, lying on its right side in an east–west orientation with the head facing west. The skeleton was identified as an infant (Figs. 3.1, 3.2).

Fig. 3.7: Area AA1, installation (F209), looking east.

REFERENCES

ʿAd, U. 2011. Ramat Gan. *Ḥadashot Arkheologiyot—Excavations and Surveys in Israel* 123. http://www.hadashot-esi.org.il/Report_Detail_Eng.aspx?id=1677&mag_id=118.

Ayalon, E. and Levy, Y. 2011. Ḥorbat Gelilot (el-Jelil): Excavations on the Fringes of a Roman–Byzantine-Period Village in the Sharon Plain. *ʿAtiqot* 66: 17*–61* (Hebrew, with English summary pp. 156–157).

Dan, Y. 1984. Eretz-Israel in the Fifth and Sixth Centuries. In: Baras, Z., Safrai, S., Tsafrir, Y. and Stern, M., eds. *Eretz-Israel from the Destruction of the Second Temple to the Muslim Conquest*, Vol. 1. Jerusalem: 265–299 (Hebrew).

Frankel, R. 1999. *Wine and Oil Production in Antiquity in Israel and Other Mediterranean Countries* (JSOT/ASOR Monograph Series 10). Sheffield.

Shavit, E. 2009. A Complex of Two Wine Presses at Rishon Le-Zion. In: Ayalon, E., Frankel, R. and Kloner, A., eds. *Oil and Wine Presses in Israel from the Hellenistic, Roman and Byzantine Periods* (BAR International Series 1972). Oxford: 239–247.

CHAPTER 4

AREA AA2 (2012–2013)

Tamar Harpak and Oren Tal

This area is divided between a northern AA2/1 area and a southern AA2/2 area; both are located to the east of Area AA1 (Fig. 1.2). Ten squares were dug during the 2012 season in Area AA2/2 and an additional four squares during the 2013 season in Area AA2/1.

In Area AA2/1, which was excavated in 2012, two segmented features were discovered, the one on the south was tagged as Locus 364, which exhibits scattered stones with some sherds and industrial glass refuse around them; the other feature is Locus 169 which reveals similar phenomena (Fig. 4.1). The finds recovered in the area were eroded. In Area AA2/2 (Fig. 4.3) a field tower was excavated along with a few additional features.

FIELD TOWER (INSTALLATION 12036)

The excavation revealed a structure built in part from well-dressed stones, identified as a field tower (at least in its later use). The structure exhibited two architectural stages, probably dated to the Byzantine and the Early Islamic periods respectively (Figs. 4.2–4.4). Its layout is similar to the field tower excavated in Area AA (Chapter 2). Walls 177 and 194 were built during the earlier stage, with Wall 185 connecting them, which seems to over-impose an earlier hidden wall (Wall 12037) that may have functioned as its foundation. During the later stage, Wall 12032 was built directly on Wall 177 and Wall 12024 was built directly on W194.

Wall 177 on the north is partially built of well-dressed stones, with three courses preserved. It is 2.50 m long, 0.70 m thick and 0.60 m high. It is parallel to Wall 194 (2 m long, 0.70 m thick and 0.50 m high) and cuts through Wall 185. The later Wall 12032 on the north and Wall 12024 on the south partially survived.

Wall 185 on the west was apparently built upon a foundation of fieldstones approximately 0.15 m wider than the wall. It is partially built of well-dressed stones, with two courses preserved; it is 1.60 m long, 0.70 m thick and 0.80 m high.

The few sherds found may attest to two stages of use for the field tower, one in the Byzantine period and the other in the Early Islamic period, although no secured (well-stratified) locus was recovered and dating is largely hypothetical.

PIT GRAVES (TOMBS 12017, 12018)

South of Wall 12024 and adjacent to it, a pit grave (Tomb 12017) was excavated (Fig. 4.5), where the deceased was found in articulation, lying on its back in a general east–west orientation, with its head towards the west. The grave post-dates the field tower (Installation 12036) and its deceased is estimated as an individual 20–30 years of age (Chapter 11). Another pit grave, Tomb 12018, was found inside the field tower (Installation 12036). The articulated body was found lying on its right side in a general east–west orientation (Fig. 4.6). The grave was assigned to a Late Islamic/modern date individual 20< years old (Chapter 11). Another pit grave was found farther northeast (Tomb 12016), but its excavation revealed no finds.

In addition, a concentration of scattered pottery from different periods was exposed beneath the collapsed stones of the field tower. In a recess hewn in the *kurkar* bedrock, pottery sherds dating to the Persian period were discovered (Chapter 13: Fig. 13.7: 1), probably representing the remains of another burial that did not survive (Fig. 4.2).

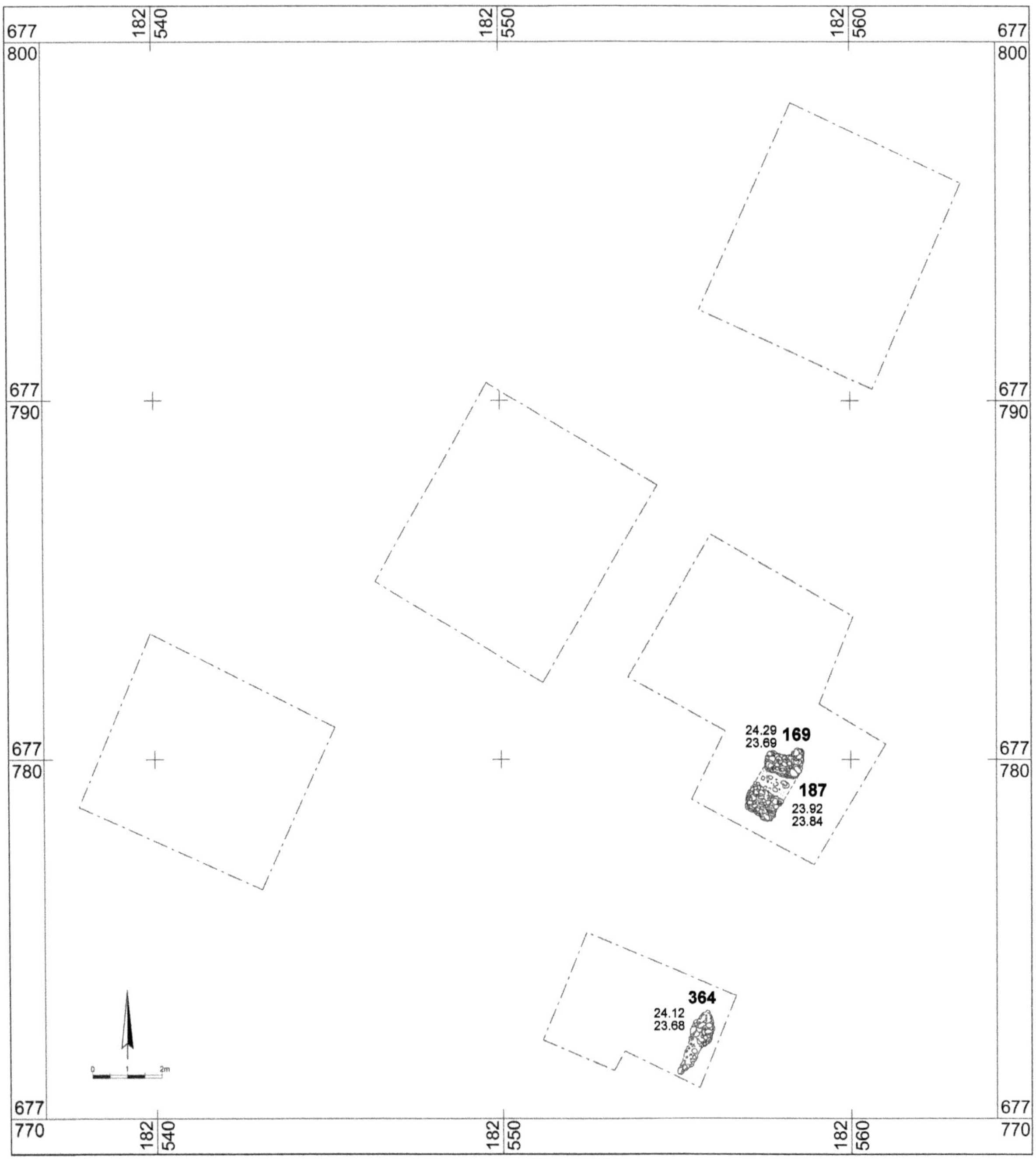

Fig. 4.1: Plan of Area AA2/1.

Fig. 4.2: Area AA2/2, aerial view.

Fig. 4.3: Plan of Area AA2/2.

Fig. 4.4: Area AA2/2, field tower (I12036), looking east.

Fig. 4.5: Area AA2/2, pit grave (T12017), looking west.

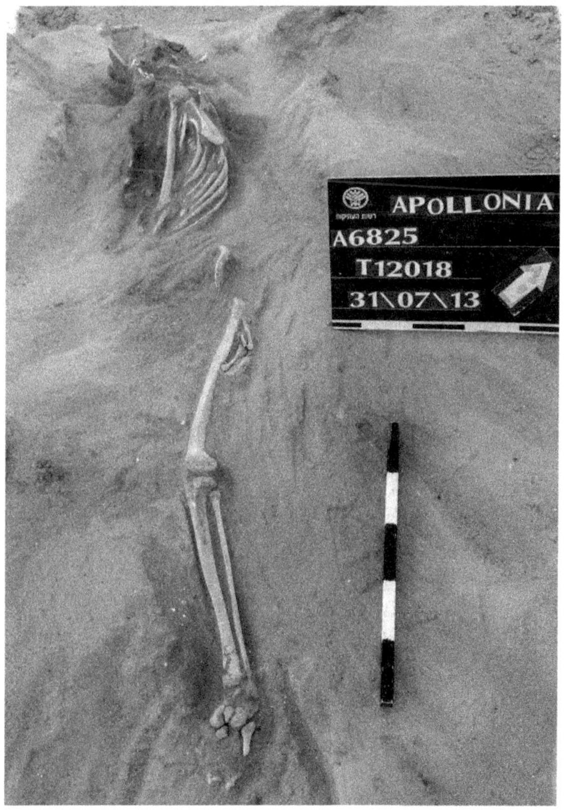

Fig. 4.6: Area AA2/2, pit grave (T12018), looking west.

CHAPTER 5

AREAS AA3, AA4 AND BB (2012–2013)

Tamar Harpak and Oren Tal

Area AA3 is located on the eastern side of the excavation (Fig. 1.2). One square was dug during the 2012 season and an extension of an additional square was made in the 2013 season. The digging revealed a built tomb in which only the bottom part had survived, containing three burial spaces; the floor of the structure is plastered and its walls are made of roughly hewn limestone, while its foundation was constructed of fieldstones (Fig. 5.1). Upon the complete removal of the built tomb fills and the clearing of landslide stones, the tomb was exposed in its full capacity. It is rectangular and constructed on top of a foundation of small fieldstones that includes three *loculi* with plastered floors: a northern (Floor 426), a central (Floor 438) and a southern (Floor 437). Their original dimensions seem to have been similar (about 1.95 × 0.45 m) as can be seen in the one more complete *loculus* (Floor 426). The inner walls of this built tomb are narrower (some 0.20 m) when compared to the external walls (some 0.60 m) (Fig. 5.2). To its southwest, a concentration of buried bones was found which may have belonged to the original burial. The bones of at least five different individuals were identified (Tomb 13001, Loci 13007–13009; Chapter 11). In the structure and the immediate surrounding area, sherds dated to the Late Roman or Early Byzantine period were found, most likely reflecting the date of use of this structure (Chapter 13). Another indication of the date of this built tomb may come from its architecture; the type is likely to be assigned to a one-room vaulted tomb type which is largely confined to the Late Roman and Byzantine southern Coastal Plain (cf. e.g., Huster and Sion 2006: 50–52, Type 1, Fig. 2; see also Jakoel 2016: 36, Fig. 5). This example may represent one of its northernmost specimens.

Area AA4 is located north of Area AA1 and characterized by glass industrial waste uncovered near the surface (Fig. 1.2). Two squares were dug during the 2012 season and an additional one during the 2013 season. As glass industrial waste was predominant during the first season, the decision to expand the area was made because of the possibility of recovering the foundations of a glass furnace. Because no archeological finds were uncovered, it appears likely that the glass industrial waste was an intentional fill (for agricultural purposes?).

Area BB is located on the eastern side of the excavation. Thirteen squares were dug during the 2012 season. In the majority of the squares, sandy fills which had accumulated above the local rock were dug out. Most squares revealed no archeological finds, but only small amounts of pottery and other remains dated mainly to the Byzantine period. In addition, stone surfaces were exposed in some of the squares. One square in the northeastern part of the area yielded a stone crater together with Byzantine-period pottery.

REFERENCES

Huster, Y. and Sion, O. 2006. Late Roman and Byzantine Period Vaulted Tombs in the Southern Coastal Plain. *Jerusalem and Eretz-Israel* 3: 49–69 (Hebrew, with English abstract p. 7*).

Jakoel, E. 2016. Tombs and Burials in Jaffa (Joppa) during the Roman Period. *Cathedra* 159: 25–56 (Hebrew, with English abstract p. 225).

Fig. 5.1: Plan of Area AA3.

Fig. 5.2: Area AA3, built tomb (T13001), looking west.

CHAPTER 6

AREA CC (2012–2013)

Tamar Harpak and Oren Tal

Area CC is the largest area excavated among those dug in the town's hinterland, located east of Byzantine Apollonia/Sozousa and the medieval fortified town of Arsuf/Arsur (Fig. 1.2). It is located northeast of Area AA2 and consisted of 92 excavation squares, 4 × 4 m each, of which 17 squares were dug during the 2012 season and an additional 75 were dug during the 2013 season (Fig. 6.1, not all squares are illustrated on the plan). The main use feature of the area is a large refuse dump, one of the central ones used during the Byzantine period. The area measures approximately 55 m long and 30 m wide; the dump extended over some 35 excavation squares (i.e., from south to north, E4–E13, F4–F13, G4–G9, H5–H8, I5–I7, J6–J7), with a maximal length of 47 m and a maximal width of 30 m (Fig. 6.2). The dump's boundaries were clearly identified prior to the excavations based on numerous sections carried out by mechanical means, which dictated the location and orientation of the excavation squares and, in addition, showed that the area beyond the dump's limits was virtually empty of archaeological materials. The digging of the topsoil revealed a sandy, yellow-brown fill some 0.50 m thick; directly beneath it was an archaeological layer (maximal thickness ca. 1 m) with large quantities of potsherds, animal bones and mollusc remains, as well as glass-production refuse and fragmented glass vessels, stone and metal objects as well as coins (cf. Chapters 13–18, 21). Below this layer, a brownish-yellow sandy layer was found that had no archaeological finds (Fig. 6.3). Thus the stratification in the area was uniform, a "sandwich" of a surface layer of sand covering a layer of potsherds (and other waste material) underlying a layer of alluvium. Given the analysis of the area's stratigraphy, it is logical to assume that the area was used almost exclusively for waste management (garbage disposal), and it was probably one of the central dumps used by the site's inhabitants during the Byzantine period. It should be borne in mind that the dump in Area CC was not only unearthed to its full perimeter and depth (leaving the baulks between its squares unexcavated), but its entire content was also dry-sifted (using a 0.50 × 0.50 cm-wide mesh).

The dump (that is, the layer of potsherds) is attributed to the main part of the Byzantine period based on the 5th–6th/7th century CE date of the great majority of the pottery types retrieved; however, parts of it may have been used for shorter periods of time within the 5th–6th/7th century CE (Fig. 6.4). The latest identifiable coins that came from the dump are dated to the mid-6th century CE, which allows a *terminus ante quem* for the dump within this period (Chapter 18). However, the possibility that the dump continued to be in use until the late 6th or even early 7th century CE cannot be excluded. To make it clear, over 260 identifiable coins were retrieved from Area CC, more than 150 from the dump; the latest coins from the dump are dated to the mid-6th century CE (two *nummia* of the Vandal king Hilderic dated to 523–530 and an anonymous Vandalic palm tree coin, attributed to the days of Justinian I, Chapter 18: Nos. 319–321). The majority of the coins (over 95%) that came from the area are dated within the 4th–6th centuries CE; this is also true for the majority of the coins that came from the dump itself (over 85%). Still, there are surface coin finds from Area CC that post-date the mid-6th century CE. It is unclear whether the two surface find 7th century CE issues (a *follis* of Phocas, 602–610 CE and an anonymous Arab-Byzantine *follis*, 647–670 CE; Chapter 18: Nos. 349, 356) were

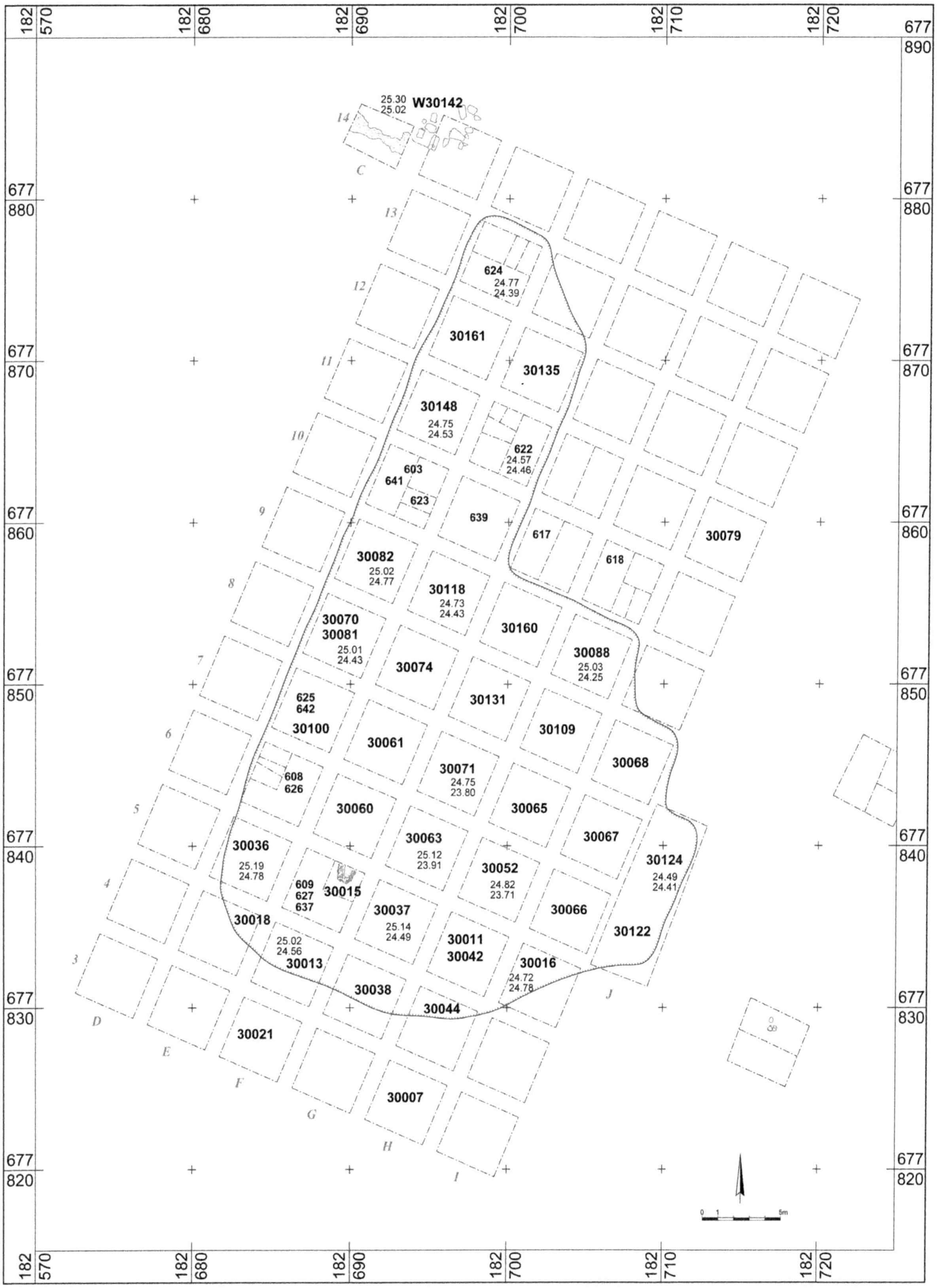

Fig. 6.1: Plan of Area CC.

Fig. 6.2: Area CC, aerial view.

somehow related to the dumping activities in the area, as there are few other later surface find coins of the 8th–19th centuries CE found in the area (Chapter 18: Nos. 359, 361, 365, 379, 380). There is also an Ayyubid *fals* (Chapter 18: No. 369) that came from a fill far from the dump area (Square I11). Most if not all of the dump's inorganic contents likely represent domestic refuse originating from the inhabited areas of the town farther to the west, though possibly also from nearby activity areas (as attested from the winepresses, field [agricultural] towers and tombs located in its vicinity, cf. chapters above and below). Since the excavated area was utilized in antiquity not only for dumping urban waste, but also for agricultural, industrial, and funerary designations, it was likely characterized by temporary and/or quasi-permanent human presence virtually year-round.

Based on the finds, it seems that the Area CC dump reflects a variety of activities and behaviors carried out in its immediate environs. These could have included, for instance, food preparation and consumption (e.g., by agricultural/industrial laborers, mourners/visitors at tombs, passers-by who stopped in the area on their way to or from the town or along the Jaffa–Caesarea road, etc.) and the storage of foodstuffs and agricultural/industrial products. A few bone objects and other miscellanea were recorded as well (Chapter 17). While the storage of foodstuffs is normally associated—from a ceramic viewpoint—with storage vessels, the former and other "domestic" behaviors are most typically reflected by various table, cooking, and utilitarian wares, as well as lamps (for the latter, cf. Chapter 14). It may be added that the distribution among the table, cooking and storage vessels in the potsherds recovered from the dump shows a statistical preference (over 70%) for the latter group (based on rim count). Among these storage vessels, two complete Gaza type amphora (Majcherek, "Gazan Amphorae," Type 4) were recovered (filled with earth) from the dump (cf. Chapter 13.1: Fig. 13.12: 11, 12); these, together with the "Samaritan" lamps, form the only pottery vessel-types that were unearthed in a complete form.

Fig. 6.3: Area CC, the refuse dump; (a) L30013, Square F4, looking northeast; (b) L30015, Square F5, looking northeast; (c) L30042, Square H5, looking northwest; (d) L30038, Square G4, looking northwest.

A breakdown of the dump's contents shows that in terms of quantity, most of the finds were potsherds (cf. Chapters 13, 14). After the potsherds were animal bones and mollusc remains (Chapters 20, 21), followed by glass production refuse and fragmented glass vessels (Chapter 16) and, finally, the metal objects (Chapter 17) and coins (Chapter 18), albeit in much smaller quantities.

Some 130 intact and complete usable "Samaritan" lamps were unearthed in the dump. All in all, 1,100 lamps and lamp fragments are recorded in the excavation diaries. Approximately 180 complete (and nearly complete) profile lamps were catalogued (cf. Chapter 14). Three were found originally intact (namely with a sealed filling hole).

In addition to the refuse dump, the remnants of a collapsed wall (Wall 30142) partially built of carved and uncarved stones was uncovered in Squares C14 and D14, in the northwestern part of the area, revealing no datable finds.

Based on the proximity, location and isolation of Area CC from any other substantially inhabited site, it has been suggested that the deposits in Area CC are related to the activity of nearby Apollonia/Sozousa and do not represent an independent feature (Pines, Sapir-Hen and Tal 2017: 200–202). Hence, the large assemblage of discarded animal bones does not represent the refuse of animals raised for their meat alone, but rather the discard of large animals used for agriculture and burden outside of the town perimeters, differing from the local disposal of consumption refuse within the town. This notion is supported by all recorded archaeozoological characteristics (Chapter 20). The transfer of refuse material out to the large dump located in the hinterland most probably required the existence of a well-organized garbage disposal mechanism, possibly supervised by a governing body.

The posited mechanism for the organized disposal of these animals outside of the town (together with other types of waste) may represent both the immediate disposal of the animals used in the hinterland and the public refuse system that aimed at emptying hazardous material from the town's inhabited areas on a regular basis (cf. for example Peña 2007: 308). Schiffer (1972: 162) suggested that with an increase

Fig. 6.4: Area CC, piles of pottery fragments from the refuse dump after being washed, counted and sorted.

in site size and population, a correlation between use and discard locations decreases, and an increase of specialized discard areas and refuse transport develops. Indeed, during the 5th, 6th and 7th centuries CE, the site of Apollonia/Sozousa reached its greatest size and became an important urban center. In accordance with Schiffer's suggestion, these results imply that communal and household dumping inside the town had been minimized to local consumption leftovers (i.e., the refuse dumps presented in Sapir-Hen, Pines and Tal 2014), probably due to the population's increase and demand for more living space. Most animals thrown in the dump in Apollonia/Sozousa's hinterland were used for plough work while a very few (mainly caprines and perhaps cattle as well) were discarded following—most probably local—consumption. This assumption agrees with the spatial-archaeological analysis of the refuse dump in Area CC and its surrounding agricultural area as previously referenced (cf. Tal and Taxel 2017).

The discard and burial of large animals in the inhabited area of the town was not only a potential health hazard, but also a waste of usable space. The centralization and transport of refuse out to the hinterland obviously served an additional agricultural purpose, well known from classical-period Latin and Jewish sources. Bone and other organic material, together with pottery sherds, reduce erosion and fasten any available nutrients into the soil; hence, it was believed to improve its fertility. The methods of fertilization of agricultural lands are detailed in some Latin sources (e.g., Cato, *De Agri Cultura*; Varro, *Rerum Rusticarum*; Columella, *De Re Rustica*), as well as Jewish ones (Feliks 1990: 82–86 with references therein). The latter, although relating in many cases to religious regulations and restrictions in the agriculture of the Land of Israel for Jews, most probably partially applied to the habits of their neighbors, the Samaritans (who have been identified as the users of the refuse dump in the hinterland), given their spiritual, mental and geographical affinity. More recurrent fertilizers are excrements of cattle, sheep, and other large domesticated animals (camels and equids), as well as poultry, sometimes mixed together with agricultural (e.g., straw and fruit and vegetable) waste and domestic rubbish. However, references are also given to blood, ash, earth (e.g., silt) and dust, which in many cases relates to potsherds and earth mixed with dismantled building materials (see, in this respect, Schnebel 1925: 87–93).

No less important are the references in the Jewish sources to the assembling of these varied fertilizers (and other waste material) in heaps in agricultural lands outside the inhabited areas of the settlement. Hence, the term *ʾšph* (ashpah) refers in many cases to the dumped waste of the household (*ʾšph šbbyt*), which included organic and inorganic material and excluded carcasses which were discarded outside the inhabited settlement (*ʾšph šbšwq*) (Feliks 1990: 91 with references therein). The latter term is appropriate for the refuse dump of Area CC, which included, as stated above, potsherds, animal bones and mollusc remains as well as glass-production refuse and fragmented glass vessels, together with metal finds, bone objects and numerous coins. Most of these components are mentioned in the sources as potential fertilizers. When buried in the soil for a lengthy period of time, these components created an upper layer of humus-compost, a mature, organic (and inorganic) decomposed and recycled soil amendment which was later dug out and spread around crop fields. The sources attest to the practice and appreciation of this method (*ibid.*)

It may be summarized that the finds analysis of Area CC enabled the performance of an in-depth analysis aimed towards the understanding of the relationship between the town and its immediate periphery during Late Antiquity. Through this understanding of the animal economic exploitation within the site's perimeters and in its hinterland, it may be concluded that waste management and utilization in agriculture and various industries were prevalent in the 5th and 6th centuries CE in Palestine (Fig. 6.5). These results reflect different aspects of identity and behavior of the Late Antiquity inhabitants of Apollonia/Sozousa (specifically the Samaritan community), highlighting their association with organic and inorganic refuse and suggesting that household and industrial waste were treated in different ways.

Fig. 6.5: Area CC, aerial view, looking south.

REFERENCES

Feliks, Y. 1990. *Agriculture in Eretz-Israel in the Period of the Bible and Talmud: Basic Farming Methods and Implements*. Jerusalem (Hebrew).

Peña, J.T. 2007. *Roman Pottery in the Archaeological Record*. Cambridge.

Pines, M., Sapir-Hen, L. and Tal, O. 2017. Consumption and Disposal Practices in the Southern Levant in Late Antiquity: Animal Bones from 'Απολλωνία/Σώζουσα's Hinterland as a Case Study. *Zeitschrift des Deutschen Palästina-Vereins* 133: 186–204.

Sapir-Hen, L., Pines, M. and Tal, O. 2014. Animal Economy and Social Diversity in Byzantine Apollonia/Sozousa. *Levant* 46: 371–381.

Schiffer, M.B. 1972. Archaeological Context and Systemic Context. *American Antiquity* 37: 156–165.

Schnebel, M. 1925. *Die Landwirtschaft im hellenistischen Ägypten*. Munich.

Tal, O. and Taxel, I. 2017. More than Trash – Cultic Use of Pottery Lamps Found in Late Antique Dumps: Apollonia (Sozousa) as a Test Case. In: Tal, O. and Weiss, Z., eds. *Expressions of Cult in the Southern Levant in the Greco-Roman Period. Manifestations in Text and Material Culture* (Contextualizing the Sacred 6). Turnhout: 181–193.

CHAPTER 7

AREAS CC2, DD1, DD2, DD3 AND TT8 (1996, 2012–2013)

Itai Elad, Tamar Harpak and Oren Tal

Area CC2, which includes three excavated squares, is located south of Area CC. One square was dug during the 2012 season and two additional squares were opened during the 2013 season. Wall 611 oriented north–south and is built of carved stones and fieldstones with two surviving courses (Fig. 7.1). It is 3 m long and 0.60 m thick. The area revealed no finds (Fig. 7.2).

Area DD1 (combined on the plan with Area DD) is in the north part of the excavated hinterland area; it is located west of Area DD2 and east of Area DD3 (Fig. 1.2). It holds 22 squares which were opened during the 2012 and 2013 seasons. The main feature is a "four-rectangular" plan winepress. The area features several other installations:

A CIRCULAR PLASTERED INSTALLATION (INSTALLATION 755)

The circular installation (Installation 755) is 4 m in diameter. The wall is 0.10 m thick wall with remnants of plaster on its inner side. A single course of stones was preserved and its function was not clarified. A few Byzantine sherds were found inside during the excavation (Figs. 7.3–7.4).

A HEARTH (INSTALLATION 40005)

The hearth is circular in plan, partially preserved and built from fieldstones bearing ash remains with no binding material. It is 1 m in diameter with two courses preserved. No datable finds were discovered (Fig. 7.3).

INSTALLATION (INSTALLATION 40007)

This installation is collapsed, circular in plan and defined as accumulation of stone without datable finds (Fig. 7.3).

WINEPRESS (INSTALLATION 769)

The remains of a winepress were unearthed, including a treading floor, an intermediary (filtration) vat and a collecting/settling (and fermentation) vat (Fig. 7.5). The treading floor (Floor 784) was partially preserved. It was built of *kurkar* stones forming an infrastructure for a plaster surface, whose remains were still visible in the northwestern corner. Based on the partially preserved walls that delimited the treading floor, the floor can be estimated at about 3 × 3 m in size. Wall 786 divides the treading floor and the two square-shaped vats located to its west. The northern vat is a shallow settling vat of a 0.60 m deep (Installation 769; about 1.35 × 1.80 m). The must would have flowed from the treading floor to the northern vat first through a channel in a wall (Wall 786), and then continued through an outlet channel in another wall (Wall 772) to the deep collecting vat located to its south. The southern collecting vat

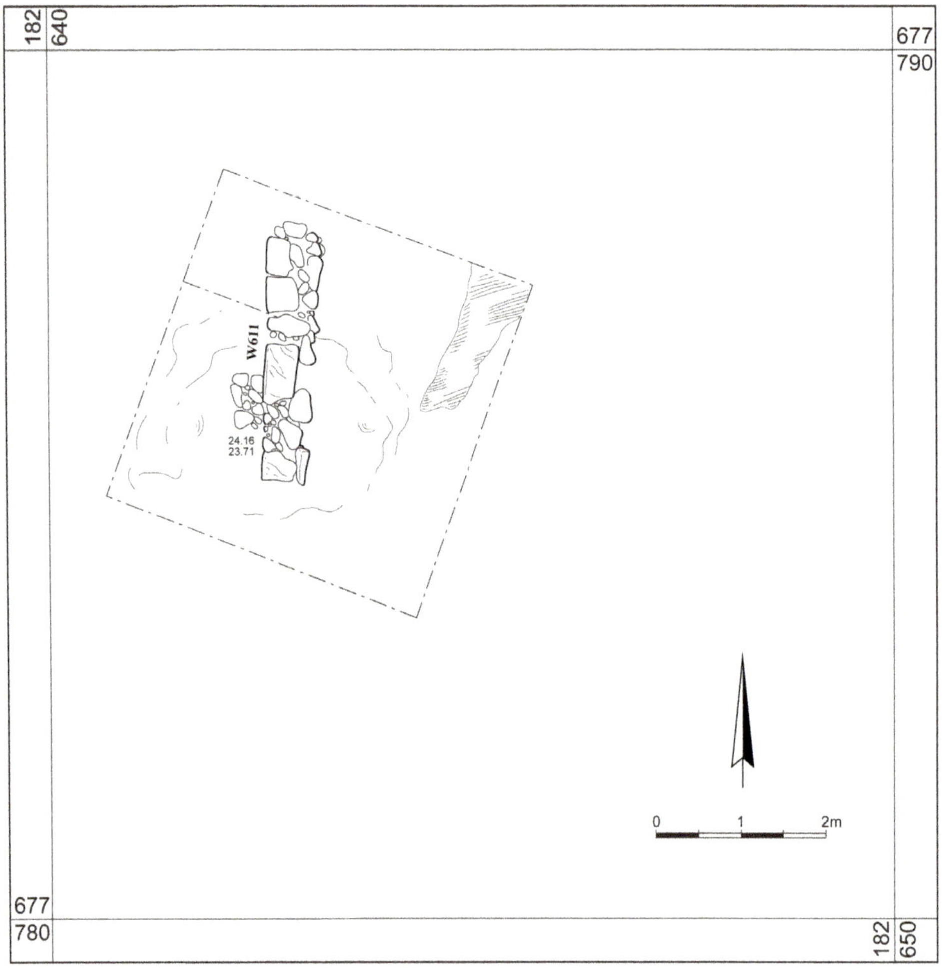

Fig. 7.1: Plan of Area CC2.

Fig. 7.2: Area CC2 and Area CC, aerial view, looking north.

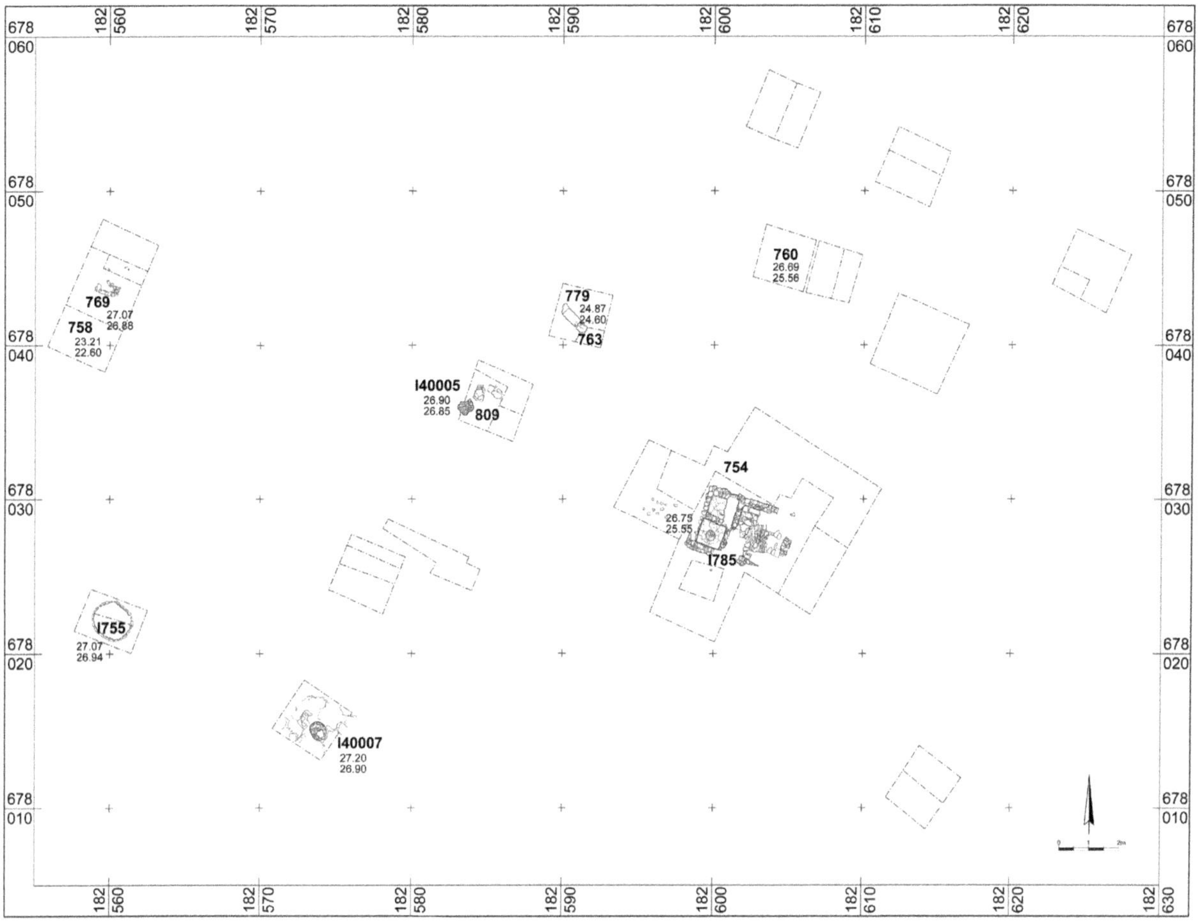

Fig. 7.3: Plan of Area DD1.

(Installation 785) is about 1.40 × 1.40 m and is approximately 1.20 m deep (capacity of which is 2,352 liters) (Fig. 7.6). A shallow circular sump was found on its floor (some 0.10 m deep). Both of the vats' inner sides and floors were coated with a layer of gray plaster.

The winepress uncovered in this area belongs to the "four-rectangular" plan, which is the most common type in the center of Israel during the Roman and Byzantine periods (Frankel 1999: 149–151) (Fig. 7.7). The use of plaster rather than mosaic floors may suggest that the winepress was built during the Roman period. Gray plaster is also known to be indicative for that period (Porath 1989: 74–75). Both the plaster and the scattered pottery sherds in the winepress attest to a date in the Late Roman or Early Byzantine period (3rd–4th centuries CE).

It may be added that anomalies in the bedrock whose function remains unclear were also exposed in Area DD1.

Area DD2 is the northernmost area excavated (Figs. 1.2, 7.8), where 15 squares were dug during the first 2012 season. Remains of poorly preserved (Gaza type) Late Roman jars were found that were used primarily for infant burials (Fig. 7.9; Chapters 11 and 13: Fig. 13.16 for the recovered jars). Although randomly scattered throughout the area, the jars were interred along a north–south axis. Part of a *kurkar* outcrop with small hewn niches was exposed to the west of the jars (Figs. 7.8, 7.10–7.12). These rectangular rock quarries adjacent to the jar burial may be a possible indication for a primary or secondary burial. The area shows some pottery fragments of Byzantine date and some animal bones, especially at its northeastern end.

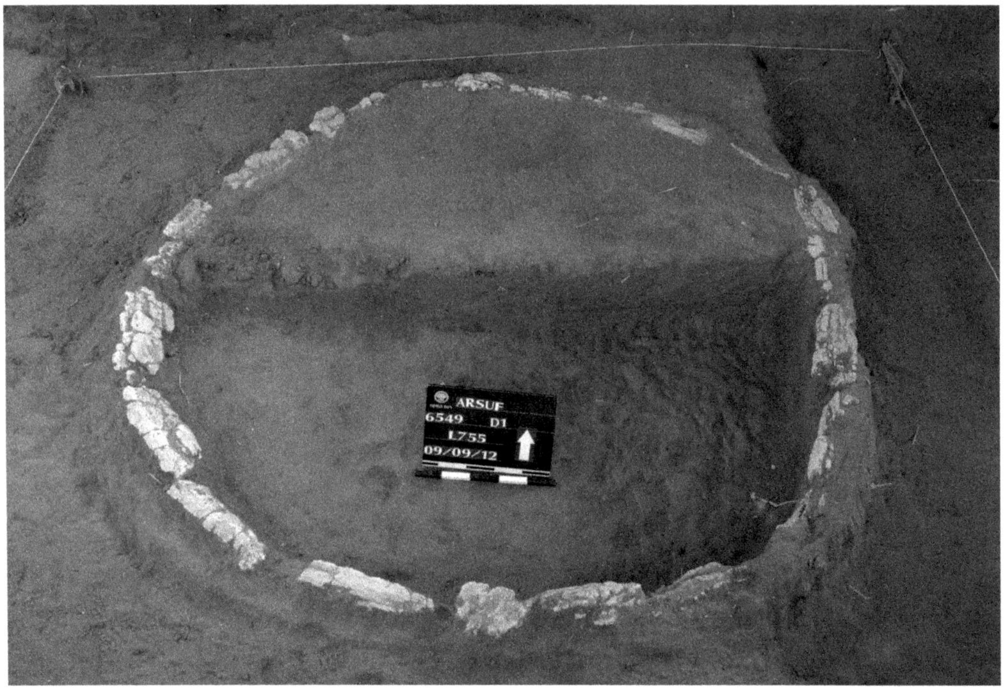

Fig. 7.4: Area DD1, installation (I755), looking north.

Fig. 7.5: Area DD1, plan of winepress (I769).

Fig. 7.6: Area DD1, winepress, the southern collecting vat (1785), looking north.

Fig. 7.7: Area DD1, aerial view of the winepress (1769), looking south.

Area DD3 is divided between a southern DD3/1 area and a western DD3/2 area; both are located to the west of Area DD2. Area DD3 is located on the north–west side of the excavation (Fig. 1.2). It includes 11 squares which were dug during the 2012 season and were deepened during the second 2013 season (especially in Area DD3/2), due to the indication of tomb finds. In addition, a winepress was also revealed in the area's southern part.

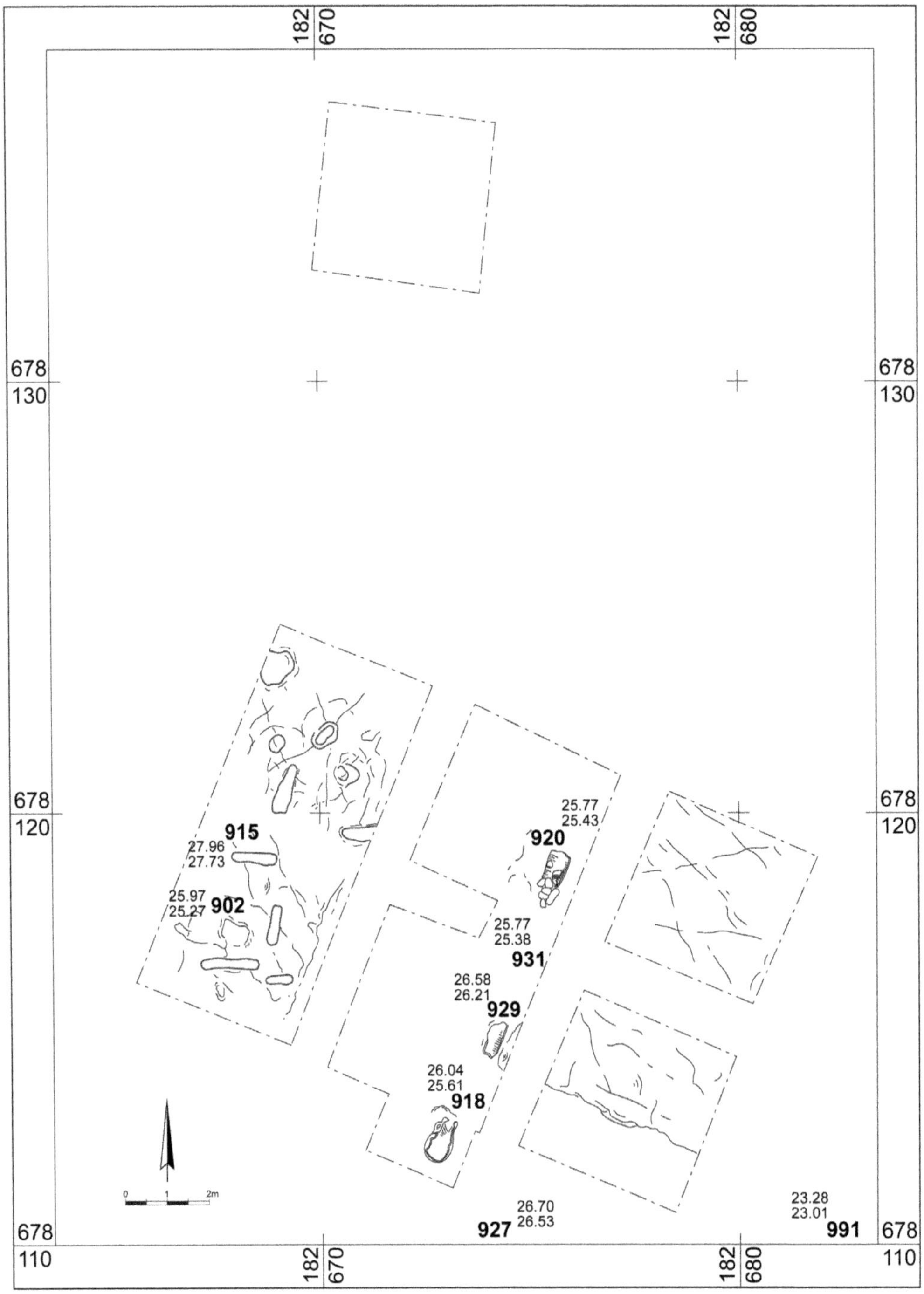

Fig. 7.8: Plan of Area DD2.

WINEPRESS (INSTALLATION 873)

The remains of a small winepress were revealed in a poor state of preservation. A 1.50 × 1 m segment of the treading floor's infrastructure has survived, comprised of small- to medium-sized *kurkar* stones (Locus 865). It is assumed that this is the infrastructure for a plaster surface, of which some scattered remnants were still visible during excavations. To the southeast of the treading floor, a circular collecting/settling

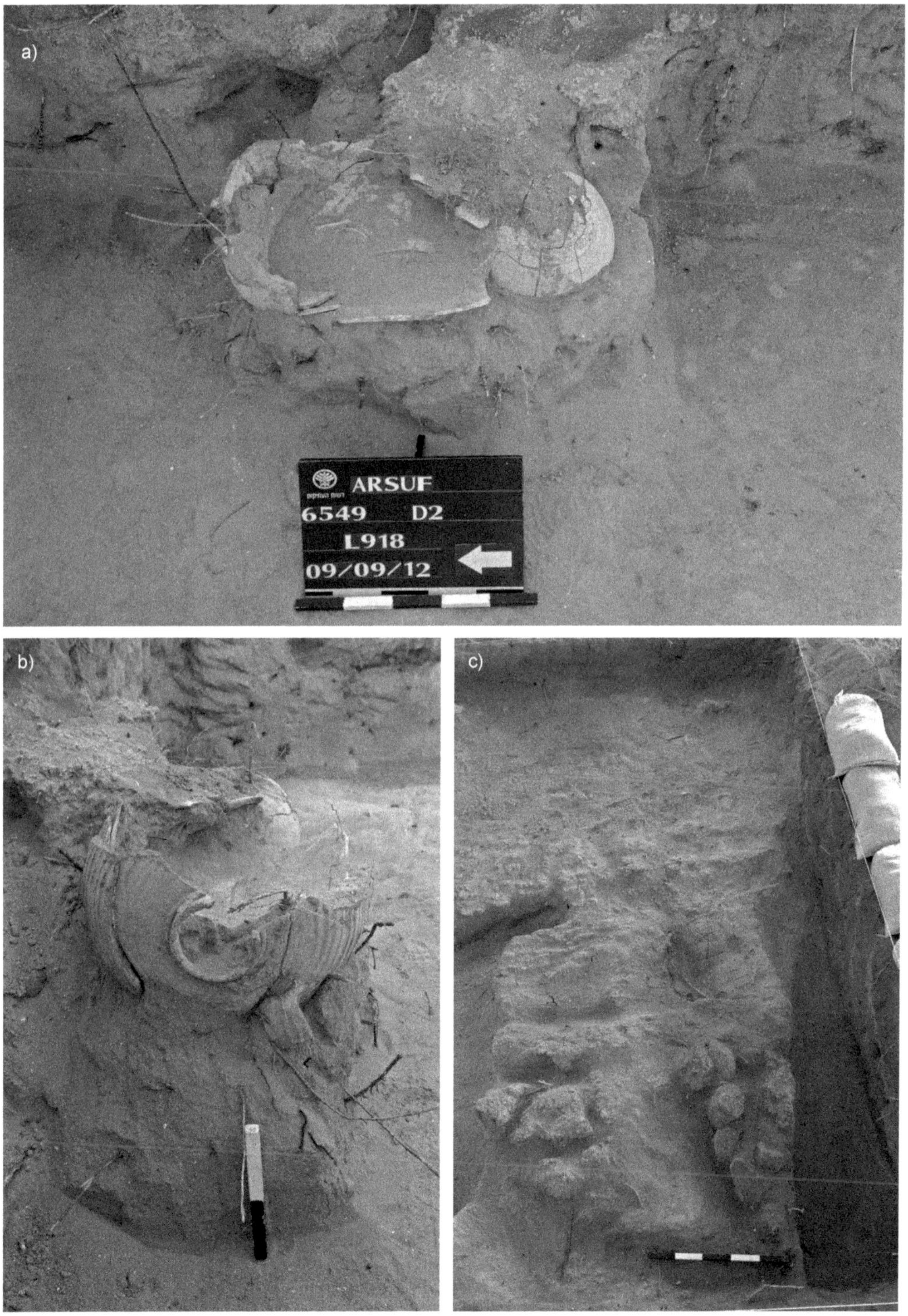

Fig. 7.9: Area DD2, jar burials; (a) L918, looking east; (b) L918, looking south; (c) L920, looking south.

(and fermentation) vat was found (Locus 873; 1.30 m in diameter, 2.25 m. deep, with a capacity of some 2,986 liters). Its walls were built of small- to medium-sized stones and the inner sides were coated with a thick layer of dense gray plaster. The plaster floor of the vat did not survive but its infrastructure did. A round shallow sump was found in its center (Figs. 7.13–7.14).

Fig. 7.10: Area DD2, hewn niches in the *kurkar* (L902), looking north.

Fig. 7.11: Area DD2, hewn niches in the *kurkar* (L902), looking west.

In the fill inside the collecting vat, a considerably large amount of Byzantine-period pottery was found, indicating that it was used as a refuse pit once the winepress ceased to function, probably late in the Byzantine or in the beginning of the Early Islamic period (Chapter 13).

The winepress belongs to the type of plain and relatively small wine-making installations. These winepresses were usually built in the area where grapevines were cultivated and used for relatively small-scale production. The exact date when the winepress was built and used is unclear, but on the basis of building technique and the use of gray plaster, it should probably be dated to either the Roman or Byzantine periods.

TOMBS (41001, 41002, 41003, 41004, 41005, 42000, 42001; FIG. 7.15)

Tomb 41005 was discovered during the 2012 season (Locus 880) and excavated in full in 2013. It is built of small and medium-sized fieldstones in an east–west orientation. It is 2.60 m long, 1 m wide and 0.70 m deep (Fig. 7.16). Primary burial of an articulated skeleton with its head towards the west facing south was found in this cist grave. The tomb yielded no finds, but was assigned to the Hellenistic period based on a similar orientation to nearby tombs of that period (Chapter 11).

Tomb 41001 was first unearthed during the 2012 season (Locus 871) and excavated in full in 2013. It is marked (or covered) by four large blocks of limestone (which is not native to the area) and encompasses a pit grave 1.50 m long, 0.70 m wide and 0.50 m deep in an east–west orientation (Fig. 7.17). Following

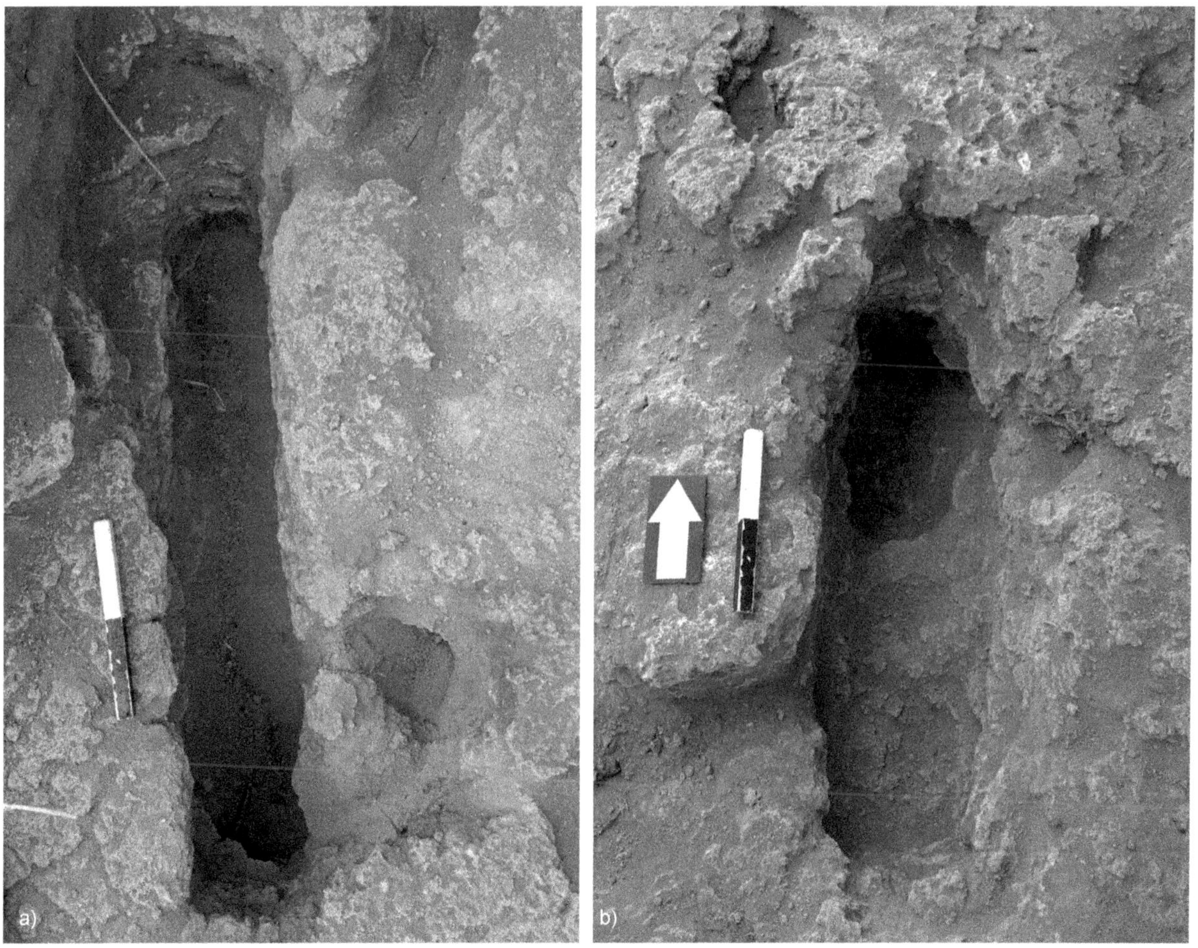

Fig. 7.12: Area DD2, hewn niches in the kurkar (L902); (a–b) in detail.

the removal of the stones, only a skull was found, and it is likely to assume that it is a secondary burial. Inside the tomb, a small Hellenistic cooking jug was found (Chapter 13: Fig. 13.19: 2).

Tomb 41003 was first recovered during the 2012 season (Locus 869) and excavated in full in 2013. It is marked (or covered) by three large blocks of limestone encompassing a pit grave of 1.50 m long, 0.80 m wide and 0.60 m deep in an east–west orientation (Fig. 7.18). Following the removal of the stones and after digging out the soil up to 1 m deep, no bones were found. However, an intact Hellenistic unguentarium was found (Chapter 13: Fig. 13.19: 4), attesting to a 3rd–early 2nd century BCE use. An additional tomb (Tomb 41004), located north of Tomb 41003, was found following the removal of the earth of the latter. It was marked (or covered) by two medium-sized blocks of limestone (Fig. 7.19). These blocks covered a 1.10 m long, 0.50 m wide and 0.50 m deep pit grave in an east–west orientation that revealed no finds. Another tomb (Tomb 41002), located south of Tomb 41003, was also found following the removal of earth of Tomb 41003. It was marked by two large blocks of limestone (Fig. 7.20). These blocks covered a 0.90 m long, 0.60 m wide and 0.50 m deep pit grave in an east–west orientation that also revealed no finds. Human bones of the deceased, if truly buried in these tombs, were probably decomposed due to soil conditions.

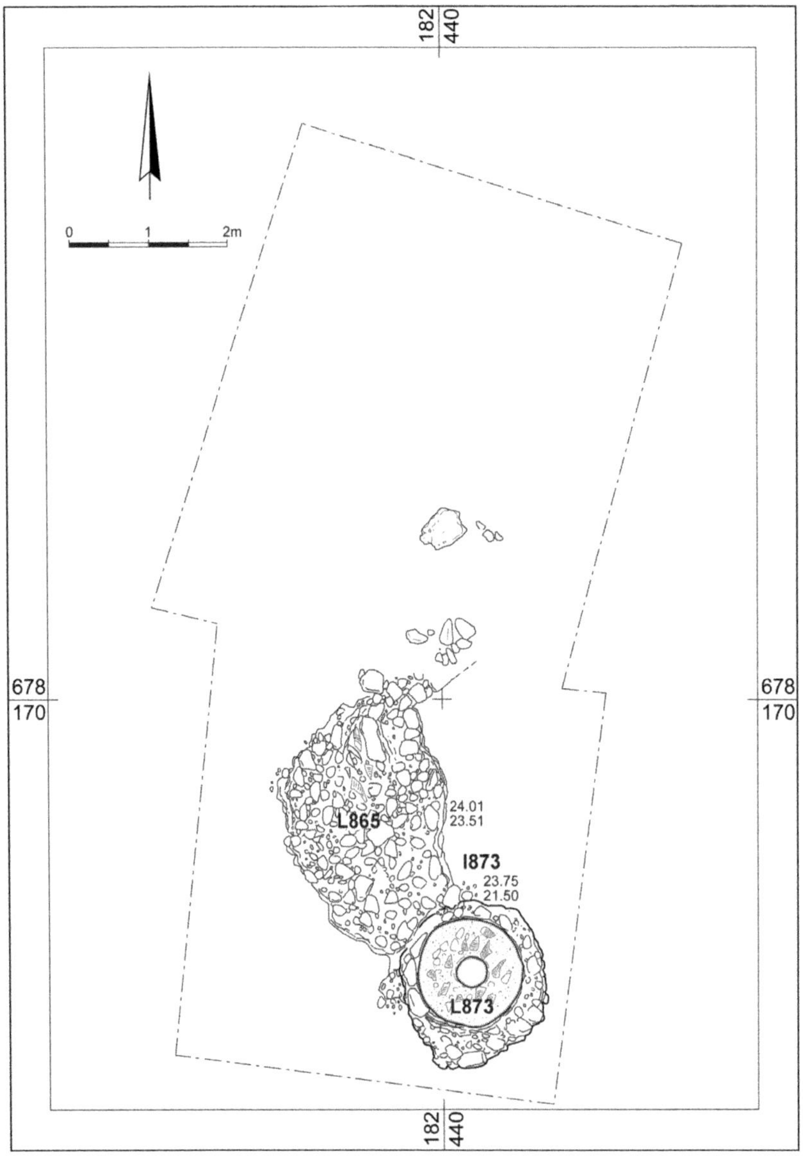

Fig. 7.13: Area DD3/1, plan of the winepress (I873).

Fig. 7.14: Area DD3/1, winepress (I873), looking north.

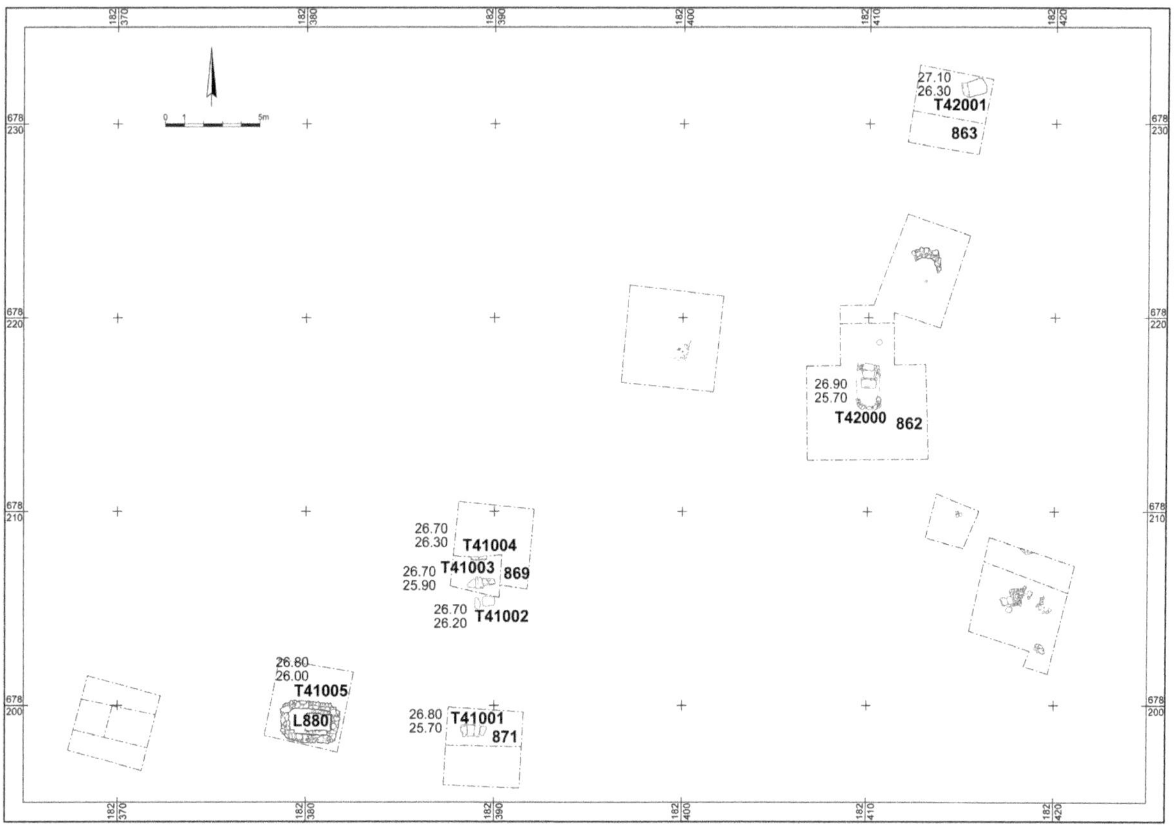

Fig. 7.15: Plan of Area DD3.

Fig. 7.16: Area DD3/2, cist grave (T41005), looking northwest.

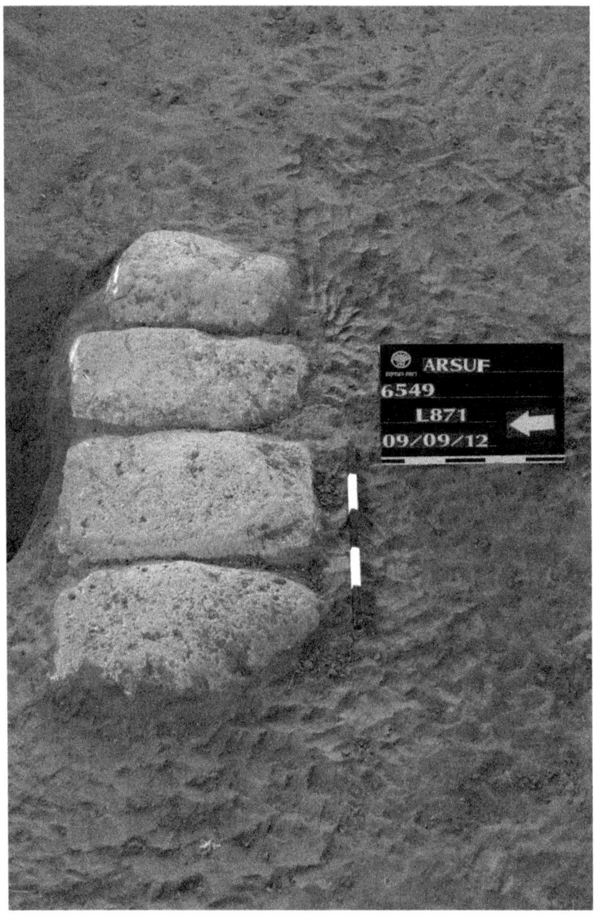

Fig. 7.17: Area DD3/2, pit grave (T41001), looking east.

Tomb 42001 (Locus 863) was discovered during the 2012 season and excavated in full in 2013. It is a 1.60 m long, 1 m wide and 0.70 m deep pit grave in an east–west orientation, partially marked (or covered) by two large blocks of limestone (0.60 × 0.35 m). It yielded non-articulated human bones (Chapter 11) together with fragments of a Hellenistic jug/jar and flask which were found close to surface level (Chapter 13: Fig. 13.19: 3, 5).

Tomb 42000 (Locus 862) was unearthed during the 2012 season and excavated in full in 2013.

It is a 2.10 m long, 1.40 m wide and 0.75 m deep cist grave built of small and medium-sized fieldstones in an north–south orientation, partially covered by three large blocks, one (on the north) of *kurkar* and two of limestone (0.60 × 0.30 m on average) (Fig. 7.21). Only a few human bones were recovered (Chapter 11).

Fig. 7.18: Area DD3/2, pit grave (T41003), looking north.

Fig. 7.19: Area DD3/2, pit grave (T869), looking north.

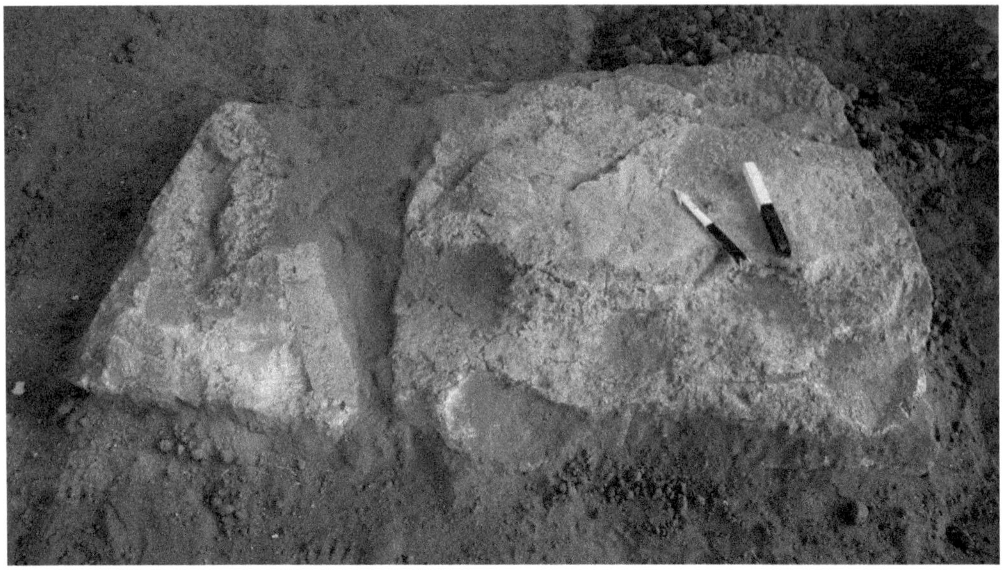

Fig. 7.20: Area DD3/2, pit grave (T41002), looking north.

Fig. 7.21: Area DD3/2, pit grave (T42000), looking north.

Overall, seven tombs were found in Area DD3 (Tombs 41001, 41002, 41003, 41004, 41005, 42000, 42001). Given the pottery evidence, they are dated either to the Hellenistic or Early Roman periods. An almost complete profile Early Roman cooking pot (Chapter 13: Fig. 13.19: 1) was found in the southern part of Area DD3 and may attest to yet another burial that did not survive.

Area TT8 is an appendage of one of the trial trenches that were excavated by means of mechanical tools in 1996, located about 70 m east of the eastern Medieval town wall (Roll 1999: 46; Fig. 7.22).

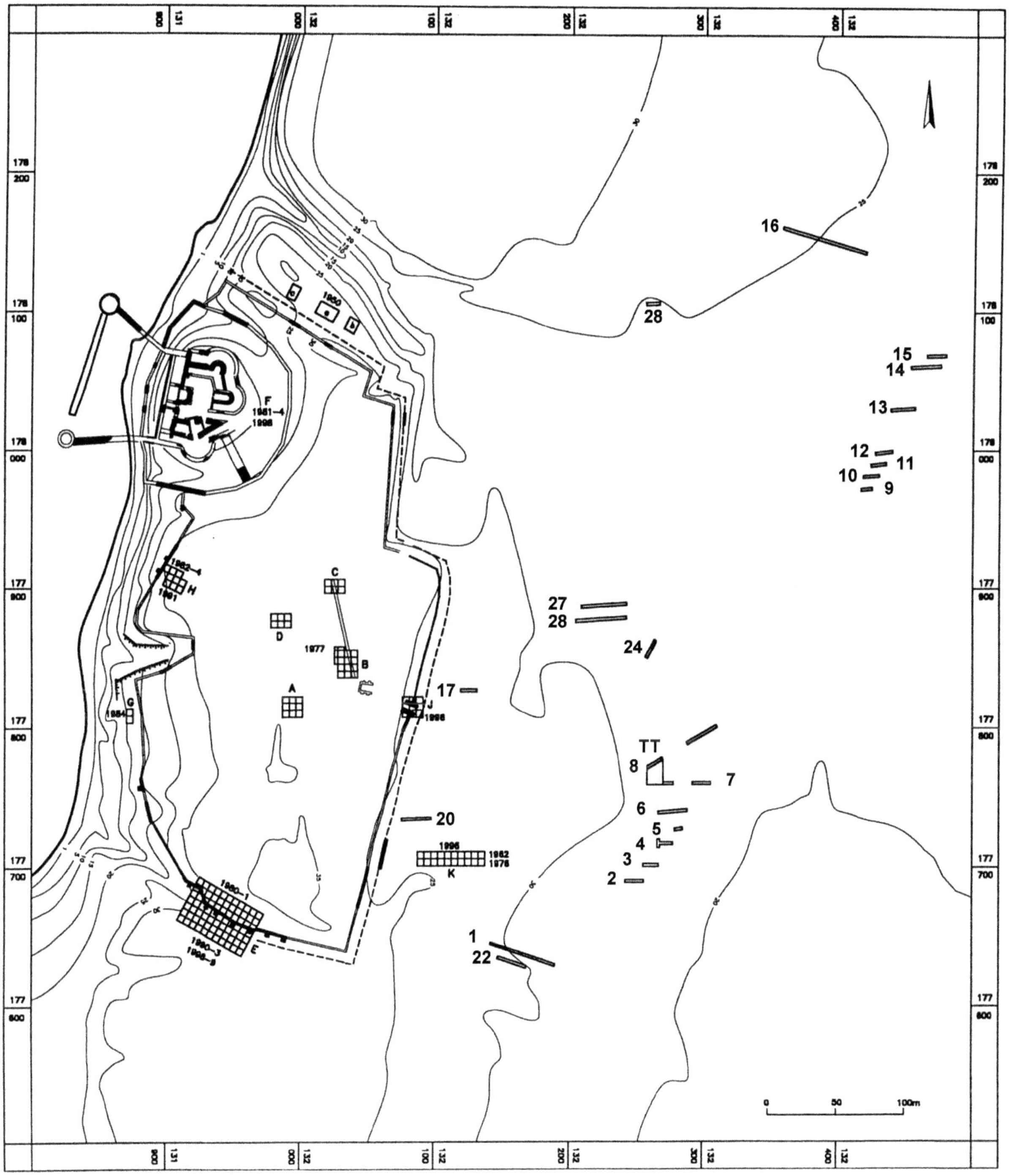

Fig. 7.22: Plan of the trial trenches excavated in the southeastern parts of Israel Military Industries Ltd. in 1996 (modified after Roll 1999: Fig. 1.2).

The trenches provided substantial archaeological finds (notably pottery), mainly from the Byzantine period, but no architectural remains. However, in the easternmost trenches no finds were unearthed. In the area between Trenches 7 and 8, four burials were located: two cist tombs, each containing a skeleton (Tomb 1 and Tomb 2); one child burial in a jar (Tomb 3); and a pit burial (Tomb 4) carved in the bedrock (Fig. 7.23). No finds were uncovered in these graves, but the pottery found in their surroundings indicates that the cist and jar burials belong to either the Late Roman or Early Byzantine times (3rd–4th century CE).

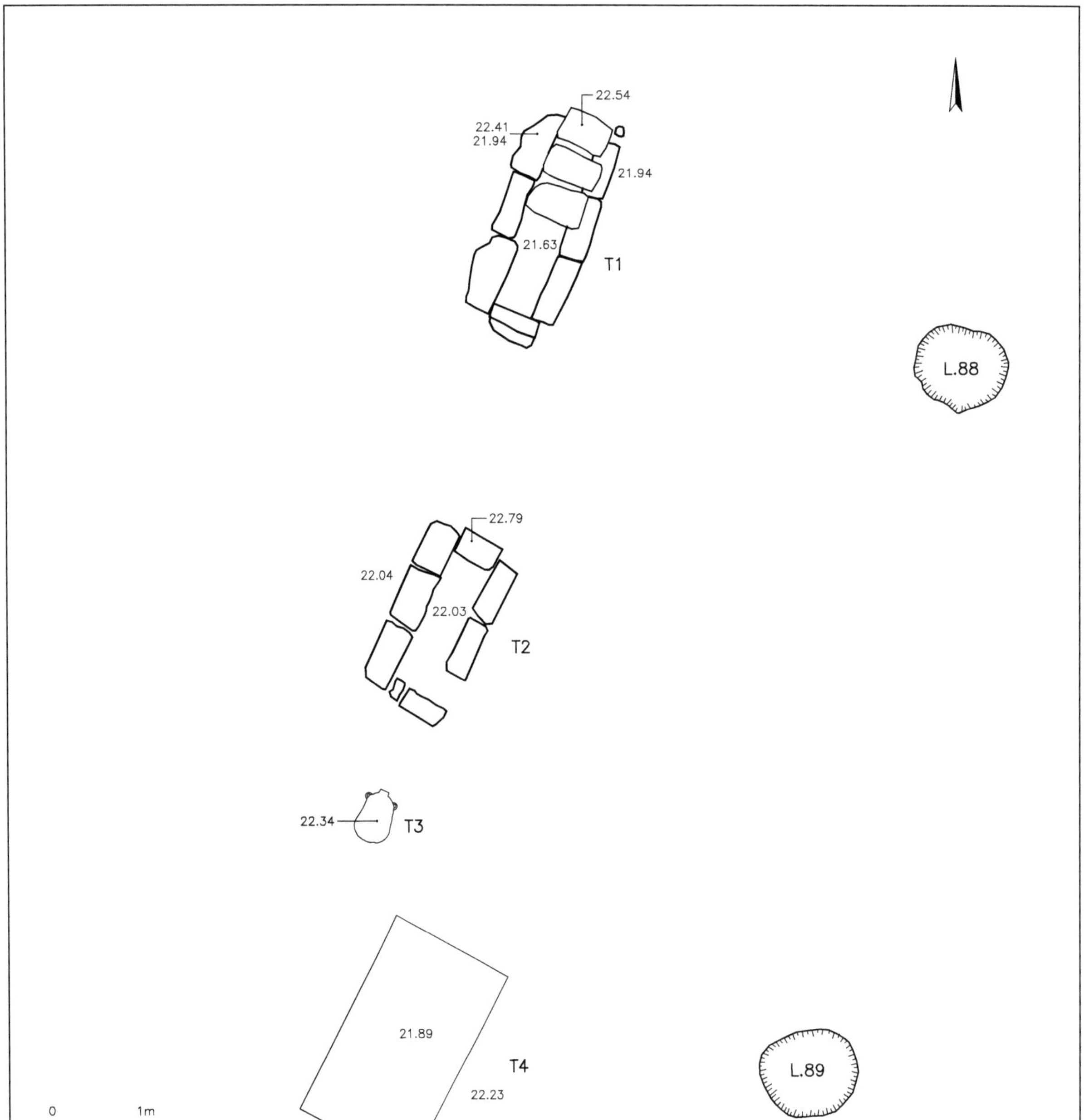

Fig. 7.23: Plan of Area TT8.

Tomb 1 is a 2.25 m long, 1.10 m wide and 0.75 m deep cist grave built of large *kurkar* blocks in a north–south orientation, discovered partially covered by three large *kurkar* blocks (0.60 × 0.35 m on average) (Fig. 7.24). The tomb included a skeleton of an adult in primary burial, oriented north–south.

Tomb 2 is a 2.05 m long, 1.10 m wide and 0.75 m deep cist grave built of large *kurkar* blocks in a north–south orientation (Fig. 7.25). The tomb included a skeleton of an adult in primary burial, oriented north–south.

Tomb 3 is a jar burial (Fig. 7.26) in a Palestinian bag-shaped ridge-necked storage jar whose upper part was detached for the purpose (for the type cf. Kingsley 1994–95: Figs. 1: 4, 2: 1), whose date can be assigned to the 4th and 5th centuries CE. The jar included the bones of two infants (Chapter 11).

Indication of probable additional tombs (Tomb 4, Tomb 5 and Tomb 6) was noted in the western section of Area TT8 (Fig. 7.26), but these were left unexcavated.

It may be added that the chief burial ground of the Late Roman and especially Byzantine period of Apollonia/Sozousa extended along the north–south sandstone ridge, located about 1.50 km further to the east (see in this respect Tal 1995; Rudin 2016; Rudin *et al.* 2018; Agmon 2017, with references to more recent excavations).

Fig. 7.24: Area TT8, Tomb 1, looking south.

Fig. 7.25: Area TT8, Tomb 2, looking south.

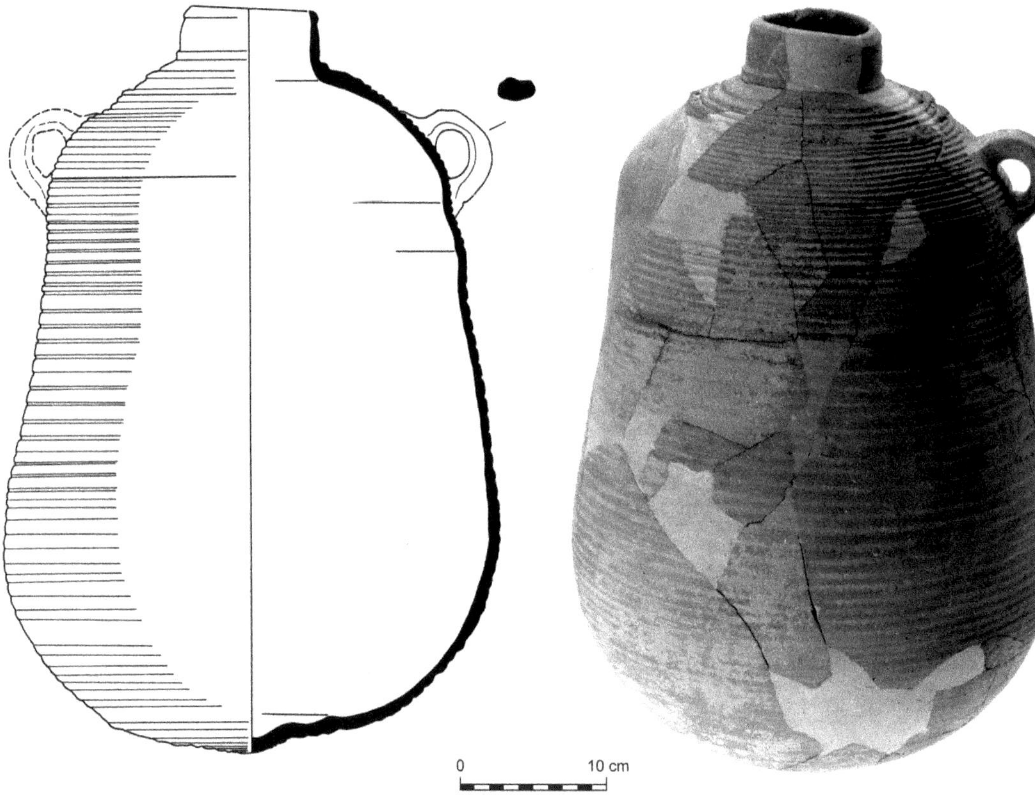

Fig. 7.26: Area TT8, jar burial (Tomb 3) after restoration.

REFERENCES

Agmon, Y. 2017. Kefar Shemaryahu. *Ḥadashot Arkheologiyot—Excavations and Surveys in Israel* 129. http://www.hadashot-esi.org.il/Report_Detail_Eng.aspx?id=25349&mag_id=125

Frankel, R. 1999. *Wine and Oil Production in Antiquity in Israel and Other Mediterranean Countries* (JSOT/ASOR Monograph Series 10). Sheffield.

Kingsley, S.A. 1994–95. Bag-Shaped Amphorae and Byzantine Trade: Expanding Horizons. *Bulletin of the Anglo-Israel Archaeological Society* 14: 39–56.

Porath, Y. 1989. Hydraulic Plaster of Aqueducts as a Chronological Indicator. In: Amit, D., Hirschfeld, Y. and Patrich Y., eds. *The Aqueducts of Ancient Palestine*. Jerusalem: 69–76 (Hebrew).

Roll, I. 1999. History of the Site, Its Research and Excavations. In: Roll, I. and Tal, O. *Apollonia-Arsuf: Final Report of the Excavations, Volume 1: The Persian and Hellenistic Periods (with Appendices on the Chalcolithic and Iron Age II Remains)* (Monograph Series of the Institute of Archaeology of Tel Aviv University 16). Tel Aviv: 1–62.

Rudin, T. 2016. *Roman–Byzantine Cemeteries and Tombs around Apollonia/Sozousa: The New Discoveries* (MA thesis, Tel Aviv University). Tel Aviv (Hebrew).

Rudin, T., Tal, O., Taxel I. and Feldstein, A. 2018. Two Burial Caves at Kefar Shemaryahu: More on Samaritan and Christian Interactions in the Byzantine-Period Central Coastal Plain. *Liber Annuus* 68: 269–302.

Tal, O. 1995. Roman–Byzantine Cemeteries and Tombs around Apollonia. *Tel Aviv* 22: 107–120.

CHAPTER 8

AREA M (2006, 2009)[1]

Oren Tal

This area is located at the far southern end of the excavated site, beyond the Roman peristyle villa (Area E) and the ravine enclosing the medieval walled town and to the west of the Mizpeh-Yam correctional facility (Fig. 1.2). The goal of the excavations here was to determine whether the Roman and Byzantine urban center of Apollonia/Sozousa had extended to this area.[2] Due to modern building activities over the years, large quantities of sandy fills were dumped in this area by bulldozers. In addition, an east–west pathway descending to the seashore was cut by a bulldozer along the southern edge of the ravine (forming the northern edge of the excavated area). Thus, prior to excavation, later fills (some 4 m thick) down to some 32 m above sea-level were removed by means of a mechanical tool (Fig. 8.1). In Squares F2, E2 and D2, two strata were identified belonging to two periods of occupation (Fig. 8.2). One was represented by a round refuse pit—entirely excavated (ca. 12 m maximum preserved diameter; 4.50 m deep)—containing substantial amounts of broken pottery (weighing some 15 tons), together with fragments of glass vessels and animal bones that had accumulated in a series of superimposed layers in Late Byzantine (6th–7th centuries CE) times (Fig. 8.3; see Chapters 13–14 and 20).[3] The date of these assemblages may be supported by the numismatic evidence; the latest coins recovered in the refuse pit of Area M belong to Maurice Tiberius (582–602 CE) (Chapter 18: Nos. 336, 337, 339–341), although there is also a post-reform (late 7th to mid-8th century) Umayyad coin (Chapter 18: No. 360) that we tend to consider as stray. The other occupational level, beneath the refuse pit, was represented by the lower end of a corner of two walls (Walls 7055 and 7058; Square D2), a small segment of another wall (Wall 7051; Square E2—a continuation of Wall 7055 to west) and a series of fallen sandstone ashlars (Square F2) (Fig. 8.4). Much of the related pottery is Late Roman/Early Byzantine. A 4th–5th century CE hoard of 21 bronze coins was also discovered in this level (see Chapter 18; Tal and Bijovsky 2017). Excavation in the two northern squares (F3 and E3) was stopped at a higher level once the natural yellow sand was reached. Excavation in the southwestern square (G3) showed that the wall uncovered there (Wall 7004) is just a one-layer retaining wall facing north, with a surface of *ḥamra* (red loam) soil behind it. This wall, together with two other walls to its north, formed a series of three descending terraces, apparently built some 4 m apart with an average height of ca. 0.40 m. Thus, Wall 7004 served as the retaining wall of the upper terrace, a robbed wall of the middle terrace (Wall 7063) and another (Wall 7054) of the lower terrace (Fig. 8.5). If there had been additional retaining walls further north, they were completely destroyed during the bulldozing of the pathway descending to the seashore. No tangible evidence has been found to indicate the nature of these terraces. The fertile *ḥamra* soil behind the upper retaining wall (Wall 7004), however, may suggest that they formed part of a terraced garden. Whether this garden was related to the peristyle villa to the north or to the buildings in the east, which have not been excavated, has not been clarified.

1 Chapter 8 is an archaeological update on earlier publication (Tal 2010: 110–112).

2 Apollonia/Sozousa is used here as reference to the Byzantine-period occupation (roughly 4th–7th centuries CE).

3 For the glass finds, cf. also Freestone, Jackson-Tal and Tal (2008); and for the animal bones Sapir-Hen, Pines and Tal (2014).

Fig. 8.1: Area M (on left), aerial view before excavation, 2006 (by courtesy of P. Bauman).

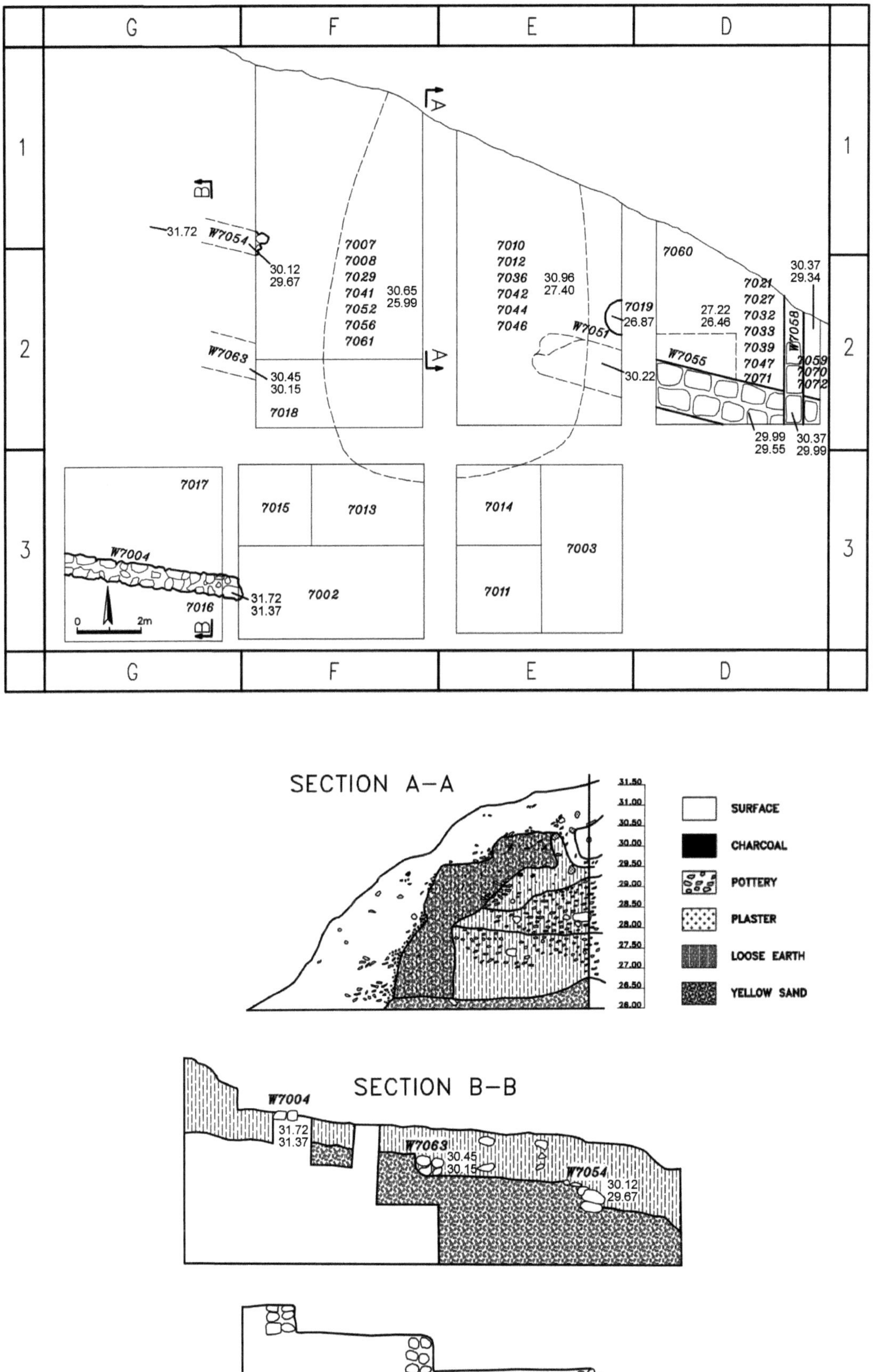

Fig. 8.2: Plan of Area M.

Fig. 8.3: Area M, the refuse pit; (a) L7010, looking west; (b) L7056, looking east.

Fig. 8.4: Area M, segmented walls; (a) 7051, looking east; (b) 7055, looking south; (c) 7058, looking north.

Fig. 8.5: Area M, segmented walls (cont.); (a) 7004, looking east; (b) 7063, looking east; (c) 7054, looking west.

REFERENCES

Freestone I.C., Jackson-Tal, R.E. and Tal, O. 2008. Raw Glass and the Production of Glass Vessels at Late Byzantine Apollonia-Arsuf, Israel. *Journal of Glass Studies* 50: 67–80.

Sapir-Hen, L., Pines, M. and Tal, O. 2014. Animal Economy and Social Diversity in Byzantine Apollonia/Sozousa. *Levant* 46: 371–381.

Tal, O. 2010. Notes and News: Apollonia-Arsuf 2006, 2009. *Israel Exploration Journal* 60: 107–114.

Tal, O. and Bijovsky, G. 2017. A Hoard of Fourth–Fifth Century CE Copper Coins from Sozousa. *Israel Numismatic Research* 12: 147–158.

CHAPTER 9

AREA N (2002) AND AREA N1 (2017)

Oren Tal

Excavations in Area N commenced in February 2002 in the context of operation works for the Apollonia National Park gate, namely the main entrance to the park southeast of the medieval town wall (Fig. 1.2). A machine-dug trench revealed a concentration of potsherds that originated in a refuse pit. A trial excavation consisting of four squares (5 × 5 m each) yielded no architectural remains except for pottery of Late Byzantine date (see Chapter 13) and lumps of melted glass, which can be supplemented by a single coin-find of the first half of the 6th century CE (Chapter 18: No. 312). Later, another trench was mechanically dug (south of the squares) in order to build a wall adjoining the newly built entrance. The excavated soil showed evidence of glass production, and mechanical excavation was halted immediately. Two squares (5 × 5 m each) were opened, and the area of the glass furnace floor was cleaned, revealing its firing area on the west end and its melting chamber on the east. The fill included lumps of melted glass, fragments of burnt *ḥamra* (red loam), vitrified and plain bricks, small chunks of charcoal, and several ribbed potsherds, stones, and a few animal bones.[1]

Additional work was performed on the glass furnace in August 2002. The goals of this activity were to identify its method of construction, to expose its firing chambers, and to determine when it was built. It became clear that the furnace is an isolated ashlar structure consisting of two parts: a melting chamber (external diameter, about 5 × 3.80 m; internal diameter, about 4.45 × 2.95 m) and a badly preserved firing area (external diameter, about 3.80 × 1.60 m) with two conical firing chambers that opened onto the melting chamber (Figs. 9.1–9.2). The layer of glass on the floor of the glass melting chamber (about 2.30 × 2.30 m; and 0.10 m thick) is located at about the center, although the western part of that chamber was probably damaged by the mechanically dug trench. A few sections, especially in the wall that divided the melting chamber from the firing area, show that the preserved stones that framed the installation were overlain by fired mudbricks of standard size (0.30 × 0.15 × 0.10 m) that were probably made from the nearby Netanya Ḥamra bed, an exposed geological unit embedded with organic (mostly straw) matter. The average dimensions of some of the ashlars (0.60 × 0.45 × 0.30 m) may indicate that they were taken from older buildings, such as the villa of Early Roman date discovered in Area E to the west of Area N. Foundation trenches of earlier walls may indicate that the entire installation was built upon an earlier one, using some of its construction materials to lower production costs.

The idea was to preserve the existing furnace due to the fact that installations for the production of raw material (primary glass) for the glass blowing industry are rare. Therefore, it was decided not to excavate below it. Exposing the furnace showed that it contained a large glass slab (about 4.45 × 2.95 m) similar to the one discovered at the site in the 1950 excavation (about 5.50 × 5.50 m) (Roll 1999: 26, Figs. 1.12, 1.14 and 1.15; Tal, Jackson-Tal and Freestone 2004: 54–56, Fig. 4) and at Bet Sheʿarim of a smaller dimension (about 3.40 × 1.95 × 0.45 m) (Brill 1967: 92–94). At the end of the production process, the extracting of the raw glass slab

1 Chapter 9 is an archaeological update on two earlier publications (Tal, Jackson-Tal and Freestone 2004: 56–61 *passim*; Tal *et al.* 2017).

required the roof of the installation to be dismantled after the glass solidified and cooled. This was done by hammering and removing chunks of various sizes, as can be seen in impressions on the preserved remains.

The high-quality raw glass was transparent blue and greenish blue, with a few bubbles (Fig. 9.3). However, glass from the preserved northwestern and southeastern corners of the melting chamber was yellowish green and yellowish brown, based on the amount of oxygen absorbed (high level = bluish/ greenish tints, and low level = yellowish tints). Numerous chunks of glass were discovered during the excavations, as well as vitrified materials from the furnace walls and ceiling (Fig. 9.4). It may be assumed that chunks of insufficient weight or size for trade were discarded; they had probably been removed from the slab while it was being extracted. Fifteen samples were analyzed (for their results, see Tal, Jackson-Tal and Freestone 2004: 61–65; and Chapter 22). A few potsherds of Byzantine date in the form of body fragments from a well-known type of Palestinian bag-shaped jar were also found (see Chapter 13; for the type cf. Kingsley 1994–95: esp. Fig. 3: Group 2). In order to establish a more exact date for this furnace, excavations were carried out below the firing area. This yielded only one rim fragment of a Palestinian bag-shaped jar type that may be dated to the 6th or 7th century CE (Fig. 9.5). Since there are no indications of Early Islamic occupation in the excavated area and in the adjacent squares excavated

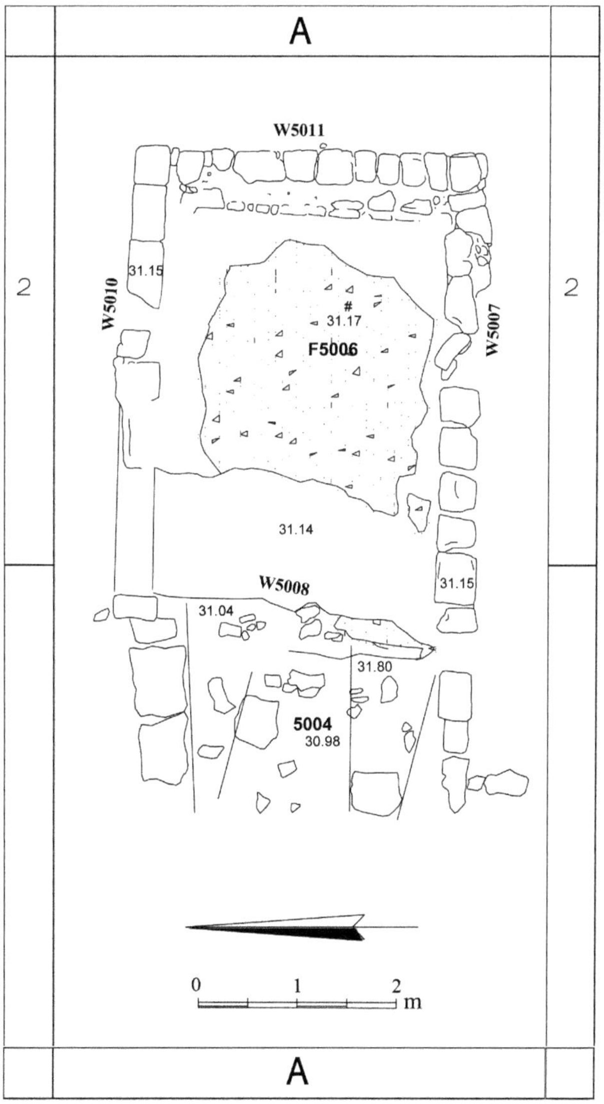

Fig. 9.1: Plan of Area N.

before the furnace was discovered, a Late Byzantine, presumably 6th century CE dating is assigned to the furnace, and this agrees with the chemical analyses of the glass. However, since this jar fragment provides a *terminus post quem* dating for the furnace, we cannot exclude a later, Early Islamic dating. The two firing chambers of the glass furnace discovered at Apollonia/Sozousa were located on the west while the melting chamber was on the east. The firing chambers, facing west, were open to sea winds, thus facilitating the airflow that would otherwise have involved the use of bellows. The Latin foot (*pes*), which measures about three-tenths of a meter, may well have been used while constructing the melting chamber, whose internal measurements are 15 × 10 *pedes* (see in this respect Adam 1999: 40–43). The roof of the melting chamber was probably vaulted with several openings (or chimneys) to provide better air circulation, although no evidence (such as concave bricks) were found to support this conjecture.

Fig. 9.2: Area N; (a) a view after excavation, 2002; (b) as at 2018.

Fig. 9.3: Area N, raw glass chunks; (a) transparent blue glass; (b) transparent greenish blue; (c) transparent yellowish brown glass (approximate scale 1:3).

Fig. 9.4: Area N, slag from the furnace walls and ceiling (approximate scale 1:3).

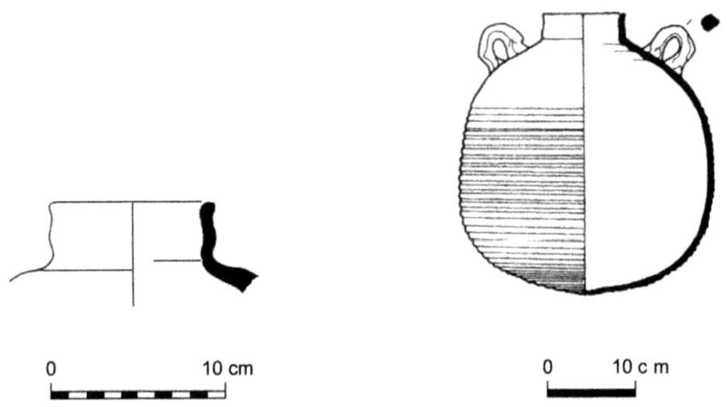

Fig. 9.5: Area N: left) fragment of a Palestinian bag-shaped jar type from the foundation of the furnace floor; right) a complete jar-type.

An ethnographic study carried out in Jalesar in northern India (Sode and Kock 2001) may assist in reconstructing the glass production process. Although glass furnaces there are circular in plan (external diameter about 5 m), they consist of firing and melting chambers, and are thus technically comparable to the one unearthed in Area N. The fuel used at Jalesar consisted of stalks from nearby mustard plants. The study showed that it took 30 days and a constant temperature of about 900°C to produce a circular glass slab. Its dimensions are not given, but according to the plan, the maximal internal diameter of the melting chamber is about 3.80 m. This chamber was filled through an opening in its wall with about three tons of sand that was free of organic impurities and stirred periodically. Every third day, about 300 kilograms of batch was added to clumps of poor-quality glass from the previous melt. This enhanced the process, since glass that has already been melted reacts at lower temperatures. An additional two weeks were needed for the glass slab to cool. It was then broken into pieces, but only a little more than half of the raw glass was acceptable for manufacturing.

Remains of an additional glassmaking furnace which dates to the Byzantine period were discovered in one of the trial trenches made in an area adjacent to Area N that henceforth was termed Area N1. The excavation area, ca. 10 m northeast of Area N, developed into a rectangle (2.50 m east–west, 5.50 m north–south; Fig. 9.6) around the furnace remains discovered in the trial trench and was excavated to a maximum depth of 1 m in accordance with the planned depth of a sewer pipe. The excavation concentrated on exposing a layer of disturbed fill that had piled up in the excavation area at the time the site was established as a national park in 2001. The fill contained building debris derived from the dismantling of structures in the nearby Israel Military Industries Ltd. (hereafter IMI) plant (earth, cement, asbestos, ceramic tiles and iron bars) as well as pottery sherds and production debris of glassmaking furnaces from the Byzantine period (Figs. 9.7).

Among the finds attributed to the debris from the area of the furnace used in the manufacture of raw glass in Area N1 were fragments of fired mudbricks used in the furnace's walls and ceiling, as well as fragments of raw glass were found on its floor (some of which were apparently *in situ*; Fig. 9.8). Additionally, fragments of raw glass deriving from the removal of the slab of glass produced for the manufacture of glass vessels, as well as a variety of finds connected to the glassmaking debris of the furnace, the most apparent being glass slag (Fig. 9.9).

The remains found in the excavation area indicate that a glassmaking furnace operated during the Late Byzantine period and was like the one that was discovered nearby (Area N). The installation was destroyed because of later disturbances, possibly in the Byzantine period, but more likely in recent years when building debris was discarded from the nearby IMI plant in the area. This debris was deposited there as part of the preparations for opening the Apollonia antiquities site and the national park to the public in 2001.

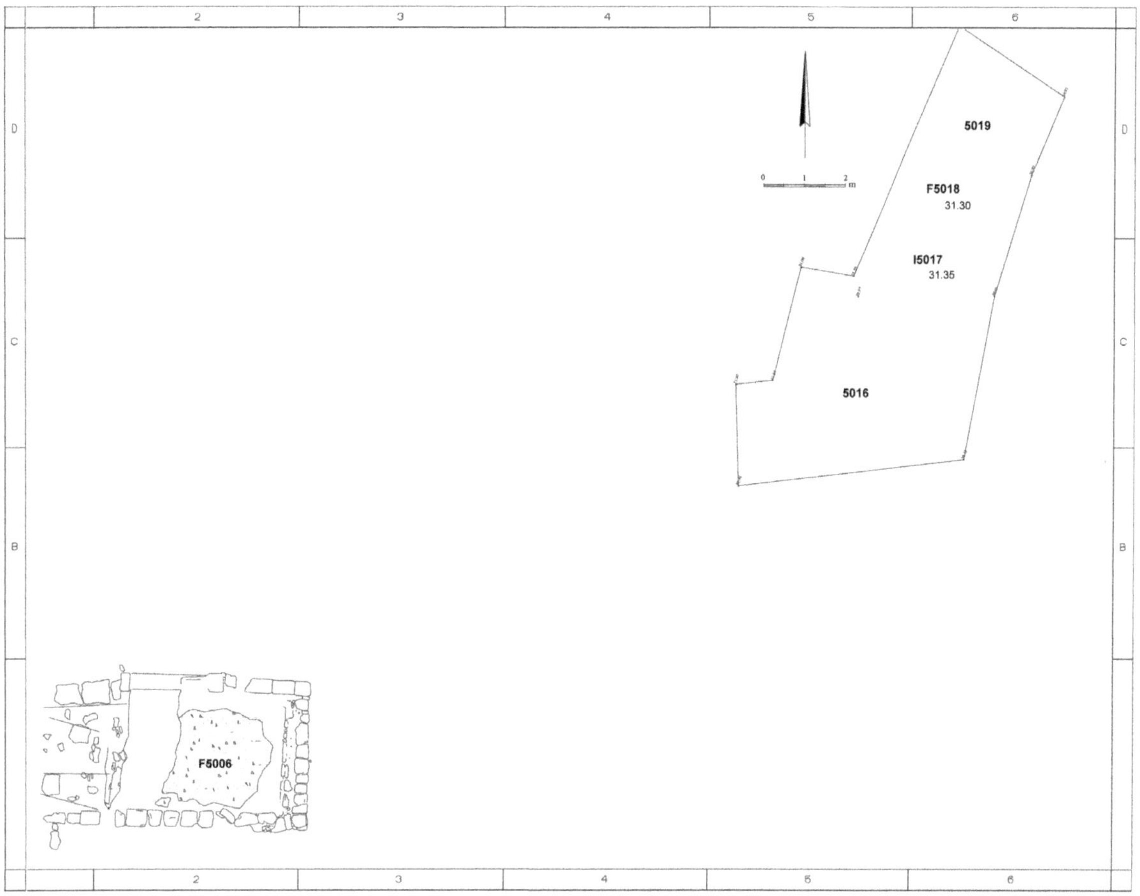

Fig. 9.6: Plan of Area N and Area N1 (on the northeast).

Fig. 9.7: Area N1, a view during excavation, 2017, looking southwest.

Fig. 9.8: Area N1, segmented furnace floor remains (*in situ*), looking north.

Fig. 9.9: Area N1, raw glass production remains (approximate scale 1:3).

The ceramic finds discovered in the excavation, especially in the context of the furnace remains, were mostly body fragments of bag-shaped jars and a few diagnostic rims, yet they were sufficient to date the furnace to the 6th–7th centuries CE, like the one nearby. Numerous modern finds, including construction debris and coins still in circulation, were found together with the ancient artifacts.

To date, two almost complete glassmaking furnaces dating to the 6th–7th centuries CE have been discovered at the Apollonia/Sozousa site, one in the northern part of the site in 1950 (near Area O) dug during salvage excavation prior to the establishment of the IMI plant, and the other, as stated, in the south of the site, in 2002 in Area N (above). The remains exposed in the excavation of Area N1 are indicative of another furnace, of which practically no vestiges were left *in situ*, and resemble one or more furnaces, whose remains were exposed in excavations in Area O (Freestone, Jackson-Tal and Tal 2008; Tal 2009; Chapter 10). The complete furnaces together with the remains of the ones discovered nearby show that these were built in clusters, like those exposed in Bet Eliᶜezer (Gorin-Rosen 1993; 2000) and operated simultaneously or for a relatively brief period because they were installations that had to be dismantled upon completion of manufacturing the raw glass to remove the product from the furnace.

The raw glass furnaces discovered at Apollonia/Sozousa are not the only ones found in Israel. Two additional sites are thought to be of later date. The first of these sites is Bet Sheᶜarim, as already stated above, located on the western edge of the Jezreel Valley some 20 kilometers from the seacoast, where a glass slab was discovered while soil was being cleared from a rock-cut cave in 1956. The remains of the furnace superstructure were probably removed during the process of removing the slab after manufacture (Brill 1967). The rather unusual findspot inside the cave suggests that such a furnace, and especially its firing area, may have benefitted from breezes entering the cave, which faces to the west. The date of the slab is uncertain, but chemical analyses suggest an Early Islamic dating, probably in the 9th century CE (Freestone and Gorin-Rosen 1999; Freestone, Gorin-Rosen and Hughes 2000: 70). The second site is Bet Eliᶜezer, east of Ḥadera and less than ten kilometers inland, on the central Sharon Plain. Salvage excavations there in 1992 revealed 17 rather poorly preserved glass furnaces (Gorin-Rosen 1993: No. 100; 2000: 52–54). Chemical analyses support an 8th-century CE dating (Freestone, Gorin-Rosen and Hughes 2000: 71–72). It should be noted that several raw glass furnaces were recently discovered in Jalame (west of Qiryat Tivᶜon) and assigned to the Late Roman period (3rd–4th century CE), but they are as yet unpublished.[2]

These glass production sites found in Israel differ in date and geography, although they made rather similar raw glass. These furnace sites may be accompanied by several glass chunks (and other remains of raw glass production) found in excavations in many sites across central and northern Israel (cf. Freestone, Gorin-Rosen and Hughes 2000: 67–69 for Dor and Banias), indicating that raw glass was produced at other places as well or alternatively imported from other sites to be re-melted locally (for the Apollonia/Sozousa region, see Roll and Ayalon 1989: 218–221 enumerating a dozen additional sites in the southern Sharon plain with remains of smaller-scale glass activity, probably related to a secondary production process).[3]

The Coastal Plain location of the Apollonia/Sozousa raw glass furnaces is probably linked to the presence of forests to provide fuel for the firing process. While present conditions hardly support

2 For a survey of such sites across the Mediterranean, see Tal, Jackson-Tal and Freestone 2004: 60.

3 The distinction between the primary production of raw glass and the secondary production of glass vessels is well attested in historical, archaeological and ethnographic studies (cf. Freestone, Gorin-Rosen and Hughes 2000: 66). It was based on the different needs for each activity (e.g., the proximity to raw materials for the glass composition and firing process and adequate winds for the production of raw glass). Therefore, at a given site, this production is located away from a residential area, while secondary production can be found in the very heart of the community, for example at Bet Sheᶜan (see Gorin-Rosen 2000: 59–60).

a forested environment, trees were probably found in the vicinity of the site, since it borders, about 1.5 kilometers to the east, a long, narrow plain filled with fertile soil. Further east are the red loam hills that cover most of the central Sharon (Tal 1999).[4] Branches may well have been used in the glass furnaces at Apollonia/Sozousa, as is indicated by ethnographic studies (above). Transporting fuel (wood) to coastal sites rather than building furnaces near the source of the fuel may suggest that the production of raw glass (glassmaking) at a given site served a secondary glass industry (glassworking) that manufactured finished products (blown vessels) (as shown in Freestone, Jackson-Tal and Tal 2008).

After 27 seasons of excavations at Apollonia, it can be concluded that furnaces found on the southern and northern fringes of the site are evidence of glass manufacturing during the Late Byzantine period.

It has been suggested in the discussion of the excavations of Apollonia (East), the immediate eastern hinterland dug during 2012 and 2013 (Haddad *et al.* 2015), that the Byzantine settlement of Apollonia/Sozousa used the area to the east primarily for agricultural and industrial purposes. This hinterland is evident in the archaeological remains of winepresses, field towers and tombs. Additionally, there are refuse pits used to deposit debris from the settlement and whose contents were used for fertilizing and improving the soil targeted for agricultural crops (below). It should be emphasized that the industrial glass waste discovered so far in the excavated areas in the eastern part of the site did not derive from additional furnaces, but to the industrial products that were dismantled from the glassmaking furnaces that were in the immediate vicinity of the Byzantine settlement and were put to secondary use as building materials, fertilizer and the like. Still, the nature of the raw glass industrial debris and lumps of raw glass recently discovered in surveys on the grounds of the IMI plant in the eastern part of the Byzantine site has not yet been sufficiently clarified; excavations there are needed in order to understand whether the debris relates to *in situ* installations or rather to a secondary use, as it was discovered in Apollonia (East).

The discovery of furnaces at Apollonia/Sozousa adds considerably to the available knowledge of glass production in Late Byzantine Palestine. It strengthens the previous assumption that the town was a major center for the making of both primary and secondary glass in the 6th and 7th centuries CE far beyond its local use. It also enhances the understanding of glass furnace construction and the production of raw glass at the site. Chemical analyses of glass samples from the Area N furnace, as well as those of glass samples recovered earlier, provide a more detailed database of ancient Near Eastern glass compositions (Tal, Jackson-Tal and Freestone 2004: 61–65). It may be that the church as the center of political and social power in Late Byzantine Apollonia/Sozousa played an important role in the production and circulation of raw glass produced at the site. Although there is no direct evidence of such a role, it is known that the church, as an administrative body, was involved in the economy and daily life of the Byzantine world (Jones 1964: 830–834 and especially 894–910). This is the place to mention that recent analytical studies have shown that the raw glass produced at the site of Apollonia/Sozousa in the Late Byzantine period was in use at relatively distant locations (e.g., in Jordan, at the sites of Umm el-Jimal, cf. Al-Bashaireha *et al.* 2016; and Jerash [Gerasa], cf. Barfod *et al.* 2018) and also in Roman Carthage (Schibille, Sterrett-Krause and Freestone 2017; see also Chapter 16 and especially Chapter 22 for a discussion on the subject).

4 In the case of the Sharon plain, this assumption may be bolstered by two historical accounts: the Septuagint, where the translation of "Sharon" in Isaiah 65:10 (וְהָיָה הַשָּׁרוֹן לִנְוֵה-צֹאן וְעֵמֶק עָכוֹר לְרֵבֶץ בָּקָר לְעַמִּי אֲשֶׁר דְּרָשׁוּנִי) appears as δρυμός (i.e., thicket, although this is more relevant to late Hellenistic times); and Strabo, *Geography* 16.2.27, where the region (or part of it) is referred to as δρομὸς μέγας (although this pertains more to early Roman times; see Stern 1974: 292). Josephus's place-name Δρυμός (*Jewish War* 1.13.2 [250]) may be another reference. Geological studies support such a flora environment for the Sharon plain (see Horowitz 1979: 205–206 and 208–209).

REFERENCES

Adam, J.P. 1999. *Roman Building: Materials and Techniques* (trans. A. Mathews). London.

Al-Bashaireh, K., Al-Mustafa, S., Freestone, I.C. and Al-Housan, A.Q. 2016. Composition of Byzantine Glasses from Umm el-Jimal, Northeast Jordan: Insights into Glass Origins and Recycling. *Journal of Cultural Heritage* 21: 809–818.

Barfod, G.H., Freestone, I.C., Lichtenberger, A., Raja, R. and Schwarzer, H. 2018. Geochemistry of Byzantine and Early Islamic Glass from Jerash, Jordan: Typology, Recycling, and Provenance. *Geoarchaeology* 33: 623–640.

Brill, R.H. 1967. A Great Glass Slab from Ancient Galilee. *Archaeology* 20: 88–95.

Freestone, I.C. and Gorin-Rosen, Y. 1999. The Great Glass Slab at Bet Sheʿarim, Israel: An Early Islamic Glassmaking Experiment? *Journal of Glass Studies* 41: 105–116.

Freestone, I.C., Gorin-Rosen, Y. and Hughes, M.J. 2000. Primary Glass from Israel and the Production of Glass in Late Antiquity and the Early Islamic Period. In: *La Route du verre: Ateliers primaires et secondaires du second millénaire av. J.-C. au Moyen Age*. Lyon: 65–83.

Freestone I.C., Jackson-Tal, R.E. and Tal, O. 2008. Raw Glass and the Production of Glass Vessels at Late Byzantine Apollonia-Arsuf, Israel. *Journal of Glass Studies* 50: 67–80.

Gorin-Rosen, Y. 1993. Ḥadera, Bet Eliʿezer. *Excavations and Surveys in Israel* 13: 42–43.

Gorin-Rosen, Y. 2000. The Ancient Glass Industry in Israel: Summary of the Finds and New Discoveries. In: *La Route du verre: Ateliers primaires et secondaires du second millénaire av. J.-C. au Moyen Age*. Lyon: 49–63.

Haddad, E., Tal, O., Ajami, M. and Harpak, T. 2015. Apollonia (East). *Ḥadashot Arkheologiyot—Excavations and Surveys in Israel* 127. http://www.hadashot-esi.org.il/report_detail_eng.aspx?id=15728&mag_id=122

Horowitz, A. 1979. *The Quaternary of Israel*. New York.

Jones, A.H.M. 1964. *The Later Roman Empire, 284–602: A Social, Economic and Administrative Survey*, vols. 1 and 2. Oxford.

Kingsley, S.A. 1994–95. Bag-Shaped Amphorae and Byzantine Trade: Expanding Horizons. *Bulletin of the Anglo-Israel Archaeological Society* 14: 39–56.

Roll, I. 1999. Introduction: History of the Site, Its Research and Excavations. In: Roll, I. and Tal, O. *Apollonia-Arsuf: Final Report of the Excavations, Volume 1: The Persian and Hellenistic Periods (with Appendices on the Chalcolithic and Iron Age II Remains)* (Monograph Series of the Institute of Archaeology of Tel Aviv University 16). Tel Aviv: 1–62.

Roll, I. and Ayalon, E. 1989. A*pollonia and Southern Sharon: Model of a Coastal City and its Hinterland.* Tel Aviv (Hebrew, with English summary pp. IV–IX).

Schibille, N., Sterrett-Krause, A. and Freestone, I.C. 2017. Glass Groups, Glass Supply and Recycling in Late Roman Carthage. *Archaeological and Anthropological Sciences* 9: 1223–1241.

Sode, T. and Kock, J. 2001. Traditional Raw Glass Production in Northern India: The Final Stage of an Ancient Technology. *Journal of Glass Studies* 43: 155–169.

Stern, M. 1974. *Greek and Latin Authors on Jews and Judaism, Volume 1: From Herodotus to Plutarch*. Jerusalem.

Tal, O. 1999. The Natural Environment. In: Roll, I. and Tal, O. *Apollonia-Arsuf: Final Report of the Excavations I: The Persian and Hellenistic Periods (with Appendices on the Chalcolithic and Iron Age II Remains)* (Monograph Series of the Institute of Archaeology of Tel Aviv University 16). Tel Aviv: 77–82.

Tal, O. 2009. A Winepress at Apollonia-Arsuf: More Evidence on the Samaritan Presence in Roman–Byzantine Southern Sharon. *Liber Annuus* 59: 319–342.

Tal, O., Jackson-Tal, R.E. and Freestone, I.C. 2004. New Evidence of the Production of Raw Glass at Late Byzantine Apollonia-Arsuf, Israel. *Journal of Glass Studies* 46: 51–66.

CHAPTER 10

AREA O (2006, 2009)[1]

Oren Tal

Area O is located near the initial excavations held in 1950 (see Fig. 1.2). The 2006 excavations were minimal and confined to the exposure of a medium-sized white *tesserae* (1.5–2 cm on average) mosaic floor adorned with a partially preserved Greek inscription that was published shortly after its discovery (Roll and Tal 2008). The 2009 excavations were conducted on a larger scale; the excavation area included eight squares, 5 × 5 m each, five of which were dug down to virgin soil. The aim was to investigate the nature of the mosaic floor with its inscription and to find out whether there had been extra-mural occupation in Early Islamic times, as previously suggested (Kahane 1951; Roll 1999: 26, 29). The inquiry shows no post-7th century CE permanent occupation; upper fills in the excavated area included pits containing pottery and fragmented glass vessels dated to the 6th–7th centuries CE. More interesting is the considerable amount of raw glass production refuse (as well as secondary glass production refuse) found below the upper fills extending over the entire excavated area. Given the amount of raw glass production refuse that was dug out (weighing some two tons), this refuse must have originated in raw glass furnaces located in the area which were dismantled while the raw glass was hammered out (for their analyses, see Freestone, Jackson-Tal and Tal 2008 and Chapters 16, 22). Previous studies were not dedicated to the examination of the cardinal role of Late Byzantine Apollonia/Sozousa as a production center of raw glass and most probably secondary glass. The above-mentioned evidence strengthens the idea that the Late Byzantine period site was instrumental in the production of raw glass (e.g., Tal, Jackson-Tal and Freestone 2004; and above Areas N and N1). The ca. 0.60 m layer of raw glass production refuse nearly covered a large winepress complex, which occupied most of the excavated area (Fig. 10.1). It became clear that the inscription discovered in 2006 occupied the central part of the preserved treading floor of the winepress (Figs. 10.2–10.4). The medium-sized white *tesserae* mosaic floor was divided into horizontal panels (five were preserved) and two of the panels in the center of the treading floor were divided into smaller frames of uneven dimensions (four were preserved). The inscription was set in the central panel (or in the center of the preserved floor, as the northern edge of the floor had washed down to the ravine below). The mosaic inscription was made of small-sized black *tesserae* (0.50–1 cm on average). Small parts of the inscription were extracted from the floor in later periods, and over time it was covered by whitewash that had accumulated on the floor. Nonetheless, the inscription was found almost complete. It could be deciphered only after conservation by a team from the Israel Nature and Parks Authority and the letters of the transcription could be transcribed in the following manner:

1. ICΘẸ[O]CMỌṆOCBỌ[HΘEI]
2. KACC[IA]NΩAMACYṂḄỊΩ̣
3. KAITẸ[K]ṆOICKAIΠCEI

1 Chapter 10 is an archaeological update of earlier publication (Tal 2009).

Fig. 10.1: Dismantled raw glass furnaces in Area O, Squares B-C/3-4 (I8019, on left; I8016, on right).

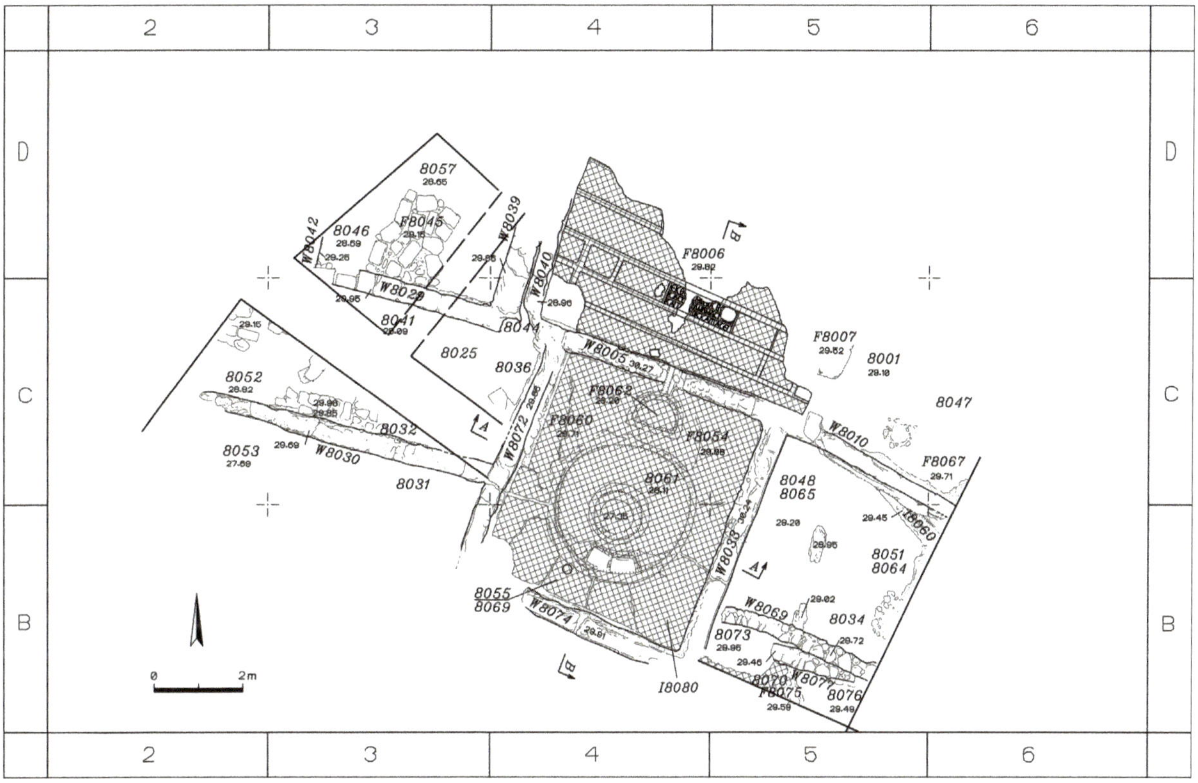

Fig. 10.2: Plan of Area O.

Hence, the transliterated and restored version of the inscription may be read as follows:

1. Εἷς θεὸς μόνος βοήθει
2. Κασσ(ι)ανῷ ἅμα συμβίῳ
3. καὶ τέκνοις καὶ πάσει

The translation is: "One God only, help / Cassianos together with (his) wife / and children and everyone."

In recent papers I have argued that it is reasonable to assume that the Εἷς θεὸς μόνος formula inscriptions in Palestine have an exclusive Samaritan provenance (e.g., Tal 2015, for another Εἷς θεὸς μόνος inscription with references therein; see also *SEG* 59, No. 1704, where my interpretation of the

Fig. 10.3: Area O, aerial view.

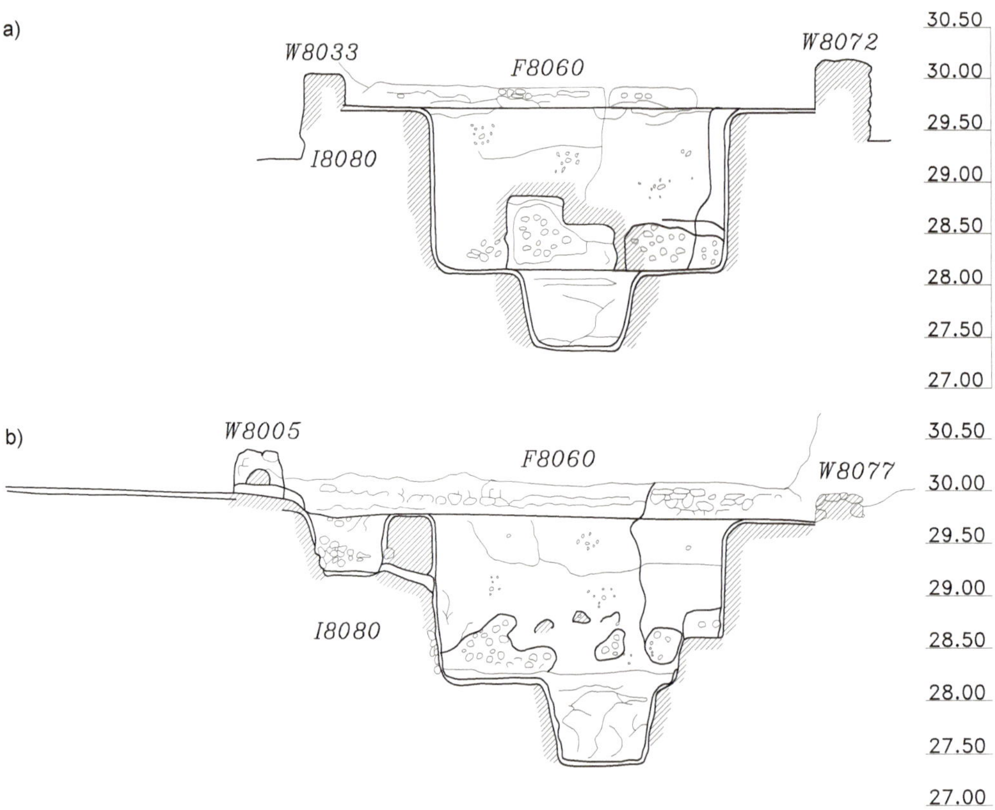

Fig. 10.4: Sections of Area O: (a) Section A-A; (b) Section B-B.

formula as Samaritan is given by the editors).[2] Indeed, Εἷς θεὸς μόνος inscriptions are far fewer than the other Palestinian Εἷς θεός formula inscriptions (Di Segni 1994: 100–101, Nos. 16, 20a, Formula C on p. 111; see also *SEG* 49, No. 2054 [from Caesarea] and *SEG* 55, No. 1731 [Ḥorvat Raqit]), but they are found in Roman and Byzantine sites in Samaria and in settlements where Samaritan communities are attested by both the archaeological finds and the written sources.[3]

Regardless of the small number of Persian, Hellenistic and Early Roman pottery fragments that were found in fills within and directly above the natural yellow sand as discovered in Square B5 (in the southeastern part of the area and possibly originating in tombs that did not survive, cf. Fig. 10.4),[4] pottery and fragments of glass vessels found below the level of the winepress complex can be dated to the 4th and 5th centuries CE (Fig. 10.6).[5] Such a date accords with the earliest coins found in the area of excavation. Notable among these coins is a bronze coin of Maximianus (286–305 CE) minted in Antioch (Syria), that came from the plaster foundation of the mosaic floor of the collecting vat (Installation 8061) which suggests that it was built sometime after 305 CE (at the latest) (cf. Chapter 18: No. 18). In any case, the use of the winepress complex was relatively short-lived. Its large, circular collecting/settling (and fermentation) vat included substantial amounts of broken pottery and glass vessels (weighing some 500 kg) accumulated in a series of superimposed layers in Late Byzantine (6th–7th centuries CE) times, showing that the winepress ceased to function sometime in the early 6th century CE, given the pottery and coin evidence (cf. Chapters 13, 18).[6] This is also the date of the several post-occupation fills found above the winepress complex and the glass refuse.[7] Moreover, excavations in the collecting vat show that once the winepress was out of use, a stone-built pier was constructed in its center (Fig. 10.7). The fact that the foundations of the pier were based upon the refuse fills and not directly upon the mosaic-paved floor of the collecting vat precludes a direct relationship between the pier and the production process of the winepress. It thus seems likely that the stone-built pier served another installation—the function of which can only be speculated. A section of stone-paved floor discovered to its northwest (Floor 8045) may have belonged to the same installation (Fig. 10.10). The wall to its northeast (Wall 8010) seems to belong to a later phase and not to the original layout of the winepress, so is the wall to its east (Wall 8069).

The winepress complex is generally oriented north–south; all its surfaces were paved with medium-sized white *tesserae*, whereas the upper and lower levels of its circular collecting vat were paved with medium-sized white *tesserae* that are unevenly "dotted" with medium-sized black *tesserae*. The delimiting walls, as well as the walls and openings of the intermediary (filtration) and collecting vats, were covered by white-grayish hydraulic plaster (Fig. 10.8). Prior to the foundation of the winepress complex, its area was dominated by natural yellow sand; once building operations began, the area was apparently covered by *ḥamra* (red loam) soil, which was then covered by layers of mortar and plaster. The latter served as the foundation for the mosaic paving. Originally, the treading floor was delimited by four walls, only two of which are preserved: Wall

2 Interestingly, this inscription was discovered in Area O and the one discussed in this paper in Area P1; these areas are located in the northern and southern parts of the excavated sites (Fig. 1.2) some 450 m apart.

3 In this context it should be noted that Ameling has recently argued in the *CIIP* II, No. 1342, while republishing an Εἷς θεὸς μόνος inscription from Caesarea Maritima, that the formula "in itself is no indication of pagan, Jewish, Christian or Samaritan adherence." However, this has no actual basis as argued in Tal 2015: 173–174.

4 E.g., cooking pots (Nos. 1–2) and bottle (No. 3) of Hellenistic date with well-stratified equivalents at Dor, cf. e.g., Guz-Zilberstein 1995: 298–299 (CP1), 304 (UG1/2) *passim*.

5 E.g., basin (No. 1), cooking pot (No. 2) and storage jars (Nos. 3–6) of Late Roman date with well-stratified equivalents at Jalame, cf. e.g., Johnson 1988: 183 (Nos. 488–493 *passim*), 195–197 (Form 12), 214–219 (Nos. 762–827 *passim*).

6 While the Late Byzantine pottery and late Samaritan oil lamps found in the refuse pit of the collecting vat can generally be dated to the 6th and 7th centuries CE, the latest coins found in the collecting vat (Locus 8061) date to the early 4th century CE.

7 Cf. Chapter 13 pottery from Locus 8015, Locus 8020, Locus 8049.

8040 in the west and Wall 8005 in the south (both walls are ca. 0.40 m thick and 0.30 m high). The maximal preserved dimensions of the treading floor are 6.50 × 3.80 m, and there is some 0.03 m height differences from north to south. The treading floor is elevated from the floor surface of the intermediary and collecting vats by some 0.15 m. It is unclear whether the inscription that occupied the central part of the preserved treading floor of the winepress was set in the center of the floor or off the center. The latter possibility would suggest that north of the inscription there may have been a stone base for the affixing of a wooden screw. Given the dimensions of the collecting vat (below), the existence of a wooden screw installation in the northern part of the treading floor (used for the second pressing of the grapes' skin and pulp) seems a more logical reconstruction. Wall 8005 divides the treading floor and the floor surface of the intermediary and collecting vats; a carved u-shaped *kurkar* stone (fossilized dune sandstone) channel fixed across this wall allowed the flow of the mashed grapes (i.e., must) into the intermediary vat (Floor 8062). This horseshoe-shaped vat is ca. 0.95 × 0.55 m and is about 0.50 m deep. A pipe (0.04 m in diameter and made of lead) was set across its lower southern wall leading into the collecting vat (8061). This vat is circular (approximately 2.90 m in diameter and about 2.35 m deep) and has two levels: an upper level, approximately 1.60 m deep, whose surface is accessible via two built beach-rock plaster-covered stairs set along the southern wall of the vat; and

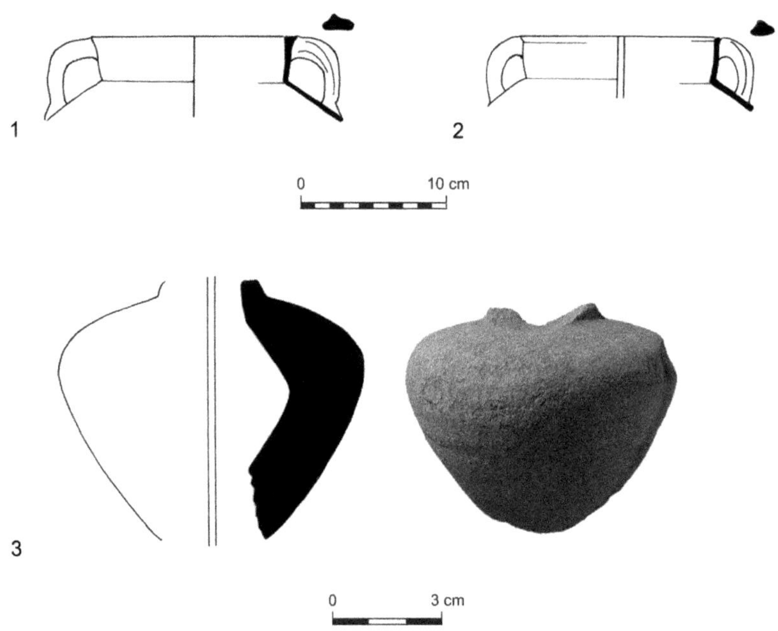

Fig. 10.5: Area O, Hellenistic and Early Roman pottery fragments from fills within and directly above the natural sand.

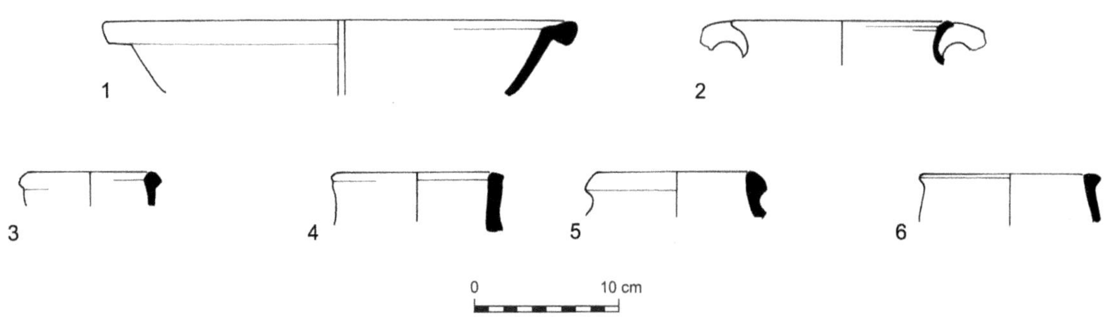

Fig. 10.6: Area O, Late Roman and Early Byzantine pottery fragments from below the level of the winepress complex.

a lower level, approximately 0.75 m deep with a smaller diameter of ca. 1.20 m top and 0.75 m bottom, serving as a sedimentation basin (Fig. 10.9). On top of the rim of the circular collecting vat, directly above the lower stair, there is a rounded dent on the mosaic surface (ca. 0.20 m in diameter), as if to allow the placement of a storage jar. The surfaces of the intermediary and collecting vats are delimited by four walls, approximately 0.30 m high (Wall 8005, Wall 8033, Wall 8074 and Wall 8072). These walls create a square mosaic-paved surface of approximately 5.50 × 5 m, which together with the treading floor encompasses an area of 9.70 × 6.50 m. However, excavations have made it clear that the winepress complex formed part of a larger complex of a yet-undiscovered nature. Wall 8005 has an integral continuation to the west (Wall 8029) and to the east

Fig. 10.7: Area O, a stone-built pier in the collecting vat, looking east.

Fig. 10.8: Area O, a view of the treading floor funneled to the intermediary vat, looking southwest.

Fig. 10.9: Area O, intermediary vat and collecting vat, looking south.

Fig. 10.10: Area O, Walls 8029, 8005 and 8010 and the northern room with its stone-paved floor (F8045) in the foreground, looking east.

(Wall 8010) (Fig. 10.10). Moreover, Wall 8030 was built together with Wall 8072 and thus reflects the same date of foundation. In fact, excavations in Squares B2, B3 and C3 (in the western part of the area) revealed two rooms with stone-paved floors that are contemporaneous with the winepress complex: a northern room (Wall 8042, Wall 8029, Wall 8039 and Floor 8045) and a southern room (Wall 8030, Wall 8072), with a badly preserved floor (8032, 8052) (Fig. 10.2). In contrast, the east side of the area (Squares A5, B5) revealed the probable remains of storage facilities of the winepress as can be seen in the southeast, where a surface of medium-sized white *tesserae* (Floor 8035) is delimited by Wall 8033 and Wall 8077 (Fig. 10.11). There are also some badly preserved plaster foundations in the northeast (Floor 8067) that may have served the same purpose. Furthermore, there is evidence of an earlier occupation layer in the northeast, where Wall 8010 of the winepress complex was built on top of a plastered channel (Installation 8060).

There are also two beach-rock, axe-shaped weights found close to surface level (Fig. 10.12). Their flattened surfaces and rounded sides may indicate that they were worked from a round burial stone ("rolling stone") such as the ones seen nowadays in the Samaritan cemetery of nearby Tel Barukh (Tal and Taxel 2015: 40, Figs. 1.8, 1.27, 1.29–1.30) or in the upper stone of a crushing basin of an oil press. Although the weights seem to be too heavy (some 200 kg each) to be used in a simple lever-and-weights press used during the second pressing of the grapes, the possibility cannot be excluded that they were used in a space and apparatus that were part of the winepress complex but did not survive. Alternatively, both the above-mentioned channel (Installation 8060) and the axe-shaped weights may have belonged to an as-yet undiscovered installation or installations.

Grapes for wine production probably came from grapevines cultivated in the narrow plain located to the east of the site between the first and second *kurkar* ridges or in the *ḥamra* hills that cover most of the central Sharon area. Rainfall water is drained by Naḥal (stream/river) Poleg to the north. This assumption accords with the viticulture of the region as is evidenced by the many Byzantine winepresses discovered in Apollonia-Arsuf and nearby sites.

The one-axis plan of the winepress complex—that is, the treading floor (together with its inscription), the intermediary and collecting vats all aligned on the same axis (Figs. 10.2–10.3)—is not commonly found

Fig. 10.11: Area O, remains of storage facilities with a surface of white *tesserae* (F8035) delimited by Walls 8033 and 8077, looking west.

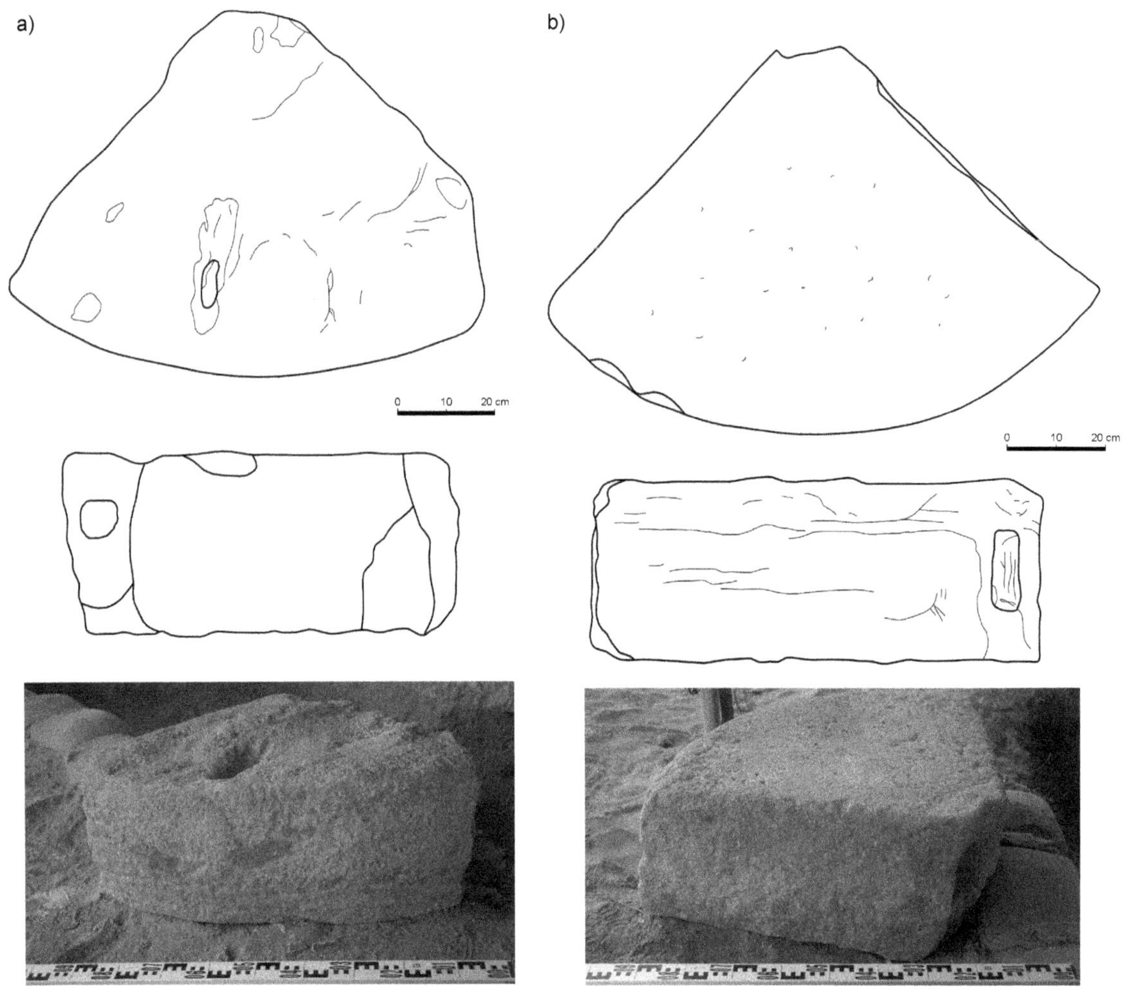

Fig. 10.12: Area O, stone axe-shaped weights (a, b).

in the Sharon Plain and is more characteristic of the Galilee, where the majority of improved wineries belong to this type (Frankel 1999: 152–153, Map 40). In contrast, the circular collecting vat is more characteristic of the Sharon Plain, although the majority of winepresses scattered in the area were built on the four-rectangle plan (Frankel 1999: 149–150, Map 39; and for the site, see Chapters 3 and 7). Nevertheless, a recently published winepress in Kfar Yaᶜabetz (Kilodia) on the eastern fringes of the Sharon Plain shows a striking resemblance to this one-axis winepress complex in both its plan, orientation and dimensions, albeit with a circular intermediate vat rather than a horseshoe-shaped one (Ayalon 2009: 161–162, Fig. 29.1).

Byzantine winepresses with inscriptions have rarely been documented in Palestine. The very few Byzantine-period dated winepresses published so far are either of Christian or Jewish orientation. Thus, for example, a Byzantine winepress adorned with a panel of a two-line Greek mosaic inscription beginning with a cross was recorded in Castra (Yeivin and Finkielsztejn 1999, 25*, Fig. 45; 2005: Finkielsztejn 2005: 448, Fig. 20). Another example is a panel of a seven-line mosaic inscription ending with a horned cross that is flanked by ivy leaves, found on a partly destroyed mosaic floor some 100 m east of Tel Ashdod (in the area of Kibbutz Hazor; see Gudovitch 2006; Tzaferis 2006). Although recently a new reading and date for the inscription was offered (Di Segni 2008), the commemoration of the foundation of a winepress (ληνός) together with a monastery (μοναστηρίον) is clearly visible. A four-line Εἷς θεὸς formula mosaic inscription that may relate to yet another Byzantine winepress of a Christian orientation is known from Bet Ḥanan, some 5 km north of Yavneh. Based on the presence of a christogram in the third line of the inscription, it was suggested that it formed part of a room of an ecclesiastical complex (monastery?) or alternatively a private (Christian) estate. The possibility of a winepress built within a monastery (or even a private estate) as was apparently the case at the site east of Tel Ashdod cannot be excluded. A Byzantine-period winepress with a Jewish orientation was the interpretation offered for the remains of what was considered a Jewish synagogue at Ḥulda because of a seven-branched *menorah*, and other Jewish motifs such as incense shovel, *shofar*, *etrog* and *lulav* depicted on the mosaic floor together with two Greek inscriptions (Fischer, Taxel and Amit 2008: 24, Figs. 15–16). These inscriptions appeared on the surface of the intermediate and collecting vats; one is a three-line inscription (ΕΥΛΟ/ΓΙΑΤΩ/ΛΑΩ) which reads "blessing to the people"; the other is a six-line inscription blessing and naming the three founders (κτίστες). However, it should be stressed that excavations at Ḥulda were limited to the area of the winepress and the possibility cannot be excluded that additional building remains in the surrounding area, together with the winepress, formed a larger (public?) complex. Such a reconstruction may agree with the previous reconstruction, that the Apollonia-Arsuf winepress complex with the inscription on its treading floor probably formed part of a large (public) compound that is yet to be discovered in the western part of the area. The probable integration of the winepress complex in a public compound notwithstanding, it is the first winepress found with a Samaritan-oriented inscription, evidence that the practice of inserting inscriptions on mosaic-paved surfaces of winepresses was done by Christians, Jews and Samaritans in Byzantine Palestine.[8] Given the fact that the use of the winepress complex was relatively short-lived, spanning the 4th/5th centuries to the early 6th century CE based on the finds recovered from fills below and above its floors, there is the possibility that the building was destroyed (that is, abandoned and intentionally filled with refuse) as a result of Justinian's law (ca. 527–531 CE) prohibiting Samaritan gatherings of any kind, thus encouraging the destruction of Samaritan synagogues (*Samaritarum synagogae destruuntur*) and other productive operations of larger scales (*Codex Iustianus* [ed. Krueger] 1.15.17). The abandonment (and/or destruction) of the winepress complex may have also been related to the edicts against the property rights of the Samaritans included in the *Novellae* enacted during the period of the Samaritan Rebellion (529 CE) (see in this respect Di Segni 2002; Rabello 2002).

Excavations show that the winepress was damaged by an earthquake, the date of which is uncertain. The southern parts of the winepress complex were cracked; notable is an east–west orientated crack off the center of Wall 8033 through Floor 8060 and one on the collecting vat (8061) ending off the center of Wall 8072 (Figs. 10.2, 10.9). However, it should be emphasized that the damage done to the winepress complex by the earthquake was relatively minor and moderate repairs could have easily made it operational again. In any case, it seems clear that the winepress complex was intentionally covered by raw glass production furnaces, which once dismantled to hammer out the raw glass, left the ca. 0.60 m layer of raw glass production refuse in the area (Fig. 10.1; Freestone, Jackson-Tal and Tal 2008: 70). Elsewhere it has been suggested that raw glass production at Apollonia-Arsuf may have been a monopoly of the Church that as an administrative body was involved in the economy and daily life of Sozousa, playing an important role in the network of trade and circulation of raw glass (Tal, Jackson-Tal and Freestone 2004: 66). If this was indeed the case, ownership over the area of the winepress complex may have been transferred from Samaritans to Christians by the second third of the 6th century CE and once the site's Byzantine occupation came to an end in the 630s CE, so did the raw glass production industry. Hence, according to this scenario, even after the turbulent regime

8 Di Segni 2008: 33* refers to yet another inscription that commemorates the building of a wine cellar in a monastery at el-Kufr in the Huran by engraving a Greek inscription on the lintel above its entrance, but this seems to relate to another practice. The same applies to the name Dosit[heos] found "cut in the side of the large winepress" in Khirbet el-Buraq in Samaria, cf. Applebaum, Isaac and Landau 1981–1982: 104–105, No. 15, which may even be a later addition to an existing winepress complex (with thanks to L. Di Segni for the latter reference). Notwithstanding the above, another Byzantine winepress of a Christian orientation with a Greek inscription commemorating its foundation in 564 CE on its mosaic treading floor was recently discovered in excavations west of Kabri (et-Tuweiri in the Plain of Akko), but is yet unpublished (D. Syon, pers. comm).

of Justinian I, the Samaritan owners of the area could not regain control over their previously-owned land. Nor were the new Islamic rulers engaged in the production of raw glass at the site (based on our current state of research). The coin evidence unearthed in this area, with the latest coins being assigned to Heraclius (610–641 CE; see Chapter 18: Nos. 350–353), lend support to our earlier assumption.

REFERENCES

Applebaum, S., Isaac, B.H. and Landau, Y. 1981–1982. Varia Epigraphica. *Scripta Classica Israelica* 6: 98–118.

Ayalon, E. 2009. A Byzantine Winepress in Kfar Yaʿabetz. In: Ayalon, E., Frankel, R. and Kloner, A., eds. *Oil and Wine Presses in Israel from the Hellenistic, Roman and Byzantine Periods* (BAR International Series 1972). Oxford: 161–162.

Di Segni, L. 2002. Samaritan Revolts in Byzantine Palestine. In: Stern, E. and Eshel, H., eds. *The Samaritans*. Jerusalem: 467–480 (Hebrew).

Di Segni, L. 2008. The Greek Inscription from Tel Ashdod: A Revised Reading. *ʿAtiqot* 58: 32*–36*.

Finkielsztejn, G. 2005. Les mosaïques de la komopolis de Porphyreon du Sud (Kfar Samir; Haïfa, Israël): Un évêché (?) entre village et cite. *La mosaïque gréco-romaine* 9: 436–452.

Fischer, M., Taxel, I. and Amit, D. 2008. Rural Settlement in the Vicinity of Yavneh in the Byzantine Period: A Religio-Archaeological Perspective. *Bulletin of the American Schools of Oriental Research* 350: 7–35.

Frankel, R. 1999. *Wine and Oil Production in Antiquity in Israel and Other Mediterranean Countries* (JSOT/ASOR Monograph Series 10). Sheffield.

Freestone I.C., Jackson-Tal, R.E. and Tal, O. 2008. Raw Glass and the Production of Glass Vessels at Late Byzantine Apollonia-Arsuf, Israel. *Journal of Glass Studies* 50: 67–80.

Gudovitch, S. 2006. Remains of a Monastery at the Foot of Tel Ashdod. *ʿAtiqot* 51: 1*–2* (Hebrew, with English summary p. 233).

Guz-Zilberstein, B. 1995. The Typology of the Hellenistic Coarse Ware and Selected Loci of the Hellenistic and Roman Periods. In: Stern, E. *et al. Excavations at Dor, Final Report I B. Areas A and C: The Finds* (Qedem Reports 2). Jerusalem: 289–433.

Kahane, P. 1951. Rishpon (Apollonia); B. *Bulletin of the Department of Antiquities of the State of Israel* 3: 42–43 (Hebrew).

Krueger, P., ed. 1877. *Codex Iustinianus, Corpus Iuris Civilis*, Vol. 2. Berlin.

Rabello, A.M. 2002. The Samaritans in Roman Law. In: Stern, E. and Eshel, H., eds. *The Samaritans*. Jerusalem: 488–495 (Hebrew).

Roll, I. 1999. Introduction: History of the Site, Its Research and Excavations. In: Roll, I. and Tal, O. *Apollonia-Arsuf: Final Report of the Excavations, Volume 1: The Persian and Hellenistic Periods (with Appendices on the Chalcolithic and Iron Age II Remains)* (Tel Aviv University, Monograph Series of the Institute of Archaeology 16). Tel Aviv: 1–62.

Roll, I. and Tal, O. 2008. A New Greek Inscription from Byzantine Apollonia-Arsuf/Sozousa: A Reassessment of the εἷς θεὸς μόνος Inscriptions of Palestine. *Scripta Classica Israelica* 28: 139–147.

SEG. *Supplementum Epigraphicum Graecum.*

Tal, O. 2015. A Bilingual Greek-Samaritan Inscription from Apollonia-Arsuf/Sozousa: Yet More Evidence of the Use of εἷς θεὸς μόνος Formula Inscriptions among the Samaritans. *Zeitschrift für Papyrologie und Epigraphik* 194: 169–175.

Tal, O., Jackson-Tal, R.E. and Freestone, I.C. 2004. New Evidence of the Production of Raw Glass at Late Byzantine Apollonia-Arsuf, Israel. *Journal of Glass Studies* 46: 51–66.

Tal, O. and Taxel, I. 2015. *Samaritan Cemeteries and Tombs in the Central Coastal Plain: Archaeology and History of the Samaritan Settlement outside Samaria (ca. 300–700 CE)* (Ägypten und Altes Testament 82). Münster.

Tzaferis, V. 2006. A Greek Inscription from Tel Ashdod. *ʿAtiqot* 51: 3*–5* (Hebrew, with English summary pp. 233–234).

Yeivin, Z. and Finkielsztejn, G. 1999. Ḥorbat Castra—1993–1997. *Excavations and Surveys in Israel* 109: 23*–27*.

CHAPTER 11

BURIALS AND SKELETAL REMAINS

Yossi Nagar

Poorly preserved human skeletal remains were uncovered in several tombs in the vast excavation area of Apollonia (East) (Areas AADD and their derivatives). The skeletal remains were found and excavated in two excavation seasons (2012 and 2013) but were analyzed by the same anthropologist (Y. Nagar) and the results were combined in the present report. The burials unearthed were attributed by the excavators to the Hellenistic, Byzantine and Early Islamic periods. The state of preservation of the bones was poor, impeding the full reconstruction of anthropological parameters. Moreover, the bones were examined only in the field and then immediately transferred to a representative of the Ministry of Religious Affairs for reburial.

DESCRIPTION OF THE REMAINS

TOMBS FROM THE HELLENISTIC PERIOD

Only a few of the skeletal remains found during the 2013 excavation season (A-6825/2013) were attributed to this period (above Chapter 7: Area DD3).

Area DD3/2

Tomb 41005. Bones of an articulated skeleton, representing primary burial, were found in a stone-lined cist grave. The deceased was put on his back in a general east–west orientation, head towards the east. The skull vault is fragmentary, the glabella and superior nuchal line are moderately pronounced, a morphology which could represent a male (Bass 1987: 82). Lower jaw: The lateral incisor shows attrition in a shape of a dentine cup, the right canine shows a deep dentine cup and the left premolar shows a dentine cup in one cusp. All the molar teeth were lost antemortem. The age at death, based upon tooth attrition rate, is estimated at 40< years (Hillson 1986).

Tomb 42000. The remains included one bone fragment found in a (stone-lined) cist grave, orientated north–south. The bone is non-diagnostic; however, it does not represent an infant.

Tomb 42001. The remains included a skull vault, teeth and postcranial fragments found in a stone-lined cist grave. Although the bones were scattered, a pattern could be noticed indicating primary burial of a single individual which had been disturbed. The deceased was put in the general north–south orientation, head towards the south. Upper teeth: Central incisors show attrition in the shape of a dentine cup; a premolar shows a deep dentine cup in one cusp. Lower teeth: A first molar shows a dentine cup in all the cusps. The age at death, based upon tooth attrition rate, is estimated at 40–50 years (Hillson 1986). The sex of this individual could not be determined.

Another grave (Tomb 41003) was dated to this period based upon its contents (Hellenistic unguentarium; Chapter 13: Fig. 13.19: 4). However, the bones were completely disintegrated.

TOMBS FROM THE LATE ROMAN AND EARLY BYZANTINE PERIODS

During an early excavation season in Apollonia (East), skeletal remains were found in jars dated to the Roman–Byzantine periods (Loci 918–929; above Chapter 7: Area DD2). These remains probably represent simple pit burials which cannot be traced. Nevertheless, a large burial structure from this period was also noticed during the current excavation phase (above Chapter 5: Area AA3) with human bones scattered outside of it (Loci 13007–13009).

Area DD2

Tomb 918. Infant bones were found inside a jar, oriented north–south. The remains included a few skull vault fragments, teeth, upper limb diaphyses and a fragment of a rib and a vertebra found in anatomical articulation indicating primary burial (Fig. 7.9a; Chapter 13: Fig. 13.16: 1–2). The deceased was put inside the jar with the legs to the inner side of it (south) and head towards the opening (north). The vertebral neural arch is still separated from the vertebral body, while the two halves of the arch are not yet fused in the midline, indicative of an infant aged <2.5 years (Yoganandan *et al.* 2011). A lower deciduous incisor tooth shows a complete root, while the permanent upper and lower first molars show a nearly complete crown. Based upon the tooth development stages, the age at death is estimated at 2–3 years (Hillson 1986).

Tomb 920. Infant bones were found inside a jar, oriented north–south. The remains included a few skull vault fragments, teeth, and a fragment of a long bone diaphysis, found in anatomical articulation indicating primary burial (Fig. 7.9c). The deceased was put inside the jar with the head to the inner side of it (north) and legs towards the opening (south). An upper deciduous incisor showed dentine exposure at one cusp. Permanent upper teeth: A central incisor and a canine show complete crowns, while a premolar tooth shows a nearly complete crown. Based upon the tooth development stages, the age at death is estimated at 4–5 years (Hillson 1986).

Tomb 927. A burial jar oriented north–south was found. However, the skeletal remains were completely disintegrated, possibly due to vegetation activity (Chapter 7; Chapter 13: Fig. 13.16: 3).

Tomb 929. Infant bones were found inside a jar, oriented north–south. The remains included a few rib fragments and a humeral diaphysis found in anatomical articulation indicating primary burial. The deceased was put inside the jar with the legs to the inner side of it (south), and the head towards the opening (north). The humeral length was measured as 100 mm. Although the ends of the bone had disintegrated, its maximum length could have been only few millimeters longer, representing an infant aged 0.5–1.5 years (Bass 1987: 149).

Area AA3

Tomb 13001, Loci 13007–13009. Bones found scattered next to a large Late Roman-period built tomb (Chapter 5: Area AA3) probably represent secondary burial related to this grave. The remains included mostly long bone fragments and teeth. The teeth were sorted and described and the age at death was estimated based upon tooth attrition stages (see IAA Anthropological Archival report for details). These teeth represent at least five individuals aged 2–7, 15–20, 20–30, 30–40, 50< years. However, the sex of the individuals could not be determined.

TOMBS LATER THAN THE EARLY ISLAMIC PERIOD

Area AA1

Tomb 11064. Bones were found in a stone-covered pit grave. The remains included an anatomically articulated skull vault, jaws, and postcranial fragments of a child, indicating primary burial. The deceased was put on its right side in a general east–west orientation, head towards the west facing south (see Fig.

3.1). Upper teeth: The deciduous central incisor had erupted, but the root is not yet complete. Lower jaw: Deciduous incisors and the first molar had erupted, a canine partially erupted, and the second molar had not erupted yet. The age at death, based upon tooth eruption stages, is estimated as 1.5–2 years (Hillson 1986). The ulnar length was measured as 94 mm. Although the ends of the bone had disintegrated, its maximum length could have been only few millimeters longer, representing an infant aged 1–2.5 years (Bass 1987: 170). The two halves of the vertebral arch, however, are fused.

Area AA2/2

Tomb 12017. Bones were found in a simple pit grave, next to a Byzantine–Early Islamic period field tower (Chapter 4: AA2). The remains included anatomically articulated postcranial fragments, indicating primary burial. The deceased was put on his back in the general east–west orientation, head towards the west. However, the head itself had been interrupted by present-day activities; therefore, it was impossible to reconstruct whether it faced south. The epiphyses in all the long bones are fused, indicative of an adult, 20< year old individual. The vertical diameter of the femoral proximal head is measured as 52 mm, indicative of a male (Bass 1987: 220). The glabella and brow ridges are relatively pronounced, a morphology typical of a male (Bass 1987: 82). Upper teeth: A central incisor and a premolar tooth show enamel attrition. Lower jaw: An incisor and a canine show slight dentine exposure, while the first and second premolars show enamel attrition. The age at death, based upon tooth attrition rate, is estimated as 20–30 years (Hillson 1986).

Tomb 12018. Bones were found in a simple pit grave, next to a Byzantine–early Arab period field structure. The remains included an anatomically articulated skull vault, teeth, and postcranial fragments, indicating primary burial. The deceased was put on his right side in the general east–west orientation, head towards the west facing south. The skull vault fragments are relatively thin; however, the glabella and brow ridges, and the mastoid process are relatively pronounced, morphology typical of a male (Bass 1987: 82). Only two teeth (a permanent canine and a premolar) were found, showing enamel attrition, indicative of an individual aged <25 years. However, the epiphyses in all the long bones and the iliac crest in the pelvis are fused, indicative of an adult, 20<year old individual (Johnston and Zimmer 1989). The vertical diameter of the femoral proximal head is measured as 45 mm. and the epicondylar width of the distal humerus is measured as 62 mm, indicative of a male (Bass 1987: 220). The femoral oblique length is 433 mm, characteristic of an individual's height of 162 cm (Feldesman, Kleckner and Lundy 1990).

DISCUSSION

In the present study, tombs from the Hellenistic, Roman and Byzantine and post-Early Islamic periods were analyzed. Despite the complications resulting from the state of preservation and the lack of laboratory study, the burial postures of the deceased were described, the age at death of all of the individuals was estimated, and the sex of 80% of the adults in the articulated graves was determined.

The region around Apollonia (East) was probably used as a burial site from the Iron Age/Persian period until the modern era. Several cases of graves dated to the Roman and Byzantine periods were reported in the past in the vicinity (Feldstein 1999). Anthropological data from these tombs are highly important, as they can be combined with data presented in the above chapter. A burial cave and cist grave in close proximity, mentioned by Ayash and Birman (2006) in Kefar Shemaryahu were dated to the Persian period, and seem to be irrelevant to the present study.

THE HELLENISTIC PERIOD

Only five graves from this period were found (Tomb 41001, Tomb 41003, Tomb 41005, Tomb 42000, Tomb 42001) and the remains of only two individuals aged 40–50, 40< years were reported. Despite the small sample, it is possible to conclude that burial in this period was performed in either pit graves or stone-lined cist graves oriented north–south, used for a single individual in a primary burial. Such burial practices were common during the Hellenistic period on the central coast, as found in Yafo (Andromeda A-2085/1995; Ganor A-3135/1999); and Gan Soreq (North A-4248/2004) (data from the IAA Anthropological Archive). These burial practices bear no indication as to the ethnicity of the dead.

The Roman and Byzantine Period

Only five graves from this period were found, four of them were pits containing jar burials and one was identified as a large built tomb (mausoleum) which had been disturbed. However, six more graves had been found in the past (Chapter 7: Area TT8), including a jar burial (T3), two cist graves (T1 and T2), and three additional graves that were left unexcavated (T4, T5 and T6). Additionally, three cist graves were excavated in 1995 by I. Ben-David and A. Krauz some 200 m south-east of this excavation (unpublished report, IAA Anthropological Archives).

Jar Burials

Articulated skeletal remains were found in three jars (Chapter 7: Area DD1; the bones of a fourth individual were completely disintegrated), indicating primary burial with the heads towards the opening of the jar. Although all four jars were oriented north–south, the positions of the heads of these individuals were either to the north or to the south. Accordingly, the interment of the deceased was either with its head to the opening of the jar or to the base. The jar of Area TT8 (T3) was also oriented north–south. Therefore, it is suggested that the general north–south orientation is the only obligated parameter in this burial type. The jars of Area DD2 included the remains of two infants (0.5–1, 2–3 years) and a child (4–5 years). However, in other cases of jar burials attributed to the Roman–Byzantine periods, such as ʿAkko (Nagar, forthcoming), Ashqelon Migdal (A-4641/2005; Nahshoni 2009), Gan Yavne, and Yavne (A-3680/2002; A-6025/2011; IAA Anthropological Archive), such vessels were used for infant burial only and no children over three years of age were reported.

Large Built Tombs

In the large built tomb (mausoleum), the deceased were originally placed in primary burial; however, the grave was found empty and the bones scattered next to it. The remains represent at least five individuals, of them a child aged 2–7 years and four adults aged 15–20, 20–30, 30–40, 50< years; sex could not be determined.

The phenomenon of using large built tombs for the common burial of several individuals is well-documented along the Israeli shore-line and Shephelah (e.g., Kogan-Zehavi 2011; Varga 2002).

Cist Graves

Three cist graves, excavated in the past by I. Ben-David and A. Krauz (A-2371/1995) have not been published; however, the bones were inspected by the current author using the same methodologies. The graves were oriented east–west. The remains from Locus 101 were characteristic of a young individual, whose age at death was estimated as 15–17 years by means of dental eruption and attrition stages (Hillson 1986). The remains from Locus 103 were characteristic of an individual aged 30–50 years (Hillson 1986). Skull and pelvic morphology were indicative of a female, whose stature, based upon femoral length, is estimated as 150 cm (Bass 1987: 24, 82). This individual was placed on her back, with the arms folded and the hands crossed above the chest. Tomb 102 yielded no skeletal remains. Two additional cist graves were reported by Roll (1999: 46; and Chapter 7: Area TT8 [T1, T2]), but the bones were not examined on-site. Nevertheless, by looking at the pictures provided by the excavator, it is possible to determine that both included skeletons in primary burial, oriented north–south, in accordance with the orientation of the jar burials. The deceased were placed on their backs. In T1, the proximal epiphysis of the humerus is fused, and the lower third molar has erupted, characteristic of an individual aged 20< years (Hillson 1986, Johnston and Zimmer 1989). In T2, the ends of the long bones are broken, but according to the bone proportions, this burial is of an adult.

Burials dated to the Roman–Byzantine periods in the vicinity of Apollonia (East) also include burial caves hewn in the *kurkar*. One such cave was excavated by H. Eliaz (1999; Kefar Shemaryahu A-2590/1996), but the osteological find was negligible and no anthropological data is available. Two more caves were excavated by A. Feldstein (1999; Rudin 2016; Kefar Shemaryahu A-1914/1992) and included the remains of at least 26 individuals (13 in each cave), among them infants, children and adults of both sexes. Based on the resemblance to the burial practices in the hill country during this period, and other finds, these caves were attributed by the excavator to a Samaritan population. Since the Kefar Shemaryahu burials are markedly different from the Apollonia (East) graves discussed above, it is possible to speculate that the Apollonia (East) population discussed in this present study represents a non-Samaritan population.

Alternatively, the three types of burials found at Apollonia (East) (jar burial, cist graves, and mausolea) are said to be common in the coastal region during the Roman and Byzantine periods and can also be found together in the same cemeteries (e.g., ʿAkko, Yavne and Ashqelon Migdal). These practices seem to follow traditions rooted in the former Hellenistic period in this area (e.g., Kastra A-3362/2001), as might also be the case at Apollonia (East).

TOMBS LATER THAN THE EARLY ISLAMIC PERIOD

Three graves dug into the ground next to Byzantine/Early Islamic period architectural remains seem to have represented burial later than this period. The pit graves were covered by stone slabs (Tomb 11064, Tomb 12017, Tomb 12018). The orientation of these graves was east–west, in contrast with most of the earlier burials at this site. The deceased were in primary burials with their heads towards the west facing south (two cases were available to arrive at such a determination), characteristic of a Muslim burial (Gorzalzcany 2007). Pit graves attributed to a Muslim population scattered around ancient architectural remains is a very common phenomenon in central Israel (e.g., Tel Sham A-6852/2013, Ksefa L-1045/2005, Emaos L-961/2002, Beqoa A-5487/2008, and Ḥorvat Ḥamoza A-2067/1993; data from the IAA Anthropological Archive). It is usually referred to as a Bedouin type of burial of uncertain date (from the Mamluk period to present day), possibly using the ancient ruins (Khirbe) as a landmark.

The skeletal sample from this period included only three individuals. These were identified as a two-year-old infant and two males aged 20–30, 20–30 years. Although the sample is small, the osteological remains were better preserved than in previous periods, allowing for more comprehensive data collection in the field. The stature of one of the adults was reconstructed as 162 cm. and no porosity was found in the orbital roofs and the skull vault of the infant and the two adults.

CONCLUSIONS

Osteological remains unearthed at Apollonia (East) included burials from several periods, differing in the type of the grave as well as the skeletal orientation and posture. During the Hellenistic period, primary burial of single individuals was performed in stone-lined cist graves oriented north-south, in accordance with the prevailing custom as seen in other coastal cemeteries. During the Roman and Byzantine period, primary burial was practiced in jars (for infants), in stone-lined cists and in large built tombs (mausolea) simultaneously. The use of jar burial for infants was probably common in the coastal region in this period; however, burying a child aged 4–5 years in this manner is an exception. Combining the current data with those retrieved in previous excavations at this site, the age at death of at least 12 individuals could be estimated. The results show the presence of at least two infants, two children, and eight adults of a wide age range. Furthermore, both sexes are represented. Hence, although the small sample is not enough for a statistical demographic analysis, it clearly demonstrates the regular, civilian nature of the cemetery. From the Mamluk period onward, simple Muslim burials were performed at this site. However, the burials are sporadic and possibly represent a Bedouin population from this region, using the ancient ruins as landmarks.

REFERENCES

Ayash, E. and Birman, G. 2006. Kefar Shemaryahu. *Ḥadashot Arkheologiyot—Excavations and Surveys in Israel* 118. http://www.hadashot-esi.org.il/report_detail_eng.aspx?id=361&mag_id=111

Bass, W.M. 1987. *Human Osteology: A Laboratory and Field Manual*. Columbia, Miss.

Feldstein, A. 1999. Kefar Shemaryahu (North). *Excavations and Surveys in Israel* 19: 39.

Gorzalzcany, A. 2007. The Kefar Saba Cemetery and Differences in Orientation of Late Islamic Burials from Israel/Palestine. *Levant* 39: 71–79.

Hillson, S. 1986. *Teeth*. Cambridge.

Johnston, F.E. and Zimmer, L.O. 1989. Assessment of Growth and Age in the Immature Skeleton. In: Iscan, M.Y. and Kenneth, A.R., eds. *Reconstruction of Life from the Skeleton*. New York: 11–22.

Kogan-Zehavi, E. 2011. Ashqelon, el-Jura. *Ḥadashot Arkheologiyot—Excavations and Surveys in Israel* 123. http://www.hadashot-esi.org.il/report_detail_eng.aspx?id=1807&mag_id=118.

Nahshoni, P. 2009. Ashqelon. *Ḥadashot Arkheologiyot—Excavations and Surveys in Israel* 121. http://www.hadashot-esi.org.il/Report_Detail_Eng.aspx?id=1041&mag_id=115

Roll, I. 1999. Introduction: History of the Site, Its Research and Excavations. In: Roll, I. and Tal, O. *Apollonia-Arsuf: Final Report of the Excavations, Volume 1: The Persian and Hellenistic Periods (with Appendices on the Chalcolithic and Iron Age II Remains)* (Tel Aviv University, Monograph Series of the Institute of Archaeology 16). Tel Aviv: 1–62.

Rudin, T. 2016. *Roman–Byzantine Cemeteries and Tombs around Apollonia/Sozousa: The New Discoveries* (MA thesis, Tel Aviv University). Tel Aviv (Hebrew).

Varga, D. 2002. Ashqelon Afridar and Barneʿa A. *Ḥadashot Arkheologiyot* 114: 87–88.

Yoganandan, N., Pintar, F.A., Lew, S.M., Rao, R.D. and Ranngarajan N. 2011. Quantitative Analyses of Pediatric Cervical Spine Ossification Patterns Using Computed Tomography. *Annals of Advances in Automotive Medicine* 55: 159–168.

CHAPTER 12

CHRONOLOGICAL SUMMARY

Oren Tal

A few flint tools of the Neolithic and Chalcolithic periods may attest to the earliest activity in the site's eastern immediate hinterland (Areas AA–DD and their derivatives; Fig. 12.1). Flint tools (especially scrapers and blades) of the Wadi Rabah and Ghassulian cultures were also found at the site itself (Area K), and although they enhance the evidence of a possible proto-historic settlement, they do not permit elaboration on its type. Storage jars of the Persian and Hellenistic periods may attest to use for burial (as found in Area DD1), as either containers for primary and secondary burials or as water jars and/or markers ("tombstones"). Other types of pottery vessels (as found in Areas DD3 and O) were most probably used as utility vessels either for burial or agricultural activity. The cist tomb (Tomb 41001) forms the earliest architectural remains (given the Hellenistic cooking jug found in it), while other tombs such as the pit graves (Tomb 41003, Tomb 42000 and Tomb 42001), and the cist grave (Tomb 41005) can be assigned to the Hellenistic period (3rd–2nd centuries BCE) as well, based on pottery found in them or in their proximity. The area of the immediate hinterland of the site during Early Roman (1st–2nd centuries CE) times seems to have maintained a similar character to that of the Hellenistic period, as the isolated pottery vessels found in these excavations were either unearthed next to tombs (in Area DD3; Chapter 13: Fig. 13.19: 1) or as isolated finds (in Area BB; Chapter 13: Fig. 13.20: 2). The Late Roman and Early Byzantine periods (3rd–4th centuries CE) illustrate burial activity as well in built tombs (as found in Area AA3), cist tombs (as found in Area TT8) or storage jars and artificial cavities in the local *kurkar* bedrock (as found in Area DD1). In addition to these burials, the early stage of activity of the winepress discovered in Area AA1, as well as the winepress discovered in Area DD1 are assigned to this period, suggesting that grapevines were cultivated at the time in the area. It is in the Late Byzantine and possibly the earliest stages of the Early Islamic period (5th–7th centuries CE) that the area of the immediate hinterland of the site shows the greatest activity. Winepresses (in Areas AA1, DD2 and O), field towers (in Areas AA and AA2), and other installations, such as the large refuse dump (in Area CC), although sparse, and small refuse pits (in Areas M and N), still exhibit a more intense agricultural and industrial activity when compared to the earlier and later periods of inhabitation (post-7th century CE). The exception to this are the working surfaces and installation (oil press?) found in the southern part of Area AA1 in addition to a few pottery finds and coins (if we overlook the few Ottoman/Mandatory period pit graves unearthed). It may also be added that the coin evidence suggests a similar trend as well. More than 1000 coins were recovered from the areas discussed in this report; they cover the Seleucid through the Ottoman periods. The vast majority are either Late Roman or Byzantine coins (4th–6th centuries CE), with a few that predate and postdate that period of time (see Chapter 18).

Fig. 12.1: Areas AA–DD and their derivatives, aerial view after excavations, as at 2018 (by courtesy of the Israel Antiquities Authority).

SECTION TWO
THE FINDS

CHAPTER 13

POTTERY

Itamar Taxel

This chapter is composed of two major parts. The first presents a selection of pottery (types and vessels) from Areas M, N and O and representative ceramic assemblages (each is represented by one or more loci) from most areas of excavation at the site. The second part discusses—typologically and chronologically —the main body of pottery found in the excavations of Areas M, N and O (within or across from the Apollonia National Park), as well as Areas AA, CC and DD located in East Apollonia (East) (aka Nof-Yam). With the exception of a handful of MB IIA pottery sherds from Apollonia (East) and a somewhat larger quantity from the Persian to Roman and ʿAbbasid to Ottoman periods found in the same area, the great majority of ceramics from the excavated areas represent the Byzantine and the beginning of the Early Islamic (Umayyad) periods. The Apollonia (East) assemblages were generally chosen due to their importance in dating the main architectural remains and other features/deposits, though selected pottery from assemblages of lesser stratigraphic importance is also presented, since it complements the main ceramic array and adds some information about the site's material culture during the discussed periods.

PROVENANCED REPRESENTATIVE ASSEMBLAGES

APOLLONIA (EAST)

Area AA

The main feature unearthed in this area is a small structure identified as a field tower (Installation 10091). The surface layer and subsurface fills (Loci 112, 122, 124, 10004, 10018, 10019, 10058, 10080) covering its remains contained a mixture of pottery sherds representing the Persian and Hellenistic periods (e.g., a black-slipped bowl and a mortarium; Fig. 13.1: 1–2); the Roman period (e.g., a Type 2 cooking pot and a Type 4 amphora; Fig. 13.1: 3–4); and the Byzantine and Early Islamic periods (e.g., an LRC/PRS Ware Form 3 bowl, a Type 4 common ware basin, Type 5 and 6 storage jar and amphora, and a Type 5 jug; Fig. 13.1: 5–9).

Another structure (Installation 11089) was found to its west; its area yielded a smaller number of pottery sherds, e.g., a Roman-period casserole and a Type 1 storage jar (Fig. 13.2).

Area AA1

The main feature unearthed in this area is a winepress complex or more accurately its two systems of mosaic-paved settling pits and collecting vats. These installations and the entire winepress area were found covered by a fill (Loci 208, 216, 223, 236, 243, 248, 258, 259, 11006) containing a relatively large number of pottery sherds. Although some of the types had already appeared in the Roman period, the actual date of the assemblage seems to fall within the Late Roman-Early Byzantine period, or more accurately the 4th to 5th centuries CE. This chronological spectrum apparently dates the use period of the winepress and provides a 5th-century CE *terminus ante quem* for its use. The discussed pottery includes mostly Roman to Early Byzantine-period Type 1 storage jars (Fig. 13.3: 3–5) and Byzantine-period Type 1A storage jars (Fig. 13.3: 6–7), in addition to a Roman to Early Byzantine-period casserole lid (Fig. 13.3: 1), an Early Byzantine to Late Roman-period Type 1 cooking pot (Fig. 13.3: 2), a Byzantine-period Type 5 storage jar (early variant; Fig. 13.3: 8), and water-wheel jars of Type 1 (Late Roman-Early Byzantine) and 2 (Byzantine) (Fig. 13.3: 9–11). Interestingly, two joint fragments of the Type 1 water-wheel jar originated in two different locations approximately 20 m apart (Loci 243 and 248, at the southeastern edge of Area AA1 and in the winepress area, respectively), probably indicating a post-depositional disturbance of the area by either human or natural agents.

Evidence for this disturbance is indicated by the presence in the same fill layer of several pottery sherds, such as a bowl with gritty glaze (Fig. 13.4: 1), an Egyptian (?) alkaline glazed bowl (Fig. 13.4: 2), a Proto-maiolica (?) glazed bowl (Fig. 13.4: 3), a soft-paste glazed bowl (Fig. 13.4: 4) and a glazed frying pan (Fig. 13.4: 5), which can all be dated to the Crusader and Mamluk periods. This is also supported by a few 13th and 14th century coins unearthed in the area (Chapter 18: 374–378).

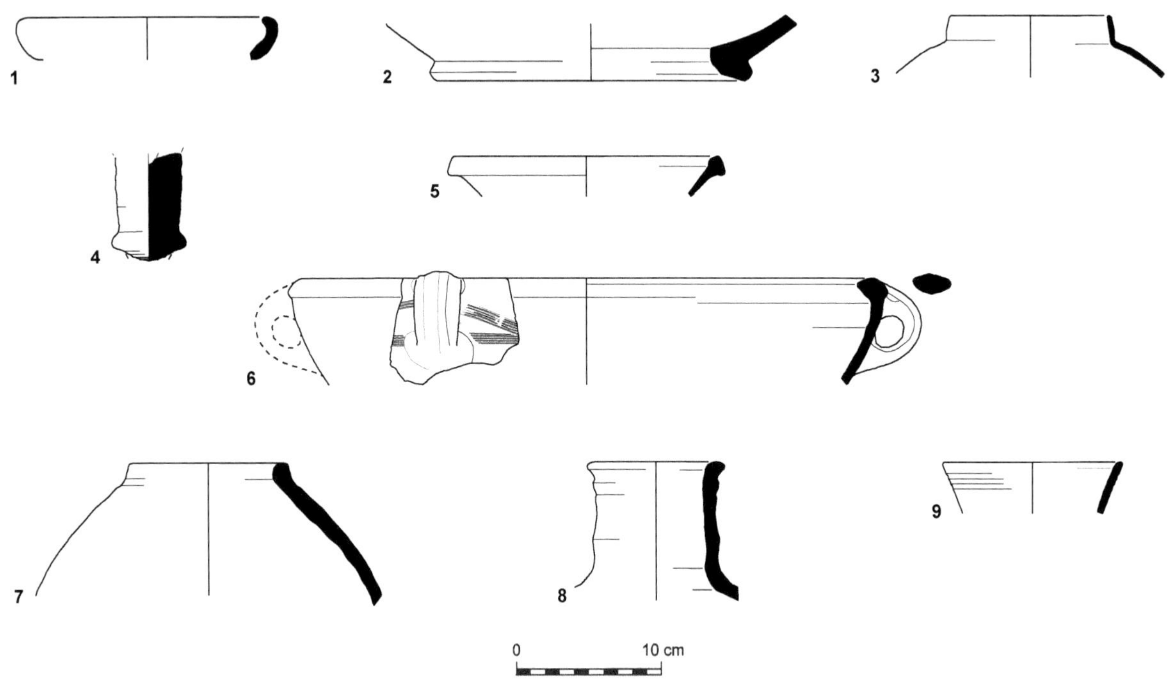

FIG. 13.1: AREA AA, INSTALLATION 11091; SELECTED POTTERY

No.	Vessel	Locus	Basket
1	Bowl	10018	100064
2	Bowl	112	1061
3	Cooking pot	10080	100404
4	Amphora (base)	10058	100411
5	Bowl	10019	100113
6	Basin	10004	100003
7	Storage jar	122	1148
8	Amphora	10004	100013
9	Jug	124	1136

The earth fill (Loci 212, 11033, 11067), which covered the remains of plastered installations (Installation 224, Installation 11066) and a stone floor (Floor 2091) at the southeastern part of Area AA1, contained some pottery sherds ranging in date from the Early Byzantine period to the Late Byzantine-beginning of Early Islamic period, such as a Type 3 common ware basin (Fig. 13.5: 1), a casserole (Fig. 13.5: 2), a Type 1 cooking pot (Fig. 13.5: 3) and a Type 2 jug (Fig. 13.5: 4).

Another noteworthy context from Area AA1 is the fill (Loci 11045, 11079) which was found between the destroyed sections of the Floor 11038. Among the pottery sherds were two neck- and upper shoulder-sections of Roman (and Early Byzantine)-period Type 1 storage jars, which had been intentionally detached by making a row of small holes across the vessels' circumference. The broken edges of the detached part were then roughly smoothed or became smooth/abraded during consequent use (Fig. 13.6: 1–2). Such detached jar necks could have been used as stands for other pottery vessels after being partially embedded upside-down in a beaten earth floor (see Taxel 2018: 94, with references). A fragment of a Late Byzantine-Early Islamic Type 3B storage jar was also found here (Fig. 13.6: 3).

AREA AA2

Two segmented features were found in the western part of Area AA2, represented by scattered stones with some sherds and industrial glass refuse around them. The recovered pottery (Loci 169, 187) included a Persian-period mortarium (Fig. 13.7: 1) and a Roman (and Early Byzantine)-period Type 1 storage jar (Fig. 13.7: 2), as well as a Late Roman-Early Byzantine lamp (for the latter, see Chapter 14). Other diagnostic pottery found in the area's surface layer (Locus 166) included a double slip glazed bowl from the Fatimid or Early Crusader period (Fig. 13.7: 3). The few sherds recovered as surface finds in Area AA22 where another field tower was identified (Installation 12036) can be attributed to the Byzantine and Early Islamic periods.

AREA AA3

Some pottery sherds were found (including some restorable fragments) over and around the remains of the built tomb (a mausoleum). With the exception of a fragment of a Hellenistic-period storage jar (not illustrated), the assemblage contained Roman (or Late Roman)-period forms, such as a Type 3 cooking pot (Fig. 13.8: 1), Type 1 and 3 storage jars and an amphora (Fig. 13.8: 2–6) and Type 1 and 2 jugs (Fig. 13.8: 7–8), which apparently provide a 4th-century CE date (i.e., the actual date may fall within the Early Byzantine period).

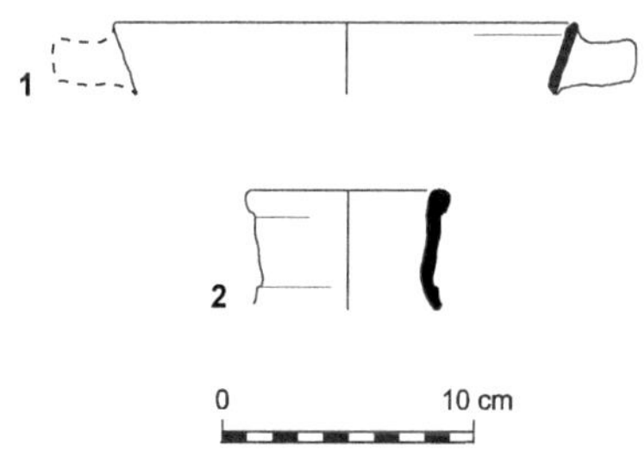

FIG. 13.2: AREA AA, INSTALLATION 11089; SELECTED POTTERY

No.	*Vessel*	*Locus*	*Basket*
1	Casserole	131	1162
2	Storage jar	111	1138

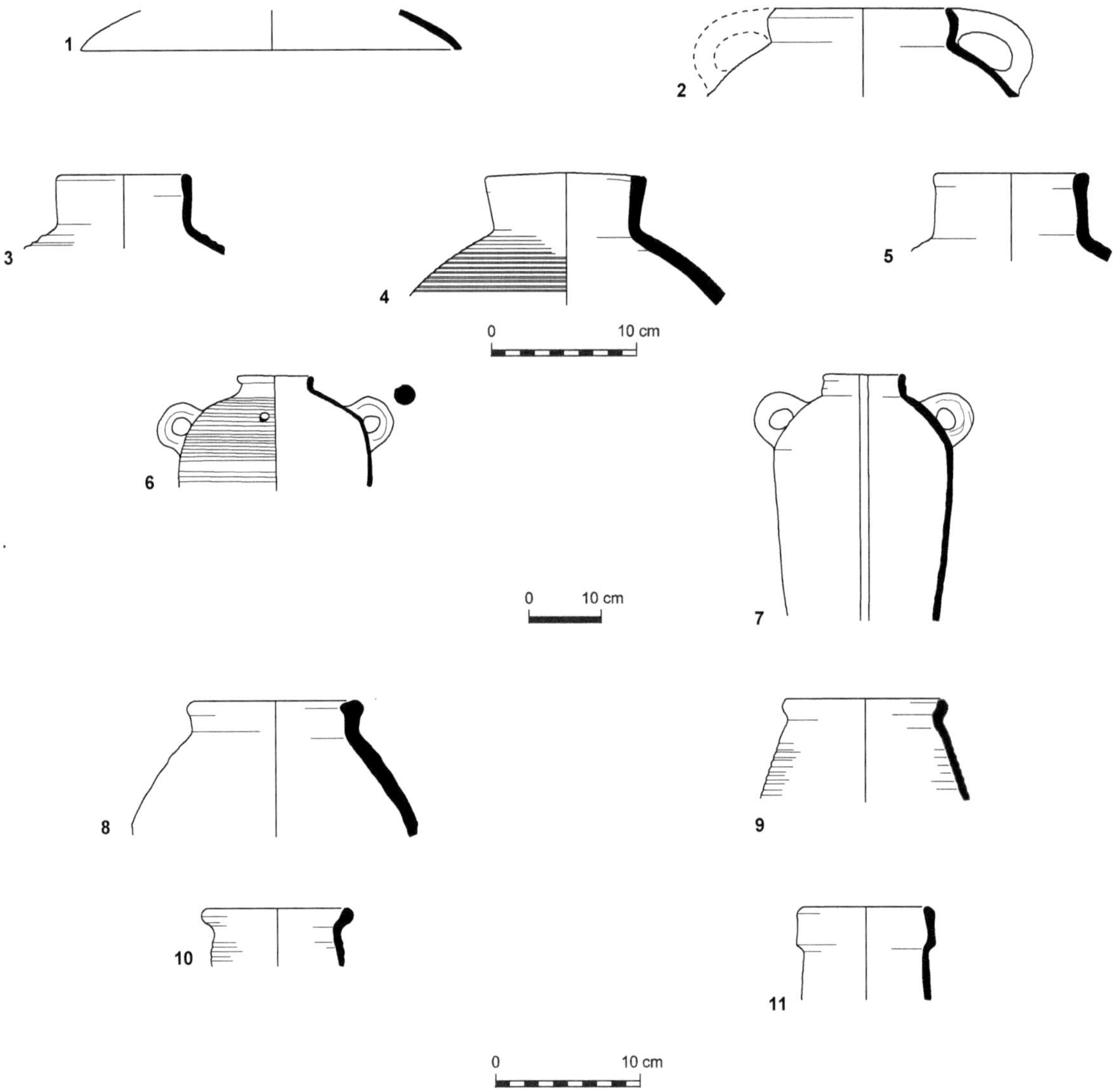

FIG. 13.3: AREA AA1, SELECTED LATE ROMAN–EARLY BYZANTINE POTTERY

No.	*Vessel*	*Locus*	*Basket*
1	Cooking ware lid	229	2063
2	Cooking pot	216	2209
3	Storage jar	216	2189
4	Storage jar	223	2089
5	Storage jar	216	2208
6	Storage jar	236	2093
7	Storage jar	236	2102
8	Storage jar	11006	101148
9	Water-wheel jar	216	2208
10	Water-wheel jar	243, 248	2088, 2098
11	Water-wheel jar	216	2135

AREA CC

The extensive refuse dump that formed the main feature of excavation in Area CC has yielded a vast amount of pottery, the great majority in fragmentary (non-restorable) state. The exceptions are two intact storage jars, two complete/nearly complete stoppers and more than 200 complete/nearly complete lamps (for the latter, see Chapter 14). The chronological range of this pottery is from the late 4th to the 7th centuries CE, though it is likely that the actual use-period of the refuse dump was shorter, namely between the 5th and 6th centuries. The latter was supported by the rich numismatic evidence (over 150 coins) that came from the dump because the latest coins are mid-6th century CE in date (Chapter 18: Nos. 319–321). Two 7th-century CE issues (Chapter 18: Nos. 349, 356) are surface finds and it is unclear whether they were related to the dumping activities in the area; this can also be said of the few other later surface find coins of the 8th–19th centuries CE found in the area but not in the dump (Chapter 18: Nos. 359, 361, 365, 379, 380). The ceramic types represented in the dump are ARS Ware Form 67, 97, 99 and 108 bowls (Fig. 13.9: 1–5), an LRC/PRS Ware Form 3 bowl (Fig. 13.9: 6), an LRD/CRS Ware Form 2 bowl (Fig. 13.9: 7), an ERS Ware A bowl (Fig. 13.9: 8), Type 1 and 5 common ware bowls and basins (Fig. 13.9: 9–12), casseroles (Fig. 13.10: 1–3), Type 1 frying pans (Fig. 13.10: 4–5), cooking ware lids (Fig. 13.10: 6–7), Type 2 and 3 cooking pots (Fig. 13.10: 8–10), Type 1A, 2, 3A, 4–8, 12 and 13 storage jars and amphorae (Figs. 13.12, 13.13), Type 1–4 and 7 jugs and juglets (Fig. 13.11: 1–6), Type 1–3 flasks (Fig. 13.11: 7–10, 14), Type 2 water-wheel jars (Fig. 13.11: 11–13), incense burners (Fig. 13.14: 1–2), Type 1 stoppers (Fig. 13.14: 3–4) and pipe sections (Fig. 13.14: 5–8).

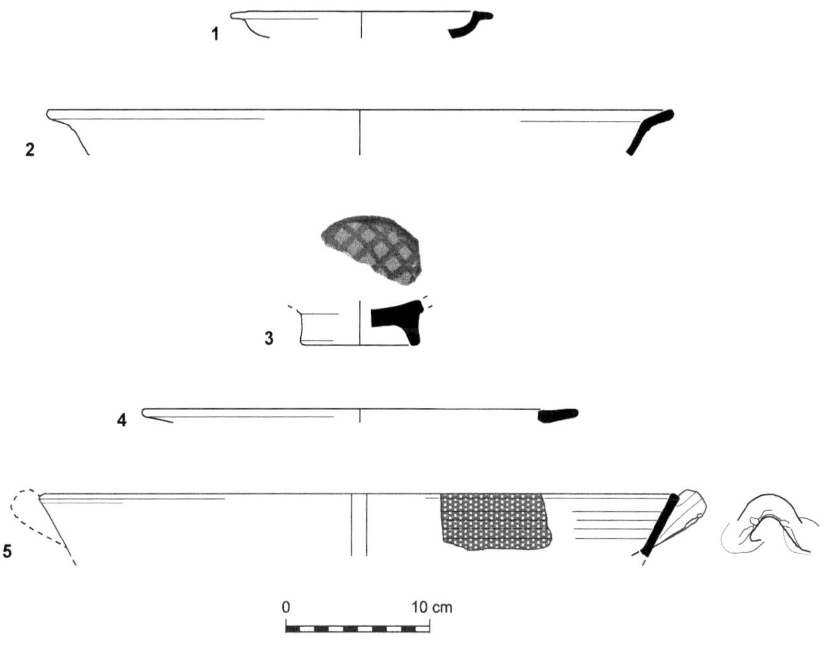

FIG. 13.4: SELECTED CRUSADER POTTERY

No.	*Vessel*	*Locus*	*Basket*
1	Bowl	216	2172
2	Bowl	223	2101
3	Bowl	258	2176
4	Bowl	208	2166
5	Frying pan	259	2182

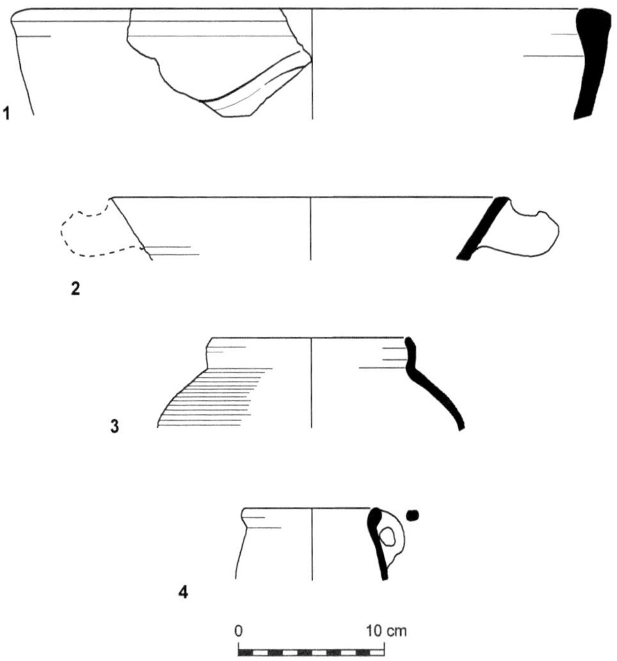

FIG. 13.5: AREA AA1, INSTALLATIONS CLUSTER; SELECTED POTTERY

No.	*Vessel*	*Locus*	*Basket*
1	Basin	11033	101218
2	Casserole	11067	101284
3	Cooking pot	212	2108
4	Jug	11033	101201

A handful of pottery sherds from earlier and later periods was also found in Area CC, such as a Persian/Hellenistic black-slipped *skyphos* (Fig. 13.14: 9) and a storage jar (Fig. 13.14: 10), an Early Roman Type 2 cooking pot (Fig. 13.14: 11), an ʿAbbasid common lead glazed bowl (Fig. 13.14: 12) and an Ottoman "Gaza" ware storage jar (Fig. 13.14: 13; represented by two joint fragments found some 10–15 m apart, in Loci 603 and 625). While the finds which pre-date the refuse dump either represent residual material from earlier activity in the area or material brought with the discarded refuse from elsewhere at the site, the later finds (which originated in the surface layer) apparently indicate some low-scale activity in the area long after the dump ceased to function.

The pottery retrieved from the dump was counted in the field by T. Harpak who classified it into functional classes and general types as illustrated in the pie chart below (Fig. 13.34):

The total number of counted fragments from the dump is 307,780, of which 108,085 fragments (body sherds, rims, bases and handles) were dated by Harpak to the dump's actual use-period (namely, the 5th to 7th centuries) and rather securely attributed to specific classes/types (lamps are excluded from this count). Of these 120,244 fragments, storage jars and amphorae constitute 73.47% (or 80,348 fragments), the cooking wares (casseroles, cooking pots and cooking ware lids) constitute 10.20% (or 12,265 fragments), the small and medium-sized containers (jugs, juglets, flasks and water-wheel jars) constitute 16.29% (or 19,586 fragments), and the bowls constitute 0.04% (or 45 fragments).[1] The high ratio of storage jars and amphorae corresponds to similar counts for such vessels from other contemporaneous

1 Harpak's count did not include basins, jar stoppers, incense burners and pipes and they were underrepresented and hence would not alter the above-mentioned figures.

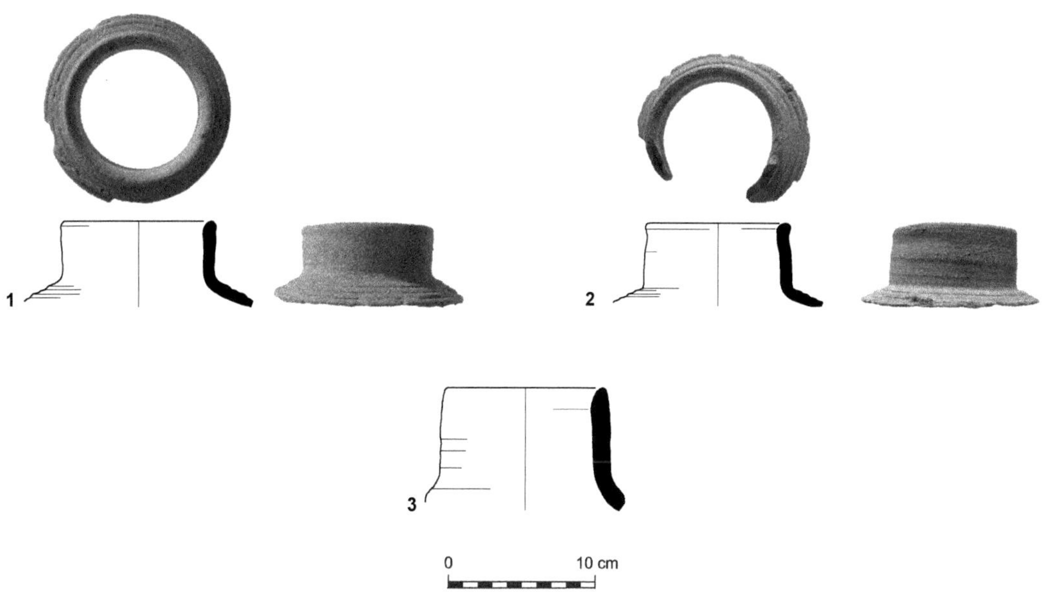

FIG. 13.6: AREA AA1, SELECTED POTTERY

No.	*Vessel*	*Locus*	*Basket*
1	Storage jar	11079	101301
2	Storage jar	11079	101301
3	Storage jar	11045	101293

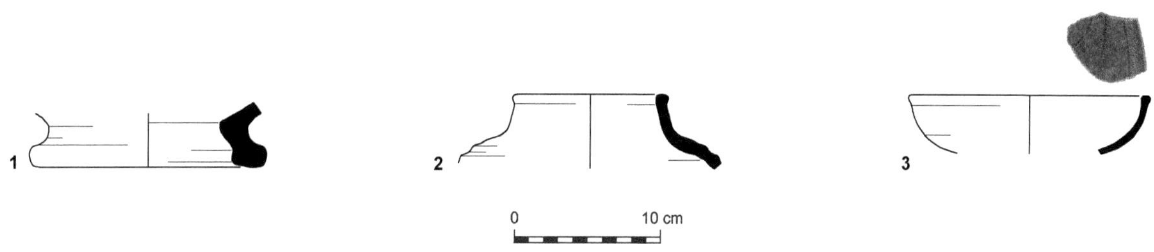

FIG. 13.7: AREA AA2/1, SELECTED POTTERY

No.	*Vessel*	*Locus*	*Basket*
1	Bowl	187	1726
2	Storage jar	187	1726
3	Bowl	166	1605

refuse disposal assemblages, e.g., from the Ramat Hanadiv farmhouse (59%, which represent complete vessels and rim fragments only; Calderon 2000: 158–160) and from a winepress at Kefar Sirkin (ca. 90%, apparently representing body sherds and the like; Singer and ʿAd 2003). The above-mentioned ratios of cooking wares are also similar to those from Ramat Hanadiv (14.7%), though in the latter assemblage the jugs constitute only 3% while the bowls and basins/kraters constitute altogether 21.8% (the remaining 1.5% are represented by lamps; Calderon 2000: 158–160). The ratio of open table and utilitarian wares from Ramat Hanadiv recalls the percentages of bowls and basins from two Early Islamic refuse deposits in Yavneh, which count for 21.07% and 29.57%, respectively.[2]

2 The refuse deposits were found in an excavation carried out at Yavneh in 2010 by E. Yannai on behalf of the Israel Antiquities Authority; the ceramic finds from this excavation have been studied for final publication by the present author.

Against these data, the meager ratio of bowls from the Nof-Yam refuse dump is especially striking and seems to correspond more with the Kefar Sirkin assemblage. In Ramat Hanadiv and Yavneh the refuse deposits can be directly associated with nearby domestic complexes, and therefore the breakdown of ceramic classes in both cases is more or less balanced with no overwhelming predominance of a certain functional class. On the other hand, the Kefar Sirkin and Nof-Yam assemblages are located on

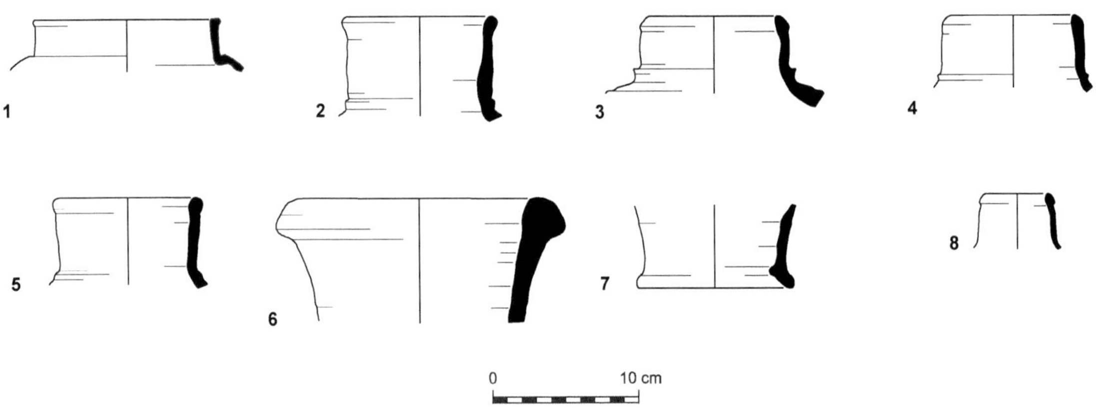

FIG. 13.8: AREA AA3, SELECTED POTTERY

No.	*Vessel*	*Locus*	*Basket*
1	Cooking pot	13008	103048
2	Storage jar	437	3090
3	Storage jar	420	3049
4	Storage jar	420	3051
5	Storage jar	408	3028
6	Amphora	426	3069
7	Jug	438	3093
8	Jug/flask	13007	103025

FIG. 13.9: AREA CC, REFUSE DUMP; BOWLS AND BASINS

No.	*Vessel*	*Locus*	*Basket*
1	Bowl	30068	302189
2	Bowl	30079	303367
3	Bowl	30071	301977
4	Bowl	30060	300721
5	Bowl	609	6079
6	Bowl	30063	302577
7	Bowl	30071	302030
8	Bowl	613	6228
9	Bowl	30007	300118
10	Basin	30067	302224
11	Basin	661	6697
12	Basin	659	6611

the agricultural and industrial outskirts of the settlements, and therefore, in theory, should be spatially and functionally related, primarily to activities carried out in the immediate environs of these dumps. Hence, it can be suggested that the majority of storage and transport containers documented in the Nof-Yam dump represent vessels whose contents – foodstuffs and/or other products – were consumed by people working (and maybe temporarily living) on the eastern fringes of the city of Apollonia/ Sozousa; similarly, the cooking wares and various smaller containers were apparently used by the same people for a variety of daily purposes. However, if food preparation was included among these activities (as indicated by the cooking wares), how was this food consumed if only a very limited

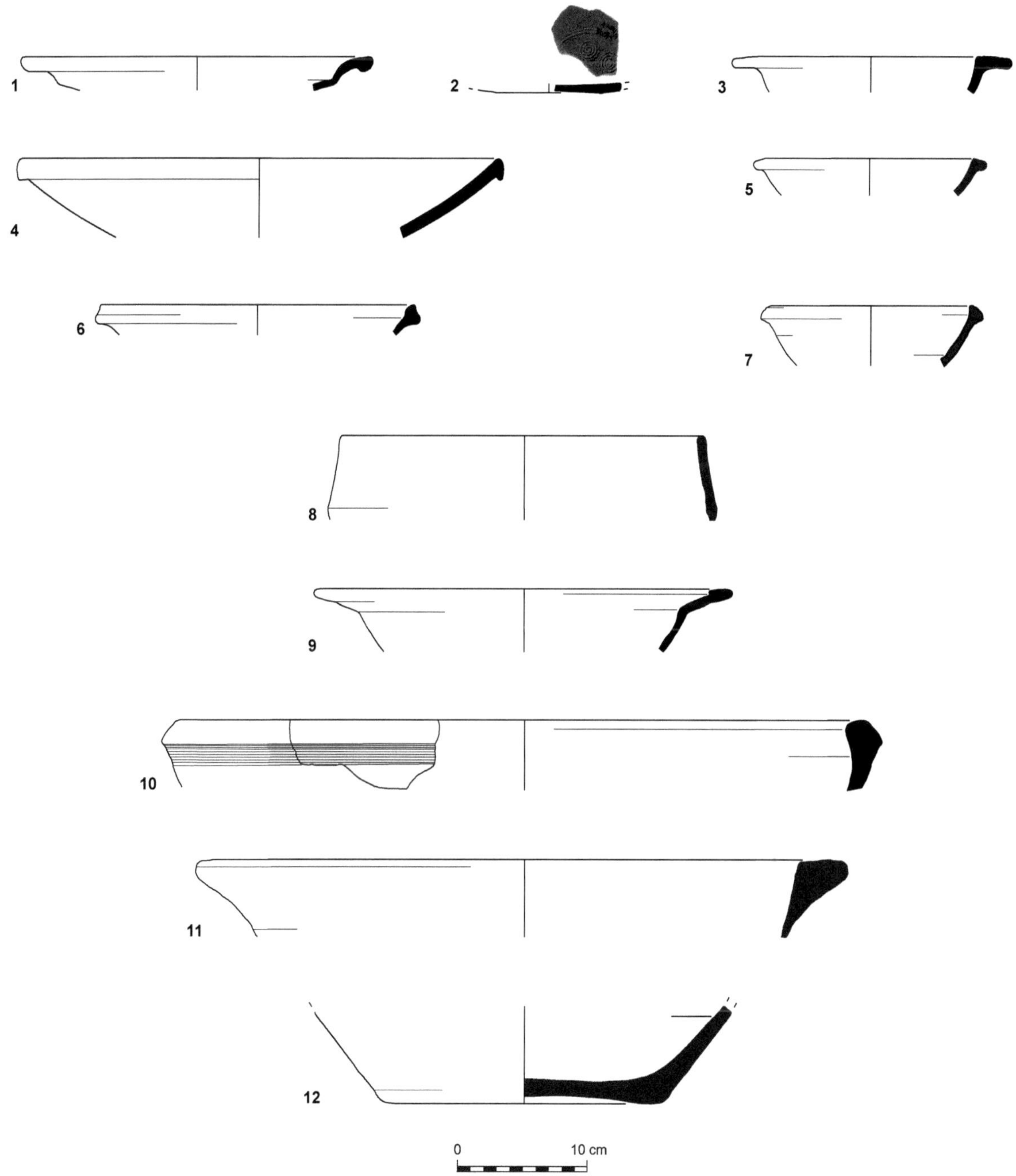

Fig. 13.9: Area CC, refuse dump; bowls and basins.

number of dining vessels were found? According to Peña, both table and cooking wares in the Roman world had a use-life of about one year (2007: 57–58). Therefore a much higher representation of bowls and plates would be expected to be found in the Nof-Yam dump, unless the people who regularly worked and acted in this part of the site did not use large quantities of table wares and consumed their food in other ways (e.g., by using wooden dishes and/or eating directly from the cooking vessels, especially in the case of casseroles).

Still, the large number of lamps found in the dump (see Chapter 14) may in fact indicate that at least some of the material it contained originated in the inhabited area of the town proper, not only in

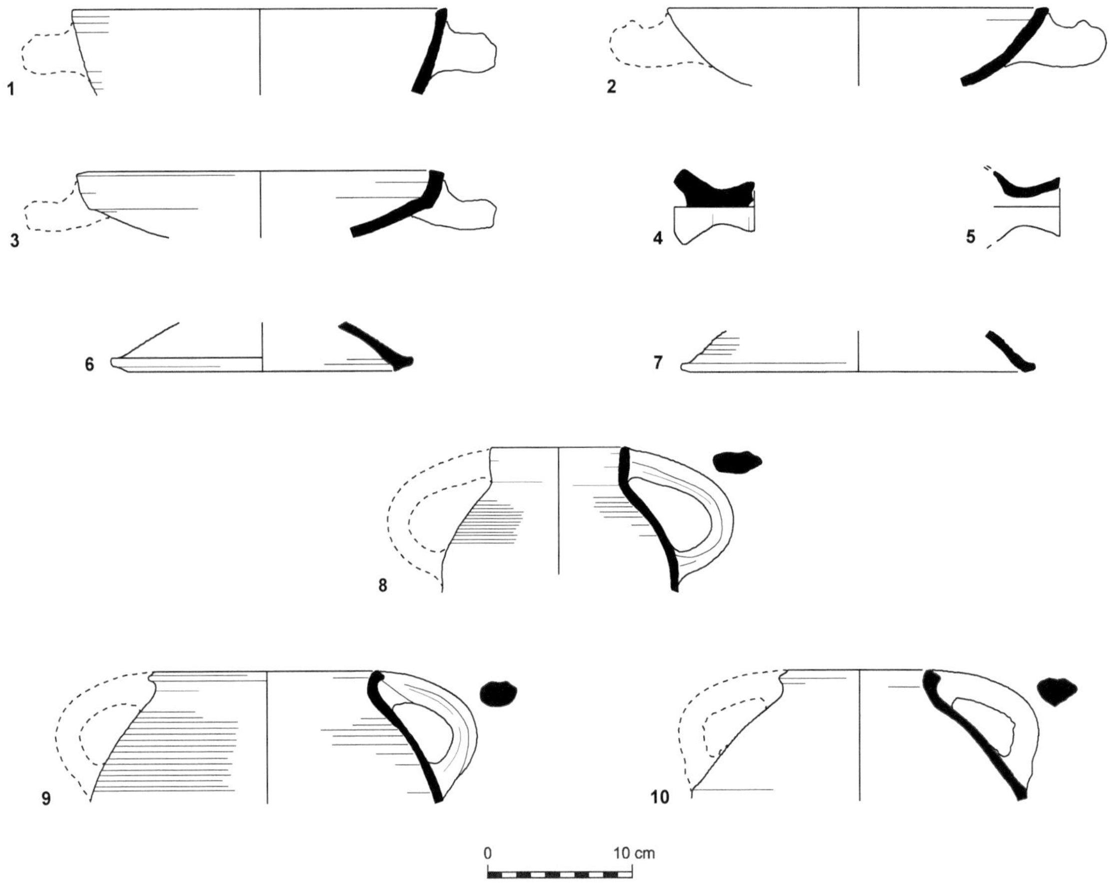

FIG. 13.10: AREA CC, REFUSE DUMP; COOKING WARE

No.	*Vessel*	*Locus*	*Basket*
1	Casserole	30067	302306
2	Casserole	30063	300666
3	Casserole	30060	301279
4	Frying pan (handle)	30060	300723
5	Frying pan (handle)	30071	303154
6	Cooking ware lid	643	6643
7	Cooking ware lid	30061	300639
8	Cooking pot	30100	303549
9	Cooking pot	30087	303707
10	Cooking pot	30060	300725

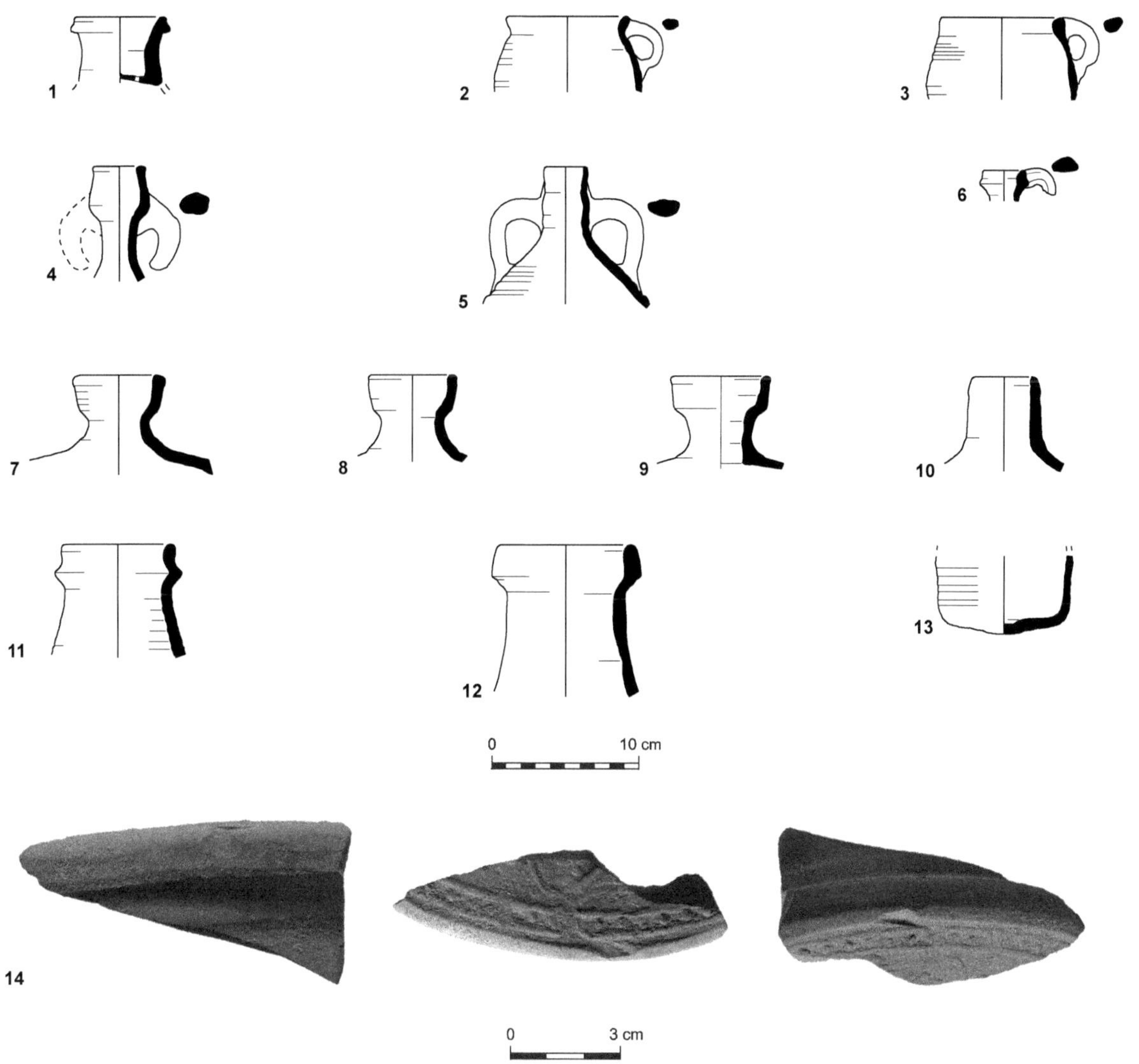

FIG. 13.11: AREA CC, REFUSE DUMP; JUGS, JUGLET, FLASKS AND WATER-WHEEL JARS

No.	*Vessel*	*Locus*	*Basket*
1	Jug	30061	303732
2	Jug	30060	301279
3	Jug	30052	301292
4	Jug	30021	30171
5	Jug	659	6573
6	Juglet	617	6308
7	Flask	30052	300927
8	Flask	3382	304624
9	Flask	30063	302165
10	Flask	30063	303114
11	Water-wheel jar	30071	301854
12	Water-wheel jar	30071	302893
13	Water-wheel jar	30063	301452
14	Flask (fragment)	30060	303135

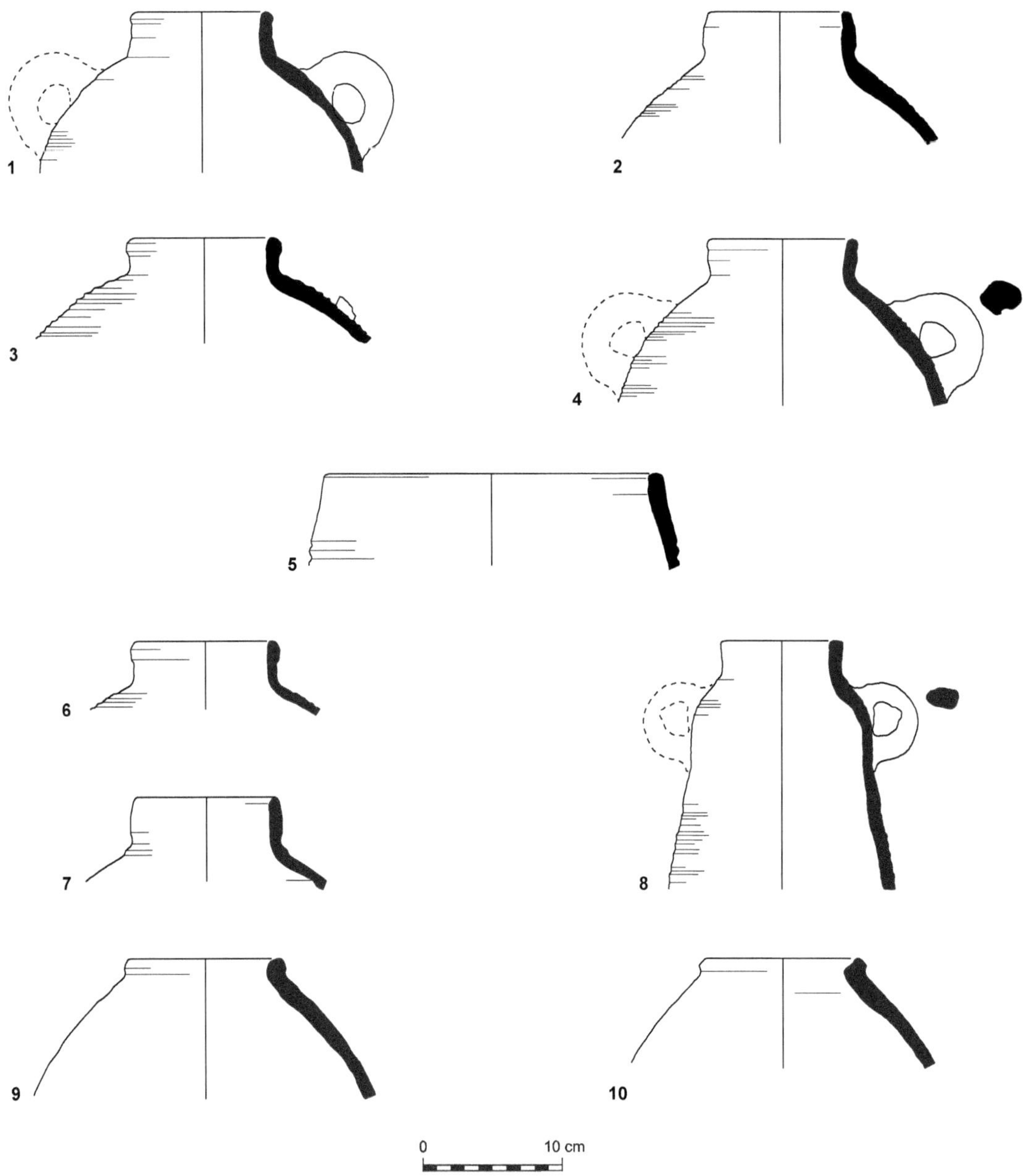

Fig. 13.12: Area CC, Refuse Dump; Storage Jars and Amphorae

No.	*Vessel*	*Locus*	*Basket*
1	Storage jar	627	6231
2	Storage jar	30060	300723
3	Storage jar	30070	302354
4	Storage jar	30118	304365
5	Storage jar (fragment)	642	6523
6	Storage jar	623	6242
7	Storage jar	637	6347
8	Storage jar	30037	301118
9	Storage jar	30037	303197
10	Storage jar	30074	303198

its agricultural/industrial fringes. This is since lamps are rarely associated with nighttime activities that usually characterize typical domestic contexts. If this indeed was the case, the question of why so few table wares were thrown to the dump not only remains open but becomes more acute.

Area DD1

A noteworthy feature excavated in this area was a refuse pit (Locus 809) which yielded three complete vessels: a Hellenistic-period krater (Fig. 13.15: 1), Hellenistic-period storage jar (Fig. 13.15: 4) and an Early Roman-period Type 1 cooking pot (Fig. 13.15: 2). The coexistence, in the same context, of vessels dated to different (albeit consecutive) periods is rather puzzling, and might be explained in three ways: 1) the discussed refuse pit was first used in the Hellenistic period, perhaps towards its end and continued in use until the very beginning of the Roman period; 2) the pit was first dug in Early Roman times but also contained earlier material which had incidentally been found and discarded during the Early Roman period; 3) the entire ceramic assemblage is contemporaneous, namely from the very end of the Hellenistic period (early 1st century BCE). The latter scenario would be plausible in case the cooking pot represents an early 1st century BCE predecessor of the "Herodian" cooking pot and the krater continued its appearance beyond the late 2nd century BCE.

Another feature possibly contemporaneous with the refuse pit is a rectangular rock-cut installation/quarry (Locus 779), whose fill (Locus 763) contained a large fragment of a Hellenistic-period storage jar (Fig. 13.15: 2).

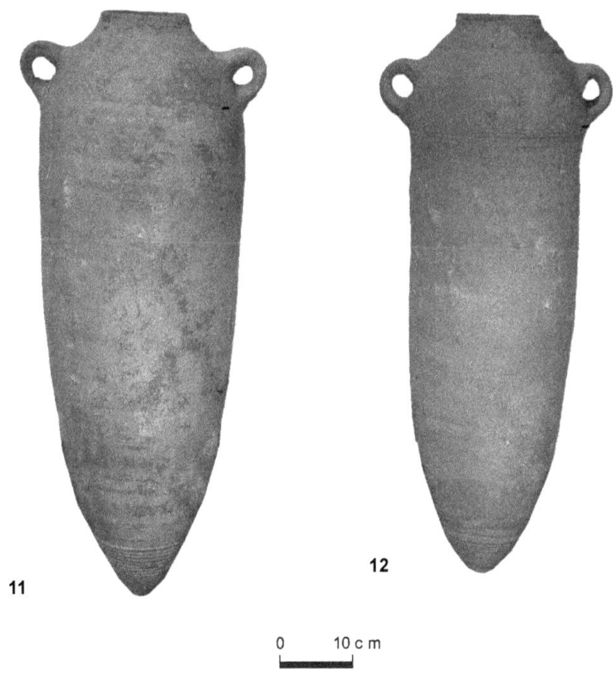

Fig. 13.12 (cont.): Area CC, Refuse Dump; Storage Jars and Amphorae

No.	*Vessel*	*Locus*	*Basket*
11	Storage jar	30011	301272
12	Storage jar	30052	301394

AREA DD2

Some of the most important remains excavated in Area DD2 (in Loci 918, 920 and 927 [to the south of the plan]) are apparently four isolated Early (to Middle?) Roman-period Type 2 storage jars which had been reused for infant burials (Fig. 13.16; Chapter 11). Two of the three examples presented here have a detached base/lower section, while the third jar has a detached upper shoulder-rim section and a missing lower section, which was either intentionally detached or became lost due to post-depositional processes.

Another feature excavated in Area DD2 is a refuse pit (Locus 991, Locus 995) that contained a small number of Byzantine-period pottery sherds. These included a casserole (Fig. 13.17: 1), a Type 4 cooking pot (Fig. 13.17: 2), a Type 1A and Type 6 storage jar and amphora (Fig. 13.17: 3–4), and a possible

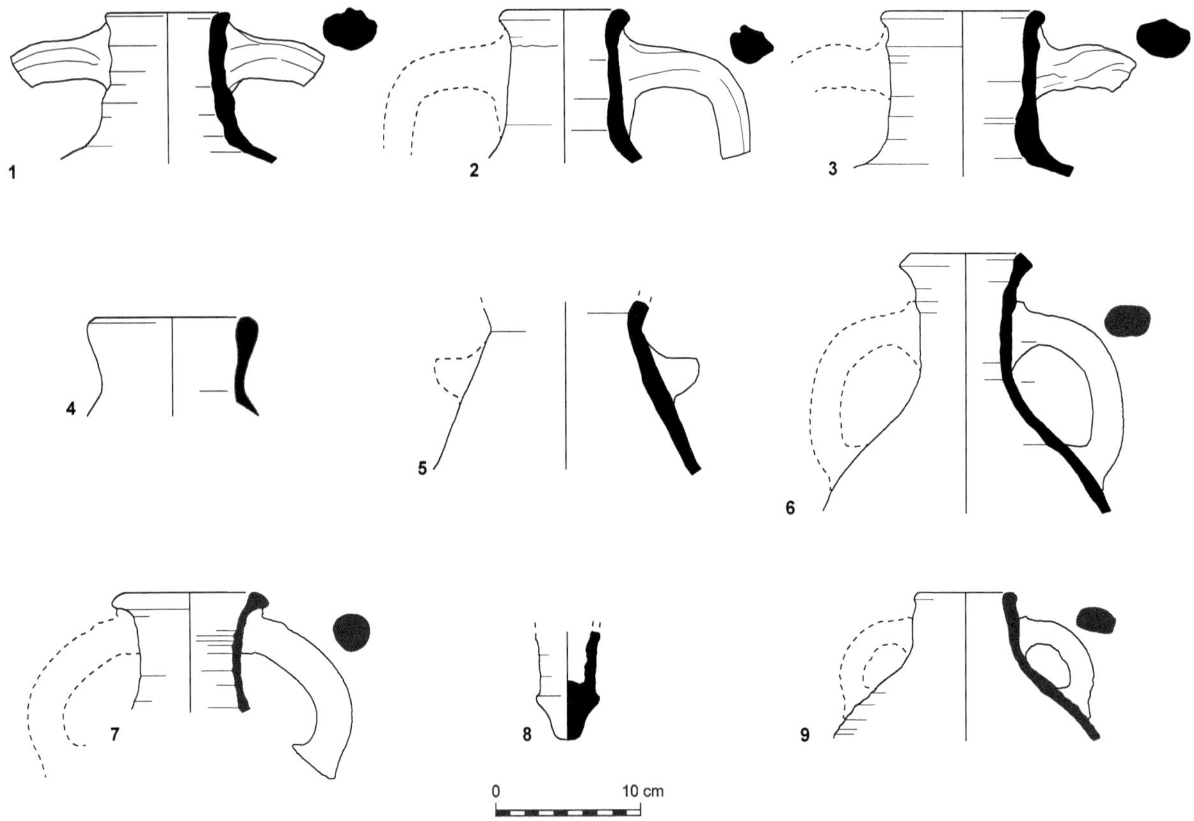

FIG. 13.13: AREA CC, REFUSE DUMP; STORAGE JARS AND AMPHORAE (CONT.)

No.	*Vessel*	*Locus*	*Basket*
1	Amphora	30052	301394
2	Amphora	30066	300746
3	Amphora	30061	300620
4	Amphora	625	6144
5	Amphora	619	6224
6	Amphora	30060	300727
7	Amphora	30037	300743
8	Amphora	30060	300727
9	Amphora(?)	30060	300721

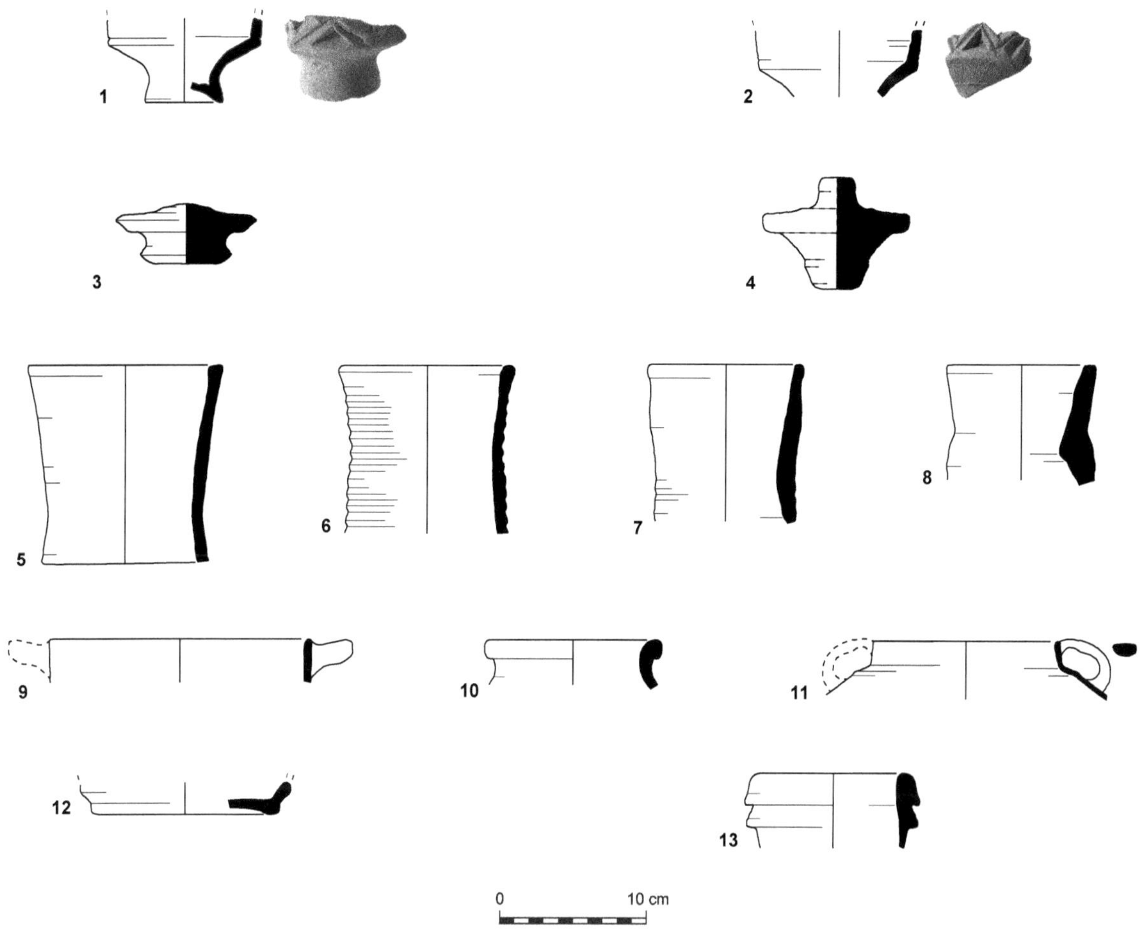

FIG. 13.14: AREA CC, REFUSE DUMP; INCENSE BURNERS, STOPPERS AND PIPE SECTIONS, AND VESSELS FROM EARLIER AND LATER PERIODS

No.	*Vessel*	*Locus*	*Basket*
1	Incense burner	30082	304534
2	Incense burner	30082	304337
3	Stopper	30066	300988
4	Stopper	30066	301396
5	Pipe section	30123	304058
6	Pipe section	30118	303914
7	Pipe section	642	6475
8	Pipe section	625	6251
9	Skyphos	Surface	-
10	Storage jar	627	6219
11	Cooking pot	30061	300620
12	Bowl	608	6170
13	Storage jar	603, 625	6004, 6210

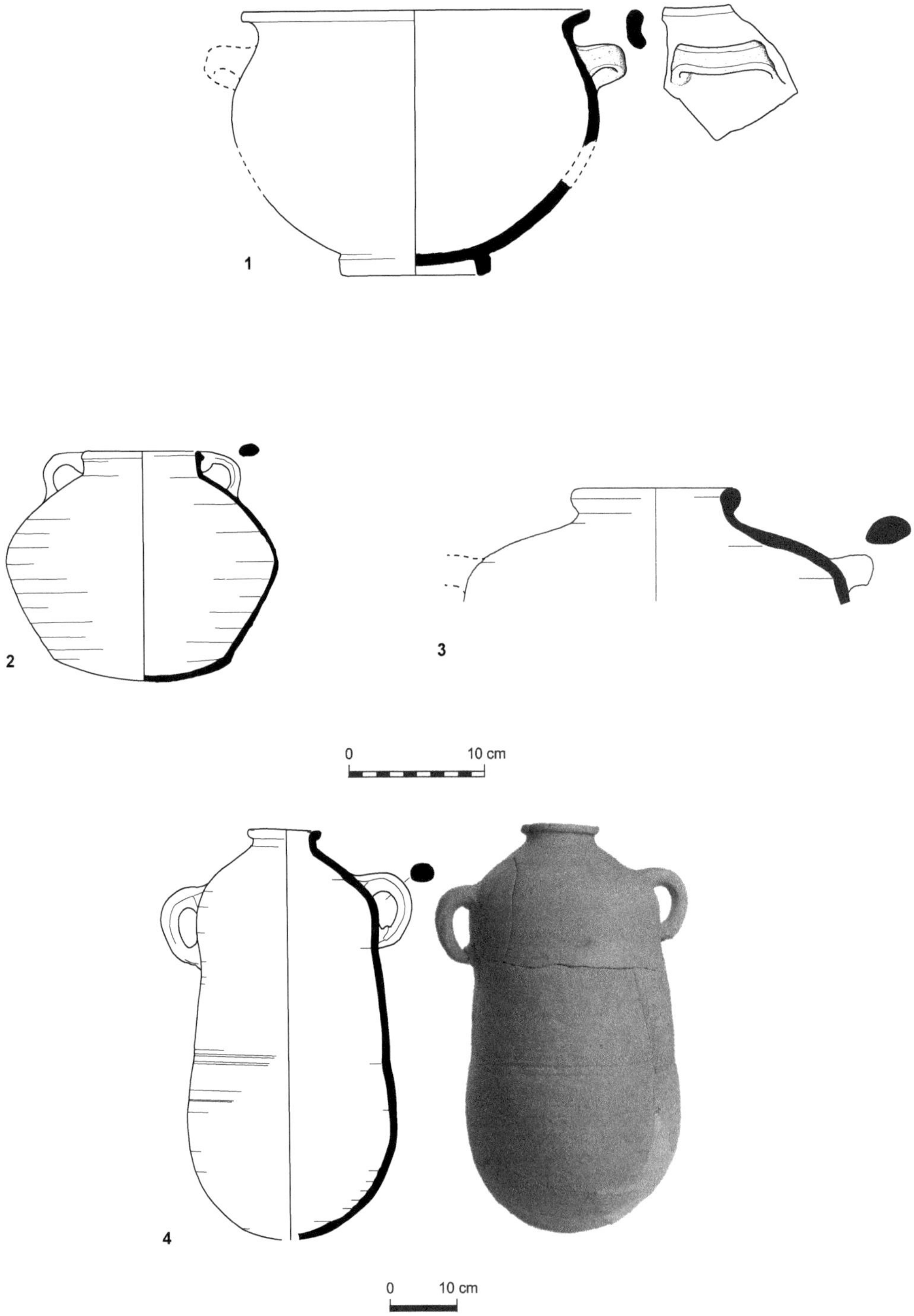

Fig. 13.15: Area DD, Rock-cut Feature (1, 2, 4) and Refuse Pit (3)

No.	*Vessel*	*Locus*	*Basket*
1	Krater	809	7220
2	Cooking pot	809	7221
3	Storage jar	763	7220
4	Storage jar	809	7076

incense burner (Fig. 13.17: 6), which provide a general 5th- to 7th-century CE date for this feature. The few pottery sherds found on the surface layer (Locus 990) covering the refuse pit included an ʿAbbasid common lead glazed bowl (Fig. 13.17: 5), which provides yet another indication for some activity in the area during Early Islamic times. Of the same period is another feature excavated in this area—an ashy accumulation (Locus 931) which contained some pottery sherds, including an Early Islamic Type 5 jug (Fig. 13.17: 7).

AREA DD3

The earliest remains excavated in this area are a few pit and cist graves, only two of which (Locus 41006 [contents of Tomb 41002] and Locus 41008 [contents of Tomb 41004]) contained intact Hellenistic-period pottery vessels—a Type 2 cooking jug (Fig. 13.19: 2) and an *unguentarium* (Fig. 13.19: 4), respectively. Inside or beside some of the other tombs (L41000, L42003 [contents of Tomb 42001] and Locus 42004 [contents of Tomb 42001]) other Hellenistic-period ceramics were found, such as a nearly complete Type 1 cooking pot (Fig. 13.19: 1) and fragments of a storage jar (Fig. 13.19: 3) and flask (Fig. 13.19: 5).

The other prominent feature unearthed in Area DD3 is a winepress (Installation 873); inside and around it (Locus 853, Locus 873) a modest assemblage of pottery fragments from the Byzantine-beginning of Early Islamic period was found. These include a Type 4 cooking pot (Fig. 13.18: 1), Type 1B, 5 and 6 storage jars and amphorae (Fig. 13.18: 2–5) and a Type 2 pithos (Fig. 13.18: 6), which suggest a 7th-century date for the assemblage. However, a single, apparently intrusive handle fragment of a Type 6 (glazed) cooking pot (Fig. 13.18: 7) points to some activity in the area long after the abandonment of the winepress, later in the Early Islamic or in the Crusader period. The date of the winepress foundation was assigned to either the Roman or Byzantine periods based on its plaster.

SELECTED SUPPLEMENTARY MATERIAL FROM TOPSOIL AND FILL LAYERS WITH NO ARCHITECTURAL RELATION

This section presents selected pottery sherds originating in various topsoil and fill loci from Apollonia (East) Areas AA, AA2, BB and DD1 (as well as in unknown provenience), which have no clear relation to architectural elements, but nevertheless provide additional information on the ceramic repertoire of the site. With the exception of a MB IIA cooking pot (Fig. 13.20: 1), the discussed material is dated to between the Roman and Ottoman periods and includes a Roman-period Type 1 storage jar (Fig. 13.20: 2), a Byzantine- and Early Islamic-period FBW Form 2B bowl (Fig. 13.20: 3), an ERS Ware A Form J bowl (Fig. 13.20: 4), Types 3 and 4 common ware basins (Fig. 13.20: 7–8), a common lead glazed bowl (Fig. 13.20: 6), a Type 2 frying pan (Fig. 13.20: 5), a Type 3B storage jar (Fig. 13.20: 11), a Type 1 pithos (Fig. 13.20: 9), a Type 8 juglet (Fig. 13.20: 10) and Type 5 stoppers/disks (Fig. 13.20: 12–14); a medieval- and Ottoman-period "Gaza" ware bowl (Fig. 13.21: 1), a Byzantine fine *sgraffito* ware bowl (Fig. 13.21: 2), a glazed frying pan (Fig. 13.21: 3) and a glazed lamp (?) (Fig. 13.21: 4).

APOLLONIA NATIONAL PARK

AREA M

The rather extensive refuse pit unearthed in Area M contained a large variety of pottery vessels, which can be ascribed to no later than the end of the Byzantine period or the very beginning of the Early Islamic period, between the mid-6th to mid-/late 7th centuries CE. Coins retrieved from the refuse support a date within the Byzantine-period. A total of 42 coins came from Area M and

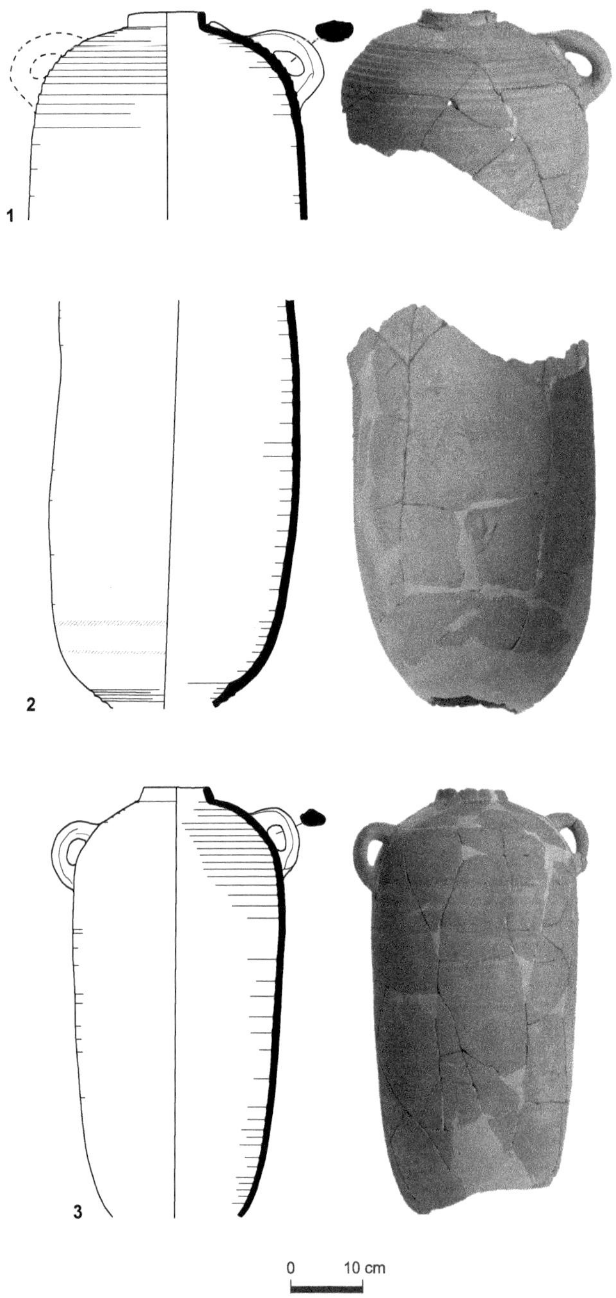

FIG. 13.16: AREA DD2, BURIAL JARS

No.	*Vessel*	*Locus*	*Basket*
1	Storage jar	918	9111
2	Storage jar	918	9094
3	Storage jar	927	9153

the latest among the 36 identifiable coins found is assigned to the regnal years of Maurice Tiberius (582–602 CE); there is also a post-reform (late 7th to mid-8th century) Umayyad coin (Chapter 18: No. 360). The ceramic types represented in the dump include ARS Ware Form 105 bowls (Fig. 13.22: 1–2), LRD/CRS Ware Forms 8 and 9 and Well-Form bowls (Fig. 13.22: 3–8), Egyptian Painted Ware bowls (Fig. 13.22: 9, 10), FBW Forms 1A, 1B and 2C bowls (Fig. 13.23: 1–5), Type 3 common ware basins (Fig. 13.23: 6–8), casseroles (Fig. 13.24: 1–2), Type 1 frying pans (Fig. 13.24: 3), cooking ware lids (Fig. 13.24: 4–5), Types 3 and 5 cooking pots (Fig. 13.24: 6–8), Types 1A, 1B, 5–7 and 10 storage jars and amphorae (Fig. 13.25: 1–7), Type 1 pithoi (Fig. 13.25: 8–10), Types 6, 7, 9 and 10 jugs and juglets (Fig. 13.26: 1–4), Type 1 flasks (Fig. 13.26: 5–8), Types 1, 2 and 4 lids and stoppers (Fig. 13.26: 9–17) and Types 3 and 4 lamps (see Chapter 14).

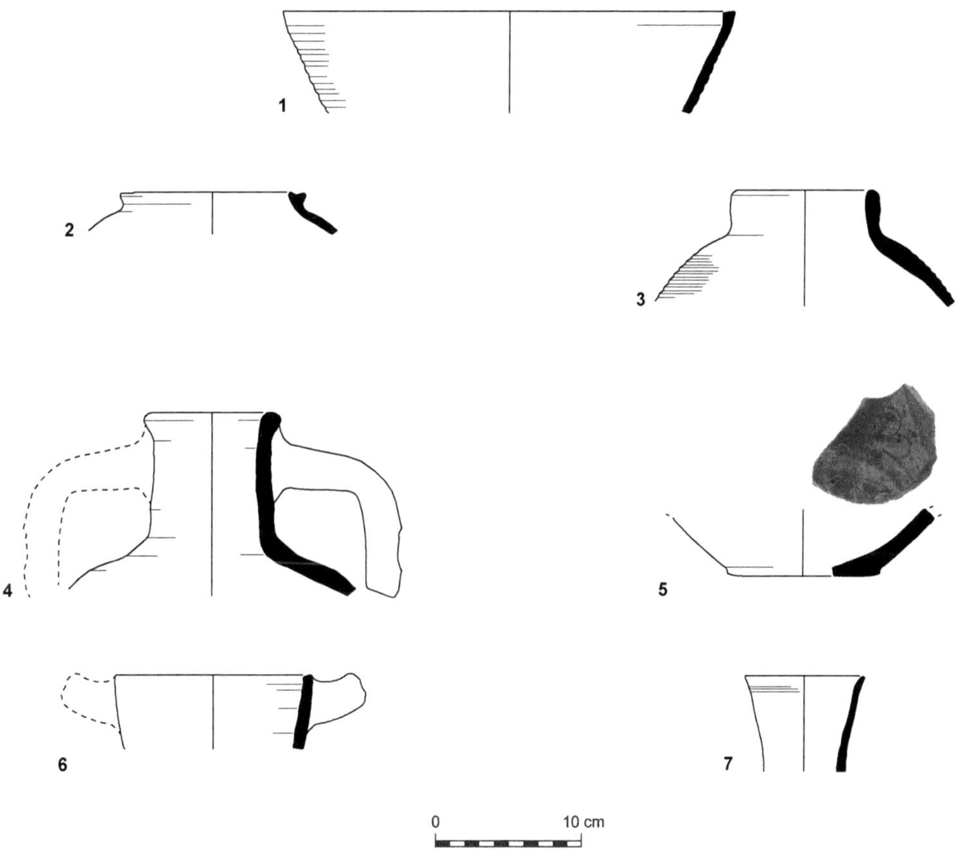

FIG. 13.17: AREA DD2, REFUSE PIT; SELECTED POTTERY

No.	*Vessel*	*Locus*	*Basket*
1	Casserole	995	9964
2	Cooking pot	991	9934
3	Storage jar	995	9964
4	Amphora	991	9936
5	Bowl	990	9926
6	Incense burner	995	9968
7	Jug	931	9152

AREA N

The smaller refuse pit excavated in Area N contained a rather modest ceramic assemblage dated to the Byzantine period. It included an LRC/PRS Ware Form 3 bowl (Fig. 13.27: 1), a Type 3 common ware basin (Fig. 13.27: 2), cooking ware lids (Fig. 13.27: 3–4), Type 1A, 1B, 2, 5–7 and 11 storage jars and amphorae (Figs. 13.27: 5–10, 13.28: 1–5), a Type 11 jug (Fig. 13.28: 6), Type 2 water-wheel jars (Fig. 13.28: 7–9), Type 1 and 3 stoppers (Fig. 13.28: 10, 11) and Type 3 lamps (see Chapter 14). Altogether, these finds allow dating the Area N refuse deposit from the 6th to early 7th centuries CE.

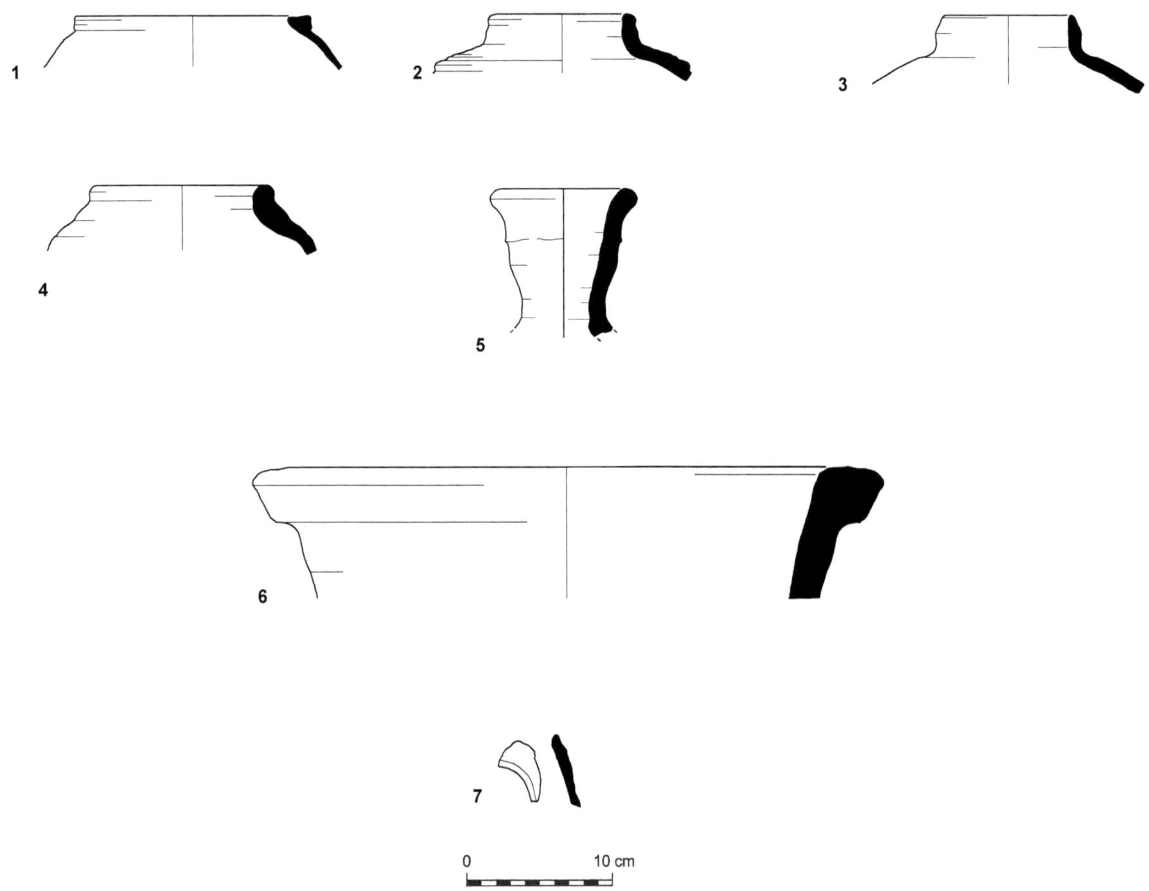

FIG. 13.18: AREA DD3/1, WINEPRESS; SELECTED POTTERY

No.	*Vessel*	*Locus*	*Basket*
1	Cooking pot	873	8010
2	Storage jar	853	8037
3	Storage jar	853	8062
4	Storage jar	853	8050
5	Amphora	853	8046
6	Pithos	873	8100
7	Cooking pot (handle)	873	8085

AREA O

The refuse deposit found inside the collecting vat of the winepress unearthed in Area O was rather abundant, though not much varied in terms of vessel types. It included a Type 2 common ware bowl (Fig. 13.29: 1), a Type 12 jug/jar (Fig. 13.29: 2), casseroles (Fig. 13.29: 3), Type 2 cooking pots (Fig. 13.29: 4–5), Types 1A, 5 and 9 storage jars and amphorae (Figs. 13.30–32, 13.33: 1–5; with storage jars Types 1A and 5 representing the overwhelming majority of pottery vessels in the assemblage), a Type 1 flask (Fig. 13.33: 6), Type 2 water-wheel jars (Fig. 13.33: 7) and Type 3 lamps (see Chapter 14). These types

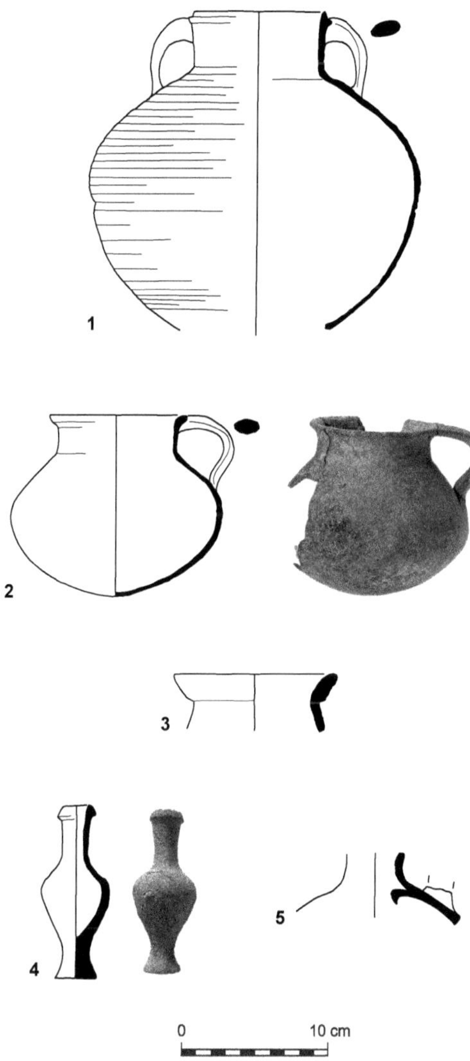

FIG. 13.19: AREA DD3/2, TOMBS; SELECTED POTTERY

No.	*Vessel*	*Locus*	*Basket*
1	Cooking pot	41000	410016
2	Cooking jug	41006	410000
3	Storage jar	42003	420000
4	Unguentarium	41008	410013
5	Flask	42001	-

allow dating the assemblages to sometime between the (late?) 6th and early/mid-7th century. This date is corroborated by the 15 identifiable coins that came from the area with the latest among them assigned to the 630s CE—the later regnal years of Heraclius (632–641 CE) (Chapter 18: Nos. 351–353).

A noteworthy detail is that most of the ceramic finds from the Area O deposit bear yellowish-brown stains and on occasion thin accretions of unidentified materials; many sherds also reflect a weathering of their exterior and/or interior surface in the form of thin, peeled off layers or shallow cavities. Staining, accretion and partial peeling are well-known characteristics of artifacts—especially pottery–originating in refuse deposits, including architectural installations used or reused to collect sewage sludge (including winepress collecting vats). Under such conditions, the organic and inorganic residues of the refuse attaches to the pottery and might even change its original color and texture.

TYPOLOGICAL AND CHRONOLOGICAL DISCUSSION

THE MB IIA

A handful of coarse-ware sherds, which seem to predate the Persian period, were found in various locations throughout the Apollonia (East) excavation areas. One of the more diagnostic of these sherds belongs to a handmade cooking pot from the MB IIA (Fig. 13.20: 1). It is made of a highly coarse low-temperature fired dark brown ware (fired to reddish-brown) and has thick straight walls, a plain perforated rim and a decorative thumb-impressed clay band on the exterior wall below the rim (cf. Yadin 2009: 113, Figs. 7.1: 6–7, 7.3: 8–11).

THE PERSIAN AND HELLENISTIC PERIODS

A negligible number of pottery sherds and a few complete vessels dated to the Persian and Hellenistic periods (5th–2nd/1st centuries BCE) were found in the Apollonia (East) excavations (as well as in Area N, Chapter 9). With the exception of several specimens—notably complete vessels found in tombs (Areas DD2, DD3) and in a refuse pit (Area DD1)—the remaining contemporaneous ceramic finds originated in mixed contexts containing later material as well.

FIG. 13.20: VARIA

No.	*Area*	*Vessel*	*Locus*	*Basket*
1	BB	Cooking pot	418	3051
2	BB	Storage jar	402	3003
3	AA	Bowl	101	1099
4	BB	Bowl	444	3116
5	BB	Frying pan	443	3131
6	AA	Bowl	118	1097
7	BB	Basin	413	3013
8	BB	Basin	417	4120
9	BB	Pithos	443	3131
10	DD1	Juglet	760	7042
11	AA2	Storage jar	12029	102097
12	Surface	Stopper/disk	-	-
13	Surface	Stopper/disk	-	-
14	Surface	Stopper/disk	-	-

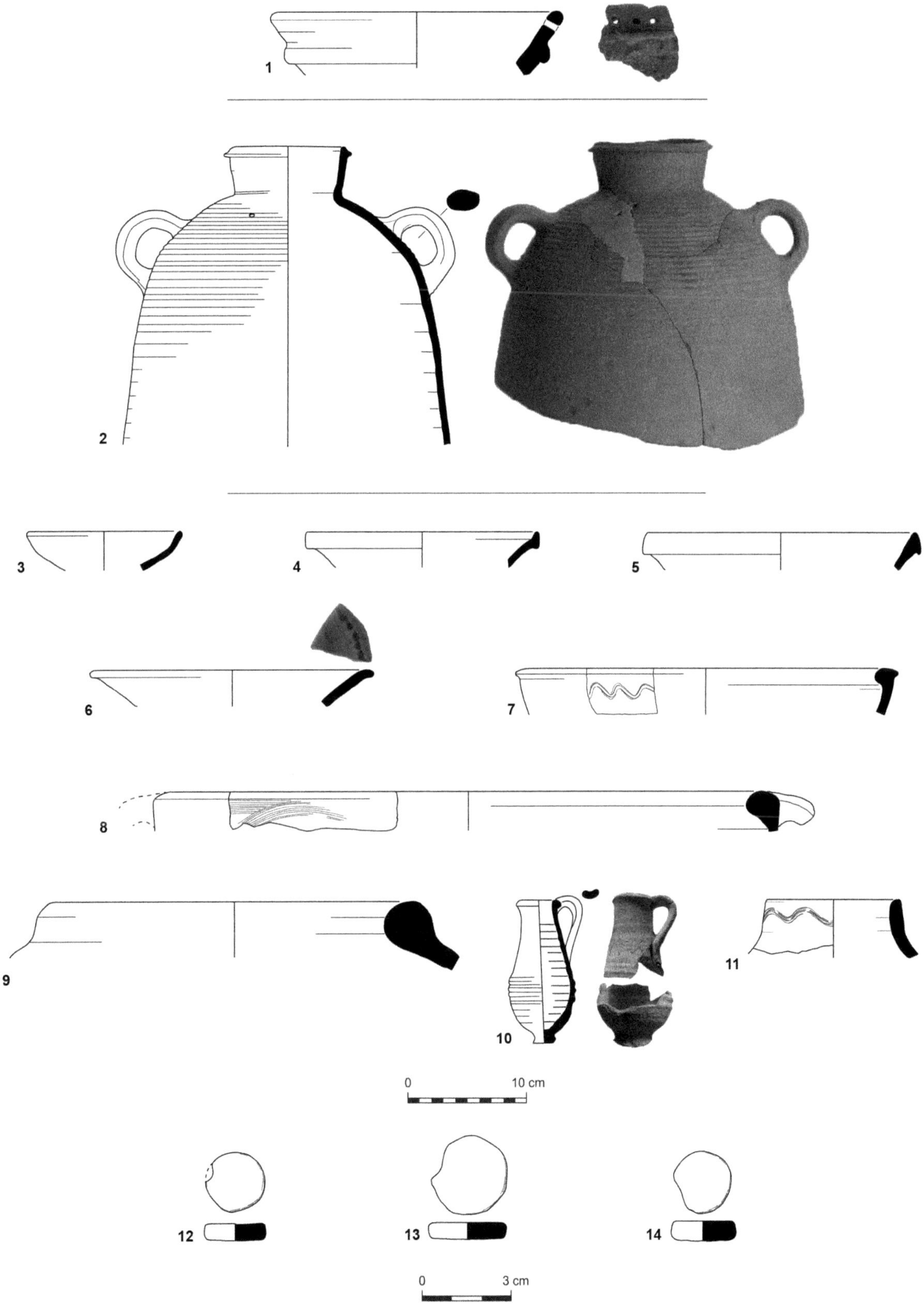

Fig. 13.20: Varia.

ATTIC SKYPHOS (FIG. 13.14: 9)

The highly fragmented example of a straight rim skyphos is an Attic Type A owl skyphos. Owl skyphoi have been discussed at length by several scholars (see e.g., Beazley 1963: 982–984). This example seems to date to mid-late 5th century BCE (on their appearance at the site and in Palestine, cf. Tal 1999: 131, 164–165). According to Guz-Zilberstein (1995: 294), the type was still common in the beginning of thc Hellenistic period (late 4th century BCE).

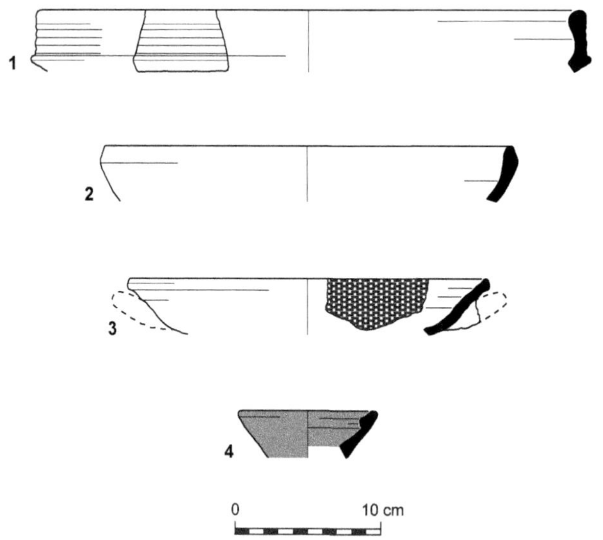

FIG. 13.21: VARIA (CONT.)

No.	*Area*	*Vessel*	*Locus*	*Basket*
1	BB	Bowl	442	3096
2	DD1	Bowl	758	7040
3	DD1	Frying pan	764	7054
4	DD1	Lamp	754	7017

FIG. 13.22: AREA M, IMPORTED BOWLS

No.	*Vessel*	*Locus*
1	Bowl	7042
2	Bowl	7034
3	Bowl	7008
4	Bowl	7029
5	Bowl	7052
6	Bowl	7029
7	Bowl	7029
8	Bowl	7007
9	Bowl	7008
10	Bowl	7052

Attic Bowl (Fig. 13.1: 1)

This bowl has an incurved rim, with rounded, convex walls. Our example seems to date to ca. 375–325 BCE (Sparkes and Talcott 1970: 130–131, 295–296, Nos. 828, 830–835, Fig. 8, Pl. 33). On the type appearance at the site and in Palestine see discussion in Tal 1999: 130–131, 164.

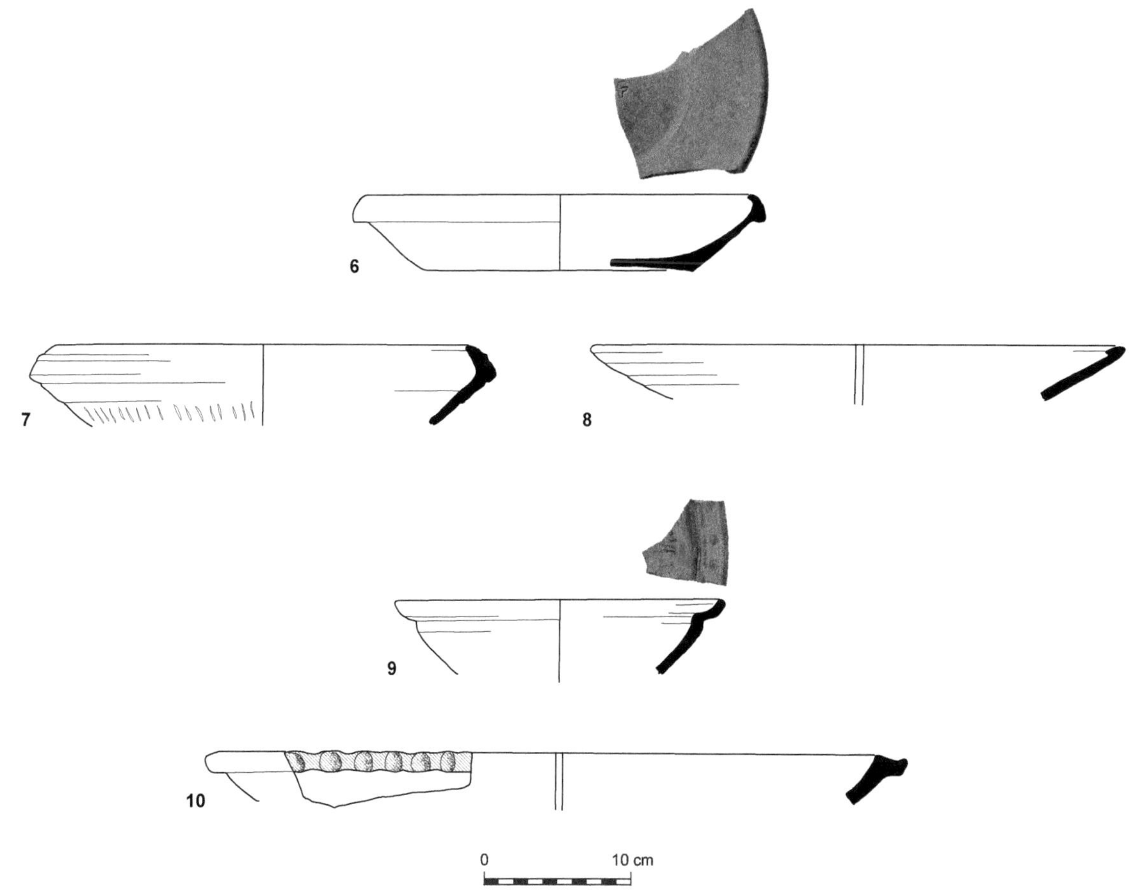

Fig. 13.22: Area M, imported bowls.

KRATER (FIG. 13.15: 1)

This vessel form is represented by a complete vessel found in a refuse pit in Area DD1. It is made of a coarse, orange-brown ware, and has a globular body, an everted rim, a low ring base and two horizontal, slightly twisted handles below the rim. The vessel corresponds to Guz-Zilberstein's "small deep krater"

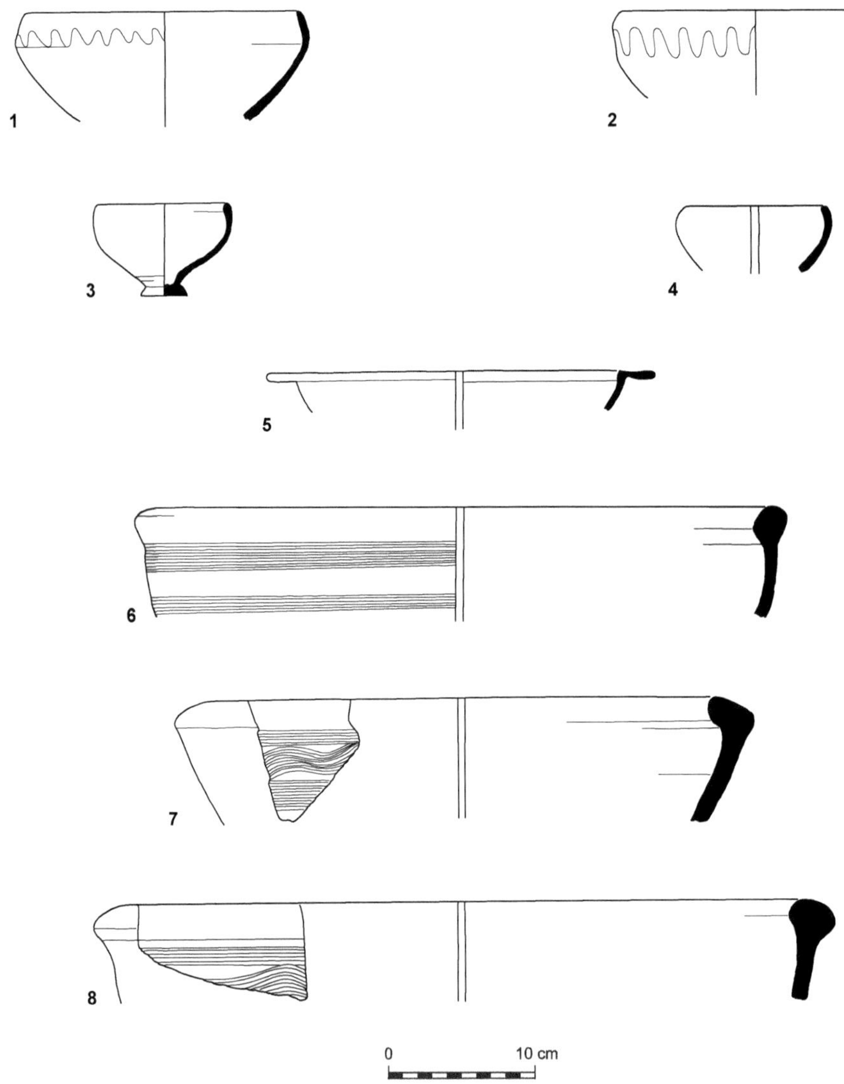

FIG. 13.23: AREA M, BOWLS AND BASINS

No.	*Vessel*	*Locus*
1	Bowl	7036
2	Bowl	7008
3	Bowl	7052
4	Bowl	7006
5	Bowl	7008
6	Basin	7031
7	Basin	7010
8	Basin	7010

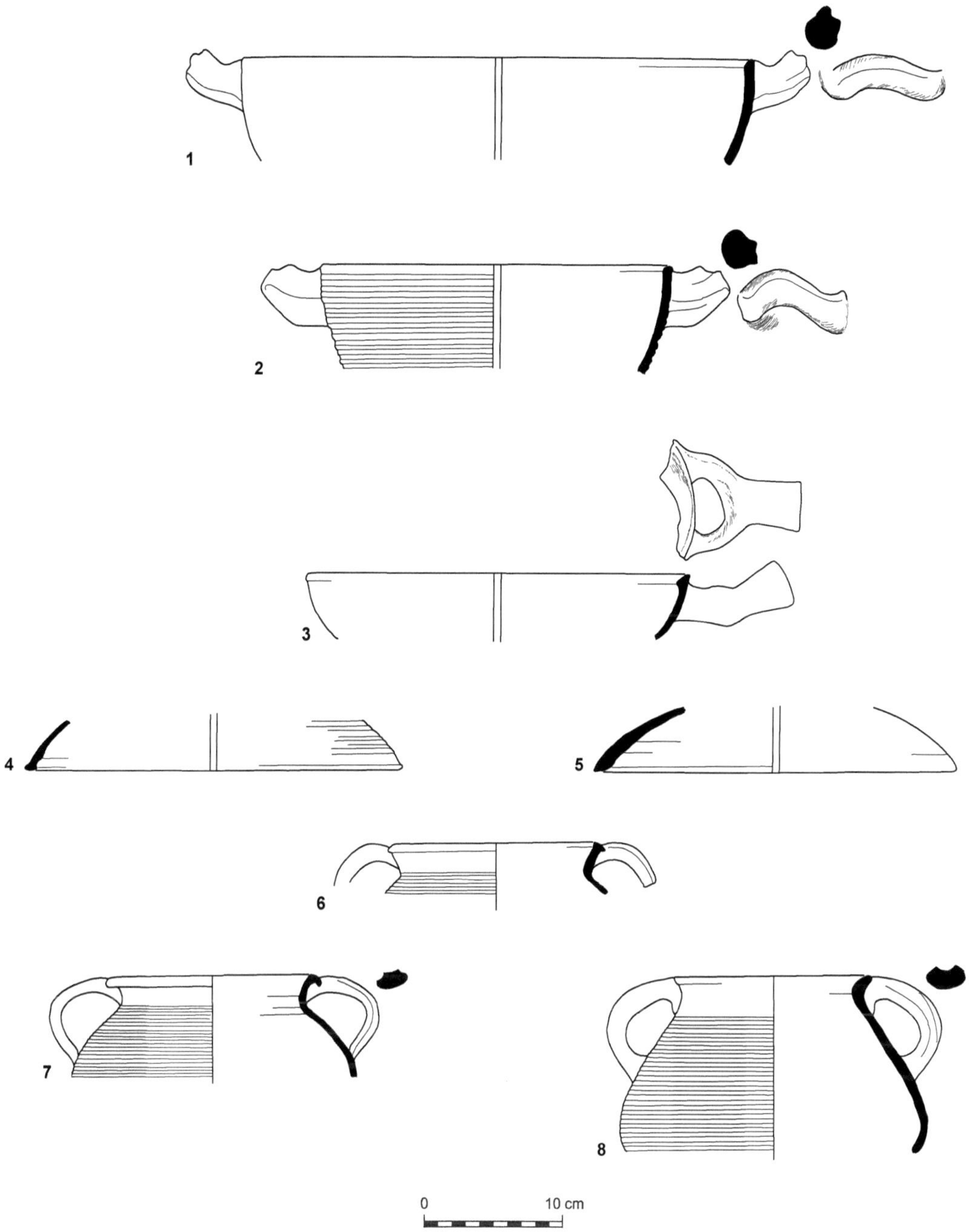

FIG. 13.24: AREA M, COOKING WARES

No.	Vessel	Locus
1	Casserole	7010
2	Casserole	7010
3	Frying pan	7010
4	Cooking ware lid	7010
5	Cooking ware lid	7007
6	Cooking pot	7007
7	Cooking pot	7007
8	Cooking pot	7010

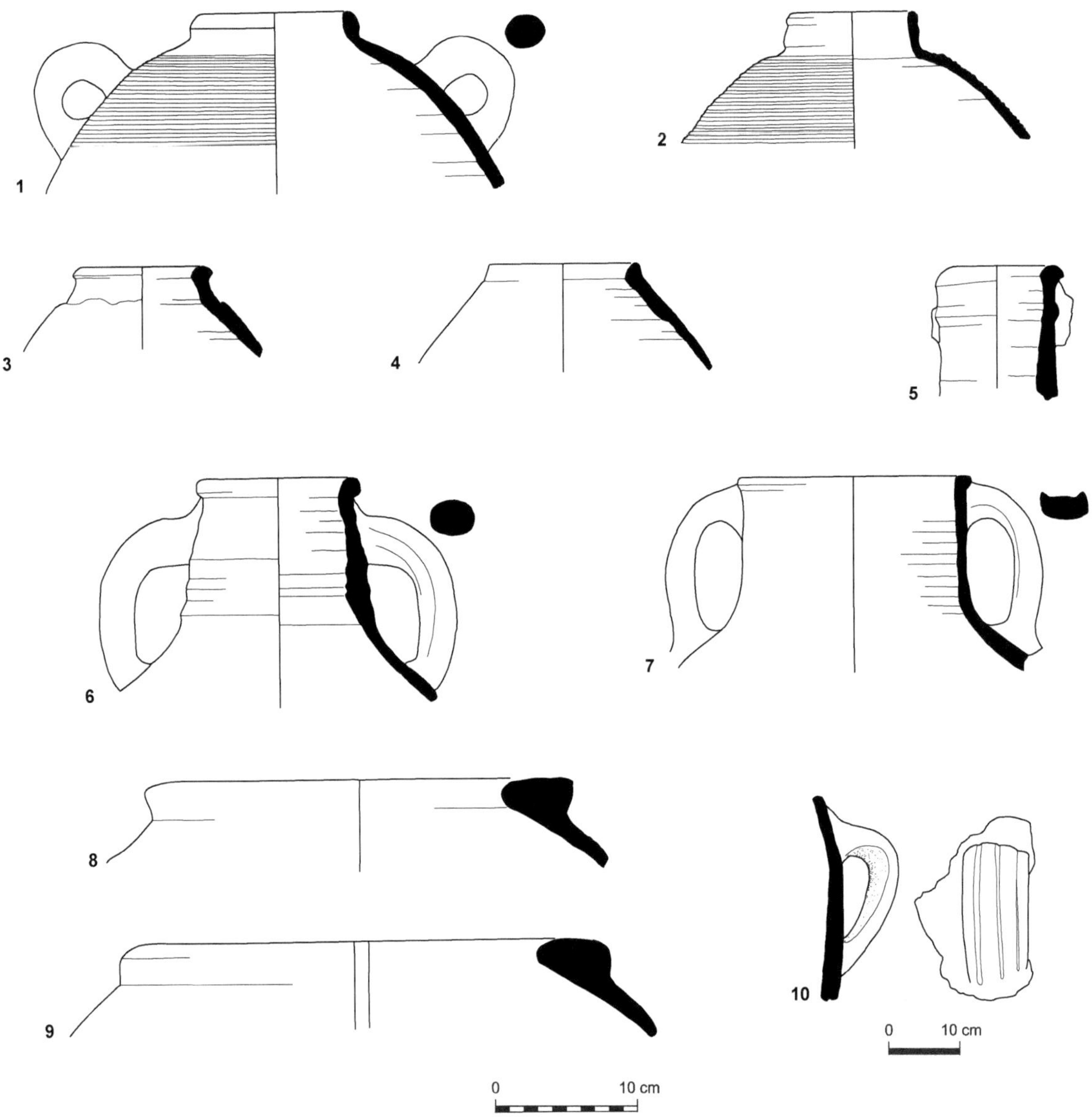

FIG. 13.25: AREA M, STORAGE JARS, AMPHORAE AND PITHOI

No.	*Vessel*	*Locus*
1	Storage jar	7010
2	Storage jar	7010
3	Storage jar	7001
4	Storage jar	7010
5	Amphora	7010
6	Amphora	7010
7	Amphora	7010
8	Pithos	7010
9	Pithos	7010
10	Pithos (handle)	7052

form (1995: 296, Fig. 6.12: 2–4), which in Dor were found mostly in contexts dated between the early 3rd and late 2nd centuries BCE.

Flask (Fig. 13.19: 5)

This type is represented by an upper body fragment of a flask made of coarse, yellowish-brown ware. The fragment includes the vessel's shoulder with a stump of one of the two handles, and the beginning of the cylindrical neck with a prominent internal ridge at its base. Similar flasks were found in rather small numbers in other Hellenistic-period assemblages dated as late as the 2nd century BCE (cf. Guz-Zilberstein 1995: 310–311, Fig. 6.34).

Mortaria (Figs. 13.1: 2, 13.7: 1)

These heavy coarse-ware bowls, typical of the Persian period, are characterized by a yellowish ware containing varied tempers. The present examples are represented by ring base fragments (see discussion in Stern 1995: 53–55; Tal 1999: 97–98).

Cooking Jug (Fig. 13.19: 2)

This small-sized cooking jug has a squat, plain body, a short vertical neck with an everted rim and a single, long strap handle from rim to shoulder. It was found inside a tomb in Area DD3 (Tomb 41001), and seems to be dated in either the 3rd or the 2nd century BCE (cf. e.g., Levine 2003: 94, Fig. 6.6: 72).

Unguentarium (Fig. 13.19: 4)

A single, intact fusiform unguentarium was found inside a tomb in Area DD3 (Tomb 41003). It is made of a coarse, yellowish-brown ware and has a string-cut base, a short rounded body and thickened rim. Given its shape, it seems to be dated within either the late 4th or 3rd century BCE (cf. Guz-Zilberstein 1995: 304–305, Fig. 6.26: 9–22).

Storage Jars (Figs. 13.14: 10, 13.15: 3, 4, 13.19: 3)

Represented by one complete and three upper body/rim fragments, this type is made of a coarse, yellowish-brown ware and has a very low, vertical neck, thickened (sometimes out-folded) rim and cylindrical or bag-shaped body. It was the most common storage jar-type in Palestine during most of the Persian and Hellenistic periods, namely between the 5th and early 1st centuries BCE (cf. e.g., Guz-Zilberstein 1995: 311, Fig. 6.35; Geva 2003: 122, Pls. 5.1: 8, 5.2: 18, 19, 24, 5.4: 5, 13, 15, 5.10: 1–2 and for in-site comparative material, see Tal 1999: 102, 127–128, 160–161).

THE ROMAN PERIOD

Compared to the previous periods, the amount of pottery attributed to the Roman period in Apollonia (East) excavations was somewhat greater, composed mostly of sherds in addition to a few complete/nearly complete vessels (the latter mostly originating in tombs). This pottery dates to between the late 1st century BCE/early 1st century CE and the 4th century CE, though some types apparently continued into the 5th century CE as well. Still, the majority of the types seems to represent the Roman period proper or the very beginning of the Byzantine period at the latest, while in most cases, they reflect Roman ceramic traditions.

Jugs

Two types of small/medium-sized jugs were attributed to the discussed period; both seem to be imports.

Type 1 (Fig. 13.8: 7)

Only one example of this type was found. It is made of a coarse, yellowish-orange ware containing numerous minute and somewhat larger brown and white grits and much mica, and has a high foot ending in a low ring base. The highly-micaceous ware of this jug indicates a Cypriot or Aegean origin; indeed, a jug with a similar base was found in Knossos in a context dated to the second half of the 2nd century CE, although no mica inclusions are mentioned in the ware description of this vessel (Hayes 1983: 108–109, Fig. 11: 142).

Type 2 (Fig. 13.8: 8)

Represented by a single example, this vessel is made of a coarse, somewhat porous reddish-brown ware, containing some mica. It has a short, thin-walled vertical neck and an out-folded rim. The ware characteristics may point to an Egyptian (or alternatively, Aegean) origin for this vessel, though its complete form and morphological determination are not clear; it could be either a jug or an exceptionally thin-walled flask. Its context allows it to be dated to the Late Roman period.

Casserole (Fig. 13.2: 1)

The present casserole type, with plain everted walls, a cut-away rim and two thin horizontal handles, appeared in the 1st century CE and remained in use throughout the Roman period and apparently during the beginning of the Byzantine period as well (cf. Magness 1993: 211–213, Form 1; Bar-Nathan 2006: 172–173, Pl. 31: 80, 82, 83), when it was gradually replaced by the somewhat coarser and larger casseroles (see below).

Cooking Pots

Four types of cooking pots were dated to the Roman period.

Fig. 13.26: Area M, Jugs, Juglet, Flasks, Lids and Stoppers

No.	*Vessel*	*Locus*
1	Jug	7041
2	Juglet	7010
3	Jug	7041
4	Jug	7010
5	Flask	7010
6	Flask	7031
7	Flask	7007
8	Flask	7012
9	Stopper	7019
10	Stopper	7010
11	Stopper	7010
12	Lid	7007
13	Lid	7007
14	Lid	7010
15	Lid	7010
16	Stopper	7016
17	Stopper	7010

Type 1 (Fig. 13.19: 1)

This cooking pot has a globular body, ribbed walls throughout, a high vertical neck with a triangular rim and two strap handles from rim to shoulder. It seems to be a transitional Hellenistic/Roman period cooking pot of the 1st century BCE/1st century CE type (cf. Lapp 1961: 187, Type 71.1L-M).

Type 2 (Fig. 13.15: 2)

This is the so-called "Herodian" cooking pot, characterized by a short, vertical neck with a triangular rim, a plain, squat body and two small strap handles from rim to shoulder. It is the most common cooking pot type in Palestinian assemblages dating between the late 1st century BCE and the first half of the 2nd century CE (Bar-Nathan 2006: 154–158, Pls. 27, 28; Taxel and Hershkovitz 2011: 350, Fig. 6.8, Pl. 248: 3–5, 7–11).

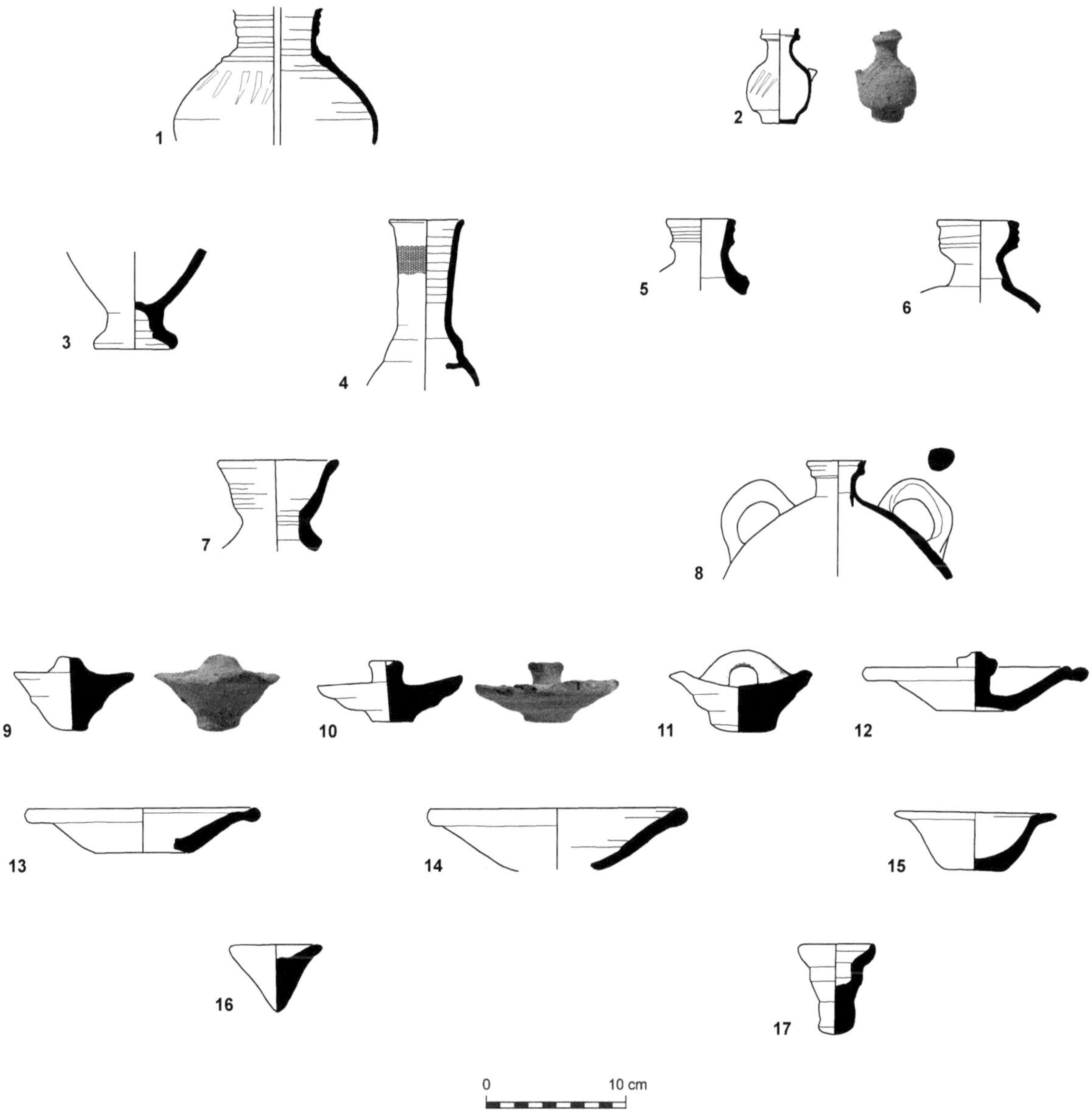

Fig. 13.26: Area M, jugs, juglet, flasks, lids and stoppers.

Type 3 (Figs. 13.1: 3, 13.14: 11)

This type has a short, vertical or slightly in-turned neck with a plain rim, a plain body with a slightly carinated shoulder, and two small loop handles from rim to shoulder. It is dated from the late 1st century BCE to the late 1st century CE (for parallels from neighboring sites, see Calderon 2011: 63*, Fig. 1: 8; Tal and Taxel 2015: 208–209, Fig. I.2.1: 2).

Type 4 (Fig. 13.8: 1)

This cooking pot has a short, vertical neck with a flattened rim and a sharp carination between the neck and shoulder. It has parallels (some with a different rim or neck profile) dated to the 2nd to 4th centuries CE (Taxel 2009: 91, Fig. 3.3: 5; Calderon 2011: 69*, 73*, Fig. 6: 12, 14).

COOKING WARE LID (FIG. 13.3: 1)

A thin-walled, plain cooking ware lid with a cut-away rim, mostly associated with casseroles, is represented at the site by a few examples. Like the above-mentioned casserole type (Fig. 13.2: 1), it too

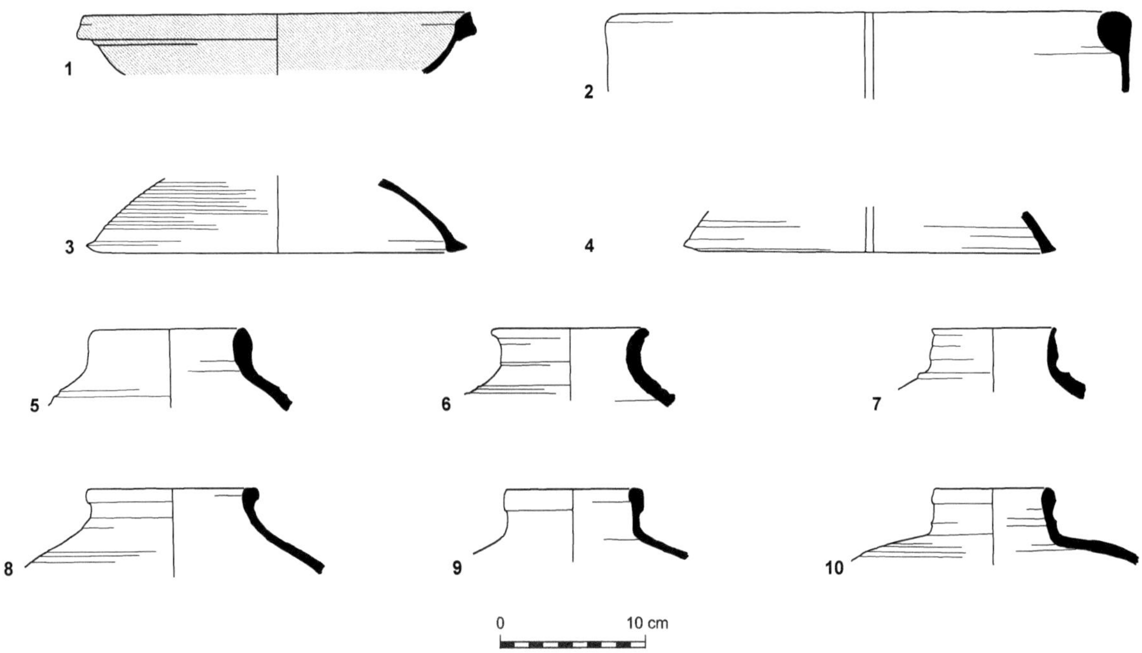

FIG. 13.27: AREA N, BOWL, BASIN, COOKING WARE LIDS AND STORAGE JARS

No.	*Vessel*	*Locus*
1	Bowl	5002/5003
2	Basin	5002/5003
3	Cooking ware lid	5002/5003
4	Cooking ware lid	5002/5003
5	Storage jar	5002/5003
6	Storage jar	5002/5003
7	Storage jar	5002/5003
8	Storage jar	5002/5003
9	Storage jar	5002/5003
10	Storage jar	5002/5003

appeared in the Early Roman period and continued well into the 4th or 5th century CE (cf. Magness 1993: 215; Bar-Nathan 2006: 172–173, Pl. 31: 81).

STORAGE JARS AND AMPHORAE

Four types of storage and transport containers are attributed to the Roman period, two of which represent local products while the other two are imported.

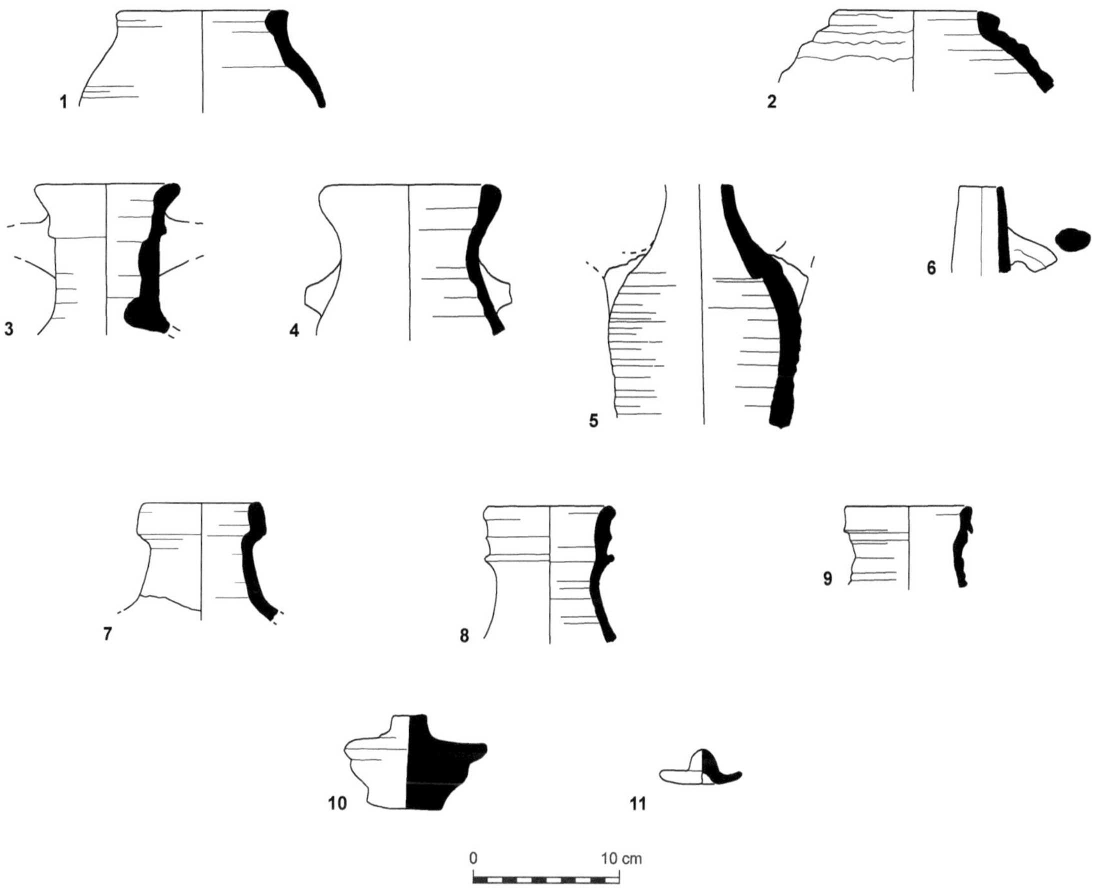

FIG. 13.28: AREA N, STORAGE JARS, AMPHORAE, JUG, WATER-WHEEL JARS AND STOPPERS

No.	*Vessel*	*Locus*
1	Storage jar	5002/5003
2	Storage jar	5002/5003
3	Amphora	5002/5003
4	Amphora	5002/5003
5	Amphora	5002/5003
6	Jug	5002/5003
7	Water-wheel jar	5002/5003
8	Water-wheel jar	5002/5003
9	Water-wheel jar	5002/5003
10	Stopper	5002/5003
11	Stopper	5002/5003

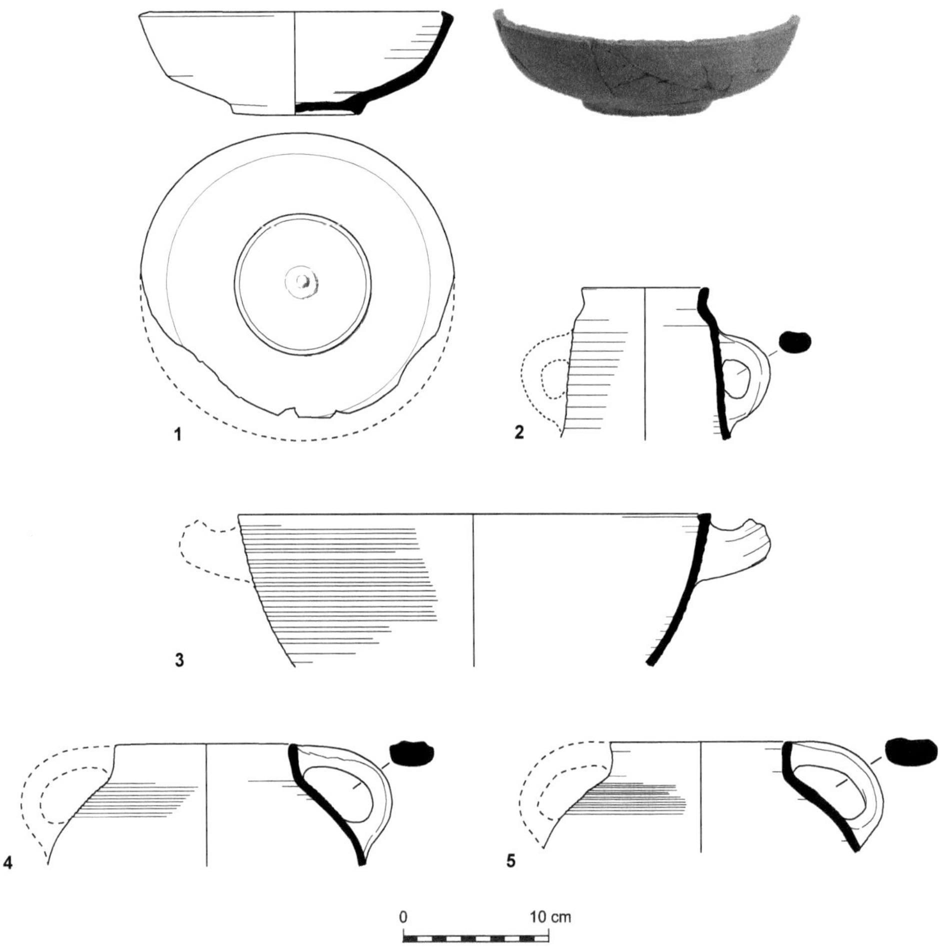

FIG. 13.29: AREA O, BOWL STORAGE JAR AND COOKING WARE

No.	*Vessel*	*Locus*
1	Bowl	8061
2	Storage Jar	8061
3	Casserole	8061
4	Cooking pot	8061
5	Cooking pot	8061

Type 1 (Figs. 13.2: 2, 13.3: 3–5, 13.6: 1, 2, 13.7: 2, 13.8: 2–5, 13.20: 2)

The most common jar type attributed to the period under discussion is the Palestinian coastal bag-shaped jar, here represented by several variants which usually differ from each other by their rim-neck profile. All are made from a coarse, orange- or yellowish-brown ware and all have a completely ribbed bag-shaped body with two loop handles on the shoulder, a short to high (ca. 3–7 cm) vertical, slightly convex or everted neck (sometimes with a ridge at its base), and a plain, rounded, out-folded or triangular rim. One variant has a prominent ridge under the rim. Most, if not all of these jars, seem to be variants of Riley's Type 1A jars, dated from the 2nd (or preferably 1st) through the 5th centuries CE (1975: 26; for parallels from sites closer to Apollonia, see Ayalon and Harpazi-Ofer 2007: 30–33, Fig. 2: 1–3; Calderon 2011: 63*, 69*, 75*, Figs. 1: 4–5; 6: 1–5, 7; Tal and Taxel 2015: 55, 143, Figs. 1.48: 1–6, 2.8: 2).

Type 2 (Fig. 13.16)

This type, represented by at least three examples from Area DD2, were reused as burial containers for infants. This is one of the earliest variants of the so-called Gaza amphora (also known, with relation to its later variants, as Late Roman Amphora/LRA 4; see below). They are made of a coarse, orange- or reddish-brown ware and are characterized by a cylindrical body (some examples are slimmer than others),

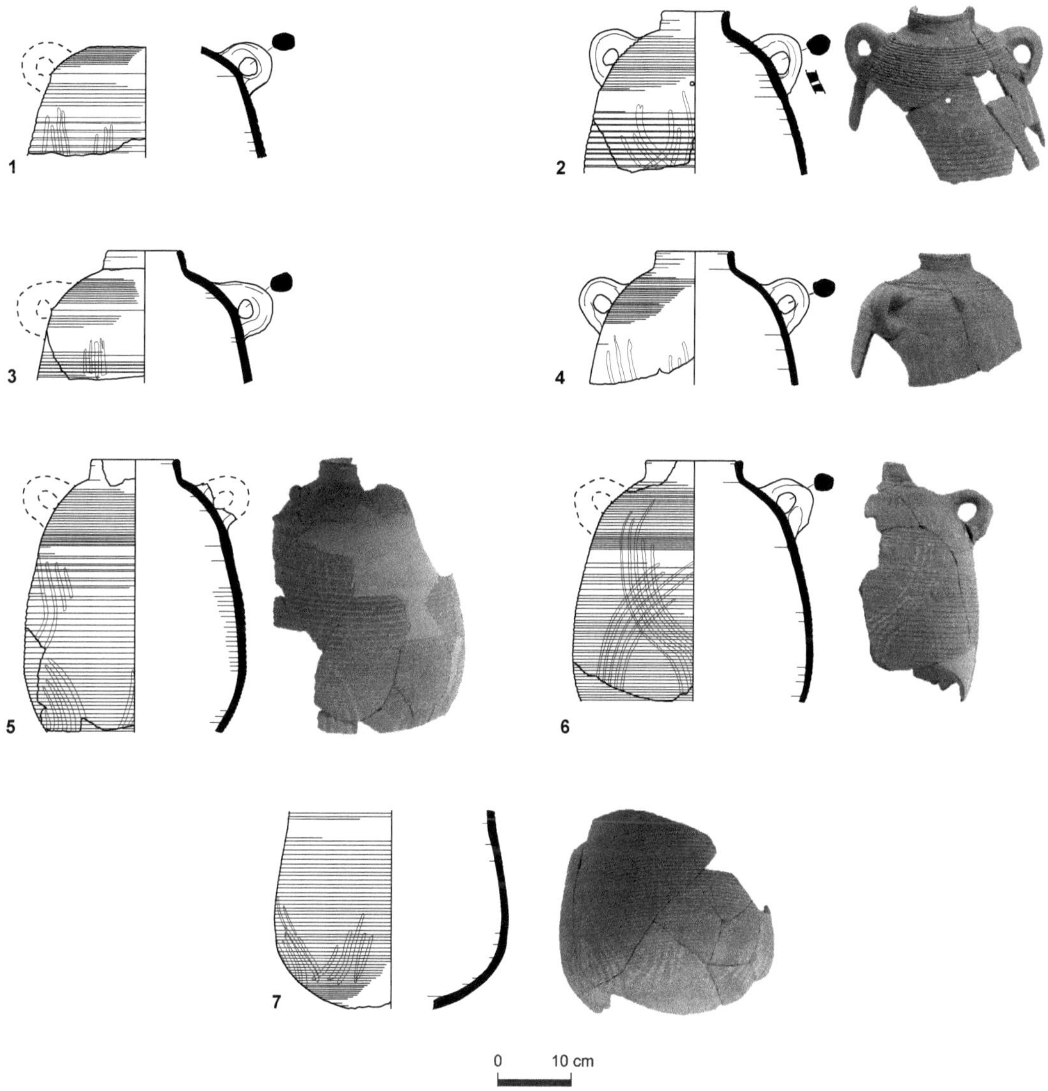

FIG. 13.30: AREA O, STORAGE WARE

No.	*Vessel*	*Locus*
1	Storage jar	8061
2	Storage jar	8061
3	Storage jar	8061
4	Storage jar	8061
5	Storage jar	8061
6	Storage jar	8061
7	Storage jar	8061

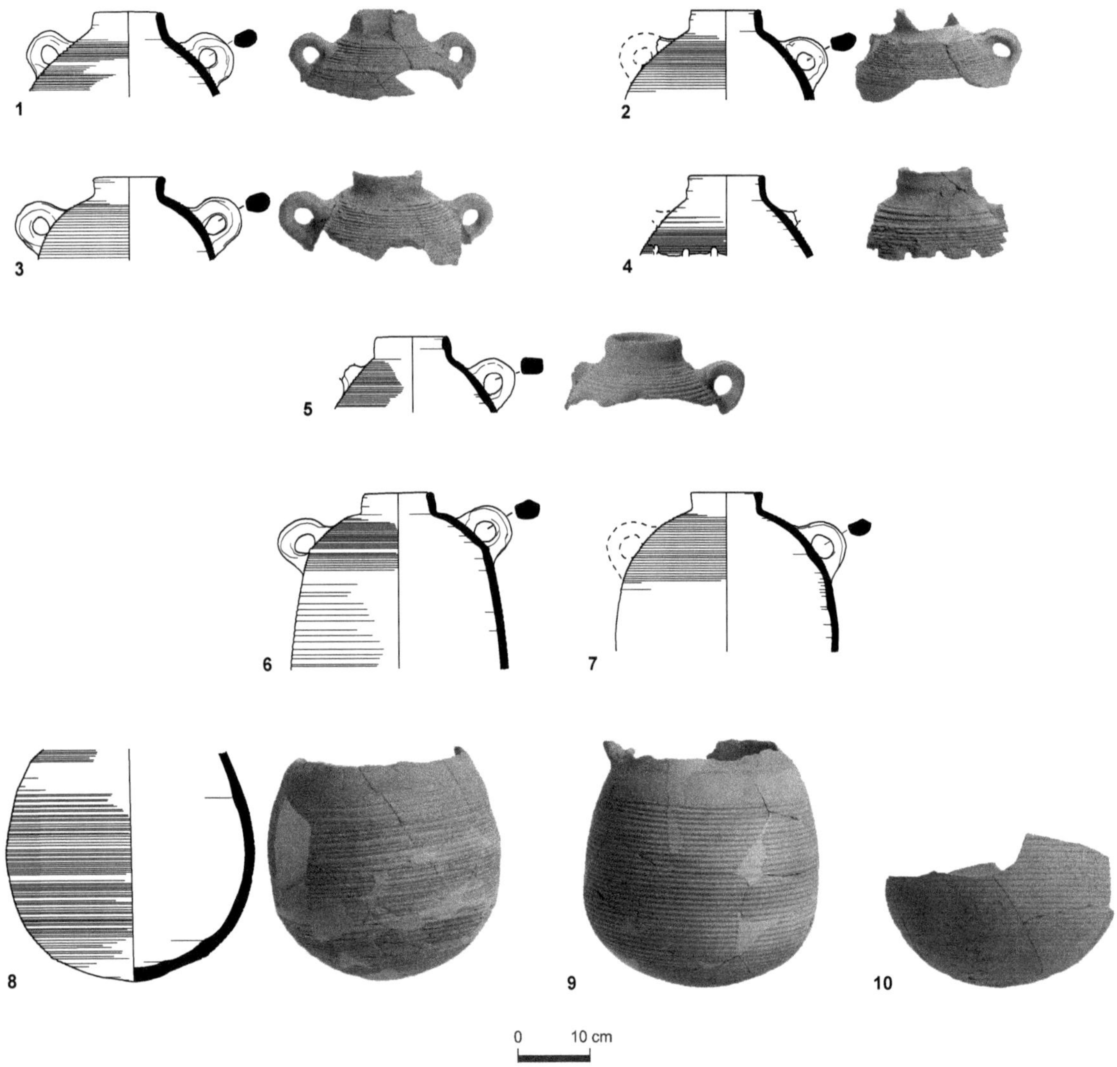

FIG. 13.31: AREA O, STORAGE WARE (CONT.)

No.	*Vessel*	*Locus*
1	Storage jar	8061
2	Storage jar	8061
3	Storage jar	8061
4	Storage jar	8061
5	Storage jar	8061
6	Storage jar	8061
7	Storage jar	8061
8	Storage jar	8061
9	Storage jar	8061
10	Storage jar	8061

a plain or ribbed shoulder with two loop handles, and a neckless opening with a vertical or slightly in-turned rim and a ridge at its base. As the present jars were reused for burial, their bases/lower sections or upper shoulder-rim sections were detached. According to Majcherek's typology of Gaza amphorae, the present variant represents his Form 1, which is dated to between the 1st and 3rd centuries CE (1995: 166). Oked, on the other hand, narrowed the dating of these variants—which belong to her Type 3—to the 1st and 2nd centuries CE (2001: 236). The reuse of contemporaneous as well as later variants of LRA 4 for burial of infants was relatively common, especially in southern coastal sites (e.g., Nahshoni 2007: 83, 88–89, Figs. 3–7, 12; and Chapter 11), with the most abundant number of such jar burials recently excavated at Yavneh (Yannai and Taxel, unpublished).[3]

*Type 3 **(Fig. 13.8: 6)***

This type is an imported amphora made of a coarse rather high-temperature fired yellowish-orange ware containing tiny white and reddish grits and some mica. It has a wide, slightly everted, thick-walled neck and a heavy, triangular rim. Although not securely identified, this amphora seems to be related to the Cypriot/Cilician pinched-handle amphora type of the 1st to 4th centuries CE, which was widely distributed across the Mediterranean (see Johnson 2008a: 153–155, Nos. 438–442, with references).

Type 4 (Fig. 13.1: 4)

Another amphora type is made of a coarse ware, whose color varies from yellowish-brown to orange-brown and contains numerous brown grits and crushed calcite. The single example of this type identified in the excavations is represented by a thick, solid toe with an acorn-like ending. This toe form is most typical of Early Roman amphorae from the Black Sea region, especially those produced in Sinope between the mid-1st century BCE and the early 2nd century CE (see Vunkov 2004: 407–411, Fig. 2).

The Byzantine and Early Islamic Periods

The greater part of the pottery retrieved in the excavations of Areas M, N and O and at Apollonia (East) can be dated between the 5th and 7th or 8th centuries CE; namely it corresponds to the main duration of the Byzantine period and to part or most of the Umayyad period. It should be noted that some of the discussed types had already appeared in the later Roman period (apparently in the 4th century CE), if not actually dated to this period; thus, a certain overlap exists between the Roman- and Byzantine-period ceramic typologies presented here. In addition, a much smaller number of pottery sherds is dated to the later part of the Early Islamic period (the mid-/late 8th to 11th centuries), namely to the ʿAbbasid and Fatimid periods.

African Red Slip (ARS) Ware Bowls

Most of the imported table wares found in the excavations were Tunisian ARS Ware bowls, represented by four types. All are made of a rather coarse, orange- or reddish-brown ware and covered with a thin layer of matte reddish-orange slip on the interior and part of or the entire exterior. The typology follows Hayes (1972: 13–299; 1980: 484–523).

ARS Ware Form 67 (Fig. 13.9: 1, 2)

This is a large bowl with a two-part (flat and curved) flaring rim ending in a thickened lip. The present subtype corresponds to Hayes' first group of this form, which he dated to ca. 360–420 CE (Hayes 1972: 112–116; 1980: 485, 503). Also related to this form is a flat base fragment; on its interior are two

3 The final report of the large-scale excavations carried out by E. Yannai on behalf of the Israel Antiquities Authority at the eastern foot of Tel Yavneh in 2010–2012 is currently being prepared by Yannai and the current author.

concentric grooves surrounding a stamped pattern composed of three concentric circles with notch-fringes. This motif belongs to Hayes' Style A (ii)-(iii) group, Type 36, dated to the late 4th to third quarter of the 5th century CE (1972: 218–219, 223, 237).

ARS Ware Form 97 (Fig. 13.9: 3)

This type is characterized by a narrow, slightly downturned ledge rim with a scalloped lip, with one deep groove following the scalloping and another groove close to the inner edge. Hayes dated this form to ca. 490–550 CE (1972: 150–151; 1980: 506).

ARS Ware Form 99 (Fig. 13.9: 4)

This bowl has rounded walls and a thickened, downturned rim. The present variant seems to belong to Hayes' Type B, which he dated to ca. 530–580 CE (1972: 152–155; 1980: 506–507).

ARS Ware Form 105 (Fig. 13.22: 1, 2)

This type is represented by a large plate with straight, everted walls, a thickened rim, and a low to high ring base; certain specimens have a slight step at the inner joint between wall and bottom. This type is dated to ca. 580/600–660 CE or later (Hayes 1972: 166–169; 1980: 508).

ARS Ware Form 108 (Fig. 13.9: 5)

This type is represented by a small bowl with rounded walls and a narrow ledge rim dated to the early 7th century CE (Hayes 1972: 171; 1980: 509).

Late Roman C (LRC)/Phocaean Red Slip (PRS) Ware Bowls

Surprisingly, very few western Asia Minor LRC/PRS Ware bowls were found in the excavations as these bowls often appear in much larger quantities in most contemporaneous assemblages (Hayes 1972: 323–370; 1980: 525–527).

LRC/PRS Form 3 (Figs. 13.1: 5, 13.9: 6, 13.27: 1)

The fragments found represent the most common Form 3, Type F, which is characterized by a semi-fine, orange-brown ware, thin, rounded walls, a square-sectioned rim and a matte, reddish-orange slip on both sides; this type is dated to the 6th century CE (Hayes 1972: 329–338; 1980: 526–527).

Fig. 13.32: Area O, Storage Ware (cont.)

No.	*Vessel*	*Locus*
1	Storage jar	8061
2	Storage jar	8061
3	Storage jar	8061
4	Storage jar	8061
5	Storage jar	8061
6	Storage jar	8061
7	Storage jar	8061
8	Storage jar	8061
9	Storage jar	8061
10	Storage jar	8061

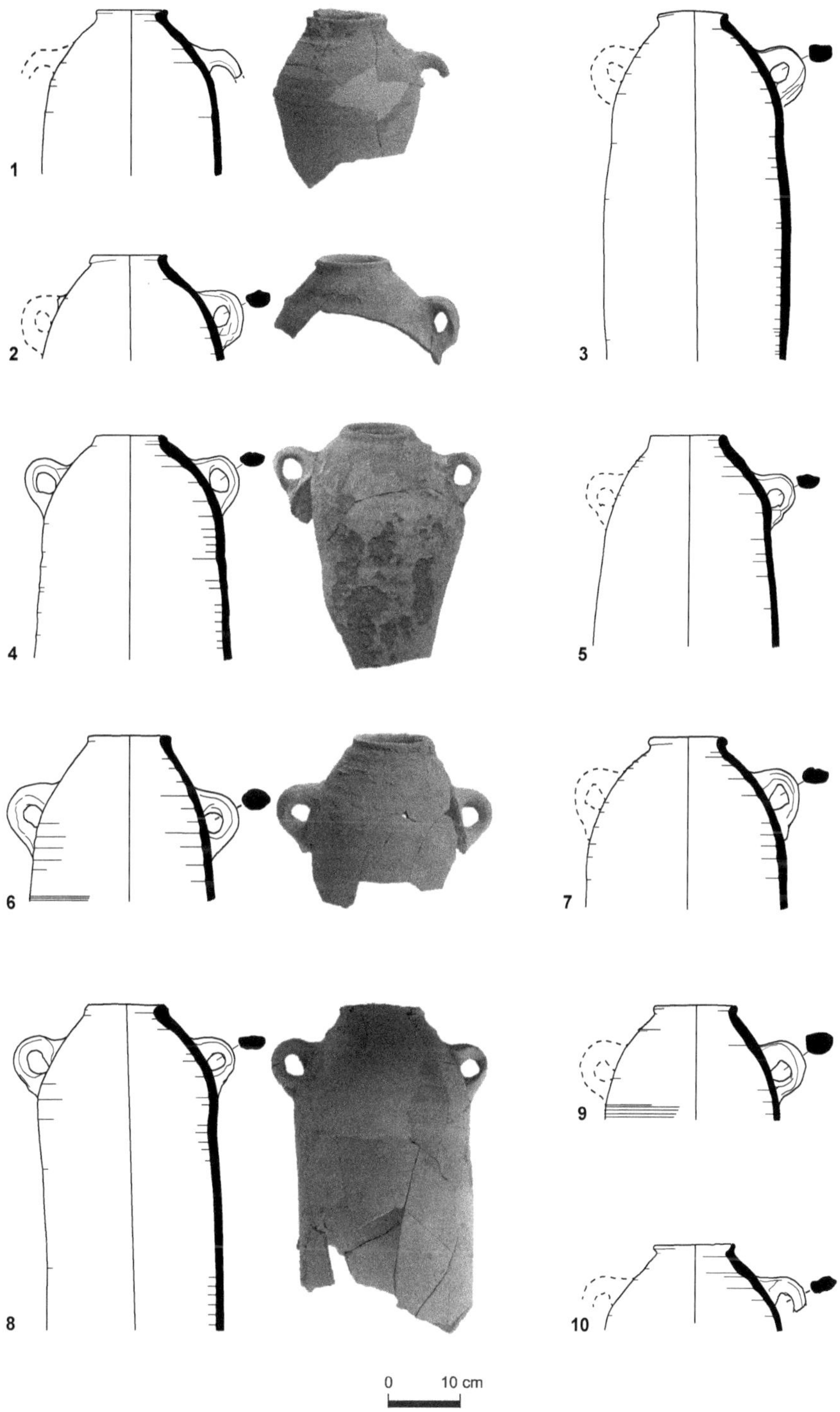

Fig. 13.32: Area O, storage ware (cont.).

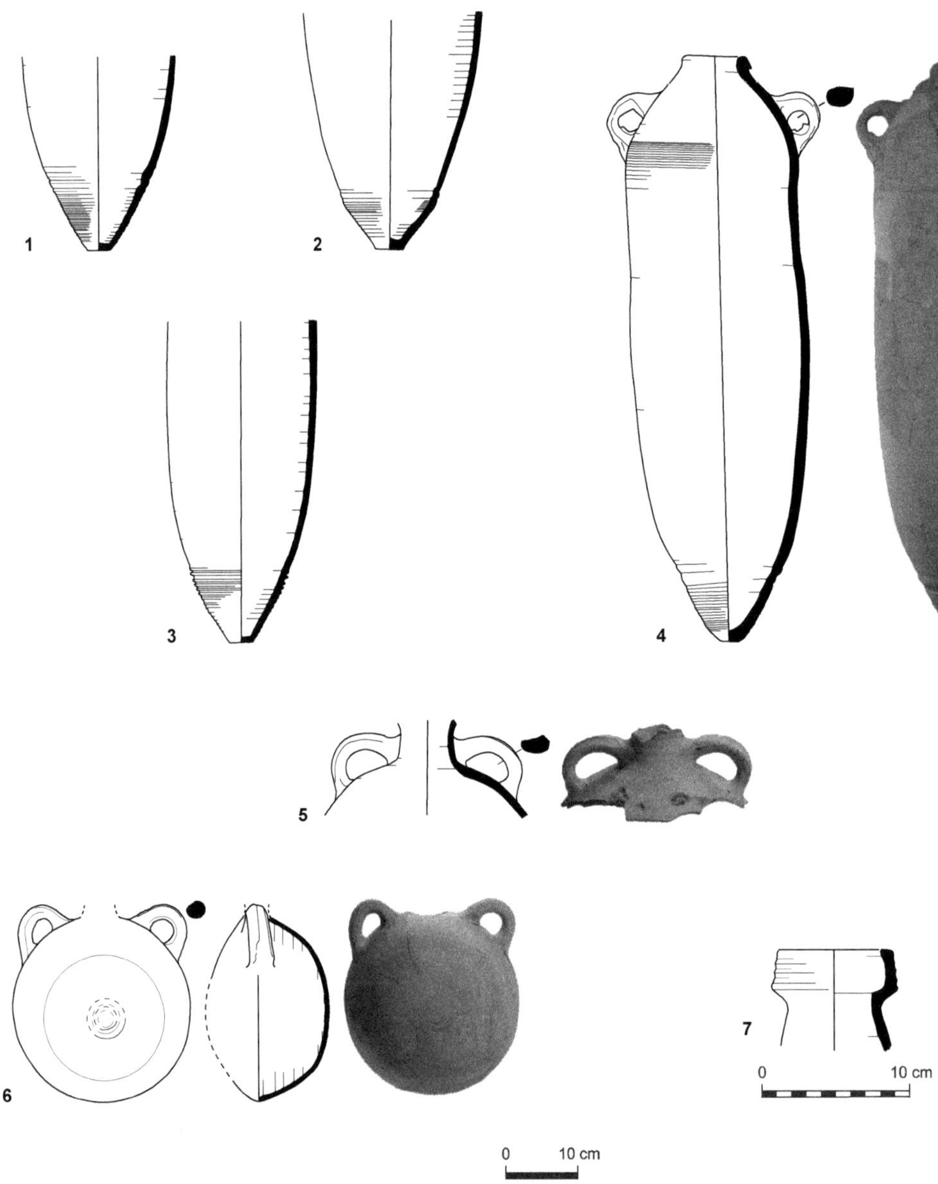

FIG. 13.33: AREA O, STORAGE JARS, AMPHORA, FLASK AND WATER-WHEEL JAR

No.	*Vessel*	*Locus*
1	Storage jar	8061
2	Storage jar	8061
3	Storage jar	8061
4	Storage jar	8061
5	Amphora	8061
6	Flask	8061
7	Water-wheel jar	8061

LATE ROMAN D (LRD)/CYPRIOT RED SLIP (CRS) WARE BOWLS

Like the ARS Ware bowls, Cypriot (Hayes 1972: 371–386; 1980: 528–529) or possibly western Asia Minor table wares (see Jackson *et al.* 2012) were also found in negligible numbers, represented here by three types.

LRD/CRS Ware Form 2 (Fig. 13.9: 7)

This small bowl is made of a fine orange-brown ware with rounded walls, a triangular, grooved rim decorated with rouletting below the rim and matt, pale brown slip on both sides. It is dated to the late 5th-early 6th century CE (Hayes 1972: 373–376).

LRD/CRS Ware Form 8 (Fig. 13.22: 3)

This rather uncommon form has a slightly concave ledge rim and a low ring base. It is dated from the 6th to early 7th centuries CE (Hayes 1972: 379; 1980: 529; Meyza 2007: 60–61).

LRD/CRS Ware Form 9 (Fig. 13.22: 4–7)

Characterized by a rounded rim, concave interior, flat base and sometimes shallow rouletted decoration on the wall, this type is represented by its three known variants—Form 9A, dated to ca. 550–600 CE, and Forms 9B and 9C (the latter sometimes has a grooved rim). Both are dated to ca. 580/600 CE until the end of 7th century (Hayes 1972: 379–383; 1980: 529). One of the Form 9C examples bears a partially-preserved impression of a small Greek cross on its inner bottom.

LRD/CRS Ware Well-Form (Fig. 13.22: 8)

This type, determined as a "Well-Form" after its discovery in a well deposit at Anamur(ium) (Asia Minor) is rare in Levantine contexts. It has everted walls and an infolded rim. According to Meyza (2007: 79–80), it appeared in the late 5th/early 6th century and continued until the late 7th century CE. The early and late variants of this type differ in the shape of the base, though determining which variant in these finds is impossible due to the lack of a base. Still, based on the chronology of the other pottery types found in the same assemblage (at Area M) it is likely that the present example is dated to not before the late 6th century CE.

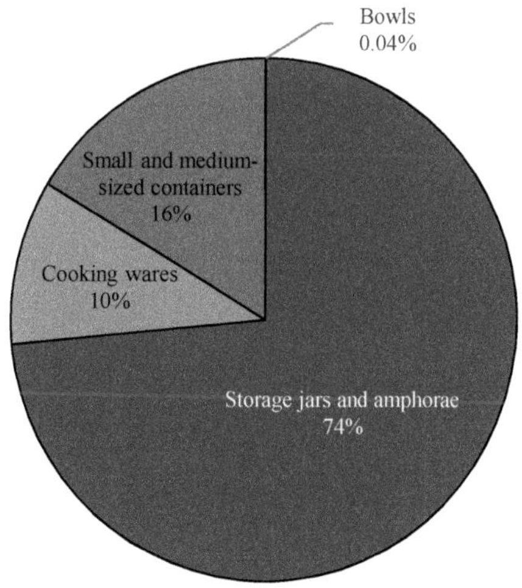

Fig. 13.34: Distribution of pottery types from Area CC.

Egyptian Red Slip (ERS) Ware Bowls (Figs. 13.9: 8, 13.20: 4)

Egyptian table wares are also rare in the discussed assemblage, with only two apparent examples; both are made of a coarse, yellowish ware and have matt, reddish-orange slip on both sides. The bowl in Fig. 13.20: 4 has everted walls and a vertical, square-sectioned rim. It belongs to Hayes' ERS A group and, more specifically to his Form J, which is dated to the 7th–8th centuries CE (1972; 1980). The bowl in Fig. 13.9: 8 has carinated walls with a vertical upper section (a typical Egyptian form) and a plain rim. A similar bowl from Ashqelon was identified by Johnson (2008a: 81, No. 249) as an unclassified form of the ERS A group, which should therefore be dated similarly to the former bowl.

Egyptian Painted Ware Bowls (Fig. 13.22: 9, 10)

Another Egyptian form is represented by two bowls. The first is made of a coarse, reddish-brown micaceous ware with a purplish core (a typical Nile fabric) with everted walls and an upturned, concave ledge rim. It is decorated on the interior with purplish-brown painted designs of dots and stripes over a thin white slip; the slip also covers the bowl's exterior. The second bowl is larger. It was made of a reddish-brown micaceous ware and has thick everted walls, a vertical ledge rim decorated with thumb impressions on its edge and thin yellowish slip on the interior and exterior. A faded painted decoration of dark-colored round dots appears on the rim surface. These bowls, sometimes called Coptic Painted Ware, are dated to the 5th to 8th centuries (see Konstantinidou 2012: 97–100, Fig. 3.26). In Palestine they appear in small quantities, mainly at sites in the northern Negev and the southern Coastal Plain (e.g., Johnson 2008a: 95–98, Nos. 296–302; Nahshoni and Seriy 2014: 42*, Fig. 17: 8), but also in more northern regions (e.g., Johnson 2008b: 57, No. 611).

Fine Byzantine Ware (FBW) Bowls

These bowls, apparently produced in the vicinity of Jerusalem, are characterized by a hard-fired, gray-brown ware, burnished from the interior and exterior; some of the variants also have incised or painted decorations. This group of local fine table wares continued well into the Early Islamic period (Magness 1993: 193–201). Its main area of distribution includes the central hill country (especially Judea) and the Shephelah, while in the Coastal Plain it appears in rather small quantities. Four types of this ceramic group are represented here.

FBW Form 1A (Fig. 13.23: 1, 2)

This is a rounded bowl/cup with a low ring base and wavy incised decoration below the rim. Magness dated it to the mid-6th to late 7th/early 8th centuries CE (1993: 193–194).

FBW Form 1B (Fig. 13.23: 3, 4)

This is a rounded bowl/cup, identical to the previous type with similar dating but lacking the wavy incision (Magness 1993: 193–195).

FBW Form 2B (Fig. 13.20: 3)

This bowl has everted, slightly carinated walls, a plain rim and traces of white painting on the interior. It is dated to the mid-7th to 9th/10th centuries CE (Magness 1992: 198–201).

FBW Form 2C (Fig. 13.23: 5)

This bowl has rounded walls and a narrow, downturned ledge rim, also dated by Magness to the mid-7th to 9th/10th centuries (1993: 198–201).

Common Ware Bowls and Basins

Two bowl and three basin types were attributed to the discussed period; all are of local origin with the exception of the fifth type, which is imported.

Type 1 (Fig. 13.9: 9)

This is a deep bowl made of a coarse, yellowish-brown ware, which has near-vertical walls and an everted rim with an infolded lip. The type originated in the western Negev (Fabian and Goldfus 2004: 14*, n 3; for a recently-excavated dump of a pottery workshop which produced these bowls, see Eisenberg-Degen 2018), and it is common mainly in the northern and western Negev and the southern coast in contexts dated to the 6th-7th centuries CE (see Taxel 2009: 96, Fig. 3.14: 2, with references).

Type 2 (Fig. 13.29: 1)

This bowl type is made of a rather coarse, yellowish-brown ware and has slightly carinated walls, a flattened, string-cut rim and a low ring base. It has no close parallels.

Type 3 (Figs. 13.5: 1, 13.9: 10, 13.20: 7, 13.23: 6–8, 13.27: 2).

This basin type is represented by a few examples. All are made of a coarse, yellowish-orange or yellowish-brown ware and have an in-turned thickened rim and near-vertical walls, which are either plain or decorated with a band of horizontal combing below the rim. The type is most common in the southern regions of the country in 6th- to 7th/early 8th-centuries CE assemblages (e.g., Taxel 2009: 97, Figs. 3.5: 7, 3.9: 2, 3.19: 1, 3.23: 1, 12, 13).

Type 4 (Figs. 13.1: 6, 13.20: 8)

This is a basin made of a coarse, orange- or reddish-brown ware, with rounded walls and a sharply-incurved—thickened or out-folded—rim. Horizontal and wavy combing or wavy incisions often appear on the exterior. Basins of this type were determined by Magness as Incurved-Rim Basins and dated to between the 8th and 10th centuries CE (1993: 210–211).

Type 5 (Fig. 13.9: 11, 12)

Represented by a few examples, this basin type (possibly a mortarium) is made of a highly coarse, yellowish-brown ware mixed with numerous white and gray/black grits, primarily crushed seashells. It has a broad, everted rim, everted walls and a flat base; according to published parallels, both the rim surface and walls of this basin type are sometimes decorated with wavy incised lines. This type is dated to the 4th to 7th centuries CE and apparently originated in the Amrit/Tartus region of the north Syrian coast, where it was produced alongside the large coarse-ware pithoi which are familiar from many coastal (and inland) sites in Palestine as well (Reynolds 2003: 544, Fig. 5: 14). Local parallels for similar basins are known especially from the north of the country and from the central Coastal Plain (e.g., Calderon 2000: 111, 150, Pls. 9: 58, 59, 25: 79; Johnson 2008b: 64–65, Nos. 734–736).

Common Lead Glazed Ware Bowls (Figs. 13.14: 12, 13.17: 5, 13.20: 6)

One of the two most prevalent glazed wares in Early Islamic Palestine, this class includes mostly bowls made of a coarse buff or orange-brown ware with everted walls, a downturned rim, and a flat disc or low ring base. They are decorated with either monochrome green or yellow glaze or with green, yellow, and/or manganese purple painted stripes and daubs under a thin transparent yellowish glaze without any slip. The glaze appears on the interior and over the rim. These apparently Palestinian/southern Levantine products prevailed between the late 8th/early 9th century and the 11th century CE (see Taxel 2014: 124, with references).

Double Slip Glazed Bowl (Fig. 13.7: 3)

This bowl type is made of a coarse, reddish-brown ware with a whitish slip completely covering the vessel and additional layer of slip on the interior. It has rounded walls and a flattened rim, and it is covered from the interior and over the rim with a monochrome green glaze with simple *sgraffito* decoration. These bowls appeared as early as the third decade of the 11th century and continued until the mid-12th century (Avissar and Stern 2005: 6), when they were replaced by a new, related type (see below). Based on petrographic analysis it has been suggested that this type originated in the south Levantine coast, perhaps in Beirut (see Waksman 2011).

Jugs and Juglets

Twelve types of small and medium-sized containers were attributed to the discussed periods (for other classes of closed forms see below).

Type 1 (Fig. 13.11: 1)

A jug made of a coarse, reddish-brown ware resembling cooking ware fabric but somewhat more porous. It has a low, vertical neck with a ridged rim, a six-hole strainer at its base (five peripheral holes, 4 mm in diameter, and a central hole, 1 cm in diameter) and one (completely missing) handle from rim to shoulder. Strainer jugs, often made of a cooking ware or similar material and presenting various neck-rim profiles, are quite common in local Byzantine-period assemblages (for a somewhat different parallel to the present type, see de Vincenz and Sion 2007: 28, Fig. 5: 4).

Type 2 (Figs. 13.5: 4, 13.11: 2, 3)

A jug/small jar made of a coarse, though rather high-temperature fired reddish-brown ware (fired to buff), characterized by a globular, ribbed, neck-less body, an everted rim and a small loop handle from rim to shoulder. This form, sometimes with a slightly higher neck/rim, is rather familiar in Roman-and Byzantine-period contexts (cf. de Vincenz and Sion 2007: 28, Fig. 5: 1–3).

Type 3 (Fig. 13.11: 4)

A jug made of a coarse, yellowish-orange ware which has a long, narrow neck with a broader upper section and a plain rim and two flat-sectioned loop handles which emerge from about the mid-neck to the neck base. This is a typical southern Palestinian form dating to the 6th and 7th centuries CE (see Gichon 1993: 148, Pl. 22: 5–6; de Vincenz 2007: 256, Pl. 25: 45–49).

Type 4 (Fig. 13.11: 5)

Another double-handled jug/table amphora made of a coarse though high-temperature fired buff ware which has a ribbed body/shoulder, a long, narrow neck with a slightly everted (?) rim and two loop handles from about mid-neck to shoulder. Published parallels to this form are not abundant and are dated generally to the Byzantine period (e.g., Peilstöcker 2009: 107, Fig. 9: 6; de Vincenz 2007: 256, 299, Pls. 25: 44, 79: 8, Fig. 131).

Type 5 (Figs. 13.1: 9, 13.17: 7)

These jugs are made of a fine or semi-fine buff ware and are characterized by a funnel-shaped neck with a plain rim; a series of low ridges or horizontal incisions may appear on the neck's exterior below the rim. This type, and its many associated variants, are commonly dated to not before the second half of the 8th century (or the middle of that century, at the earliest), while their heyday occurred between the 9th and 11th/early 12th centuries (see Walmsley 2001: 308–310, Type ICW-B2; cf. Cytryn-Silverman 2010: 106–107; 2013: 172–174, with references).

Type 6 (Fig. 13.26: 1)

This is a jug belonging to the FBW group (above). It is made of a fine, yellowish-orange ware and has an everted, ridged neck (the rim is missing) and biconical body with decoration of short gouged lines on shoulder. It belongs to Magness's Form 1B (1993: 237–239), and is dated to the mid-6th to early 8th centuries CE.

Type 7 (Figs. 13.11: 6, 13.26: 2)

Also of the FBW group, this is a small juglet with a short neck, triangular rim, globular body, flat base and a loop handle from rim to shoulder; the body is decorated with groups of three parallel gouged lines. It is dated the same as the previous type (Magness 1993: 239–241, Form 2A).

Type 8 (Fig. 13.20: 10)

This is a juglet made of a coarse, orange-brown ware with a short neck that forms a direct continuation of an elongated ribbed body; it has a triangular rim, a thickened, string-cut base and a loop handle from rim to shoulder. It belongs to a type which was dated by Magness to the 3rd–8th centuries CE (1993: 246–247, Form 6A), and the poor stratigraphic value of the context from which the present vessel was retrieved does not allow more accurate dating.

Type 9 (Fig. 13.26: 3)

One of three types of imported jugs found in Areas M and N, this jug is made of a reddish-brown, micaceous ware and has a high trumpet base with a concave edge and globular (?) body; a thick white slip covers the vessel's exterior, including the underneath part of the base. The ware and morphology of this jug indicate Egyptian origin. Such jugs were often decorated in reddish-brown or purplish painting, similarly to the Egyptian/Coptic Painted Ware bowls discussed above. They too are basically dated to the 5th to 8th centuries CE (see Konstantinidou 2012: 97–98, 111–112, Fig. 3.29: 211–214; for a Palestinian parallel, see Johnson 2008b: 57, No. 613 [identified as a bowl base]).

Type 10 (Fig. 13.26: 4)

Made of a fine, dark brown micaceous ware (fired to a yellowish hue), this jug has a long, narrow neck widening toward the rim, an everted rim, sloping shoulder and an internal ridge at the neck-shoulder joint. No handles are attached to the neck and its upper part is decorated with a horizontal painted band in reddish-brown. No secure parallels were found for this type; its ware may point to either an Egyptian or Aegean origin (cf. a similar jug from Caesarea, albeit made of a somewhat different ware and with two handles from neck to shoulder; Johnson 2008b: 58, No. 615).

Type 11 (Fig. 13.28: 6)

This jug (?) is made of an orange-brown, micaceous ware fired to a yellowish hue from the exterior. It has a narrow, conical neck with a plain rim and one handle which emerges from the neck. No parallels were found to this rare form, though its ware seems to be most typical to the Aegean region.

Type 11 (Fig. 13.29: 2)

A jug/small jar made of a coarse, yellowish ware. It has a slightly ribbed, bag-shaped (?) body which tapers towards the rim with no actual neck. Its rim is either plain and separated from the body by a shallow depression, or it is everted; there are two small loop handles slightly below the rim. The exact geographic origin of this jar is unknown, though the closest parallels to this type were found in contexts dated to the 363 CE earthquake at the ʿEn Ḥazeva fortress, in a 4th-century CE context at the Yotvata fortress and in early 5th-century CE contexts at Oboda/Avdat, where they were termed "ration jars" and were associated with a military presence at these sites (Erickson-Gini 2010: 131, 165, Figs. 4.39, 6.33, 6.34; Magness 2015: 76, Fig. 2.21: 1, Color Fig. 17: 12). Another parallel comes from a 6th- to 7th-century CE context at Yavneh (Yannai and Taxel, unpublished; see above, n 2 and n 3).

Flasks

Three types of flasks were found; one is local and the other two are imported.

Type 1 (Figs. 13.11: 7–9, 13.26: 5–8, 13.33: 6)

This flask, of which several examples were found, is made of a coarse, yellowish, yellowish-orange or yellowish-brown ware; a few specimens are made of a coarse though rather high-temperature fired orange-brown ware with a yellowish self-slip. It has a vertical neck with a broad upper section (either plain or slightly ribbed) and a plain rim, and is dated to the (Late?) Byzantine and beginning of Early Islamic periods (e.g., Johnson 2008b: 52, Nos. 528–530).

Type 2 (Fig. 13.11: 10)

Represented by a single example, this flask is made of a semi-fine, micaceous orange ware and has a slightly conical neck and an out-folded rim. This is a well-known type of a handle-less, melon-shaped Egyptian flask related to the ERS A Ware group and dated to the late 4th to 5th centuries (see Egloff 1977: 172–173, Pls. 29: 15, 16, 90: 2, Type 338; Tréglia 2003: 441, Fig. 138). Only a few examples of this type have been published from Palestinian assemblages, e.g., from Caesarea (Johnson 2008b: 55, No. 577) and Paneas (Israeli 2008: 115, Fig. 7.10: 20).

Type 3 (Fig. 13.11: 14)

This is another imported flask, here represented by one body fragment. It is made of a fine high-temperature fired yellowish-brown ware and is characterized by a mold-made, carinated body. One of its broader faces is decorated with a marginal motif of protruding dots between two parallel lines surrounding an unidentified central decoration, which—based on a published parallel—likely described a mythological scene. This is a well-known type of wine flask—*oinophoros*—produced in Sagalassos (southwest Turkey) in the 4th and 5th centuries (see Talloen 2011: 579, Fig. 1). A few similar vessels (all fragmentary) are known from other Palestinian sites such as Caesarea (Johnson 2008b: 65, No. 749) and Ramat Raḥel (Gadot *et al.* 2016: 128, Fig. 8.30: 11); in both cases the flasks are decorated with a marginal herringbone motif. It is likely that these isolated examples were personal belongings of pilgrims or travelers from Asia Minor rather than true imported wares (the same may also be true for the above-mentioned Egyptian flasks).

Casseroles

The casseroles, as the other cooking ware vessels of the discussed periods, are made of a coarse, reddish-brown cooking pot ware, and are represented here by two variants. The most common variant has everted—plain or ribbed—walls, cut-away rim and thick horizontal handles (Figs. 13.5: 2, 13.10: 1–2, 13.17: 1, 13.24: 1–2, 13.29: 3). This is the most widespread casserole form in assemblages dated mainly to the 6th to 8th centuries CE, although it is already known from the Late Roman and Early Byzantine periods (Magness 1993: 211–213, Form 1). The second variant has plain, everted walls with a sharp carination below the rim (Fig. 13.10: 3) and is typical mostly to northern Palestine (see Calderon 2000: 140, Pl. 23: 50).

Frying Pans

Two types of frying pans—one plain and the other glazed—have been attributed to the discussed periods.

Type 1 (Figs. 13.10: 4, 5, 13.24: 3)

These frying pans are dated to the 6th–7th centuries CE (Magness 1993: 212, Form 2), and they differ from the contemporaneous casseroles by their (usually) shallower profile and by their single horizontal hollow wishbone handle.

Type 2 (Fig. 13.21: 3).

This is a shallow frying pan with everted walls, a triangular rim, and splashes of brown-purple glaze on its interior. The first appearance of glazed frying pans seems to vary from site to site, or from region to region, though they probably did not appear before the late 9th century (see Avissar 1996: 139, Fig. XIII.100).

Cooking Ware Lids (Figs. 13.10: 6, 7, 13.24: 4, 5, 13.27: 3, 4)

Usually associated with casseroles and frying pans, these shallow lids have rounded, ribbed walls, commonly ending in a knob handle, and a cataway rim. Similar to casseroles, the form continues from the Late Roman period well into Early Islamic times (see Magness 1993: 215).

Cooking Pots

Six types of closed cooking pots are dated to the discussed periods.

Type 1 (Figs. 13.3: 2, 13.5: 3)

This type has a very short, convex neck and a triangular rim. It has close parallels in assemblages dated to the 4th–5th centuries CE (e.g., Ayalon and Harpazi-Ofer 2007: 33, Fig. 3: 7–8; Tal and Taxel 2015: 55, Fig. 1.48: 10). Such cooking-pots may have been produced during the Early Byzantine period at Khirbat el-Niʿana (south of Lod), as indicated by their presence in contemporary pottery workshop dumps found at the site (de Vincenz and Sion 2007: 24, Fig. 2: 5–8, 11).

Type 2 (Figs. 13.10: 8, 13.29: 4, 5)

With a short, vertical—straight or slightly convex—neck and a plain rim, this cooking pot type apparently appeared as early as the Late Roman or Early Byzantine period (around the 4th century CE) and continued until the 7th century CE (see Magness 1995: 133–134, Fig. 1: 15).

Type 3 (Figs. 13.10: 9, 10, 13.24: 6, 7)

This type has a very short, vertical or slightly everted neck and a hooked rim and is dated to the 5th/6th to late 7th/early 8th centuries CE (Magness 1993: 219–220, Form 4B).

Type 4 (Figs. 13.17: 2, 13.18: 1)

This is a neckless cooking pot, characterized by an out-folded, ridged rim. Such cooking pots are mostly typical to northern Palestine (and Transjordan), though they do appear as well in small quantities in more southern regions; the present type is dated mostly to the 6th and 7th centuries, though its production apparently continued into the first half of the 8th century as well (see Bar-Nathan 2011: 260–262, Fig. 11.22: 11; Watson 1992: 235, Fig. 2: 12).

Type 5 (Fig. 13.24: 8)

This type is also a neckless cooking pot differing from the previous type by its broader, everted rim; it dates from the same period (Bar-Nathan 2011: 260–262, Fig. 11.22: 10; Watson 1992: 235, Fig. 2: 15).

Type 6 (Fig. 13.18: 7)

The latest cooking pot type found in the excavations is represented here by a single fragment of a wide, horizontal strap handle with splashes of purplish-brown glaze on its interior and exterior. Apparently, globular, glazed cooking pots appeared in the local ceramic repertoire not before the late 9th century (like to the glazed frying pans, above) and continued well into medieval times (see Avissar 1996: 132–136; Avissar and Stern 2005: 91–92). Judging by the present fragment, therefore, it is hard to determine whether it represents an Early Islamic- (ʿAbbasid-Fatimid) or Crusader-period variant.

Storage Jars and Amphorae

Fifteen types of locally-produced and imported storage jars and amphorae were found.

Type 1A (Figs. 13.3: 6, 7, 13.12: 1–5, 13.17: 3, 13.25: 1, 13.27: 5, 6, 13.30, 13.31, 13.35)

One of the two most widespread types of Late Byzantine- to Umayyad-period storage jars found at the site is represented by a certain variant of the Palestinian coastal bag-shaped jar. These jars are made of a coarse and sandy, orange- or yellowish-brown ware and have a bag-shaped body with two loop handles on the shoulder and a short (ca. 2–3 cm) vertical (slightly convex) neck with a plain or thickened rim. The body is completely or nearly completely ribbed with the shoulder ribbing somewhat denser than the body ribbing. Some of the jars have a slight carination at the body-shoulder joint. Some of the jars are decorated with whitish painting of vertical and wavy parallel stripes, arranged in groups of three to five, which start at the lower shoulder or upper body and end slightly above base. These jars are dated from the 5th through the 7th centuries CE (Calderon 2000: 127–129, Pl. 17, Figs. 16–18; Riley 1975: 26–27, Type 1B; cf. Tal and Taxel 2015: 143, Fig. 2.8: 1), if not slightly later, and are especially widespread in the Carmel area, the central Coastal Plain (the Sharon) and the northern part of the southern Coastal Plain (as south as the area of Yavneh). A round hole (ca. 0.50 cm in diameter) pierced in the lower shoulder on some of these jars (Fig. 13.3: 6) indicates that this specific vessel—and probably many others of this type—contained wine during its initial stage of usage, since such holes are commonly interpreted as either fermentation or decanting openings typical of wine containers in antiquity.

One (lower) body fragment of such a jar (from Apollonia [East] Area CC) has a highly worn and smoothed edge, which may represent a jar with a detached upper section (Fig. 13.12: 5). The lower body of jars whose upper part was removed might have been used for a variety of secondary purposes (including burial, see Tal and Taxel 2015: 57, 143, Figs. 1.46: 1–2, 2.8: 1) and they are often characterized by a horizontal smoothed edge. A neck-shoulder section of another jar (from Area O) was detached by drilling round holes (ca. 1 cm in diameter, ca. 3 cm apart) in a radial line below its handles (Fig. 13.31: 4). This operation was followed by the removal of the upper part of the vessel by creating a more or less horizontal break (perhaps by using a hammer/punch) which ran through the holes; the jar's handles were also removed. Detached upper parts of storage jars and amphorae might have been reused, for instance, as funnels and as fixed stands (for a thorough discussion on the various reuse practices of bag-shaped and other jar types with a detached upper or lower part, see Taxel 2018: 78–99).

Type 1B (Figs. 13.18: 2, 3, 13.25: 2, 13.27: 7)

Much less common in the discussed assemblages, this is the typical southern coast bag-shaped jar. It is made of a coarse, yellowish- or reddish-brown ware and has a very short (less than 2 cm), vertical (slightly convex) neck with a plain rim and densely combed shoulder. It should be noted that in terms of morphology (at least of the upper section), these jars are often identical to some of those determined as Type 1A, with the exception of the combed versus ribbed shoulder. Noteworthy is the fact that Type 1B is documented in much larger quantities elsewhere in Apollonia/Sozousa and other sites in the Sharon. This might be only a matter of coincidence; however, if we accept Kingsley's claim (1994–95: 42) that the combed-shoulder variant appeared in large quantities not before the late 6th or early 7th century CE, it would not be unreasonable to assume that these specific areas of Apollonia's immediate hinterland were largely abandoned not later than the early 7th century CE. At this time the southern bag-shaped jars had only started to appear in the Sharon region in large numbers (see in this respect Tal and Taxel 2012: 500–501, where such a scenario is suggested for the entire site based on historical accounts and coin finds due to the site Persian-Sasanian occupation).

Type 2 (Figs. 13.12: 6, 13.27: 8–10)

Another type of bag-shaped jar, represented by several examples, is of northern Palestinian origin. It is made of a coarse high-temperature fired ware which might be either gray or (more often) orange-brown with a pale gray self-slip; it has a short, vertical neck with a thickened or out-folded rim and a ribbed shoulder. This variant of the northern Palestinian bag-shaped jar has 6th- to 7th-century CE parallels (Młynarczyk 2013: 480–481, Figs. 21–32; Watson 1992: 239, Fig. 9: 64, 65).

Type 3A (Fig. 13.12: 7)

This bag-shaped jar type is also represented by several specimens. It is typical mainly to Judea and the southern Samaria Hills and is characterized by a rather fine, yellowish-brown high-temperature fired ware with a yellowish-buff self-slip, a short, vertical neck with a ridge at its base and a plain rim. It was dated by Magness to the late 6th to 7th centuries CE (1993: 223–226, Form 4C).

Type 3B (Figs. 13.6: 3, 13.20: 11)

Related to the above-mentioned group, this is a larger and heavier bag-shaped jar, characterized by either a short or long, vertical neck with a ridge at its base and a plain rim; some specimens have a wavy combing on the neck. It was dated by Magness to the late 6th/7th to 8th centuries (1993: 227–230, Form 6), though it continued well into the Early Islamic period, apparently until the 10th century (e.g., Arnon 2008: 159, 222, 252, Types 822, 831, 841; Cytryn-Silverman 2010: 101–102, Pls. 9.1: 10, 9.2: 1, 3–4, 9, 9.10: 2, 9.13: 3, 9.20: 6, 9.35: 5).

Type 4 (Fig. 13.12: 8)

This rare form seems to be an atrophied version of a Palestinian bag-shaped jar, made of a highly-coarse, pinkish ware (fired to a yellowish hue from the interior and to yellowish-green from the exterior) rich with small to large inclusions. It has a slim cylindrical body, short, vertical neck with

Fig. 13.35: Area O, Palestinian coastal bag-shaped jars and other pottery types recovered from the collecting vat of the winepress.

a slight ridge at its base and a flattened rim, sharply-sloped, almost unnoticeable shoulder, and small loop handles extending from it. A slight ridge marks the transition from shoulder to body; both are ribbed. Identical parallels, made of the same ware as the southern coast bag-shaped jars, were found in 6th- to 7th-century CE contexts at Ḥorvat Zikhrin (Taxel 2005: 68, Fig. 41: 14) and even at overseas locations, such as Corinth (e.g., Warner Slane and Sanders 2005: 263, 271, 278, 286, Figs. 5: 23, 8: 21, 13: 20).

Type 5

Alongside Type 1, the present storage jar—the so-called Gaza amphora or Late Roman Amphora 4 (LRA 4)—is the most frequent in Byzantine- and beginning of Early Islamic-period contexts at the site, including two intact specimens found in the Area CC dump and one complete (restorable) jar from Area O (Fig. 13.36). These were the standard commercial containers for wines (and probably other foodstuff) produced along the southern Palestinian coast and the northwestern Negev since the Roman period. The jars are made of a coarse orange-brown ware (sometimes fired to a yellowish hue from the exterior), and are represented here by two of their latest variants. The first variant, with a vertical, concave rim (Figs. 13.3: 8, 13.25: 3, 13.28: 1), is dated to the 5th and 6th centuries CE (Majcherek 1995: 168–169, Form 3; Pieri 2005: 105–106, Form B1). The second and most common variant has a plain rim that continues the line of the shoulder and has a pointed ribbed base (Figs. 13.1: 7, 13.12: 9–12, 13.18: 4, 13.25: 4, 13.28: 2, 13.32, 13.33: 1–4); it is dated to between the late 6th/7th to the 8th century (Majcherek 1995: 169, Form 4; Pieri 2005: 106–107, Forms B2 and B3).

Type 6 (Figs. 13.1: 8, 13.13: 1–3, 13.17: 4, 13.18: 5, 13.25: 5, 6, 13.28: 3)

This is one of the many types of imported amphorae found in the excavations dated to the discussed period, representing the most common group among the imports. It is made of a coarse orange-brown ware (on occasion fired to a yellowish hue) which contains numerous tiny and small inclusions, including mica; it is fired at a high temperature. This amphora—the well-known Late Roman Amphora 1 (LRA 1)—is characterized by a vertical neck with a thickened rim and a ridge slightly beneath it from which emerge two long, oval-sectioned ridged handles. It was produced in various locations in

Fig. 13.36: Area O, Gaza amphora / Late Roman Amphora 4 (LRA 4) recovered from the collecting vat of the winepress.

Cyprus, the northern Syrian coast and the southern Anatolian coast and was the most common wine (and olive oil?) commercial container in the eastern Mediterranean between the 5th and 7th centuries CE. The present variant belongs to Pieri's Type LRA 1B1, which is dated to not before the (mid-?) 6th century until the mid-7th century CE (Pieri 2005: 75–76, Pls. 15–18; cf. also Peacock and Williams 1986: 185–187, Class 44B).

Type 7

Another imported amphora is the Late Roman Amphora 2 (LRA 2). It is made of a semi-fine, high-temperature fired orange-brown ware, containing numerous tiny and small white and orange inclusions, including mica. It has a tall broad conical neck with two long oval-sectioned handles extending from the neck's upper section to the shoulders and a broad, everted rim with a thickened lip (Figs. 13.13: 4–5, 13.28: 4). This variant corresponds to Pieri's LRA 2B, dated to the second half of the 6th century CE (2005: 88).

Type 8 (Fig. 13.13: 8)

A third type of imported container is the LRA 3, a small Aegean amphora made of a fine, highly-micaceous reddish-brown ware. The present example is represented by its typical solid pointed base; it is dated to the 4th to 6th centuries CE (Pieri 2005: 95–101).

Type 9 (Fig. 13.33: 5)

Another type of amphora, represented by a single example, is made of a coarse, yellowish-brown ware with a buff self-slip. It has a globular body, a rather short, vertical neck with an everted (missing) rim and two flat/concave-sectioned loop handles extending from the neck base to the shoulder. Although the rim of the present example is missing, it seems to correspond to a rare type of globular amphora with a hooked rim documented thus far in only a few southern Levantine contexts. The largest number of such vessels was found at Yavneh in contexts dated to the mid-/late 7th to the early 8th century CE. Other single finds are known from sites in the vicinity of Yavneh and from two sites in northern Sinai and Egypt, mainly in contexts dated to the second half of the 7th century CE (Taxel and Cohen-Weinberger 2019: 7–13, Figs. 5, 6: 1–5). It should be mentioned that all of the known examples of such amphorae, whose shoulder was preserved, have a ribbed shoulder, contrary to the plain shoulder of the Apollonia example. It should also be noted that the context of the Apollonia amphora is dated earlier than the other, above-mentioned examples, which may indicate that it was a forerunner of the latter. Interestingly, no secure parallels for this amphora type have been found in published studies on sites located elsewhere in the Mediterranean and neighboring regions, including the Aegean and Cyprus, which theoretically precludes a foreign origin for this type. Furthermore, petrographic analysis was carried out on three of the amphora fragments from Yavneh, one of which was retrieved from an accumulation inside a pottery kiln together with many other similar amphora fragments. The fact that some present production defects (a deformed body) indicates without doubt that these vessels were produced somewhere in the area stretching between the northern Negev and the southern Shephelah/southern coast, with a high probability of production at Yavneh proper. However, the petrographic analysis of the Apollonia amphora could not pinpoint with certainty at its area of production, though there is a slight possibility that it was somewhere along the Mediterranean coast of Israel (Taxel and Cohen-Weinberger 2019: 14–18).

Type 10 (Fig. 13.25: 7)

This amphora (?) is made of a highly coarse, brittle yellowish-grayish ware and has a broad thin-walled vertical neck with a flattened rim and two (?) broad, concave-sectioned handles from rim to shoulder. Dark gray slip or painting appears on the vessel's rim, handle surface and part of the neck. This amphora seems to be a variant of the Aegean (Samian?) type known as Agora M273 or Late Roman Amphora 8 which appeared in the 5th century CE (see Pieri 2005: 132–137); it was produced in various fabrics, with some of the variants dated to as late as the early to mid-6th century (see Reynolds 2010: 97, Fig. 6: c-h).

Type 11 (Fig. 13.28: 5)

This small amphora type is made of a rather fine, orange-brown micaceous ware and has an external buff self-slip. The preserved fragment has a thick-walled, slim conical body with ribbing at least on its upper part, a narrow neck and two handles attached to the shoulder; a slight step appears on the interior at the shoulder-neck joint. This is most probably a representative of the carrot-shaped Sinopean amphora, produced at Sinop in the Black Sea region between the 3rd and 7th centuries CE (see Kassab Tezgör 2010). The present example seems to be a variant of Kassab Tezgör's Type D, dated to the 6th century CE (2010: 134–137). However, parallels from elsewhere in the Black Sea and the Mediterranean indicate that similar amphorae appeared as late as the early/mid-7th century CE (e.g., Calderon 2000: 133–135, Pl. 20, Figs. 26–29; Reynolds 2013: 102, Pl. 68: AM324; Waksman *et al.* 2014: 920, Fig. 2).

Type 12 (Fig. 13.13: 9)

This unusual vessel is made of a semi-fine, high-temperature fired yellowish-brown ware containing tiny brown/black and white inclusions and some mica. It has a short, vertical neck with a slightly convex profile, an out-folded, rounded rim, a ribbed shoulder and short loop handle/s from neck to shoulder. Most of these characteristics generally recall the Palestinian bag-shaped jar, except for the location of the handle and the neck's diameter, which is narrower than that of the average Palestinian containers. In addition, the micaceous ware points to a foreign origin for this type, apparently in the Aegean region or Cyprus. However, no exact parallels to this form have been found, and it is also uncertain whether it served as a commercial container or domestic storage/serving vessel (e.g., as a table amphora).

Type 13 (Fig. 13.13: 6, 7)

Represented by two examples, this is probably the only type of western Mediterranean amphora found in the excavations. It has a narrow neck, a pronounced triangular rim and round- or oval-sectioned handles which extend from below the rim or from mid-neck to the shoulder. One of the vessels is made of a coarse, though still high-temperature fired, yellowish ware with numerous tiny to medium-sized white, brown and black inclusions and mica; this vessel also has two thumb impressions on the upper end of its preserved handle (Fig. 13.13: 6). The second example is made of a semi-fine, high-temperature fired yellowish-brown ware with numerous tiny black inclusions and mica (Fig. 13.13: 7). These amphorae seem to be variants of a south Italian amphora known as Keay Type 52 (Keay 1984: 267–268; cf. Reynolds and Pavlidis 2017: 656, Fig. 7: 2), dated to the 5th century.

Pithoi

Two types of exceptionally large storage containers—pithoi—were found.

Type 1 (Figs. 13.20: 9, 13.25: 8–10)

Made of a coarse, reddish-brown ware, this pithos type has a wide holemouth opening with a thick flattened rim and two large grooved handles on shoulder. It belongs to a well-known type, whose geographical distribution in neighboring regions and petrographic analyses point to its origin on the northern Syrian coast or Cyprus (see Reynolds 2003: 544, Fig. 5: 14). Its date falls between the 5th/6th to early 8th centuries CE and, in Palestine, it is especially common in the harbor towns from Caesarea in the north to Yavneh-Yam in the south (see Ayalon 1991).

Type 2 (Fig. 13.18: 6)

Represented by a single example, this pithos is made of a coarse, though high-temperature fired yellowish-brown ware with a broad, everted neck and a square-sectioned rim. Similar pithoi were found in a 7th-century CE context in Cyprus (Catling 1972: 13, 66–67, Figs. 6: P1, P11, P16, P323). In early-to mid-7th century contexts, other pithoi, with somewhat different rim profiles, were found at Ras el-Bassit on the Syrian coast (one of which determined as a local ware [Mills and Beaudry 2010: 857, Fig. 4a: N32, N34]), and in Caesarea (where its ware was identified as similar to that of the north Syrian mortaria [Johnson 2008b: 54, No. 554]).

Water-Wheel Jars

The excavation has yielded a few fragmentary water-wheel (*sāqiya*) jars, represented by two types.

Type 1 (Fig. 13.3: 9, 10)

This type is made of a coarse, reddish-brown ware (resembling cooking-pot ware) and is characterized by a neck-less, ribbed bag-shaped body and an everted, internally-concave rim. It is dated to the 4th and 5th centuries CE (Ayalon 2000: 223, Fig. 3: 2–3).

Type 2 (Figs. 13.3: 11, 13.11: 11–13, 13.28: 7–9, 13.33: 7)

Somewhat more common at the site, this type is made of a coarse, yellowish-orange ware, and has a partially-ribbed bag-shaped body, a short, vertical neck with a plain rim, and a rounded base. This type is dated to between the 5th/6th and 7th centuries CE (Ayalon 2000: 223, Fig. 3: 4).

Incense Burners (Figs. 13.14: 1, 2, 13.17: 6)

One of the less common types of ceramic vessels found in the excavation (in the Area CC dump) is represented by two fragmentary lower parts of bowls belonging to two-part incense burners which were originally accompanied by a matching lid. They are made of a coarse, yellowish-orange ware and have a rather high ring base with a carinated body decorated with chip-carving (Kerbschnitt) geometric motifs; some of these knife-cuts possibly formed the holes through which the odiferous fumes produced by the melting resins inside the bowls were drawn off. Another possible fragment of such a vessel (from the Area DD2 refuse pit) represents the bowl's upper part, with a cutaway rim and a horizontal handle.

This vessel type was recently discussed in a comprehensive study of the published (and some unpublished) examples of such incense burners (Taxel and Iserlis 2014; see also Tal and Taxel 2015: 53–54). Such burners were made in the form of a single closed bowl; a single horizontal or loop handle was produced separately and after initial drying was joined to the bowl's body. The bowl's broader upper section was then fenestrated and/or decorated using various techniques. At this stage the lid (concave, with either a knob or a high loop handle and fenestrated and decorated like its matching bowl) was cut at an oblique angle with a knife through the upper third in order to produce the body and ensure a close fit, similar to the technique used in the production of contemporaneous casseroles and casserole lids. This study shows that the distribution of these incense burners is almost entirely restricted to certain regions in Palestine, namely the ʿAkko Plain, the Carmel Ridge and its surroundings, the northern Samaria Hills and the Sharon, with the exception of a few examples found farther to the south and east. It was also found that their date ranges between the late 2nd or 3rd century to the 6th or 7th century CE, though they were probably most prevalent during the 4th and 5th centuries CE. Based on the geographical distribution of these vessels and on certain aspects of the Samaritan religion, it is likely that these incense burners were in use mainly among the rural Samaritan population of Late Roman and Byzantine Palestine. The great majority of incense burners documented originated at sites located in regions inhabited by a substantial, if not a predominantly Samaritan population, and the present examples provide yet additional evidence for this.

LIDS AND STOPPERS

Five types of lids and stoppers and related objects were found.

Type 1 (Figs. 13.14: 3, 4, 13.26: 9–11, 13.28: 10)

These are jar stoppers (ca. 10–15 cm in diameter) made of a highly coarse, low-temperature fired, orange- or reddish-brown ware, which on occasion resemble cooking ware material. They have solid, conical bodies with flattened upper faces broader than the bodies and solid knobs or (rarely) loop handles. This type is known from many Late Byzantine and Early Islamic (6th to 8th century CE) assemblages (e.g., Magness 1993: 248, Form 2; de Vincenz and Sion 2007: 28, Fig. 4: 3–10, 12–15; Yannai 2010: 133, Fig. 22: 5).

Type 2 (Fig. 13.26: 12–15)

This type of lid/stopper (ca. 15–25 cm in diameter) has a shallow, bowl-shaped body, a flat or slightly concave base, a thickened, everted or ledge rim, and, on occasion, a solid knob handle. It is made of a rather coarse reddish-brown, micaceous ware, sometimes mixed with organic tempers represented by thin, straight cavities in the clay. Although this lid/stopper form is known throughout the eastern Mediterranean and was certainly produced in Palestine as well, the ware of the present examples points to their Egyptian origin. Indeed, Egyptian parallels are known, though they were sometimes determined to be saucer lamps, as some of the examples from the Monastery of Baramus, which are dated to between the 5th and 9th/10th centuries CE (Konstantinidou 2012: 237, 240–241, Figs. 3.78: 597–601, 3.79: 609–616). Another parallel from a local context—the Dor 2006 shipwreck—was dated to the mid-6th to early 7th century CE, namely, it is more or less contemporaneous with the present finds; its Egyptian origin was confirmed by an Instrumental Neutron Activation Analysis/INAA (Barkan *et al.* 2013: 129–130, Fig. 17).

Type 3 (Fig. 13.28: 11)

This small lid/stopper (ca. 7 cm in diameter) has a disk-shaped body with a concave base and a central, rectangular knob handle. It is made of pale brown, micaceous ware with traces of organic tempers and it too is likely an Egyptian import. A parallel from the Monastery of Baramus was dated to the 5th–9th centuries CE (Konstantinidou 2012: 241, Fig. 3.79: 620).

The foreign (Egyptian) origin of Type 2 and 3 lids/stoppers is quite remarkable, since such crude, utilitarian ceramic forms are neither fine/decorated tableware (similar to the above-mentioned Egyptian Red Slip and Painted Ware bowls and the Egyptian jug), nor are they commercial containers. Most reasonably, these lids/stoppers were not true imports, but were probably attached to closed vessels of some kind (amphorae, large jugs and the like) imported from Egypt with their contents.

Type 4 (Fig. 13.26: 16, 17)

This type is actually represented by two modified bases of unidentified amphorae reused as stoppers. The first is made of a reddish-brown ware and has a solid conical profile. The fact that it is highly abraded throughout allows the suggestion that this amphora base is an old (Roman-period?) artifact found somewhere at the site during the Byzantine period and converted into a stopper. The second amphora base is made of a yellowish-brown, micaceous ware indicating its foreign origin and has a somewhat stepped profile with a solid, conical point. It is slightly worn and the uneven surface of its upper edges indicates that it was roughly removed by hammering from the original vessel. Reworked amphora bases reused as stoppers are known from elsewhere in the Roman and Byzantine world (Peña 2007: 157–158; for local examples, see Taxel 2018: 103, with references).

Type 5 (Fig. 13.20: 12–14)

These are three small round objects (ca. 2 cm in diameter) fashioned out of reused storage jar body sherds. One example has an incised mark, apparently the letter E, made after firing (and thus could represent either the object itself or the original vessel from which it was cut). The custom of making disc-shaped objects out of pottery sherds is well-known in this region since early times up until the Late Islamic period. They are commonly interpreted as stoppers,[4] but also as counters, weights, loom weights, tokens, gaming pieces and toys (see Peña 2007: 153–160, Fig. 6.12; for a discussion on the local finds of this kind, see Taxel 2018: 100–102).

Pipe Sections (Fig. 13.14: 5–8)

A few fragmentary pipe sections were found, all made of a highly coarse, reddish-brown ware with a straight or slightly concave plain or ribbed body. Only one fragment is preserved to its full length (13.30 cm). Some fragments bear remains of white mortar, which indicate that they were incorporated into the walls or floors of structures or installations.

THE MEDIEVAL AND OTTOMAN PERIODS

A relatively small number of pottery sherds dated to the Crusader/Ayyubid period (mainly) and the Ottoman period (roughly the 12th–13th and 18th–19th centuries CE) were also found in the excavations within the Nof-Yam compound, mainly in mixed and/or surface contexts.

Bowls with a Gritty Glaze (Fig. 13.4: 1)

This bowl type apparently developed from the glazed bowls with a double slip of the eleventh to mid-12th centuries CE (above). It is made of a coarse, reddish-brown ware and has shallow, rounded walls and a ledge rim. Gritty monochrome green or yellow glaze, applied directly on the clay with no slip underneath, covers the interior and the exterior just over the rim; the bowls' interiors are decorated with fine *sgraffito*. This type is dated to the Crusader/Ayyubid period, between the second half of the 12th century to the first half of the 13th century CE. It was probably manufactured in Lebanon, as were its Fatimid- to early Crusader-period predecessors (Avissar and Stern 2005: 8; cf. Waksman 2011).

Egyptian (?) Alkaline Glazed Bowl (Fig. 13.4: 2)

This bowl type, like the following three, is represented by a single fragment. It is made of a coarse, pale brown ware, with rounded walls and an upturned ledge rim with a slight ridge below; it is covered from the interior and over the rim with an opaque, crazed turquoise alkaline glaze applied on a white slip. The small dimensions of the present fragment and poor preservation of the glaze do not allow a secure typological identification of this bowl, though it seems quite close to two related types of Egyptian glazed table ware: the first has a transparent lead-alkaline glaze and is decorated with over- or under-

4 In that case, the smallest examples, as those presented here, could have been used for narrow-mouthed containers such as certain jugs and juglets.

glaze dark painting, and the second has an opaque alkaline glaze; both are dated to the late 11th to late 12th centuries CE (Avissar and Stern 2005: 35–38).

BYZANTINE FINE *SGRAFFITO* BOWL (FIG. 13.21: 2)

This bowl is an import from the Byzantine Empire (with production centers identified in western Asia Minor and Greece). It is made of a coarse, orange-brown ware and has everted walls and a vertical, thickened rim with white slip on the interior and a thinner layer of slip on the exterior. A transparent lead glaze covers the interior and rim, originally accompanied by thin *sgraffito* decoration. This type is dated to ca. 1140–1190 CE and, according to Avissar and Stern (2005: 42), it is the most common type of Byzantine glazed ware found in Crusader-period assemblages in Palestine.

PROTO-MAIOLICA (?) GLAZED BOWL (FIG. 13.4: 3)

The present bowl is made of a coarse, yellowish-brown ware (fired to grayish-buff) and has a low ring base and an internal grid-pattern decoration painted in dark brown over an opaque white tin (?) glaze. The glaze and decoration characteristics are reminiscent of a certain group of Italian Proto-maiolica bowls dated to the second half of the 13th century CE, although the latter are made of a paler clay (Avissar and Stern 2005: 63–64).

SOFT-PASTE GLAZED BOWL (FIG. 13.4: 4)

Made of a coarse, yellowish soft-paste/frit, this bowl has a narrow ledge rim and painted decoration in blue under a transparent colorless glaze. It represents a well-known ceramic family manufactured in Ayyubid- to Mamluk-period Syria, though the small dimensions of the present fragment do not allow an accurate classification; it seems most likely that this bowl belongs to one of three groups decorated with blue painting (usually combined with other colors) which were common between the late 12th and 14th centuries CE (Avissar and Stern 2005: 26–29).

GLAZED FRYING PANS (FIGS. 13.4: 5, 13.21: 3)

Clearly developed from the Early Islamic glazed frying pans of the late 9th century CE on (above), this type has everted walls, a plain rim and small horizontal handles with a dark brown glaze covering the interior. It is dated to the second half of 12th to the first half of the 13th centuries CE (Avissar and Stern 2005: 96).

"GAZA" WARE BOWL (FIG. 13.21: 1)

This bowl is made of coarse though high-temperature fired dark gray "Gaza" ware typical of ceramics produced in Gaza and along the southern Palestinian coast throughout the Ottoman and British Mandate periods. It has carinated, everted walls and a vertical, thickened rim with a slightly ridged external surface; a sharp, thumb-impressed ridge indicates the carination at the wall-rim junction. This is one of the most common "Gaza" Ware bowl forms documented in Ottoman- to British Mandate-period assemblages in Palestine (e.g., Avissar 2009: 11–12, Figs. 2: 8, 10: 9, 10; Boas 2000: 551, Pl. 2: 8–10; for a general discussion, see Israel 2006: 201–218).

"GAZA" WARE STORAGE JAR (FIG. 13.14: 13)

Like the above-mentioned bowl, this storage jar is made of a coarse, dark gray "Gaza" ware fabric. The present type has a somewhat convex, ribbed neck with an out-folded rim and a prominent, thumb-impressed ridge below. It has numerous parallels dated to the 18th to mid-20th centuries CE (e.g., Boas 2000: 548, Pl. 2: 1–5; cf. Israel 2006: 86–111).

CONCLUSIONS

The above-discussed pottery finds form a rather reliable reflection of the main periods during which the site of Apollonia-Arsuf/Sozousa was permanently occupied, namely the Persian to Crusader periods (5th century BCE to 13th century CE), while it also represents lesser-known eras in the history of the site, namely the MB II and the Ottoman period. The main period of activity in the immediate northern, southern and eastern outskirts of the town occurred during the Roman and mainly Byzantine/beginning of the Early Islamic periods (roughly between the 2nd and 7th centuries CE) based on the amount and distribution of contemporaneous ceramics. Apparently, the volume of activity and presence in the area sharply diminished after the 7th century CE, despite the fact that Early Islamic- and Crusader-period Arsuf/Arsur remained an important center. It seems that in these periods the main off-site agricultural and industrial activity took place in areas farther to the east, north or south. Finally, the apparent absence of typical Mamluk-period pottery and the negligible amount of Ottoman-period sherds echo the decline and abandonment of the town starting in the late 13th century CE.

The great majority of the discussed pottery is fragmentary and rather worn, as it originated in disturbed and/or secondary (if not tertiary) deposits and fills ("death assemblages"). In other words, it is likely that few if any of these contexts represent primary/de-facto deposits, or "life assemblages" (see Schiffer 2010: 34–38) which can be directly attributed to activities carried out at the artifacts' very location of discovery. This includes, of course, the vast Byzantine-period dump excavated in Nof-Yam Area CC and the smaller refuse dumps in Areas M, N and O. Most if not all of their contents—including the numerous pottery items—likely represent domestic refuse originating in the inhabited areas of the town, though possibly also in nearby activity areas.

This is also true for at least some of the other, more restricted refuse pits and deposits from the Hellenistic to the Byzantine/beginning of Early Islamic periods discovered in Nof-Yam Areas AA1, AA2, DD1, DD2 and DD3. Since the excavated area was utilized in antiquity not only for dumping urban waste, but also for agricultural, industrial and funerary designations, and was therefore characterized by temporary and/or a quasi-permanent human presence virtually year-round, much of the ceramic (and other) objects found with and without relation to architectural elements must reflect a variety of activities and behaviors carried out in the immediate environs. These could have included, for instance, food preparation and consumption (e.g., by agricultural/industrial laborers, mourners/visitors at tombs, passers-by who made intermediate stops in the area on their way to or from the city, etc.) and the storage of foodstuffs and agricultural/industrial products. While the latter activity is normally associated with storage vessels (jars, amphorae and pithoi), the former and other domestic behaviors are most typically reflected by table, cooking and various utilitarian wares.

REFERENCES

Avissar, M. 1996. The Medieval Pottery. In: Ben-Tor, A., Avissar, M. and Portugali, Y. *Yoqneʿam I: The Late Periods* (Qedem Reports 3). Jerusalem: 75–172.

Avissar, M. 2009. Ottoman Pottery Assemblages from Excavations in Israel. In: Walker, B.J., ed. *Reflections of Empire: Archaeological and Ethnographic Studies on the Pottery of the Ottoman Levant* (*AASOR* 64). Boston: 7–14.

Avissar, M. and Stern, E.J. 2005. *Pottery of the Crusader, Ayyubid, and Mamluk Periods in Israel* (IAA Reports 26). Jerusalem.

Ayalon, E. 1991. The Giant Jars from Yavneh-Yam. In: Fischer, M., ed. *Yavneh-Yam and its Surroundings*. Palmahim: 80–88 (Hebrew).

Ayalon, E. 2000. Typology and Chronology of Water-Wheel (*sāqiya*) Pottery Pots from Israel. *Israel Exploration Journal* 50: 216–226.

Ayalon, E. and Harpazi-Ofer, S. 2007. A Late Roman Burial Cave and Dump at Tell Qasile. *ʿAtiqot* 55: 29–36 (Hebrew).

Barkan, D., Yasur-Landau, A., Mommsen, H., Ben-Shlomo, D. and Kahanov, Y. 2013. The 'Dor 2006' Shipwreck: The Ceramic Material. *Tel Aviv* 40: 117–143.

Bar-Nathan, R. 2006. *Masada VII, The Yigael Yadin Excavations 1963–1965, Final Reports: The Pottery of Masada*. Jerusalem.

Bar-Nathan, R. 2011. The Pottery Corpus. In: Bar-Nathan, R. and Atrash, W. *Bet Sheʾan II: Baysān. The Theater Pottery Workshop* (IAA Reports 48). Jerusalem: 229–343.

Beazley, J.D. 1963. *Attic Red-figure Vase-painters*. Oxford.

Boas, A.J. 2000. Pottery and Small Finds from the Late Ottoman Village and Early Zionist Settlement. In: Hirschfeld, Y. *Ramat Hanadiv Excavations. Final Report of the 1984–1988 Seasons*. Jerusalem: 547–580.

Calderon, R. 2000. Roman and Byzantine Pottery. In: Hirschfeld, Y. *Ramat Hanadiv Excavations. Final Report of the 1984–1988 Seasons*. Jerusalem: 91–165.

Calderon, R. 2011. The Pottery from Ḥorbat Gelilot. *ʿAtiqot* 66: 63*–78* (Hebrew).

Catling, H.A. 1972. An Early Byzantine Pottery Factory at Dhiorios. *Levant* 4: 1–82.

Cytryn-Silverman, K. 2010. The Ceramic Evidence. In: Gutfeld, O. *Ramla. Final Report on the Excavations North of the White Mosque* (Qedem 51). Jerusalem: 97–211.

Egloff, M. 1977. *Kellia III: La poterie Copte*. Geneva.

Eisenberg-Degen, D. 2018. Tel ʿIrit. *Ḥadashot Arkheologiyot–Excavations and Surveys in Israel* 130. http://www.hadashot-esi.org.il/Report_Detail_Eng.aspx?id=25388&mag_id=126

Erickson-Gini T. 2010. *Nabataean Settlement and Self-Organized Economy in the Central Negev: Crisis and Renewal* (BAR International Series 2054). Oxford.

Fabian, P. and Goldfus, H. 2004. A Byzantine Farmhouse, Terraces and Agricultural Installations at the Goral Hills near Beʾer Sheva. *ʿAtiqot* 47: 1*–14* (Hebrew).

Gadot, Y., Freud, L., Tal, O. and Taxel, I. 2016. Sub-Sector ACS2: Squares W-AA/15–22. In: Lipschits, O., Gadot, Y. and Freud, L. *Ramat Raḥel III: Final Publication of Yohanan Aharoni's Excavations (1954, 1959–1962)*, Vol. 1 (Monograph Series of the Institute of Archaeology of Tel Aviv University 35). Tel Aviv: 97–129.

Gichon, M. 1993. *En Boqeq: Ausgrabungen in einer Oase am Toten Meer I: Geographie und Geschichte der Oase. Das spätrömisch–byzantinische Kastell*. Mainz am Rhein.

Guz-Zilberstein, B. 1995. The Typology of the Hellenistic Coarse Ware and Selected Loci of the Hellenistic and Roman Periods. In: Stern, E. *et al. Excavations at Dor, Final Report Volume I B. Areas A and C: The Finds* (Qedem Reports 2). Jerusalem: 289–433.

Hayes, J.W. 1972. *Late Roman Pottery*. London.

Hayes, J.W. 1980. *A Supplement to Late Roman Pottery*. London.

Hayes, J.W. 1983. The Villa Dionysos Excavations, Knossos: The Pottery. *Annual of the British School at Athens* 78: 97–169.

Israel, Y.M. 2006. *Black Gaza Ware from the Ottoman Period* (Ph.D. dissertation, Ben-Gurion University of the Negev). Beer Sheva (Hebrew).

Israeli, S. 2008. Area F: Stratigraphic Analysis of the 'Burnt' Street of Shops and Its Pottery. In: Tzaferis, V. and Israeli, S. *Paneas, Volume I: The Roman to Early Islamic Periods. Excavations in Areas A, B, E, F, G and H* (IAA Reports 37). Jerusalem: 105–127.

Jackson, M., Zelle, M., Vandeput, L. and Köse, V. 2012. Primary Evidence for Late Roman D Ware Production in Southern Asia Minor: A Challenge to "Cypriot Red Slip Ware." *Anatolian Studies* 62: 89–114.

Johnson, B.L. 2008a. *The Leon Levy Expedition to Ashkelon. Ashkelon 2: Imported Pottery of the Roman and Late Roman Periods*. Winona Lake.

Johnson, B.L. 2008b. The Pottery. In: Patrich, J. *Archaeological Excavations at Caesarea Maritima: Areas CC, KK and NN, Final Report*. Jerusalem: 13–206.

Kassab Tezgör, D. 2010. *Les fouilles et le matériel de l'atelier amphorique de Demirci près de Sinope* (Varia Anatolica 22). Istanbul.

Keay, S.J. 1984. *Late Roman Amphorae in the Western Mediterranean. A Typology and Economic Study: The Catalan Evidence* (BAR International Series 196). Oxford.

Kingsley, S.A. 1994–95. Bag-Shaped Amphorae and Byzantine Trade: Expanding Horizons. *Bulletin of the Anglo-Israel Archaeological Society* 14: 39–56.

Konstantinidou, A. 2012. *Pots for Monks. Ceramics and Life in the Old Monastery of Baramūs in the Wādī al-Natrūn, Egypt (4th–9th c.)* (Ph.D. dissertation, Leiden University). Leiden.

Lapp, P.W. 1961. *Palestinian Ceramic Chronology 200 B.C. – A.D. 70*. New Haven.

Levine, T. 2003. Pottery and Small Finds from Subterranean Complexes 21 and 70. In: Kloner, A. *Maresha Excavations Final Report I: Subterranean Complexes 21, 44, 70* (IAA Reports 17). Jerusalem: 73–130.

Magness, J. 1993. *Jerusalem Ceramic Chronology, circa 200–800 CE* (JSOT/ASOR Monograph Series 9). Sheffield.

Magness, J. 1995. The Pottery from Area V/4 at Caesarea. *AASOR* 52: 133–145.

Magness J. 2015. The Pottery. In: Davies, G. and Magness, J. *The 2003–2007 Excavations in the Late Roman Fort at Yotvata*. Winona Lake: 74–141.

Majcherek, G. 1995. Gazan Amphorae: Typology Reconsidered. In: Meyza, H. and Młynarczyk, J., eds. *Hellenistic and Roman Pottery in the Eastern Mediterranean: Advances in Scientific Studies, Acts of the Second Workshop at Nieborow*. Warsaw: 163–178.

Meyza, H. 2007. *Nea Paphos V. Cypriot Red Slip Ware: Studies on a Late Roman Levantine Fine Ware*. Warsaw.

Mills, P.J.E. and Beaudry, N. 2010. Pottery from Late Roman Ras el Bassit, Syria. In: Menchelli, S. *et al.*, eds. *LRCW3. Late Roman Coarse Wares, Cooking Wares and Amphorae in the Mediterranean. Archaeology and Archaeometry Comparison between Western and Eastern Mediterranean* (BAR International Series 2185 II). Oxford: 857–866.

Młynarczyk, J. 2013. Wine for the Christians in Early Islamic Susita (Hippos of the Decapolis). *Études et Travaux* 26: 473–485.

Nahshoni, P. and Seriy, G. 2014. A Byzantine Monastery and Islamic-Period Settlement Remains at Ḥorbat Maᶜon. *ᶜAtiqot* 78: 13*–62* (Hebrew).

Peacock, D.P.S. and Williams, D.F. 1986. *Amphorae and the Roman Economy, an Introductory Guide*. London.

Peilstöcker, M. 2009. Tel ᶜAfar: A Byzantine Site South of Caesarea. *ᶜAtiqot* 61: 95–118.

Peña, J.T. 2007. *Roman Pottery in the Archaeological Record*. Cambridge.

Pieri, D. 2005. *Le commerce du vin oriental à l'époque byzantine (Vᵉ-VIIᵉ siècles). Le témoignage des amphores en Gaule*. Beirut.

Reynolds, P. 2003. Lebanon. In: Bakirtzis, Ch., ed. *VIIᵉ congrés international sur la céramique médiévale en méditeranée, 11–16 Octobre 1999, Thessaloniki*. Athens: 536–546.

Reynolds, P. 2010. Trade Networks of the East, 3rd to 7th Centuries: The View from Beirut (Lebanon) and Butrint (Albania) (Fine Wares, Amphorae and Kitchen Wares). In: Menchelli, S. *et al*., eds. *LRCW3. Late Roman Coarse Wares, Cooking Wares and Amphorae in the Mediterranean. Archaeology and Archaeometry Comparison between Western and Eastern Mediterranean* (BAR International Series 2185 I). Oxford: 89–114.

Reynolds, P. 2013. Transport Amphorae of the First to Seventh Centuries: Early Roman to Byzantine Periods. In: Aylward, W., ed. *Excavations at Zeugma, Conducted by Oxford University*, Vol. 2. Los Altos: 93–161.

Reynolds, P. and Pavlidis, E. 2017. An Early 5th Century AD Pottery Deposit from a *Cloaca* Cleaning Shaft of the *Cardo* Next to Basilica A, Nicopolis (Greece). In: *Speira: A Festschrift in Honor of Angelika Douzougli and Konstantinos Zachos*. Athens: 651–666.

Riley, J.A. 1975. The Pottery from the First Season of Excavation in the Caesarea Hippodrome. *Bulletin of the American Schools of Oriental Research* 218: 25–63.

Schiffer, M.B. 2010. *Behavioral Archaeology: Principles and Practices*. London and Oakville.

Singer, K. and ᶜAd, U. 2003. The Pottery from the Winepress at Kefar Sirkin. *ᶜAtiqot* 44: 267–270.

Sparkes, B.A. and Talcott, L. 1970. *The Athenian Agora XII: Black and Plain Pottery of the 6th, 5th and 4th Centuries B.C.* Princeton.

Stern, E. 1995. Local Pottery of the Persian Period. In: Stern, E. *et al. Excavations at Dor, Final Report Volume I B. Areas A and C: The Finds* (Qedem Reports 2). Jerusalem: 51–92.

Tal, O. 1999. The Persian Period. In: In Roll, I. and Tal, O. *Apollonia-Arsuf: Final Report of the Excavations, Volume 1: The Persian and Hellenistic Periods (with Appendices on the Chalcolithic and Iron Age II Remains)* (Monograph Series of the Institute of Archaeology of Tel Aviv University 16). Tel Aviv: 83–222.

Tal, O. and Taxel, I. 2012. Socio-Political and Economic Aspects of Refuse Disposal in Late Byzantine and Early Islamic Palestine. In: Matthews, R., Curtis, J., *et al.* eds. *Proceedings of the 7th International Congress on the Archaeology of the Ancient Near East, 12–16, April 2010*. Wiesbaden: 497–518.

Tal, O. and Taxel, I. 2015. *Samaritan Cemeteries and Tombs in the Central Coastal Plain: The Archaeology and History of the Samaritan Settlement outside Samaria (ca. 300–700 CE)* (Ägypten und Altes Testament 82). Münster.

Talloen, P. 2011. From Pagan to Christian: Religious Iconography in Material Culture from Sagalassos. In: Lavan, L. and Mulryan, M., ed. *The Archaeology of Late Antique 'Paganism'* (Late Antique Archaeology 7). Leiden: 575–607.

Taxel, I. 2005. *The Transition between the Byzantine and the Early Islamic Periods (the 7th Century CE) as Seen through Rural Settlement – Horvat Zikhrin as a Case Study* (MA thesis, Tel Aviv University). Tel Aviv (Hebrew).

Taxel, I. 2009. *Khirbet es-Suyyagh: A Byzantine Monastery in the Judaean Shephelah* (Salvage Excavation Reports 6). Tel Aviv.

Taxel, I. 2014. Luxury and Common Wares: Socio-Economic Aspects of the Distribution of Glazed Pottery in Early Islamic Palestine. *Levant* 46: 118–139.

Taxel, I. 2018. *Fragile Biography: The Life Cycle of Ceramics and Refuse Disposal Patterns in Late Antique and Early Medieval Palestine* (BABESCH Supplements 35). Leuven.

Taxel, I. and Cohen-Weinberger, A. 2019. A Newly-Identified Type of Late Antique Palestinian Amphora: Production, Evolution and Use of the Mediterranean Globular Amphora. *Journal of Mediterranean Archaeology* 32: 3–31.

Taxel, I. and Hershkovitz, M. 2011. The Hellenistic and Early Roman Pottery. In: Thareani, Y. *Tel ʿAroer. The Iron Age II Caravan Town and the Hellenistic-Early Roman Settlement. The Avraham Biran (1975–1982) and Rudolph Cohen (1975–1976) Excavations* (Annual of the Nelson Glueck School of Biblical Archaeology, Hebrew Union College–Jewish Institute of Religion 8). Jerusalem: 343–368.

Taxel, I. and Iserlis, M. 2014. Two-Part Ceramic Incense Burners in Late Roman and Byzantine Palestine: Technological, Regional and Ethno-Religious Aspects. In: Fischer-Genz, B., Gerber, Y. and Hamel, H., eds. *Roman Pottery in the Near East. Local Production and Regional Trade. Proceedings of the Round Table Held in Berlin, 19–20 February 2010* (Roman and Late Antique Mediterranean Pottery 3). Oxford: 159–169.

Tréglia, J.-Ch. 2003. *La céramique imperial et romaine tardive. Secteur 5 et la fouille du pont de Gabbari.* In: Emperur, J.-Y. and Nenna, M.-D. *Nécropolis 2* (Études alexandrines 7). Cairo.

de Vincenz, A. and Sion, O. 2007. Two Pottery Assemblages from Khirbat el-Niʿana. *ʿAtiqot* 57: 21–52.

Vunkov, S.Y. 2004. Pan-Roman Amphora Types Produced in the Black Sea Region. In: Eiring, J. and Lund, J., eds. *Transport Amphorae and Trade in the Eastern Mediterranean. Acts of the International Colloquium at the Danish Institute at Athens, September 26–29, 2002*. Arhus: 407–415.

Waksman, S.Y. 2011. Ceramics of the 'Serçe Limanı Type' and Fatimid Pottery Production in Beirut. *Levant* 43: 201–212.

Waksman, S.Y., Morozova, Y., Zelenko, S. and Çolak, A. 2014. Archaeological and Archaeometric Investigations of the Amphorae Cargo of a Late Roman Shipwreck Sunk near the Cape of Plaka (Crimea, Ukraine). In: Poulou-Papadimitriou, N., Nodarou, E. and Kilikoglou, V., eds. *LRCW 4. Late Roman Coarse Wares, Cooking Wares and Amphorae in the Mediterranean: Archaeology and Archaeometry. The Mediterranean: A Market Without Frontiers*, Vol. 1 (BAR International Series 2616). Oxford: 919–929.

Walmsley, A. 2001. Turning East. The Appearance of Islamic Cream Ware in Jordan: The "End of Antiquity"? In: Villeneuve, E. and Watson, P.M., eds. *La céramique byzantine et proto-islamique en Syrie-Jordanie (IVe-VIIIe siècles apr. J.-C.)*. Beirut: 305–313.

Warner Slane, K. and Sanders, G.D.R. 2005. Corinth: Late Roman Horizons. *Hesperia* 74: 243–297.

Watson, P.M. 1992. Change in Foreign and Regional Economic Links with Pella in the Seventh Century A.D.: The Ceramic Evidence. In: Canivet, P. and Rey-Coquais, J.-P., eds. *La Syrie de Byzance à l'Islam VIIe-VIIIe siècles: Actes du colloque international, Lyon-Maison de l'Orient Méditerranéen, Paris – Institute du Monde Arabe, 11–15 septembre 1990*. Damascus: 233–248.

Yadin, E. 2009. Middle Bronze Age Pottery. In: Gadot, Y. and Yadin, E. *Aphek-Antipatris II. Remains on the Acropolis. The Moshe Kochavi and Pirhiya Beck Excavations* (Monograph Series of the Institute of Archaeology of Tel Aviv University 27). Tel Aviv: 111–181.

Yannai, E. 2010. A Salvage Excavation at Ḥorbat Roẓeẓ. *ʿAtiqot* 62: 107–137.

CHAPTER 14

LAMPS

Oren Tal, Itamar Taxel and Marcio Teixeira Bastos

Most of the oil lamps discussed in this chapter (with the exception of Types 5–7) are typologically defined as made by Samaritans or primarily for the use by Samaritans (Sussman 1983; 2017: 128–190). These lamps emerged as a cultural entity within the power vacuum created by the changes of political entities that controlled the Roman Empire. The presence of "Samaritan" lamps in large Roman and Byzantine cities may suggest that Jews, Christians and other ethno-religious groups were using the same types of lamps. "Samaritan" lamps were fashioned according to the legal part of the Jewish literature – the *Halacha* – with a filling hole completely sealed during manufacture; consequently, a lamp could became useable only after breaking the filling hole seal.

The "Samaritan" lamps were manufactured using two molds whose products were joined together. The manufacture of these lamps with a sealed filling hole (namely, with a thin, sunk discus that is intended to be broken upon use) is one of the major characteristics of their production and identification as Samaritan. The outline of the decoration was incised on the upper mold. The designs (mostly geometric) cover virtually the entire surface of the lamps' upper body and this was probably the easiest method to decorate the products. All of these lamps were manufactured with similarity in shape, fabric, decorative style and with a completely flat upper discus with a dot in its center—a sort of a pinpoint in both the upper and lower body parts of the lamps as can be seen in their bases (with a protruding dot in their center). The disc could certainly be a reminder of the Roman discus lamp type and the idea of breaking it upon use seems to be related to the intentional breaking of the disc of Roman discus lamps as known in the country in a variety of contexts in Roman times (Tal and Teixeira Bastos 2012; 2015).

There is no perfect typology and the lamp classifications presented here could not with any certainly bear the same ideas and thoughts as those employed by the persons producing them. Typology is necessary as a classificatory device to order large quantities of material and to simplify communication and comparison. Thus, the attributes selected to define lamps here are based on Sussman's previous classification (1983; 2017: 128–190) with a few modifications, as recently published in a rather large collection of such lamps from burial contexts (Tal and Taxel 2015). The main decorative elements of the groups discussed below are radial lines, ladders, herringbone patterns, circles, semicircles, concentric circles and dots. These patterns are combined with great diversity giving each lamp an almost particular identity. Moreover, despite the large number of lamps, attempts to find two or more lamps made from the same pair of molds were unsuccesful.

TYPOLOGY

The great majority of lamps discovered in the discussed excavation areas came from Area CC. Smaller quantities of lamps were found in Areas M, N and O. All are presented below; they comprise seven types (and a few sub-types) of the Late Roman, Byzantine and Crusader periods. Type 1, 2, 3 and 4 are "Samaritan" lamp types; Type 5 belongs to the "candlestick" lamp type and Type 6 is of an unknown workshop but may well be a "Samaritan" lamp despite the lack of the intentional breaking of the filling hole. Type 7 belongs to the slipper (shoe-shaped) Crusader/Mamluk lamp type.

TYPE 1 (FIG. 14.1)

These lamps are made of a sandy, yellowish-orange or orange-brown ware. Until recently, lamps of Type 1 were considered as the earliest "Samaritan" lamp type, characterized by a rounded receptacle, an arched (bow-shaped) nozzle, a ring base with a protruding dot in the center and a star-shaped (four-armed) handle (which seems to be more decorative than functional). Recently Sussman suggested an earlier "Samaritan" lamp type known in the literature as the "Yavneh North" lamp, which she considers as a transitional late 3rd and 4th centuries CE predecessor (2017: 73–80, II. LR11; 128–137, V. LR18). This idea may be corroborated by thin-section analysis carried out on one such lamp recovered from Tel Barukh that shows identical fabric to some of the "Samaritan" lamps recovered (Tal and Taxel 2015: 44–47, Type 6 and Table II.2 on p. 226). The nozzles of some of these lamps are outlined both on the underside and upper side with two parallel curved lines. The decoration of Type 1 lamps is either geometric (ladder patterns, dotted circles, semicircles, concentric circles and the combination of all these motifs, herringbone patterns and net patterns) or floral (stylized branches, vine tendrils and rosettes). A few bear a central motif on the nozzle (such as a kantharos and a plain basket/washing basin). According to Sussman's typology, this lamp type is dated to the late 3rd/4th to 6th centuries CE (1983: 73–78, 85 [Type 1 lamps]; 2002: 341, Fig. 1: 12; 2017: 140–173, V. LR20)—a date which is strongly corroborated by the coins found together with the Type 1 lamps in Area CC.

TYPE 2 (FIGS. 14.2–14.5)

These lamps are made of a sandy and coarser, orange-brown ware. It normally has a pear-shaped body that in many cases tends to become almost ovoid with a channel between the filling hole and the wick hole and a tongue handle on the lamp's rear part. The base of this lamp type is a shallow ring or concave with a protruding dot in the center. These Type 2 lamps have been divided into three sub-types based on body characteristic or decoration. The first sub-type includes three lamps considered "transitional" between Type 1 and 2 as they are pear-shaped but have no channel between the filling hole and the wick hole (Fig. 14.2); one is adorned with alternating radial patterns and dots and a central motif on the nozzle (a five-branch menorah?) and the other two are plain (undecorated). The second sub-type is illustrated by five lamps with an arched ladder and/or net pattern (Fig. 14.3) and the third comprises 23 lamps usually with arched ladders across the two sides of the nozzle and ladder and herringbone patterns, concentric semicircles and circles, as well as protruding dots in various combinations on top of the receptacles (Figs. 14.4–14.5). Type 2 lamps belong to Sussman's Type 2 of her 1983 typology of the "Samaritan" lamps (1983: 73–74, 78–79, 85 [Type 2 lamps]; cf. also 2002: 342, Fig. 1: 5–6) and Type V. LR21A of her recent classification (Sussman 2017: 174–177)—a transitional type between the former classification (Type 1) and the next (Type 3) types that normally has a coarser and larger appearance, as well as an ovoid shape. Type 2 is dated to the 5th and 6th century CE, as based on the chronology of the other ceramic types found together with them, as well as coins. Both types 1 and 2 were found in Area CC; a single specimen of the "transitional" sub-type between Type 1 and 2 came from Area AA1 (Fig. 14.2: 3).

TYPE 3 (FIGS. 14.6–14.21)

This is the most common lamp type found in the excavations (over 60% of all the lamps recovered from Area CC).[1] These lamps are made of a sandy and coarse, yellowish, yellowish-orange, yellowish-brown or

1 Only those fragments of lamps identified as belonging to defined types (which were about half of the ca. 1,100 lamps and fragments recovered from Area CC) were counted.

Fig. 14.1: Area CC, Lamps

No.	*Vessel*	*Locus*	*Basket*	*Inventory No.*	*Type*
1	Lamp	30061	301882	013	1
2	Lamp	30037	301121	042	1
3	Lamp	30052	301013	075	1
4	Lamp	30060	302725	114	1
5	Lamp	30037	300689	081	1
6	Lamp	30061	304242	190	1
7	Lamp	30066	300749	082	1
8	Lamp	30052	301133	006	1
9*	Lamp	30074	303127	067	1

* Lamp sampled for petrography.

reddish-brown ware and have a broad piriform or ovoid body with a broad channel between the filling hole and the wick hole, a shallow ring or concave base (with a protruding dot in the center) and a tongue handle. Type 3 lamps have been divided into four sub-types (and two derivatives) based on body decoration.

The first sub-type includes 19 lamps that are adorned with a herringbone pattern across the two sides of the channel that runs between the filling hole and the wick hole, while the rest of the upper body is decorated with of the following: radial lines, palm branches, arched ladders or a herringbone pattern with protruding dots, or a combination (Figs. 14.6–14.8). Noteworthy are the first two lamps (Fig. 14.6: 1–2) which were never in use as indicated by their sealed filling holes and lack of soot remains on their nozzle tips (as found on other lamps recovered from Area CC). One of these two lamps has an intentionally-made hole in the side wall (Fig. 14.6: 2), which was probably designated to prevent any use, at least as a lighting implement. Intentionally-made holes on either the side wall or bases are attested on many of the complete lamps recovered from Area CC (cf. e.g., Figs. 14.5: 12, 14.7: 3, 14.10: 6, 14.15: 2).

The second sub-type is illustrated by 28 lamps with a radial decoration across the channel and body (Figs. 14.9–14.11) and a derivative sub-group of 16 lamps whose radial decoration is combined with other geometric patterns (arches, ladders, a herringbone and/or protruding dots) (Figs. 14.12–14.13).

The third sub-type includes 19 lamps with sparsely decorated geometric patterns—usually exhibiting arched ladders across the two sides of the channel that runs between the filling hole and the wick hole and radial lines, palm branches, arched ladders, concentric circles and protruding dots on the rest of the upper body parts (Figs. 14.14–14.15). Based on the sparse decoration of this sub-type two plain (undecorated) lamps (Fig. 14.15: 11, 12) have also been assigned to it.

The fourth sub-type shows 31 lamps that resemble the third sub-type in terms of geometric decoration yet this decoration appears in a dense fashion (Figs. 14.16–14.18). This sub-type has a derivative sub-group of 26 lamps whose decoration is similar but combined with protruding dots (Figs. 14.19–14.21). Noteworthy is one (broken) lamp (Fig. 14.18: 2) which was never in use, as indicated by its sealed filling hole. It is the third sealed lamp recovered from Area CC.

All in all 139 Type 3 lamps (intact, complete or nearly complete) have been assembled that largely correspond with Sussman's Type 3 of her 1983 typology of the "Samaritan" lamps (1983: 74, 80, 85 [Type 3 lamps]; cf. also 2002: 342, Fig. 1: 7) and Type V. B22 and V. B22A of her recent classification (Sussman 2017: 178–180), which she dates to between the 5th and 7th centuries CE. While on occasion, there was hesitation to differentiate lamps of Type 2 and Type 3—those assigned to Type 3 are in general coarser and have a broader channel between the filling hole and the wick hole.

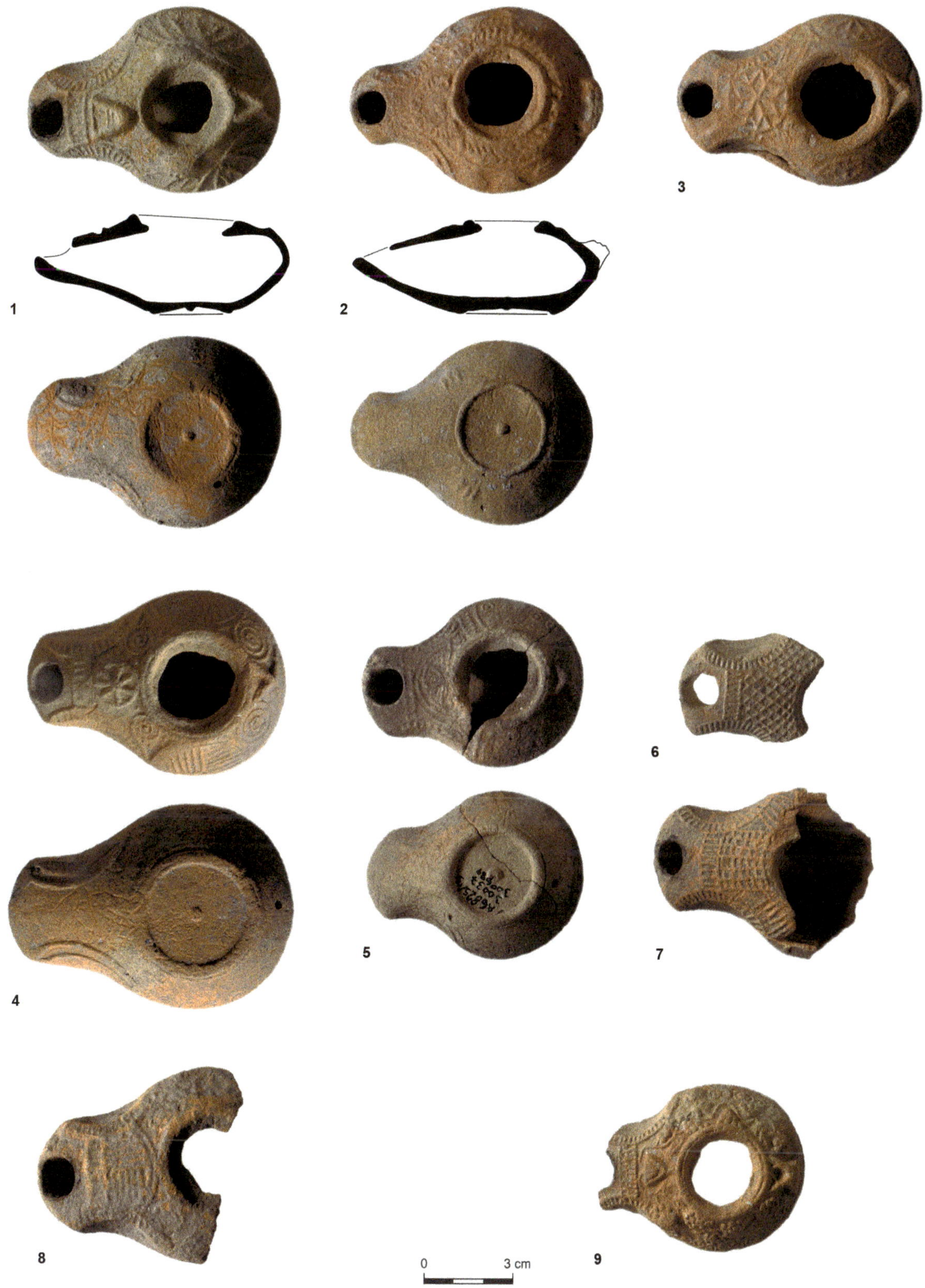

Fig. 14.1: Area CC, lamps.

TYPE 4 (FIG. 14.22)

This type is made of a coarse, orange-brown ware, egg-shaped with a broad channel, a tongue handle and lentoid in cross section (convex tops). These three lamps are decorated with palm branches across the two sides of the channel and radial lines on the upper body. They belong to Sussman's Type 4 of her 1983 typology of the "Samaritan" lamps (1983: 80 [Type 4 lamps]; cf. also her recent classification; Sussman 2017: 180–181, V. B23)—whose date is assigned to the 6th century CE—which is in full alignment with the context of all the specimens that came from Area CC.

All types of "Samaritan" lamps recorded in this chapter (Types 1–4, above) seem to have been manufactured with a sealed filling hole (in the form of a flat, plain disc) which was later broken—apparently by the lamps' buyers—in order to make them useable. The edges around the broken disc were only rarely smoothed over as can be seen by some of the present examples. The custom of producing lamps with a closed filling hole was interpreted as an apparent religious demand of the contemporaneous Samaritan communities to preserve the lamps' purity prior to use (Sussman 1983: 71).

TYPE 5 (FIG. 14.25: 4, 5)

This type is represented by two examples that came from Area M. These lamps are made of a coarse, yellowish or yellowish-gray ware, have an ovoid body, a ring base and a simple linear decoration. They belong to the large candlestick lamp type, adorned with radial strokes on the shoulder (upper receptacle) and a palm branch on the nozzle. This type is dated to the mid-6th to mid-8th centuries CE (Magness 1993: 251–255, Form 3A; Hadad 2002: 66–68, Type 28; Sussman 2017: 99–101, III. B14.1–2) which were produced in various locations in Judea and the central/southern Coastal Plain.

TYPE 6 (FIGS. 14.23: 1, 14.24: 1)

These lamps are made of a coarse light brown ware, piriform in shape and decorated with a horizontal ladder across the mid-body. The lamp is closely related to the Type 2 lamps (in terms of shape and ware) but lacks the intentional breaking of the filling hole as it was produced with a large filling hole from the start. Attempts to assign this lamp type to a known workshop were unsuccessful though resemblance to the so-called Jerusalem workshop lamps is apparent (Sussman 2017: 81–89, III.

Fig. 14.2: Areas AA1 and CC, lamps (cont.)

No.	*Vessel*	*Locus*	*Basket*	*Inventory No.*	*Type*
1	Lamp	30063	301705	110	2
2	Lamp	30036	302445	085	2
3	Lamp	11067	101286	071	2

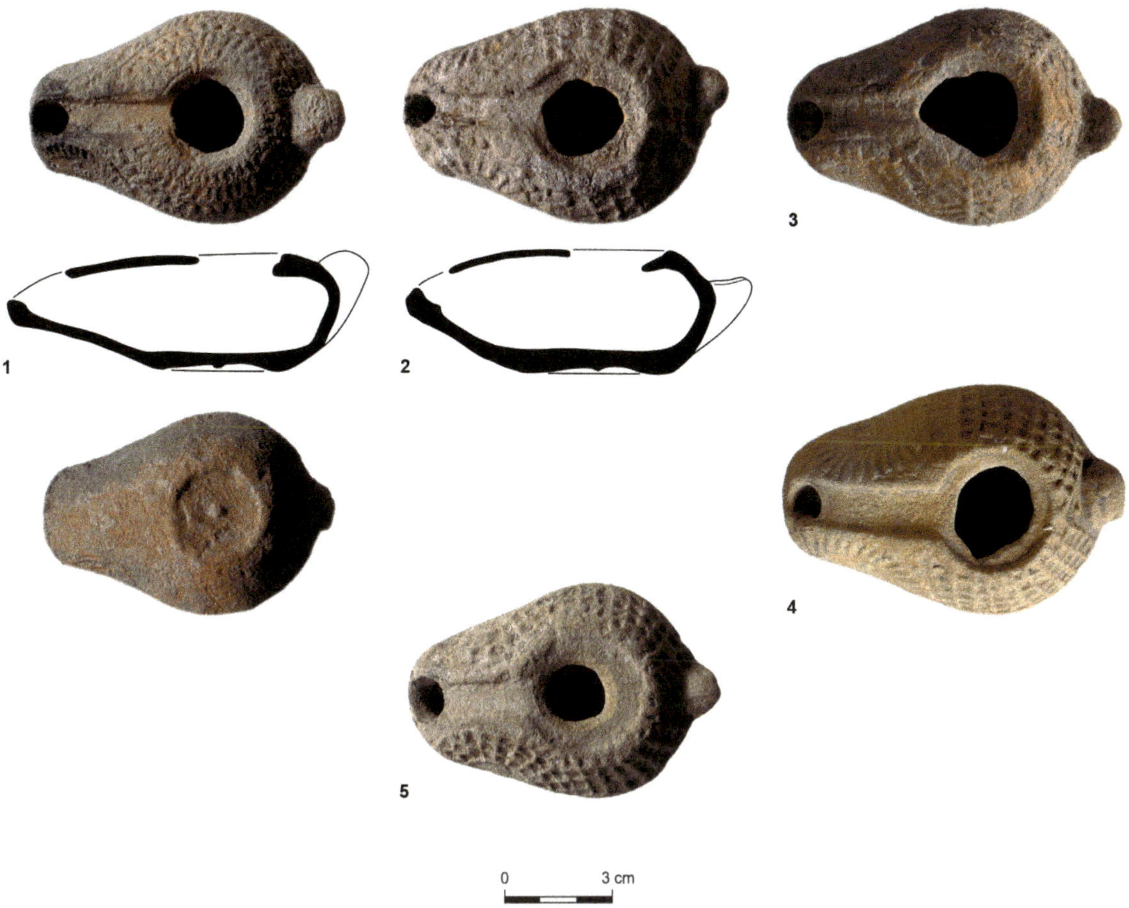

Fig. 14.3: Area CC, Lamps (cont.)

No.	*Vessel*	*Locus*	*Basket*	*Inventory No.*	*Type*
1	Lamp	30060	301508	036	2
2	Lamp	30060	300918	090	2
3	Lamp	30061	301858	108	2
4	Lamp	30082	303277	118	2
5	Lamp	30148	305395	189	2

LR12–III.B15, esp. Nos. 1500–1505, whose handles however are more delicate). Still the tendency is to assign these lamps to "Samaritan" workshops despite the production of the lamps with an open filling hole.

TYPE 7 (FIG. 14.23: 2)

This is a slipper lamp made of a coarse light brown ware, with a bent handle (a pulled up and folded-over tongue handle with the tip of the handle attached to the top of the lamp). It is mold-made, decorated with geometric linear patterns and dated from about the mid-13th century to the end of the 14th century CE (and perhaps even later) (cf. Avissar and Stern 2005: 128, Type III.2.1.2, Fig. 53: 4). It may be added that most lamps of this type at the site came from the Crusader castle (Area F) from a mid-13th century context.

PROVENANCE

Lamps discussed in this chapter came from Areas AA1, CC, DD3, M, N and O.

AREA AA1

The area is mostly characterized by several facilities, among them round and square plastered collecting vats belonging to a winepress complex. The single specimen of the "transitional" sub-type lamp between Type 1 and 2 came from a fill in the vicinity of Installation 224.

AREA CC

All the lamps came from an extensive refuse dump that formed the main feature of excavation in the area. It yielded a vast amount of pottery mostly in fragmentary (non-restorable) state, comprising table, cooking and storage vessels (in addition to the lamps) (Chapter 13). The 1100 lamps and lamp fragments (recorded in the excavation diaries) can be supplemented by the huge number of coins recovered from the dump, over 800 bronze (and one gold) coins. Over 260 identifiable coins were retrieved from Area CC, more than 150 coming from the dump; the latest coins from the dump are dated to the mid-6th century CE (two *nummi* of the Vandal king Hilderic dated to 523–530 and an anonymous Vandalic palm tree coin, attributed to the days of Justinian I, Chapter 18: Nos. 319–321). The majority of the coins (over 95%) that came from the area are dated within the 4th to 6th centuries CE; this is also true for the majority of the coins that came from the dump itself (over 85%). Still there are surface coin finds from Area CC that post-date the mid-6th century CE. It is unclear whether the two surface find 7th-century CE issues (a *follis* of Phocas, 602–610 CE and an anonymous Arab-Byzantine *follis*, 647–670 CE; Chapter 18: Nos. 349, 356) were somehow related to the dumping activities in the area. There are several other later surface find coins of the 8th–19th centuries CE that have been found in the area (Chapter 18: Nos. 359, 361–365, 379, 380), as well as an Ayyubid fals (Chapter 18: No. 369) that came from a fill far from the dump area (Sq. I11). As stated in Chapter 6 approximately 130 intact and complete usable "Samaritan" lamps were unearthed in the dump and are divided between Types 1, 2, 3 and 4. The date of the majority of coins found in the dump are dated between the 4th to 6th centuries CE which may reflect on the prevalence of the use of Type 3 lamps (which represent over 60% of the total number of dumped lamps in Area CC) within this time period. Approximately 220 complete (and nearly complete) lamp profiles were catalogued during the first stage of this work, but in order to produce a coherent chapter some 180 lamps have been illustrated in the respective Area CC lamp

FIG. 14.4: AREA CC, LAMPS (CONT.)

No.	*Vessel*	*Locus*	*Basket*	*Inventory No.*	*Type*
1	Lamp	30063	301704	027	2
2	Lamp	30063	301314	103	2
3	Lamp	30061	301178	116	2
4	Lamp	30073	301971	094	2
5	Lamp	30081	304383	188	2
6	Lamp	30052	301511	041	2
7	Lamp	623	6267	203	2
8	Lamp	627	6334	230	2
9	Lamp	30015	300227	039	2
10	Lamp	30061	302269	051	2
11	Lamp	30011	300279	060	2

Fig. 14.4: Area CC, lamps (cont.).

Fig. 14.5: Area CC, Lamps (cont.)

No.	*Vessel*	*Locus*	*Basket*	*Inventory No.*	*Type*
1	Lamp	30036	300790	069	2
2	Lamp	30070	302362	055	2
3	Lamp	30063	302371	097	2
4	Lamp	30061	302271	030	2
5	Lamp	30061	302159	026	2
6	Lamp	30071	302017	050	2
7	Lamp	30118	303793	168	2
8	Lamp	30061	302084	076	2
9	Lamp	30037	301709	101	2
10	Lamp	30013	300377	002	2
11	Lamp	30037	301899	087	2
12	Lamp	30061	301888	074	2

figures, where intact, complete and nearly complete lamps are exhibited. A breakdown of these lamps provide the following numbers: in addition to the approximately 130 intact and complete lamps, three were found originally intact (namely with a sealed filling hole, Figs. 14.6: 1–2, 14.18: 2); approximately 50 were found nearly complete and 40 were found in large fragments (usually with more than half of the body preserved). With the exception of the three originally intact lamps, all the approximately 130 complete lamps were found with their discus broken out; most of them bear soot marks (14 complete lamps were found clean of soot marks, as were the three intact lamps; hence more than 10% of the complete and intact lamp assemblage may have related to lamps that had not been lit). Moreover, among these non-lit lamps three bear holes on their left sidewalls made after firing. Interestingly, one of the "Samaritan" lamps found in the Area M refuse pit (Chapter 8) also presents a lack of soot marks on its tip and a hole intentionally made in its base after firing (cf. Fig. 14.25: 2).[2] It may be added that the original number of complete or usable lamps would probably been much higher as their deposition in the ground caused some of the complete lamps to be broken into pieces. Given the porous nature of many lamps, restoring the broken pieces seemed to be superfluous. It may also be added that all 13 analyzed samples of "Samaritan" lamps from the dump belong to Sample A fabric whose matrix characteristics suit the environment of the southern Sharon Plain (namely the environs of the site of Apollonia-Arsuf, see appendix below).

AREA DD3

The area is characterized by a few pit and cist graves of the Hellenistic and Roman periods. The discovery of a fragment of Crusader-period lamp type may be accidental.

AREA M

The lamps came from a refuse pit of a considerable size that yielded a rather large ceramic assemblage dated to the 6th and early/mid-7th centuries CE, comprising table, cooking and storage vessels (Chapter 13). The latest coins recovered in the refuse pit of Area M belong to Maurice Tiberius (582–602 CE) (Chapter 18: Nos. 336, 337, 339–341); although there is also a post-reform (late 7th to mid-8th century) Umayyad

2 This latter phenomenon recalls the Jewish and Edomite "holed" or "punctured" vessels and probably marked the lamps for a certain (religious/ritualistic?) purpose, possibly to visually demonstrate that they were no longer to be used (similar to pierced vessels sometimes found in tombs); see, in this respect, Grossberg 2002; Stern and Noam 2015.

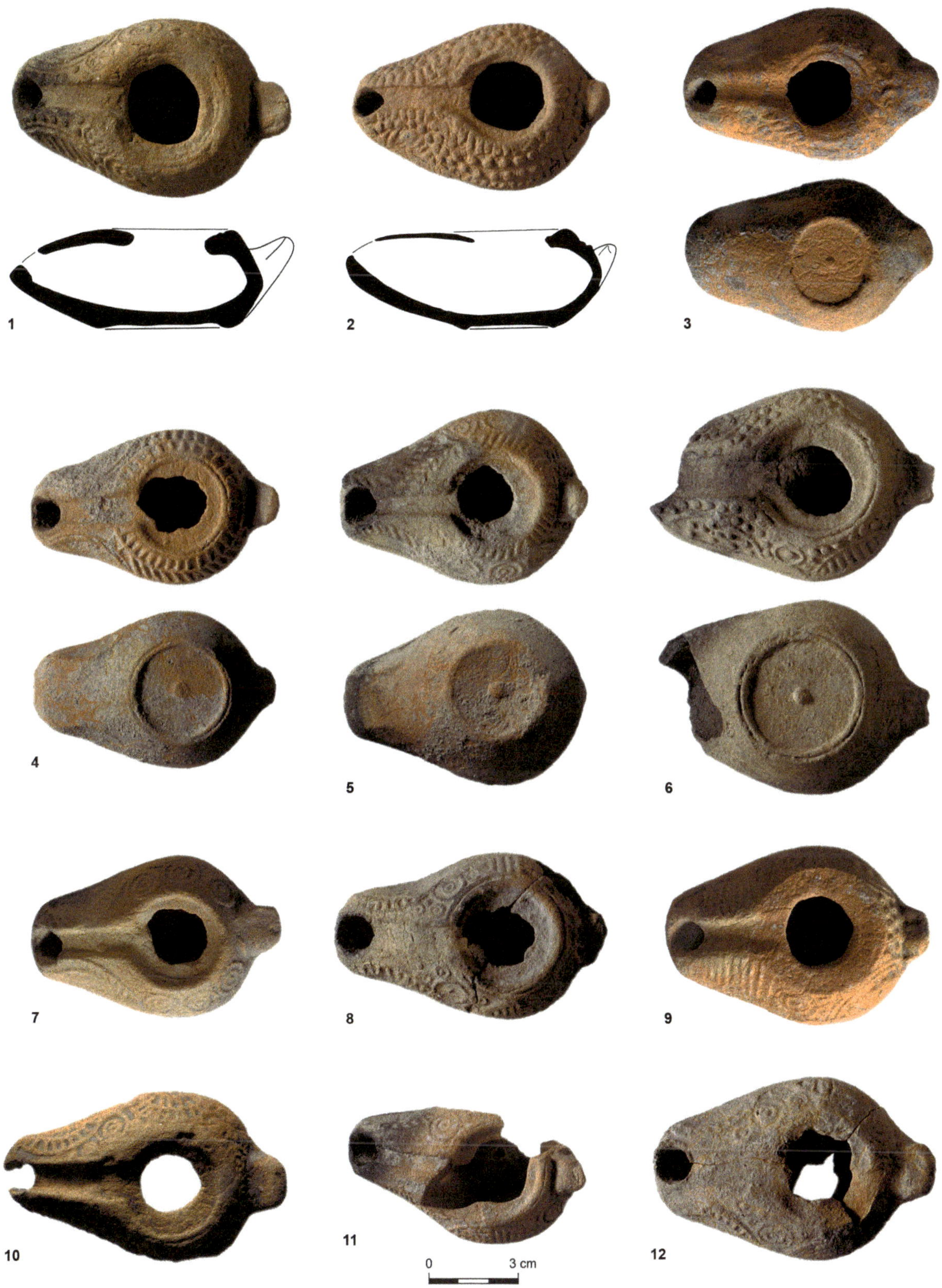

Fig. 14.5: Area CC, lamps (cont.).

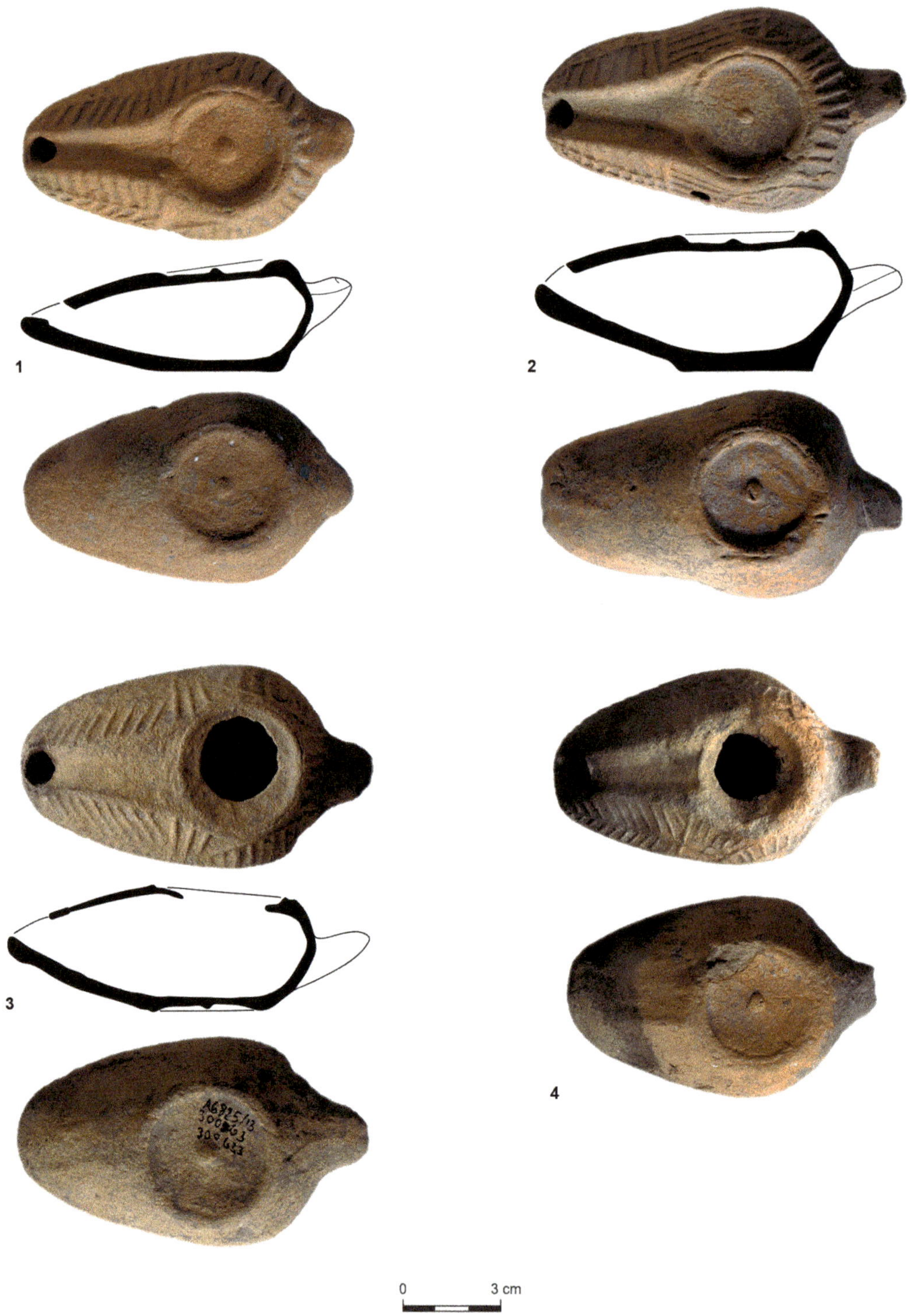

Fig. 14.6: Area CC, Lamps. (cont.)

No.	*Vessel*	*Locus*	*Basket*	*Inventory No.*	*Type*
1	Lamp	30066	305443	143	3
2	Lamp	30118	304361	161	3
3	Lamp	30063	300633	045	3
4	Lamp	30060	301509	102	3

coin (Chapter 18: No. 360) that we tend to consider as stray. Thirteen complete (and nearly complete) lamps were documented in Area M. These are divided between Types 2, 3, 5 and 6.

AREA N

Only two lamps of Type 3 from Area N were recorded and they supplement the assemblage recovered from the area—a small refuse pit that yielded a modest ceramic assemblage dated to the 6th to early 7th centuries CE comprising table, cooking and storage vessels (Chapter 13).

AREA O

The lamps recovered from Area O came from the dump accumulated inside the circular collecting vat (Installation 8061) which went out of use in the early 6th century CE. Six complete (and nearly complete) "Samaritan" lamps that were documented exclusively belong to Type 3. It may be added that with the exception of an early 4th century coin CE that came from the plaster foundation of the mosaic floor of the collecting vat, no other identifiable coins came from it. Furthermore, the latest coin that came from the area belongs to the later regnal years of Heraclius (631–639 CE) (Chapter 18: No. 353).

DISCUSSION

During the Late Roman and Byzantine period, a fundamental increase in the number of regional types of clay lamps throughout the country is apparent. The far-flung vibrant international exchange economy during the Byzantine period clearly illustrates the correlation between increased interconnectivity and the development of networks (Lavan 2012). The Byzantine market can be seen as an economic system of transactions for the exchange of goods and services as part of fragmented, unconnected markets within the more restrictive framework of a tributary state or a comprehensive network of relatively dependent demands and markets. When it comes to lamps in Palestine, it seems that Darom-type lamps reflected local popular artistic expression that followed the classic Roman discus lamps which gradually faded away (Sussman 2017: 1–8). The lamp manufacture in the East helped shape new and different cultural entities after the end of Bar Kokhba Revolt (132–135 CE), which changed the balance of ethnic entities in the region. This stormy cultural change was precipitated by the influence coming from eastern artistic centers, such as Palmyra and the Parthians with changes in architecture, sculpture, mosaic pavements, coins and clay lamps. The lamps were intended to be produced in vast quantities to satisfy local market needs. From the second half of the 4th century CE onwards when Christianity surrounded the life of pagans, Jews and Samaritans, during the time of Constantine I onward, a significant cultural change occurred. The lamps were now manufactured to suit different ethno-religious customers through the choice of decorative motifs and symbols (among other functions), while imported lamps from North Africa offered new prototypes.

LAMPS IN DUMPS[3]

The lamps that came from Areas CC, M, N and O were found in small (Areas M, N, O) and large (Area CC) domestic and industrial refuse dumps. It has long been acknowledged by scholars that oil lamps—mostly made of clay—had a rather central role in various cultic activities in the greater Greco-Roman (including Late Roman/Byzantine) world, as evidenced by textual and archaeological materials alike. Lamps were widely used as votive offerings in official and non-official cultic places, including temples, sacred fountains and other water sources (often incorporated into temples or bathhouse complexes) and cave sanctuaries, where they were either placed in or thrown into designated locations (see, with additional

3 The following is an update of an earlier publication (Tal and Taxel 2017).

Fig. 14.7: Area CC, Lamps (cont.)

No.	*Vessel*	*Locus*	*Basket*	*Inventory No.*	*Type*
1	Lamp	625	6298	208	3
2	Lamp	30070	302086	054	3
3	Lamp	625	6205	224	3
4	Lamp	30074	303890	179	3
5	Lamp	30061	301510	020	3
6	Lamp	30083	303469	119	3
7*	Lamp	30061	302037	112	3
8	Lamp	30071	302446	117	3
9*	Lamp	30070	303011	111	3
10	Lamp	30100	303595	122	3
11	Lamp	30123	304017	182	3
12	Lamp	30118	305136	150	3

* Lamps sampled for petrography.

references, Bouras and Parani 2008; Karivieri 2010: 417–240, 427–429; Nilsson 1950; Zissu *et al.* 2017). In typical Christian contexts, lamps and candles had a central role in Byzantine-period community and monastic churches in manipulating the liturgical atmosphere by creating a special equilibrium between light and shadow. Furthermore, lamps were lit on or near saints' tombs and other holy sites and in front of saints' icons (Bouras and Parani 2008: 23–24, 26–29; Nesbitt 2012). And of course, lamps were also commonly used in ordinary funerary contexts, both for functional and ritual purposes. The latter seem to include the placing and lighting of lamps inside and outside tombs and near the bier of the deceased in order to respect and commemorate the dead (such as in the Jewish custom of the lamp/candle of the soul) and to light his/her way to the afterlife. Customs such as these were common among most religious and ethnic groups in Roman times and, in particular, late antiquity, and in Palestine related particularly to polytheists, Christians, Jews and Samaritans (Tal and Taxel 2015: 195, 198–199, with references; and cf. for the Jewish and Christian perspectives, Brand 1953: 365–366; Bouras and Parani 2008: 22–23).

Archaeological activity in Palestine has yielded several examples of lamp (and other artifact) deposits attributed to ritual practices which were usually associated with polytheist rites but also with pan-religious popular beliefs. These include the Paneas temples (Berlin 1999: 32–36), the Ḥammat Gader baths (Coen Uzzielli 1997: 319), the ʿEin Tzur spring (which apparently functioned as a wishing well) (Hirschfeld 2000: 336–337), the Teʾomim Cave (Zissu *et al.* 2017) and the sacred well at the sanctuary of Mamre/Terebinthus (Mader 1957). The latter case is especially interesting, as can be seen in the detailed description by the 5th-century monk Sozomen of this site and the activities it hosted, including the following:

> Here the inhabitants of the country and of the regions round Palestine, the Phoenicians and the Arabians, assemble annually during the summer season to keep a brilliant feast; and many others, both buyers and sellers, resort there on account of the fair. [...] The place is open country and arable and without houses, with the exception of the buildings around Abraham's old oak and the well he prepared. No one during the time of the feast drew water from that well; for according to Pagan usage, some placed burning lamps near it; some poured out wine, or cast in cakes; and others, coins, myrrh or incense (Sozomen, *Ecclesiastical History* 2.4).[4]

4 And cf. the description given by Cyril of Jerusalem in the 4th century CE, apparently with relation to the contemporaneous Palestinian reality: "The devil's worship consists of prayers in the temples of idols, honors paid to lifeless idols, the lighting of lamps or burning of incense by springs and rivers" (Cyril of Jerusalem, *Catecheses*, trans. by Yarnold, Mystagogic Catechesis I.8).

Strikingly, this literary evidence for lamp offerings can be securely identified with the numerous lamps discovered by Mader in his excavations at the site, especially around and inside the well identified with the one mentioned by Sozomen.

Lamps, it must be noted, were also used for lychnomancy—divination in sacrificial rituals during which "Chtonic demons were summoned with the help of lamps to prophecy and send dreams and diseases" (Karivieri 2010: 416). These rites, which were practiced by a variety of religious groups,

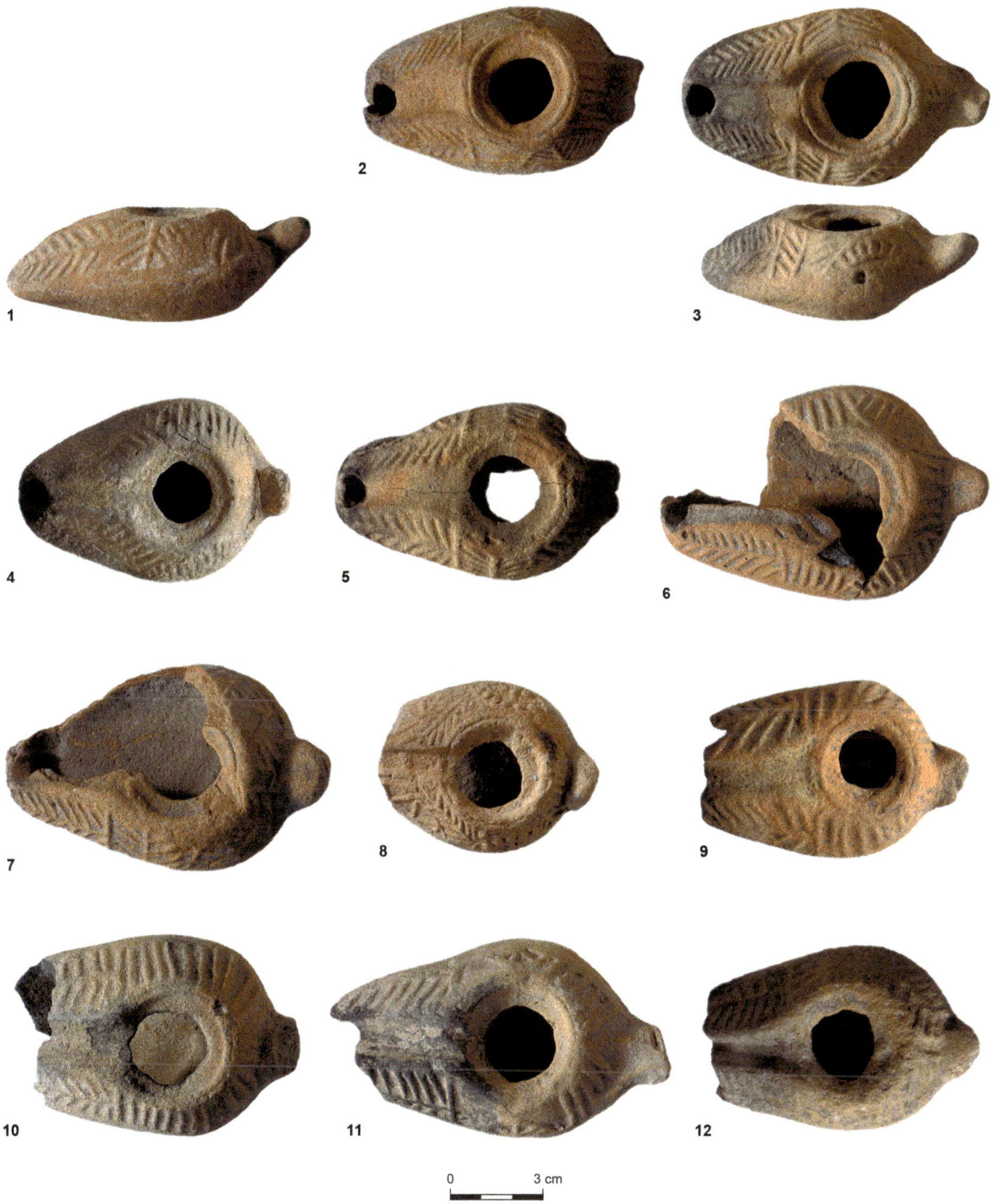

Fig. 14.7: Area CC, lamps (cont.).

could have taken place virtually anywhere, and especially in designated cult places and domestic and other contexts. Textual and archaeological evidence for such activities indicate that ceramic lamps were sometimes inscribed with magical texts or lit with wicks made of unusual materials and/or with special kinds of oils. The Greek magical papyri from Egypt frequently refer to the practice of lighting a lamp and praying or reciting a divination text to them (see e.g., Karivieri 2010: 416–420; and cf. also Berlin 1999: 36–37, who attributed a similar use to the numerous votive lamps found in the latest phase [3rd–5th centuries CE] of the Paneas temples).

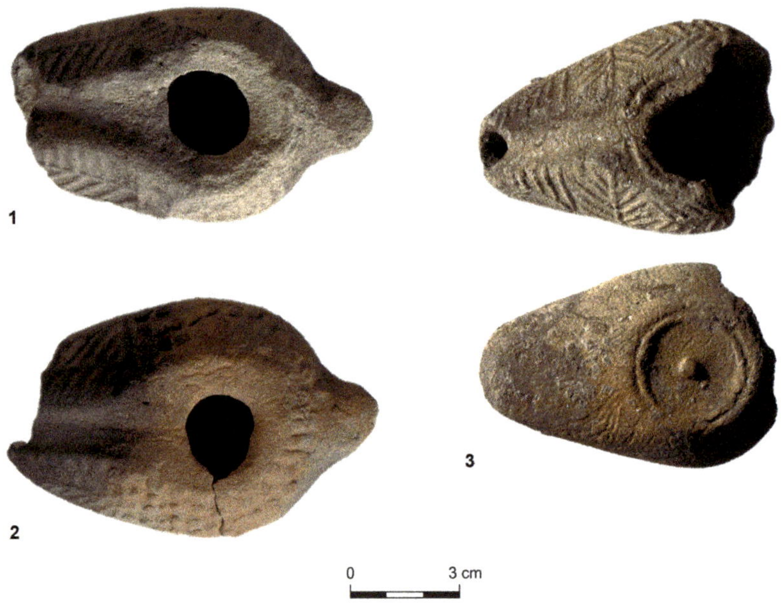

Fig. 14.8: Area CC, Lamps (cont.)

No.	*Vessel*	*Locus*	*Basket*	*Inventory No.*	*Type*
1	Lamp	30081	304495	170	3
2	Lamp	30074	303509	137	3
3	Lamp	30066	301524	016	3

Fig. 14.9: Area CC, Lamps (cont.)

No.	*Vessel*	*Locus*	*Basket*	*Inventory No.*	*Type*
1	Lamp	30036	300755	065	3
2	Lamp	643	6525	227	3
3	Lamp	30074	303589	132	3
4	Lamp	643	6527	226	3
5	Lamp	627	6380	214	3
6	Lamp	627	6365	217	3
7	Lamp	30061	302877	021	3
8	Lamp	30036	300593	029	3
9	Lamp	30052	300653	044	3
10	Lamp	30036	300736	052	3

In accordance with earlier attempts to discuss various socioeconomic and behavioral aspects of refuse disposal and utilization in late antique and Early Islamic Palestine (Tal and Taxel 2012; Tal, Taxel, and Jackson-Tal 2013; Taxel 2018: 132–155), it is suggested here that refuse dumps can be included among the places where lamps were utilized for various magic (and cultic) purposes. This hypothesis is based on two kinds of evidence.

The first is the substantial number of complete or near-complete and seemingly useable lamps that are on occasion found in refuse assemblages in Palestine, especially from the Late Roman, Byzantine

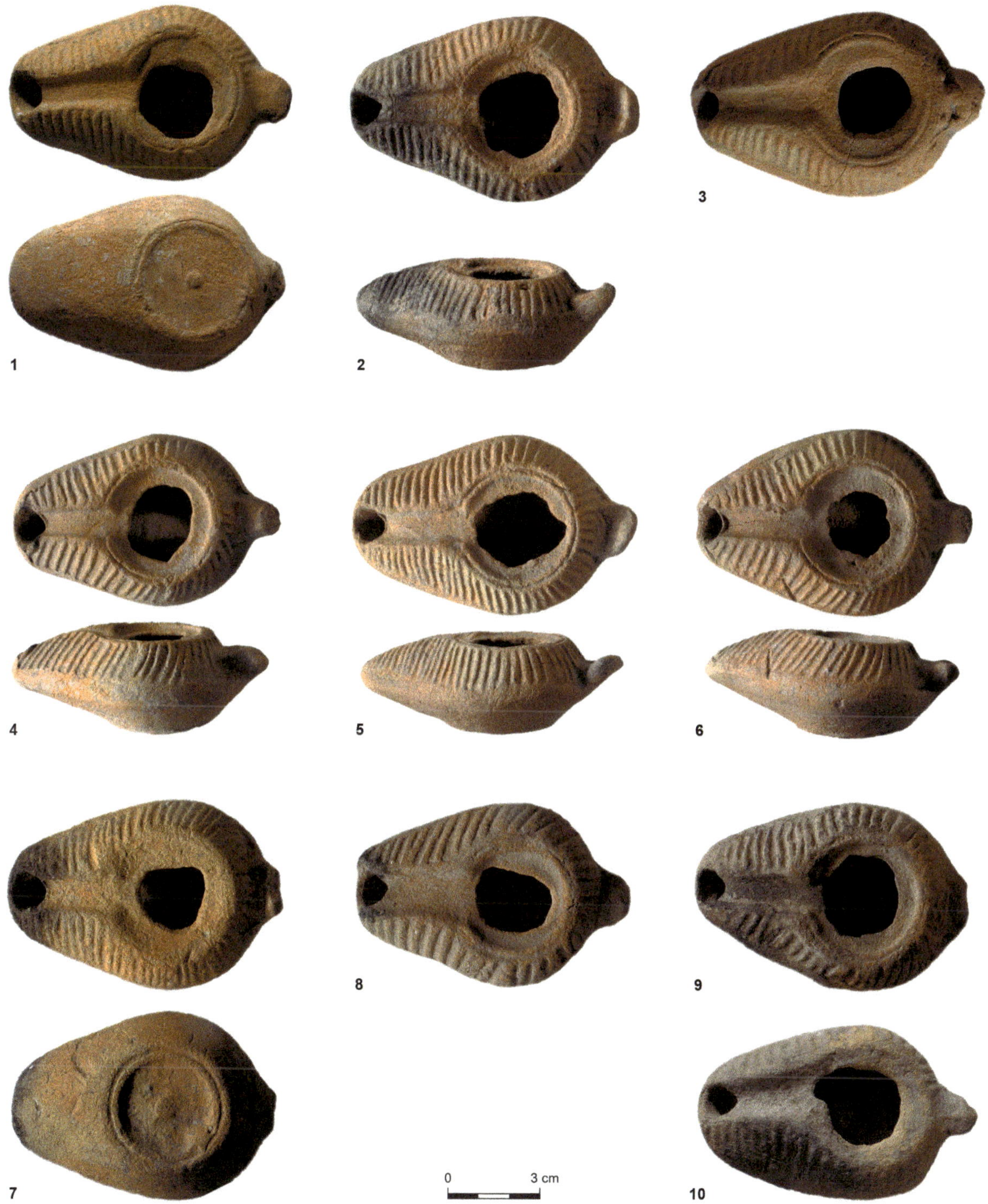

Fig. 14.9: Area CC, lamps (cont.).

Fig. 14.10: Area CC, Lamps (cont.)

No.	*Vessel*	*Locus*	*Basket*	*Inventory No.*	*Type*
1	Lamp	30060	302245	059	3
2	Lamp	30100	303298	141	3
3	Lamp	30148	305253	145	3
4	Lamp	30118	304148	187	3
5	Lamp	627	6289	218	3
6	Lamp	30060	303170	134	3
7	Lamp	627	6257	200	3
8	Lamp	659	6576	205	3
9	Lamp	30052	301411	096	3
10	Lamp	30082	304730	178	3

and Early Islamic periods. In this article, the argument is based on the discovery of numerous lamps in the Apollonia-Nof Yam refuse dump (in the immediate hinterland east of Apollonia/Byzantine Sozousa), one of the largest refuse dumps ever to be excavated in Palestine in a systematic and controlled manner. Moreover, a relative abundance of lamps has also been documented from other refuse disposal assemblages in the country, as demonstrated by a number of examples. At least two lamp-rich dumps (accumulated inside abandoned structures) of the Late Roman and Byzantine periods were excavated at Ḥorvat Migdal/Tsur Natan (Matthews, Neidinger and Ayalon 1990: 26, Fig. 28). A partially excavated Byzantine-period bathhouse at Baqa el-Gharbiya was found covered by refuse deposits that yielded about fifty mostly complete 5th- to 7th-century CE lamps (Badhi 2001: 61*–69*, Figs 6–9). At Kefar Sava, a large refuse dump was found with numerous complete lamps, including two with originally intact sealed filling holes (Ayalon 1998: 114–116, Fig. 11). At Mishmar David, a large refuse deposit from the beginning of the Early Islamic period (mid-7th to mid-8th centuries CE), which had accumulated over the remains of abandoned structures, yielded about a dozen complete and near-complete lamps. In a thick refuse dump from the same period, excavated on the south-eastern fringes of Yavneh, more than twenty complete and near-complete lamps were found; some never used before being discarded, in a few cases due to production defects (the excavations revealed evidence for a local lamp industry).[5] Finally, in Apollonia itself, numerous lamps—often complete—were found in a number of extensive Roman and Byzantine-period dumps in several locales in the town and on its fringes. Among the notable examples of such refuse is a group of Roman discus lamps with intentionally broken discs (of which more than 30 specimens were unearthed complete). These were recovered from Area E (south) (right below the southern medieval fortification wall), mostly from a dump (of ca. 20 m maximum preserved diameter; and up to 5 m deep) that had accumulated on top of a Roman villa, and that has been dated to the late 1st and early 2nd centuries CE (Tal and Teixeira Bastos 2012; 2105). A group of some 90 "Samaritan" lamps came from a refuse pit (ca. 4 m deep and at least 4 m in diameter) located east of the medieval town gate, but this was subject to looting, as most of the lamps collected from this dump were in the hands of a private collector who was present there throughout development work (Sussman 1983).[6]

5 The excavations at Mishmar David and Yavneh were directed by Eli Yannai on behalf of the Israel Antiquities Authority in 2006 and in 2010–2012, respectively. The ceramic finds from both excavations have been studied for the final publication by Taxel.

6 Etan Ayalon, personal communication, October 2015. Smaller dumps such as those excavated in Areas M, N and O that are above-mentioned are excluded from this discussion. For other pan-Mediterranean classical-period examples of deposition of lamps in large quantities, see Zissu *et al.* 2017: 125–126.

The second piece of evidence is a yet-unpublished Cairo Genizah text in the form of a magical recipe written in eloquent Palestinian Aramaic. Although dated to the early 10th century CE, this text is likely a copy of an earlier, apparently late antique recipe that originated in Palestine. It reads:

> An amulet for a spirit ṬBḤYTH [from the root TBḤ, to slaughter]. Take a new cooking pot [QDWRH ḤDTH/קדורה חדתה] and put in it salt and wine and [two more ingredients] from a grapevine and bury it in a dunghill [BQYQLH DZBL/בקיקלה דזבל], and wr[ite upon it] ᵓYŠTH QYQLY the angel, I adjure you [by] the name, and by the "watcher and holy one who went down from hea[ven] and

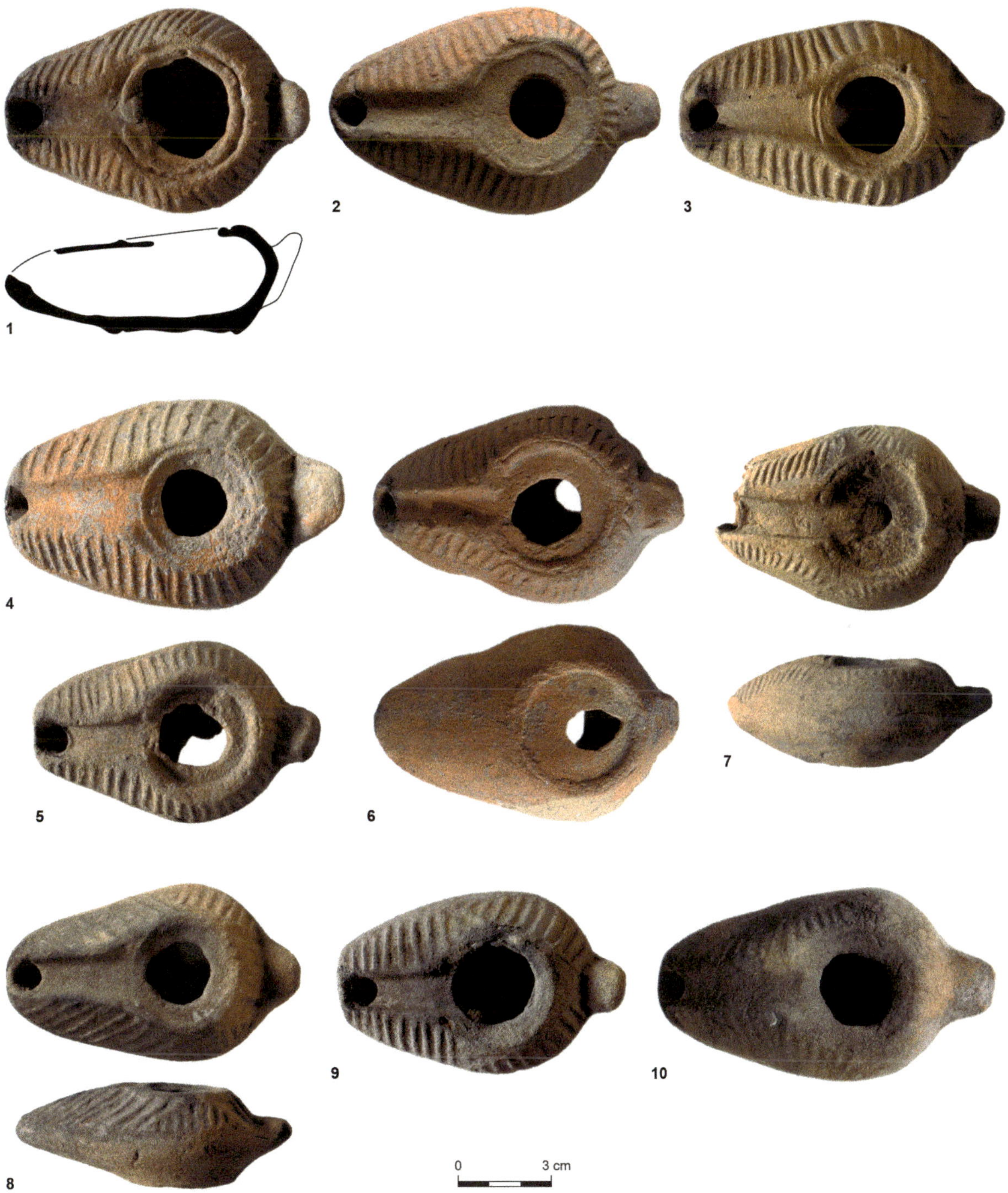

Fig. 14.10: Area CC, lamps (cont.).

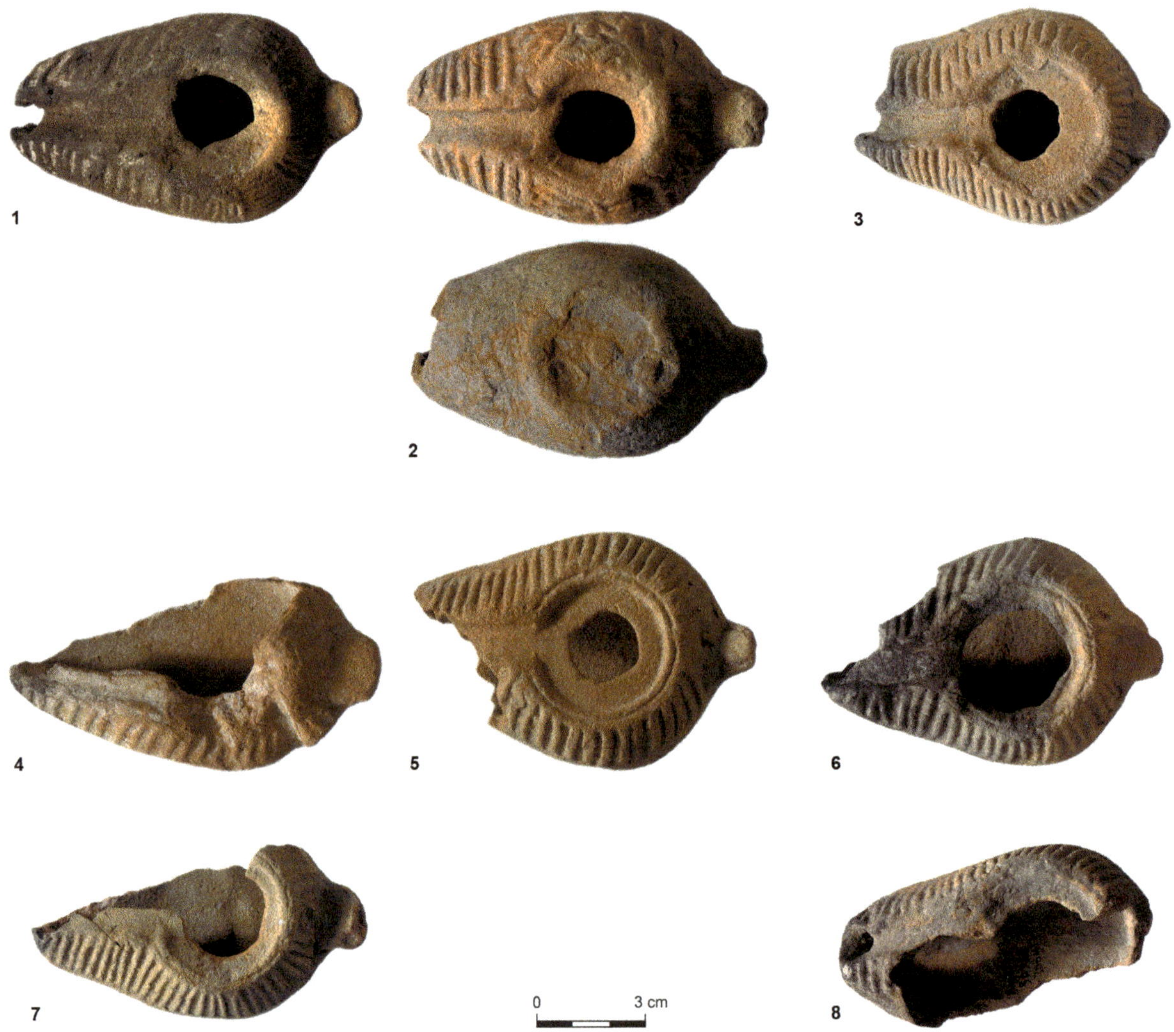

Fig. 14.11: Area CC, Lamps (cont.)

No.	*Vessel*	*Locus*	*Basket*	*Inventory No.*	*Type*
1	Lamp	30037	302636	017	3
2	Lamp	30060	301117	095	3
3	Lamp	30060	304120	185	3
4	Lamp	30061	301276	061	3
5	Lamp	30037	301859	066	3
6	Lamp	643	6466	213	3
7	Lamp	643	6541	222	3
8	Lamp	30052	300417	014	3

said, surround the tree and destroy it" [Daniel 4:20], so shall you surround [and destroy] and stop up the buttocks of NN from his buttocks [to his heart] and from his heart to his head, and it shall be subdued and humbled until QWSTᶜ the angel shall come and loosen it.[7]

7 Translated from the Genizah fragment Bodleian Heb. a 3.31, for which see Bohak 2011; we are indebted to Gideon Bohak for bringing this text to our attention and for his translation.

Indeed, this recipe specifically refers to a cooking pot (QDWRH; apparently a miscopying of the more common version QDYRH/קדירה), since a relatively large vessel with considerable volume was required in this case.[8] Still, the intensive usage of lamps in ritual and magic activities, so deeply rooted in the eastern Mediterranean world in Roman times (if not earlier, see above), allows for the suggestion that pottery lamps were equally used for magic rites of the kind described in the above Genizah document.

According to Peña, who referred to the use-life of lamps in the Roman world: "it seems reasonable to assume that they [lamps] normally remained in use for a relatively brief period of time, in all likelihood substantially less than one year. After a short period of use lamps likely became saturated with oil, rendering them a nuisance to handle and prone to being dropped and broken. Further, [...] lamps were exceedingly inexpensive, making replacement cost much less of a consideration than it would have been for vessels belonging to the other functional categories [storage/transport, table, cooking and utilitarian wares]. Also worth noting is the fact that lamps were regularly employed as votive and grave offerings, meaning that substantial numbers would have been employed in depositional use applications prior to their wearing out or breaking" (Peña 2007: 56–57).[9]

Regarding the latter point, it is agreed that the abundance of lamps in certain refuse dumps more often than not reflects merely the discarding of objects retired from regular daily use. Nevertheless, the idea is not rejected that at least a small percentage of lamps found in dumps (including those with an intact disc) could have been intentionally deposited there after fulfilling a role in magic rituals that took place at the same spots or in their immediate area, given the arguments in the lines above.

But why dumps? Apparently throughout human history (present-day societies included), people had a complex and rather ambivalent attitude towards refuse, and animal and human excrement alike. A plethora of historical, social, ethnographic, archaeological and ethno-archaeological studies are fully or partially dedicated to the practices people employed to manage the waste produced daily by domestic, industrial, and commercial activities, namely the various methods of refuse disposal and utilization, and norms of hygiene and sanitation.[10] These works, as well as ancient sources, demonstrate both the repulsion and attraction of people to refuse (in the broader sense of the word). On the one hand, waste is something one wishes to get rid of, and people, avoid staying near dumps and other provisional or terminal locations of refuse accumulation. On the other hand, various components of waste can be treated as highly useful, as a source for materials worthy of reuse and recycling, as fertilizers spread in agricultural land, and as ingredients in certain industries (such as tanneries). Indeed, people's visits to dumps for the purpose of scavenging and salvaging/reclaiming artefacts or seeking fertilizers and the like is not an unfamiliar phenomenon which was likely common also in Palestine and elsewhere during Roman, late antique and

8 The magic use of cooking pots is already documented in the rabbinic sources (see Brand 1953: 477–478, with references), which supports the above assumption that the Genizah recipe in question is based on an earlier text.

9 Cf. Brand 1953: 359 for references in the rabbinic sources about the difference between new and old/used lamps, with respect to the latter being saturated with oil and even considered inappropriate to be used in the *sukkah* during the Tabernacles (*Sukkot*) festival.

10 A comprehensive bibliography of the subject is well beyond the scope and aims of the present chapter. Basic noteworthy works include Rathje and Murphy 1992; Schiffer 1995, *passim*; 1996: 47–98, *passim*; Lambton 1997; Strasser 1999; Laporte 2000. In regard to the greater Roman world, these aspects were dealt with, for instance, by Scobie 1986: 407–422; Peña 2007: 272–318; and Koloski-Ostrow 2015; and in various site-specific studies (e.g., Ballet, Cordier and Dieudonné-Glad 2003, *passim*). The Palestinian perspective of personal hygiene and refuse disposal practices in the Roman, Byzantine and Early Islamic periods was discussed by Baruch and Amar 2004; by Magness 2011: 130–144; and in Tal and Taxel 2012; Tal, Taxel, and Jackson-Tal 2013; Taxel 2018: 132–155.

Fig. 14.12: Area CC, Lamps (cont.)

No.	*Vessel*	*Locus*	*Basket*	*Inventory No.*	*Type*
1	Lamp	30060	302801	024	3
2	Lamp	30118	304295	181	3
3	Lamp	30074	303379	121	3
4	Lamp	30036	300549	088	3
5	Lamp	627	6238	204	3
6	Lamp	30118	304233	184	3
7	Lamp	30037	301647	154	3
8	Lamp	30074	304112	169	3
9	Lamp	30060	302393/1	032	3
10	Lamp	30118	303780	167	3
11	Lamp	30063	301705	022	3
12	Lamp	30061	301107	034	3

early medieval times.[11] Within this context—and with the above-mentioned archaeological and Genizah document evidence in mind—it is suggested that dumps sometimes fulfilled yet another behavioral necessity, and an essential requirement of a ritual (or rituals)—that is, as the locale in which magic/cultic rites have been carried out.

The rather large number of lamps found in the dump suggested that an additional type of behavior might be explained by a hitherto overlooked practice, namely the use of lamps in magical or ritual activities carried out specifically in locations of refuse discard. These ideas may be strengthened by the fact that the mapping of the lamps within the excavated dump in Area CC shows that most of them were exposed in certain squares/loci related to the major parts of the dump, i.e., E9/Locus 30082; F6–F9/Loci 30060, 30061, 301131, 30160; G6–G7/Loci 30063, 30071, while the number of lamps in the surrounding squares was considerably smaller. The fact that the dump was overwhelmed by (almost) a single group of oil lamps ("Samaritan"), together with the near absence of pig bones, and the presence of two inscribed Samaritan rings,[12] suggest that the dump was used (mostly) by a Samaritan population, as was seen for example in the refuse dug out from the winepress collecting vat discovered in Area O (Tal 2009; and Chapter 10).

11 See, in general, Koloski-Ostrow 2015; Peña 2007: 12, 317–318; Schiffer 1996: 99–120, *passim*. Textual evidence for this practice in the southern Levant region is given in the *Life* of the 6th-century CE monk George of Choziba (3.1A), where Anthony of Choziba noted that the former used to search in the monastery's dump for torn pieces of cloth from which he prepared new garments. The complex feeling of contemporaneous populations towards waste and the like is well reflected by the numerous references in the rabbinic sources (notably those associated with Palestine itself, namely the Mishnah, Tosefta and Jerusalem Talmud) to terms such as ʾŠPH/אשפה (refuse), GLL/גלל (dung), ZBL/זבל (manure) and ṢWʾH/צואה (excrement, though also filth in general). See Kasovski 1932–1961: *I*, 619; II, 247; III, 7, 572; 1956–1961: I, 276, 451; II, 587–88, 881; Kosovsky 1979–2002: II, 181–82, 204; III, 349; VII, 1–2.

12 For the animal bones, see Pines, Sapir-Hen and Tal 2017 and Chapter 20, below. These are divided between 26.2% of cattle (*Bos Taurus*; NISP: 488), 4.7% of camel (*Camelus*; NISP: 87); 6.3% of horse/donkey (*Equuid*; NISP: 116); and most of the remainder 47.6% (NISP: 888) are large ungulates that belong to one of these species. Other identified species (such as sheep/goats, deer, gazelle, pigs, chickens, and wild animals) are under-represented (below 1.2% per species). For the Samaritan rings, see Ashkenazi, Taxel and Tal 2015: 199–200, Table 1, Rings C and G. For the reading of Ring C, see Tal and Taxel 2015: 169, n 16 and Chapter 17.

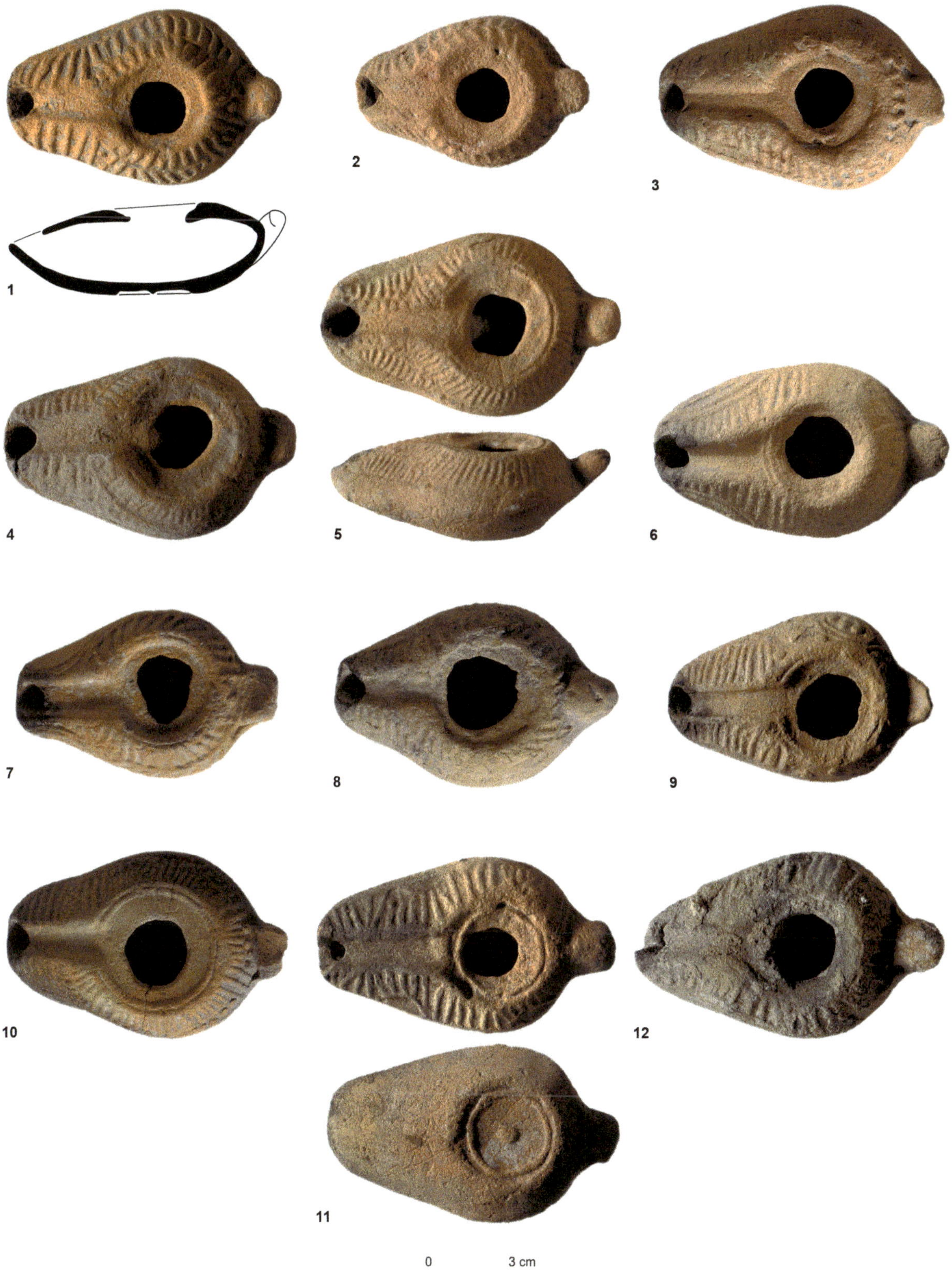

Fig. 14.12: Area CC, lamps (cont.).

FIG. 14.13: AREA CC, LAMPS (CONT.)

No.	*Vessel*	*Locus*	*Basket*	*Inventory No.*	*Type*
1	Lamp	30036	300247	099	3
2	Lamp	30065	302172	109	3
3	Lamp	30148	305333	146	3
4	Lamp	30061	304250	173	3

In regard to the large number of lamps (including unused ones), the authors are of the opinion that these lamps could not all represent an ordinary discard of unusable material, and think that the explanation for this phenomenon lies in the realm of an overlooked behavioral practice. Therefore, three possible scenarios are suggested:

Scenario 1

An unknown portion of the dumped lamps attesting to the material remains of a magical ritual (based on a recipe?) whose practice was carried out in the dump area—notably, though not exclusively by professional magicians. The lamps would have been used as containers for (organic) substances that had decomposed (similar to the Genizah recipe presented in the lines above), and/or were lit while a divination text was prayed or recited (as described in the Greek magical papyri from Egypt).

Scenario 2

An unknown portion of the dumped lamps attesting to a repository of old religious/cultic items which were in use in the town's Samaritan synagogue/s,[13] and were discarded due to religious or practical needs. Clearly, this interpretation blurs the boundaries between the sacred and the mundane nature of lamps (or any other class of artifacts), but it nonetheless allows speculation that a special significance was attributed to some discarded/deposited lamps.

13 On a possible location of one such synagogue, see Tal 2015. Excavation in the inscription area (Area P1) in the summer season of 2015 revealed the foundation of what was likely the southeastern corner and eastern wall of a building in which the inscription was located. Still, given the disturbance by remains from later periods elaborating on the building's plan seems superfluous.

Scenario 3

An unknown portion of the dumped lamps, attesting to a repository of the personal belongings of deceased individuals from among the town's inhabitants, were—due to fear of impurity or for other reasons—discarded and not buried with the dead or kept by their relatives. Such a scenario can also explain the existence of other typical personal accessories in the dump, among them the two inscribed

Fig. 14.14: Area CC, Lamps (cont.)

No.	*Vessel*	*Locus*	*Basket*	*Inventory No.*	*Type*
1	Lamp	30061	302518	062	3
2	Lamp	30052	300508	091	3
3	Lamp	30013	300105	104	3
4	Lamp	30052	300551	092	3
5	Lamp	30060	301876	107	3
6	Lamp	30118	305051	157	3
7	Lamp	30108	304147	177	3

Fig. 14.15: Area CC, Lamps (cont.)

No.	*Vessel*	*Locus*	*Basket*	*Inventory No.*	*Type*
1	Lamp	30050	302532	018	3
2	Lamp	30060	303000	019	3
3	Lamp	30067	300884	106	3
4	Lamp	30074	303560	142	3
5	Lamp	641	6434	072	3
6	Lamp	30070	300899	012	3
7	Lamp	30061	305496	023	3
8	Lamp	30060	302460	105	3
9	Lamp	30073	302085	037	3
10	Lamp	30131	304676	175	3
11	Lamp	30071	302267	064	3
12	Lamp	30063	301704	098	3

Samaritan rings (similarly, ceramic vessels which were in direct contact with menstruating women were considered impure—by Jews and likely by Samaritans as well—and therefore could commonly have been discarded).

Each of these scenarios may be valid, either individually or even together.[14] All these scenarios may have been associated with the exceptional number of coins, at least some of which may have played a part in a different ritual or practice.[15]

CONCLUSIONS

The site of Apollonia-Arsuf has (after 25 seasons of continuous excavations) produced a large number of complete lamps from three considerable dumps. The first dump, where some ninety complete "Samaritan" lamps were discovered in the mid-1970s, is located east of the medieval town gate; however, because it was excavated illicitly and published selectively, we are unable to elaborate on their discovery (Sussman 1983). The second dump is the one in Area E (south), excavated intermittently between 1980 and 2000, with some 30 complete Roman discus lamps that had accumulated on top of a Roman villa dated to the late 1st and early 2nd centuries CE (Tal and Teixeira Bastos 2012; 2015). The third dump is the one in Area CC of the site's eastern hinterland, where some 130 complete "Samaritan" lamps were discovered.

The function of lamps as lighting utensils led to their use as votive offerings, being either placed or thrown into designated locations for either functional or ritual purposes. They were used by both

14 Regardless of the reason/s behind their sometimes mass deposition in dumps, though with relevance to the suggested herewith understanding of the formation of the archaeological record, the fact is that lamps are often found in dumps in a complete or only partially broken state. This can be explained by the small, compact dimensions of lamps, which made them relatively durable to depositional and post-depositional agents compared with most other (usually larger and more vulnerable) vessel forms.

15 Suffice is here to mention other such non-hoarded coin discoveries whose "cultic" function may be postulated; e.g., Hirschfeld 2000: 336–337 (identifying the ʿEin Tzur spring as a wishing well based on the discovery of over 2000 coins from the 4th to 7th centuries inside it). See, however, Hirschfeld and Ariel 2005: 72, n 7, who reject—at least regarding the specific coin assemblage they discuss—a ritual explanation for its deposition. Still other cultic- or ritual-orientated accumulations of copper/bronze coins (normally of low-value) in foundation deposits, especially of synagogues (see in this respect, Bijovsky 2012: 90–91), but also of other buildings are quite a common phenomenon in the southern Levant.

Fig. 14.15: Area CC, lamps (cont.).

Fig. 14.16: Area CC, Lamps (cont.)

No.	*Vessel*	*Locus*	*Basket*	*Inventory No.*	*Type*
1	Lamp	30070	300891	028	3
2	Lamp	30066	300748	035	3
3	Lamp	627	6203	201	3
4	Lamp	643	6476	223	3
5	Lamp	30061	301001	068	3
6	Lamp	30052	301353	056	3
7	Lamp	30052	301894	053	3
8	Lamp	30016	300226	100	3
9	Lamp	30074	303484	126	3
10	Lamp	30074	303176	140	3

monotheists and polytheists. All these aspects of lamp use have been dealt with in the scientific literature dealing with lamps in various periods and locales. However, the function of lamps in disposed dumps has not hitherto been dealt with, as far as we know, in terms of the explanation that we have tried to put forward for their "post-functional" use—as refuse yet usable material found in considerable quantities in dumps. Our approach, being post-processual in nature, suggests yet another neglected aspect regarding the presence of lamps in the dumps of late antiquity.[16]

16 For similar and other aspects of the use-life of lamps in late antique Palestine, see Taxel 2018: 27–28, 108–109.

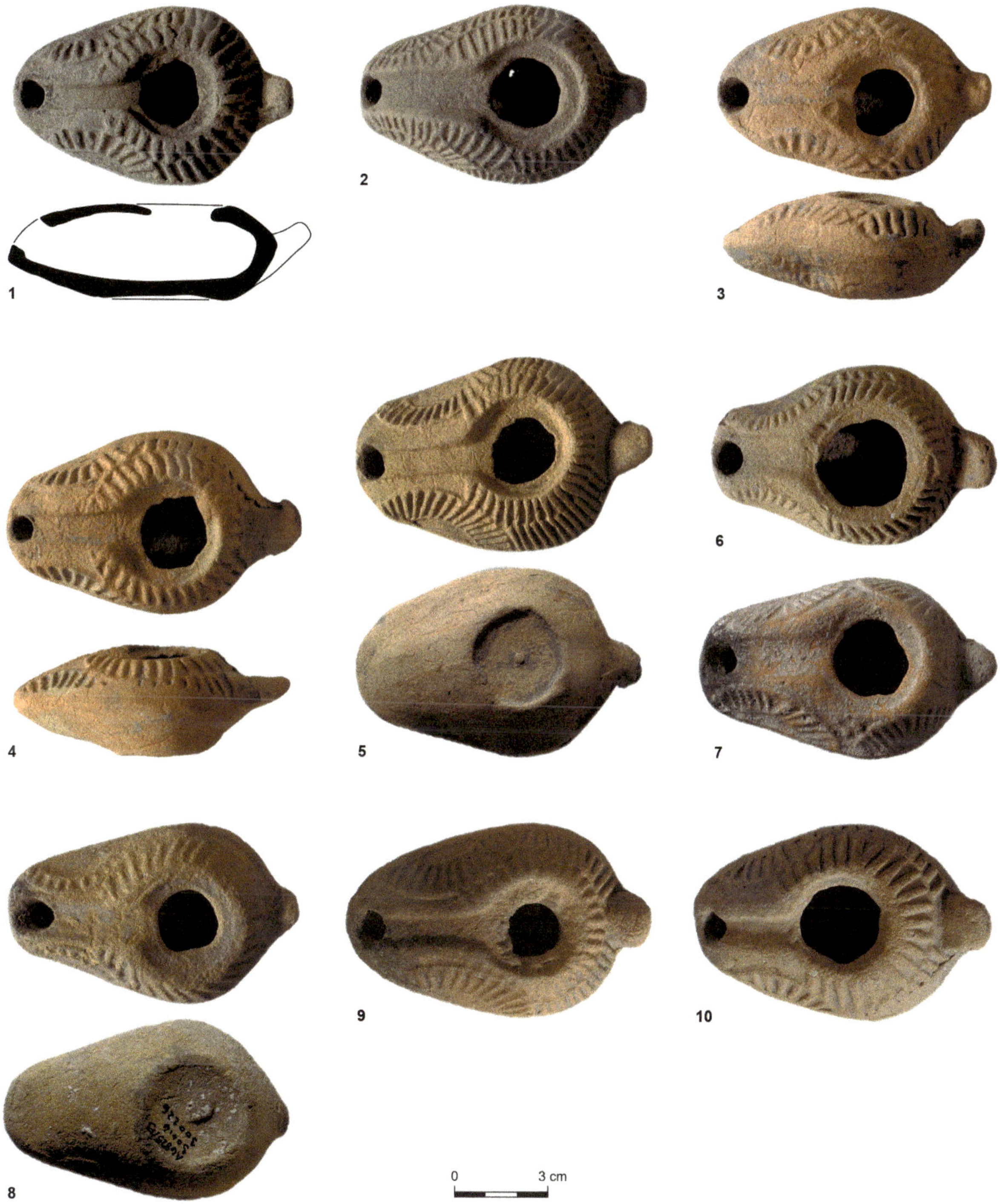

Fig. 14.16: Area CC, lamps (cont.).

Fig. 14.17: Area CC, Lamps (cont.)

No.	*Vessel*	*Locus*	*Basket*	*Inventory No.*	*Type*
1	Lamp	30082	303502	129	3
2	Lamp	627	6239	211	3
3	Lamp	30060	302393/2	033	3
4	Lamp	30082	304890	163	3
5	Lamp	30118	303956	162	3
6	Lamp	30118	304675	164	3
7	Lamp	30074	303496	131	3
8	Lamp	643	6564	215	3
9	Lamp	30061	301912	031	3

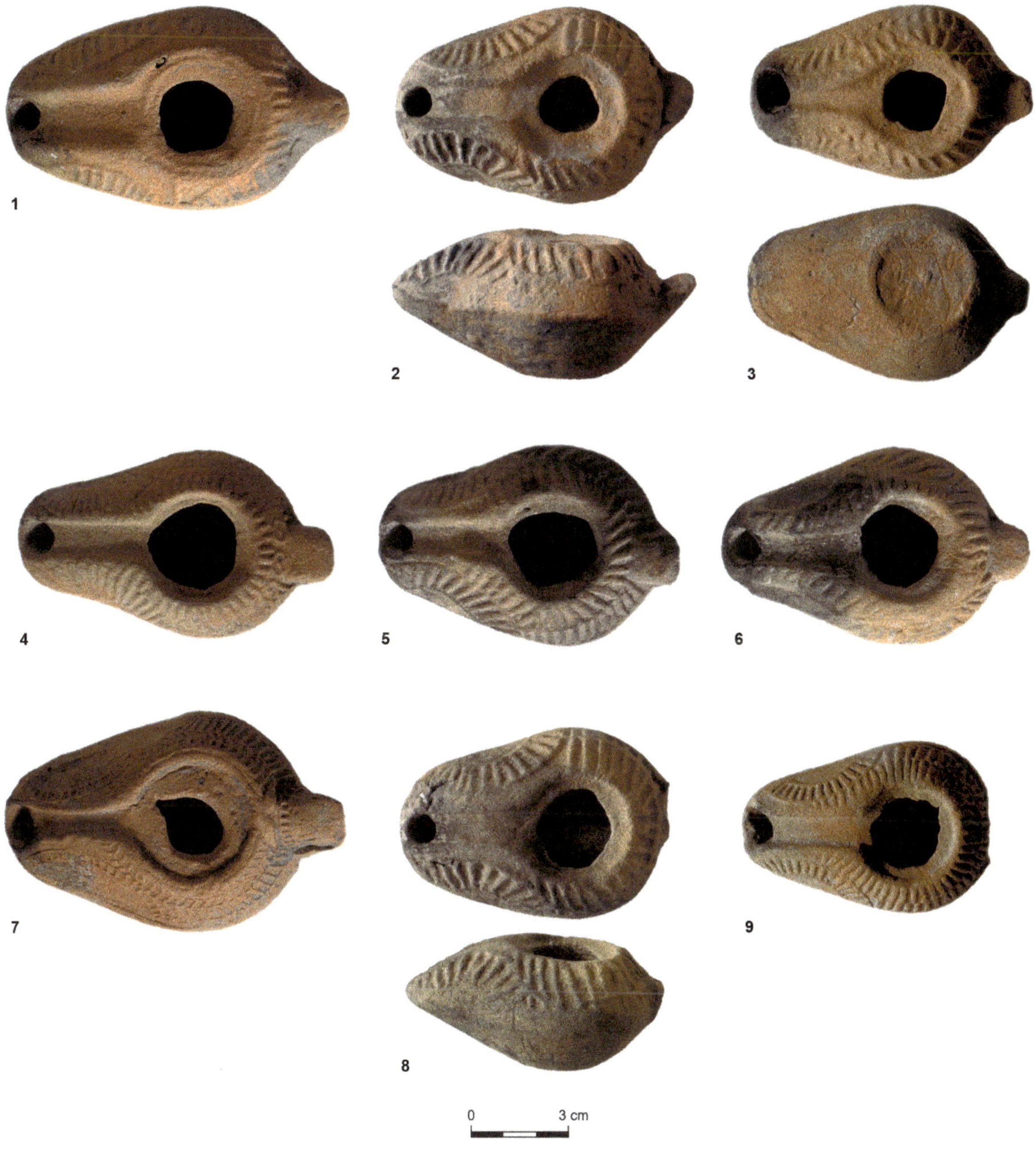

Fig. 14.17: Area CC, lamps (cont.).

FIG. 14.18: AREA CC, LAMPS (CONT.)

No.	*Vessel*	*Locus*	*Basket*	*Inventory No.*	*Type*
1	Lamp	30074	303669	125	3
2*	Lamp	30074	302880	079	3
3*	Lamp	30060	302016	040	3
4	Lamp	30036	300346	078	3
5	Lamp	623	6173	207	3
6*	Lamp	30066	301140	113	3
7	Lamp	30148	305282	155	3
8	Lamp	30061	305321	148	3
9	Lamp	30036	300242	080	3
10	Lamp	30148	305251	149	3
11	Lamp	30063	302927	077	3
12	Lamp	627	6258	073	3

Fig. 14.18: Area CC, lamps (cont.).

FIG. 14.19: AREA CC, LAMPS (CONT.)

No.	*Vessel*	*Locus*	*Basket*	*Inventory No.*	*Type*
1	Lamp	30061	301108	093	3
2	Lamp	30118	304413	186	3
3	Lamp	643	6601	206	3
4	Lamp	643	6700	221	3
5	Lamp	30074	303571	120	3
6	Lamp	643	6607	216	3
7	Lamp	30060	304256	166	3
8	Lamp	30037	303234	124	3
9	Lamp	30061	302087	115	3
10	Lamp	30063	303004	089	3
11	Lamp	30036	300336	063	3
12	Lamp	30123	303833	180	3

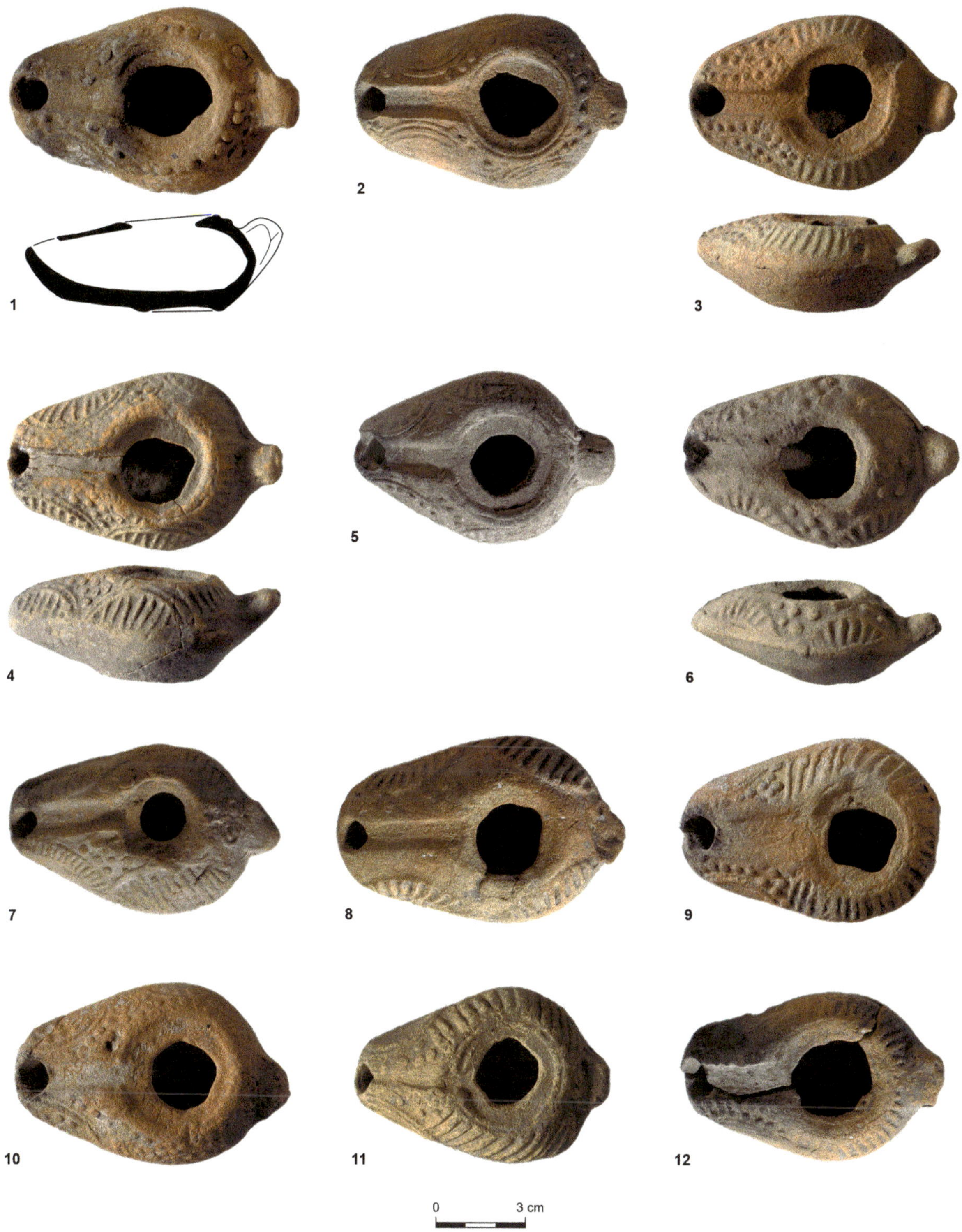

Fig. 14.19: Area CC, lamps (cont.).

Fig. 14.20: Area CC, Lamps (cont.)

No.	*Vessel*	*Locus*	*Basket*	*Inventory No.*	*Type*
1	Lamp	30071	302783	084	3
2	Lamp	625	6265	209	3
3	Lamp	30052	301894	053	3
4	Lamp	641	6616	229	3
5	Lamp	643	6468	220	3
6	Lamp	627	6382	228	3
7	Lamp	30074	303675	128	3
8	Lamp	30082	305224	135	3
9	Lamp	30067	303442	123	3
10	Lamp	30082	305146	158	3
11*	Lamp	30071	303225	127	3
12	Lamp	622	6175	210	3

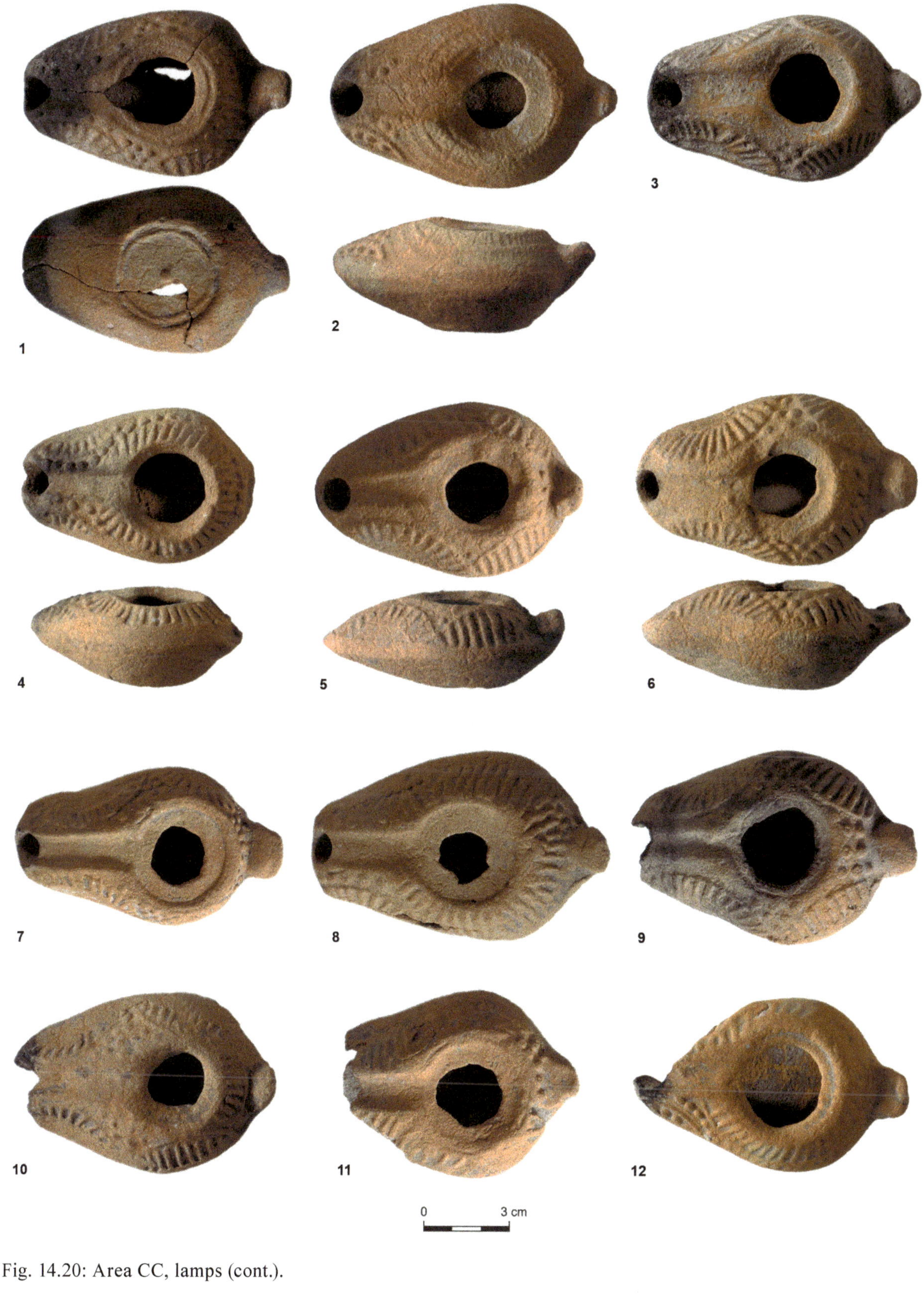

Fig. 14.20: Area CC, lamps (cont.).

Fig. 14.21: Area CC, Lamps (cont.)

No.	*Vessel*	*Locus*	*Basket*	*Inventory No.*	*Type*
1	Lamp	641	6618	219	3
2	Lamp	627	6270	225	3

Fig. 14.22: Area CC, Lamps (cont.)

No.	*Vessel*	*Locus*	*Basket*	*Inventory No.*	*Type*
1	Lamp	30066	300747	049	4
2	Lamp	30052	301135	070	4
3	Lamp	30071	301512	038	4

1

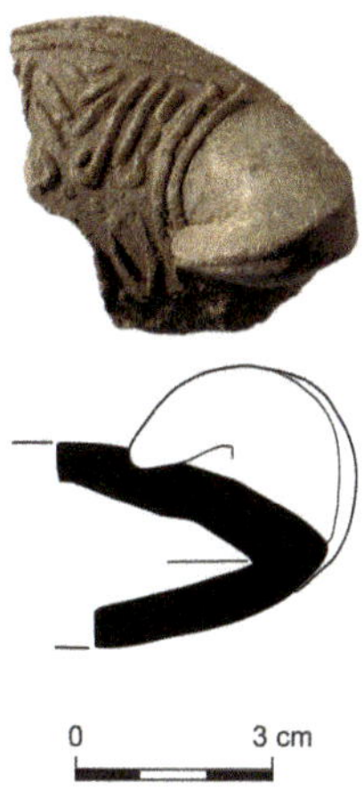

2

Fig. 14.23: Area CC and DD3, Lamps (cont.)

No.	*Vessel*	*Locus*	*Basket*	*Inventory No.*	*Type*
1	Lamp	627	6391	202	6
2	Lamp	853	8037	212	7

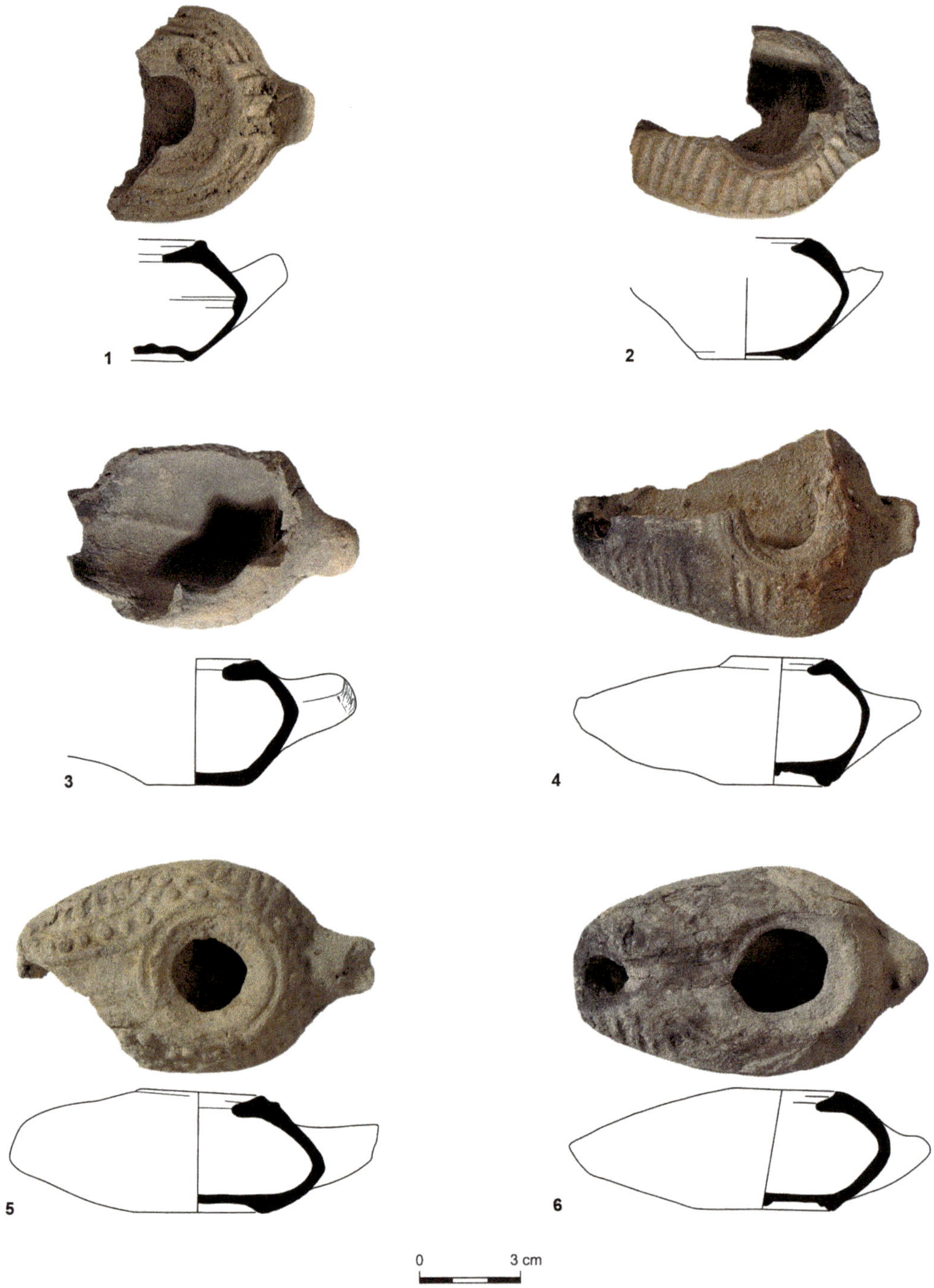

Fig. 14.24: Area M, Lamps

No.	*Vessel*	*Locus*	*Basket*	*Type*
1	Lamp	7049	71160	2/6
2	Lamp	7049	71095	3
3	Lamp	7007	70121	3
4	Lamp	7047	71032	3
5	Lamp	7044	71278	3
6	Lamp	7044	71043	3

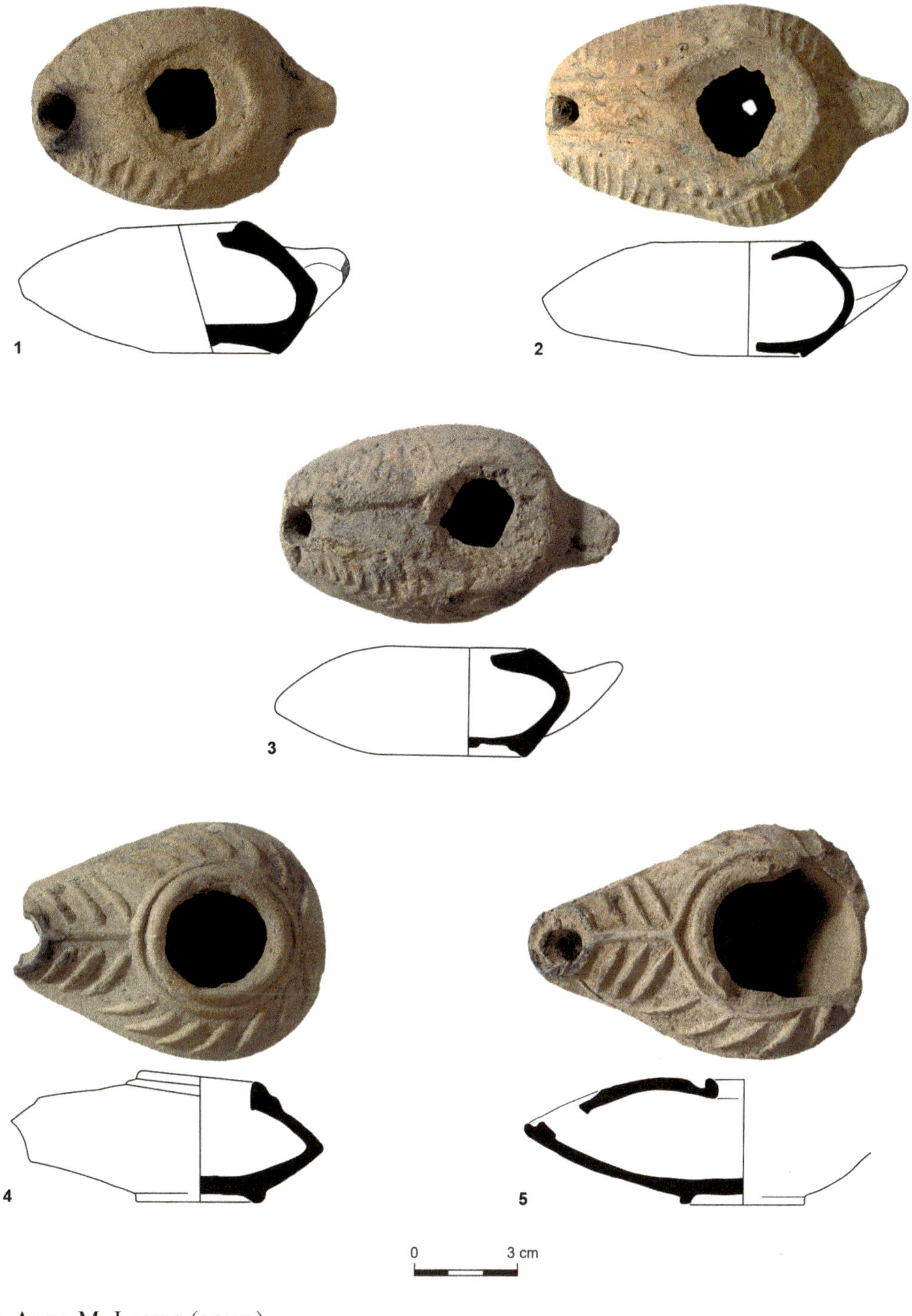

Fig. 14.25: Area M, Lamps (cont.)

No.	*Vessel*	*Locus*	*Basket*	*Type*
1	Lamp	7019	70287	3
2	Lamp	7010	70412	3
3	Lamp	7044	71015	3
4	Lamp	7044	71278	5
5	Lamp	7029	70973	5

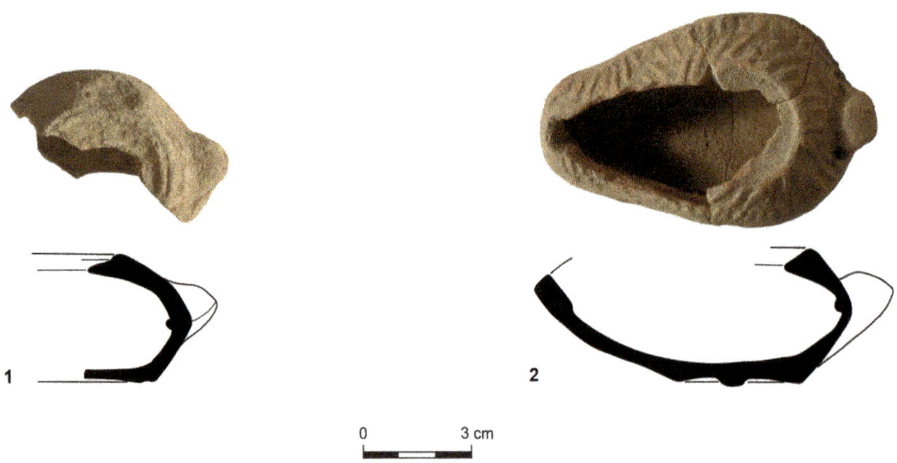

Fig. 14.26: Area N, Lamps

No.	*Vessel*	*Locus*	*Basket*	*Type*
1	Lamp	5002	50025	3
2	Lamp	5002	50032	3

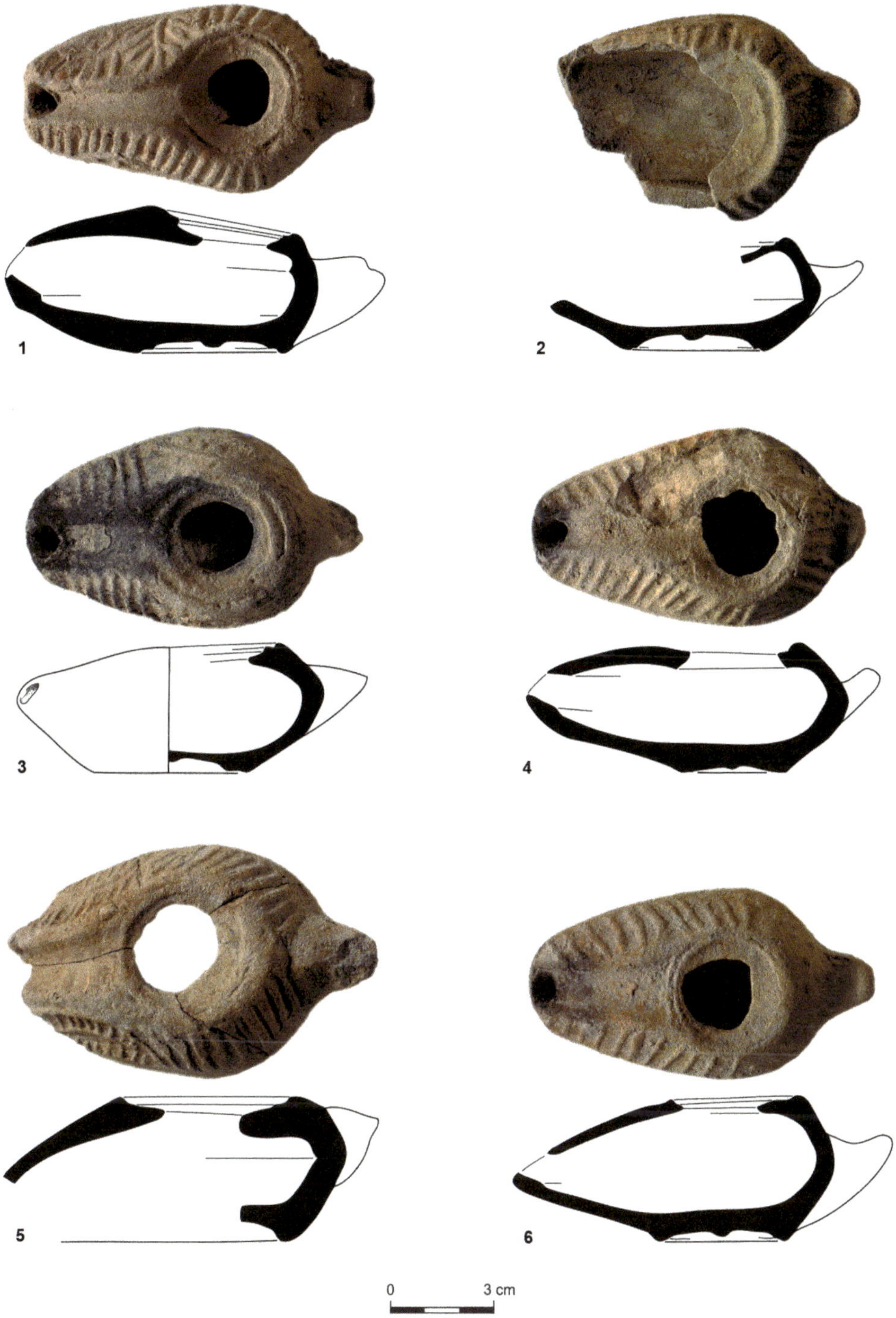

Fig. 14.27: Area O, Lamps

No.	*Vessel*	*Locus*	*Basket*	*Type*
1	Lamp	8061	80359	3
2	Lamp	8061	80391	3
3	Lamp	8061	80344	3
4	Lamp	8061	80414	3
5	Lamp	8061	80415	3
6	Lamp	8061	80359	3

APPENDIX 14.1

OPTICAL MINERALOGY ANALYSIS OF SAMARITAN OIL LAMPS

Mark Iserlis

METHOD

The Optical Mineralogy (OM) analysis used in this study follows standard procedures (Bishop, Rands and Holley 1982; Goren, Finkelstein and Na'aman 2004; Porat 1989; Whitbread 1995). Slices taken from lamps were impregnated with epoxy resin in vacuum and allowed to cure for nine hours. Samples were polished on the grinding machine and affixed to glass slides with epoxy resin. Thin sectioning system was used to grind the samples to a standard thickness of 30 µm. The slides were covered with microscope cover glass.

The samples were examined and described under a Zeiss Axiolab-POL polarising microscope in the Laboratory for Comparative Microarchaeology of the Institute of Archaeology, Tel Aviv University. Color and orientation patterns of the matrix were identified and described according to Bullock *et al.* (1985). The minerals in the silt and the temper were identified and their frequency, sorting, shape and roundness were described with the aid of visual charts (FitzPatrick 1980; Bullock *et al.* 1985). Temper in this study is non-plastic coarse (larger than 62 µm) particles, added by a potter as well as occurring naturally in the clay.

Thin-sections from Apollonia-Arsuf were compared with thin-sections of lamps from Khirbet al-Ḥadra and Tel Barukh (Tal and Taxel 2015), and with thin-sections from the collection in the Laboratory for Comparative Microarchaeology of the Institute of Archaeology, Tel Aviv University. The lithology of the thin-sections was compared to the geological maps (Sneh, Bartov and Rosensaft 1998).

RESULTS

A sample of 13 lamps from Apollonia-Arsuf was selected for OM analysis. The main conclusions of the OM analysis are presented in Table 14.1. A detailed description of all the sherd samples is presented in Table 14.2. One fabric group (A) was identified.

FABRIC A

Characterization: The matrix is marly and foraminiferous. The silt (<1–<3%) includes mainly quartz and accompanied by opaque minerals, plagioclase, calcite, epidote and zircon particles. The non-plastic assemblage (<7–<30%) of this group includes rounded to sub-angular quartz grains (>5–>15%) up to 390 µm (sometimes up to 530 µm), feldspar (<1–3%) up to 250–330 µm, rounded to sub-rounded chalk and limestone grains (<1–3%) up to 500–900 µm (rarely up to 2300 µm) and shell fragments up to 300–500 µm (rarely up to 2300 µm). Sometimes occasional chert fragments and soil balls were observed.

FABRICS FROM TEL BARUKH, KHIRBET AL-ḤADRA AND TELL QASILE: INTERPRETATION AND COMPARATIVE ANALYSIS

Seventeen analyzed lamps from Tell Qasile, Khirbet al-Ḥadra and Tel Barukh belong to three fabric groups, A, B and C. Most of the analyzed lamps (12 samples) belong to fabric group A, two to fabric group B and three samples were defined as belonging to fabric group C (Table 14.1).

Table 14.1: Distribution of Examined Samples According to Fabrics

Fabric/ Site	*A*	*B*	*C*	*Total*
Lamps, Apollonia-Arsuf	13			13
Lamps, Tel Barukh (reference group)	8	1	1	10
Lamps, Khirbet al-Ḥadra (reference group)	2		2	4
Lamps, Tell Qasile (reference group)	2	1		3
Total sampled lamps	*25*	*2*	*3*	*30*

Table 14.2: Examined Samples from Apollonia (East)—Area CC (A-6825/2013)

Figure	*Locus/Basket*	*Matrix*	*Temper*	*Fabric*
14.1: 9	30074/303127 (Sample 67)	Marly, foraminiferous, inactive	Quartz <20%, feldspar <1%, chalk and shell <3%	A
14.7: 9	30070/303011 (Sample 111)	Marly, foraminiferous, inactive	Quartz >5%, feldspar <1%, chalk and limestone >3%	A
14.20: 11	30071/303225 (Sample 127)	Marly, foraminiferous, weak orientation	Quartz >15%, feldspar <3%, chalk >1%, limestone and shell >1%, very rare chert	A
14.18: 2	30074/302880 (Sample 79)	Marly, foraminifera	Quartz >7%, feldspar <1%, chalk >1%, shell >1%	A
Not illustrated	30071/302038 (Sample 46)	Marly, foraminiferous, weak orientation	Quartz >7%, feldspar <1%, chalk >1%	A
14.18: 9	30060/302016 (Sample 40)	Marly, foraminifera, inactive, porosity >3%	Quartz <15%, feldspar 1%, chalk >1%, shell >1%, oxide 1%	A
Not illustrated	30131/309138 (Sample 152)	Marly, inactive, foraminiferous, <3% silt, porosity 3%	Quartz 7%, l >3	A
Not illustrated	30060/303317 (Sample 138)	Marly, foraminiferous, weak optical orientation, porosity 1%	Quartz >10%, feldspar <1%, chalk <3%	A
Not illustrated	30061/302892 (Sample 86)	Calcareous, foraminiferous, inactive, silt <3%, porosity >3%	Quartz >10%, feldspar >1%, limestone and chalk up to 2.30 mm 3%, shell up to 2.30 mm <1%	A
14.18: 6	30066/301140 (Sample 113)	Foraminiferous, marly, weak optical orientation, porosity <5%	Quartz <10%, feldspar 1%, chalk >1%, limestone <1%, shell fragments <1%	A
14.7: 7	30061/302037 (Sample 112)	Foraminiferous, marly, inactive	Quartz >7%, feldspar 1%, chalk and limestone >1%	A
Not illustrated	30052/303071 (Sample 47)	Foraminiferous, marly, porous <3%	Quartz 7%, feldspar >1%, chalk <3%, shell	A
Not illustrated	30036/301543 (Sample 10)	Foraminiferous, marly, very weak orientation, porous <3%	Quartz >5%, feldspar <1%, chalk, limestone and shell <3%	A

FABRIC B

The matrix is marly and foraminiferous. The silt (<1–>1%) includes quartz, accompanied by opaque minerals, plagioclase, calcite, epidote and zircon particles. The non-plastic assemblage (>1–>3%) includes chalk and limestone (>1–<3%) grains up to 90 μm and a few rounded to sub-rounded quartz grains up to 80 μm.

FABRIC C

The matrix is ferruginous, optically active and rich in opaque bodies of iron minerals. The silt (>1–>3%) includes mainly quartz grains. Plagioclase, calcite, epidote, rutile and zircon particles were also observed. The non-plastic assemblage (>5–>25%) includes rounded to sub-angular quartz up to 400 or 530 μm (>7–<15%), feldspar (<3–>5%, plagioclase and microcline) up to 400–480 μm, oxide particles (<1–>1%), milky calcareous rock fragments (<1–>1%), a few calcite crystals and very rare chert fragments up to 100 or 180 μm. Sometime rare *kurkar* and shell fragments were observed.

Based on the extensive body of reference material, Fabric C is identified as quaternary *ḥamra* soil mixed with coastal sand. *Ḥamra* occurs along the Coastal Plain between Ashdod and the Carmel (Dan *et al.* 1976; Goren, Finkelstein and Na'aman 2004, 292–293; Singer 2007). The *ḥamra* soil from the Carmel coast contains up to 50% calcareous component (Nir 1989: 12). The *ḥamra* soil between Ashdod and Caesarea contains mainly quartz. Based on the geological map and published data, the matrix and inclusions indicate a depositional environment peculiar to the central Coastal Plain (Apollonia-Arsuf, Tel Barukh, Khirbet al-Hadra and Tell Qasile) and its immediate surroundings (Ravikovitch 1969; 1981; Sneh, Bartov and Rosensaft 1998; Singer 2007). The fabric is well known from pottery assemblages from sites of different periods in the central Coastal Plain. It has been documented at the Middle Bronze Age workshops at Naḥal Śoreq, in Tel Aviv and at Tel Michal (Singer-Avitz and Levy 1992; Kletter and Gorzalczany 2001; Gorzalczany 2006b). In the Persian period this group was found to be common in assemblages from Tel Michal, Naḥal Tut, Ḥorbat Malta, Tel Yaʿoz and Apollonia-Arsuf (Gorzalczany 1999; 2006a; 2006b; 2006c; 2008).

INTERPRETATION AND COMPARATIVE ANALYSIS

Based on the extensive body of reference material, Fabric C is identified as Quaternary *ḥamra* soil mixed with coastal sand. *Ḥamra* occurs along the Coastal Plain between Ashdod and the Carmel (Dan *et al.* 1976; Goren, Finkelstein and Na'aman 2004, 292–293; Singer 2007). The *ḥamra* soil from the Carmel coast contains up to 50% calcareous component (Nir 1989: 12). The *ḥamra* soil between Ashdod and Caesarea contains mainly quartz. Based on geological map and published data, the matrix and inclusions indicate a depositional environment peculiar to the central coastal plain (Apollonia-Arsuf, Tell Qasile, Khirbet al-Ḥadra and Tel Barukh) and its immediate surroundings (Ravikovitch 1969; 1981; Sneh, Bartov and Rosensaft 1998; Singer 2007). The fabric is well known from pottery assemblages from sites of different periods in the central Coastal Plain. It has been recorded from the Middle Bronze Age workshops at Naḥal Śoreq, in Tel Aviv and at Tel Michal (Singer-Avitz and Levy 1992; Kletter and Gorzalczany 2001; 2006b). In the Persian period this group was found to be common in assemblages from Tel Michal, Naḥal Tut, Ḥorbat Malta, Tel Yaʿoz and Apollonia-Arsuf (Gorzalczany 1999; 2006a; 2006b; 2006c; 2008).

Fabric A and its non-plastic assemblage suit the environment of both Apollonia-Arsuf, Tell Qasile, Khirbet al-Ḥadra and Tel Barukh, but for the marly matrix. Based on the extensive reference material,

Fabric A non-plastic assemblage is identified as sand from the central Coastal Plain. Since the samples of Fabric A are mineralogically similar to the samples of Fabric C and to the Quaternary *ḥamra* (red sand and loam) soil occurs along the coastal plain between Ashdod and the Carmel coast, they may be identified as originating nearby. The principal difference between these two fabrics is a marly or calcareous (and non-ferruginous) character of the matrix and the presence of rounded to sub-rounded chalk and limestone grains in the temper assemblage of Fabric A. The quality of Fabric A matrix suggests that it was collected some distance from the outcrop of the marl or mixed with alluvial sediment by potters. Outcrops of Eocene, Turon and Upper Cenoman limestone, chalk and marl are located at a distance of 10–15 km from Apollonia-Arsuf (Sneh, Bartov and Rosensaft 1998). Area west of the Shephelah and east of the central Coastal Plain is covered by Quaternary alluvium, colluvium and soil. These sediments are rich in calcareous components. Fabric A is therefore a product of marly alluvial-colluvial sediments and artificially added coastal sand. Based on geological map this fabric is identified as alluvial-colluvial soil of the eastern Coastal Plain.

Since the samples of the Fabric B are mineralogically similar to the samples of Fabric A, they may be identified as originating nearby. The difference between these two groups is an absence of rounded to sub-angular quartz and feldspar grains up to 530 µm temper assemblage of fabric group B. The quantity and quality of rare rounded to sub-rounded quartz grains suggests that they are integral part of the clay. Fabric B is therefore a product of alluvial-colluvial soil.

REFERENCES

Ashkenazi, D., Taxel, I. and Tal, O. 2015. Archeometallurgical Characterization of Late Roman- and Byzantine-Period Samaritan Magical Objects and Jewelry Made of Copper Alloys. *Materials Characterization* 102: 195–208.

Avissar, M. and Stern, E.J. 2005. *Pottery of the Crusader, Ayyubid, and Mamluk Periods in Israel* (IAA Reports 26). Jerusalem.

Ayalon, E. 1998. Ancient Kefar Sava in the Light of Recent Excavations. *ʿAtiqot* 34: 107–120 (Hebrew).

Badhi, R. 2001. Remains of a Bathhouse and Other Structures in Baqa el-Gharbiya. *ʿAtiqot* 42: 57*–71* (Hebrew).

Ballet, P., Cordier, P. and Dieudonné-Glad, N., eds. 2003. *La ville et ses déchets dans la monde romain: rebuts et recyclages*. Actes du Colloque de Poitiers (19–21 Septembre 2002). Montagnac.

Baruch, E. and Amar, Z. 2004. The Latrine in the Land of Israel in the Roman–Byzantine Period. *Jerusalem and Eretz-Israel* 2: 27–50 (Hebrew).

Berlin, A.M. 1999. The Archaeology of Ritual: The Sanctuary of Pan at Banias/Caesarea Philippi. *Bulletin of the American Schools of Oriental Research* 315: 27–45.

Bijovsky, G. 2012. *Gold Coin and Small Change: Monetary Circulation in Fifth–Seventh Century Byzantine Palestine* (Polymnia Numismaticaantica e medievale. Studi 2). Trieste.

Bishop, R.L., Rands, R.L. and Holley, G.P. 1982. Ceramic Composition Analysis in Archaeological Perspective. *Advances in Archaeological Method and Theory* 5: 275–325.

Bohak, G. 2011. The Magical Rotuli from the Cairo Genizah. In: Bohak, G., Harari, Y. and Shaked, S., eds. *Continuity and Innovation in the Magical Tradition* (Jerusalem Studies in Religion and Culture 15). Leiden: 321–340.

Bouras, L. and Parani, M.G. 2008. *Lighting in Early Byzantium* (Dumbarton Oaks Byzantine Collection Publications 11). Washington.

Brand, Y. 1953. *Ceramics in Talmudic Literature*. Jerusalem (Hebrew).

Bullock, P., Fedoroff, N., Jongerius, A., Stoops, G. and Tursina, T. 1985. *Handbook for Soil Thin Section Description*. Albrington.

Coen Uzzielli, T. 1997. The Oil Lamps. In: Hirschfeld, Y., ed. *The Roman Baths of Hammat Gader*. Jerusalem: 319–346.

Cyril of Jerusalem. 2000. *Catecheses*. Translated by Edward S.J. Yarnold, in *Cyril of Jerusalem*. London.

Dan, J., Yaalon, D.H., Koyumdjisky, H. and Paz, Z. 1976. *The Soils of Israel*. Bet Dagan: The Volcani Institute of Soil, Water and Environmental Sciences.

FitzPatrick, E.A. 1980. *The Micromorphology of Soils*. London.

Goren, Y., Finkelstein, I. and Na'aman, N. 2004. *Inscribed in Clay: Provenence Study of the Amarna Tablets and other Near Eastern Texts* (Monograph Series of the Institute of Archaeology of Tel Aviv University 23). Tel Aviv.

Gorzalczany, A. 1999. Petrographic Analysis of the Persian-Period Pottery—A Preliminary Report. In: Roll, I. and Tal, O. *Apollonia-Arsuf, Final Report of the Excavations 1: The Persian and Hellenistic Periods* (Monograph Series of the Institute of Archaeology of Tel Aviv University 16). Tel Aviv: 185–189.

Gorzalczany, A. 2006a. Petrographic Analysis of the Persian-Period Pottery from Tel Yaʿoz. *ʿAtiqot* 52: 39*–45* (Hebrew).

Gorzalczany, A. 2006b. Petrographic Analysis of the Tel Mikhal (Tel Michal) Pottery. *ʿAtiqot* 52: 57–65.

Gorzalczany, A. 2006c. Petrographic Analysis of the Pottery from Naḥal Tut. *ʿAtiqot* 52: 191–195.

Gorzalczany, A. 2008. Petrographic Analysis of the Persian-Period Pottery from Ḥorbat Malta. *ʿAtiqot* 59: 82–86.

Grossberg, A. 2002. Cooking Pots with Holes Found in Jerusalem and the Customs of Haverim and Amei Ha-Aretz. *New Studies on Jerusalem* 8: 59–71 (Hebrew).

Hadad, S. 2002. *The Oil Lamps from the Hebrew University Excavations at Bet Shean* (Qedem Reports 4). Jerusalem. http://www.hadashot-esi.org.il/report_detail_eng.aspx?id=15728&mag_id=122

Hirschfeld, Y. 2000. Architecture and Stratigraphy. In: Hirschfeld, Y., ed. *Ramat HaNadiv Excavations: Final Report of the 1984–1988 Seasons*. Jerusalem: 13–87.

Hirschfeld, Y. and Ariel, D.T. 2005. A Coin Assemblage from the Reign of Alexander Jannaeus (104–76 BCE) Found on the Shore of the Dead Sea. *Israel Exploration Journal* 55: 66–89.

Karivieri, A. 2010. Magic and Syncretic Religious Culture in the East. In: Gwynn, D.M. and Bangert, S., eds. *Religious Diversity in Late Antiquity* (Late Antique Archaeology 6). Leiden: 401–434.

Kasovski, Ḥ.Y. 1932–1961. *Thesaurus Tosephthae: Concordantiae verborum quae in sex Tosephthae ordinibus reperiuntur*. Jerusalem (Hebrew).

Kasovski, Ḥ.Y. 1956–1961. *Thesaurus Mishnae: Concordantiae verborum quae in sex Mishnae ordinibus reperiuntur*. Jerusalem (Hebrew).

Kletter, R. and Gorzalczany, A. 2001. A Middle Bronze Age II Type of Pottery Kiln from the Coastal Plain of Israel. *Levant* 33: 95–104.

Koloski-Ostrow, A.O. 2015. *The Archaeology of Sanitation in Roman Italy: Toilets, Sewers, and Water Systems*. Chapel Hill.

Kosovsky, M. 1979–2002. *Concordance to the Talmud Yerushalmi (Palestinian Talmud)*. Jerusalem (Hebrew).

Lambton, L. 1997. *Temples of Convenience, Chambers of Delight*. London.

Laporte, D. 2000. *History of Shit*. (Trans. from the French *Histoire de la merde* by N. Benabid and R. el-Khoury). Cambridge.

Lavan, L. 2012. From Polis to Emporion? Retail and Regulation in the Late Antiquity City. In: Morrisoon, C., ed. *Trade and Markets in Byzantium*. Washingtion, D.C.: 340–350.

Mader, E. 1957. *Mambre: Die Ergebnisse der Ausgrabungen im heiligen Bezirk Ramet el-Halil in Südpalästina*. Freiburg.

Magness, J. 1993. *Jerusalem Ceramic Chronology, circa 200–800 CE* (JSOT/ASOR Monograph Series 9). Sheffield.

Magness, J. 2011. *Stone and Dung, Oil and Spit: Jewish Daily Life in the Time of Jesus*. Grand Rapids.

Matthews, E., Neidinger, W. and Ayalon, E. 1990. *Preliminary Report on the Excavation at Zur Natan: 1989 and 1990 Seasons*. Houston.

Nesbitt, C. 2012. Shaping the Sacred: Light and the Experience of Worship in Middle Byzantine Churches. *Byzantine and Modern Greek Studies* 36/2: 139–160.

Nilsson, M.P. 1950. Lampen und Kerzen im Kult der Antike. *Opuscala Archaeologica* 6: 96–111.

Peña, J.T. 2007. *Roman Pottery in the Archaeological Record*. Cambridge.

Pines, M., Sapir-Hen, L. and Tal, O. 2017. Consumption and Disposal Practices in the Southern Levant in Late Antiquity: Animal Bones from ’Απολλωνία/Σώζουσα’s Hinterland as a Case Study. *Zeitschrift des Deutschen Palästina-Vereins* 133: 186–204.

Porat, N. 1989. *Composition of Pottery—Application to the Study of the Interrelations between Canaan and Egypt during the Third Millennium B.C.* (Ph.D. dissertation, Hebrew University of Jerusalem). Jerusalem.

Rathje, W. and Murphy, C. 1992. *Rubbish! The Archaeology of Garbage*. New York.

Schiffer, M.B. 1995. *Behavioral Archaeology: First Principles*. Salt Lake City.

Schiffer, M.B. 1996. *Formation Processes of the Archaeological Record*. Salt Lake City.

Scobie, A. 1986. Slums, Sanitation, and Mortality in the Roman World. *Klio* 68: 399–433.

Singer, A. 2007. *The Soils of Israel*. Berlin.

Singer-Avitz, L. and Levy, Y. 1992. An MBIIa Kiln at the Naḥal Śoreq Site. *ʿAtiqot* 21: 9*–14* (Hebrew).

Sneh, A., Bartov, Y. and Rosensaft, M. 1998. *Geological Map of Israel* 1:200.000. Jerusalem: Geological Survey of Israel.

Sozomen. 1890. *The Ecclesiastical History of Sozomen, Comprising a History of the Church from AD 323 to AD 425*. Translated by Chester D. Hartranft. Buffalo.

Stern, I. and Noam, V. 2015. Holey Vessels of Maresha. *Aram* 27: 343–364.

Strasser, S. 1999. *Waste and Want: A Social History of Trash*. New York.

Sussman, V. 1983. The Samaritan Oil Lamps from Apollonia-Arsuf. *Tel Aviv* 10: 71–96.

Sussman, V. 2002. Samaritan Oil Lamps. In: Stern, E. and Eshel, H., eds. *The Samaritans*. Jerusalem: 339–371 (Hebrew).

Sussman, V. 2017. *Late Roman to Late Byzantine/Early Islamic Period Lamps in the Holy Land: The Collection of the Israel Antiquities Authority*. Oxford.

Tal, O. 2009. A Winepress at Apollonia-Arsuf: More Evidence on the Samaritan Presence in Roman–Byzantine Southern Sharon. *Liber Annuus* 59: 319–342.

Tal, O. 2015. A Bilingual Greek-Samaritan Inscription from Apollonia-Arsuf/Sozousa: Yet More Evidence of the Use of εἷς θεὸς μόνος Formula Inscriptions among the Samaritans. *Zeitschrift für Papyrologie und Epigraphik* 194: 169–175.

Tal, O. and Taxel, I. 2012. Socio-Political and Economic Aspects of Refuse Disposal in Late Byzantine and Early Islamic Palestine. In: Matthews, R. and Curtis, J., eds. *Proceedings of the 7th International Congress of the Archaeology of the Ancient Near East, 12th–16th April 2010, the British Museum and UCL, London, 1: Mega-cities and Mega-sites: The Archaeology of Consumption & Disposal, Landscape, Transport & Communication.* Wiesbaden: 497–518.

Tal, O. and Taxel, I. 2015. *Samaritan Cemeteries and Tombs in the Central Coastal Plain: Archaeology and History of the Samaritan Settlement outside Samaria (ca. 300–700 CE)* (Ägypten und Altes Testament 82). Münster.

Tal, O. and Taxel, I. 2017. More Than Trash – Cultic Use of Pottery Lamps Found in Late Antique Dumps: Apollonia (Sozousa) as a Test Case. In: Tal, O. and Weiss, Z., eds. *Expressions of Cult in the Southern Levant in the Greco-Roman Period: Manifestations in Text and Material Culture* (Contextualizing the Sacred 6). Turnhout: 181–193.

Tal, O., Taxel, I. and Jackson-Tal, R. 2013. Khirbet al-Ḥadra: More on Refuse Disposal Practices in Early Islamic Palestine and their Socio-Economic Implications. *Bulletin of the Anglo-Israel Archaeological Society* 31: 117–148.

Tal, O. and Teixeira Bastos, M. 2012. Intentionally Broken Discus Lamps from Roman Apollonia: A New Interpretation. *Tel Aviv* 39: 105–115.

Tal, O. and Teixeira Bastos, M. 2015. More on the Intentionally Broken Discus Lamps from Roman Palestine: Mutilation and Its Symbolic Meaning. In: Blömer, M., Lichtenberger, A. and Raja, R., eds. *Religious Identities in the Levant from Alexander to Muhammed: Continuity and Change* (Contextualizing the Sacred 4). Turnhout: 345–368.

Ravikovitch, S. 1969. *Manual and Map of Soils of Israel*. Jerusalem (Hebrew).

Ravikovitch, S. 1981. *The Soils of Israel: Formation, Nature and Properties*. Tel Aviv (Hebrew).

Taxel, I. 2018. *Fragile Biography: The Life Cycle of Ceramics and Refuse Disposal Patterns in Late Antique and Early Medieval Palestine* (BABESCH Supplements 35). Leuven.

Whitbread, I.K. 1995. *Greek Transport Amphorae: A Petrological and Archaeological Study* (The British School at Athens; Fitch Laboratory Occasional Paper 4). Exeter.

Zissu, B., Klein, E., Davidovich, U., Porat, R., Langford, B. and Frumkin, A. 2017. Votive Offerings from the Late Roman Period in the Teʾomim Cave, Western Jerusalem Hills. In: Tal, O. and Weiss, Z., eds. *Expressions of Cult in the Southern Levant in the Greco-Roman Period: Manifestations in Text and Material Culture* (Contextualizing the Sacred 6). Turnhout: 111–130.

CHAPTER 15

STONE VESSELS

Itamar Taxel

The excavated areas discussed in this report yielded relatively few stone vessels. They are presented below according to the type of stone they are made of, namely basalt or marble.

BASALT VESSELS

MORTARS/GRINDING BOWLS

Represented by one complete and several fragmentary examples, this category includes three vessel forms. The first is a small hourglass-shaped mortar (ca. 16 cm high, 11 cm deep and 18 cm in diameter) fashioned as a deep conical bowl with a solid conical base (Fig. 15.1: 1). The second form, represented by a large fragment, is a massive grinding bowl (or a bowl-shaped mortar; ca. 13 cm high, 11 cm deep and 39 cm in diameter) with a flat base, straight everted walls and what appears to be two rounded lug handles (Fig. 15.1: 2). The third and most common vessel form is a smaller bowl with rounded walls, a three-footed base and (originally) four rounded lug handles (Fig. 15.2: 1–3). All these vessels, and especially the three-footed bowls, were common milling and grinding implements used for the processing of grains/seeds/nuts, spices, medicinal and make-up materials, dyes and the like, and they are documented in numerous contexts dated to various periods, including those represented in the current excavations (cf. Patrich and Shadmi 2008: 348–351, Nos. 20–64).

MARBLE VESSELS

GRINDING BOWLS

Functionally related to the previous class are fragments of marble bowls (up to 35 cm in diameter) with rounded walls, (originally) flat bases and four lug handles. Fig. 15.3: 1 shows a fragmented vessel with two preserved handles; one is rounded and decorated with simple incisions on its upper surface (two abstracted volutes across a dividing line/arrow) and the other is shaped like an elongated shallow spout. Two thin concentric lines are incised on the bowl's upper rim surface. Fig. 15.3: 2 illustrates a rim and handle fragment – the latter is similarly designed like the above incised handle but it is larger. Marble grinding bowls/mortars of this type (and of various dimensions) are frequently found in Byzantine-period, and sometimes later contexts, in Palestine and elsewhere, and their local production out of imported marble blocks or reused architectural marble items has also been documented in Caesarea (Patrich and Shadmi 2008: 351–354, Nos. 76–122).

BOWLS

This category is represented by several fragments of fine-carved bowls. All have thin, rounded and highly polished walls. The upper body parts preserve a flattened, slightly everted rim (Fig. 15.4: 1–2). One of these bowls has a high pedestal base with a concave bottom and a rounded ridge at its upper

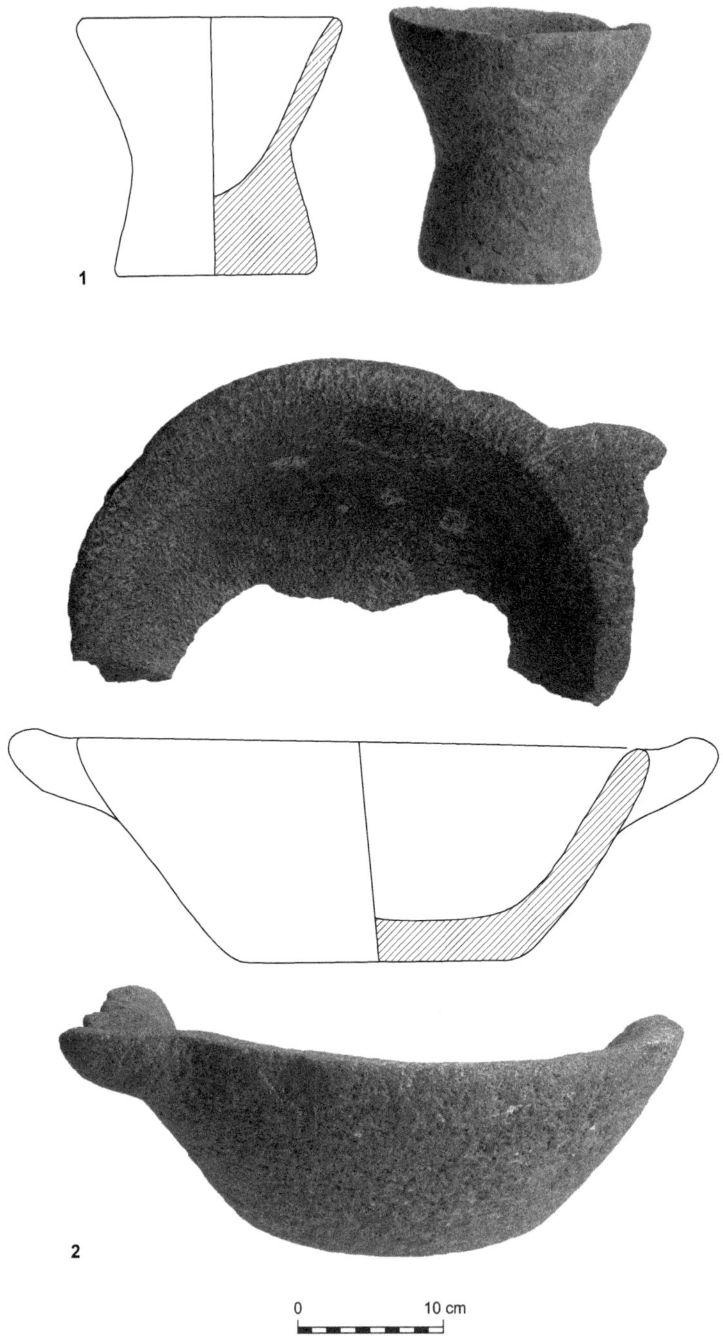

Fig. 15.1: Basalt Mortars/Grinding Bowls

No.	*Type*	*Area*	*Locus*
1	Mortar	AA	106
2	Grinding bowl	BB	Surface

section (Fig. 15.4: 1). Other examples are lower body parts with broad high ring bases (Fig. 15.4: 3–4). These fine bowls were most likely used as table (eating/serving) dishes and/or—in religious contexts (churches and synagogues alike)—as liturgical vessels designated to hold water, oil and/or wine. In either case, they are relatively common in local contexts of the Byzantine period (e.g., Patrich and Shadmi 2008: 351, Nos. 68–72).

PLATTERS/TABLETOPS

Two fragments of marble items were found which can be identified either as platters or round/sigma-shaped tabletops with thick, flat bottoms. The first has a broad, plain ledge rim whose edges are decorated with a carved bead-and-reel/astragal motif (Fig. 15.4: 5), which likely continued

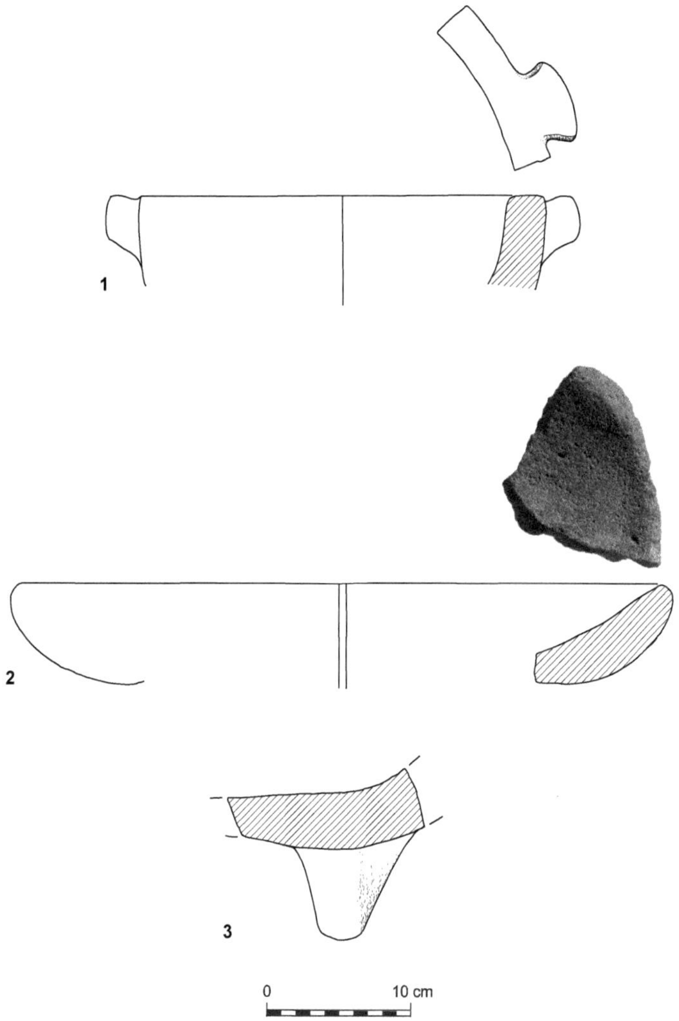

FIG. 15.2: BASALT MORTARS/GRINDING BOWLS (CONT.)

No.	*Type*	*Area*	*Locus*	*Basket*
1	Grinding bowl	AA	10034	100238
2	Grinding bowl	CC	30060	303672
3	Grinding bowl	CC	30074	303584

along the entire perimeter of the rim. This type is known from a number of Byzantine-period sites in Palestine and other regions (e.g., Fiema and Frösén 2008: 213, Fig. 11: 1; Taxel 2009: 166, Fig. 6.3: 3), though it is less common than most types of contemporaneous platters/tabletops. The second has a thickened edge/rim, with a profile convex from the exterior and a diagonal from the interior (Fig. 15.4: 6). Platters/tabletops with similar profiles, either plain throughout or decorated with the bead-and-reel/astragal and other motifs on their rim surface and/or edges, were rather common in the Byzantine period across the Mediterranean (see Chalkia 1991: 28–49, Pl. 1, Figs. 1, 7, 9, 32). Although such objects are usually associated with ecclesiastical contexts, they could have equally been used by non-Christians in both religious/public and domestic contexts (cf. the marble "tabletops" found in a dwelling structure at the Jewish village of En-Gedi; Sidi 2007: 557, Figs. 24–26, Pl. 14).

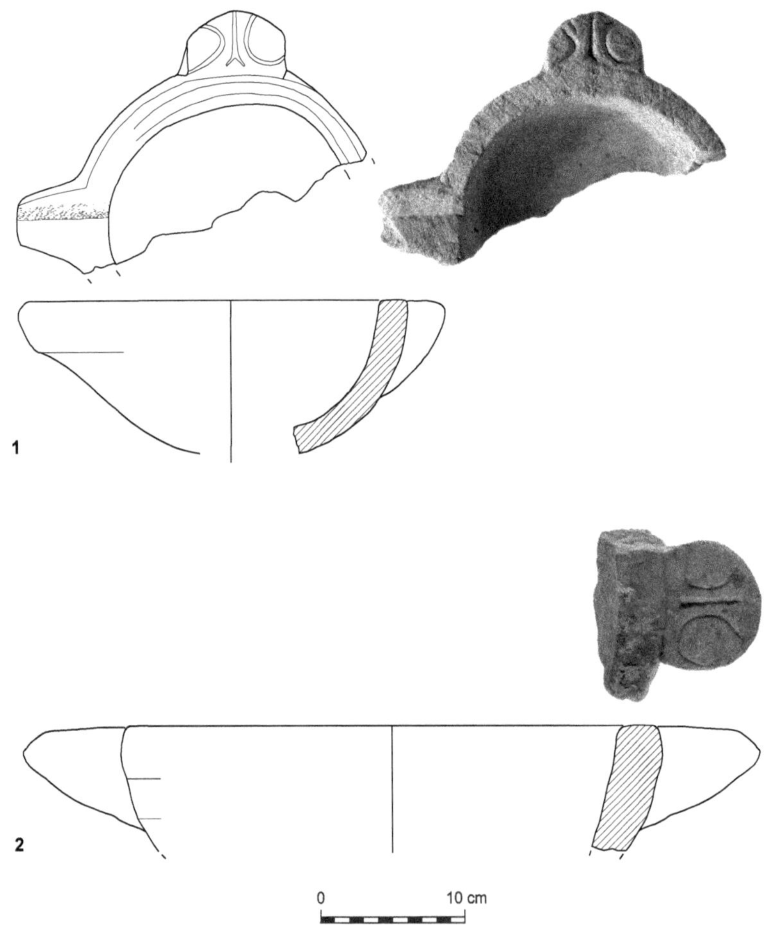

Fig. 15.3: Marble Grinding Bowls

No.	*Type*	*Area*	*Locus*	*Basket*
1	Grinding bowl	CC	30074	303584
2	Grinding bowl	CC	30061	302232

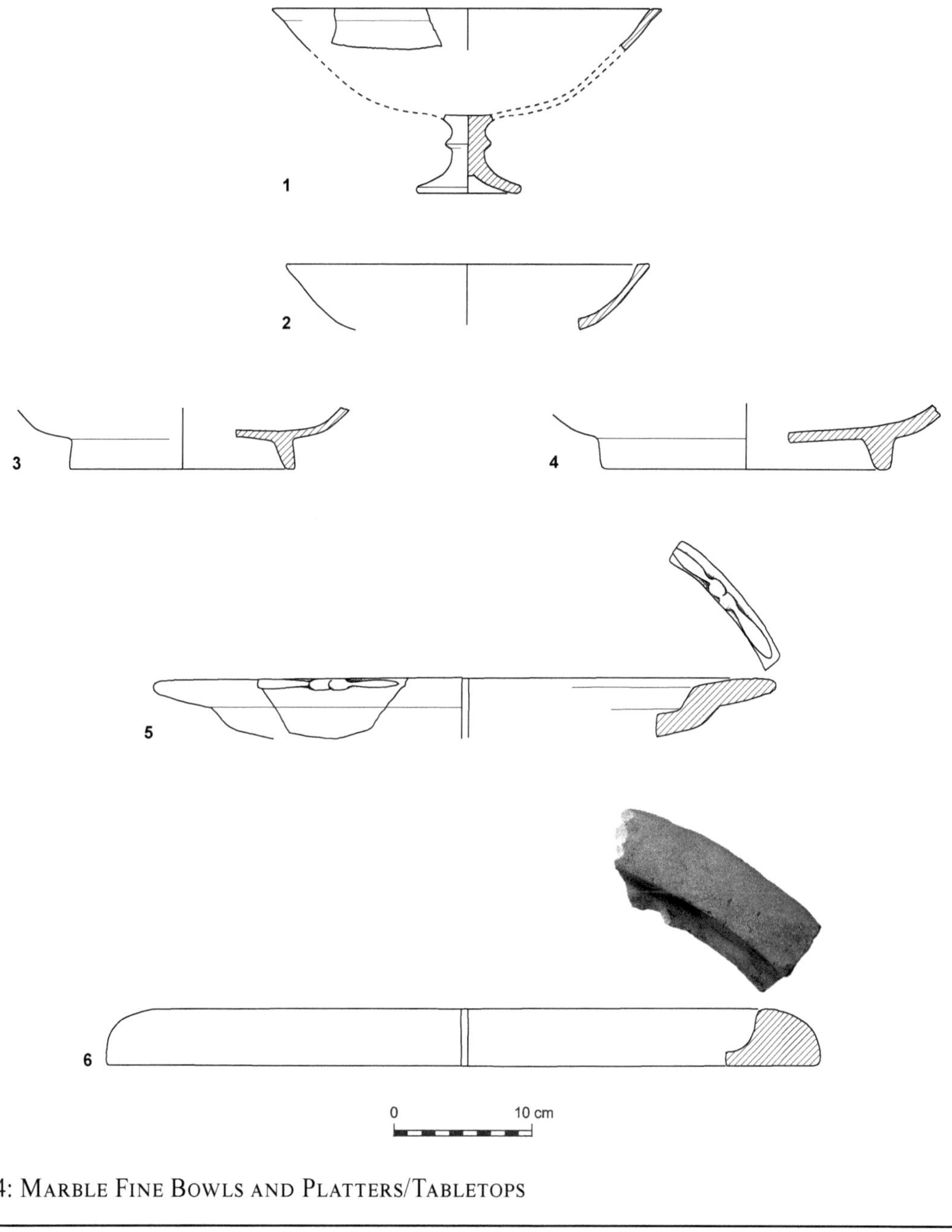

FIG. 15.4: MARBLE FINE BOWLS AND PLATTERS/TABLETOPS

No.	*Type*	*Area*	*Locus*	*Basket*
1	Footed bowl	CC	30063	303856
2	Bowl	CC	30052	300592
3	Bowl (base)	CC	30052	300592
4	Bowl (base)	O	8065	-
5	Platter/tabletop	CC	30037	301795
6	Platter/tabletop	CC	30071	303673

REFERENCES

Chalkia, E. 1991. *La mense paleocristiane. Tipologia e funzioni della mense secondary nel culto paleocristiano*. Rome.

Fiema, Z.T. and Frösén, J. 2008. *Petra—The Mountain of Aaron. The Finnish Archaeological Project in Jordan, Volume I: The Church and the Chapel*. Helsinki.

Patrich, J. and Shadmi, T. 2008. The Stone Vessels. In: Patrich, J. *Archaeological Excavations at Caesarea Maritima: Areas CC, KK and NN, Final Report*. Jerusalem: 347–365.

Sidi, N. 2007. Stone Utensils. In: Hirschfeld, Y. *En-Gedi Excavations II, Final Report (1996–2002)*. Jerusalem: 544–573.

Taxel, I. 2009. *Khirbet es-Suyyagh: A Byzantine Monastery in the Judaean Shephelah* (Salvage Excavation Reports 6). Tel Aviv.

CHAPTER 16

GLASS

Ruth E. Jackson-Tal

Thousands of fragments of glass vessels, as well as a large amount of production debris, were found in the various areas at the site of Apollonia (Byzantine Sozousa). The quantity, diversity and context provide information on the production and use of glass vessels during the Late Roman and especially Byzantine periods at the site. The site is extremely significant for the study of glass production and vessels in the country because of the Byzantine glass furnaces recovered and the vast numbers of Byzantine glass finds unearthed (Tal, Jackson-Tal and Freestone 2004; Freestone, Jackson-Tal and Tal 2008). These indicate the important role of the site as a major production center for raw glass and glass vessel production. The current report deals with glass finds from the areas excavated outside the medieval town walls, which are dominated by finds dated to the Byzantine period. The areas of excavation are located to the east of the town (Areas AA–DD and their derivatives), to the south (Areas M, N and its derivative) and to the north (Area O). The glass finds from all these areas can be dated to the Byzantine period based on their typology and contexts. In many cases, vessels were recovered together with coins that provide a chronological frame which is generally dated from the 4th century to the 6th century CE. The glass vessels are presented according to areas of excavations and are followed by a presentation of the glass production refuse. Parallels were given when possible from the vicinity of the site or from other sites throughout Israel. Parallel glass assemblages were studied from several sites with similarly dated contexts, mostly identified as Samaritan given the nature of the current evidence. These parallel assemblages come mostly from burials, but also settlements and industrial glass production remains and furnaces, such as Khirbet al-ʿAura/Tel Barukh cemetery (Jackson-Tal 2015a) and a burial cave in Khirbet al-Ḥadra (Jackson-Tal 2015b), burials and settlement remains at Shechem/Neapolis (Magen 2009; Sarig 2009) and Samaria (Crowfoot 1957), refuse pits with glass industrial refuse remains at Khirbat el-Fatuna (Jackson-Tal 2007a), a glass workshop at Ramla (South) (Tal, Jackson-Tal and Freestone 2008), burials and glass industrial refuse remains at Khirbat el-Niʿana (Gorin-Rosen and Katsnelson 2007) and the glass factory dump at Jalame (Weinberg and Goldstein 1988).

PROVENANCE AND AMOUNTS

AREA AA

Some 640 fragments of glass vessels and production refuse were found during the excavations in Area AA. Of these one production fragment of a flattened test piece was chosen for presentation (Fig. 16.1: 1).

AREA AA1

Some 250 fragments of glass vessels and production refuse were found during the excavations in Area AA1. Of these one vessel fragment of a free-blown beaker was chosen for presentation according to its state of preservation. The glass production refuse consists of a large number of primary product

Fig. 16.1: Areas AA, AA1 and AA2, Selected Glass Finds

No.	*Area*	*Locus*	*Basket*	*Descriptiom*	*Notes*
1	AA	141	1243	Refuse fragment	Light green. Silver weathering and iridescent film. Elongated flattened and thickened piece with tooled marks. Thickness: 0.5–1 cm
2	AA1	205	2078	Rim and wall fragment	Colorless. Thick silver weathering and iridescent film. Flaring rounded rim, straight wall. Rim diameter: 7.4 cm
3	AA1	266	2221	Furnace wall remains	White. Silver weathering and iridescent film, lime deposits. Uneven thick chunk of mudbrick with a thin layer of glazed smoothed white glass. Thickness: 6.5 cm
4	AA2	227	2170	Four glass lumps	Black with porous white limy layer. Small uneven lumps of porous dark glass covered with a thick layer of limy/ashy material. Thickness: 1–2 cm
5	AA2	168	1672	Base and wall fragment	Greenish-blue. Thick silver weathering and iridescent film. Concave base with solid base-ring (pontil mark 1 cm), beginning of splaying out wall. Base diameter: 2–4 cm
6	AA2	162	1636	Refuse fragment	Light blue. Silver weathering and iridescent film. Elongated flattened drop with rounded base. Base diameter: 1 cm

remains, around 140 raw glass chunks in various sizes and a few furnace remains (e.g., Fig. 16.1: 3). In most cases glass recovered came from fills while production debris seems to have been in secondary use for building/agricultural purposes. The fragments of vessels recovered at the area are dated to the Late Roman–Byzantine periods (e.g., Fig. 16.1: 2).

AREA AA2

Some 750 fragments of glass vessels and production refuse were found during the excavations in Area AA2. Of these one vessel fragment of a free-blown bowl was chosen for presentation according to its state of preservation. The glass production refuse consists of primary and secondary product remains, around 600 raw glass chunks in various sizes and a few vessel production remains (e.g., Fig. 16.1: 4, 6). The fragments of vessels recovered at the area are dated to the Late Roman–Byzantine periods (e.g., Fig. 16.1: 5).

AREA BB

Some 40 fragments of glass vessels and production refuse were found during the excavations in Area BB. No vessels were chosen for presentation according to their state of preservation, but they included free-blown bowls and bottles. The glass production refuse consists of primary product remains, around 30 raw glass chunks in various sizes. The fragments of vessels recovered at the area are dated to the Late Roman–Byzantine periods.

AREA CC

Over 10,000 fragments of glass vessels and production refuse were found during the excavations in Area CC. Of these vast numbers, seventy indicative vessel fragments, representing the main and reoccurring types, were chosen for presentation according to their state of preservation. They include free-blown bowls, beakers, bottles and jugs, wineglasses, lamp bowls and a window-pane (e.g., Figs. 16.2–16.6). The glass production refuse consists of around 2000 remains of the floor, wall and ceiling of glass furnaces as well as primary and secondary product remains (e.g., Figs. 16.7–16.10). The glass finds unearthed in the dump layer of Area CC are generally dated to between the 4th and 6th centuries CE. This date is supported by the analysis of some 150 coins that came from the dump, where most of the earliest among the identifiable coins found are dated to the mid-4th century CE and the latest to the mid-6th century CE (Chapter 18: Fig. 18.1).

AREA DD2

Some 100 fragments of glass vessels and production refuse were found during the excavations in Area DD2. Eight vessels were chosen for presentation according to their state of preservation. They include free-blown bowls, bottles and jug. The glass production refuse consists of primary product remains and approximately 70 raw glass chunks in various sizes. The fragments of vessels recovered at the area are dated to the Late Roman–Byzantine periods (e.g., Fig. 16.11: 1–8).

AREA DD3

Some 180 fragments of glass vessels and production refuse were found during the excavations in Area DD3. Of these two furnace remains were chosen for presentation (Fig. 16.11: 10–11).

AREA M

Some 100 fragments of glass vessels and production refuse were found during the excavations in Area M. Some 42 vessels were chosen for presentation according to their state of preservation. They include free-blown bowls, beakers, bottles and lamp bowls (e.g., Figs. 16.12–16.15). The glass production refuse consists of few primary and secondary product remains, approximately 10 raw glass chunks in various sizes and a single moil (e.g., Fig. 16.16). The fragments of vessels recovered from the area can be assigned to the Late Roman through the Late Byzantine period. The coins recovered in the area support this date, where the earliest among the 36 identifiable coins found are dated to the mid-4th century CE (Chapter 18: Nos. 38–39; if one ignores an earlier Augustan-period coin, No. 6) and latest is assigned to the regnal years of Maurice Tiberius (582–602 CE); there is also a post-reform (8th century) Umayyad coin (Chapter 18: No. 360) that the excavators tend to consider intrusive.

AREAS N AND N1

Some 750 fragments of glass production refuse were found during the excavations in Areas N (2002) and Area N1 (2017). The glass production refuse consists of chunks of the furnaces floors *in situ*, and mud-bricks from the walls and ceilings of the raw glass furnaces, as well as primary product remains (Figs. 16.22–16.25 and see Chapter 9: Figs. 9.3–9.4, 9.8). Most of the finds recovered at these areas were found with pottery of the 6th–7th centuries CE.

AREA O

Some 435 fragments of glass vessels and production refuse were found during the excavations in Area O. Twenty vessels were chosen for presentation according to their state of preservation (e.g., Figs. 16.17–16.18). The glass production refuse consists of approximately 100 remnants of the floors, walls and ceilings of glass furnaces, as well as primary and secondary product remains (e.g., Figs. 16.19–16.21 and see Chapter 10: Fig. 10.1). Most of the fragments of vessels recovered at the area came from the refuse in the collecting vat of the winepress that was likely filled in the second half of the 6th century CE.

FIG. 16.2: AREA CC, REFUSE DUMP; BOWLS

No.	*Locus*	*Basket*	*Description*	*Notes*
1	30060	302708	Rim and wall fragment	Colorless with bluish tinge. Silver weathering and iridescent film. Flaring rounded rim, curving in rounded wall. Rim diameter: 12.2 cm
2	30082	304789	Rim and wall fragment	Colorless. Silver weathering and iridescent film. Curving in rounded rim, tapering wall. Rim diameter: 11 cm
3	30082	304789	Rim and wall fragment	Colorless with greenish tinge. Thick silver weathering and iridescent film. Slightly curving in rounded rim, curving in shallow wall. Rim diameter: 16.6 cm
4	30061	301104	Rim and wall fragment	Colorless. Silver weathering and iridescent film. Curving in cut-off rim, thin tapering wall. Rim diameter: 10.6 cm
5	30037	300680	Rim and wall fragment	Colorless with bluish tinge. Thick silver weathering and iridescent film. Straight cut-off rim, curving in carinated wall. Rim diameter: 13 cm
6	30061	301276	Rim and wall fragment	Colorless with bluish tinge. Thick silver weathering and iridescent film. Straight cut-off rim, curving in thick carinated wall. Rim diameter: 13.2 cm
7	30074	303132	Rim and wall fragment	Colorless. Thick silver weathering. Straight rounded rim, with applied fused thin horizontal blue trails. Tapering thin wall. Rim diameter: 12.4 cm
8	30082	303383	Rim and wall fragment	Colorless with bluish tinge. Thick silver weathering and iridescent film. Flaring rounded rim, with applied fused thin horizontal blue trails. Tapering thin wall. Rim diameter: 16 cm
9	30060	303235	Rim and wall fragment	Colorless. Silver weathering. Straight folded-out rim, with applied fused horizontal blue trails. Straight wall. Rim diameter: 14.2 cm

TYPOLOGY

THE GLASS VESSEL ASSEMBLAGE

BOWLS/BEAKERS WITH ROUNDED RIMS (FIGS. 16.2: 1–3; 16.12: 1; 16.17: 1–2)

Bowls with flared or curved-in rounded rims are well known in Israel from the Late Roman–Byzantine periods and can be identified as plain bowls or beakers, lamp bowls or wineglasses. Similar vessels were found in such contexts at Ḥorvat Ḥermeshit (Winter 1998: 174, Fig. 1: 2), Khirbat el-Fatuna (Jackson-Tal 2007a: Fig. 3: 2), Khirbat el-Niʿana (Gorin-Rosen and Katsnelson

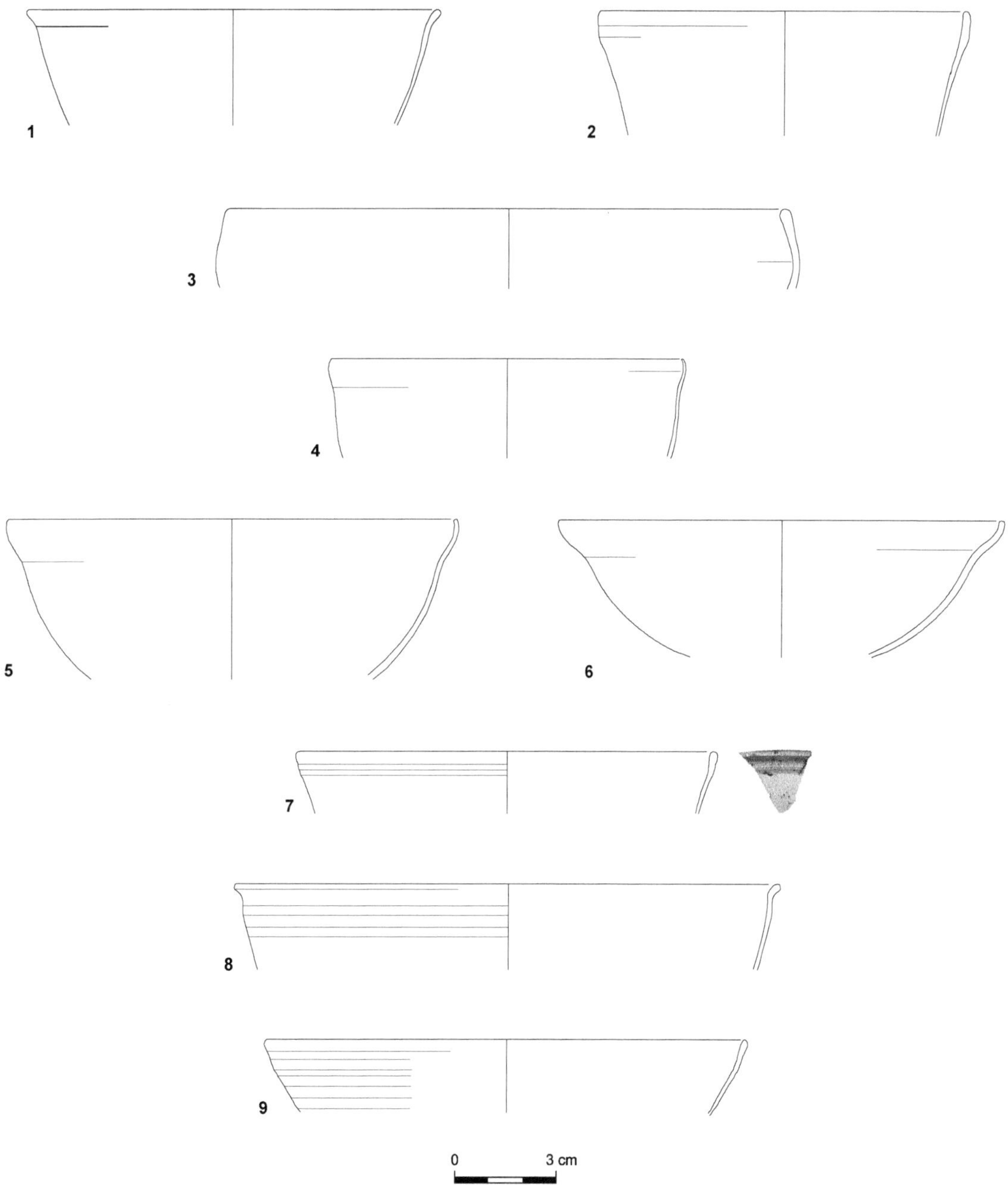

Fig. 16.2: Area CC, refuse dump; bowls.

2007: 116–117, Fig. 22: 7), Ḥorbat Roẓeẓ (Winter 2010: 148–149, Fig. 2: 1), Tel Shiqmona (Barash 2012: 131, Figs. 1: 8) and the factory dump at Jalame (Weinberg and Goldstein 1988: 40, 50, Figs. 4-1: 4, 4-10: 83).

BOWLS WITH CUT-OFF RIMS (FIG. 16.2: 4–6)

Such bowls, plain or decorated with horizontal or geometric wheel-cut incisions, are known in Late Roman contexts in several sites in the country. For example, similar bowls were found at the Khirbet al-ᶜAura/Tel Barukh cemetery (Jackson-Tal 2015a: 57, Fig. 1.49: 1), Samaria (incised, Crowfoot 1957b: 407, Fig. 93: 8), Ras el-ᶜEin, Shechem/Neapolis (Sarig 2009: 26–27, Pl. 17: 1) and Khirbat el-Niᶜana (Gorin-Rosen and Katsnelson 2007: 129, 132, Fig. 29: 1–2).

BOWLS/WINEGLASSES WITH HORIZONTAL BLUE TRAILS (FIGS. 16.2: 7–9; 16.11: 1–2; 16.12: 7; 16.17: 6)

Wineglasses or bowls with applied and fused trails, blue or in the color of the vessel, are well known in this region from the Late Roman–Byzantine periods. Similar bowls were found in the refuse pits at Khirbat el-Fatuna (Jackson-Tal 2007a: Fig. 3: 3), the workshop at Ramla (South) (Tal, Jackson-Tal and Freestone 2008: 87, Fig. 10: 1), at Khirbat el-Niᶜana (Gorin-Rosen and Katsnelson 2007: 84–85, Fig. 5: 1, 3, with discussion and additional references), at Ḥorbat Roẓeẓ (Winter 2010: Fig. 2: 3–4) and in the factory dump at Jalame (Weinberg and Goldstein 1988: 55–56, Fig. 4-17: 129).

FIG. 16.3: AREA CC, REFUSE DUMP; BOWLS (CONT.)

No.	*Locus*	*Basket*	*Description*	*Notes*
1	30074	303132	Rim and wall fragment	Colorless with bluish tinge. Thick silver weathering and iridescent film. Folded-out straight rim, beginning of thin straight wall. Rim diameter: 15.6 cm
2	30037	300680	Rim and wall fragment	Colorless. Thick silver weathering. Folded-out curving-in rim, beginning of curving in wall. Rim diameter: 15.6 cm
3	30100	303382	Rim and wall fragment	Colorless with greenish tinge. Thick silver weathering. Folded-out flaring rim, straight wall. Rim diameter: 20 cm
4	30074	303132	Rim and wall fragment	Colorless. Silver weathering. Folded-out straight rim, straight wall. Rim diameter: 20.6 cm
5	643	6549	Rim and wall fragment	Colorless with greenish tinge. Thick silver weathering and iridescent film. Folded-out straight rim, beginning of straight thin wall. Rim diameter: 25 cm
6	30069	302714	Rim and wall fragment	Colorless. Thick silver weathering and iridescent film. Flaring rounded rim, straight wall with hollow fold. Rim diameter: 9.8 cm
7	30123	304312	Rim and wall fragment	Colorless. Thick silver weathering and iridescent film. Straight rounded rim, straight wall with hollow fold. Rim diameter: 8.4 cm
8	30118	303735	Rim and wall fragment	Colorless. Thick silver weathering and iridescent film. Straight rounded rim, straight wall with hollow fold. Rim diameter: 9.8 cm
9	30071	301938	Rim and wall fragment	Colorless. Thick silver weathering and iridescent film. Straight rounded rim, straight wall with double hollow fold
10	30062	302703	Rim and wall fragment	Colorless. Thick silver weathering and iridescent film. Flaring rounded rim, straight wall with double hollow fold. Rim diameter: 12.6 cm
11	30061	301104	Base and wall fragment	Colorless with bluish tinge. Thick silver weathering and iridescent film. Convex base with folded high base-ring (pontil mark 1 cm), beginning of splaying out wall. Base diameter: 8 cm
12	30061	300899	Base and wall fragment	Colorless with bluish tinge. Thick silver weathering and iridescent film. Convex base with high uneven trailed base-ring (pontil mark 1 cm), beginning of splaying out wall. Base diameter: 6.8 cm

BOWLS WITH FOLDED-OUT RIMS (FIGS. 16.3: 1–5; 16.12: 2–3; 16.17: 3–4)

Bowls with folded-out rims are the most common glass finds in Late Roman and Byzantine levels, although they have also been found in earlier contexts. A single bowl is adorned with a fused blue trail (Fig. 16.17: 6). Similar bowls were found at Khirbet al-ʿAura/Tel Barukh cemetery (Jackson-Tal 2015a: 57, Fig. 1.49: 5–7), in burial caves near Ḥorbat Zikhrin (Jackson-Tal 2007b: 76*, Fig. 1: 1), at Ras el-ʿEin, Shechem/Neapolis (Sarig 2009: 23, Pl. 15: 1–4), in Caesarea (Israeli 2008: 376–377, Nos. 78–82), at Ḥorbat Roẓeẓ (Winter 2010: 147, Fig. 1: 2–4), at Khirbat el-Fatuna (Jackson-Tal 2007a: Fig. 3: 5) and at Khirbat el-Niʿana (Gorin-Rosen and Katsnelson 2007: 80, 129, Figs. 2: 1–5, 27: 3–8).

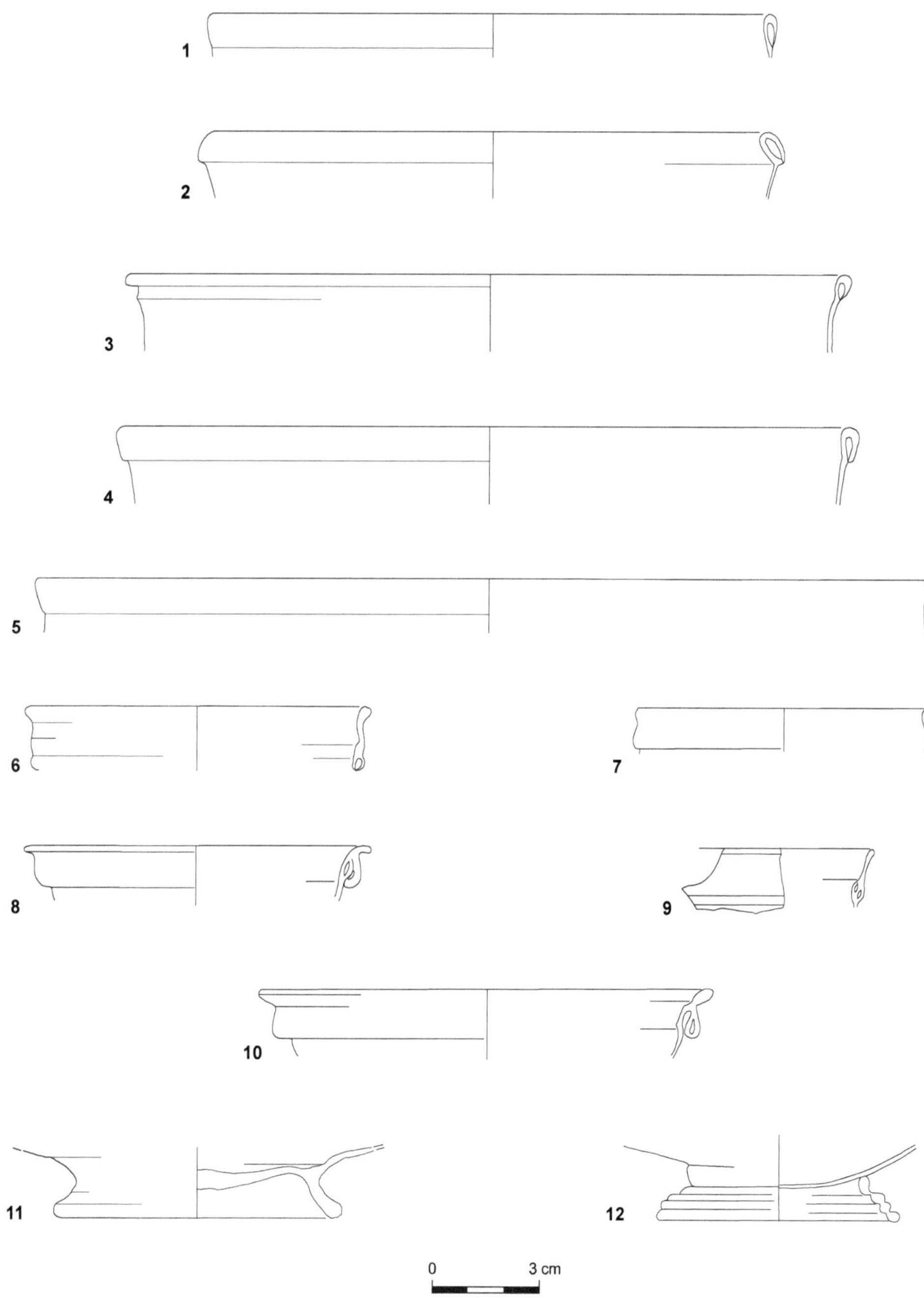

Fig. 16.3: Area CC, refuse dump; bowls (cont.).

Bowls with Tubular Folded Rims (Figs. 16.3: 6–10; 16.12: 4)

Such bowls with single or double tubular folds are well known throughout the Roman period. Bowls with tubular folds were found at Khirbet al-ᶜAura/Tel Barukh cemetery (Jackson-Tal 2015a: 57, Fig. 1.49: 4), in Samaria (trailed, Crowfoot 1957b: 414–415, Fig. 96: 4), at Ras el-ᶜEin, Shechem/Neapolis (Sarig 2009: 24, Pl. 15: 9–12), in Caesarea (Israeli 2008: 377, Nos. 84–85), at Khirbat el-Niᶜana (Gorin-Rosen and Katsnelson 2007: 81–83, 129, Figs. 3: 5–8, 28: 1–5) and in Ashqelon (Katsnelson 1999: 67*, Fig. 1: 1).

Bowls with Horizontal Ribs (Figs. 16.12: 5; 16.17: 5)

Bowls with a horizontal ribs below the rim are very common in Late Roman contexts in Israel. Similar bowls were found in the factory dump at Jalame (Weinberg and Goldstein 1988: 45, 47, Fig.

Figs. 16.4: Area CC, Refuse Dump; Beakers, Jugs and Bottles

No.	*Locus*	*Basket*	*Description*	*Notes*
1	30037	301043	Rim and wall fragment	Colorless. Thick silver weathering and iridescent film. Flaring rounded rim, straight wall with applied fused light blue trail below the rim. Rim diameter: 7.2 cm
2	30063	302	Base and wall fragment	Bluish-green. Thick silver weathering and iridescent film. Concave solid thick base (pontil mark 1.2 cm), beginning of curving out wall. Base diameter: 3.2 cm
3	691	6149	Base and wall fragment	Bluish-green. Thick silver weathering and iridescent film. Concave solid thick base (pontil mark 1 cm). Base diameter: 3.2 cm
4	659	6560	Base and wall fragment	Bluish-green. Thick silver weathering and iridescent film. Concave solid thick base (pontil mark 1 cm), beginning of curving up wall. Base diameter: 4 cm
5	30061	301104	Base and wall fragment	Light blue. Thick silver weathering and iridescent film. Concave tubular base-ring (pontil mark 1.4 cm), beginning of curving up wall. Base diameter: 4.2 cm
6	30061	301104	Base and wall fragment	Light greenish. Thick silver weathering and iridescent film. Concave tubular base-ring (pontil mark 1.4 cm), beginning of curving up wall. Base diameter: 5 cm
7	643	6549	Rim and neck fragment	Colorless with bluish tinge. Silver weathering and iridescent film. Flaring rounded rim, cylindrical neck. Rim diameter: 4 cm
8	30037	300650	Rim and neck fragment	Colorless. Thick black and silver weathering. Folded-in uneven straight rim, tapering neck. Rim diameter: 2.6 cm
9	30037	300650	Rim fragment	Colorless with bluish tinge. Thick silver weathering. Folded-in funnel-shaped rim. Rim diameter: 2.6 cm
10	30061	301104	Rim and neck fragment	Light bluish. Iridescent film. Folded-in funnel-shaped rim and beginning of cylindrical neck. Rim diameter: 5 cm
11	30061	301104	Rim and neck fragment	Light bluish. Silver weathering and iridescent film. Straight rounded rim, tapering into a cylindrical neck. Rim diameter: 4.2 cm
12	30074	303734	Rim fragment	Yellow-green. Silver weathering and iridescent film. Straight rounded rim, curving in cup-shaped. Rim diameter: 5.6 cm
13	30074	303237	Rim and neck fragment	Colorless. Thick silver weathering and iridescent film. Straight rounded rim and neck. Rim diameter: 4 cm
14	30100	303382	Rim and neck fragment	Colorless. Thick silver weathering. Straight rounded rim and neck. Rim diameter: 4.6 cm
15	30118	304014	Rim and neck fragment	Colorless. Thick silver weathering. Straight rounded rim and neck. Rim diameter: 4.6 cm

4–6), at Sumaqa (Lehrer-Jacobson 1999: 333, Fig. 1: 2–3), at Ḥorbat Roẓeẓ (Winter 2010a: 145, Fig. 1: 1) and in a winepress at Akhziv (Syon 1998: 94, Fig. 14: 2). Others were found in Late Roman burial caves in the Western Galilee, at Ḥanita (Barag 1978: 15, 17, Fig. 8: 26), near Kabri (Stern and Gorin-Rosen 1997: 19–20, Fig. 10: 6–7), near Ḥ. Sugar (Gorin-Rosen 1997a: 96–97, Fig. 5: 2–3), at Kisra (Stern 1997: 109, Fig. 2: 12), and in burial caves at Khirbat el-Shubeika (Gorin-Rosen 2002a: 290, Fig. 1: 2–3).

BOWLS WITH A SHALLOW SOLID BASE (FIG. 16.1: 5)

This type of base was used for bowls during the Late Roman–Byzantine periods. No exact parallel has been found for this base, as most bases common in these periods are tubular or pad-based.

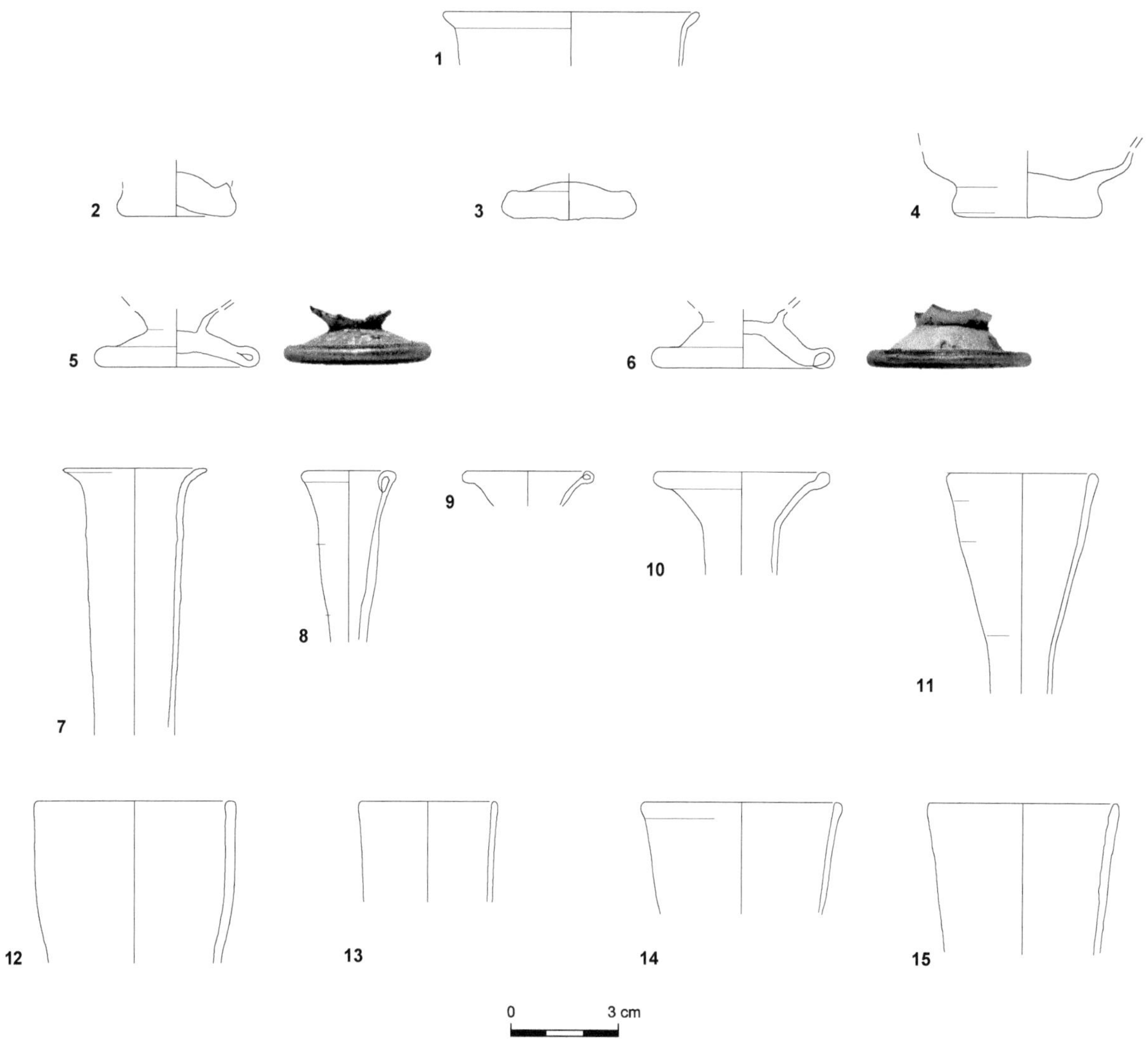

Figs. 16.4: Area CC, refuse dump; beakers, jugs and bottles.

Bowls with High Solid Base-Ring (Pad-Base) (Fig 16.3: 11)

High ring bases were a common type of bowl base found in Late Roman contexts at sites in Israel. Similar bases were found at Khirbet al-ᶜAura/Tel Barukh cemetery (Jackson-Tal 2015a: 60, Fig. 1.50: 1, with additional references), at Ras el-ᶜEin, Shechem/Neapolis (Sarig 2009: 28, Pl. 18: 1–3), in Caesarea (Israeli 2008: 376–377, Nos. 80–81), at Kefar ᶜAra (Sussman 1976: 99, Fig. 4: 12–15), at Khirbat el-Niᶜana (Gorin-Rosen and Katsnelson 2007: 86, 88, 132, 134, Figs. 6, 30) and in many burial caves in the Galilee, for example at Ḥurfeish (Gorin-Rosen 2002b: 144*–153*, Figs. 4–8, with additional references).

Bowls with High Tubular Base-Rings (Fig. 16.12: 12–13; 16.17: 10–12)

These pushed-in, tubular high bases are the most common feature in Late Roman and Byzantine deep or shallow bowls found in Israel. Similar bases were uncovered in large numbers at Khirbat el-Niᶜana, dated to the 4th–5th century CE (Gorin-Rosen and Katsnelson 2007: 86, 88, 132, 134, Figs. 6, 30: 1–3), in the factory dump at Jalame (Weinberg and Goldstein 1988: 41, Fig. 4-4), in a burial cave at Ḥanita (Barag 1978: 11, 13, 17, 21, 23, Figs. 6: 1, 5, 7: 9–10, 21, 8: 26, 10: 33–34, 11: 37–39), in a burial cave near Kabri (Stern and Gorin-Rosen 1997: 10, 12, Figs. 6: 2–3, 7: 9–10), at Asherat (Gorin-Rosen 1997b: 62, 66, Figs. 1: 2, 4: 1–2), in a burial cave at Kisra (Stern 1997: 106, Fig. 1: 1–2), in a burial cave at Khirbat el-Shubeika (Gorin-Rosen 2002a: Cave 1, 290, Fig. 2: 9, Cave 2, 303–304, Fig. 1: 1), at Ḥurfeish (Aviam and Gorin-Rosen 1997: 29–30, 32, Figs. 4: 5, 5: 9–10; and in Burial Cave D, Gorin-Rosen 2002b: 144*, 146*, 149*, Figs. 4: 10–11; 5, 7).

Bowls with High Trailed Base-Rings (Figs. 16.3: 12; 16.11: 3–5; 16.17: 9)

Trail bases were made by winding glass trails around a thickened flattened base to create a ring base for beakers and bowls. This base type is very common in Late Roman Palestine. Similar bases were

Fig. 16.5: Area CC, Refuse Dump; Bottles

No.	*Locus*	*Basket*	*Description*	*Notes*
1	30060	303235	Rim and neck fragment	Light blue. Silver weathering and iridescent film. Straight rounded rim and neck. Applied horizontal trail on the neck. Rim diameter: 5 cm
2	641	655	Rim and neck fragment	Colorless. Thick silver weathering and iridescent film. Straight rounded rim and neck. Applied multiple horizontal trail on the neck. Rim diameter: 3.8 cm
3	30061	301104	Rim and neck fragment	Colorless. Silver weathering and iridescent film. Straight rounded rim and neck. Applied multiple horizontal trail on the neck. Rim diameter: 5 cm
4	30061	301104	Rim fragment	Light bluish. Thick silver weathering and iridescent film. Flaring rounded funnel-shaped rim. Applied single thick horizontal trail below rim. Rim diameter: 8.4 cm
5	30074	628	Rim fragment	Colorless with bluish tinge. Thick silver weathering and iridescent film. Flaring rounded funnel-shaped rim. Applied multiple thick horizontal trails. Rim diameter: 5.8 cm
6	30036	300278	Rim and neck fragment	Colorless with bluish tinge. Thick silver weathering and iridescent film. Slightly flaring rounded funnel-shaped rim. Applied multiple thick horizontal trails to the rim, cylindrical neck. Rim diameter: 5.8 cm
7	30148	305266	Complete base and wall, neck fragment	Light blue. Silver weathering and iridescent film. Pear-shaped wall, concave base (no pontil mark). Beginning of cylindrical neck. Base diameter: 4.4 cm
8	30060	301784	Base and wall fragment	Colorless with greenish tinge. Silver weathering and iridescent film. Concave base (pontil mark 1 cm). Base diameter: 6.6 cm

found in Late Roman contexts such as Khirbet al-ᶜAura/Tel Barukh cemetery (Jackson-Tal 2015a: 61, Fig. 1.50: 3), at Ras el-ᶜEin, Shechem/Neapolis (Sarig 2009: 29, Pl. 18: 6–10), in Caesarea (Israeli 2008: 391, No. 259), at Khirbat el-Fatuna (Jackson-Tal 2007a: Fig. 3: 6), in large numbers at Khirbat el-Niᶜana (Gorin-Rosen and Katsnelson 2007: 88–90, 134, Figs. 7, 31) and in Ashqelon (Katsnelson 1999: 120*, Fig. 9: 5).

BEAKERS WITH FLARING RIMS AND SOLID BASES (FIGS. 16.1: 2; 16.4: 1–4; 16.12: 6, 8, 10–11; 16.17: 7–8)

Beakers with flaring rims, cylindrical or bag-shaped bodies and solid bases are well known in Late Roman Palestine. Similar rims of such vessels were found in such contexts at Ras el-ᶜEin, Shechem/Neapolis (Sarig 2009: 29, Pl. 18: 12–13), at Khirbat el-Niᶜana (Gorin-Rosen and Katsnelson 2007: 93, Fig. 8: 3), at Tel Shiqmona (Barash 2012: 131, Figs. 1: 8, 2: 15–16) and in the factory dump at Jalame (Weinberg and Goldstein 1988: 60, 62, 63, Figs. 4-23, 4-25). Similar bases were found in Late Roman contexts in large numbers at Khirbat el-Niᶜana, dated to the 4th–5th century CE (Gorin-Rosen and Katsnelson 2007: 93, 135, Figs. 8: 3–9; 32: 1–2, with additional references).

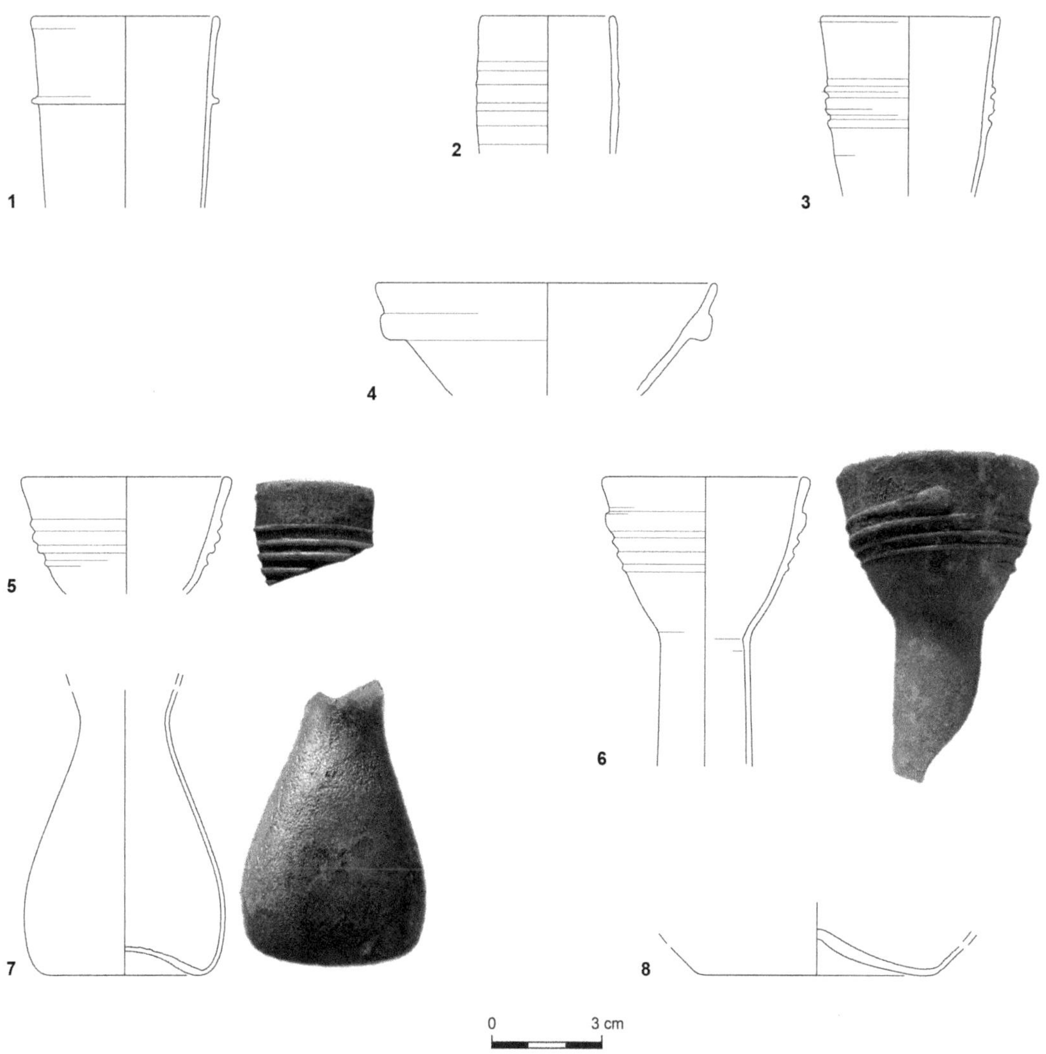

Fig. 16.5: Area CC, refuse dump; bottles.

BOWLS/JUGS WITH TUBULAR BASE-RINGS (FIGS. 16.4: 5–6; 16.11: 8)

Bowls and jugs with high tubular ring bases were very common during the Late Roman period. Similar vessels were found at Khirbet al-ᶜAura/Tel Barukh cemetery (Jackson-Tal 2015a: 61, Fig. 1.49: 8), at Ras el-ᶜEin, Shechem/Neapolis (Sarig 2009: 30, Pl. 18: 16–21), at Khirbat el-Niᶜana (Gorin-Rosen and Katsnelson 2007: 93, 135, Figs. 8: 11–12, 32: 5–6) and in the factory dump at Jalame (Weinberg and Goldstein 1988: Fig. 4-29: 229–231).

A BOTTLE WITH A FLARING RIM (FIG. 16.4: 7)

No exact parallel has been found for this vessel. The style and fabric indicate a general Late Roman–Byzantine date.

BOTTLES WITH FOLDED-IN RIMS (FIGS. 16.4: 8–10; 16.12: 9; 16.13: 9–11)

Bottles with folded-in rims, tapering (Fig. 16.4: 8), funnel-shaped (Fig. 16.4: 9–10; 16.13: 9–11) or straight (Fig. 16.12: 9) are known during the Late Roman and Byzantine periods. Similar bottles were found at Khirbet al-ᶜAura/Tel Barukh cemetery (Jackson-Tal 2015a: 61, Fig. 1.53: 1–2), at Ras el-ᶜEin, Shechem/Neapolis (Sarig 2009: 32, Pl. 19: 12–15), at Rafidiya, Shechem (Hizmi 1997: 126, Fig. 6: 14), at Khirbat el-Fatuna (Jackson-Tal 2007a: Fig. 3: 7) and at Khirbat el-Niᶜana (Gorin-Rosen and Katsnelson 2007: 98, 135, Figs. 11: 1–2, 33: 3).

FIG. 16.6: AREA CC, REFUSE DUMP (AND SURFACE FIND [L30053]); WINE GLASSES, LAMP BOWLS, WINDOW AND MISCELLANEA

No.	*Locus*	*Basket*	*Description*	*Notes*
1	30063	303302	Base and foot fragment	Colorless. Thick silver weathering and iridescent film. Concave tubular base, pushed in hollow cylindrical foot. Base diameter: 4 cm
2	30082	303383	Base, foot and wall fragment	Colorless. Thick silver weathering and iridescent film. Concave tubular base, pushed in short hollow cylindrical foot. Beginning of curving out wall. Base diameter: 3.4 cm
3	627	6241	Base, foot and wall fragment	Colorless. Thick silver weathering and iridescent film. Concave tubular base, pushed in short solid cylindrical foot. Beginning of curving up wall. Base diameter: 4 cm
4	30053	302728	Base, foot and wall fragment	Colorless. Thick silver weathering and iridescent film. Concave tubular base, pushed in short solid cylindrical foot. Beginning of curving up wall. Base diameter: 3.5 cm
5	623	6249	Base, foot and wall fragment	Colorless. Thick silver weathering and iridescent film. Concave tubular base, pushed in short solid beaded foot. Beginning of curving out wall. Base diameter: 5 cm
6	623	6189	Base and stem fragment	Light green. Silver weathering and iridescent film. Hollow cylindrical stem with flat base. Base diameter: 1 cm
7	30074	303132	Base and stem fragment	Colorless with bluish tinge. Silver weathering and iridescent film. Hollow cylindrical stem with flat base. Base diameter: 1.2 cm
8	643	6549	Base and stem fragment	Bluish-green. Silver weathering and iridescent film. Hollow cylindrical stem with flat base. Base diameter: 1.2 cm
9	30060	301784	Wall fragment	Yellow-green. Thick silver weathering and iridescent film. Curved wall with wide horizontal groove above four applied blue spots
10	30063	301936	Wall fragment	Colorless with greenish tinge. Silver weathering and iridescent film. Flat wall with little remains of rounded edge. Rim diameter: 26 cm

BOTTLES WITH STRAIGHT AND TAPERING RIMS AND NECKS (FIGS. 16.4: 11–15; 16.13: 2–4, 7–8; 16.18: 1–3)

Bottles with straight or tapering rims and necks and usually rounded or barrel-shaped walls are very well known from during the Late Roman and Byzantine periods. Similar bottles were found at Khirbet al-ᶜAura/Tel Barukh cemetery (Jackson-Tal 2015a: 67, Figs. 1.54: 2–3, 1.55: 1–2, with additional references), a burial cave in Khirbet al-Ḥadra (Jackson-Tal 2015b: 61, Figs. 2.10–2.11) and at Ras el-ᶜEin, Shechem/Neapolis (Sarig 2009: 31, Pl. 19: 1–3).

BOTTLES WITH STRAIGHT AND TAPERING TRAILED RIMS (FIGS. 16.5: 1–3; 16.13: 5–6)

Adding horizontal trails to the rim and neck of bottles was a very common motif during the Late Roman and Byzantine periods. Similar bottles were found at Khirbet al-ᶜAura/Tel Barukh cemetery (Jackson-Tal 2015a: 61, 67, Figs. 1.54: 1, 1.55: 1, with additional references) and at Ras el-ᶜEin, Shechem/Neapolis (Sarig 2009: 31, Pl. 19: 4–5).

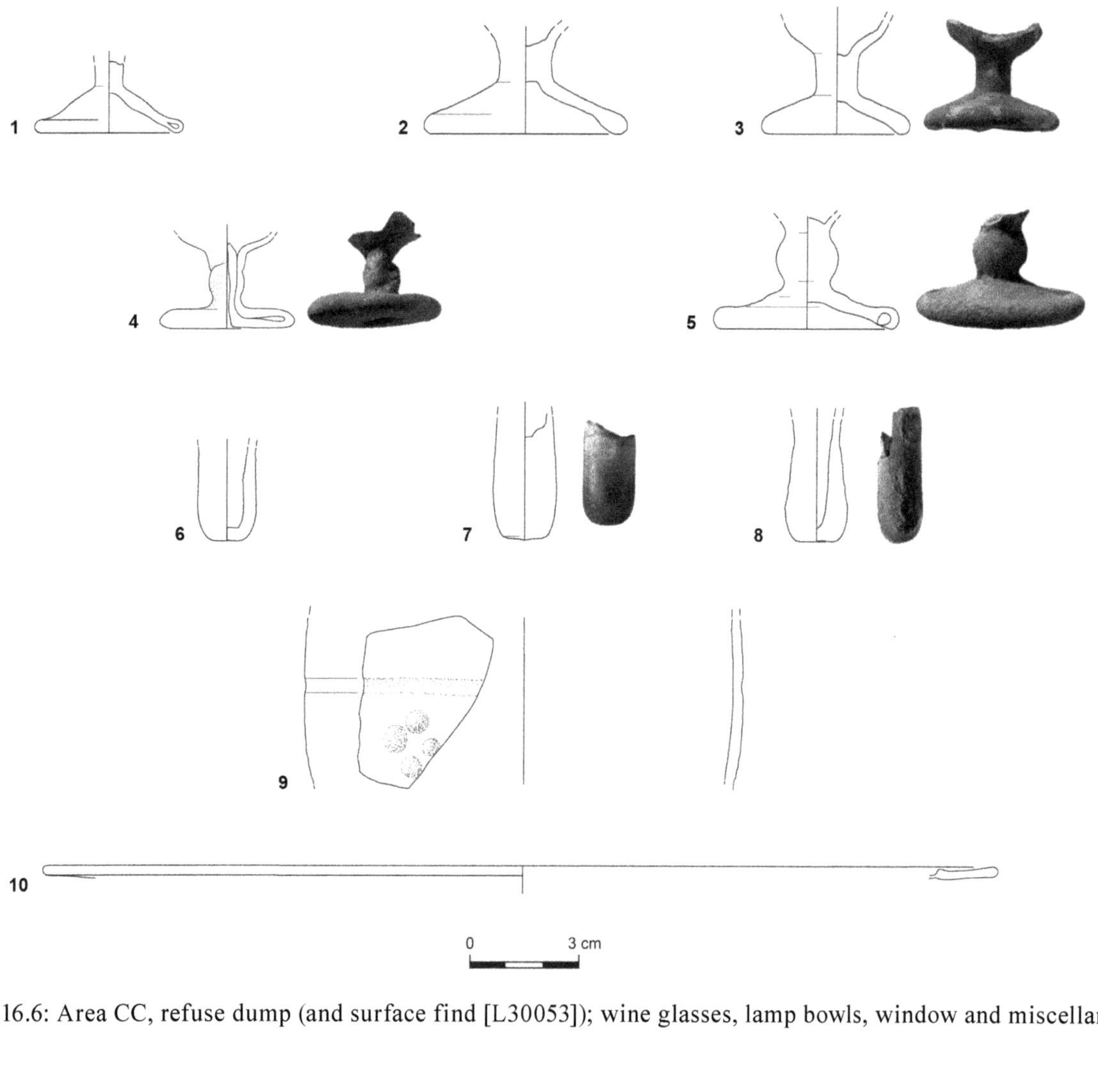

Fig. 16.6: Area CC, refuse dump (and surface find [L30053]); wine glasses, lamp bowls, window and miscellanea.

Bottles with Funnel-Shaped Trailed Rims (Figs. 16.5: 4–6; 16.11: 6–7; 16.13: 1; 16.18: 4)

These bottles are wide or narrow mouthed, decorated with single or multiple trails. Similar bottles with a single trail were found at Khirbet al-ʿAura/Tel Barukh cemetery (Jackson-Tal 2015a: 61, Fig. 1.53: 3, with additional references), at Ras el-ʿEin, Shechem/Neapolis (Sarig 2009: 31–32, Pl. 19: 7–11), at Khirbat el-Niʿana, dated to the 4th–5th centuries CE (Gorin-Rosen and Katsnelson 2007: 98, 135, 139, Figs. 11: 6, 13: 1, 33: 11) and in the factory dump at Jalame (Weinberg and Goldstein 1988: 69–70, Fig. 4-31: 265). Similar bottles with multiple trails were found at Khirbat el-Fatuna (Jackson-Tal 2007a: Fig. 3: 8) and at Khirbat el-Niʿana, dated to the 4th–5th centuries CE (Gorin-Rosen and Katsnelson 2007: 100–101, 103,139, Figs. 13: 34, 34: 5, with additional references).

Fig. 16.7: Area CC, Glass Furnace Remains

No.	*Locus*	*Basket*	*Description*	*Notes*
1	30060	302708	Seven wall furnace remains	Green. Silver weathering and iridescent film, lime deposits. Uneven chunks of mudbricks with a thin layer of glazed smoothed green glass in several shades. Thickness: 1.5–3.5 cm
2	30060	302708	Three chunks of furnace floor remains	Light blue. Silver weathering and iridescent film, lime deposits. Uneven chunks of mudbrick with a thick pointed and smoothed layer of translucent light blue glass mixed with the mudbricks and lime unevenly. Thickness: 2–3.5 cm

A BOTTLE WITH PEAR-SHAPED BODY (FIG. 16.5: 7)

Bottles with pear-shaped walls are known from Late Roman period sites, but are less common than their rounded counterparts. Similarly shaped bottles were found at Khirbet al-ᶜAura/Tel Barukh cemetery (Jackson-Tal 2015a: 61, Fig. 1.54: 1, with additional references) and in a burial cave at Khirbet al-Ḥadra (Jackson-Tal 2015b: 149, Fig. 2.12: 1).

FIG. 16.8: AREA CC, REFUSE DUMP; GLASS FURNACE REMAINS (CONT.)

No.	*Locus*	*Basket*	*Description*	*Notes*
1	30060	302708	Three chunks of furnace floor remains	Light blue and light green. Silver weathering and iridescent film, lime deposits. Uneven chunks of mudbrick with a thick pointed and smoothed layer of translucent light blue and green glass mixed with the mudbricks and lime unevenly. Thickness: 3–4.5 cm
2	30081	304153	Twenty-one chunks of furnace floor remains	Light green and yellow-green. Silver weathering and iridescent film, lime deposits. Uneven chunks of mudbrick with a thick pointed and smoothed layer of translucent light green and yellow-green glass mixed with the mudbricks and lime unevenly. Thickness: 2–4.5 cm

FIG. 16.9: AREA CC, REFUSE DUMP (AND SURFACE FIND [L30029]); PRIMARY PRODUCT REMAINS; RAW GLASS CHUNKS

No.	*Locus*	*Basket*	*Description*	*Notes*
1	30074	303132	Raw chunk	Green. Thick silver weathering and iridescent film, lime deposits. Uneven thick chunk. Thickness: 2 cm
2	30082	303510	Raw chunk	Bluish-green. Thick silver weathering and iridescent film, lime deposits. Uneven thick chunk. Thickness: 2 cm
3	30148	305280	Three raw chunks	Light blue. Silver weathering and iridescent film. Uneven small chunks. Thickness: 2 cm
4	30148	305280	Five raw chunks	Light blue, the central chunk with yellow-green streaks. Silver weathering and iridescent film. Uneven small chunks. Thickness: 1 cm
5	30029	300373	Thirteen raw chunks	Light blue. Silver weathering and iridescent film. Uneven small chunks. Thickness: 1–2 cm

BOTTLES WITH CONCAVE BASES (FIGS. 16.5: 8; 16.13: 12; 16.18: 5–6)

Concave bases were very common in bottles of the types discussed here. Parallels were found at Khirbet al-ʿAura/Tel Barukh cemetery (Jackson-Tal 2015a: Figs. 1.53–1.55).

WINE GLASSES (FIGS. 16.6: 1–5; 16.15: 1–5; 16.18: 7)

Wine glasses are one of the most common finds at Byzantine sites in the region, but have also been found in Late Roman contexts. The fragments found at the site are the lower parts of a straight and beaded foot and base. Similar fragments were found in Samaria (Crowfoot 1957: 416, Fig. 96: 11), at Khirbat el-Niʿana (Gorin-Rosen and Katsnelson 2007: 93–94, Fig. 8: 16–17), in Ashqelon (Katsnelson 1999: 71*, Fig. 2: 12–14), at Ḥorbat Roẓeẓ (Winter 2010: 149, Fig. 2: 2) and at Tel Shiqmona (Barash 2012: 131, Fig. 2: 19–21).

FIG. 16.10: AREA CC, PRIMARY PRODUCT REMAINS; GLASS LUMPS AND SECONDARY PRODUCTION REMAINS

No.	*Locus*	*Basket*	*Description*	*Notes*
1	30060	302708	Nine glass lumps	Black with porous limy white layer. Small uneven lumps of porous dark glass covered with a thick layer of limy/ashy material. Thickness: 1–3 cm
2	30060	302708	Refuse fragment	Light green. Silver weathering and iridescent film. Elongated flattened narrow drop with rounded base and marks of pincers on the elongation. Base diameter: 0.4 cm
3	643	6549	Two refuse fragments	Light blue. Thick silver weathering and iridescent film. Uneven deformed and twisted small fragments
4	30074	303384	Refuse fragment	Light blue. Thick silver weathering and iridescent film. Uneven deformed and twisted fragment with tooled side
5	30156	305318	Refuse fragment	Light green. Silver weathering and iridescent film. Uneven deformed and twisted small fragment

Kohl Tubes (Fig. 16.15: 6–7)

Cosmetic tubes were probably used to store kohl. They are known to have been used in the region during the Late Roman and the Byzantine period. The cosmetic tubes found at the site are double tubes, made by tooling a single tube into two usually uneven tubes. Many similar finds have been found in the region, to name a few: at Khirbet al-ᶜAura/Tel Barukh cemetery (Jackson-Tal 2015a: 75, Figs. 1.59: 1, 1.60: 1–3), in the Khirbet al-Ḥadra burial cave (Jackson-Tal 2015b: 160, Fig. 2.13: 2), in the Tell Qasile burial cave (Jackson-Tal 2015c: 184, Fig. 3.3: 3) and at Khirbat el-Niᶜana (Gorin-Rosen and Katsnelson 2007: 108–111, 114, 143, Figs. 17–21; 36).

Oil Lamps (Figs. 16.6: 6–8; 16.14: 1–8; 16.18: 8)

Suspended lamp bowls were hung from the ceiling by metal chains attached to three handles (Fig. 16.14: 1–3). An inner wick tube was used to hold the oil and burning thread. Such lamp bowls were extremely common in the area during the Byzantine period. Similar vessels were found in Samaria (Crowfoot

Fig. 16.11: Areas DD2 and DD3, Selected Glass Finds

No.	*Area*	*Locus*	*Basket*	*Description*	*Notes*
1	DD2	995	9957	Rim and wall fragment	Colorless with greenish tinge. Silver weathering. Slightly flaring rounded rim, with applied fused horizontal blue trail. Curving in, rounded wall. Rim diameter: 11 cm
2	DD2	995	9957	Rim and wall fragment	Colorless. Thick silver weathering. Flaring rounded rim, with applied fused thin horizontal blue trails. Tapering thin wall. Rim diameter: 13.2 cm
3	DD2	995	9957	Base and wall fragment	Colorless with greenish tinge. Silver weathering and iridescent film. Convex base with wound trailed base (pontil mark 1 cm), beginning of curving out wall. Base diameter: 6 cm
4	DD2	995	9957	Base and wall fragment	Yellowish-green wall and light blue base. Silver weathering and iridescent film. Convex base with wound trailed base (pontil mark 1.1 cm), beginning of curving out wall. Base diameter: 6 cm
5	DD2	994	9952	Base and wall fragment	Greenish-blue. Silver weathering and iridescent film. Convex base with wound trailed base (pontil mark 1 cm), beginning of curving up wall. Base diameter: 7 cm
6	DD2	991	9942	Rim and wall fragment	Colorless with greenish tinge. Silver weathering and iridescent film. Wide funnel-shaped rim with applied trails in the middle. Rim diameter: 8.2 cm
7	DD2	901	9935	Rim fragment	Colorless. Thick silver weathering and iridescent film. Flaring rounded funnel-shaped rim. Applied multiple thick horizontal trails, upper ones colorless, lower ones blue. Rim diameter: 7 cm
8	DD2	996	9972	Base and wall fragment	Bluish-green. Thick silver weathering and iridescent film. Concave tubular base (pontil mark 1 cm), beginning of curving up straight wall. Base diameter: 4.2 cm
9	DD2	904	9075	Furnace floor remains	Light blue. Silver weathering and iridescent film, lime deposits. Uneven large chunk of mudbrick with a thick pointed layer of translucent light blue glass mixed with the mudbricks and lime unevenly. Thickness: 2.5 cm
10	DD3	853	8053	Furnace wall and ceiling remains	Green. Silver weathering and iridescent film, lime deposits. Uneven chunk of mudbrick with a thin layer of glazed smoothed green glass in several shades. Dripping glass, indicates it was probably a ceiling part. Thickness: 2 cm
11	DD3	873	8087	Furnace wall and ceiling remains	White and green. Silver weathering and iridescent film, lime deposits. Uneven chunk of mudbrick with a thin layer of glazed smoothed white glass in the center, bordered by green glass, dripping in one corner-probably a ceiling part. Thickness: 3.5 cm

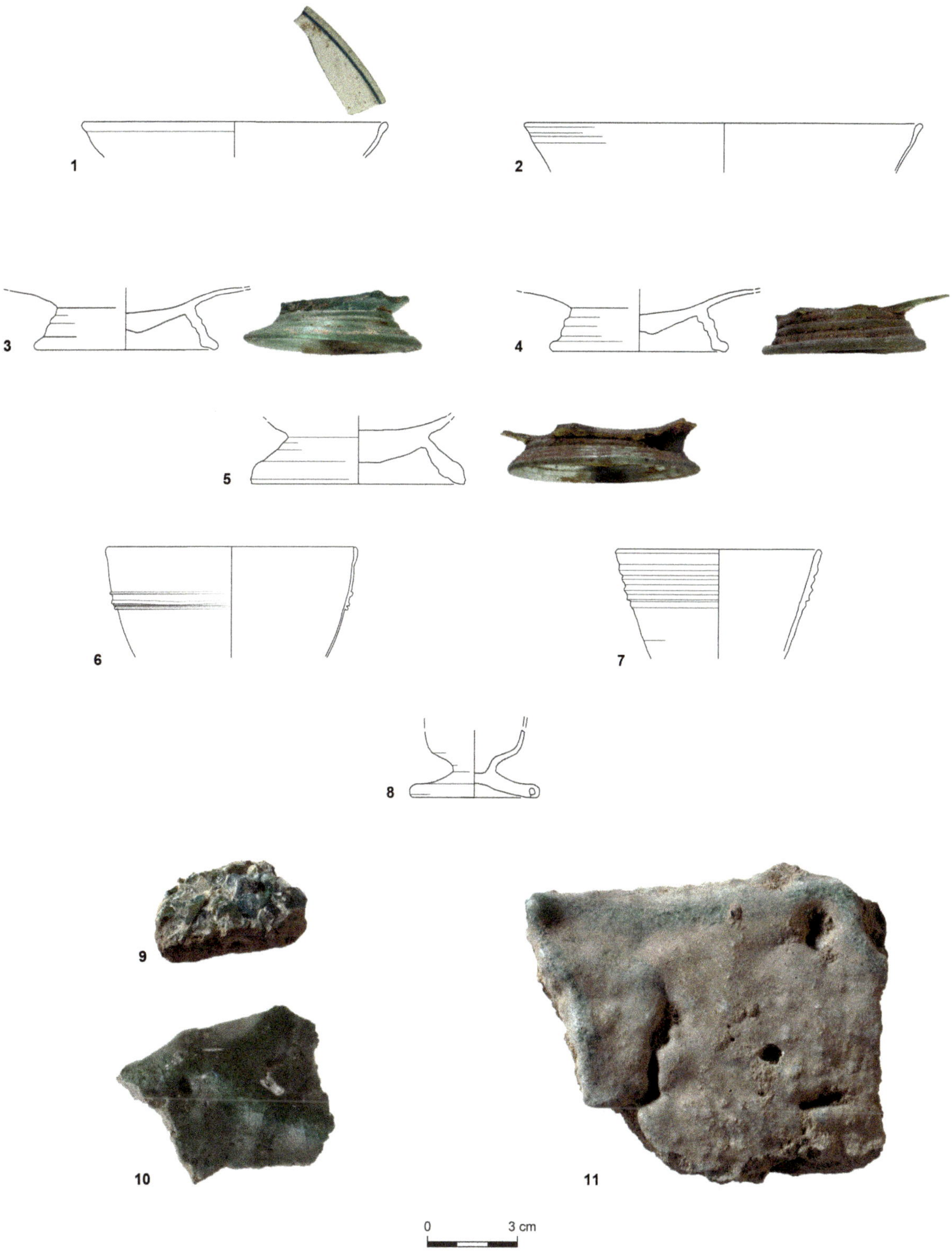

Fig. 16.11: Areas DD2 and DD3, selected glass finds.

1957: 418–419, Fig. 99: 2–3), at the workshop at Ramla (South) (Tal, Jackson-Tal and Freestone 2008: 87, Fig. 10: 2), at Khirbat el-Niᶜana (Gorin-Rosen and Katsnelson 2007: 116, 145, Figs. 22: 4–5; 37: 2–3), in Ashqelon (Katsnelson 1999: 78*, Fig. 5: 4), in Jerusalem, International Convention Center (Gorin-Rosen 2005: 205, Fig. 2: 34–35), in Jerusalem, City Wall (Gorin-Rosen 2006: 116* Fig. 14: 6–7) and many other sites.

Stemmed lamp bowls were placed in metal candelabra (Figs. 16.6: 6–8; 16.14: 4–8; 16.18: 8). They are well known in Israel in contexts dated to the Late Roman period and, most commonly, to the Byzantine period. The fragments from the site include only the lower hollow stem fragment. Similar fragments have been found in numerous excavations throughout the country, for example at Khirbet al-ᶜAura/Tel Barukh cemetery (Jackson-Tal 2015a: 75, Fig. 1.61), at Ras el-ᶜEin, Shechem/Neapolis (Sarig 2009: 35, Pl. 20: 23), at Rafidiya, Shechem (Hizmi 1997c: 126, Fig. 6: 3–4), at the workshop at Ramla (South) (Tal, Jackson-Tal and Freestone 2008: 87, Fig. 10: 3), at Khirbat el-Niᶜana (Gorin-Rosen and Katsnelson 2007: 116–117, 145, Figs. 22: 6–8, 37: 4), in Ashqelon (Katsnelson 1999: 78*–79*, Fig. 5: 5; Katsnelson and Jackson-Tal 2004: 107, Fig. 3: 3–4) and at many other sites.

Fig. 16.12: Area M, Selected Glass Vessels

No.	*Locus*	*Basket*	*Description*	*Notes*
1	7029	70922	Rim and wall fragment	Light blue. Silver weathering and iridescence. Flaring thickened rounded rim and curing in wall. Rim diameter: 16.4 cm
2	7050	71225	Rim and wall fragment	Light green. Silver weathering and iridescence. Folded out rim and tapering wall. Rim diameter: 12.4 cm
3	7010	70209	Rim and wall fragment	Colorless. Silver weathering and iridescence. Folded out rim and straight wall. Rim diameter: 22 cm
4	7000	70010	Rim and wall fragment	Colorless with greenish tinge. Silver weathering and iridescence. Slightly flaring rounded rim with tubular double fold on the straight wall. Rim diameter: 20 cm
5	7059	71320	Rim and wall fragment	Colorless with greenish tinge. Silver weathering and iridescence. Straight rounded rim with horizontal rib on the tapering wall. Rim diameter: 24 cm
6	7010	70567	Rim and wall fragment	Colorless. Silver weathering and iridescence. Flaring rounded rim and straight wall. Rim diameter: 8 cm
7	7029	70922	Rim and wall fragment	Colorless with bluish tinge. Silver weathering and iridescence. Flaring thickened rounded rim with applied deep blue horizontal trail. Curving in wall. Rim diameter: 10.2 cm
8	7059	71320	Rim and wall fragment	Colorless. Silver weathering and iridescence. Flaring thickened rounded rim, slightly tapering wall with applied horizontal trail. Rim diameter: 8 cm
9	7044	71002	Rim and wall fragment	Colorless. Thick white and silver weathering. Folded-in thick rim and straight wall. Rim diameter: 4 cm
10	7052	71241	Base and wall fragment	Yellow-green. Silver weathering and iridescence. Thick solid base and beginning of wall. Base diameter: 3.4 cm
11	7059	71320	Base and wall fragment	Yellow-green. Silver weathering and iridescence. Thick solid base and beginning of wall. Base diameter: 4 cm
12	7010	70271	Complete base and wall fragment	Light blue. Silver weathering and iridescence. Tubular flaring base with flat bottom and beginning of wall. Pontil scar 1 cm. Base diameter: 6.2 cm
13	7010	70374	Complete base and wall fragment	Light blue. Silver weathering and iridescence. Tubular flaring base with flat bottom and beginning of wall. Large pontil scar 1.5 cm. Base diameter: 8 cm

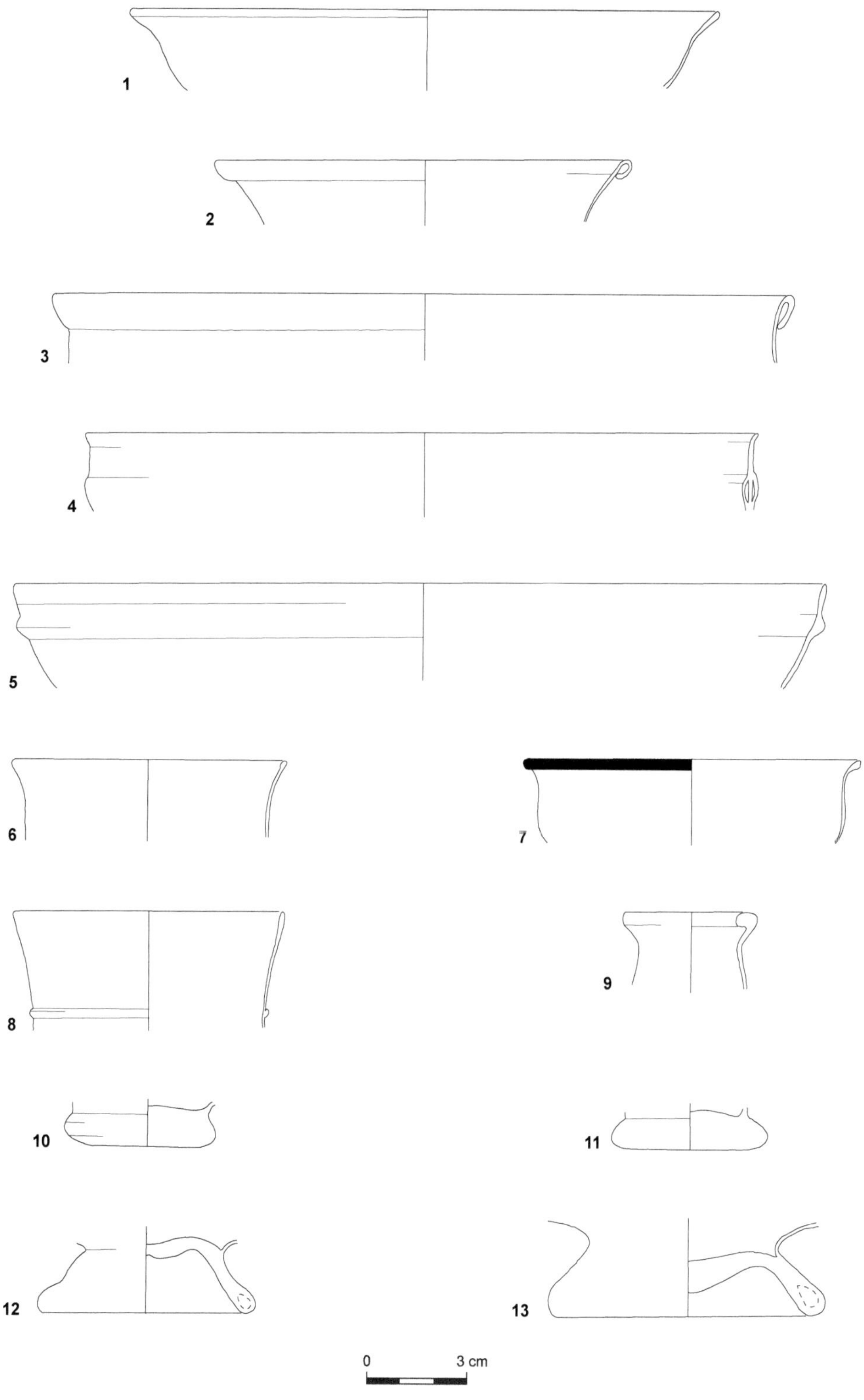

Fig. 16.12: Area M, selected glass vessels.

A DECORATED WALL FRAGMENT (FIG. 16.6: 9)

This wall fragment has a wide horizontal groove above four applied blue circular blobs. Vessels decorated in such a way are usually conical with cut-off rims and dated to the Late Roman and beginning of the Byzantine periods. They functioned as lamps or beakers, with many parallels in the eastern and western parts of the Roman Empire (Weinberg and Goldstein 1988: 89–91). Similar vessels were found in large numbers in the factory dump at Jalame where they were produced (Weinberg and Goldstein 1988: 87–94, Figs. 4-45–4-47), at Ras el-ʿEin, Shechem/Neapolis (Sarig 2009: 26–28, Pl. 17: 5, 7, 10–12), and at Khirbat el-Niʿana (Gorin-Rosen and Katsnelson 2007: 90, 92–93, Fig. 8: 1–2, with additional references).

A WINDOW PANE (FIG. 16.6: 10)

Glass window panes are known mostly in Byzantine contexts. They were placed in plaster frames in public and private buildings. Glass window panes are divided according to their shape, into rounded windows (the so-called bullseye type) and to square windows. The rounded type predominated with a variety in diameters and rim designs: folded, curving up or thickened (for a detailed discussion of techniques and chronology, see Meyer 1989). The window pane found at the site is probably rounded with

FIG. 16.13: AREA M, SELECTED GLASS VESSELS (CONT.)

No.	*Locus*	*Basket*	*Description*	*Notes*
1	7042	70958	Rim fragment	Colorless. Thick black and silver weathering and iridescence. Funnel-shaped rounded rim with applied thick horizontal trail. Rim diameter: 9.2 cm
2	7005	70042	Complete rim and neck and beginning of wall	Light blue. Silver weathering and iridescence. Uneven funnel-shaped rounded rim, tapering neck and beginning of sloping shoulder. Rim diameter: 3 cm
3	7050	71225	Complete rim and neck and beginning of wall	Colorless with bluish tinge. Silver weathering and iridescence. Straight funnel-shaped rounded rim, tapering elongated neck and beginning of shoulder. Rim diameter: 3 cm
4	7010	70209	Rim and wall fragment	Colorless with bluish tinge. Silver weathering and iridescence. Straight rounded rim, tapering elongated neck. Rim diameter: 4 cm
5	7010	70374	Rim fragment	Colorless with bluish tinge. Silver weathering and iridescence. Straight rounded rim with applied thin horizontal trails. Rim diameter: 4 cm
6	7029	70922	Rim fragment	Colorless with bluish tinge. Silver weathering and iridescence. Straight rounded rim, with applied blue horizontal trails, thick on the rim, thin below. Rim diameter: 4.6 cm
7	7044	71002	Rim fragment	Colorless with bluish tinge. Silver weathering and iridescence. Flaring rounded rim, tapering in. Rim diameter: 8 cm
8	7042	71009	Rim fragment	Colorless with bluish tinge. Silver weathering and iridescence. Folded in funnel-shaped rim. Rim diameter: 5 cm
9	7050	71225	Rim fragment	Colorless with bluish tinge. Silver weathering and iridescence. Folded in funnel-shaped rim. Rim diameter: 3.6 cm
10	7059	71320	Rim fragment	Colorless with greenish tinge. Silver weathering and iridescence. Folded in rim, tapering in. Rim diameter: 8 cm
11	7042	70958	Rim fragment	Colorless with greenish tinge. Silver weathering and iridescence. Folded in funnel-shaped rim. Rim diameter: 6.6 cm
12	7007	70207	Base and wall fragment	Colorless with bluish tinge. Silver weathering and iridescence. Concave base and curving wall. Base diameter: 4.6 cm

a rounded rim. Rounded window panes were found in a monastic building and settlements at Yavneh Yam (Vitto 1998: 111–112, Fig. 4: 1–2), at Khirbat Tabaliya (Gorin-Rosen 2000a: 92*–93*, Fig. 3: 40) and at Jerusalem, City Wall (Gorin-Rosen 2006: 116*–117* Fig. 14: 8). Others were found in South Sinai (Gorin-Rosen 2000b: 238–240, Figs. 3, 4: 1–8, with additional references).

Bracelets (Fig. 16.15: 8–9)

Two ribbed and twisted bracelets were found in Area M. Ribbed bracelets are known from the Byzantine period (Spaer 2001: 195–196, 199–200, No. 449) and twisted bracelets from the Late Roman and Byzantine periods (Spaer 2001: 194, 201, Nos. 462–465).

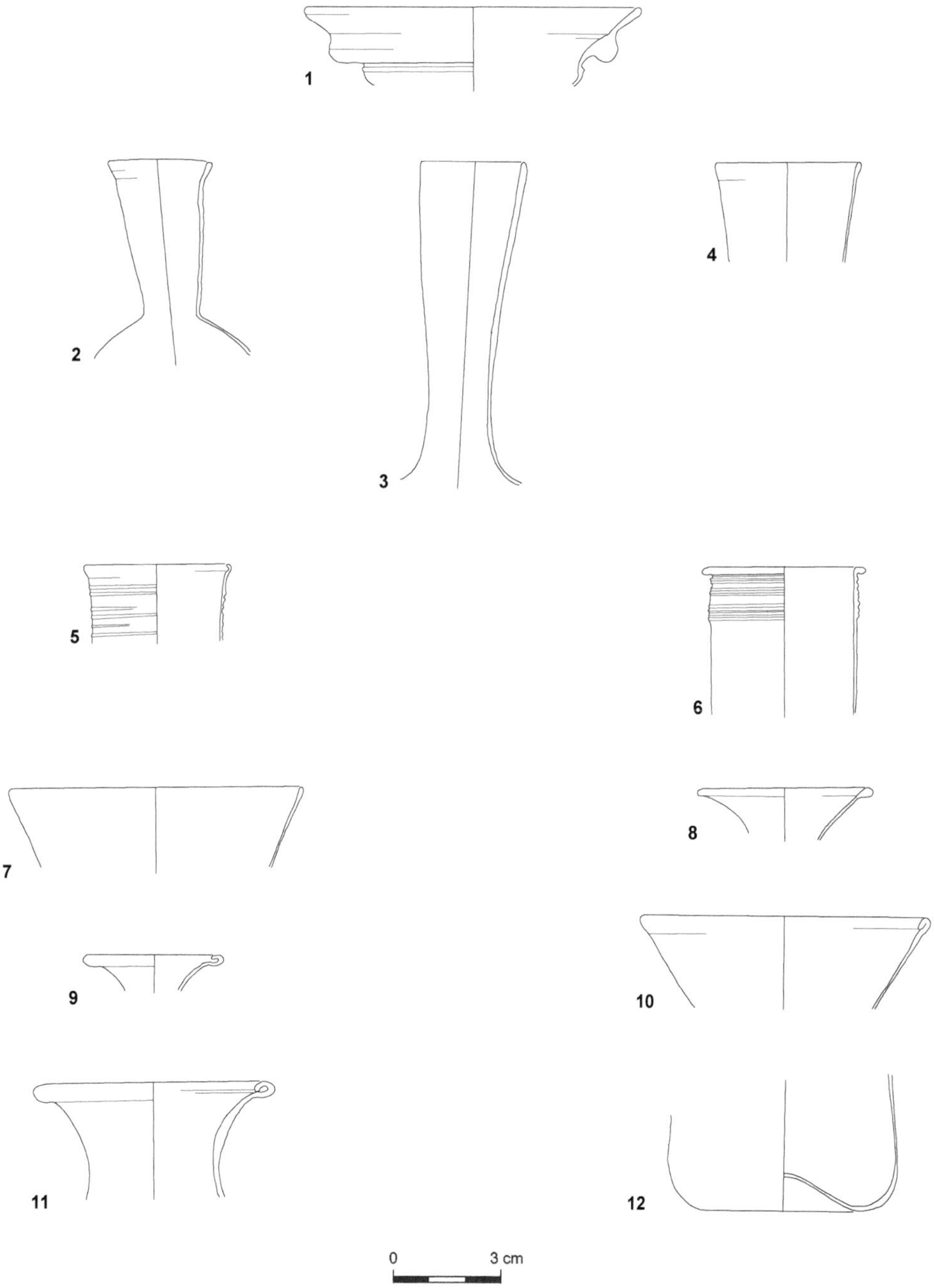

Fig. 16.13: Area M, selected glass vessels (cont.).

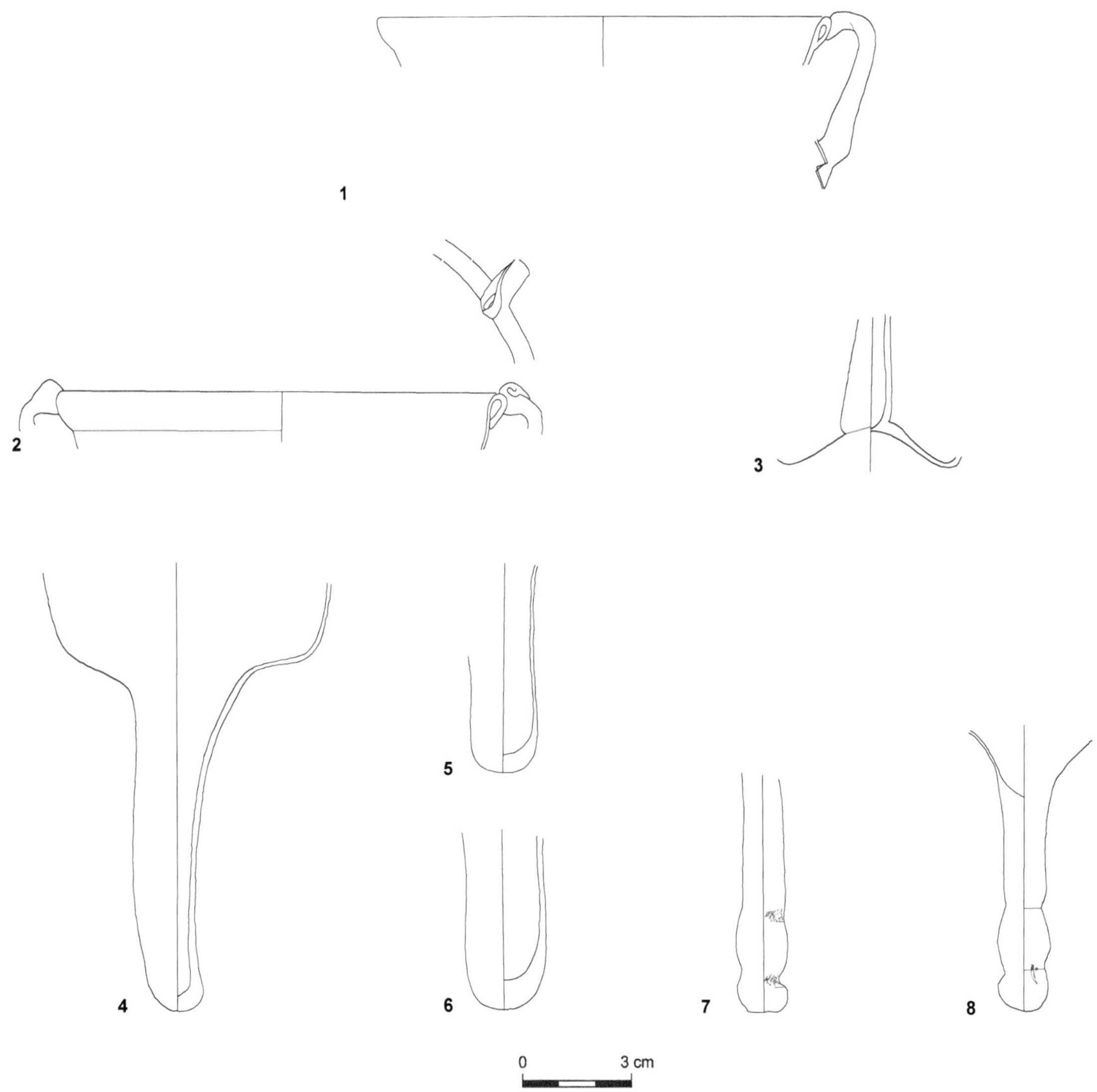

FIG. 16.14: AREA M, SELECTED GLASS VESSELS (CONT.)

No.	*Locus*	*Basket*	*Description*	*Notes*
1	7007	70207	Rim and wall fragment	Light blue. Silver weathering and iridescence. Folded out rim with rounded uneven handle, beginning of wall. Rim diameter: 12.2 cm
2	7029	70825	Rim and wall fragment	Light green. Silver weathering and iridescence. Folded out rim with beginning of handle. Rim diameter: 12.2 cm
3	7010	70675	Base and wick tube fragment	Light blue. Silver weathering and iridescence. Concave base with pontil scar (1 cm). Small uneven hollow wick tube
4	7010	70374	Complete stem and bowl fragment	Light blue. Silver weathering and iridescence. Uneven hollow stem and beginning of rounded bowl. Base diameter: 0.6 cm
5	7007	70207	Stem fragment	Light green. Silver weathering and iridescence. Cylindrical hollow stem. Base diameter: 0.8 cm
6	7024	70531	Stem fragment	Light blue. Silver weathering and iridescence. Cylindrical hollow stem. Base diameter: 0.8 cm
7	7010	70374	Stem fragment	Light blue. Silver weathering and iridescence. Solid stem pinched unevenly near the base. Base diameter: 1 cm
8	7010	70374	Stem and wall fragment	Light blue. Silver weathering and iridescence. Solid stem pinched unevenly near the base. Beginning of curving wall. Base diameter: 1 cm

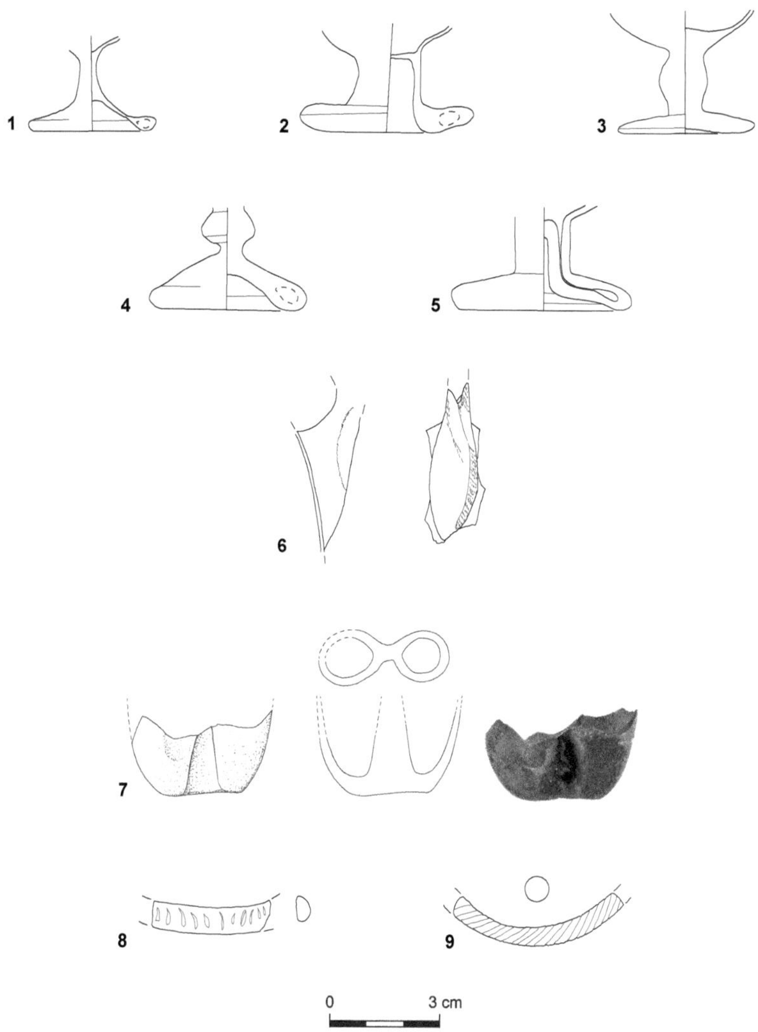

FIG. 16.15: AREA M, SELECTED GLASS VESSELS (CONT.)

No.	*Locus*	*Basket*	*Description*	*Notes*
1	7010	70209	Complete base and foot, wall fragment	Light blue. Thick silver weathering and iridescence. Concave tubular base, narrow foot and beginning of curving wall. Base diameter: 3.2 cm
2	7029	70097	Complete base and foot, wall fragment	Light blue. Thick silver weathering and iridescence. Concave tubular base, wide foot and beginning of curving wall. Base diameter: 2.4 cm
3	7010	70209	Complete base and foot, wall fragment	Light blue. Thick silver weathering and iridescence. Flat base, rounded foot and beginning of curving wall. Base diameter: 4 cm
4	7010	70209	Complete base and foot	Light blue. Thick silver weathering and iridescence. Concave tubular base, beaded foot. Base diameter: 4 cm
5	7042	71136	Complete base and foot	Light blue. Thick silver weathering and iridescence. Flat tubular base, straight foot. Base diameter: 4.6 cm
6	7010	70209	Handle and wall fragment	Light blue. Thick silver weathering and iridescence. Beginning of curving up handle and curving wall
7	7010	70567	Complete base and tubes fragment	Light blue. Thick silver weathering and iridescence. Flat base, double uneven tubes. Base diameter: 2.2 cm
8	7046	71142	Bracelet fragment	Opaque appearing black. Flattened semi-circular section ribbed bracelet
9	7042	71202	Bracelet fragment	Opaque appearing black. Rounded section twisted bracelet

THE GLASS REFUSE

Glass refuse indicating primary and secondary glass production was discovered in the areas surrounding the Byzantine-period town. The finds include furnace remains as well as primary and secondary product remains. The furnace remains that came from Areas CC and M were found in dumps, indicating a dismantling of the furnace structure whose original location remains unknown. The finds from Area O include remains of a dismantled furnace *in situ*. Additional furnace remains were found in the *in situ* furnace discovered in Area N and in the disturbed furnace remains in Area N1 (see below and Chapter 9, above).

The primary and secondary glass refuse unearthed in the different areas comprises a large part of the glass assemblage. It consists of approximately 3000 fragments with an estimated weight of around 150 kg. These remains include refuse from the floors, walls and ceilings of glass furnaces, raw chunks and vessel production remains.

Glass Furnace Remains

Around 750 small, medium and large chunks and fragments of bricks (ranging from 3.5 × 2 cm to 12 10 cm) from the melting chamber/tank floor, walls and vaulted ceiling were found (Figs. 16.1: 3; 16.7–16.8; 16.16: 1–2; 16.19; 16.22–16.25). The wall and ceiling remains include thick mudbricks with a thin layer of glazed smoothed glass ranging from white to light green and deep green glass (Fig. 16.1: 3; 16.7: 1; 16.11: 10–11; 16.19: 1–3). Several large chunks and fragments of bricks (ranging from 3.50 × 2.00 cm to 12 × 10 cm) from the melting chamber walls with a thin layer of glazed either rough or smoothed glass were found in Area N (16.22–16.23). The texture of the glass and color are probably the result of heating the glass to very high temperatures and points of different oxidation throughout the furnace. The floor remains (Fig. 16.7: 2; 16.8: 1–2; 16.11: 9; 16.16: 1–2; 16.19: 4–7; 16.24–16.25) include thick mudbricks with a layer of smoothed translucent glass or more often a pointed layer of translucent glass mixed unevenly with the mudbricks and lime. The glass colors vary from light green to bluish-green and yellowish-green. Similar remains were found in other areas at Apollonia, in Area N (and Area N1), where a glass furnace was unearthed (Chapter 9; see also Tal, Jackson-Tal and Freestone 2004) and in Area O (Chapter 10, above) where remains of what is likely another dismantled furnace was excavated (Freestone, Jackson-Tal and Tal 2008: 70). Other similar furnace remains were found at Khirbat el-Niᶜana (Gorin-Rosen and Katsnelson 2007: 127, 129, Fig. 25: 21–22). Primary furnaces with similar remains were found at several sites in Israel, at Bet Eliᶜezer and at Bet Sheᶜarim (see discussion in Gorin-Rosen 2000c: 52–56).

Fig. 16.16: Area M, Glass Furnace Remains; Secondary Production Remains

No.	*Locus*	*Basket*	*Description*	*Notes*
1	7010	70566	Five chunks of furnace floor remains	Light blue. Silver weathering and iridescent film, lime deposits. Uneven chunks of mudbrick with a thick pointed and smoothed layer of translucent light blue glass mixed with the mudbricks and lime unevenly. Thickness: 3–4.5 cm
2	7019	70568	Three chunks of furnace floor remains	Light blue. Silver weathering and iridescent film, lime deposits. Uneven chunks of mudbrick with a thick pointed and smoothed layer of translucent light blue glass mixed with the mudbricks and lime unevenly. Thickness: 3–4.5 cm
3	7033	70252	Moil fragment	Light green. Silver weathering and iridescence. Cylindrical fragment cut straight on one end and uneven on the other. Diameter: 2 cm

Primary Product Remains

Around 1,700 small and medium raw glass chunks (ranging from 2.50 × 1.50 cm to 7 × 6 cm) were found (Fig. 16.9: 1–5; 16.20; 16.21: 1–2). They are made mostly of bluish-green but also of yellowish-green and light green glass, covered with a layer of silver weathering. They were either broken from larger chunks, used to produce vessels or melted in the furnace as cullet. Some have already been published in the past from the furnace unearthed in Area N (Tal, Jackson-Tal and Freestone 2004: 57, Fig. 7), from the refuse pit of Area M and the dismantled furnace remains in Area O (Freestone, Jackson-Tal and Tal 2008: 67–68, 70, Fig. 2). Similar remains were found in several secondary workshops in the country, at Samaria, Sepphoris and Bet Shean (Gorin-Rosen 2000c: 52–60, with additional references), in Ramla (South) (Freestone, Jackson-Tal and Tal 2008: 84–85, Fig. 6) and at Khirbat el-Niʿana (Gorin-Rosen and Katsnelson 2007: 127, 127, Fig. 25: 9–20).

About 450 small (1–4 cm) rounded and uneven lumps of porous dark glass covered with a thick layer of limy/ashy material were found (Figs. 16.1: 4; 16.10: 1). These lumps may be waste from the mixing of raw glass in the furnace. They may have been left on the floor and sides of the furnace, thus becoming contaminated with lime, or they may have been re-melted with cullet. The material covering these lumps may be ash or a fuel-ash slag as discovered in Ramla (South) (Tal, Jackson-Tal and Freestone 2008: 85–86, Fig. 7).

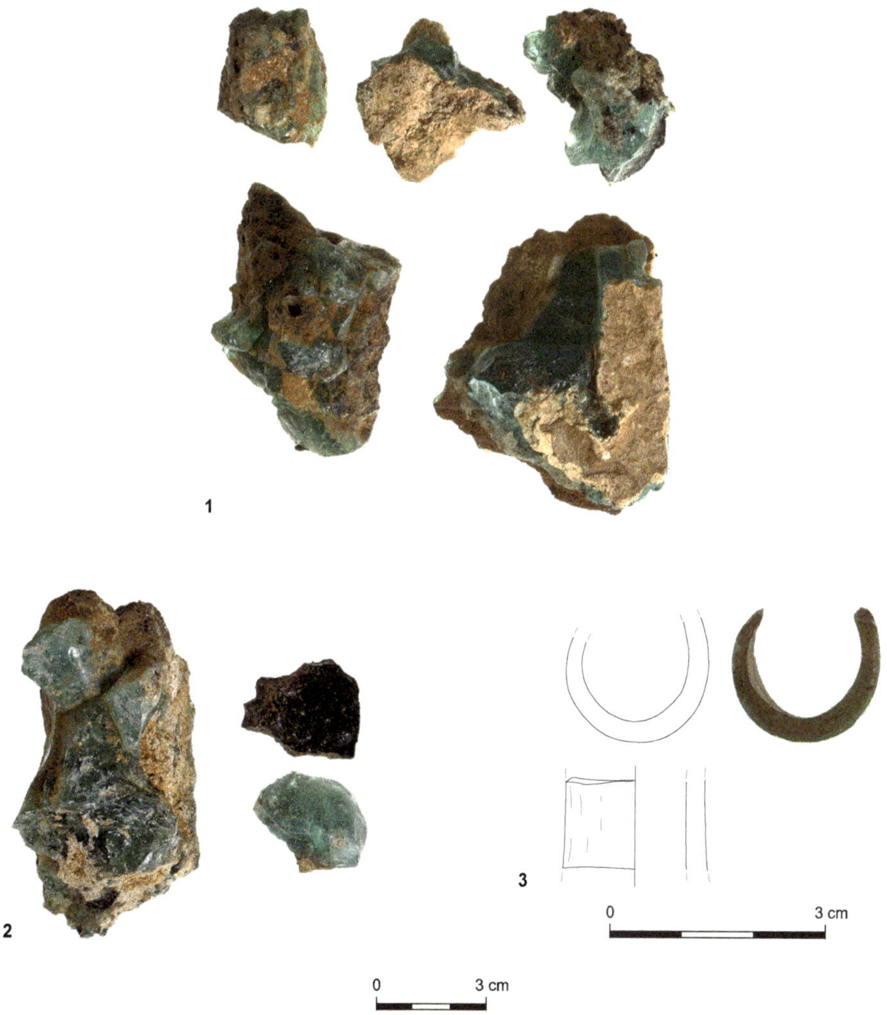

Fig. 16.16: Area M, glass furnace remains; secondary production remains.

SECONDARY PRODUCTION REMAINS

About 100 fragments of working debris: flattened drops, deformed melted pieces, and threads made of bluish-green glass and moils were found in Areas CC, M and O; these were covered with silver weathering and iridescent film (Figs. 16.1: 1, 6; 16.10: 2–5; 16.16: 3; 16.21: 3–4). These objects are typical byproducts of the making of glass vessels. The drops (Figs. 16.1: 6; 16.10: 2) are probably an indication of testing the properties of the glass before starting the forming process. Another indication of glass testing is evident in the flattened piece (Fig. 16.1: 1) that is pinched in the center. A small gob of glass was gathered from the furnace on the end of a pontil, hung down to form an elongated flattened drop and tested by pincers to determine its viscosity and quality and therefore suitability for glass vessel formation (Weinberg 1988: 36). Similar drops were found in the factory dump refuse at Jalame (Weinberg 1988: 36, Pl. 3-8: B, with discussion) and at Khirbat el-Niᶜana (Gorin-Rosen and Katsnelson 2007: 127, 145, Figs. 25: 5–8; 38). Small deformed pieces, representing by-products of the blowing process, were also found (Figs. 16.10: 3–5; 16.21: 3). Similar pieces were found in the factory dump refuse at Jalame (Weinberg 1988: 35, Pl. 3-8: A) and in a glass workshop at Ramla (South) (Tal, Jackson-Tal and Freestone 2008: 87, Fig. 9). Two moils were found as well (Figs. 16.16: 3; 16.21: 4). Moils are waste glass that remains around the end of the blowing tube after the vessel has been removed. These moils were found in Areas M and O and are fragments of cylindrical rods, with one end cut off straight and the other end left rounded and uneven. The moils (diameter 2–2.2 cm) clearly indicate the use of blowing tubes for the production of glass at the site. Similar moils were found at Jalame (Weinberg 1988: 35, Pl. 3-5: E), at Ramla (South) (Tal, Jackson-

FIG. 16.17: AREA O (LOCUS 8061), SELECTED GLASS VESSELS

No.	*Description*	*Notes*
1	Rim and wall fragment	Light blue. Silver weathering and iridescence. Curving in thickened rim and curving in wall. Rim diameter: 16.4 cm
2	Rim and wall fragment	Colorless with bluish tinge. Silver weathering and iridescence. Curving in thickened rim and curving in wall. Rim diameter: 18.4 cm
3	Rim and wall fragment	Light blue. Silver weathering and iridescence. Folded out straight rim and tapering wall. Rim diameter: 13.4 cm
4	Rim and wall fragment	Colorless. Silver weathering and iridescence. Folded out straight rim and curving in S shaped wall. Rim diameter: 16.4 cm
5	Rim and wall fragment	Light blue. Silver weathering and iridescence. Slightly flaring rim and tapering wall with horizontal rib. Rim diameter: 16.5 cm
6	Rim and wall fragment	Bluish-green. Silver weathering and iridescence. Folded out rim with fused in blue trails and curving wall. Rim diameter: 20.2 cm
7	Base and wall fragment	Bluish-green. Silver weathering and iridescence. Thick solid base and beginning of wall. Base diameter: 3.4 cm
8	Base and wall fragment	Bluish-green. Silver weathering and iridescence. Thick solid base and beginning of wall. Base diameter: 3.2 cm
9	Base and wall fragment	Colorless with bluish tinge. Silver weathering and iridescence. Applied trail base and beginning of wall. Base diameter: 5.2 cm
10	Base and wall fragment	Bluish-green. Silver weathering and iridescence. High tubular base-ring and beginning of wall. Base diameter: 6.8 cm
11	Base and wall fragment	Colorless with bluish tinge. Silver weathering and iridescence. High tubular base-ring, flat base and beginning of wall. Base diameter: 7.2 cm
12	Base and wall fragment	Bluish-green. Silver weathering and iridescence. High tubular base-ring, flat base with pontil mark (1 cm) and beginning of wall. Base diameter: 8 cm

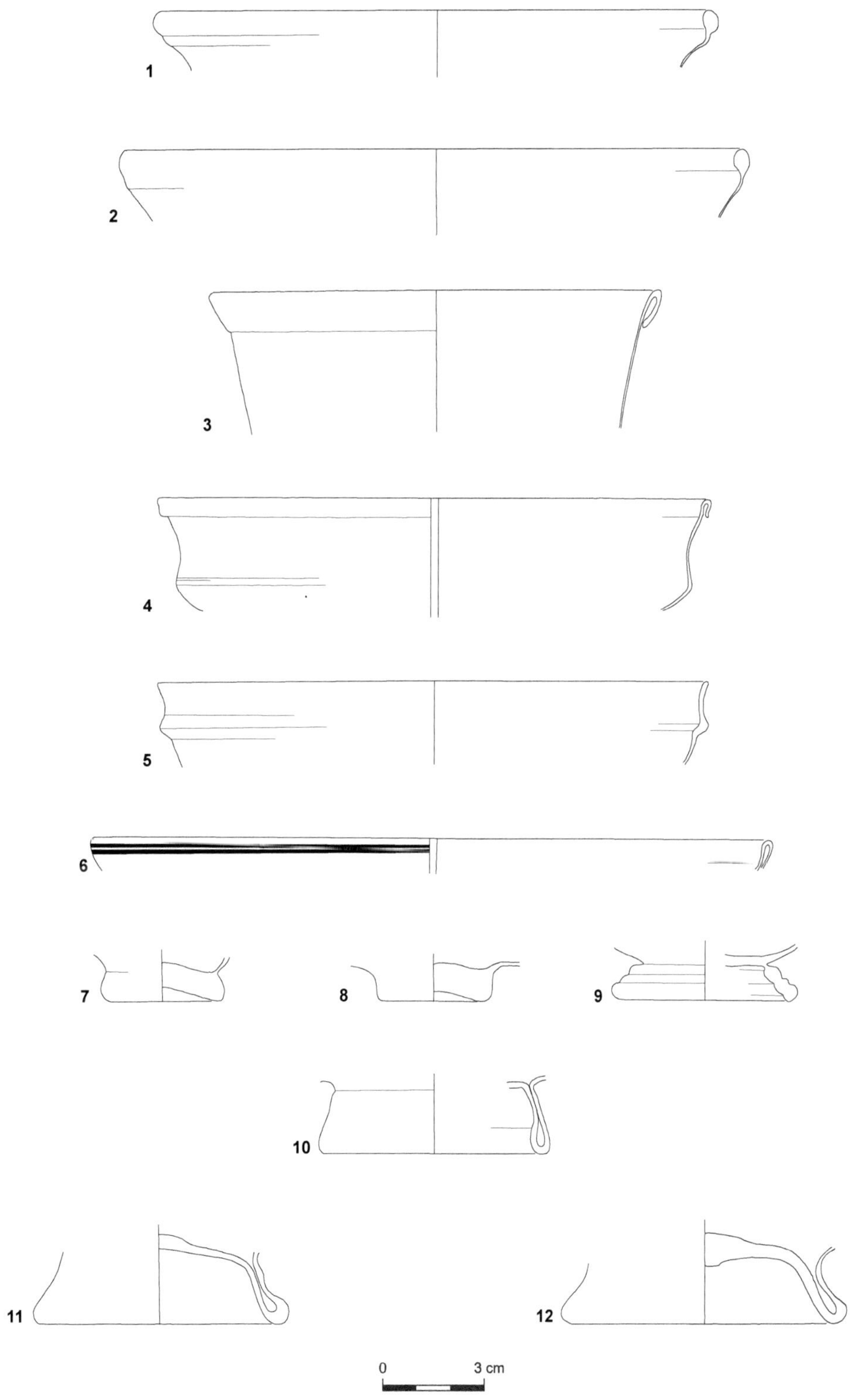

Fig. 16.17: Area O (Locus 8061), selected glass vessels.

Tal and Freestone 2008: 86–87, Fig. 8) and at Tel Aviv, Khirbet al-Ḥadra (Freestone *et al.* 2015: 48, Fig. 7, although in an Early Islamic context). Although only two moils were found, the overall evidence of test drops and deformed glass pieces clearly indicate that glass vessel production took place at the site.

DISCUSSION

Large numbers of glass vessels and as well as considerable amounts of production refuse were found in the various areas surrounding the site of Apollonia (Byzantine Sozousa). This extensive glass vessel and glass production evidence is a clear indication of the important role of glass vessel consumption and production at the site during the Late Roman–Byzantine periods. It shows the vast extent of glass vessel use in everyday life and the major role of the site in production of raw glass and in forming glass vessels especially during the Byzantine period. Analytical studies comparing the composition of vessels found at the site and raw glass produced at the site have shown a correlation which means glass vessels used at Apollonia (Byzantine Sozousa) were made of the raw glass produced there (Freestone, Jackson-Tal and Tal 2008: 79). The few moils and other vessel production remains discovered in several areas at the site indicate vessel production probably occurred at the site, but in a much more limited scale than the raw glass production.

The new evidence from the different areas at the site published herewith strengthens the assumption of a large-scale manufacture of raw glass at the site, making Apollonia/Sozousa one of the most important and interesting sites for reconstruction of the ancient glass industry in the southern Levant. It may be added that while quantifying the number of glass finds discovered at the site in Late Byzantine period contexts, the ratio between glass vessels and glass refuse is about 1:4. This ratio clearly validates the dominant role of mostly raw (and secondary) glass production at the site at the time. This is also demonstrated in recent analytical studies that exhibit the extent of use of raw glass produced at the site of Apollonia/Sozousa in the Late Byzantine period at sites far away from Apollonia. Interestingly the results of the analytical studies concur with the historical documentation

FIG. 16.18: AREA O (LOCUS 8061), SELECTED GLASS VESSELS (CONT.)

No.	*Description*	*Notes*
1	Rim and wall fragment	Colorless. Silver weathering and iridescence. Elongated funnel-shaped rim, tapering neck. Rim diameter: 3.2 cm
2	Rim and wall fragment	Colorless with bluish tinge. Silver weathering and iridescence. Rounded funnel-shaped rim, curving out neck. Rim diameter: 4 cm
3	Rim and wall fragment	Colorless. Silver weathering and iridescence. Beginning of funnel-shaped rim. Rim diameter: 5.2 cm
4	Rim and wall fragment	Bluish-green. Silver weathering and iridescence. Funnel-shaped rim with applied multiple horizontal trails. Rim diameter: 5.2 cm
5	Base and wall fragment	Colorless with bluish tinge. Silver weathering and iridescence. Concave base, curving out rounded wall. Rim diameter: 6 cm
6	Base and wall fragment	Colorless with bluish tinge. Silver weathering and iridescence. Concave base, curving out rounded wall. Rim diameter: 6 cm
7	Base and foot fragment	Bluish-green. Silver weathering and iridescence. Tubular base, cylindrical foot. Base diameter: 3.8 cm
8	Stem and wall fragment	Bluish-green. Silver weathering and iridescence. Solid pinched cylindrical stem, beginning of curving out wall. Base diameter: 0.6 cm

on the differences between Alexandrian and Judean glass. Freestone suggests (Chapter 22) that the composition of the Egyptian glass was easier to melt and work than the Levantine I glass. He also differentiates between them according to their colors, yellow-green Egyptian glass and bluish-green Levantine I glass. Fragments of the Dioclatian edict dated to 301 CE found in Asia Minor include the price list of Alexandrian and Judean raw glass, glass vessels and glass window-pane prices (Erim and Reynolds 1973). The prices of the Alexandrian glass products are higher than the Judean ones and refer to greenish Judean glass and probably to colorless Alexandrian glass, which seem to reflect the analytical results (with the exception of the Egyptian glass color). However, the term Judean in the

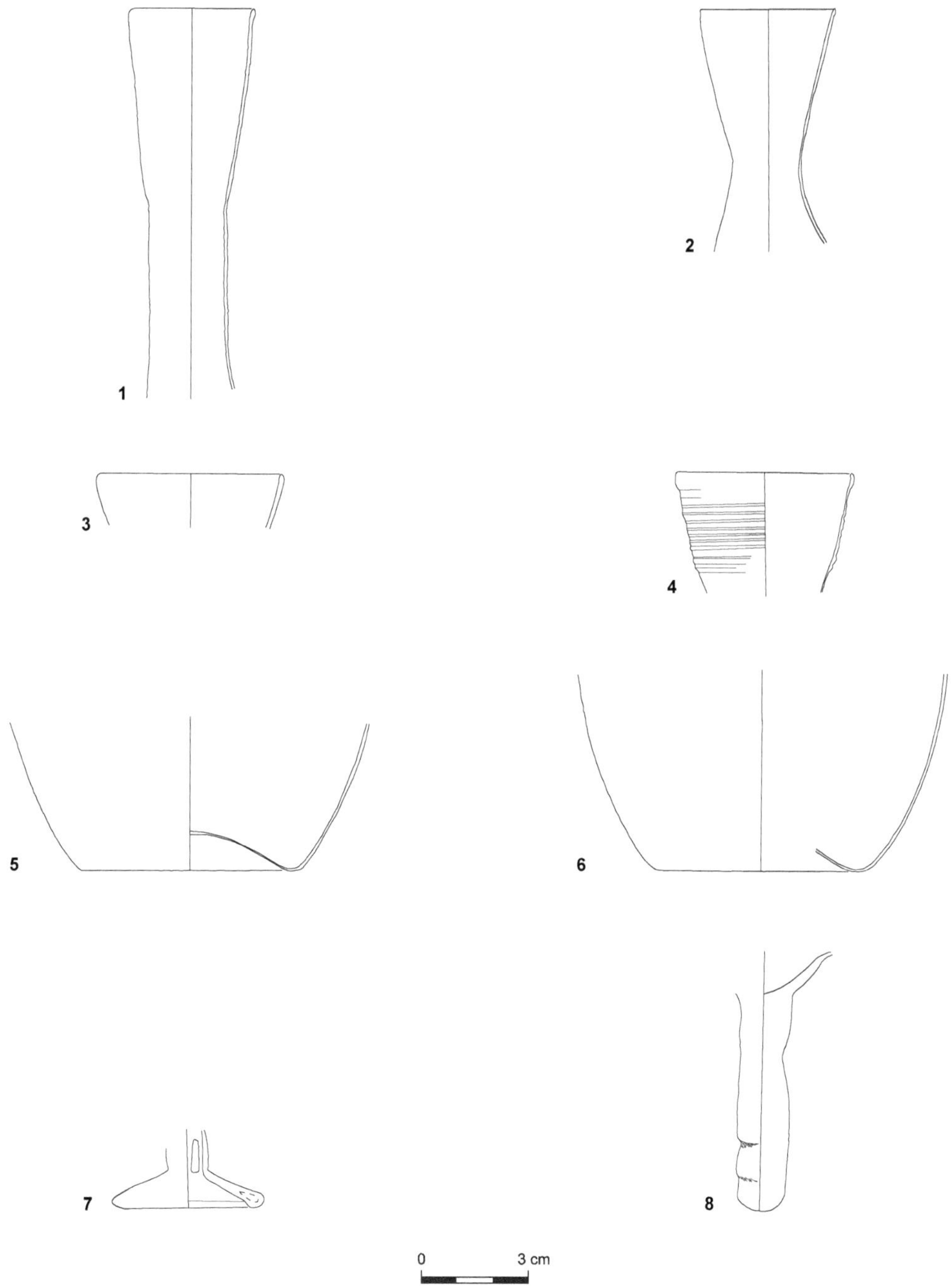

Fig. 16.18: Area O (Locus 8061), selected glass vessels (cont.).

beginning of the 4th century CE is ambiguous, as the Province of Judea ceased to exist under that name in the early 2nd century CE (ca. 135 CE), following the Jewish rebellion against the Romans the province was renamed Syria-Palestina. Two different approaches were used to interpret the term Judean glass. Dorothy Charlesworth suggested Judea is a geographic term referring to Sidon (Charlesworth 1973). She was supported by others with the correction of the Province of Judea instead of Sidon on the basis of chemical analysis (Jackson, Cool and Wager 1998: 60–61 and Whitehouse 2004). Dan Barag suggested Judea as a generic term for a specific type of naturally colored bluish-green glass (1987; 2005), supported by Stern (2007: 374–375, 377–378). It seems that the Apollonia-made raw glass was one of the main production sources in the southern Levant, used in many sites in order to create glass vessels, proving its importance as a major raw glass supplier. Although the Apollonia-made raw glass is dated later than the 4th century CE it could suggest that together with the recent finds from Jalame (Gorin-Resen, Freestone, yet unpublished), the Dioclatian edict does reflect a geographical reality where the two main production centers for manufacturing raw glass were in Egypt and Judea/Syria-Palaestina and that they differ in their quality and color as seen through their chemical compositions.

FIG. 16.19: AREA O, GLASS FURNACE REMAINS

No.	*Locus*	*Description*	*Notes*
1	8019	Furnace wall and ceiling remains	White and bluish-green. Silver weathering and iridescent film, lime deposits. Six uneven chunks of mudbrick with layers of glazed smoothed white and bluish-green glass. Thickness: 3.5–8 cm
2	8025	Furnace wall remains	White and bluish-green. Silver weathering and iridescent film, lime deposits. Seven uneven chunks of mudbrick with layers of smoothed white and bluish-green glass. Thickness: 3.5–8 cm
3	8019	Furnace wall and ceiling remains	Bluish-green. Silver weathering and iridescent film, lime deposits. Four uneven chunks of mudbrick with layers of smoothed bluish-green glass. Thickness: 3–6 cm
4	8025	Furnace floor remains	Light blue. Silver weathering and iridescent film, lime deposits. Uneven large chunk of mudbrick with a thick pointed layer of translucent light blue glass mixed with the mudbricks and lime unevenly. Thickness: 9 cm
5	8025	Furnace floor remains	Light blue. Silver weathering and iridescent film, lime deposits. Six uneven chunks of mudbrick with smoothed and pointed layers of translucent light blue glass mixed with the mudbricks and lime unevenly. Thickness: 3–8 cm
6	8016	Furnace floor remains	Light blue. Silver weathering and iridescent film, lime deposits. Eleven uneven chunks of mudbrick with pointed layers of translucent light blue glass mixed with the mudbricks and lime unevenly. Thickness: 2–6 cm
7	8019	Furnace floor remains	Light blue. Silver weathering and iridescent film, lime deposits. Six-teen uneven chunks of mudbrick with pointed layers of translucent light blue glass mixed with the mudbricks and lime unevenly. Thickness: 2–8 cm

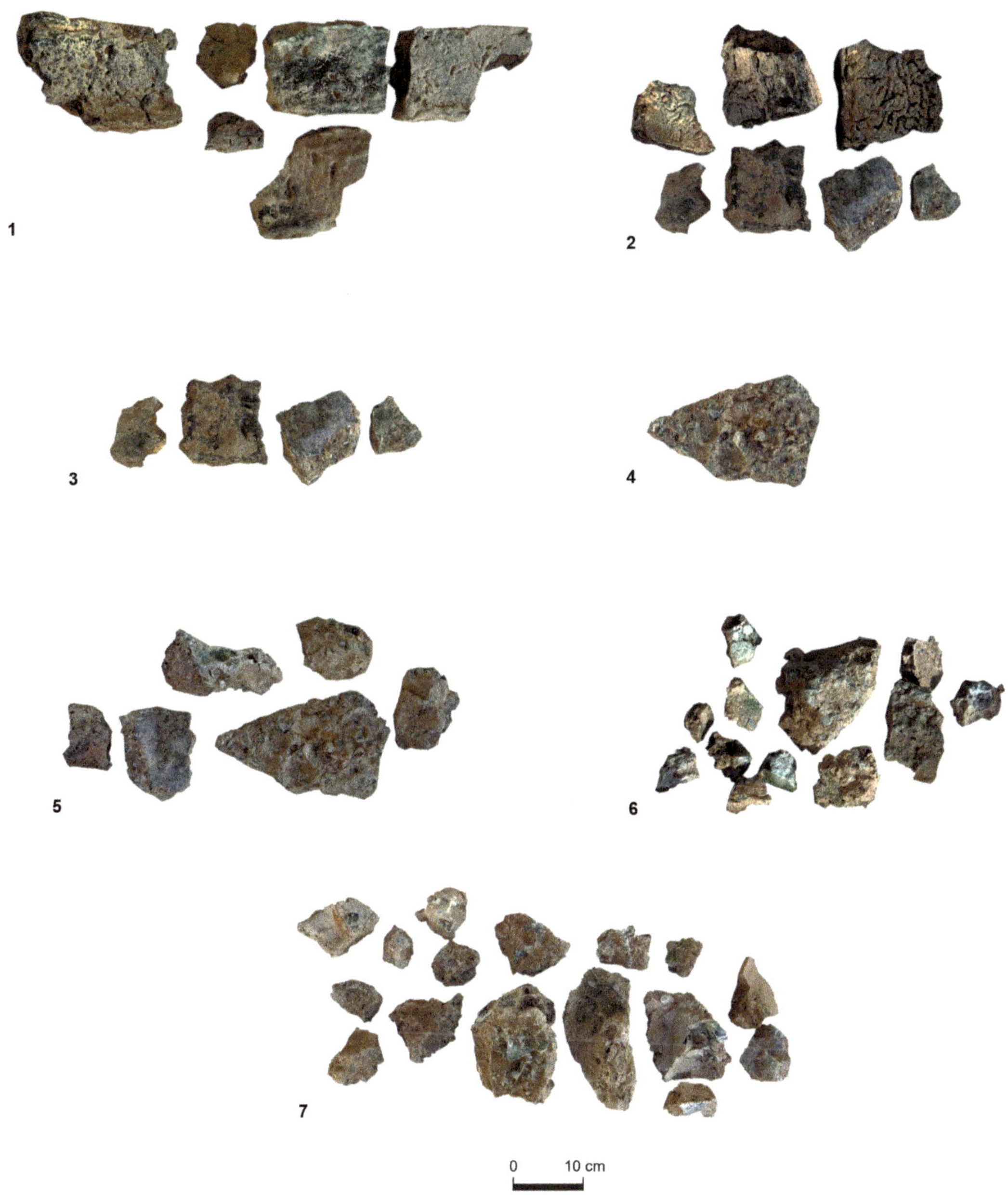

Fig. 16.19: Area O, glass furnace remains.

Fig. 16.20: Area O, primary product remains (Locus 8020).

Fig. 16.21: Area O, Primary Product Remains; Raw Glass Chunks and Secondary Production Remains

No.	*Locus*	*Basket*	*Description*	*Notes*
1	8016	-	Around 40 raw chunks	Green, light blue and bluish-green. Thick silver weathering and iridescent film, lime deposits. Around forty small uneven chunks. Thickness: 1–6 cm
2	8025	-	Raw chunks	Light blue and bluish-green. Thick silver weathering and iridescent film. Six uneven raw chunks. Thickness: 2–4 cm
3	8004	80008	Refuse fragment	Light blue. Silver weathering and iridescent film. Five rounded, elongated, flattened and twisted pieces with tooled marks. Thickness: 0.5–2 cm
4	8026	80148	Moil fragment	Light blue. Silver weathering and iridescence. Uneven cylindrical fragment, cut straight on one end and uneven on the other. Diameter: 2.2 cm

Fig. 16.21: Area O, primary product remains; raw glass chunks and secondary production remains.

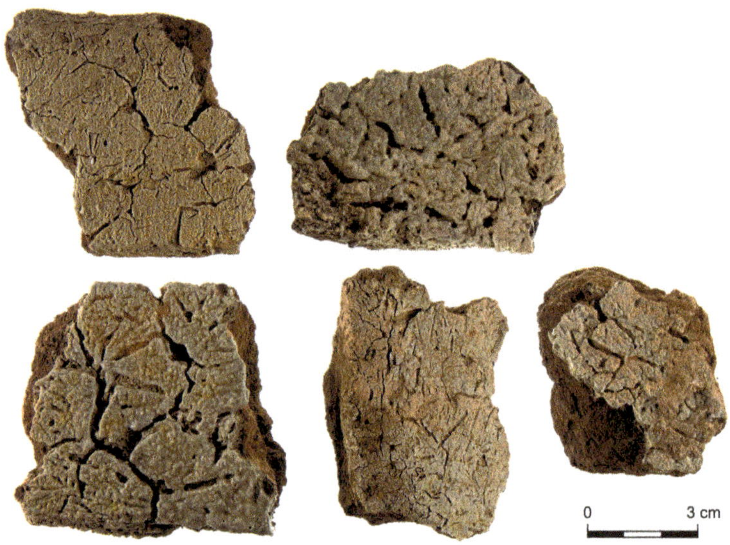

Fig. 16.22: Area N, glass furnace remains (bricks) (Wall 5011).

Fig. 16.23: Area N1, glass furnace remains (bricks) (Locus 5019).

Fig. 16.24: Area N1, glass furnace remains (floor) (Locus 5018).

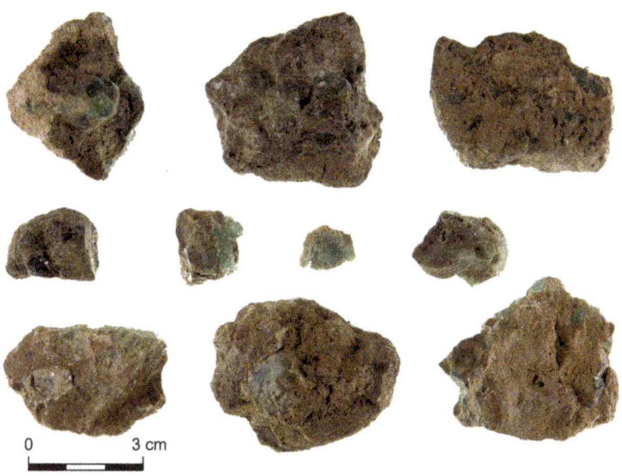

Fig. 16.25: Area N1, glass furnace remains (floor) (Locus 5017) (cont.).

REFERENCES

Aviam, M. and Gorin-Rosen, Y. 1997. Three Burial Caves from the Roman Period at Ḥurfeish. *ʿAtiqot* 33: 25–37 (Hebrew, with English summary pp. 9*).

Barag, D. 1987. Recent Important Epigraphic Discoveries Related to the History of Glassmaking in the Roman World. *Annales de l'Association Internationale pour l'Histoire du Verre* 10: 109–116.

Barag, D. 2005. Alexandrian and Judaean Glass in the Price Edict of Diocletian. *Journal of Glass Studies* 47: 184–186.

Barash, I. 2012. Glass Vessels from the Late Byzantine Buildings along the Eastern Fringes of Tel Shiqmona. *ʿAtiqot* 72: 131–134.

Charlesworth, D. 1973. In: Erim, K.T. and Reynolds, J. The Aphrodisias Copy of Diocletian's Edict on Maximum Prices. *Journal of Roman Studies* 63: 108–109.

Crowfoot, G.M. 1957. The Glass. In: Crowfoot, J.W., Crowfoot, G.M. and Kenyon, K.M. *Samaria-Sebaste III: The Objects from Samaria*. London: 403–422.

Erim, K.T. and Reynolds, J. 1973. The Aphrodisias Copy of Diocletian's Edict on Maximum Prices. *Journal of Roman Studies* 63: 99–110.

Freestone, I.C., Jackson-Tal, R.E. and Tal, O. 2008. Raw Glass and the Production of Glass Vessels at Late Byzantine Apollonia-Arsuf, Israel. *Journal of Glass Studies* 50: 67–80.

Freestone, I.C., Jackson-Tal, R.E., Taxel, I. and Tal, O. 2015. Glass Production at an Early Islamic Workshop in Tel Aviv. *Journal of Archaeological Science* 62: 45–54.

Gorin-Rosen, Y. 1997a. The Glass Vessels. In: Aviam, M. and Stern, E. Burial Caves near Ḥ. Sugar. *ʿAtiqot* 33: 96–98 (Hebrew, with English summary p. 16*).

Gorin-Rosen, Y. 1997b. Glass Vessels from Burial Caves in Asherat. *ʿAtiqot* 33: 61–67 (Hebrew, with English summary pp. 12*–13*).

Gorin-Rosen, Y. 2000a. The Glass Vessels from Kh. Tabaliya (Givʿat Hamatos). *ʿAtiqot* 40: 81*–94* (Hebrew, with English summary pp. 165–166).

Gorin-Rosen, Y. 2000b. Glass from Monasteries and Chapels in South Sinai. In: Dahari, U. *Monastic Settlements in South Sinai in the Byzantine Period: The Archaeological Remains* (IAA Reports 9). Jerusalem: 233–245.

Gorin-Rosen, Y. 2000c. The Ancient Glass Industry in Israel: Summary of the Finds and New Discoveries. In: Nenna, M.-D., ed. *La route du verre, ateliers primaries et secondaires du second millénaire av. J.-C. au Moyen Âge*. Lyon: 49–63.

Gorin-Rosen, Y. 2002a. Excavations at Khirbet el-Shubeika 1991, 1993; The Glass Vessels. In: Gal, Z., ed. *Eretz Zafon: Studies in Galilean Archaeology*. Jerusalem: 288–322 (Hebrew).

Gorin-Rosen, Y. 2002b. The Glass Vessels from Burial Cave D at Ḥurfeish. In: Gal, Z., ed. *Eretz Zafon: Studies in Galilean Archaeology*. Jerusalem: 140*–166*.

Gorin-Rosen, Y. 2005. The Glass. In: Arubas, B. and Goldfus, H., eds. *Excavations on the Site of the Jerusalem International Convention Center (Binyanei Haʿuma): A Settlement of the Late First to Late Second Temple Period, the Tenth Legion's Kilnworks, and a Byzantine Monastic Complex, the Pottery and Other Small Finds (Journal of Roman Archaeology Supplementary Series* 60). Portsmouth: 195–210.

Gorin-Rosen, Y. 2006. Glass Finds. In: Weksler-Bdolah, S. The Old City Wall of Jerusalem. *ʿAtiqot* 54: 115*–117* (Hebrew, with English summary pp. 163–164).

Gorin-Rosen, Y. and Katsnelson, N. 2007. Local Glass Production in the Late Roman – Early Byzantine Periods in Light of the Glass Finds from Khirbat el-Niʿana. *ʿAtiqot* 57: 73–154.

Hizmi, H. 1997. Two Burial Caves in Rafidiya (Shechem). *ʿAtiqot* 32: 125–130 (Hebrew, with English summary p. 45*).

Israeli, Y. 2008. The Glass Vessels. In: Patrich, J. *Archaeological Excavations at Caesarea Maritima, Areas CC KK and NN, Final Reports 1: The Objects*. Jerusalem: 367–418.

Jackson, C.M., Cool, H.E.M. and Wager, E.C.W. 1998. The Manufacture of Glass in Roman York. *Journal of Glass Studies* 40: 55–61.

Jackson-Tal, R.E. 2007a. The Glass Finds. In: Sari, C. Khirbat el-Fatuna. *Ḥadashot Arkheologiyot—Excavations and Surveys in Israel* 119: http://www.hadashot-esi.org.il/Report_Detail_Eng.aspx?id=639&mag_id=112

Jackson-Tal, R.E. 2007b. Early Roman and Early Byzantine Glass Vessels from Tombs T2 and T4 near Ḥorbat Zikhrin. *ʿAtiqot* 56: 59–63 (Hebrew, with English summary on p. 76*).

Jackson-Tal, R.E. 2015a. Glass Vessels [Tel Barukh Cemetery]. In: Tal, O. and Taxel, I. *Samaritan Cemeteries and Tombs in the Central Coastal Plain: Archaeology and History of the Samaritan Settlement outside Samaria (ca. 300–700 CE)* (Ägypten und Altes Testament 82). Münster: 57–80.

Jackson-Tal, R.E. 2015b. Glass Vessels [Khirbet al-Ḥadra]. In: Tal, O. and Taxel, I. *Samaritan Cemeteries and Tombs in the Central Coastal Plain: Archaeology and History of the Samaritan Settlement outside Samaria (ca. 300–700 CE)* (Ägypten und Altes Testament 82). Münster: 149–160.

Katsnelson, N. 1999. Glass Vessels from the Painted Tomb at Migdal Ashqelon. *ʿAtiqot* 37: 67*–82*.

Katsnelson, N. and Jackson-Tal, R.E. 2004. The Glass Vessels from Ashqelon, Semadar Hotel. *ʿAtiqot* 48: 99–109.

Lehrer-Jacobson, G. 1999. The Glass Vessels from Horvat Sumaqa. In: Dar, S. *Sumaqa: A Roman and Byzantine Jewish Village on Mount Carmel, Israel*. (BAR International Series 815). Oxford: 333–344.

Magen, Y. *Flavia Neapolis: Shechem in the Roman Period* (Judea and Samaria Publications 11). Jerusalem.

Meyer, C. 1989. Crown Window Panes: Constantinian or Justinian? In: Leonard, A. and Williams, B.B., eds. *Essays in Ancient Civilizations Presented to Helen J. Kantor*. Chicago: 213–219.

Sarig, S. 2009. Glass Vessels from Ras el-ʿEin. In: Magen, Y. *Flavia Neapolis: Shechem in the Roman Period* (Judea and Samaria Publications 11). Jerusalem: 23–37.

Spaer, M. 2001. *Ancient Glass in the Israel Museum: Beads and Other Small Objects*. Jerusalem.

Stern, E. 1997. Burial Caves at Kisra. *ʿAtiqot* 33: 103–135 (Hebrew, with English summary p. 17*).

Stern, E. and Gorin-Rosen, Y. 1997. Burial Caves near Kabri. *ʿAtiqot* 33: 1–22 (Hebrew, with English summary pp. 7*–8*).

Stern, E.M. 2007. Ancient Glass in a Philological Context. *Mnemosyne* 60: 341–406.

Sussman, V. 1976. A Burial Cave at Kefar ʿAra. *ʿAtiqot* 11: 92–101.

Syon, D. 1998. A Winepress at Akhziv. *ʿAtiqot* 34: 85–99 (Hebrew, with English summary p. 7*).

Tal, O., Jackson-Tal, R.E. and Freestone, I.C. 2004. New Evidence of the Production of Raw Glass at Late Byzantine Apollonia-Arsuf, Israel. *Journal of Glass Studies* 47: 51–66.

Tal, O., Jackson-Tal, R.E. and Freestone, I.C. 2008. Glass from a Late Byzantine Secondary Workshop at Ramla (South), Israel. *Journal of Glass Studies* 50: 81–95.

Vitto, F. 1998. Maḥoza D-Yamnin: A Mosaic Floor from the Time of Eudocia. *ʿAtiqot* 35: 109–134.

Weinberg, G.D. and Goldstein, S.M. 1988. The Glass Vessels. In: Weinberg, G.D., ed. *Excavations at Jalame: Site of a Glass Factory in Late Roman Palestine.* Columbia, Miss.: 38–102.

Whitehouse, D. 2004. Glass in the Price Edict of Diocletian. *Journal of Glass Studies* 46: 189–191.

Winter, T. 1998. The Glass Vessels from Ḥorbat Ḥermeshit (1998–1990). *ʿAtiqot* 34: 173–177 (Hebrew, with English summary p. 10*).

Winter, T. 2010. The Byzantine-Period Glass Vessels from Ḥorbat Roẓeẓ. *ʿAtiqot* 62: 145–155.

CHAPTER 17

SMALL FINDS

Oren Tal

The small finds discussed below include a variety of items from different periods that span the last two millennia. They include a stamped proto-Knidian amphora handle of the Early Hellenistic period, inscribed Samaritan rings of the Byzantine period, metal weights of the Early Islamic period, as well as bone figurine, spindle whorls (or buttons), beads and inlay, and various metal objects.

STAMPED PROTO-KNIDIAN HANDLE (FIG. 17.1)

License: A6825/2013 (Apollonia [East])

Area: CC (Sq. D5)

Locus: 30069

Basket: 302689

ZH

Φ

The reading of this stamp is partial but given the ware and the few legible letters, it is likely to be assigned to the so-called Zenon-Group A stamps. The group probably originated in the Datça peninsula which belonged to the polis of Knidos; consequently it belongs to one of the Proto-Knidian groups that is datable to ca. 285–270 BCE (cf. Palaczyk and Schönenberger 2003: 199). The reading, which shows an abbreviated name, ZH (Zή)νων, is followed by a horizontal Φ which may stand for another name abbreviation (unknown at the present time). The context of this example is, however, Byzantine; hence, it is an intrusive find. Proto-Knidian stamp handles are numbered in this region (for an overview, see Ariel 1990: 76–77, S464; 2017: 47; see also Fischer and Tal 2017: 94, No. 92). This Zenon-Group A example may supplement two other published 3rd-century BCE stamped handles from Amman (Russell 1997: 51, No. 49) and Sinai (Ariel 2017: 47).

INSCRIBED SAMARITAN RINGS

The three inscribed Samaritan rings found at the site and discussed below may supplement a previously published inscribed Samaritan ring of the polygonal (octagonal) type that was accidently found at the site as stray (cf. Reich 2002: 301–302, No. 17).

The three rings may be categorized into three distinct types: an octagonal ring, a ring with an oval bezel and a ring with a circular bezel.

All finger rings are made of brass.

OCTAGONAL RING (FIG. 17.2: 1)

License: A6825/2013 (Apollonia [East])

Area: CC (Sq. H6)

Fig. 17.1: Stamped Proto-Knidian handle.

Locus: 30052

Basket: 301518

Description and measurements: Fair preservation. Weight 1.75 g; hoop thickness is 0.9–1.5 mm; hoop width is 3.8–4.2 mm; internal diameter is 16.3–16.6 mm; and external diameter is 19.2–19.4 mm. The legend letter thickness is 400–600 µm.

Production technique: Lost-wax casting followed by heat-treatments.

Script and reading: A short legend on each facet, usually two lines per facet, written in the Samaritan script. According to the prevalent view, the legends probably originated in verses of the Samaritan Pentateuch. Some of the letters are carelessly written (possibly intentionally), and, therefore, the following reading is suggested:

(a)	**(b)**	**(c)**	**(d)**	**(e)**	**(f)**	**(g)**	**(h)**
lh	*yhwh*	*yhwh*	*ʾyn*	*yšr*	*yhwh*	*ky*	*yhwh*
	šmw	*ʾḥd*	*kʾl (?)*	*wn (?)*	*šmw/h*	*ʾny*	*nṣḥ*

Context/Date: 5th–7th centuries CE; Byzantine.

References: Preliminary publication in Tal and Taxel 2014: 169, n 16; and in Ashkenazi, Taxel and Tal 2015: "Ring C," where its chemical analysis was reported. Similar finger rings bearing Samaritan legends are known from other sites in the Samaria hills, the southern Carmel region and the central Coastal Plain (Reich 2002), including from nearby Ḥorbat Gelilot (Reich 1994) and Khirbet al-Ḥadra (HaGolan Street) (Tal and Taxel 2014: 168–169; 2015: 170–172). Others are known from collections (e.g., Berger-Lober 2012).

RING WITH A CIRCULAR BEZEL (FIG. 17.2: 2)

License: A6825/2013 (Apollonia [East])

Area: CC (Sq. G7)

Locus: 30071

Basket: 302639

Description and measurements: Well preserved. Weight 1.32 g; hoop thickness is 0.5–0.9 mm; hoop width is 1.7–2.5 mm. The bezel diameter varies between 10.9 and 12.0 mm and its thickness is 1.1–1.2 mm. The inscription on the bezel is well preserved. The thickness of the letters varies between 500 and 900 μm.

Production technique: Brazing marks and remains of the brazing metal were observed on the back of the ring bezel. The wavy design of the bezel inscription letters indicates they were probably engraved. The ring was made of two cast parts (shank and bezel) that were brazed together. Hammering and annealing cycles were applied to shape the shank to its final design (a long incision is visible on one of its sides).

Script and reading: A three-line legend is written in the Samaritan script; it reads: *ʾyn kʾl yšr[wn]* (after Deut. 33:26)

Context/Date: 5th–7th centuries CE; Byzantine.

References: Preliminary publication in Ashkenazi, Taxel and Tal 2015: "Ring G", where it was also chemically analyzed; cf. also Reich 2002: 299, No. 12, with a full *yšrwn* rather than abbreviated *yšr* (from Caesarea).

RING WITH AN OVAL BEZEL (FIG. 17.2: 3)

License: G46/2012 (Apollonia National Park)

Area: X

Locus: 5100

Basket: 51010

Description and measurements: This ring came from the Apollonia National Park and for the sake of completeness of the site repertoire of Samaritan rings, it was decided to include it in the current chapter. Well preserved. Weight 0.95 g; hoop thickness is 0.5–0.9 mm; hoop width is 1.8–2.8 mm. The diameter

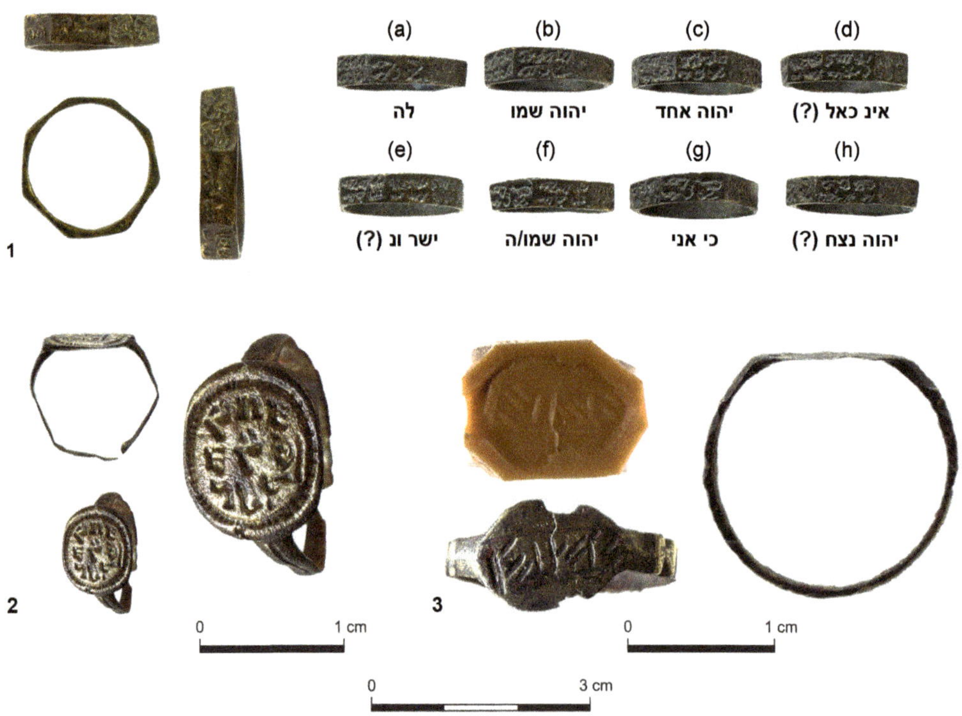

Fig. 17.2: Inscribed Samaritan rings.

of the bezel varies between 7.5 and 11 mm and its thickness is 0.4–0.7 mm. The inscription on the bezel is well preserved. The thickness of the letters varies between 400 and 600 μm.

Production technique: Brazing marks and remains of the brazing metal were observed on the back of the ring bezel. The design of the inscription letters on the bezel indicates they were probably engraved. The ring was made of two cast parts (shank and bezel) that were brazed together. Hammering and annealing cycles were applied to shape the hoop to its final design. The hoop was adorned with "s-coil" incisions on its sides and bottom.

Script and reading: a one-line legend written in the Samaritan script reads: *yhwh*.

Context/Date: Surface find; Byzantine/Early Islamic.

DISCUSSION

The relatively high number of inscribed Samaritan rings from Apollonia/Sozousa and its periphery cannot be used to determine the actual frequency of the daily use of such objects (i.e., inscribed rings as well as inscribed amulets/pendants) by members of the local Samaritan community in Byzantine times. The inscribed Samaritan rings found in the dump (Area CC; Fig. 17.2: 1–2) may have been the personal belongings of the deceased, who had worn them regularly. Their discovery in a dump may suggest that they were intentionally thrown away (or buried) in the dump as an act of cultic or practical nature as they were either considered contaminated or too personal to be used by family members of the deceased. If the former was indeed the case, this intentional act seems to have been meant for the protection of the living from the dead (see, in this respect, Härke's 2014: 51, but in Anglo-Saxon milieu).

EARLY ISLAMIC WEIGHTS (FIG. 17.3)

Seven weights were retrieved during the excavations; all are made of copper alloy. Most of the weights were found with the aid of a metal detector operating during most stages of the 2013 excavations. The weights were cleaned in the IAA laboratory and weighed before and after cleaning by Mettler PE 200; they were measured by an OMC caliper. All appear in Fig. 17.3 in 1:1 scale.

SPHEROID-SHAPED WEIGHT (FIG. 17.3: 1)

License: A6825/2013 (Apollonia [East])

Area: CC (Sq. F8)

Locus: 30074

Basket: 304026

Description: A well-preserved spheroid-shaped weight with convex sides and flat upper and lower surfaces decorated with concentric circles and dots (bird's eyes). The sides are rhombus-shaped and the upper and lower surfaces each have a central dot.

Measurements: Height 10.2 mm; maximal diameter 15 mm

Material and weight (before and after cleaning): AE, 14.23 g, 14.19 g

Value: 3 *dinars*

Context/Date: 7th–8th centuries CE; Early Islamic.

References:[1] Holland 1986: 195, No. 115, Pl. 34; Kletter 2005: 117, No. 1

1 References refer to comparanda of the weight's shape, design and actual weight/units.

Fig. 17.3: Early Islamic weights.

SPHEROID-SHAPED WEIGHT (FIG. 17.3: 2)

Area: AA

Locus: 100

Basket: 1250

Description: A fairly preserved spheroid-shaped weight with convex sides and flat upper and lower surfaces decorated with concentric circles and dots (bird's eyes). The sides are rhombus-shaped and the upper and lower surfaces each have a central dot.

Measurements: Height 10.2 mm; maximal diameter 15 mm

Material and weight (before and after cleaning): AE, 14.28 g, 14.08 g

Value: 3 *dinars*

Context/Date: 7th–8th centuries CE; Early Islamic (the weight was lost after the excavations).

References: Holland 1986: 195, No. 115, Pl. 34; Kletter 2005: 117, No. 1

SPHEROID-SHAPED WEIGHT (FIG. 17.3: 3)

Area: AA1

Locus: 201

Basket: 2006

Description: A fairly preserved spheroid-shaped weight with convex sides and flat upper and lower surfaces decorated with concentric circles and dots (bird's eyes). The sides are rhombus-shaped and the upper and lower surfaces each have a central dot.

Measurements: Height 6 mm; maximal diameter 11 mm

Material and weight (before and after cleaning): AE, 4.55 g, 3.21 g

Value: 1 *dinar*

Context/Date: 7th–8th centuries CE; Early Islamic.

References: Holland 1986: 195, No. 156, Pl. 34; Tal 2008: 206, No. 3

BRICK-SHAPED WEIGHT (FIG. 17.3: 4)

Area: CC2

Locus: 31000

Basket: 310008

Description: A well-preserved brick-shaped weight with plain sides.

Measurements: 14 × 11 mm; maximal height 25 mm

Material and weight (before and after cleaning): AE, 3.00 g, 2.88 g

Value: 1 *dirham*

Context/Date: 7th–8th centuries CE; Early Islamic.

References: Zelinger 2000: 57*, Fig. 108: 2; Tal 2008: 207, No. 10

BRICK-SHAPED WEIGHT (FIG. 17.3: 5)

Area: AA2

Locus: 12018

Basket: 102045

Description: A well-preserved brick-shaped weight with plain sides. The upper surface is partially concave and bears an inscription that reads: [ا/ك]لمزال

Measurements: 12.5 × 9 mm; maximal height 60 mm

Material and weight (before and after cleaning): AE, 3.00 g, 2.88 g

Value: 1 *dirham*

Context/Date: 7th–8th centuries CE; Early Islamic.

References: Tal 2008: 207, No. 10

BRICK-SHAPED WEIGHT (FIG. 17.3: 6)

Area: CC (Sq. F13)

Locus: 30138

Basket: 305406

Description: A well-preserved brick-shaped weight with plain sides.

Measurements: 7.7 × 6.9 mm; maximal height 22 mm

Material and weight (before and after cleaning): AE, 1.49 g, 1.42 g

Value: 1/2 *dirham*

Context/Date: 7th–8th centuries CE; Early Islamic.

References: Tal 2008: 207, No. 11

BRICK-SHAPED WEIGHT (FIG. 17.3: 7)

Area: CC (Sq. F13)

Locus: 30138

Basket: 305406

Description: A well-preserved brick-shaped weight with plain sides. The upper surface is partially concave and bears an illegible inscription.

Measurements: 6.3 × 6 mm; maximal height 29 mm

Material and weight (before and after cleaning): AE, 1.47 g, 1.40 g

Value: 1/2 *dirham*

Context/Date: 7th–8th centuries CE; Early Islamic.

DISCUSSION

Most of the weights from Apollonia (East) came from different loci that mainly represent Early Islamic fills. Thus, there is no indication that they functioned as one (or more) set/s, nor that they functioned contemporaneously. The weights were cast in molds; however, some details in the decoration of the spheroid- (roughly polygonal) shaped weights, such as the dot on the upper and lower surfaces, were added after completion by punching. In the same manner, inscriptions were added to the upper surfaces in two of the four brick-shaped examples. Small copper alloy weights of the types retrieved from Apollonia (East) are common in occupation layers of the Early Islamic period of Palestinian sites and are normally assigned to the late 8th, 9th or 10th centuries based on their context, typology and metrology. Only a few studies discuss these weights in their Palestinian contexts thoroughly, and that of Holland's (1986) on weights of Caesarea Maritima and Kletter's (2005) and Tal's (2008) on weights of Ramla are the most worthy recent attempts on the subject.[2]

It is a well-known fact that the basic weight units of the Early Islamic period are the *dinar* and the *dirham* (Lewis, Pellat and Schact 1965: s.v. Dīnār; Dirham). These weight units underwent standard variations under different dynasties, rulers and in different regions, as is attested from coins, inscribed weights and historical documentation. Based on these sources of evidence, it is clear that the copper alloy weights of Apollonia (East) were produced according to Late Umayyad and ʿAbbasid standards. Their actual weight shows that the three spheroid-shaped weights (or polyhedra, as classified by Holland 1986) correspond to the system of the *dinar*, whereas the four brick-shaped weights correspond to that of the *dirham*. The Early Islamic *dinar* (from Greek, δηνάριον), which followed the weight standard of the Byzantine *solidus* (ca. 4.55 g), had a value of ca. 4.25 g after ʿAbd al-Malik Ibn Marwan's reforms in 696 CE (77 H.) and was used for the following centuries (Miles 1964: 78*–82*). The weights from Apollonia thus correspond to three units (Fig. 17.3: 1–2) and one unit (Fig. 17.3: 3). The weights recovered are slightly above and below the average theoretical value of ca. 4.25 g for a *dinar*. The slightly below average weight (Fig. 17.3: 2) may be explained by its wear and tear and the cleaning process involved.

In contrast, the Early Islamic *dirham* (from Greek, δραχμή) was mainly used in Egypt until the Fatimid came to power (Balog 1970: 239). Metrological studies suggest that the *dirham kail* unit corresponds to ca. 2.95 g. Therefore, these weights correspond to one unit (Fig. 17.3: 4–5) and 1/2 unit (Fig. 17.3: 6–7). All weights are slightly below the average theoretical value of ca. 2.95 g for a *dirham* and this may be explained by their wear and tear and the cleaning process involved.

2 More than 600 bronze weights of questionable provenance are recorded by Holland (1986) as coming from Caesarea Maritima. Kletter (2005) published four from the ʿOpher Park at Ramla. Tal studied an additional 11, and the contemporaneous excavation carried out at Ramla (South) by the Israel Antiquities Authority unearthed several more (yet unpublished). All the published bronze weights of Ramla originated in controlled archaeological excavations. Those from Apollonia supplement several more found in excavation areas within the walled town.

The function of these copper alloy weights (sometimes referred to as "bronze weights") is open to speculation. Balog referred to the weights he published as "coin weights" (1970), but this sole function was rightfully refuted by Holland due to the fact that "true coin weight is intended specifically for weighing coins of a particular denomination, ... and usually bears an inscription to that effect, identifying the denomination, the weight standard, and the issuing authority" (1986: 185–186). Because of documentary and archaeological evidence (cut gold and silver coins) for the use of fractions of *dinars* in transactions, Holland suggested that these weights would be needed for almost all cash transactions ("money weights" in a sense) and that their abundance at Palestinian sites rules out the exclusive use by officials, metal-smiths or other specialists (1986: 186–192). However, one cannot exclude the possibility that these copper alloy weights were used as coins and transacted at their face value.

CARVED BONE FIGURINE (FIG. 17.4)

License: A6825/2013 (Apollonia [East])

Area: CC (Sq. F6)

Locus: 30060

Preservation and measurements: Fair. Height 106 mm; width 330 mm; thickness 20 mm.

Description: Carved tablet (probably made of *Bos femur*) with high relief figure of *Aphrodite Pudica*. The back is roughly worked and smoothed. The carving of the figure (that is the front part) follows the lines of the body and garment. Aphrodite stands to the front leaning on her right leg. The left leg and part of the left hand are missing. Locks of long hair may be seen behind the neck. The right hand, with a bracelet above the elbow, covers the left breast and the arm covers the right breast. The left hand covers the genitalia. The belly, with its navel, is slightly rounded and the pelvis is relatively narrow. No perforation holes are visible.

Context/Date: 5th–7th centuries CE; Byzantine.

References: Ayalon 2005: 91, No. 339, Fig. 35, with earlier bibliography (from Caesarea Maritima, said to be "the only object of its type").

SPINDLE WHORLS/BUTTONS (FIG. 17.5)

License: A6825/2013 (Apollonia [East])

Area: CC (Sq. G7)

Locus: 30071

Basket: 302883

Description: Low domed whorl/button with a flat plain bottom and decorated dome with two concentric circles on top and circle-and-dot designs in two concentric rows.

Preservation, weight and measurements: Fair. Bone. 9.21 g. Height 70 mm; dimeter 333 mm

License: A6825/2013 (Apollonia [East])

Area: CC (Sq. E7)

Locus: 625

Basket: 6323

Description: high domed whorl/button, with a flat plain bottom and plain dome.

Preservation, material, weight and measurements: Fair. Stone. 21.87 g. Height 160 mm; dimeter 318 mm

Two round spindle whorls were found, one made of bone and the other of polished, blackish stone (probably basalt). These spherical objects are relatively heavy (weighing 9.21, 21.87 g accordingly) in relation to their size. In the context of daily life, they normally attest to (wool?) weaving, given the fact that whorls were fitted onto a spindle in order to increase speed and steadiness of the spin, hence a shortened weaving time. It is commonly accepted that weaving was women's work in ancient households (cf. Reich 2001: 149–150, [basing his arguments on Jewish sources]; and also Magness 2002: 176–185). Both examples were retrieved from Byzantine contexts.

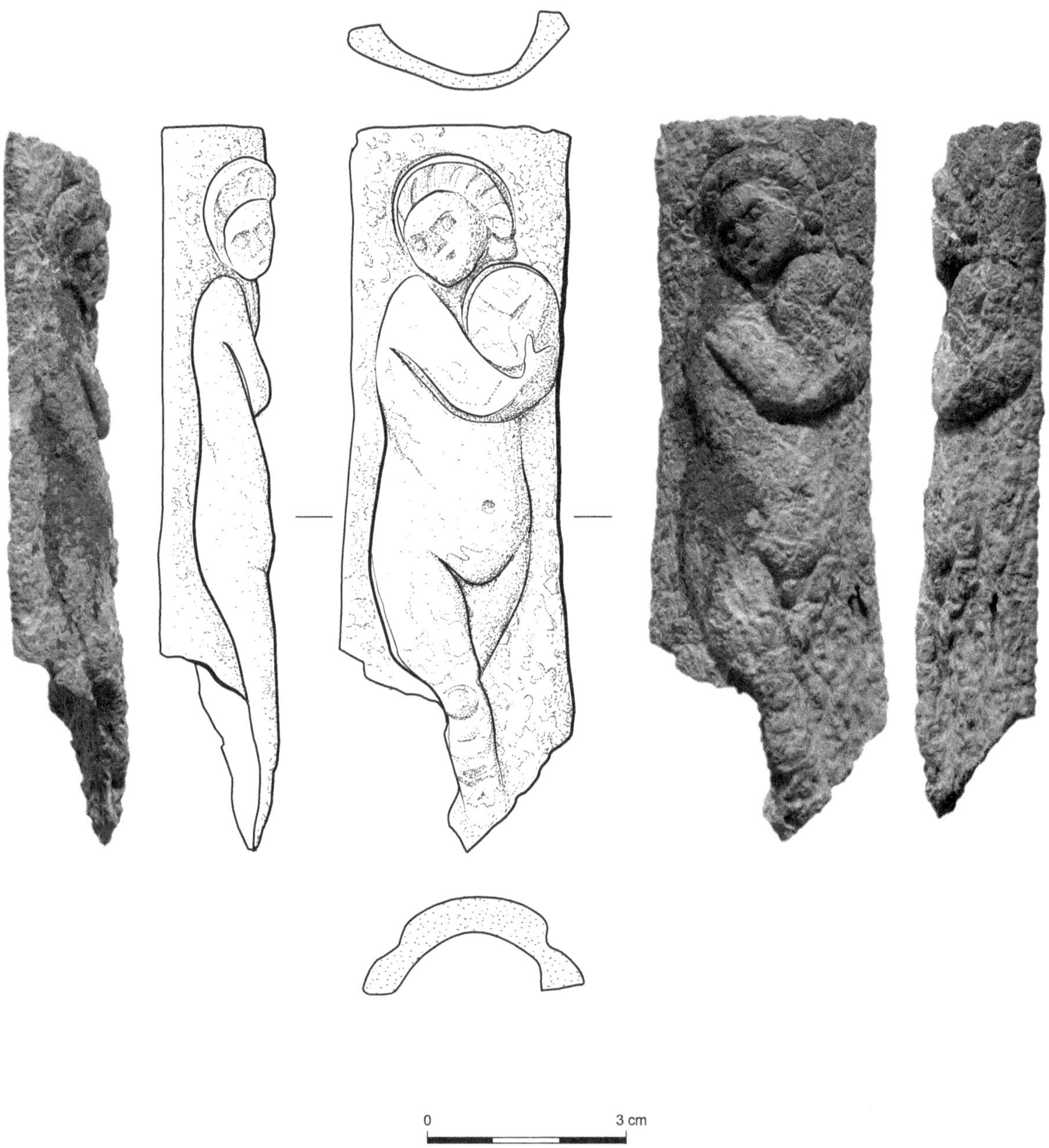

Fig. 17.4: Carved bone figurine.

BEADS AND INLAY (FIG. 17.6)

The very few beads and inlay recovered during the excavations were made of varied materials (faience, glass, alabaster and carnelian) and mostly came from Byzantine contexts. They were probably used as jewelry and ornaments and consist of common types of the period that are mostly known from burial caves (cf. e.g., Jackson-Tal 2015).

Fig. 17.5: Spindle whorls/buttons.

FIG. 17.6: BEADS AND INLAY

No.	Area	Locus	Basket	Object	Material/Shape	Context/Date
1	CC	30050	302203	Bead	Faience/Rounded	Surface/Byzantine(?)
2	AA2	167	1622	Bead	Glass/Rounded	Fill/Byzantine
3	DD2	Surface	9149	Bead	Alabaster/Bi-conical	-
4	BB2	641	6544	Bead	Carnelian/Rounded	Fill/Byzantine
5	CC	30071	3012150	Inlay	Carnelian/Scaraboid	Fill/Byzantine

VARIOUS METAL OBJECTS (FIGS. 17.7–17.8)

PERSONAL ACCESSORIES

These are usually made of copper alloy and can be categorized as rings, an earring(?), a fibula, kohl sticks and cosmetic spoons (spatulae) and buckles (Fig. 17.7: 1–19). The copper alloy and brass finger rings are varied in both type and date. The brass-made finger ring shown in Fig. 17.7: 1 has a 17 mm loop internal diameter and a plain oval bezel. The ring was made of two cast parts (shank and bezel) that were brazed together. Hammering and annealing cycles were applied to shape the hoop to its final design. The hoop is adorned with incisions on its sides and bottom. Although it is a surface level find, it is likely to be assigned to either the Byzantine or Early Islamic period based on material and design. A similar ring with an inscribed bezel is discussed above (Chapter 17: No. 3, Fig. 17.2: 3). The copper alloy ring illustrated in Fig. 17.7: 2 has a 15.5 mm loop internal diameter and an oval bezel that has a decoration that seems to have suffered deterioration. It is likely that the ring was manufactured by lost-wax casting technique with no further heat or worked treatments. The ring came from a well-secured locus of a Byzantine date and it resembles similar rings of the period (cf. Tal and Taxel 2015: 102, Fig. 1.67: 5). The copper alloy ring shown in Fig. 17.7: 3 has a 16.5 mm loop internal diameter and an oval bezel with a decoration of a radiated sphere with a two-line inscription in Arabic that may be read as بسم الله (*bi-sm illāhi*). It is likely that the ring was manufactured by lost-wax casting technique, with no further heat or worked treatments. Although it is a surface level find, it is likely to be assigned to the Early Islamic period based on the epigraphy. The copper alloy ring exhibited in Fig. 17.7: 4 is circular in shape with a plain continuous loop (with no bezel), a 17 mm loop internal dimeter and has a shank that is triangular in section. It is likely that the ring was manufactured by lost-wax casting technique with no further heat or worked treatments. It is a surface level find that is likely to be assigned to either the

Fig. 17.7: Various Metal Objects

No.	*Area*	*Locus*	*Basket*	*Object*	*Material*	*Context/Date*
1	CC	30137	305471	Ring	Brass	Surface/Byzantine-Early Islamic(?)
2	CC	30060	-	Ring	Copper alloy	Fill/Byzantine
3	CC	30077	303709	Ring	Copper alloy	Surface/Early Islamic(?)
4	DD	40003	400040	Ring	Copper alloy	Surface/Byzantine-Early Islamic(?)
5	AA2	12019	102059	Ring	Copper alloy	Surface/Byzantine-Early Islamic(?)
6	CC	619	6153	Ring (fragment)	Copper alloy	Fill/Byzantine
7	CC	637	6400	Ring (fragment)	Copper alloy	Fill/Byzantine
8	DD3	853	8034	Ring	Brass	Mixed fill/Ottoman(?)
9	AA3	13008	103047	Earrings (fragments)	Gold	Fill/Late Roman-Early Byzantine
10	CC	620	6347	Bell/phylactery (fragment)	Copper alloy	Fill/Byzantine(?)
11	AA2	183	1727	Bell/phylactery (fragment)	Copper alloy	Fill/Byzantine-Early Islamic
12	DD1	Surface		Fibula	Copper alloy	Surface/Hellenistic
13	CC	30104	303993	Kohl stick	Copper alloy	Surface/Byzantine(?)
14	CC	30060	302090	Spatula	Copper alloy	Fill/Byzantine
15	CC	30050	302089	Spatula	Copper alloy	Surface/Byzantine(?)
16	CC	617	6313	Buckle	Copper alloy	Fill/Ottoman(?)
17	AA	10000	100416	Buckle	Copper alloy	Surface/Ottoman(?)
18	AA1	204	2038	Buckle	Copper alloy	Surface/Ottoman(?)
19	CC	608	6118	Buckle	Copper alloy	Surface/Ottoman(?)

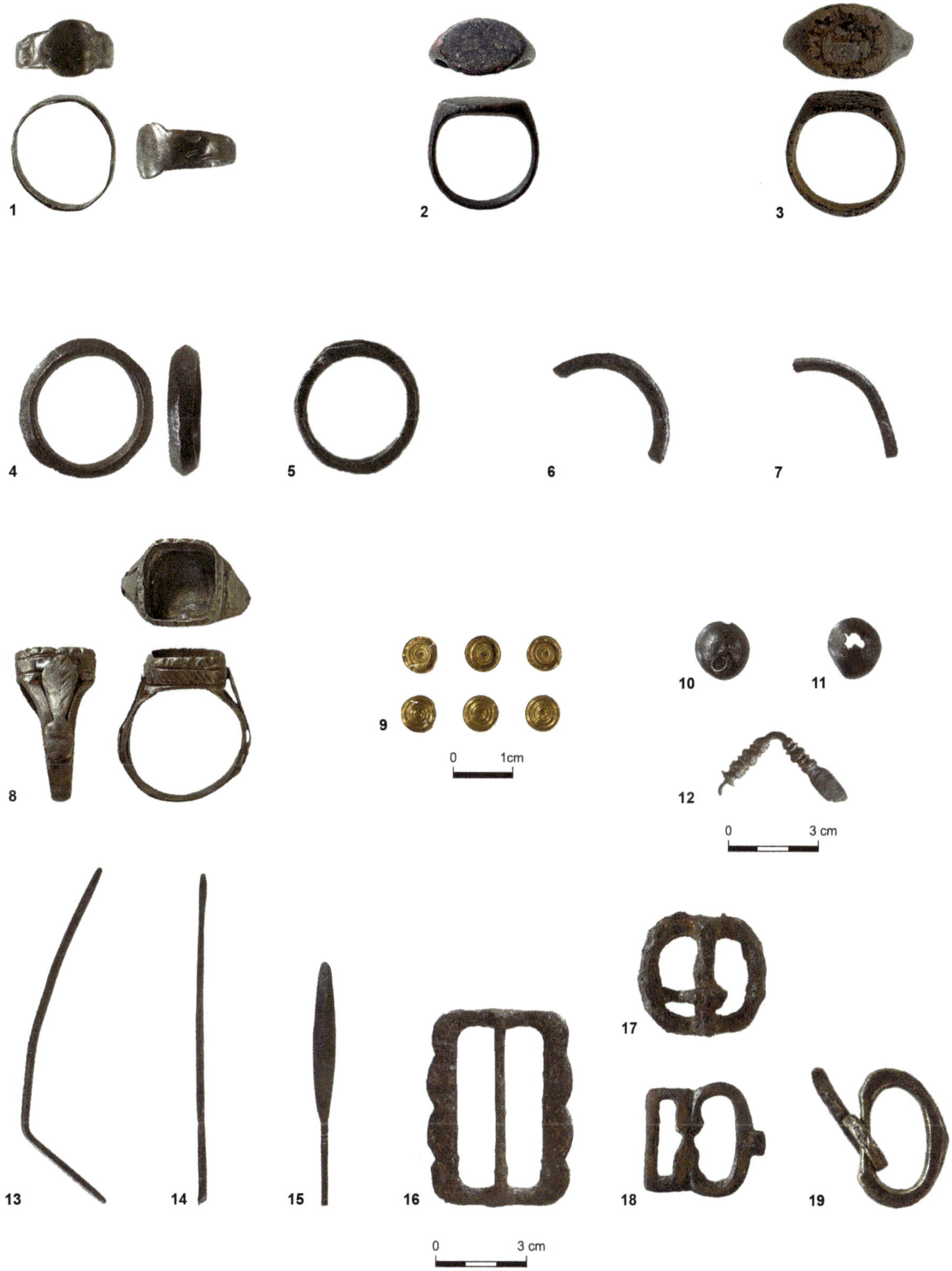

Fig. 17.7: Various metal objects.

Byzantine or Early Islamic period based on the design. The copper alloy rings illustrated in Fig. 17.7: 5–7 form the simplest type found at the site (in either complete or broken state)—a plain, continuous loop (ca. 15–20 mm internal diameter) with a round cross-section. The brass ring shown in Fig. 17.7: 8 with its leaf-shaped ornaments on both sides of the loop (17 mm internal diameter) has a deep square-shaped bezel (with herringbone decorative design on its exterior) where a gem had been set. Despite being found in a mixed fill, it seems to have originated in a Bedouin tomb.

The three gold-made disks illustrated in Fig. 17.7: 9 seem to be ornamental parts of either an earring, bracelet or a necklace. The fact that the disks came from Area AA3, where a disturbed built tomb of Late Roman or Early Byzantine date was unearthed, may suggest that this jewelry was originally worn by one of the deceased buried there.

The copper alloy dome-shaped objects illustrated in Fig. 17.7: 10–11 seem to belong to either small bells or, more likely, the edges of phylactery containers (cylindrical tubes with two pierced lugs) similar to those recently published from nearby Tel Barukh (Tal and Taxel 2015: 120–121, Figs. 180–181).

FIG. 17.8: VARIOUS METAL OBJECTS (CONT.)

No.	*Area*	*Locus*	*Basket*	*Object*	*Material*	*Context/Date*
1	CC	30082	304850	Fish weights (2)	Lead	Fill/Byzantine
2	CC	30065	301521	Fish weights (2)	Lead	Fill/Byzantine
3	CC	30061	302092	Fish weight	Lead	Fill/Byzantine
4	CC	30063	302568	Fish weight	Lead	Fill/Byzantine
5	CC	30061	302597	Fish weight	Lead	Fill/Byzantine
6	CC	30015	300042	Fish weight	Lead	Fill/Byzantine
7	CC	30067	-	Fish weight	Lead	Mixed fill/Byzantine(?)
8	AA1	11031	101234	Fish weight	Lead	Mixed fill/Byzantine(?)
9	AA1	11006	10151	Fish weight	Lead	Mixed fill/Byzantine(?)
10	CC	643	6566	Fish weight	Lead	Fill/Byzantine
11	AA1	207	2013	Fish weight (2)	Lead	Surface/Byzantine(?)
12	AA2	12023	102066	Arrowhead	Iron	Mixed fill/Byzantine(?)
13	CC	601	6017	Spearhead	Iron	Surface/Byzantine-Early Islamic(?)
14	DD2	900	9009	Chisel/hoof pick	Iron	Surface/Byzantine-Early Islamic(?)
15	CC	627	6395	Plough	Iron	Fill/Byzantine
16	CC	30000	300011	Horseshoe	Iron	Surface/Ottoman(?)
17	CC	30037	300767	Nails (2)	Iron	Fill/Byzantine
18	CC	30067	302597	Nail	Iron	Mixed fill/Byzantine(?)
19	CC	30071	302607	Nail	Iron	Fill/Byzantine
20	CC	30118	304733	Nails (5)	Iron	Fill/Byzantine
21	AA	134	1244	Nail	Iron	Fill/Byzantine
22	CC	30048	300544	Nail	Iron	Surface/Byzantine-Early Islamic(?)
23	CC	30061	302151	Nail	Iron	Fill/Byzantine
24	CC	30015	300156	Nail	Iron	Fill/Byzantine
25	CC	30037	301352	Clasp	Iron	Fill/Byzantine
26	AA1	201	2006	Tack	Copper alloy	Surface/Byzantine-Early Islamic(?)
27	BB	-	-	Tack	Copper alloy	Surface/Byzantine-Early Islamic(?)
28	DD1	Surface	-	Tack	Copper alloy	Surface/Byzantine-Early Islamic(?)

Fig. 17.8: Various metal objects (cont.).

The beaded bow copper alloy fibula (Fig. 17.7: 12) was retrieved as a surface find, yet seems to generally belong to the Persian and Hellenistic periods (cf. Muhly and Muhly 1989: 288, Fig. 25.13: No. 244–247). The bent copper alloy kohl stick (Fig. 17.7: 13) is also a surface find but seems to belong to the Byzantine period (cf. Tal and Taxel 2015: 161, Fig. 2.16: 1). The two spatulae illustrated in Fig. 17.7: 14–15, although only partially preserved, seem to belong to a single type, with a leaf-shaped spoon. The joint between the shaft and the spoon is usually decorated with ridges as a molded design (cf. Tal and Taxel 2015: 104, Fig. 1.70). The remainder are simple copper alloy buckles of varied types that came from mixed contexts (Fig. 17.7: 16–19). They may be connected to the site's World War I activity (cf. Chapter 19; and see, in respect, Turner 2006). There are additionally a few fragmented bracelets, pins, chains and partially preserved objects (mostly badly preserved and hence not illustrated) that might also be mentioned in this context. All these may be classified (in the main) as personal utility vessels used by the site's inhabitants and visitors.

OBJECTS OF FISHING, HUNTING, CARPENTRY AND AGRICULTURAL ACTIVITIES

The fish weights retrieved are mechanically reformed sinkers made from cast pieces of lead that were cut, folded, bent or rolled into the desired shape. All our examples are plain and belong to the so-called double-folded rectangular sheets. They are varied in size and this may relate to the function of the lead line to which the sinkers were attached. In Fig. 17.8: 1–11 the better-preserved specimens have been assembled, representing some 90% of the finds recovered. Generally they can be characterized as medium-sized sinkers, with a hole diameter (determined by the width of the folded lead line) of 1.5–2.8 mm and this may attest to their use in gill or trammel nets (cf. Galili, Rosen and Sharvit 2010: 90–92, Fig. 41). Fish weights of the type recovered in Apollonia (East) form the most common type of net sinker recovered from archaeological sites along the Israeli coast, especially in Roman and Byzantine contexts (cf. also Sharvit and Planer 2015: 49, Fig. 1). The fragmented iron arrowhead that was identified (Fig. 17.8: 12) seems to belong to a medieval-period type found in large quantities in the Crusader castle of Area F (cf. Ashkenazi, Golan and Tal 2012). As the current example is carbonized in a similar manner to most arrowheads recovered from Area F, it may have originated in the context of the site's Mamluk conquest of 1265 CE. The fragmented (socketed?) spearhead (Fig. 17.8: 13) came from a mixed context. The complete iron object (Fig. 17.8: 14) with a tang and a blade that narrows toward the center and then widens slightly and ends with a rounded point (14 cm in length) is apparently a chisel. It is a surface find that may be related to carpentry work, given its dimensions and narrow tang. A similar object (but with a much wider tang) was found in the Samaritan cemetery of Tel Barukh in an Early Byzantine context (Tal and Taxel 2015: 107, Fig. 1.72: 7); the latter may have been related to the rock cutting of burial caves. Alternatively this object may have been used as a hoof pick used to clean horses' hooves. The plough (Fig. 17.8: 15), on the other hand, originated from a well-secured locus of a Byzantine date—a relatively unique find for the period and region. The horseshoe (Fig. 17.8: 16) is a surface level find. It seems likely that it is a 20th century artifact that may be related to the militaria discussed in Chapter 19.

STRUCTURAL (AND ORNAMENTAL) FITTINGS

These mostly relate to nails and a few tacks. It is safe to say that most of the metal finds retrieved during the excavations are structural fittings made of iron and originally related to building activities. These are dominated by large nails (over 50 mm long) and clasps, as well as plaques and waste that are commonly known in Roman and Byzantine period sites. In Fig. 17.8: 17–28 the better preserved specimens have been catalogued, which represent some 10% of the finds recovered. The few rounded head (when preserved) tacks found are made of bronze and may originally have belonged to sandals and belts or other kinds of leather-worked items.

REFERENCES

Ariel, D.T. 1990. *Excavations at the City David 1978–1985 Directed by Yigal Shiloh II: Imported Stamped Amphora Handles, Coins, Worked Bone and Ivory, and Glass* (Qedem 30). Jerusalem.

Ariel, D.T. 2017. Imported Hellenistic Stamped Amphora Handles and Fragments from the North Sinai Survey. *Journal of Hellenistic Pottery and Material Culture* 2: 20–67.

Ashkenazi, D., Golan, O. and Tal, O. 2012. An Archaeometallurgical Study of 13th-Century Arrowheads and Bolts from the Crusader Castle of Arsuf/Arsur. *Archaeometry* 55: 235–257.

Ashkenazi, D., Taxel, I. and Tal, O. 2015. Archeometallurgical Characterization of Late Roman- and Byzantine-Period Samaritan Magical Objects and Jewelry Made of Copper Alloys. *Materials Characterization* 102: 195–208.

Ayalon, E. 2005. *The Assemblage of Bone and Ivory Artifacts from Caesarea Maritima, Israel 1st–13th Centuries CE* (Bar International Series 1457). Oxford.

Balog, P. 1970. Islamic Bronze Weights from Egypt. *Journal of the Economic and Social History of the Orient* 13: 233–256.

Berger-Lober, S. 2012. JHWH erhebe Dich! Zwei samaritanische Schriftamulette und ihre Schutzfunktion. *Zeitschrift des Deutschen Palästina-Vereins* 128: 26–42.

Fischer, M. and Tal, O. 2017. Stamped Amphora Handles. In: Greenberg, R., Tal, O. and Daᶜadli, T. *Bet Yeraḥ, Volume III: Hellenistic Philoteria and Islamic al-Ṣinnabra* (IAA Reports 61). Jerusalem: 77–96.

Galili, E., Rosen, B. and Sharvit J. 2010. Artifact Assemblages from Two Roman Shipwrecks off the Carmel Coast. *ᶜAtiqot* 63: 61–110.

Härke, H. 2014. Grave Goods in Early Medieval Burials: Messages and Meanings. *Mortality* 19: 41–60.

Holland, L. 1986. Islamic Bronze Weights from Caesarea Maritima. *American Numismatic Society, Museum Notes* 31: 171–201.

Jackson-Tal, R.E. 2015. Beads, Pendants and Inlays. In: Tal, O. and Taxel, I. 2015. *Samaritan Cemeteries and Tombs in the Central Coastal Plain: Archaeology and History of the Samaritan Settlement outside Samaria (ca. 300–700 CE)* (Ägypten und Altes Testament 82). Münster: 108–114.

Lewis, B., Pellat, C. and Schacht, J., eds. 1965. *The Encyclopedia of Islam*, Vol. II. Leiden.

Kletter, R. 2005. Early Islamic Bronze Weights from Ramla. *ᶜAtiqot* 49: 117–119.

Magness, J. 2002. *The Archaeology of Qumran and the Dead Sea Scrolls*. Grand Rapids and Cambridge.

Miles, G.C. 1964. On the Varieties and Accuracy of Eighth Century Arab Coin Weights. *Eretz-Israel* 7: 78*–87*.

Muhly, J.D. and Muhly, P. 1989. Metal Artifacts. In: Herzog, Z., Rapp, G. Jr. and Negbi, O., eds. *Excavations at Tel Michal, Israel* (Tel Aviv University, Publications of the Institute of Archaeology 8). Minneapolis and Tel Aviv: 267–295.

Palaczyk, M. and Schönenberger, E. 2003. *Eretria Ausgrabungen und Forschungen XII: Amphorenstempel, Grabungen 1965–2001*. Gollion.

Reich, R. 1994. Two Samaritan Rings from Gelilot (el-Jalil), Near Herzliyya. *ᶜAtiqot* 25: 135–138.

Reich, R. 2001. Women and Men at Masada – Some Anthropological Observations Based on the Small Finds (Coins, Spindles). *Zeitschrift des Deutschen Palästina-Vereins* 117: 149–163.

Reich, R. 2002. Samaritan Amulets from the Late Roman and Byzantine Periods. In: Stern E. and Eshel, H., eds. *The Samaritans*. Jerusalem: 289–309 (Hebrew).

Russel, K.W. 1997. Stamped Amphora Handles (with revisions by G. Finkielsztejn and A. Koutsoukou). In: Koutsoukou, A., Russel, K.W., Najjar, M. and Momani, A. *The Great Temple of Amman: The Excavations*. Amman: 39–54.

Sharvit, J. and Planer, D. 2015. A Roman-Period Fishing Station at Yavne-Yam (North). *ᶜAtiqot* 81: 49–58 (Hebrew, English summary pp. 118*–119*).

Tal, O. 2008. Early Islamic Weights. In: Tal, O. and Taxel, I. *Ramla (South): An Early Islamic Industrial Site and Remains of Previous Periods* (Salvage Excavation Reports 5). Tel Aviv: 205–209.

Tal, O. and Taxel, I. 2014. Samaritan Burial Customs Outside Samaria: Evidence from Late Roman and Byzantine Cemeteries in the Southern Sharon Plain. *Zeitschrift des Deutschen Palästina-Vereins* 130: 155–180.

Tal, O. and Taxel, I. 2015. *Samaritan Cemeteries and Tombs in the Central Coastal Plain: Archaeology and History of the Samaritan Settlement outside Samaria (ca. 300–700 CE)* (Ägypten und Altes Testament 82). Münster.

Turner, P. 2006. *Soldiers' Accoutrements of the British Army 1750–1900*. Ramsbury.

Zelinger, Y. 2000. Ramla, Yeḥezqel Street. *Ḥadashot Arkheologiyot – Excavations and Surveys in Israel* 111: 57*.

CHAPTER 18

COINS (AREAS AA–DD, M, N, O)

Gabriela Bijovsky (with a contribution by Issa Baidoun)

Nine hundred and sixty-three coins were discovered during the excavations at Apollonia (East) (Areas AA–DD) and Apollonia National Park (Areas M, N and O). All are registered at the Israel Antiquities Authority (hereafter IAA) Coin Department. However, due to budget limitations, only around a third of the total number of coins were selected for cleaning and identification. These coins were carefully chosen according to their stratigraphic importance (diagnostic loci and installations), their state of preservation and their numismatic value. Three hundred and eighty-two were eventually identifiable and they appear in the catalogue below.[1] The coins are arranged chronologically and typologically as retrieved from the entire excavated site (in 2002, 2009, 2012 and 2013) and not by areas of excavation. The following discussion will describe the numismatic evidence in general and specifically in comparison to the refuse dump unearthed in Area CC. In addition, there is a hoard of 21 small coins discovered in Area M. These coins, only 12 of which were identifiable, were dated to the second half of the 5th century CE. The hoard was fully published (Tal and Bijovsky 2017) and its contents appear at the end of this coin report.

The isolated coins date from the Seleucid up to the Ottoman periods, but the bulk consists primarily of Late Roman and Byzantine coins (4th to 6th centuries CE). All the coins are made of bronze with a few exceptions: three silver *denarii* of Vespasian (No. 7), Hadrian (No. 9) and Julia Domna (No. 10), a gold *solidus* of Zeno (No. 209), an ʿAbbasid silver *dirham* and a fraction of *dirham* (Nos. 362–363) and three silver *deniers* (Nos. 370–372).

Coins dated before the Byzantine period (Nos. 1–17) are normally residual. Nevertheless, a few exceptions may be apparent; No. 8 came from Area DD3 where cist tombs of the Hellenistic and Early Roman period were documented; No. 13 came from Area AA1, the winepress complex, where activity as early as the 3rd century CE is plausible. The earliest coins are two worn Seleucid coins (Nos. 1–2), two *prutot* of Alexander Janneus (Nos. 3–4) and a coin of Herod the Great (No. 5). These are followed by a group of coins of the Roman period (from the first to the 3rd centuries CE), which include the above-mentioned three silver imperial *denarii* minted in Rome (Nos. 7, 9 and 10). Three bronze coins are Roman Provincial issues: an autonomous Tyrian coin dated to 98/99 CE (No. 8) and two coins minted in Neapolis: one of Elagabalus (No. 11) and the other of Volusian (No. 12). Geographically, Apollonia is relatively close to Neapolis and is likely to have been within the radius of coin distribution of this mint. Only two coins of the second half of the 3rd century were discovered: an *antoninianus* of Claudius II (No. 16) and another two of Maximianus minted in Cyzicus (Nos. 17–18).

A large number of coins are dated to the first half of the 4th century CE, from which 32 have been assigned with certainty to this period. Those assigned to the last quarter of the 4th century are three times more in number, representing the highest peak of coins recovered from the excavation in the discussed areas. This is, in fact, the usual picture in most classical-period sites in Palestine (Bijovsky 2000–2002:

1 The coins were cleaned at the IAA laboratories under the direction of L. Kupperschmidt and were photographed by C. Amit of the IAA.

196–197). The coin types are conventional and do not warrant special discussion. The leading types for the first half of the 4th century are: GLORIA EXERCITVS with one standard (Nos. 20–24) and *Vota* types (Nos. 27–32); and for the second half of the 4th century: FEL TEMP REPARATIO fallen horseman (Nos. 33–41, 45–50), SECVRITAS REIPVBLICAE (Nos. 52–58) and SALVS REIPVBLICAE Victory dragging captive (Nos. 69–71, 73–80, 85–119).

Coins of the 5th century CE are numerous in Apollonia-Arsuf (Byzantine Sozousa). The types dated to the first half are: VIRTVS EXERCITI Victory crowning emperor (Nos. 180–181); CONCORDIA AVGGG cross (Nos. 182–185) and its imitations (Nos. 195–196); GLORIA ROMANORVM three emperors (Nos. 186–188); cross within wreath (No. 190); and VICTORIA AVGGG Victory with palm branch and wreath—the official one struck by Honorius in Rome (No. 189) and its varied imitations (Nos. 191–194).

Coin types dated to the second half of the 5th century CE are: one imitation bearing a monogram of Marcian (No. 203), five *nummi* of Leo I of different types (Nos. 204–208) and four coins of Zeno: three *nummi* (Nos. 210–212) and a *solidus* (No. 209). Interestingly and for no clear reason, this gold coin was found in the refuse dump of Area CC (see below).

A typical characteristic of Byzantine sites in Israel is the mass of worn unidentifiable *minimi* that circulated up to the end of the 6th century CE (Bijovsky 2012: 173, 340–341, 352). This phenomenon occurs in Apollonia-Arsuf as well. Most of these coins are Late Roman *minimi* dated to the 4th–5th centuries—60 coins (Nos. 120–179)—and additional 60 coins which can be attributed to the period between the mid-5th to the mid-6th centuries (Nos. 216–235; 241–280).

Foreign coinage such as Vandalic, Ostrogothic and Axumite are a regular component in the monetary currency in circulation in Palestine during this period. These coins appear also in Apollonia-Arsuf. A number of Vandalic *nummi* from Carthage were identified: a proto-Vandalic type dated to ca. 455–484 showing the symbol ⳨ (No. 215); two coins of King Trasamund (496–523) showing a stylized figure of Victory holding a palm branch and wreath (Nos. 236–237); two *nummia* of King Hilderic (523–530) of the cross within wreath type (Nos. 319–320); and last, an anonymous *nummus* of the palm tree type (No. 321). Likewise, there are three small cast Axumite imitations minted in Egypt and roughly dated to 450–550 (Nos. 238–240; Bijovsky 2012: 148–152).

The last foreign coin in the sequence is a *nummus* weighing 0.98 g depicting a bust facing right on the obverse and the letters BD on the reverse (No. 214). The letters are very clear and they do not seem to be intertwined as in a monogram. So far, no proposed identification seems convincing. It might be an unpublished type of the Ostrogothic king Baduila (541–552) or Odovacar (476–493), or even a coin of the Burgundian Gundobad (472–474).[2]

Official imperial Byzantine coins of the 6th century CE constitute a significant group in Apollonia (Byzantine Sozousa). The earliest are copper coins of Anastasius I (491–518): two *folles* of the large module (Nos. 281–282); a *decanummium* dated to 507–512 (No. 283); a half *follis* (No. 294); and eleven *nummia* all from Constantinople with one exception from Antioch (Nos. 285–295). Next are those of Justin I: five *folles* (Nos. 296–300); a *decanummium* from Antioch (No. 301); and a *dodecanummium* from Alexandria (No. 302). Ten coins of Justinian I were identifiable: seven *folles*, all undated (Nos. 305–311); a half *follis* from Nicomedia (No. 312); and six *nummia* minted in Carthage (Nos. 313–318).

A poor local imitation of a ☧ *chi-rho pentanummium* was also discovered (No. 322). This type is tentatively dated to ca. 522–540 and based on frequency and archaeological contexts. Such coins are attributed to a mint somewhere in the area of Ashqelon (Bijovsky 2012: 291–297). Six coins of Justin II were identified: four are *folles* from Constantinople bearing dates between 568 and 575 (Nos. 323–326) and two are half *folles* (Nos. 327–328). Seven coins of Maurice Tiberius were discovered: five *folles* (Nos. 335–339) and two half *folles* (Nos. 340–341).

2 As proposed by N. Schindler (personal communication).

Coins dated to the 7th century CE are relatively few. They include a *follis* of Phocas from Antioch dated to 607/608 (No. 349) and four *folles* of Heraclius (Nos. 350–353). In addition, there are two coppers of Constans II from Constantinople: a *follis* dated to 655/656 (No. 354) and a half *follis* dated to 656/657 (No. 355). The latter is an overstrike upon an earlier type of the same emperor. From approximately the same period are three Arab-Byzantine coins of the earliest series dated to ca. 647–670. No. 356 belongs to the most common type imitating issues of Constans II, while No. 358 is a mule combining an imperial bust on the obverse with a cursive **m** on the reverse. This combination is rare (Pottier, Schulze and Schulze 2008: Class III).

A number of Islamic coins have been identified.[3] The earliest are three post-Reform Umayyad *fūlus* (Nos. 359–361). An interesting group of five ʿAbbasid coins is next; among them is a silver *dirham* of al-Mahdī dated to 778 CE and struck in al-Muḥammadiya (No. 362) and a fraction of *dirham* of Muḥammad al-Amīn dated to 811 CE (No. 363). Legends on both coins were carefully reconstructed by comparison with similar issues from Lowick (1996, see coin catalogue).

Three Ayyubid *fūlus* (Nos. 367–369) are more or less contemporary to a Crusader silver *denier* of Baldwin III of the Tower of David type (No. 371). Five Mamluk *fūlus* are next, four of Bybars (Nos. 374–377) and one of Barqūq from Aleppo (No. 378). The latest identified coins are Ottoman: an *akçe* of Selim I (No. 379) and a *para* of Maḥmūd II (No. 380).

Figure 18.1 shows the numismatic profile of the excavated site in comparison to that of the refuse dump in Area CC. This area was located in the town's immediate hinterland to the east (Apollonia [East]), intended for garbage disposal. A breakdown of the dump's contents shows that most of the finds in the pit were potsherds, animal bones and mollusc remains, glass and metal object fragments, some 130 intact oil lamps and a high concentration of coins, of which 144 were identifiable (Chapters 6 and 14, above).

The graph presents an almost complete correspondence between both ensembles showing the same peaks and chronology. This picture may suggest that the dump had been filled with refuse disposed from the site and therefore its contents reflect the profile of the coinage in circulation at the site and the same periods of occupation.[4]

Most striking in Fig. 18.1 is the rise in the number of coins towards the last quarter of the 4th century and the large quantities of worn 4th–5th century *minimi*. The number of coins decreases drastically by the mid-6th century. The latest datable coins from the refuse dump are a *nummus* of the Vandal king Hilderic dated to 523–530 (Nos. 319–320) and the anonymous Vandalic palm tree coin, attributed to the days of Justinian I (No. 321). According to these coin finds, the refuse dump in Area CC went out of use by the mid-6th century (Nos. 343–344), while the Byzantine settlement probably continued up to the early/mid-7th century.[5]

The excavators speculate that all magic practices and rituals involving the discarding of personal property of the deceased may have been associated with the exceptional number of coins (Chapter 14). They also suggest that the place functioned not only for refuse disposal but also for magical or ritual practices based on the complete lamps found and postulated sequence or development of events: 1) the material remains of a magical recipe whose practice was carried out in the dump area where the lamps were used as containers for organic substances; 2) a repository of old religious/cultic items which were in use in the town's Samaritan synagogue and discarded due to religious or practical needs; 3) a repository of personal belongings of deceased individuals from among the town's inhabitants discarded rather than

3 The Islamic coins were identified by Issa Baidoun.

4 Moreover, the correspondence between both coin evidence in the graph indicates that the preliminary selection of coins for cleaning was accurate and does not distort the numismatic profile of the excavation.

5 This conclusion, however, is relative since it is based only on those coins which have been selected for identification and analysis.

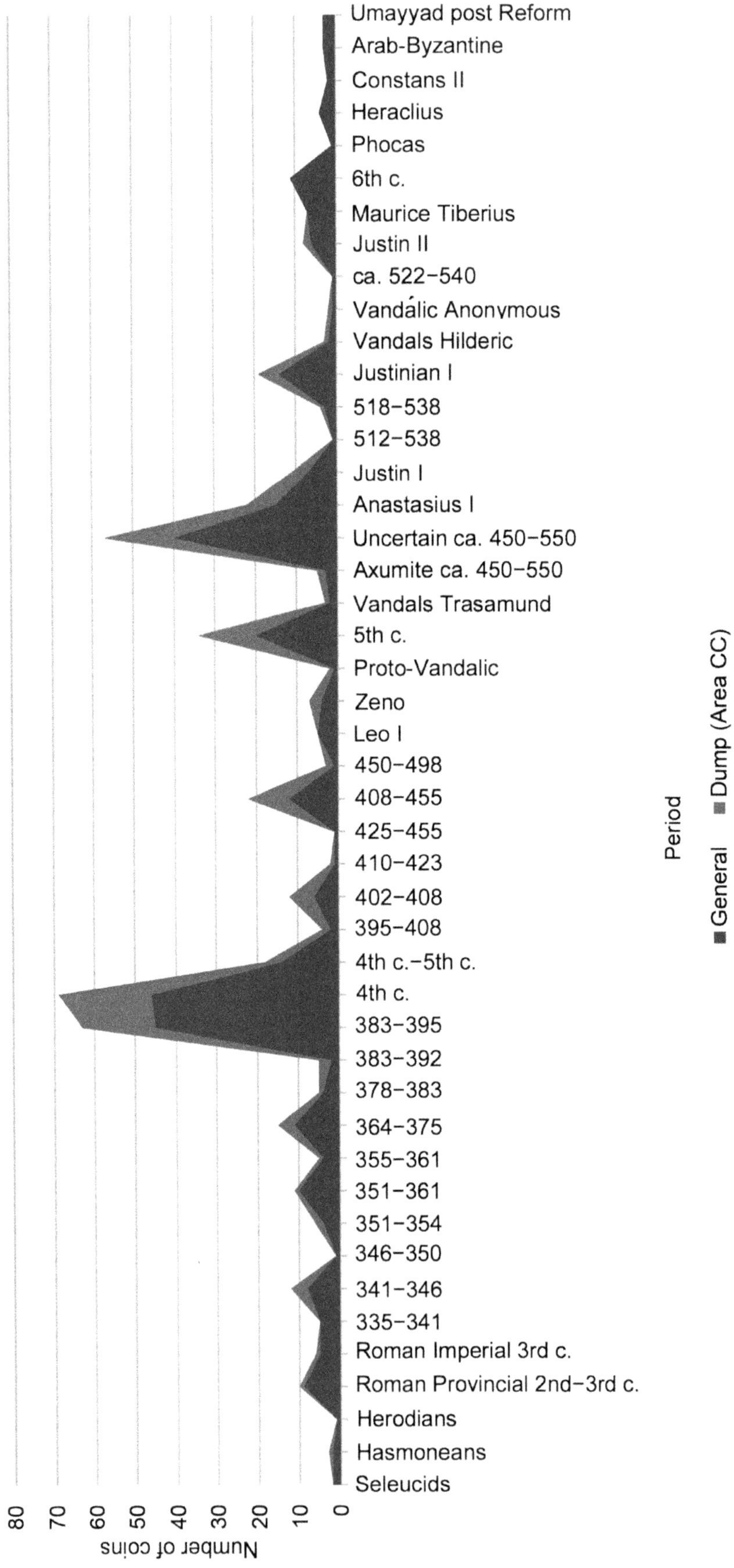

Fig. 18.1. The general numismatic profile at Apollonia (East) in comparison to the refuse dump unearthed in Area CC.

buried with the dead or kept by their relatives. The excavators speculate that all these scenarios may have been associated with the exceptional number of coins, some of which may have functioned in a ritual or a societal practice (Tal and Taxel 2017: 188–190; see also Chapter 14 above).

Accumulations of tiny low-value copper coins in archaeological contexts are a common phenomenon in Byzantine Palestine and the Levant. Many of these accumulations are of ritual or apotropaic character, such as foundation deposits in synagogues and other buildings, accumulations in wishing wells, etc.[6] Occasionally, gold coins were included in such ensembles, such as the floor foundation deposits in the synagogues at Deir ʿAziz, Dabiyye, Umm el Qanatir and Ḥorvat Rimmon (Bijovsky 2012: 90–91). As mentioned above, a solidus of Zeno was discovered within the dump of Area CC at the site. The possibility that this coin reached the dump by mistake or distraction is valid. Still, the question remains of why anyone would throw such valuable property into a dump if not for ritual reasons such as a votive offering. As in the case of floor foundation deposits, the owner must have realized that the gold coin would not be retrieved.

6 This subject was comprehensively studied by the author. See the index entry "foundation deposits" for the many references (Bijovsky 2012). See also Ahipaz 2013.

Coins from Excavations in Apollonia (East) (Areas AA–DD and Their Derivatives) and Apollonia National Park (Areas M, N, O) (License Nos. G-59/2006 and G-56/2009; Permits Nos. A-6549/2012 and A-6825/2013) Catalogue of the Isolated Coins (Figs. 18.2–18.4)*

Cat. No.	*Loc. No.*	*Basket*	*W. (gr)*	*Diam. (mm)*	*Axis*	*Obverse*	*Reverse*	*Date (CE)*	*Mint*	*References and Notes*	*IAA No.*
Seleucids: Antiochus III (223–187 BCE)											
1	30114	303867	1.70	10	↑	Head of Apollo r.	[ΒΑΣΙΛ]ΕΩΣ [ΑΝΤΙΟΧΟΥ] Apollo stg. l., holding bow and arrow		Antioch	*SC* 1: 404, No. 1064	148677
Seleucids: Uncertain											
2	30089	303324	1.48	13		Obliterated	Obliterated			Serrated?	148648
Hasmoneans: Alexander Jannaeus (103–76 BCE) – *Prutah*											
3	30082	302377	0.83	12		[---] Anchor within wreath	[---] Star	After 80/79 BCE	Jerusalem	*TJC*: 210, Nos. L7–L17	148634
4	30054	303034	0.69	12		Same	Same	Same	Same	Same	148408
Herodians: Herod I (37–4 BCE) – *Prutah*											
5*	111	1245	1.38	14	↑	[---] Anchor	Double cornucopia, with caduceus between horns		Jerusalem	*TJC*: 223, No. 59	148745
Roman Procurators in Judea: Under Augustus											
6	7033	70798	1.66	16	↑	[KAICA]POC Ear of grain	Palm tree flanked by date: L–M	9/10?	Jerusalem	*TJC*: 256, No. 314	117346
Roman Provincial: Vespasianus (69–79 CE) – silver *Denarius*											
7*	13008	103042	3.04	18	↓	IMP CAESAR VESPASIANVS AVG Head l., laureate	Pair of oxen stg. l. In exergue: COS VIII	77–78	Rome	*CRE* 2: 38, Nos. 206–209	148283
Roman Provincial: Autonomous											
8*	Surface	8018	1.54	13	↑	Head of Tyche r.	Tyche stg. l. on galley. To l. date: ΔΚΣ; to r.: ΜΡ	98/99	Tyre	*BMC Phoen.*: 261, No. 303	148782
Roman Provincial: Hadrian (117–138 CE) – silver *Denarius*											
9*	13008	103043	3.13	18	↓	HADRIANVS AVG COS III PP Head r., laureate	HISPANIA Hispania reclining to l., behind her a hare	134–138	Rome	*CRE* 3: 346, No. 849	148284

* Loci prefixed by 10X–15X, 37X and by 100XX came from Area AA; by 20X–26X, and by 110XX came from Area AA1; by 16X–19X, 35X–36X and by 120XX came from Area AA2; by 130XX came from Area AA3; by 40X–45X came from Area BB; by 60X–65X, and by 300XX came from Area CC; by 310XX came from Area CC2; by 400XX came from Area DD; by 75X–81X came from Area DD1; by 90X-99X came from Area DD2; and 85X–88X and by 410XX came from Area DD3. Coins from Area M are prefixed by 70XX and 72XX; coins from Area N by 50XX and coins from Area O by 80XX. Description for the loci appears in the List of Loci. Cat. Nos. marked with * appear in Figs. 18.2–18.4.

Fig. 18.2: Coins from excavations at Apollonia (Areas AA–DD, M, N, O).

Cat. No.	Loc. No.	Basket	W. (gr)	Diam. (mm)	Axis	Obverse	Reverse	Date (CE)	Mint	References and Notes	IAA No.
Roman Provincial: Julia Domna (w. of Septimius Severus) – silver *Denarius*											
10*	165	1621	3.18	19	↑	IVLIA PIA FELIX AVG Head r., laureate	VESTA Vesta seated to l., holding simpulum and scepter	211–217	Rome	*CRE* 5: 435, Nos. 31–32	148748
Roman Provincial: Elagabalus (218–222 CE)											
11*	10022	100137	8.73	21	↓	AY KAI MAP ANTWNEINOC CEB Bust r., laureate	ΦΛ NEAC ΠΟΛEWC CYΠAΛ Tyche stg. l. within tetrastyle temple		Neapolis	*CHL*: 55, No. 104	148260
Roman Provincial: Volusian (251–253 CE)											
12*	10030	100166	9.57	25	↑	[AYT KAIC ΓOYI] TPEBO YOΛ Y CIANOC Bust r., radiate	ΦΛ NEAC ΠΟΛEWC Eagle facing holding Mount Gerizim between wings		Neapolis	Rosenberger 1977: 25, No. 123	148266
Roman Provincial: Uncertain											
13	205	2002	4.88	19–24		[---] Bust r.	Obliterated	2nd–3rd ca.			148752
14	30118	304691	4.50	30		Same	Same	3rd ca.			148688
Roman Imperial: Gallienus (253–268 CE) – *Antoninianus*											
15	8070	80337	3.91	20–22	↓	GALLIENVS AVG Bust l., radiate, cuirassed and draped	LV[NA L]VCIF Diana adv. r. holding torch. In ex.: PXV	267	Antioch	*RIC* 5/1: 185, No. 609	140258
Roman Imperial: Claudius II (268–270 CE) – *Antoninianus*											
16*	30000	304669	3.35	20–22	↓	IMP C CLAVDIVS AVG Bust l., radiate, cuirassed and draped	NEPTV N AVG Neptune stg. l. with trident and dolphin		Antioch	*RIC* 5/1: 229, No. 214	148287
Roman Imperial: Maximianus (286–305, 306–308, 310 CE)											
17	30061	301748	2.74	20–22	↓	IMP C MA MAXIMIANVS PF AVG Bust r., radiate, cuirassed and draped	CONCORDIA MILITVM Emperor receiving Victory on globe from Jupiter. Below: KB	295–299	Cyzicus	*RIC* 6: 581, No. 15b	148430
18*	8061	80315	6.96	21–23	↑	IMP C GAL VAL MAXIMIANVS PF AVG Bust r., radiate, cuirassed and draped	GENIO E[X]ERCITVS Genius sacrificing on altar. To l.: ∪; to r.: H; in ex.: ANT	310	Antioch	*RIC* 6: 638, No. 147	140252

Fig. 18.3: Coins from Excavations in Apollonia (Areas AA–DD, M, N, O) (cont.).

Cat. No.	Loc. No.	Basket	W. (gr)	Diam. (mm)	Axis	Obverse	Reverse	Date (CE)	Mint	References and Notes	IAA No.
ROMAN IMPERIAL: Licinius I (307–324 CE)											
19	Surface	b	1.33	19	↓	]LICIN[Bust r., laureate, cuirassed and draped	]VR[Figure stg?				140260
LATE ROMAN: Uncertain											
20	30020	300163	1.47	14	↑	DN CONSTAN[---] Bust r., pearl-diademed, cuirassed and draped	[GLORIA EXERCITVS] Two soldiers stg. facing with shields and spears. Between them a standard. Mintmark illegible	335–341		Cf. *LRBC* 1: 31, Nos. 1391–1393	148299
21	601	6032	1.04	17	↓	[---] Same	Same	Same		Same	148758
22	30074	302898	0.87	15–17		Same	Same	Same		Same	148606
23	30062	302567	0.96	15	↑	Same	Same	Same		Same	148567
24	608	6297	0.49	12	↓	Same	Same	Same		Same	148760
LATE ROMAN: Constantine I deified											
25	30148	305242	1.24	15	↑	]CONSTAN[Bust r., veiled and draped	VN–MR Emperor stg. facing, veiled and draped. Mintmark illegible	341–346		Cf. *LRBC* 1: 31, No. 1397	148713
26	10030	100371	1.20	11–15	↓	Same	Same	Same		Same	148267
LATE ROMAN: Constans I (337–350 CE)											
27	10023	100099	1.37	15	↓	[DN CONS]TANS PF AVG Bust r., pearl-diademed, cuirassed and draped	Within wreath: VOT/XX/MVLT/XXX In exergue: SMANT	341–346	Antioch	Cf. *LRBC* 1: 31, No. 1398	148262
28	11079	101302	2.06	15	↓	CONSTAN[---] Same	Same	Same	Same	Same	148659
29	12012	102057	1.29	15	↑	Same	Same, but mintmark illegible	Same		Same	148276
30	30081	303332	1.21	13–15		Same	Same	Same		Same	148630
31	30037	301558	0.90	12–14	↑	Same	Same	Same		Same	148386
32	30118	305004	0.92	15	↑	Same	Same	Same		Same	148701
LATE ROMAN: Constantius II (337–361 CE)											
33	30011	300160	4.34	20–23	↑	DN CONSTAN TIVS PF AVG Bust l., pearl-diademed, cuirassed and draped, holding globe.	FEL TEMP REPARATIO Emperor stg. l. holding standard with ☧, to l. two captives facing r. In ex.: AL[EA]	346–350	Alexandria	Cf. *LRBC* 2: 103, No. 2816	148297

Fig. 18.4: Coins from Excavations in Apollonia (Areas AA–DD, M, N, O) (cont.).

Cat. No.	Loc. No.	Basket	W. (gr)	Diam. (mm)	Axis	Obverse	Reverse	Date (CE)	Mint	References and Notes	IAA No.
34*	---	1115	5.26	22	↑	DN CONSTAN TIVS PF AVG Bust r., pearl-diademed, cuirassed and draped	FEL [TEMP REPA]RATIO Virtus spearing fallen horseman, embracing the horse's neck (FH4). In l. field: • In exergue: CONSΘ	351–354	Constantinople	Cf. *LRBC* 2: 87, No. 2043 (but FH3)	148784
35	Surface	a	2.36	18	↓	Same	FEL [TEMP REP]ARATIO Virtus spearing fallen horseman, raising arm (FH3). In ex.: AQP	352–354	Aquilea	Cf. *LREC* 2: 66, No. 930	140259
36	253	2138	2.10	17	←	Same	[FEL] TEMP REPA]RATIO Virtus spearing fallen horseman, raising arm (FH3). Mintmark illegible	351–361		Cf. *LRBC* 2: 100, No. 2632	148756
37	Surface	g	2.42	19	↑	Same	Same	Same		Same	140265
38	7041	70038	2.06	16	↓	Same	Same	Same		Same	117347
39	7008	70307	1.33	17	↑	Same	Same	Same		Same	117337
40	10029	100202	1.96	15	↑	Same	Same	Same		Same	148265
41	30071	302107	1.39	13	↑	Same	Same	Same		Same	148591
42	201	2017	2.04	15	↓	DN CONSTANTIVS PF AVG Bust r., pearl-diademed, cuirassed and draped	SPES REI–PVBLICE Virtus stg. facing, holding spear and globe. Mintmark illegible.	355–361		Cf. *LRBC* 2: 100, No. 2638	148751
43	636	6405	1.70	14	↑	Same	Same	Same		Same	148765
44	30071	302417	0.95	14	↑	Same	Same	Same		Same	148596
LATE ROMAN: Constantius Gallus (351–354 CE)											
45*	30063	302566	4.97	22	↓	DN FL CONSTAN TIVS NOB CAES Bust r., bare-headed, cuirassed and draped	FEL [TEMP REPA]RATIO Virtus spearing fallen horseman, raising arm (FH3). In exergue: SMKB		Cyzicus	*LRBC* 2: 96, No. 2491	148566
46	30118	304853	3.61	21	↑	Same	Same, but mintmark illegible			Same	148696
LATE ROMAN: 351–361 CE											
47	30081	304380	3.07	18	↓	[---] Bust r., bare-headed, cuirassed and draped	[FEL TEMP REPARATIO] Virtus spearing fallen horseman, raising arm (FH3). In exergue: ALE?		Alexandria	Cf. *LRBC* 2: 103, Nos. 2841 or 2847	148632
48	12019	102055	2.03	20		Obliterated	Same, but mintmark illegible			Same	148280
49	30037	300774	1.27	16		Same	Same			Same	148372
50	12019	102054	1.26	16	↓	[---] Bust r.	Same			Same	148281

Cat. No.	Loc. No.	Basket	W. (gr)	Diam. (mm)	Axis	Obverse	Reverse	Date (CE)	Mint	References and Notes	IAA No.
LATE ROMAN: Julian II (360–363 CE)											
51	10046	100037	1.34	15	↑	DN IVLIANVS NOB CAES Bust r., bare-headed, cuirassed and draped	SPES REI–PVBLICE Virtus stg. facing, holding spear and globe. Mintmark illegible.	355–361		Cf. *LRBC* 2: 100, No. 2639	148268
LATE ROMAN: Uncertain emperor											
52	11078	101304	1.95	11–13	↑	[---] Bust r., pearl-diademed, cuirassed and draped	SECVRI[TAS REIPVBLICAE] Victory adv. l., holding palm branch and wreath. Mintmark illegible	364–375		Cf. *LRBC* 2: 100, Nos. 2656–57	148661
53	30081	304482	1.82	15	↑	Same	Same	Same		Same	148633
54	30070	302128	1.80	14	↓	Same	Same	Same		Same	148584
55	12004	102011	1.28	15	↓	Same	Same	Same		Same	148274
56	30036	300714	1.15	12	↑	Same	Same	Same		Same	148313
57	30061	302588	1.10	11–13	↓	Same	Same	Same		Same	148435
58	643	6677	1.01	13	↓	Same	Same	Same		Same	148775
59	30000	302584	1.12	17	↓	[---] Bust r., pearl-diademed, cuirassed and draped	[GLORIA ROMANORVM] Emperor advancing r., holding standard and dragging captive. Mintmark illegible	Same		Cf. *LRBC* 2: 100, Nos. 2658–62	148285
60	8021	80129	1.78	15	↑	Same	Same	Same		Same	140247
61	30071	302207	0.65	12	↑	Same	Same	Same		Same	148592
62	10022	100167	0.65	10–13	↓	Same	Same	Same		Same	148261
LATE ROMAN: Valentinian II (375–392 CE)											
63	30070	302127	1.10	12	↑	DN VALENT[INIANVS PFAVG] Bust r., pearl-diademed, cuirassed and draped	Within wreath: VOT/X/MVLT/XX Mintmark illegible	378–383		Cf. *LRBC* 2: 101, No. 2733	148583
LATE ROMAN: 378–383 CE											
64	30000	304363	0.61	13	↓	[---] Bust r., pearl-diademed, cuirassed and draped	Within wreath: VOT/X/MVLT/XX In exergue: ANΓ		Antioch	Cf. *LRBC* 2: 101, Nos. 2740–43	148286
65	30081	303333	1.22	10–11	↑	Same	Same, but mintmark illegible			Same	148631
66	30050	302113	1.07	13		Same	Illegible *Vota* type				148403

Cat. No.	*Loc. No.*	*Basket*	*W. (gr)*	*Diam. (mm)*	*Axis*	*Obverse*	*Reverse*	*Date (CE)*	*Mint*	*References and Notes*	*IAA No.*
Late Roman: Arcadius (383–408 CE)											
67	30060	303037	1.10	14	↑	DN ARCADIVS PF AVG Bust r., pearl-diademed, cuirassed and draped	Within wreath: VOT/V Mintmark illegible	383		Cf. *LRBC* 2: 101, No. 2736	148426
Late Roman: 383–392 CE											
68	30148	305281	0.99	13	↑	[---] Bust r., pearl-diademed, cuirassed and draped	GLORIA REIPVBLICE Camp gate. Mintmark illegible			Cf. *LRBC* 2: 82, No. 1862	148717
Late Roman: Valentinian II (375–392 CE)											
69*	212	2195	1.47	12–14		DN VALENTINIANVS PF AVG Bust r., pearl-diademed, cuirassed and draped	SALVS REI PVBLICAE Victory advancing l., dragging captive, holding trophy. In l. field, ⳨. In exergue: ANTA	383–392	Antioch	*LRBC* 2: 102, No. 2768	148755
70	30071	301747	0.93	12	↑	Same	Same, but mintmark illegible	Same		Same	148589
71	30071	---	0.90	14	↑	Same	Same	Same		Same	148585
Theodosius I (379–395 CE)											
72	30061	302600	1.11	13	↑	[DN THEODO[SIVS PF AVG] Bust r., pearl-diademed, cuirassed and draped	Within wreath: VOT/X/MVLT/XX In exergue: ALEΓ	378–383	Alexandria	Cf. *LRBC* 2: 104, No. 2882	148437
73	30041	300699	1.40	14	↓	[DN THE]ODO[SIVS PF AVG] Bust r., pearl-diademed, cuirassed and draped	SA[LVS REI]PVBLI[CAE] Victory advancing l., dragging captive, holding trophy. In l. field, ⳨. In exergue: C[ONS]	383–395	Constantinople	*LRBC* 2: 89, No. 2178	148401
74	30007	300167	1.17	14	5	Same	Same, but mintmark illegible	Same		Cf. *LRBC* 2: 89, No. 2178	148291
75	30148	305325	1.07	13	↑	Same	Same	Same		Same	148719
76	643	6673	0.57	12	↗	Same	Same	Same		Same	148774
Late Roman: Arcadius (383–408 CE)											
77	30114	304128	1.35	12	↑	DN ARCADIVS PF AVG Bust r., pearl-diademed, cuirassed and draped	SALVS REI PVBLICAE Victory advancing l., dragging captive, holding trophy. Mintmark illegible	383–395		Cf. *LRBC* 2: 89, No. 2185	148678
78	30071	302210	0.93	11	↓	Same	Same	Same		Same	148593

Cat. No.	Loc. No.	Basket	W. (gr)	Diam. (mm)	Axis	Obverse	Reverse	Date (CE)	Mint	References and Notes	IAA No.
79	30060	302113	0.93	14	↑	Same	Same	Same		Same	148417
80	30071	301746	0.77	14	↑	Same	Same	Same		Same	148588
81	11052	101271	2.76	15	↑	Same	GLORIA ROMANORVM Emperor riding horse r. In exergue: ALEA	Same	Alexandria	Cf. *LRBC* 2: 105, No. 2915	148658
82	30118	303945	0.69	10–13		DN AR[CADIVS PF AVG] Bust r., pearl-diademed, cuirassed and draped	Obliterated				148680
Late Roman: Honorius (393–423 CE)											
83	10028	100203	0.98	11–13	7	DN HONORIVS PF AVG Bust r., pearl-diademed, cuirassed and draped	SALVS REI PVBLICAE Victory advancing l., dragging captive, holding trophy. Mintmark illegible	393–395		Cf. *LRBC* 2: 89, No. 2194	148263
84	30060	302586	1.44	10		Same	Obliterated				148422
Late Roman: 383–395											
85	Dump	9960	0.98	12	↓	[---] Bust r., pearl-diademed, cuirassed and draped	[SALVS REI PV]BLICAE Victory advancing l., dragging captive, holding trophy. In l. field, ⳩. In exergue: ANTA		Antioch	Cf. *LRBC* 2: 102, Nos. 2768–2771	148783
86	12019	102053	0.72	11	↑	Same	Same, but in exergue: CON		Constantinople	Cf. *LRBC* 2: 89, Nos. 2183–2185	148279
87	641	6600	1.40	12	↓	Same	Same, but mintmark illegible			Same	148767
88	Surface	e	1.36	12	↓	Same	Same			Same	140270
89	12015	102047	1.27	11	↓	Same	Same			Same	148277
90	30061	302601	1.27	12	↓	Same	Same			Same	148438
91	30037	301766	1.23	13	↑	Same	Same			Same	148392
92	178	1730	1.18	11x14	↓	Same	Same			Same	148749
93	12012	102056	1.12	12	↓	Same	Same			Same	148275
94	30134	304732	1.13	13	↑	Same	Same			Same	148710
95	30074	304231	1.12	12	↑	Same	Same			Same	148627
96	30055	302123	1.11	12	-	Same	Same			Same	148409
97	30068	302519	1.10	12	↑	Same	Same			Same	148579
98	30034	300940	1.07	11	4	Same	Same			Same	148375
99	30130	304706	1.02	11	↑	Same	Same			Same	148708

Cat. No.	Loc. No.	Basket	W. (gr)	Diam. (mm)	Axis	Obverse	Reverse	Date (CE)	Mint	References and Notes	IAA No.
100	30101	303327	1.01	12	↓	Same	Same			Same	148671
101	11043	101229	1.01	13	↓	Same	Same			Same	148270
102	30037	300772	0.98	12	↑	Same	Same			Same	148316
103	30040	300703	0.98	12	3	Same	Same			Same	148400
104	30060	301513	0.97	12x15	↓	Same	Same			Same	148413
105	30060	302888	0.97	11	↑	Same	Same			Same	148411
106	30071	302740	0.97	13	↑	Same	Same			Same	148597
107	163	1651	0.96	13	↓	Same	Same			Same	148747
108	30037	300971	0.95	16	↑	Same	Same			Same	148376
109	30074	303836	0.93	14	↓	Same	Same			Same	148621
110	30038	300290	0.83	14	↑	Same	Same			Same	148398
111	---	102044	0.82	11	↑	Same	Same			Same	148727
112	30015	300154	0.81	12	↓	Same	Same			Same	148298
113	30118	304938	0.78	12	↑	Same	Same			Same	148699
114	30037	301381	0.77	10	↑	Same	Same			Same	148382
115	30023	300151	0.77	13	!	Same	Same			Same	148301
116	30071	301745	0.75	12	↑	Same	Same			Same	148587
117	30052	301520	0.69	14	↓	Same	Same			Same	148405
118	30037	300771	0.65	13	↑	Same	Same			Same	148315
119	30074	303681	0.50	12	↑	Same	Same			Same	148617
Late Roman: Uncertain 4th century CE											
120	30087	301907	1.51	13		[---] Bust r., pearl-diademed, cuirassed and draped	Obliterated				148643
121	30059	302557	1.30	14		Same	Same				148410
122	30118	304581	1.28	10		Same	Same				148685
123	30100	303331	1.26	11		Same	Same				148664
124	30003	300165	1.25	15		Same	Same				148293
125	30088	303036	1.19	13		Same	Same				148644
126	30037	301530	1.17	12		Same	Same				148662
127	11042	101210	1.14	10		Same	Same				148655
128	30071	---	1.14	11		Same	Same				148586
129	30087	303324	1.13	14		Same	Same				148645

Cat. No.	*Loc. No.*	*Basket*	*W. (gr)*	*Diam. (mm)*	*Axis*	*Obverse*	*Reverse*	*Date (CE)*	*Mint*	*References and Notes*	*IAA No.*
130	30060	302587	1.10	13		Same	Same				148423
131	30036	300368	1.08	10		Same	Same				148308
132	6671	643	1.08	12		Same	Same				148773
133	11041	101270	1.04	10		Same	Same				148269
134	30060	303085	1.04	13		Same	Same				148425
135	30118	304722	1.02	13		Same	Same				148690
136	30082	303314	1.01	13		Same	Same				148637
137	30061	302559	0.99	13		Same	Same				148436
138	30089	302328	0.95	13		Same	Same				148649
139	30060	302112	0.93	14		Same	Same				148416
140	30007	300168	0.92	13		Same	Same				148292
141	30060	301514	0.89	15		Same	Same				148414
142	30005	300166	0.88	13		Same	Same				148290
143	30074	303507	0.87	13		Same	Same				148615
144	30065	302565	0.87	12		Same	Same				148576
145	30032	301903	0.85	13		Same	Same				148302
146	30065	301091	0.85	15		Same	Same				148570
147	30060	303549	0.81	13		Same	Same				148427
148	30036	300370	0.80	12		Same	Same				148309
149	30036	300365	0.76	12		Same	Same				148306
150	30118	304392	0.74	10		Same	Same				148682
151	617	6115	0.72	14		Same	Same				148761
152	30036	300594	0.67	12		Same	Same				148310
153	30036	---	0.64	10		Same	Same				148303
154	13002	103021	0.60	12		Same	Same				148282
155	30037	301083	0.54	12		Same	Same				148378
156	643	6693	0.52	11		Same	Same				148777
157	30074	302904	0.46	13		Same	Same				148609
158	30100	303475	0.39	11		Same	Same				148667
159	11078	305303	1.46	13	↑	Same	Victory to l.?				148660
160	11044	101232	1.91	14		Same	Same				148656
161	30087	304863	1.39	15	↓	Same	Same				148638
162	30068	302220	1.30	12	↓	Same	Two figures stg.?				148578

Cat. No.	Loc. No.	Basket	W. (gr)	Diam. (mm)	Axis	Obverse	Reverse	Date (CE)	Mint	References and Notes	IAA No.
163	11037	101228	1.40	10		Obliterated	Figure to l.?				148654
164	30065	302522	1.34	10		Same	Same				148575
165	Surface	i	1.05	11		Same	Same				140267
Late Roman: Uncertain 4th–5th centuries CE											
166	30036	300364	0.94	10		[---] Bust r., pearl-diademed, cuirassed and draped	Figure to l.?				148305
167	643	6664	0.47	11		Same	Wreath?				148772
168	7042	71338	1.08	14		Same	Obliterated				117350
169	30060	300008	0.99	10		Same	Same				148412
170	30083	303324	0.95	11		Same	Same				148641
171	30074	302099	0.91	10		Same	Same				148605
172	30083	303032	0.85	10		Same	Same				148640
173	30038	300452	0.77	10		Same	Same				148399
174	30061	301509	0.71	11		Same	Same				148429
175	Surface	k	0.59	9		Same	Same				140269
176	30071	302789	0.58	10		Same	Same				148598
177	30074	302931	0.51	12		Same	Same				148611
178	30112	303823	0.46	10		Same	Same				148675
179	30082	304904	1.30	10		Obliterated	Same				148639
Late Roman: 395–408 CE											
180	30065	301744	1.35	12	↓	[---] Bust r., pearl-diademed, cuirassed and draped. In l. field star	[VIRTVS EXERCITI] Victory crowning Victory with wreath. Mintmark illegible			Cf. *LRBC* 2: 102, Nos. 2791–2794	148573
181	30118	304571	1.07	13	↑	Same	Same			Same. Imitation?	148684
Late Roman: Honorius (393–423 CE)											
182	30118	304685	0.37	10	↑	DN HONO[RIVS PF AVG] Bust r., pearl-diademed, cuirassed and draped. In l. field star	[CONCORDIA AVGGG] Cross, mintmark illegible	402–408		Cf. *LRBC* 2: 95, No. 2452	148687

Cat. No.	*Loc. No.*	*Basket*	*W. (gr)*	*Diam. (mm)*	*Axis*	*Obverse*	*Reverse*	*Date (CE)*	*Mint*	*References and Notes*	*IAA No.*
Late Roman: 402–408 CE											
183	30100	303330	0.51	11	↑	[---] Bust r., pearl-diademed, cuirassed and draped. In l. field star	[CONCORDIA AVGGG] Cross, in exergue: CO[NS		Constantinople	Cf. *LRBC* 2: 90, No. 2221	148663
184	30160	305428	0.54	10		Same	Same, but mintmark illegible			Same	148721
185	30118	303984	0.40	9	↓	Same	Same			Same	148681
Late Roman: 403–408 CE											
186	30061	300709	1.11	13	↑	[---] Bust r., pearl-diademed, cuirassed and draped. In l. field star	GLORIA ROMANORVM Three emperors stg. facing. Mintmark illegible			Cf. *LRBC* 2: 102, Nos. 2801–2804	148428
187	11026	101190	1.16	13		Same	Same			Same	148651
188	30060	302585	1.06	14	↓	Same	Same	Same		Same	148421
Late Roman: Honorius (393–423 CE)											
189*	30037	301765	1.16	11	↑	DN HONORIVS PF AVG Bust r., pearl-diademed, cuirassed and draped	VICT[ORIA AVGGG] Victory advancing l., holding palm branch and wreath. In l. field: S In exergue: RM	410–423	Rome	*LRBC* 2: 63, No. 828	148391
Late Roman: 425–455 CE											
190	643	6592	0.90	12	↑	[---] Bust r., pearl-diademed, cuirassed and draped.	Cross within wreath. Mintmark illegible			Cf. *LRBC* 2: 103, No. 2810	148768
Imitative issues: First half of 5th century CE											
191	30037	301186	1.33	12	↓	[---] Bust r., pearl-diademed, cuirassed and draped.	[VICTORIA AVGGG] Victory advancing l., holding palm branch and wreath. In l. field: T			Bijovsky 2012: 108–109, Nos. 1–2	148380
192	30037	301554	1.09	12	↓	Same	Same, but in l. field: S			Same	148385
193	30037	301078	0.60	9	↓	Same	Same, but no letters in field			Same	148377
194	30036	300602	0.75	9		Obliterated	Same			Same	148312
195	30118	304462	0.52	9		Same	Cross			Bijovsky 2012: 113–117	148683
196	30036	300598	0.37	10		Same	Same			Same	148311
197	30074	303071	0.67	10		Same	Illegible *Vota* inscription			Bijovsky 2012: 110–113	148612

Cat. No.	Loc. No.	Basket	W. (gr)	Diam. (mm)	Axis	Obverse	Reverse	Date (CE)	Mint	References and Notes	IAA No.
198	30074	304108	0.56	10		[---] Bust r., pearl-diademed, cuirassed and draped.	Same?			Same	148626
199	30036	300291	0.36	12		Obliterated	Same?			Same. Cast	148304
200	30060	302537	0.93	12	←	]IN[Bust r., pearl-diademed, cuirassed and draped.	Figure stg. to r.: A			Barbaric style	148418
201	30037	301768	0.34	10		Obliterated	Wreath?			Cast	148393
202	30037	300969	0.20	11		Same	Same			Same	148373
Imitative issue (Marcian?): Second half of 5th century CE											
203*	30118	304764	0.81	9	↓	]IV[Bust r., pearl-diademed, cuirassed and draped.	Imitation of monogram of Marcian with ഗ above and circle below				148691
Leo I (457–474 CE) – *Nummus*											
204	30148	305260	1.15	11	!	[---] Bust r., pearl-diademed, cuirassed and draped.	Lion crouching l., head to r.			Cf. *LRBC* 2: 91, Nos. 2260–2261	148714
205	30074	303508	1.21	10		Same	Same?			Same	148616
206	608	6296	0.83	10		Same	Same			Same	148759
207*	30000	305255	1.06	10–12	!	DN L[EO--- Bust r., pearl-diademed, cuirassed and draped.	[b] / E Verina stg. facing, holding transversal scepter			Cf. *LRBC* 2: 91, Nos. 2272–2275	148288
208	30	305	0.69	10		Obliterated				Cf. *LRBC* 2: 91, Nos. 2262–2264	148256
Zeno (476–491 CE) – Gold *Solidus*											
209*	30065	301070	4.07	20	↓	DN [ZENO AVC] Bust ¾ profile, helmeted, cuirassed and draped.	VICTORI–A AVGGGE Victory stg. l., holding long cross. In r. field: star; in exergue: CONOB		Constantinople	*RIC* 10: 307, Nos. 910–912	148569
Nummus											
210*	30074	303889	0.87	9	!	DN ZENO PERP AVC Bust r., pearl-diademed, cuirassed and draped	 within wreath		Constantinople	*LRBC* 2: 91, No. 2279	148625
211	30037	301579	0.86	10	↓	Obliterated			Same	Same	148387

Cat. No.	Loc. No.	Basket	W. (gr)	Diam. (mm)	Axis	Obverse	Reverse	Date (CE)	Mint	References and Notes	IAA No.
212	30071	302790	0.80	8		Same	Same		Same	*LRBC* 2: 91, No. 2281	148599
Uncertain, *Nummus*											
213	Surface	j	0.12	8		Obliterated	Monogram?	ca. 450–498?			140268
Unknown ruler: Burgundian? Gundobad (472–474 CE)? Ostrogoths? Baduila (541–552 CE): *Nummus*											
214*	30065	301093	0.98	10	↓	]VA[? Bust r., pearl-diademed, cuirassed and draped.	**BD** or monogram?		Italy?	Cf. *RIC* 10: 464, No. 3785. Identification proposed by N. Schindler	148571
Vandals: Proto Vandalic											
215	30037	301185	0.18	9		Bust r.	⳩?	ca. 455–484	Carthage	Bijovsky 2012: 143–144	148379
Uncertain: 5th century CE											
216	30118	304842	1.37	12		Bust r.	Two figures stg.?				148694
217	30041	300701	0.53	12		Same	Same				148402
218	30118	305017	0.48	9		Same	Wreath?				148702
219	30061	302603	0.84	10	↑	[---] Bust r., pearl-diademed, cuirassed and draped	Victory to l.?				148440
220	30118	304787	1.12	12		Same	Obliterated				148693
221	30100	303489	1.11	9		Same	Same				148668
222	30037	300769	1.03	9		Same	Same				148314
223	30074	302903	0.88	10		Same	Same				148608
224	3007	300146	0.85	11		Same	Same				148259
225	30071	302792	0.84	10		Same	Same				148600
226	30037	300773	0.83	11		Same	Same				148371
227	608	6295	0.79	7		Same	Same				148741
228	30087	303588	0.77	10		Same	Same				148647
229	30100	303465	0.74	10		Same	Same				148666
230	30118	304843	0.67	12		Same	Same				148695
231	30065	301742	0.61	9		Same	Same				148572
232	30118	304768	0.54	8		Same	Same				148692

Cat. No.	Loc. No.	Basket	W. (gr)	Diam. (mm)	Axis	Obverse	Reverse	Date (CE)	Mint	References and Notes	IAA No.
233	30071	302102	0.53	10		Same	Same				148590
234	30037	301873	0.38	10		Same	Same				148394
235	30089	303691	0.35	9		Same	Same				148650
Vandals: King Trasamund											
236	30074	303499	0.60	10	←	Bust r.	Victory to l. with wreath and palm branch	496–523	Carthage	Bijovsky 2012: 311–312, Table 57, Fig. 116	148614
237*	30060	302643	0.27	9	↑	Same	Same	Same	Same	Same Pierced	148424
Axumite: Imitations of Ezana											
238*	30060	302621	0.46	10		Blundered inscription. Bust to r. within circle	Blundered inscription. Cross within circle	ca. 450–550	Egypt	Bijovsky 2012: 148–152 Cast	148420
239	30074	303779	0.36	9		Same	Same	Same	Same	Same	148619
240	30118	304937	0.26	10		Same	Same	Same	Same	Same	148700
Byzantine: Uncertain											
241	30074	302095	1.15	11		Obliterated	Monogram?	ca. 450–550			148602
242	30114	303746	1.10	10		Same	Same	Same			148676
243	30061	302117	1.03	12		Same	Same	Same			148434
244	30148	305262	0.99	10		Same	Same	Same			148715
245	30100	303666	0.97	8		Same	Same	Same			148669
246	30037	301763	0.83	9		Same	Same	Same			148389
247	30037	301380	0.77	10		Same	Same	Same			148381
248	30036	300366	0.72	10		Same	Same	Same			148307
249	30083	305421	0.71	11		Same	Same	Same			148642
250	10029	10165	0.70	9		Same	Same	Same			148264
251	30148	305268	0.69	11		Same	Same	Same			148716
252	30061	302602	0.65	10		Same	Same	Same			148439
253	30037	301762	0.53	10		Same	Same	Same			148388
254	30074	302900	0.53	8		Same	Same	Same			148607
255	30071	302214	0.45	10		Same	Same	Same			148594
256	30037	301550	0.45	9		Same	Same	Same			148383
257	30060	302569	0.44	10		Same	Same	Same			148419
258	30074	303853	0.42	10		Same	Same	Same			148622

Cat. No.	Loc. No.	Basket	W. (gr)	Diam. (mm)	Axis	Obverse	Reverse	Date (CE)	Mint	References and Notes	IAA No.
259	30037	301552	0.39	11		Same	Same	Same			148384
260	30100	303669	0.39	8		Same	Same	Same			148670
261	30137	301908	0.38	9		Same	Same	Same			148396
262	30037	301905	0.37	10		Same	Same	Same			148395
263	30118	304716	0.33	8		Same	Same	Same			148689
264	30118	304612	0.29	7		Same	Same	Same			148686
265	643	6628	0.85	7		[---] Bust r., pearl-diademed, cuirassed and draped	Obliterated	Same			148771
266	163	1659	0.87	10		Same	Same	Same			148746
267	30074	302096	0.71	9		Same	Same	Same			148603
268	30082	303233	0.65	10		Same	Same	Same			148635
269	30021	302743	0.57	9		Same	Same	Same			148300
270	30100	303299	0.44	9		Same	Same	Same			148613
271	30074	303855	0.42	11		Same	Same	Same			148623
272	30037	303830	0.37	10		Same	Same	Same			148397
273	30037	301764	0.33	8		Same	Same	Same			148390
274	30061	302115	0.78	11		Same	Same	Same		Cast imitation. Bijovsky 2012: 124–127	148432
275	30074	303866	0.26	11		Obliterated	Inscription?	Same		Cast imitation. Bijovsky 2012: 110–113	148624
276	30115	305261	0.49	12		Blank	Blank	Same		Cast. Bijovsky 2012: 129	148679
277	30070	302124	0.35	11		Same	Same	Same		Same	148581
278	30061	302114	0.29	12		Same	Same	Same		Same	148431
279	30037	301071	0.22	10		Same	Same	Same		Same	148374
280	30313	304288	0.41	11		Same	Same	Same		Same Pierced	148722
Byzantine: Anastasius I (491–518 CE) – *Follis*											
281*	641	6589	15.08	30	↓	DN ANASTA[SI]VS PP AVC Bust facing r., diademed, cuirassed and draped	**M** flanked by eight pointed stars; above, cross; below: Є; in exergue: CON	512–518	Constantinople	*MIBE*: 87, No. 27.3	148766

Cat. No.	Loc. No.	Basket	W. (gr)	Diam. (mm)	Axis	Obverse	Reverse	Date (CE)	Mint	References and Notes	IAA No.
282*	30052	301520	17.28	32	↓	Same	**M** flanked by six pointed stars with dots above and below; above, cross; below: Є; in exergue: C[ON]	512–517	Same	*MIBE*: 87, No. 28b	148406
BYZANTINE: *Decanummium*											
283*	627	6288	1.82	17	↓	[DN ANASTA]SIVS PP AVC Bust facing r., diademed, cuirassed and draped	CON–CORD **I** flanked by dots	507–512	Constantinople	*MIBE*: 89, No. 35	148763
BYZANTINE: Half *follis*											
284	8048	80234	9.14	25–29	↓	DN ANASTASIVS PP AVC Bust facing r., diademed, cuirassed and draped	**K** To l. long cross; to r.: Γ	512–518	Constantinople	*DOC* 1: 23, No. 24d	140249
BYZANTINE: *Nummus*											
285	623	6266	0.88	9	↗	[DN ANASTASIVS PP AVC] Bust facing r., diademed, cuirassed and draped		491–518	Constantinople	*DOC* 1: 10, No. 15	148762
286*	30118	305159	0.82	10	↓	Same	Same	Same	Same	Same	148704
287	30074	303817	0.58	9		Same	Same	Same	Same	Same	148620
288	12019	102051	0.48	9	7	Same	Same	Same	Same	Same	148278
289	30131	304936	0.94	10		Obliterated	Same	Same	Same	Same	148709
290	30118	304914	0.68	8		Same	Same	Same	Same	Same	148698
291	30118	305023	0.64	10		Same	Same	Same	Same	Same	148703
292	627	6291	0.63	7		Same	Same	Same	Same	Same	148764
293	30074	302102	0.57	8		Same	Same	Same	Same	Same	148604
294	643	6681	0.44	7		Same	Same	Same	Same	Same	148776
295	30071	303744	0.62	9	↑	[DN ANASTASIVS PP AVC] Bust facing r., diademed, cuirassed and draped		Same	Antioch	*MIBE*: 93, No. 64	148618
BYZANTINE: Justin I (518–527 CE) – *Follis*											
296	30037	300774	16.66	31	↓	DN IVSTI–NVS PP AVC Bust facing r., diademed, cuirassed and draped	**M** flanked by six pointed stars; above, cross; below: Γ; in exergue: CON	518–522	Constantinople	*MIBE*: 96, No. 11	148255

Cat. No.	Loc. No.	Basket	W. (gr)	Diam. (mm)	Axis	Obverse	Reverse	Date (CE)	Mint	References and Notes	IAA No.
297	8063	80360	15.23	28	↓	Same	**M** to l. six pointed star; above, cross; below: A; in exergue: CON	518–527	Constantinople	Same?	140256
298*	30060	301515	16.69	34	↓	Same	**M** to l. star and to r. cross; above, cross; below: Δ; in exergue: [CO]N	Same	Same	*MIBE*: 96, No. 12	148415
299	30065	302521	15.98	35	↓	Same	**M** to l. eight pointed star and to r. C; above, cross; in exergue: ANTIX	Same	Antioch	*MIBE*: 103, No. 60	148574
300*	8063	80290	14.38	32	↓	Same	**M** to l. eight pointed star and to r. ∪; below: reversed Γ; in exergue: ANTX	Same	Same	Same	140254
Byzantine: *Decanummium*											
301	30061	302116	3.13	23	↑	DN IVST[INV]S PP AVC Bust facing r., diademed, cuirassed and draped	CONCORDIA **I** flanked by dots. In exergue: ANTX	518–527	Antioch	*MIBE*: 104, No. 62	148433
Byzantine: *Dodecanummium*											
302	10018	100098	2.59	16		[DN IVSTINVS PP AVC Bust facing r., diademed, cuirassed and draped	**I*B** In exergue: AΛE[Ξ]	518–527	Alexandria	*MIBE*: 105, No. 68	148257
Byzantine: Uncertain – *Follis*											
303	30011	300159	13.91	23		Obliterated	**M** details illegible; below: Є Mintmark illegible	512–538			148296
304	30070	302125	16.44	30	↓	DN IVST[Bust facing r., diademed, cuirassed and draped	**M** to l. star, to r. illegible; above, cross; below: Γ. Mintmark illegible	518–538			148582
Byzantine: Justinian I (527–565 CE) – *Follis*											
305*	30151	305314	17.76	30	↓	DN IVSTINIANVS PP AVC Bust facing r., diademed, cuirassed and draped	**M** flanked by six pointed stars; above, cross; below: A; in exergue: CON	527–532	Constantinople	*DOC* 1: 80, No. 30	148718
306	30082	303313	16.70	30	↓	Same	**M** on l. star, on r. cross; above, cross; below: A; in exergue: CON	532–538	Same	*MIBE*: 126, No. 84	148636
307	Surface	n	16.06	30	↓	Same	Same, but below: Δ	Same	Same	Same	140272
308	30065	300719	15.49	30	↓	Same	Same, but below illegible	Same	Same	Same	148568
309	30118	305160	15.48	30	↓	Same	Same	Same	Same	Same	148705
310	7000	70017	14.02	30	↓	Same	**M** to l.: ∪; above, cross; in exergue: ANTIX	527–532	Antioch	*MIBE*: 142, No. N125	117331

Cat. No.	Loc. No.	Basket	W. (gr)	Diam. (mm)	Axis	Obverse	Reverse	Date (CE)	Mint	References and Notes	IAA No.
311	8063	80356	13.52	27–30	↓	Same	**M** flanked by eight pointed stars; above, cross; in exergue: ΘY[ΠOΛϚ]	537–539	Same	Cf. *MIBE*: 143, No. 131	140255
Byzantine: Half *follis*											
312	5004	50036	6.78	24–26	↙	DN IVSTINIANVS PP AVC Bust r., diademed, cuirassed and draped	**K** to l. long cross flanked by N–I	527–538	Nicomedia	*MIBE*: 135, No. N109	117296
Byzantine: *Nummus*											
313	30000	305257	0.63	8		Obliterated		534–539	Carthage	Bijovsky 2012: 233–235	148289
314	30074	302906	0.62	8		Same	Same	Same	Same	Same	148610
315	30100	303351	0.31	8		Same	Same	Same	Same	Same	148665
316	30118	304869	0.56	9		Bust r.	 within two concentric circles	538–542	Same	Bijovsky 2012: 237, Fig. 77	148712
317	30148	305171	0.60	7		Bust r.	Same	Same	Same	Same	148697
318*	30068	302632	0.31	8	-	Bust facing		542–552	Same	Bijovsky 2012: 240–242	148580
Vandals: Hilderic (523–530 CE) – *Nummus*											
319*	30063	301566	0.95	10	-	Bust r.	Cross within wreath with medallion		Carthage	Bijovsky 2012: 313–314	148441
320	643	6614	0.64	9		Same	Same		Same	Same	148770
Vandalic Anonymous – *Nummus*											
321	30067	302110	0.50	8		Obliterated	Palm tree	534–565	Carthage	Bijovsky 2012: 317–321	148577
Byzantine: Uncertain imitation – *Pentanummium*											
322	31002	310014	1.61	12	↓	Bust facing r.		ca. 522–540	Ashqelon?	Bijovsky 2012: 291–297	148725
Byzantine: Justin II (565–578 CE) – *Follis*											
323*	30127	304712	11.78	28	↓	DN IVSTI–NVS PP AVC Justin and Sophia seated facing on double throne	**M** to l.: ANNO; above, cross; below: Δ; to r. date: II/II; in exergue: CON	568/569	Constantinople	*DOC* 1: 206, No. 26c	148707

Cat. No.	*Loc. No.*	*Basket*	*W. (gr)*	*Diam. (mm)*	*Axis*	*Obverse*	*Reverse*	*Date (CE)*	*Mint*	*References and Notes*	*IAA No.*
324	30143	305420	11.19	29	↓	Same	**M** Same, but below: B and to r. date: ꟼ	570/571	Same	*DOC* 1: 207, No. 28	148720
325	100	1127	11.99	28	↑	Same	**M** Same, but below: Є and to r. date: ꟼI	571/572	Same	*DOC* 1: 208, No. 32	148744
326	8063	80289	11.25	30	↓	DN IVSTI–NVS PP AVC Justin and Sophia seated facing on double throne with cross between them	**M** to l.: ANNO; below: Γ; to r. date: X; in exergue: tHEUP	574/575	Antioch	*DOC* 1: 245, No. 157	140253
Byzantine: Half *Follis*											
327	7041	70969	5.14	17–22	↓	DN [---] Justin and Sophia seated facing on double throne	**K** details illegible; above, cross		Thessalonica?	Cf. *DOC* 1: 221, No. 66	117349
328	600	6114	4.56	20	↓	DN IVSTI–NVS PP AVC Justin and Sophia seated facing on double throne	**K** details illegible; above, cross; to r. Δ				148757
Byzantine: Uncertain – *Follis*											
329	30087	303352	4.90	29		Obliterated	**M** details illegible. In exergue: CON	6th ca.			148646
Byzantine: *Dodecanummium*											
330	Surface	8017	4.03	15	↓	[DN IVSTIN]VS PP [AVC] Bust facing r., diademed, cuirassed and draped	**I+B** In exergue: [AΛEΞ]	6th ca.	Alexandria		148781
Byzantine: *Pentanummium*											
331	30071	303089	2.02	13	↓	Blundered inscription. Bust r.	**Є** to r.: A	6th ca. ?			148601
332	643	6596	0.60	10		Same	Same	Same			148769
Byzantine: *Nummus*?											
333	30071	302218	0.51	8		[---] Bust r.	Obliterated	First half 6th ca.			148595
334	620	6154	1.03	9		Obliterated	Same	Same			145747

Cat. No.	Loc. No.	Basket	W. (gr)	Diam. (mm)	Axis	Obverse	Reverse	Date (CE)	Mint	References and Notes	IAA No.
BYZANTINE: Maurice Tiberius (582–602 CE) – *Follis*											
335	8027	80154	12.43	28	↓	dNmA[---] Bust facing, wearing crown, cuirassed and draped, holding globe with cross	**M** to l.: ANNO; above, cross; to r. date: X/ϛ; below: E; in exergue: CON	598/599	Constantinople	*DOC* 1: 309, No. 40	140248
336	7008	70344	8.32	28	↓	[---]PP Same	**M** to l.: ANNO; above, cross; to r. date: ϛ/II; below: B; in exergue: NIKO	589/590	Nicomedia	*DOC* 1: 325, No. 98	117339
337*	7005	70030	11.71	29	↓	]INYOP[Same	**m** to l.: ANNO; above, cross; to r. date: II; in exergue: tHEUP'	583/584	Antioch	*DOC* 1: 338, No. 153	117334
338*	8013	80061	11.24	30	↓	]NOCY VΛΓNTA Same	**m** to l.: ANNO; above, cross; to r. date: ϛ; in exergue: tHEUP'	586/587	Same	*DOC* 1: 339, No. 156	140244
339	7202	73123	10.55	28	↓	[---] Same	**M** to l.: [ANNO]; above, cross; to r. date: X/ϛII; in exergue: tHEUP'	598/599	Same	*DOC* 1: 344, No. 169	140240
BYZANTINE: Half *Follis*											
340	7002	70127	4.85	20	↓	[---] Same	**K** to l.: ANNO; above, cross; to r. date: II?; below: TES	583/584	Thessalonica	*DOC* 1: 320, No. 72	117333
341	7010	70328	5.01	20–24	↑	[ON mAVRT] IbER[PPA] Same	**K** to l.: ANNO; above, cross; to r. date: ϛIII; below: A	590/591	Cyzicus	*DOC* 1: 335, No. 141	117342
BYZANTINE: Uncertain – *Follis*											
342	7007	70295	9.44	27–30	↓	[---] Bust r.	**M** details illegible	518–538			117335
343	7061	71324	5.35	---	---	DNIV[---] Bust r.	**M** to l., star. All other details illegible	Same		Fragment	117352
344	7010	70398	3.32	27		Obliterated	**M** to l.: ANNO; above, cross; to r.: II/II; below: B; in ex.: CON	6th ca.			117343
BYZANTINE: Half *Follis*											
345	7041	70968	5.28	21		Obliterated	**K** to l.: ANNO; above, cross; to r.: ϛ	6th ca.			117348
346	7008	70249	3.42	21–28		Bust facing	**K** all details illegible	Same			117336
BYZANTINE: *Dodecanummium*											
347	Surface	m	2.66	15		Obliterated	**I+B** in ex.: AΛEΞ	6th ca.		Cf. *MIBE*: 105, No. 68	140271
348	7008	70345	2.69	15		Same	Same	6th – 7th ca.			117340

Cat. No.	Loc. No.	Basket	W. (gr)	Diam. (mm)	Axis	Obverse	Reverse	Date (CE)	Mint	References and Notes	IAA No.
BYZANTINE: Phocas (602–610 CE) – *Follis*											
349	30050	302119	10.10	28	↓	[ON FOC]A NEPE AV[Phocas and Leontia stg. facing	**m** to l.: ANNO; above, cross; to r. date: ꟼI; in exergue: tHEUPO	607/608	Antioch	*DOC* 2/1: 188, No. 88	148404
BYZANTINE: Heraclius (610–641 CE) – *Follis*											
350	8056	80291	13.03	32	↓	[ddNNhERACLI ЧSEt] hERACON[StPAV] Heraclius and sons stg. facing, holding cross on globe and long cross	**M** to r. date: Ч; all other details are illegible	614/615	Constantinople	Overstruck. *DOC* 2/1: 283, No. 80	140251
351*	8063	80361	6.42	25	↓	[---] Heraclius and son stg. facing, holding cross on globe and long cross	**M** to l.: ☧; above: NNO; to r. date: X/ꟼ; below: A; in ex.: CON	624/625	Same	*DOC* 2/1: 292, No. 99	140257
352*	8048	80316	6.11	25		Original strike: Heraclius in military dress stg. facing. Upper strike: Three imperial figures stg. facing	Upper strike: **M** below: Γ; in ex.: CON Original strike: **M** to l.: NNO	629–631 over 624–628	Same	Overstruck *DOC* 2/1: 297, No. 108	140250
353*	8015	80069	4.97	22–25	↑	Heraclius and son stg. facing between them a cross	**M** to l.: [A]NNO; above: ⳨; below B	631–639	Same	Cf. *DOC* 2/1: 298, No. 112	140245
BYZANTINE: Constans II (641–668 CE) – *Follis*											
354*	201	2015	2.80	20	↑	[---] Imperial figure stg. facing, holding cross on globe and long cross	**M** to l.: ANNO; above, K; to r. date: XЧ; illegible inscription in exergue	655/656	Constantinople	*DOC* 2/2: 453, No. 77	148750
BYZANTINE: Half *Follis*											
355*	11054	101274	1.86	24	7	Constans II and son stg. facing	**K** to l.: ANN[O]; above, cross; to r. date: [XЧ/I] Original strike: Bust facing	656/657	Constantinople	Overstruck on Constans II's earlier half *follis*. *DOC* 2/2: 463, No. 94	148273

Cat. No.	Loc. No.	Basket	W. (gr)	Diam. (mm)	Axis	Obverse	Reverse	Date (CE)	Mint	References and Notes	IAA No.
ARAB-BYZANTINE 1: Anonymous – *Follis*											
356*	31000	310013	3.74	23	4	[---] Imperial figure stg. facing, holding cross on globe and long cross	**m** to l.: Λ/I; above, cross; to r. A/N	ca. 647–670		Cf. *SICA* 1: Type E	148724
357	Surface	f	1.33	17–20	↓	Same, but in l. field: I/X	**m** above: ANNO?; to r. A/N	Same		Same. Poligonal cut	140264
358*	10019	100199	3.28	24	↓	ThqЄO–COHƆ Imperial bust with crown, facing	**m** to l.: ANN; to r. ANI; in exergue: CΛOC	Same		Cf. Pottier, Schulze and Schulze 2008: Class III, mule	148724
UMAYYAD: Post-Reform, Anonymous, *Fals*											
359	31000	310010	1.83	13		لا اله \ الا الله \ وحده	محمد \ رسول \ الله	8th ca.		Walker 1956: 212, No. 657	148723
360*	7013	70213	3.27	18		Same	Same	Same		Same	117344
361*	30104	303964	1.54	16		Center: لا اله ا \ لا الله \ وحده له Margin: لله الملك فلس وا ف	Center: ضرب بفلسطين Margin:] ضـر [ب فلـ [سطين [	After 90 H / 709	Filasṭīn	Walker 1956: 276, No. 911; Ilisch 1993: 10, No. 21	148674
ʿABBASID: al-Mahdī (158–169 H = 775–785 CE), Silver *Dirham*											
362*	30125	304282	1.20	23		Center: لا اله الا \ الله وحده \ لا] شريك له] Margin: ...هذا الدرهم بالمحمدية سنة اثنتين وستين ومئة	Center: محمد رسول الله صلي الله عليه وسلم الخاليفة المهدي Margin: Quran ix:33	162 H / 778	al-Muḥammadiya	Cut fragment of a *dirham*. Lowick 1996: 195, No. 1639	148706
ʿABBASID: Muḥammad al-Amīn (193–198 H = 809–813 CE), Silver fraction of *Dirham*											
363*	30078	303690	0.42	11		Center: لا اله الا \ الله وحده \ لا [شريك له] Margin: Mint missing, date: ... سنة ست ...	Center: محمد رسول الله صلي الله عليه وسلم مما امريه الأمير الأمين محمد بن امير المؤمنين Margin: Quran ix:33	(19)6 H / 811	Missing	Reconstructed according to comparison with: Lowick 1996: xlvii, type (k4c)	148629

Cat. No.	Loc. No.	Basket	W. (gr)	Diam. (mm)	Axis	Obverse	Reverse	Date (CE)	Mint	References and Notes	IAA No.
ʿAbbasid: Anonymous, *Fals*											
364	30104	303963	2.55	18–22		لا اله الا \ الله وحده \ لا شريك له Margin illegible	Center: لله \ محمد \ رسول \ الله Margin illegible	After 170 H / 786		Cast	148673
ʿAbbasid: al-Maʾmūn (198–218 H = 813–833 CE), *Fals*											
365	30141	305057	3.17	20		Center: لا اله الا \ الله وحده \ لا شريك له Margin illegible	Center: محمد \ رسول \ الله \ بخ Margin illegible	217 H / 832	al-Ramlah?	Cast. Cf. Ilisch 1993: 10, Nos. 96–102	148711
ʿAbbasid: Uncertain, *Fals*											
366	8020	80109	2.77	15–24		Center: لا اله الا \ الله وحده \ [لا شريك له] Margin: بسم الله ضرب هذا الفلس مدينة [- - -]	Center: [محمد \ رسول \ الله]	9th ca.		Half a coin	140246
Ayyubids: al-Nāṣir Ṣalāḥ al- Dīn Yūsuf ibn Ayyūb (564–589 H = 1169–1193 CE), *Fals*											
367*	42002	420003	1.56	15		Center: صلاح \ الدين يوسف Margin illegible	Center: الملك \ الناصر	Illegible	Illegible but Syrian type?	Cf. Balog 1980: 95, Nos. 151–153	148726
368	Surface	d	3.58	25		Doublestruck	Doublestruck	Same	Dimashq	Cf. Balog 1980: 93, Nos. 145	140262
Ayyubids: Uncertain, *Fals*											
369	30077	303688	0.50	16		Illegible	Illegible	12th–13th		Worn fragment	148628
Medieval: Henry, Silver *Denier*											
370	Surface	c	0.71	16		+ IHPERATOR H within circle	+ ENRICVS In center: LVCA	End 10th ca.	Lucca	Metcalf 1983: #11, Pl. 1	140261
Crusader: Latin Kingdom of Jerusalem, Baldwin III (1143–1162 CE), Silver *Denier*											
371*	10000	---	0.74	17		+ REX BALDVINVS Cross within circle	+ DE IERVSALEM Tower of David within circle		Acre	Metcalf 1995: Nos. 156–164	148738
Crusader: Uncertain, *denier*											
372	Surface	e	0.20	13		Illegible	Illegible	12th–13th		Worn fragment	140263

Cat. No.	Loc. No.	Basket	W. (gr)	Diam. (mm)	Axis	Obverse	Reverse	Date (CE)	Mint	References and Notes	IAA No.
MAMLUKS: al-Zāhir Rukn al- Dīn Bybars citing caliph al-Hakim (658–676 H = 1260–1277 CE), *Fals*											
373	Surface	h	0.80	20		Center: Lion to l. Segments: [السلطان \ الملك \ الظاهر]	Center: الامام الحاكم امير المؤمنين			Balog 1964: 104, No. 96.	140266
MAMLUKS: al-Zāhir Rukn al- Dīn Bybars (658–676 H = 1260–1277 CE), *Fals*											
374	11054	101249	2.01	18		Center: Lion to l. Segments: السلطان \ الملك \ الظاهر \ ركن الدين	Center: لا اله الا \ الله محمد \ رسول الله Segments: mint and date	671 H / 1272 CE	Dimashq	Balog 1964: 105, No. 100.	148271
375*	11034	101200	1.11	16		Same, but above and below: السلطان \ الملك الظاهر	Center: لا اله الا الله \ محمد رسول الله Segments: mint and date	missing	Same	Balog 1964: 105, No. 99.	148652
376	11031	101205	2.09	17		Same	Same	Missing	Same	Same (var.)	148653
377	11061	101269	1.51	18		Same	Center: لله \ لا اله ا \ محمد رسول ا \ لله Segments: mint and date	Missing	Same	Balog 1964: 105, No. 98	148657
MAMLUKS: al-Zāhir Sayf al-Dīn Barqūq first reign (784–791 H = 1382–1389 CE), *Fals*											
378	11061	101267	2.16	13x18		Illegible	Traces of octagonal star in field (Syrian type)		Aleppo?	Fragment. Cf. Balog 1964: 259, No. 563	148272
OTTOMANS: Selim I (918–928 H = 1512–1520 CE), *Akçe*											
379	30054	303033	0.68	13x15		Center: السلطان \ سليم \ شاه	Illegible			Père 1968: 105, No. 124	148407
OTTOMANS: Maḥmūd II (1223–1255 H = 1808–1839 CE), *Para*											
380	30104	303692	0.38	15		Center: Tuğra	Center: ضرب في \ مصر ١٢٢٣	1223–1255 H / 1808–1839 CE	Misr	Pierced. Cf. Père 1968: 252, No. 844	148672

A Byzantine Hoard from Apollonia National Park (Area M) (License Nos. G-59/2006 and G-56/2009)* Catalogue (Fig. 18.5)**

Cat. No.	*Loc. No.*	*Basket*	*W. (gr)*	*Diam. (mm)*	*Axis*	*Obverse*	*Reverse*	*Date (CE)*	*Mint*	*References and Notes*	*IAA No.*
Late Roman											
351–361											
H1	7070	72016	1.39	12×14		Obliterated	[FEL TEMP REPARA]TIO Virtus spearing fallen horseman. Details obscure. Mintmark illegible			Cf. *LRBC* 2: 100, No. 2632	140235
Constantius II (337–361)											
H2*	7059	71340	0.73	10×14	↓	]CON[Bust r., pearl-diademed, cuirassed and draped	SPES REI–PVBLICE Virtus stg. facing, holding spear and globe. Mintmark illegible.	355–361		Cf. *LRBC* 2: 100, No. 2638	117353
Julian II (360–363)											
H3*	7059	71326	7.64	26×29	↓	DN FL CL IVLI-ANVS PF AVG Bust r., bearded, pearl-diademed, cuirassed and draped	SECVRITAS REIPVB Bull stg. r., above, two stars. In ex.: SCONST	361–363	Arles	*RIC* 8: 299, No. 317	117354
H4*	7059	71318	7.40	28	.	Same	Same, but in ex.: ANTΓ	Same	Antioch	*LRBC* 2: 100, Nos. 2640–2641	117355
House of Valentinian Uncertain											
H5	7059	71337	1.23	12	↑	[---] Bust r., pearl-diademed, cuirassed and draped	[SECVRITAS REIPVBLICAE] Victory adv. l., holding palm branch and wreath. Mintmark illegible	364–375		Cf. *LRBC* 2: 100, Nos. 2656–2657	117357
H6*	7059	71333	1.59	13×15	5	[---] Bust r., pearl-diademed, cuirassed and draped	[GLORIA ROMANORVM] Emperor advancing r., holding standard and dragging captive. Mintmark illegible	Same		Cf. *LRBC* 2: 100, Nos. 2653–2654	117356
Theodosius I (379–395 CE)											
H7*	7072	72025	1.06	14	↑	[DN T]HEODO[S]IVS [PF] AVG Bust r., pearl-diademed, cuirassed and draped	SALVS REIPVBLICAE Victory advancing l., dragging captive, holding trophy. In l. field, ☧. In exergue: CONS	383–395	Constantinople	*LRBC* 2: 89, No. 2184	140236

* Nine coins were unidentifiable and are not included in the catalogue. The coins are in a poor state of preservation.

** Previously published in Tal and Bijovsky 2017. Cat. Nos. marked with * appear in Fig. 18.5.

Cat. No.	*Loc. No.*	*Basket*	*W. (gr)*	*Diam. (mm)*	*Axis*	*Obverse*	*Reverse*	*Date (CE)*	*Mint*	*References and Notes*	*IAA No.*
383–395											
H8	7059	71334	1.13	14	↓	[---]IV[---] Bust r., pearl-diademed, cuirassed and draped	[SALVS REI PVBLICAE] Victory advancing l., dragging captive, holding trophy. In l. field, ☧. In exergue: ALEA(?)		Alexandria?	Cf. *LRBC* 2: 105, Nos. 2907–2909	117358
H9	7070	72014	0.76	10	↑	Same	Same, but mintmark illegible				140234
Uncertain 4th century											
H10	7059	71335	1.80	14×16		[---] Bust r., pearl-diademed, cuirassed and draped	Obliterated				117360
H11	7059	71335	0.81	14		Same	Same				117359
Leo I (457–474 CE) – *Nummus*											
H12	7072	72027	1.49	11		Obliterated	Emperor stg. facing, hand on captive			Cf. *LRBC* 2: 91, Nos. 2265–2267	140237

Fig. 18.5: A Byzantine Hoard from Apollonia (Area M).

REFERENCES

Ahipaz, N. 2013. Floor Foundation Coin Deposits in Byzantine-Period Synagogues. In: Guri-Rimmon, O., ed. *Hoards and Genizot as Chapters in History* (Hecht Museum Catalogue 33). Haifa: 62*–69*.

Balog, P. 1964. *The Coinage of the Mamlūk Sultans of Egypt and Syria* (Numismatic Studies 12). New York.

Balog, P. 1980. *The Coinage of the Ayyūbids* (Royal Numismatic Society Special Publication 12). London.

Bijovsky, G. 2000–2002. The Currency of the Fifth Century C.E. in Palestine—Some Reflections in Light of the Numismatic Evidence. *Israel Numismatic Journal* 14: 196–210.

Bijovsky, G. 2012. *Gold Coin and Small Change: Monetary Circulation in Fifth–Seventh Century Byzantine Palestine* (Polymnia Numismatica antica e medievale. Studi 2). Trieste.

BMC Phoen.: Hill, G.F. 1910. *Catalogue of the Greek Coins of Phoenicia*. London.

CHL: Meshorer, Y., Bijovsky, G. and Fischer-Bossert, W. 2013. *Coins of the Holy Land: The Abraham and Marian Sofaer Collection at the American Numismatic Society and the Israel Museum* (Ancient Coins in North American Collections 8). Edited by D. Hendin and A. Meadows. New York.

CRE 2: Mattingly, H. 1930. *Coins of the Roman Empire in the British Museum II*: *Vespasian to Domitian*. London.

CRE 3: Mattingly, H. 1936. *Coins of the Roman Empire in the British Museum III*: *Nerva to Hadrian*. London.

CRE 5: Mattingly, H. 1950. *Coins of the Roman Empire in the British Museum V: Pertinax to Elagabalus* (2 vols.). London.

DOC 1: Bellinger, A.R. 1966. *Catalogue of the Byzantine Coins in the Dumbarton Oaks Collection and in the Whittemore Collection 1*: *Anastasius I to Maurice, 491–602*. Washington, D.C.

DOC 2/1: Grierson, P. 1968. *Catalogue of the Byzantine Coins in the Dumbarton Oaks Collection and in the Whittemore Collection 2/1*: *Phocas and Heraclius (602–641).* Washington, D.C.

DOC 2/2: Grierson, P. 1968. *Catalogue of the Byzantine Coins in the Dumbarton Oaks Collection and in the Whittemore Collection 2/2*: *Heraclius Constantine to Theodosius III (641–717).* Washington, D.C.

Ilisch, L. 1993. *Sylloge Numorum Arabicorum. Palästina IVa Bilād aš-Šam I.* Tübingen.

Lowick, N. 1996. *Early ʿAbbasid Coinage: A Type Corpus*. London.

LRBC I: Hill, P.V. and Kent, J.P.C. 1965. The Bronze Coinage of the House of Constantine, A.D. 324–346. In: *Late Roman Bronze Coinage A.D. 324–498*. London: 4–40.

LRBC II: Carson, R.A.G. and Kent, J.P.C. 1965. Bronze Roman Imperial Coinage of the Later Empire, A.D. 346–498. In *Late Roman Bronze Coinage A.D. 324–498*. London: 41–114.

Metcalf, D. M. 1995. *Coinage of the Crusades and the Latin East in the Ashmolean Museum, Oxford* (2nd ed.). London.

MIBE: Hahn, W. 2000. *Money of the Incipient Byzantine Empire (Anastasius I–Justinian I, 491–565)* (Veröffentlichungen des Instituts für Numismatik und Geldgeschichte der Universität Wien 6). Wien.

Père, N. 1968. *Coins of the Ottoman Empire*. Istanbul (Turkish).

Pottier, H., Schulze, I. and Schulze, W. 2008. Pseudo-Byzantine Coinage in Syria under Arab Rule (638–c. 670): Classification and Dating. *Revue Belge de Numismatique et de Sigillographie* 154: 87–155.

RIC 5/1: Webb, P.H. 1927. *The Roman Imperial Coinage V, I*. London.

RIC 6: Sutherland, C.H.V. 1967. *The Roman Imperial Coinage VI: From Diocletian's Reform (A.D. 294) to the Death of Maximinus (A.D. 313).* London.

Rosenberger, M. 1977. *City-Coins of Palestine (The Rosenberger Israel Collection) III: Hippos–Sussita, Neapolis, Nicopolis, Nysa–Scythopolis, Caesarea–Panias, Pelusium, Raphia, Sebaste, Sepphoris–Diocaesarea, Tiberias*. Jerusalem.

SC I: Houghton, A. and Lorber, C. 2002. *Seleucid Coins. A Comprehensive Catalogue I*: *Seleucus I through Antiochus III*. London.

SICA 1: Album, S. and Goodwin, T. 2002. *Sylloge of Islamic Coins in the Ashmolean 1*: *The Pre-Reform Coinage of the Early Islamic Period*. Oxford.

Tal, O. and Bijovsky, G. 2017. A Hoard of Fourth–Fifth Century CE Copper Coins from Sozousa. *Israel Numismatic Research* 12: 147–158.

TJC: Meshorer, Y. 2001. *A Treasury of Jewish Coins: From the Persian Period to Bar Kochba*. Jerusalem.

CHAPTER 19

TWENTIETH CENTURY MILITARIA

Alexander Glick

The militaria discussed in this chapter came from Apollonia (East) during the TAU-IAA excavations' second season (A6826/2013). The finds attest to some military activity at the site's immediate hinterland during World War I (hereafter WWI) and possibly also during Israel's War of Independence in 1948. They supplement many such artifacts unearthed in other areas of excavations in the context of the Apollonia-Arsuf Excavation Project within the Apollonia National Park (e.g., Areas P, R, S, T, U, which will be published in the future in a more comprehensive manner). The discovery of these finds is much connected to the fact that British troops camped at the site from December 1917 to September 1918 (Falls and Beck 1930: 275, Sketches 20–21).[1] While the 157th Brigade of the 52nd Division, the XXI Corps, occupied the site from December 1917 to March 1918 and was probably replaced by troops of the 7th Division, the British attack from Arsuf northeastward in September 1918 (the so-called Battle of Sharon) was carried out by troops of the 60th Division, XXI Corps (179th, 180th, 181st Brigades). The WWI militaria retrieved from the site are most likely connected to all these forces and possibly to the Ottoman forces that camped nearby as well.[2]

The finds discussed below are divided between accessories (buttons) and ammunition (bullets and shrapnel/musket balls). All are shown in Fig. 19.1.

BUTTONS

Two British military buttons are present in this assemblage; one of them is the so-called General Service Button (Bull 1998: 18) and another is a standard army button with four holes. They dated from the end of the 19th century to the middle of the 20th century. The General Service Button appeared on uniforms of most British units during WWI. Following the reforms in the 1920s, new unit buttons were introduced. The General Service Button did not completely disappear and was brought back into broad use due to the shortage of uniforms with the advent of WWII. It is occasionally possible to date finds combining the button to the time of the producers' activity. Firmin & Sons Ltd of London continued in business at least until the 1970s and they probably produced the button illustrated in Fig. 19.1: 2. W. Deakin & Co of Birmingham is less well-known. The company produced military wares as early as the 1830s until the WWI period (and even later) and they probably produced the button exhibited in Fig. 19.1: 1. Although the context of the buttons (in fills in Area CC) do not provide sufficient dating, it is reasonable to date these items to WWI.

1 For the entrenchment of the troops at the site "... in formidable trench systems" cf. Falls and Beck's testimony (1930: 351).

2 The selective reference below may be supplemented by photos stored in the online archive of the Imperial War Museum (www.iwm.org.uk; to be found under "arsuf"), as well as a few YouTube videos on the troops stationed at the site (cf. https://www.youtube.com/watch?v=7WL1HMp1HRE; https://www.youtube.com/watch?v=qLmMk0V1dTk) to be found under "arsf" and "arsf1."

BULLETS

Our identification was done without the sophisticated equipment usually available in police laboratories and on artifacts that were not cleaned and had suffered some corrosion, facts which may hamper potential accuracy.

The bullet from Area CC (Basket 30399; Fig. 19.1: 3) belongs to a small caliber weapon. Based on its shape and size it is probably a .22 Standard Velocity Long Rifle type. Such bullets were used in pistols and rifles from the end of the 19th century and still are in use today. However, contrary to the WWI period, when they were widely distributed, they are in rather limited use at present and usually in arms not commonly used in the country. They were already quite rare in WWII, and during that time used mostly for sport rather than on the battlefield. It seems thus that this bullet was shot from a small caliber weapon during WWI.

The 7.8 mm bullets from Area CC (Baskets 300164, 305407, 300708; Fig. 19.1: 4–6) probably belong to British .303 ammunition, which was common in both WWI and WWII. They were widely used during Israel's War of Independence when they were also locally produced.

The bullet from Area AA1 (Basket 101150; Fig. 19.1: 7) is probably part of Mauser 7.92 × 57 ammunition. It is extremely corroded. Some Israeli collectors believe that strong corrosion is characteristic of the Czech Mauser bullets but at present this view has no substantiation in research.

MUSKET/SHRAPNEL BALLS (FIG. 19.1: 8–17)

It is very difficult to distinguish lead musket balls from shrapnel shell ammunition. The reason is simple: shrapnel shells were loaded with musket balls. At first actual musket balls were inserted. Later, shrapnel

FIG. 19.1: TWENTIETH CENTURY MILITARIA

No.	*Area*	*Locus*	*Basket*	*Number and Type*	*Maker*	*Date*
1	CC	30122	303992	British army button type "General Service Button"	W. Deakin & Co, Birmingham, GB	From 1871 – WWII
2	CC	30154	305405	Standard army button, 4 holes	Firmin (Firmin & Sons Ltd), London, GB	WWI(?)
3	CC	30104	303993	Bullet 5.6 mm caliber; 11.5 mm long. Fired. Possible ".22 Long Rifle standard velocity"	Not identifiable	Late 19th – present day
4	CC	30020	300164	Rifle bullet caliber circa 7.8 mm; 32.6 mm long. Not fired (manually extracted?)	GB(?)	WWI – 1948
5	CC	30000	305407	Rifle bullet caliber circa 7.8 mm; 32.1 mm long. Fired	GB(?)	WWI – 1948
6	CC	30048	300708	Rifle bullet caliber circa 7.8 mm; 33.1 mm long. Fired	GB(?)	WWI – 1948
7	AA1	11010	101150	Rifle bullet caliber circa 8.2 mm; 28.4 mm long. Corroded.	Czechoslovakia (?)	1948(?)
8	AA2	12019	102059	a) Musket/shrapnel ball, lead, 11.5 mm caliber b) Musket/shrapnel ball, lead, 13 mm caliber, with cast gate remains. c) Damaged musket/shrapnel ball, lead, 11.5 mm caliber	Not identifiable	Not identifiable
9	AA1	11034	101221	Half of a musket/shrapnel ball, lead, 8 mm in diameter.	Not identifiable	Not identifiable
10	CC	30005	300049	Musket/shrapnel ball, lead, 12 mm caliber	Not identifiable	Not identifiable
11	CC	30071	300055	Two musket/shrapnel balls, lead, 12 mm caliber	Not identifiable	Not identifiable
12	CC	30007	300147	Musket/shrapnel ball, lead, 12 mm caliber	Not identifiable	Not identifiable
13	CC	30055	300706	Musket/shrapnel ball, lead, 12 mm caliber	Not identifiable	Not identifiable
14	CC	30057	301096	Musket/shrapnel ball, lead, 12 mm caliber	Not identifiable	Not identifiable
15	CC	600	6031	Musket/shrapnel ball, lead, 12 mm caliber	Not identifiable	Not identifiable
16	CC	30000	305407	Four musket/shrapnel balls, lead, 12 mm caliber	Not identifiable	Not identifiable
17	DD2	-	9961	Two musket/shrapnel balls, lead, 12 mm caliber	Not identifiable	Not identifiable

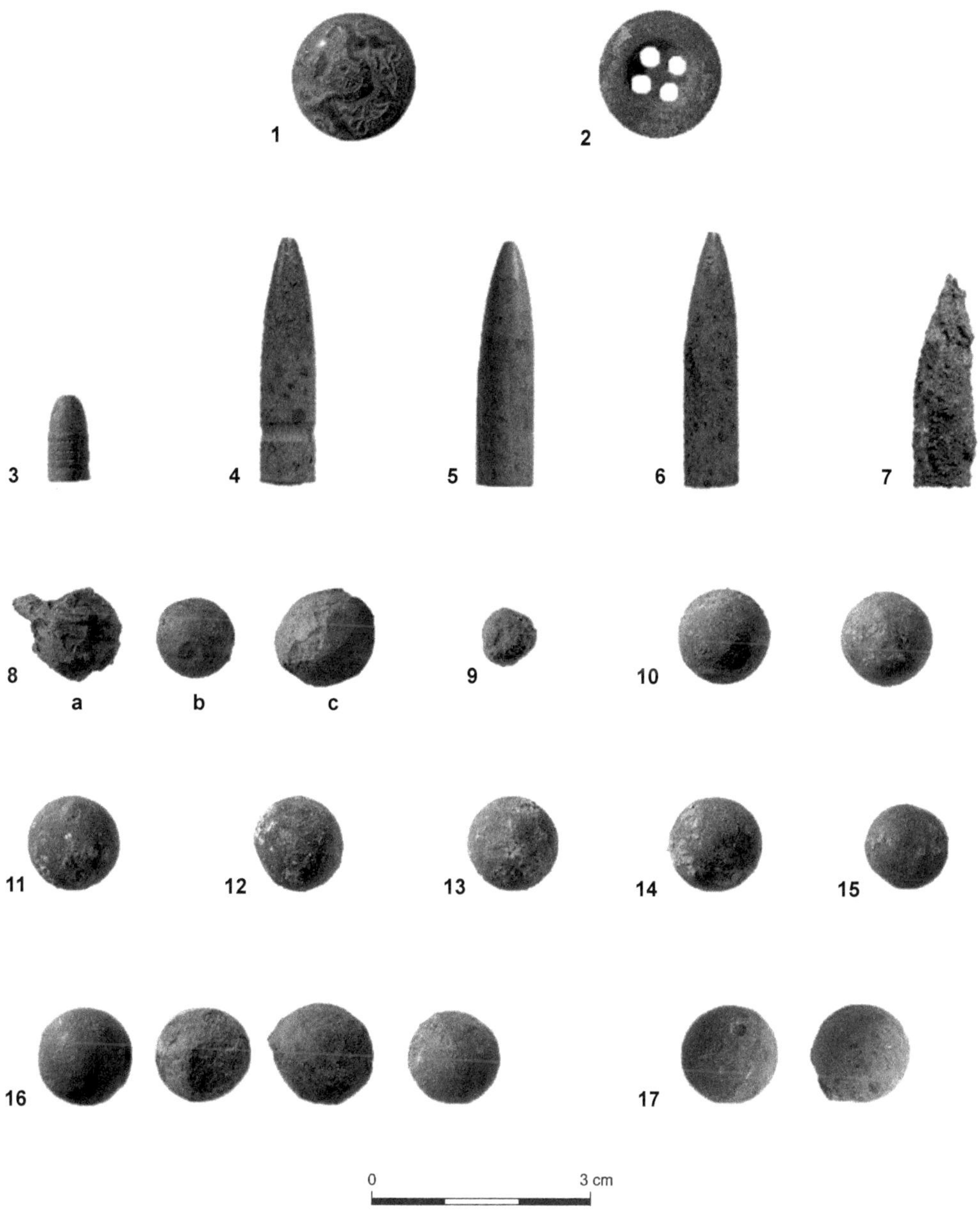

Fig. 19.1: Twentieth century militaria.

balls underwent standardization and were produced exclusively as such, and yet no significantly noticeable difference evolved between them and lead musket balls. Most balls from the current excavation are of identical size (slightly over 12 mm) and of very precise industrial production with no hints of manual involvement. The balls' size, about half of an inch in diameter, fits well with shrapnel shell ammunition. It is therefore likely that the balls are from shrapnel shells. The exceptions are the balls from Area AA (Basket 102059; Fig. 19.1: 8) that are of irregular size with one ball even having a "tail"—a clear mark of manual production by mold. These may be actual musket balls. It should be noted however that such balls were used in this country from the 15th century up to the British Mandate. Several guns that made use of such balls were discovered in a hoard of weapons confiscated by the British and found at the Jaffa Kishleh (police compound) yard.

REFERENCES

Barnes, F. 1993. *Cartridges of the World.* Northbrook.

Bull, S. 1998. *World War One British Army.* Hong Kong.

Falls, C. and Becke, A.F. 1930. *History of the Great War: Military Operations, Egypt and Palestine, from June 1917 to the end of the War.* London.

Glick, A. Forthcoming. A Hoard of Weapons from the Late Nineteenth-Early Twentieth Centuries. In: Arbel, Y. Excavations at the Ottoman Military Compound (Qishle) of Jaffa. In: Peilstöcker, M. and Burke, A.A., eds. *The History and Archaeology of Jaffa,* 3.

Hamilton, D. 1915. *Shrapnel Shell Manufacture.* New York.

SECTION THREE

FAUNA

CHAPTER 20

THE ANIMAL ECONOMY OF BYZANTINE SOZOUSA AND ITS IMMEDIATE HINTERLAND (AREAS M, O, AA1 AND CC)

Miriam Pines and Lidar Sapir-Hen

This study presents the faunal remains collected from Areas M, O, AA1 and CC during four seasons of excavation at Apollonia/Arsuf (Sozousa). Areas M and O assemblages, derived from two refuse pits located in the northern and southern extremities of the site (respectively), were excavated during the 2006 and 2009 seasons headed by O. Tal. Areas AA1 and CC assemblages are derived from the refuse deposits located east of the town limits in its immediate hinterland, unearthed during excavations in 2012 and 2013 headed by E. Haddad (in 2012), O. Tal and M. Ajami (in 2013) (see Chapter 2).

The faunal samples put forward are derived from confined refuse deposits attributed to the main part of the Byzantine period (5th to 6th/7th-century CE). They enable us to reconstruct the patterns of animal exploitation at Apollonia/Sozousa and its hinterland and to enhance understanding of the Byzantine economies of the southern Levant.

This report presents the full raw data for these assemblages. A detailed discussion of the identity and diversity of the population of Late Byzantine Apollonia/Sozousa and the garbage disposal patterns identified in the town and its hinterland have already been discussed by the authors of this chapter (see Sapir-Hen, Pines and Tal 2014; 2017) and, therefore, only an overview of the conclusions will be presented here.

METHODS

The faunal remains were identified using the comparative collection of the Steinhardt Museum of Natural History and National Research Center, and the Laboratory of Archaeozoology of the Institute of Archaeology at Tel Aviv University. Bones were retrieved by hand in Areas M and O and through dry sieving in Areas AA1 and CC (using 1 × 1 cm wide mesh). All animal bones presented in this report were recorded and analyzed using a unified protocol in the Laboratory of Archaeozoology at TAU. Completeness percentages of identified fragments were coded according to five element zones in the case of long bones (proximal epiphysis, proximal shaft, shaft, distal shaft and distal epiphysis) and completeness percentages of two element zones for others (dorsal and ventral or cranial and caudal).

Bone fragments were identified to the lowest taxonomic level possible. Fragments that could not be identified to species were assigned to one of four body size groups: A (i.e., camel/cattle/horse/donkey), B (i.e., caprines/pig), C (i.e., dog) and D (i.e., fox/cat/hare).

Taxonomic frequencies were based on NISP (number of identified specimens) and MNI (minimum number of individuals), that is, the highest figure of a particular element (with consideration of body side) for a given taxon. The relative abundance of skeletal elements (MAU%; minimum animal units) was calculated based on MNE (minimum number of elements). MNE was quantified by adding together the percentages of completeness of each element with consideration of body side. MAU% was calculated by dividing the MNE value of an element per species, by its expected value in the skeleton, multiplied by the taxon's MNI (following Lyman 2008: 238–239).

Identification of caprine bones down to the genus level (sheep or goat) was not always possible according to the criteria presented in Zeder and Lapham (2010). Therefore, for the sake of the analysis, they were grouped into a sheep/goat (caprine) category. Domestic pigs were distinguished from wild boar (*Sus scrofa*) by comparison to wild boar measurements taken by Hongo and Meadow (1998). Distinguishing horses from donkeys was accomplished by examining morphological differences present in the equids' molar teeth, described in Johnstone (2004 with references therein) and Motro (2004). Camel species (dromedary or bactrian) were distinguished when possible, based on morphological criteria of selected bones described in Wapnish (1984), although all of the camel bones in this assemblage are likely to belong to dromedaries based on their geographical distribution (von den Driesch and Boessneck 1995: 85 with references therein; Dayan 1999: 481).

Recorded bones were inspected for various modifications. Butchery marks were classified according to Binford's (1981) typology for the three stages of the preparation for consumption: removal of the skin, dismemberment of the carcass and filleting. Signs of animal activity (i.e., rodent gnawing and carnivore punctures, scoring, and digestion) were recorded as well (Lyman 1994), along with weathering damage (rated between 0–5 following Behrensmeyer 1978). Burning signs were coded according to changes in bone color. Bone pathologies were recorded only in Area M and were discussed in Sapir-Hen, Pines and Tal (2014).

The age at death of the main livestock was analyzed based on bone epiphyseal sequences (following Silver 1969 for cattle, equids and pigs; Zeder 2006 for caprines) and dental eruption and attrition stages (following Grant 1982 and Lemoine *et al.* 2014 for pigs; Zeder 2006 for caprines).

Standardized morphometric measurements were taken on all fused bones according to von den Driesch (1976). Metrical data are presented in the Appendix (below). Sex ratios of the main livestock were not determined lacking sufficient samples to measure for that aim.

RESULTS

A total of 5,467 bones were recovered from the Late Byzantine deposits at the site, of which 41% (2254) were attributed to skeletal element and to the lowest taxonomic level possible. The majority of the bones were recovered from Area CC followed by the assemblages collected from Areas M, O and AA1. These comprised, in total, 12 mammal taxa and one bird taxa:

Cattle	(*Bos taurus*)	Domestic chicken	(*Gallus gallus domesticus*)
Sheep	(*Ovis aries*)	Mountain gazelle	(*Gazella gazella*)
Goat	(*Capra hircus*)	Red deer	(*Cervus elaphus*)
Donkey	(*Equus asinus*)	Roe deer	(*Capreolus capreolus*)
Horse	(*Equus caballus*)	Red Fox	(*Vulpes vulpes*)
Dromedary camel	(*Camelus dromedaries*)	Syrian brown Bear	(*Ursus arctos*)
Pig	(*Sus scrofa domesticus*)		

Most of the species were domesticated; however, there were several wild species as well (Table 20.1 for NISP and MNI). Weathering signs on the bones in Areas M, O and CC are low and no carnivore damage is evident, implying that the bones were quickly covered after their disposal in the refuse pit (Table 20.2). Bones in Area A1 are more fragile and display higher weathering signs (see below).

Table 20.1: Species Frequencies by Assamblage/Area

Species	*Area AA1*		*Area CC*		*Area M*		*Area O*	
	NISP (MNI)	*NISP%*	*NISP (MNI)*	*NISP%*	*NISP (MNI)*	*NISP%*	*NISP (MNI)*	*NISP%*
Cattle	13 (1)	62%	488 (5)	26.2%	62 (3)	21.2%	26 (5)	34.2%
Sheep/ Goat (Caprines)	1	5%	136 (11)	7.3%	66 (4)	22.6%	40 (4)	52.6%
Sheep			6 (2)	0.3%	6 (1)	2.1%		
Goat			2 (1)	0.1%	3 (1)	1.0%	1	1.3%
Horse/ Donkey (Equids)	1	5%	102 (9)	5.5%			2	2.6%
Donkey			9 (1)	0.5%				
Horse			5 (3)	0.3%				
Dromedary camel			87 (4)	4.7%				
Pig			22 (2)	1.2%	23 (1)	7.9%	1	1.3%
Domestic chicken			6 (1)	0.3%	63 (7)	21.6%	2	2.6%
Other birds					12	4.1%		
Mountain gazelle			1	0.1%	3	1.0%		
Red deer			5 (1)	0.3%	1	0.3%		
Roe deer			1	0.1%				
Red fox			1	0.1%				
Syrian brown bear					1	0.3%		
Body size A	1	5%	888	47.6%	9	3.1%	4	5.3%
Body size B	5	24%	105	5.6%	24	8.2%		
Body size C, D					18	6.2%		
Rodent			1	0.1%	1	0.3%		
Total	*21*	*0.9%*	*1865*	*82.7%*	*292*	*13.0%*	*76*	*3.4%*

Table 20.2: Weathering Signs Rated Above Level 3 (Following Behrensmeyer 1978 Criteria), Animal Gnawing and Burning Marks (NISP/NISP%)

Area	*Weathering*	*Animal gnawing*	*Burn marks*
Area AA1	21 (100%)		1 (5%)
Area CC	165 (14.4%)	2 (0.04%)	10 (0.2%)
Area M		1 (0.3%)	
Area O	2 (2.6%)		

5TH–6TH/7TH CENTURY CE APOLLONIA/SOZOUSA

The assemblages from the town of Apollonia/Sozousa were unearthed from two refuse pits located at the southern (Area M) and northern (Area O) extremities of the site, which consequently represent the southern and northern limits of the Late Byzantine town (for a further discussion concerning the limits of Byzantine-period Apollonia/Sozousa, see Tal and Taxel 2012: 500).

AREA M

A total of 323 bones were recovered from the round pit (Locus 7061) in Area M (see Chapter 8), of which 292 (NISP; NISP% = 90) bones were identified. The majority of the bones belong to caprines (26%; N = 75) and cattle (21.3%; N = 62). Other species include domestic chicken (22%; N = 63) and pigs (8%, N = 23). Only one bone (tibia) was available for measurements of pig's status (wild or domesticated) and yielded smaller measurements than that of a wild boar (*Bd* = 28.61 mm, *Dd* = 24.5 mm). Three wild species were found, but represented poorly: mountain gazelle (N = 3), red deer (N = 1), and a single first phalange of a Syrian brown bear (N = 1) (See below). Butchering marks (Table 20.3) are abundant on the bones in the Area and display all stages of preparation for consumption. Age profiles based on tooth wear analysis (Table 20.4) and epiphyseal fusion (Table 20.5) of caprines yielded varied results; although both samples are small, it can be assumed that they complement each other. It appears that caprines were slaughtered at two culling points: at a very young age of several months as well as at an advanced age. This pattern fits the model of milk/wool production suggested by Payne (1973: 281–284, Fig. 2–3). Cattle mortality profiles were not calculated due to the small sample.

Table 20.3: Frequency (NISP) of Butchery Marks (Identification to Stage Following Binford 1981)

Species	*Body part*	*Stage*	*Area CC*	*Area M*	*Area O*
Cattle	Humerus	Dismembering	1		
		Filleting		1	
	Tibia	Filleting	1		
	Vertebrae: axis	Dismembering		1	
	Vertebrae: Thoracic	Filleting	1		
	Metatarsal	Dismembering		1	
	Metatarsal	Filleting		1	
	Tarsal: Astragalus	Dismembering		1	
	First phalange	Undefined		2	
Caprines	Mandible: Mandibular hinge	Dismembering		1	
	Mandible: Ramus	Dismembering			1
	Scapula	Dismembering	1		
	Humerus	Dismembering	1		
	Radius	Dismembering	1		
	Metatarsal	Dismembering		1	
	Rib	Filleting		1	
	Rib	Filleting		1	
	Skull: Parietal	Skinning			1
	Vertebrae: Sacrum	Dismembering			1
Pig	Femur	Undefined		1	
	Tibia	Dismembering		1	
	Metatarsal	Dismembering		1	
Gazelle	Tibia	Undefined		1	
Body size B	Pelvis: Ilium	Dismembering		1	
	Tibia	Undefined		1	
Total			*6*	*17*	*3*

AREA O

The bone sample from Area O was derived from a refuse deposit (Locus 8061) accumulated inside the round collecting vat of a winepress after its use was discontinued during the early 6th century (Tal 2009; Tal and Taxel 2012 and above Chapter 10). The small sample of 76 (NISP) bones is comprised predominantly of sheep and goats (54%; N=41) and cattle (34%; N=26). In addition, two chicken bones were identified (3%) and one pig bone (1%). Age profiles based on tooth wear analysis of caprines display an exploitation of prime age (for meat) as well as older individuals. Skeletal element frequencies (MAU%; Fig. 20.1) display high proportions of meat-rich parts for caprines and cattle.

Table 20.4: Tooth wear Stage of Caprines' Mandibular M3 and dP4 (Following Payne 1974)

Tooth	*Stage*	*Area M*	*Area O*	*Estimated Age*
dP4	D	1		19–25m
M3	D	1	1	12–24m
	E		1	2–3y
	F	2	1	3–4y
	G/H		1	6y
	I		1	8+y

Table 20.5: Aging of Caprines Based on Epiphyseal Fusion (Following Zeder 2006)

		Area M		*Area O*		*Area CC*	
Age in Months	*Body part*	*Fused*	*Unfused*	*Fused*	*Unfused*	*Fused*	*Unfused*
0–6	Proximal Radius					6	1
6–12	Distal Humerus	4				9	3
	Pelvis	2	1	2		13	2
	Scapula	5	1	2		23	1
Total		*11*	*2 (15%)*	*4*		*51*	*7 (12%)*
12–18	2nd Phalanges	3				1	
	1st Phalanges	3		1		3	
18–30	Distal Tibia	2				10	
	Distal Metacarpal			1	1	10	
	Distal Metatarsal					4	
Total		*8*		*2*	*1 (33%)*	*28*	
30–48	Calcaneum		1			3	
	Distal Femur					3	
	Proximal Ulna	2					2
	Distal Radius	1				7	
	Proximal Tibia	1				12	1
Total		*4*				*25*	*3 (11%)*
>48	Proximal Humerus					4	
Grand Total		*23*	*2 (8%)*	*6*	*1 (14%)*	*108*	*10 (8%)*

5TH–TO 6TH/7TH CENTURY CE HINTERLAND OF APOLLONIA/SOZOUSA

The faunal assemblage from the agricultural hinterland of Apollonia/Sozousa derived from two refuse deposits located approximately 400 (Area AA1) and 700 meters (Area CC) east of the Late Byzantine town. The scarcity of remains found in proximity to these two features suggest their relation to the town and imply that the refuse pit in Area CC was used as a central refuse dump by the town inhabitants and the users of the agricultural installations in the hinterland (cf. Pines, Sapir-Hen and Tal 2017; Tal and Taxel 2017). The small refuse deposit in Area AA1 displays human behavior related to the agricultural activities in the hinterland (see below).

AREA AA1

A small sample of 21 (NISP) bones was retrieved in Area AA1, from a winepress complex (see Chapter 3) (Table 20.1). The bones were collected from a round collecting vat (Installation 214) and from a secondary, rectangular-shaped collecting vat located to its south (Installation 215) (Loci 227, 258, 259,

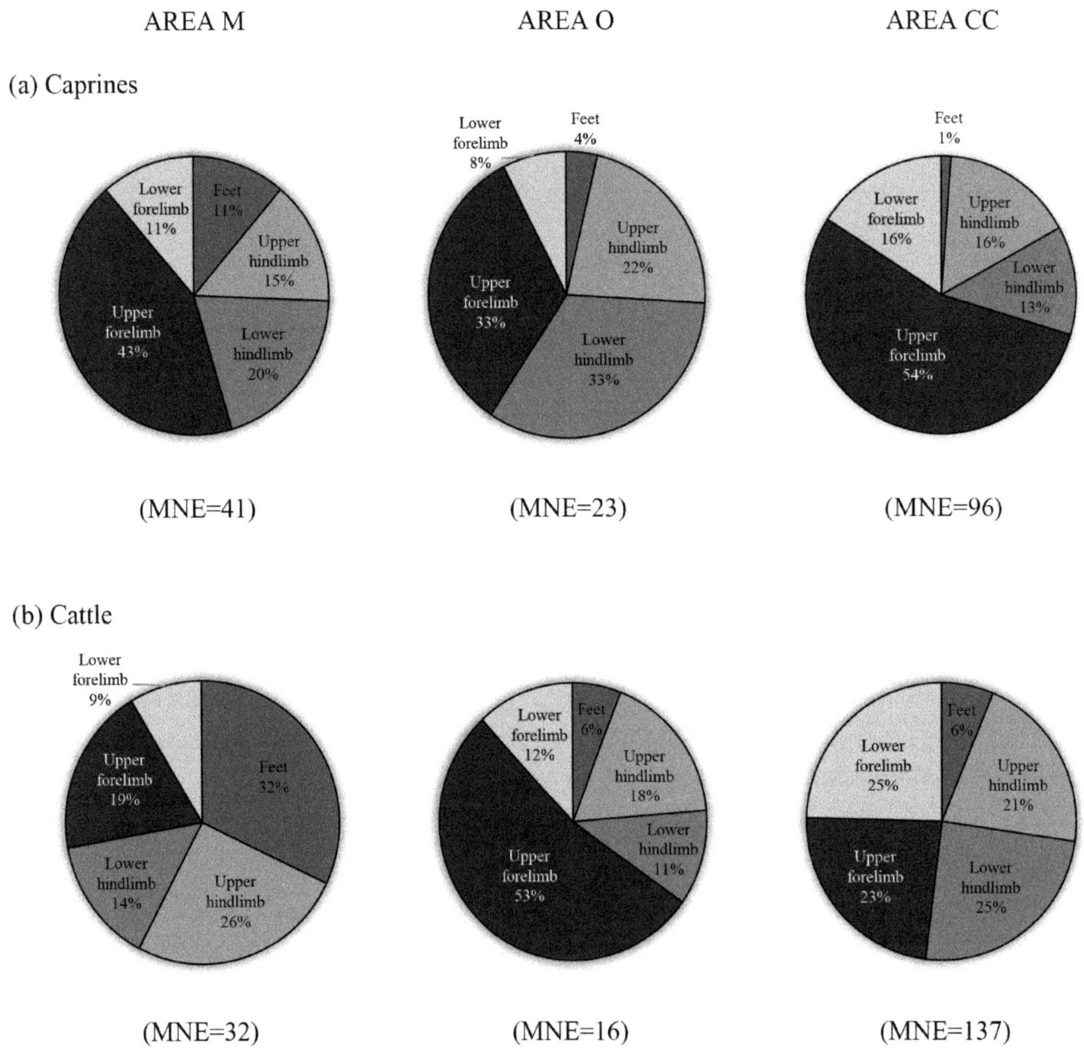

Fig. 20.1: Body Part Representation (MAU%) in Areas M, O and CC for Caprine and Cattle. Body part key Upper forelimbs: scapula and humerus; Lower forelimbs: ulna, radius, metacarpal and carpals; Upper hindlimbs: pelvis, sacrum, femur; Lower hindlimbs: tibia, metatarsal, astragalus, calcaneum and tarsals; Feet: 1st, 2nd and 3rd phalanges.

262 and 216 respectfully). Weathering stages recorded were high (at above level 3; Table 20.2), suggesting that the bones were not immediately covered when discarded. The poor state of the bones, along with the evidence of other materials found with them (Chapter 3), imply that the round and rectangular vats were used, after ceasing to function as winepress facilities, to discard mainly dry objects such as pottery sherds and building material (specifically tesserae stones). The discarded materials were then possibly covered with earth gathered from the surrounding area of the complex. Due to the small sample, a further analysis of the bones is not available, although it is worth noting that an abundance of large animals (80%) was recorded in the sample, the majority of which belonged to cattle (N = 13), followed by equids (N = 1) and a bone classified as belonging to body size A (N = 1).

AREA CC

A total of 4,622 bones were collected in Area CC, of which 1865 (40%) were identified (Table 20.1). Animal remains from Area CC were collected throughout the area of the refuse dump (Locus 30052 /Sq. H6, Locus 30060 /Sq. F6, Locus 30061 /Sq. F7, Locus 30063 /Sq. G6, Locus 30071 /Sq. G7, Locus 30037 /Sq. G5 and Locus 30160 /Sq. G9), all from localities belonging to the same strata of garbage disposal dated to the 5th-to 6th/7th-century CE (Chapter 6). Large ungulates (84%) including cattle (26%; N = 488), equids and donkeys (6%; N = 116), and camels (5%; N = 87) predominate Area CC. Due to the high rate of fragmentation, the remaining bones (48%) could only be classified as a large body size animal (i.e., size A). Both sheep (N = 6) and goats (N = 2) are present in the assemblage (total caprines; 7.3%, N = 136). Other species found in the refuse dump include pig (1%, N = 22), whose domestic or wild status could not

TABLE 20.6: AGING OF CATTLE BASED ON EPIPHYSEAL FUSION (FOLLOWING SILVER 1969)

		Area M		*Area O*		*Area CC*	
Age in Months	*Body Part*	*Fused*	*Unfused*	*Fused*	*Unfused*	*Fused*	*Unfused*
7–10	Scapula			3		28	1
12–18	Distal Humerus		1			8	9
	Proximal Radius					18	
18	1st Phalanges			1		9	
	2nd Phalanges					2	
Total			*1 (100%)*	*4*		*65*	*10 (13%)*
24–36	Distal Metacarpal					14	
27–36	Distal Metatarsal		2			20	2
36–42	Distal Tibia		1			18	1
36–42	Calacaneus			1			
Total			*3 (100%)*	*1*		*52*	*3 (5.5%)*
42–48	Proximal Femur		1		1	12	
	Distal Femur	1	1			24	
	Proximal Ulna			1		12	5
	Distal Radius					6	1
	Proximal Tibia					21	3
	Proximal Humerus	1				2	1
Total		*2*	*2 (50%)*	*1*	*1 (50%)*	*77*	*10 (11.5%)*
<54	Pelvis					15	9 (37.5%)
Grand Total		*2*	*6 (75%)*	*6*	*1 (14%)*	*209*	*32 (13%)*

be determined due to the lack of measurable bones. Two bones representing wild animals were recorded: roe deer (N = 1), and mountain gazelle (N = 1). A single unidentified rodent bone was also present in the sample. The rodent probably burrowed into the strata; therefore this bone will not be discussed further.

Age profiles for main livestock in Area CC demonstrate that caprines were kept primarily until adulthood (>48 months) in the hinterland of Apollonia/Sozousa. Only 5% (N=6) of caprines were culled at a prime age (24–36 months) for their meat (Payne 1973: 281–282, Fig. 1), while the rest of the animals were slaughtered when older than 30–48 months, fitting a culling pattern of secondary product management, possibly that of wool (Table 20.5).

Mortality profiles of large ungulates in Area CC indicate that nearly all of the animals (87%) were kept until an advanced age and were most probably exploited primarily for agricultural work and

Table 20.7: Fused and Unfused Elements of Camel in Area CC

Body part	*Fused*	*Unfused*	*%Unfused*
Distal Metacarpal	7		-
Distal Metatarsal	3		-
1st Phalanges	11	1	8%
2nd Phalanges	1		-
Proximal Calcaneum	2	1	33%
Distal Scapula	4		-
Proximal Ulna	1	1	50%
Pelvis (Ilium)		1	100%
Proximal Femur		1	100%
Proximal Radius	2		-
Proximal Tibia		1	100%
Total	*31*	*6*	*16%*

Table 20.8: Aging of Equids Based on Epiphyseal Fusion (Following Silver 1969)

Age in Months	*Body Part*	*Fused*	*Unfused*	*%Unfused*
9–12	2nd Phalanx	1		-
13–15	1st Phalanx	2		-
15–18	Distal Humerus	3		-
15–18	Proximal Radius	2	1	33%
15–18	Distal Metacarpal	5		-
16–20	Distal Metatarsal	4	1	20%
20	Distal Scapula	5		-
20–24	Distal Tibia	3		-
36–42	Proximal Tibia	7		-
36–42	Distal Femur	1		-
36–42	Proximal Humerus	1		-
42	Distal Radius	4		-
42	Proximal Ulna	1	1	50%
54–60	Pelvis	1		-
Total		*40*	*3*	*7%*

secondary products before being slaughtered for consumption (Grigson 1995: 256; Horwitz 1989: 51; Sasson 2008: 46). Only 14% of the cattle were slaughtered under the age of 36 months (Table 20.6), the prime age for cattle meat culling (Grigson 1995: 256; Horwitz 1989: 51; Sasson 2008: 40). Furthermore, fusion closure observations on the bones of camels and equids revealed that 16% of camels and 7% of equids were immature at death (Tables 20.7, 20.8).

All body parts of all major livestock (caprines, cattle, equids and camels) were present in the sample, yet they differ in their relative frequency. For large mammals, the identification to species level was based primarily on teeth rather than on the fragmented long bones. Thus, in order to avoid an identification-based bias, cranial parts were not included in the skeletal remains analysis per species. MAU% values show a high frequency of meat-rich upper forelimb parts in caprines (MAU% = 47%). Skeletal element frequencies (MAU%) of cattle and equids are similar—all body parts are represented in equal proportions—upper and lower limbs and feet (Fig. 20.2).

DISCUSSION

The Late Byzantine animal economy in Apollonia/Sozousa was based primarily on livestock husbandry, accompanied by occasional hunting of wild animals. While the two assemblages from Areas M and O of the town are relatively small and probably reflect local domestic disposals, the assemblage recovered from Area CC in the hinterland of Apollonia/Sozousa is notably larger and derives from a central area dump and differs significantly from the assemblage found within the perimeters of the Late Antiquity town to its west.

As reflected in the site and hinterland assemblages, draft animals and secondary products were an important part of the town's economy, suggesting that during the Byzantine period Apollonia/Sozousa's agricultural produce was a primary source of the diet, supplemented by meat of smaller animals (along with prime cuts of cattle).

Comparison of the assemblages located inside the town perimeters reveals some economic and cultural differences among them. In Area M, caprines, cattle and chickens are represented in relatively equal proportions, in addition to domestic pig and a few wild species, whereas in Area O, caprines and cattle were abundant, and only one pig bone and two chicken bones were recorded.

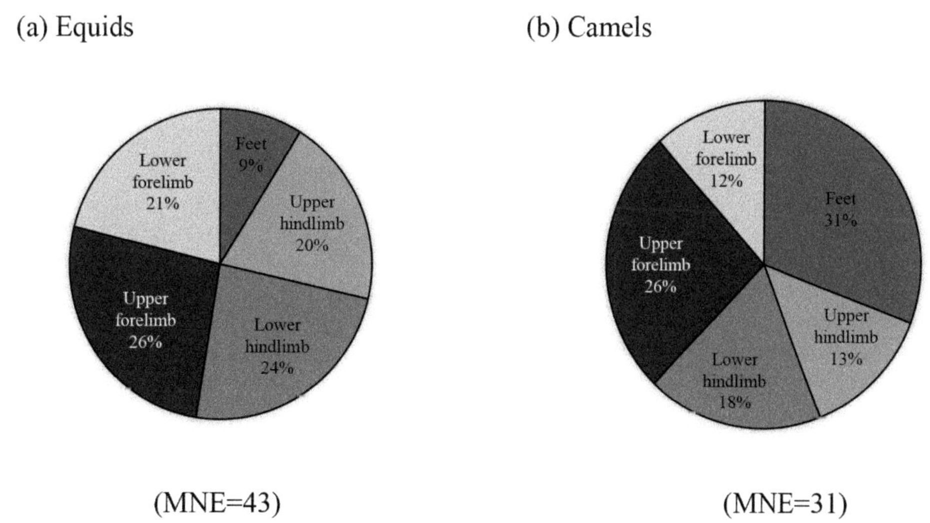

Fig. 20.2: Body Parts Representation (MAU%) in Area CC for Equids and Camels. Body part key Upper forelimbs: scapula and humerus; Lower forelimbs: ulna, radius, metacarpal and carpals; Upper hindlimbs: pelvis, sacrum, femur; Lower hindlimbs: tibia, metatarsal, astragalus, calcaneum and tarsals; Feet: 1st, 2nd and 3rd phalanges.

Pig and chicken require low investment in comparison to the common grazing animals since they mature quickly and can be fed with scraps of garbage and low-cost food (Sapir-Hen, Pines and Tal 2014 with references therein). Thus, the lower quantities of rich meat (caprines and cattle) and the dominance of chicken remains in Area M may suggest that the inhabitants of this area were of a lower social status when compared to those in Area O. Furthermore, although the frequency of hunted game animals is very low in both areas, their presence in the Area M assemblage and absence from that of Area O might also stem from the different status (Sapir-Hen, Pines and Tal 2014 with references therein).

In addition to species frequencies, the representation of body parts of the major species and their mortality profiles suggest caprines and cattle were exploited differently in the two areas. Caprines and cattle from Area M display a representation of all body parts, butchery waste together with meaty parts. However, the skeletal representation of caprines and cattle from Area O include only the meaty parts and reveal a greater emphasis on animals of prime age. In addition, all stages of preparing the animal for consumption are evident in Area M. Along with the differing species frequencies (above), these characteristics imply that the food consumption practices were different; whereas the inhabitants in Area M may have kept and slaughtered their own livestock on site, the inhabitants of Area O enjoyed a higher status and were supplied with meat.

In addition to the economic differences, the presence of pigs in Area M and their near absence in Area O, along with other supporting evidence (Tal 2009 and above Chapters 8 and 10), may reflect the diets of two separate ethnic groups using the two refuse dumps: the Samaritans in the north (i.e., the more affluent) and Christians in the south (i.e., those of a lower status; cf. Sapir-Hen, Pines and Tal 2014 for a wider discussion).

Comparing the refuse dumps' faunal assemblages from the town with the one from its hinterland reveals differences in species frequencies as well as in their manner of exploitation and discard. While the refuse dump assemblages from the town are dominated by caprines, cattle, pig and chicken that were butchered at optimal ages for meat consumption, large ungulates, slaughtered at a relatively advanced age and probably exploited for labor and secondary products, are prevalent in the hinterland assemblage. Body part representation in both areas adds supporting evidence for these differences; while evidence of prime cuts dominated the town samples, the hinterland assemblage displayed all body parts of the animals discarded. Furthermore, pack animals such as horse/donkey were found in very small numbers in Area O inside the town (N=2) and camel was completely absent. Butchery mark frequencies were also different in the town and its periphery. While the number of butchery marks on the bones in the hinterland was low, the bones from Area M in the town displayed a high number of marks attesting to all stages of preparation for consumption, suggesting that the consumers (identified as Christians, see above) had a direct connection to the herders and/or possibly produced their own food.

The assemblages from within the town are largely similar to other assemblages from the same period. In contrast, the hinterland sample differs significantly from other contemporaneous faunal assemblages in the southern Levant. The dominance of draft animals stands out markedly from findings of other Byzantine assemblages such as Tell Hesban (von den Driesch and Boessneck 1995), Tel Bet Shean (Horwitz 2006), Tel Yokneʾam (Cope 1999), Kh. Sumaqa on Mount Carmel (Horwitz, Tchernov and Shimon 1990), Ḥorvat Rimmon (Horwitz 1998) and Ḥorvat Karkur ʿIllit in the Negev (Horwitz 2004). This may reflect differences in the localities studied at the different sites, considering excavations were carried out in residential dwellings at Tell Hesban, Tel Bet Shean and Tel Yokneʾam, and in religious buildings at Ḥorvat Karkur ʿIllit (a church and associated structures), Kh. Sumaqa and Ḥorvat Rimmon (synagogues). Accordingly, the findings from inside the limits of the town of Apollonia/Sozousa are consistent with the domestic and cultic Byzantine assemblages and display a dominance of sheep and goats.

WILD SPECIES

Only a few wild animals were recorded in the Apollonia/Sozousa samples; red deer, roe deer, mountain gazelle, red fox and the Syrian brown bear are each represented by a few specimens. Interestingly, red and roe deer were both considered to have been extinct in the area of the Sharon plain during the Byzantine period (cf. Tsahar *et al.* 2009), though this assertion might result from the low number of Byzantine assemblages studied in the region. Gazelles are common in the area to this day and can still be seen roaming the national park of Apollonia-Arsuf, probably due to intensive cultivation of the surrounding fields, which increased the availability of green leaves and fresh water in the summer (Mendelssohn and Yom-Tov 1999: 42).

Of special interest is the presence of the brown bear in the sample. The last specimens of brown bear have been hunted during the 19th and 20th centuries in the Galilee, the Jordan Valley and eastern Jordan (Masseti 2009: 230 and Tsahar *et al.* 2009: with references therein). Additional archaeological evidence for brown bears in contemporary Byzantine sites in Northern Israel and Jordan is lacking (cf. Wapnish and Hesse 1979; Horwitz, Tchernov and Shimon 1990; Horwitz 1996; 1998; 2004; 2006; 2008; von den Driesch and Boessneck 1995; Grantham 1992; 1996; Manor, Rabinovich and Horwitz 1997; Rephael and Lernau 1996; Rielly 1993; Sade 2007; 2012),[1] therefore the addition of the identified specimen to the archaeozoological record is important.

CONCLUSIONS

With limited living space and food, a complex urban society may have formed in Apollonia/Sozousa enabling only the affluent (such as the Samaritan community) to obtain the meat of costly livestock animals, accounting for the vast differences found between the two assemblages in Areas M and O, situated only 450 meters from each other.

Considering the large increase in population and site size in Apollonia/Sozousa during the Byzantine period, the importance of agriculture and crops growing in the immediate vicinity of the town was probably elevated for logical economic reasons. This is perhaps why cattle, along with other beasts of burden, comprised the vast majority of the species in the hinterland assemblage. Massive herding of caprines would have damaged the crops during growing seasons, while cattle have a less mobile feeding regime and may also be used for plow and other toil-related tasks in addition to the secondary products produced (Broshi 1986).

In summary, our results reveal that there is great value in studying intra-site faunal assemblages along with contemporary assemblages from the site's periphery. Future studies should consider this important relationship when assessing a site's whole economy, which depends a great deal on its hinterland.

1 In a report from Khirbat es-Suyyagh, Sasson accounts for six (NISP) bones identified as "*Ursus*," although it is not clear whether the bones derived from Late Byzantine or ʿAbbasid period contexts (Sasson 2009: 185).

APPENDIX 20.1

MEASURMENTS
(STANDARDIZED MEASURMENTS TAKEN ACCORDING TO VON DEN DRIESCH 1976)

AREA A1

A. Equids

Body Part	*Measurements*	
	Bd	*SD*
1st Phalanges	40.05	24.11

AREA CC

A. Cattle

Body Part	*Measurements*															
	Bp	*Bd*	*SD*	*Dl*	*Dm*	*GL*	*GLl*	*Glm*	*MBS*	*DLS*	*Ld*	*GLpe*	*BFd*	*BFp*	*GB*	*Ld*
Astragalus		51.5		39.51	39.75		75.52	67.13								
		42.21		38.54	39.22		71.94	66.79								
							70.14									
		46.78						66.45								
		43.94		37.36	39.84		69.43	62.97								
		40.67			37.75		66.51	62.01								
							64.25	60.85								
							68.42	63.93								
Metacarpal	51.1															
	52.48		32.87													
Metatarsal	55.97															
Patella						62.52									53.5	
1st Phalanges						59.51						59.69				
												63.24				
	22.39	23.68	21.55									62.19				
2nd Phalanges	17.23	22.92	22.52			37.43						38.12				
3rd Phalanges									19.19	60.77						48.58
					37.7		70.1	65.1								
									23.16	68.2	55.12					
									21.78	61.96	46.7					
Radius	91.11	67.49											63.26	85.38		
	78.36													73.27		
Tibia		60.53														
	46.48															

b. Camels

Body Part	*Measurements*		
	SD	*GL*	*GLI*
Astragalus			79.93
1st Phalanges	21.39	87.37	
	26.31		
	25.13		
	23.55		

c. Equids

Species	*Body Part*	*Measurements*						
		Bp	*Bd*	*SD*	*GL*	*LmT*	*GH*	*Dp*
Equus	Astragalus					45	49.54	
	Metacarpal		46.36					
	Metatarsal		38.22					
	2nd Phalanges	44.5		38.33	46			37.63
Equus Asinus	1st Phalanges			20.93				

d. Caprines

Species	*Body Part*	*Measurements*					
		Bp	*Bd*	*SD*	*Gd*	*GLpe*	*BT*
Ovis aries/ Capra hircus	Tibia	38.06	25.85				
	Calcaneum				19.57		
	1st Phalanges	10.8	9.28	9.57		33.23	
	Metatarsal	23.43					
Capra hircus	Humerus		29.61	17.86			30.32
Ovis aries	Tibia	24.69		17.17			

e. Red Deer

Body Part	*Measurements*
	Bp
Tibia	69.16

AREA M

a. Caprines

Body Part	*Measurements*		
	Bd	*Bfd*	*BT*
Humerus			31.26
			30.39
			33.89
			32.16
Radius	31.93	26.7	

B. CATTLE

Body Part	*Measurements*		
	Bd	*GLl*	*GLm*
Astragalus	39.44	67.28	63.01
	46.77	72.63	67.05
Metatarsal	45.01		

C. PIGS

Body part	*Measurements*			
	Bp	*Bd*	*Dd*	*GL*
Metatarsal	13.9		16.27	
Radius	29.28			
Tibia	49.68	32.25	27.86	200.01

AREA O

A. CAPRINES

Species	*Body Part*	*Measurements*		
		Bp	*Bd*	*GL*
Ovis aries/ Capra hircus	Metacarpal	26.92		
		24.56		
		25.91		
	Metatarsal	20.3		
		21.22		
Capra hircus	1st Phalanges	14.27	14.38	43.06

B. CATTLE

Body Part	*Measurements*		
	Bd	*GB*	*GLP*
Calcaneum		35.44	
Scapula			64.39
1st Phalanges	26.57		

C. EQUIDS

Body Part	*Measurements*		
	Bp	*Bd*	*GL*
2nd Phalanges	58.81	58.25	46.96
Radius	52.17	43.19	

REFERENCES

Behrensmeyer, A.K. 1978. Taphonomic and Ecologic Information from Bone Weathering. *Paleobiology* 4: 150–162.

Binford, L.R. 1981. *Bones: Ancient Men and Modern Myths*. New York.

Broshi, M. 1986. The Diet of Palestine in the Roman Period–Introductory Notes. *Israel Museum Journal* 5: 41–56.

Cope, C.R. 1999. Faunal Remains and Butchery Practices from Byzantine and Islamic Contexts (1993–1994 Seasons). In: Holum, K.G., Raban, A. and Patrich, J., eds. *Caesarea Papers II* (Roman Archaeology Supplement 35). Portsmouth: 405–418.

Dayan, T. 1999. Faunal Remains: Areas A-G. In: Beit-Arieh, I., ed. *Tel ʿIra: A Stronghold in the Biblical Negev* (Monograph Series of the Institute of Archaeology of Tel Aviv University 15). Tel Aviv: 480–488.

Driesch, A. von den. 1976. *A Guide to the Measurement of Animal Bones from Archaeological Sites: As Developed by the Institut für Palaeoanatomie, Domestikationsforschung und Geschichte der Tiermedizin of the University of Munich*. Massachusetts.

Driesch, A. von den and Boessneck, J. 1995. Final Report on the Zooarchaeological Investigation of Animal Bone Finds from Tell Hesban, Jordan. In: LaBianca, Ø.S. and von den Driesch, A., eds. *Hesban 13: Faunal Remains: Taphonomical and Zooarchaeological Studies of the Animal Remains from Tell Hesban and Vicinity*. Berrien Springs: 65–109.

Grant, A. 1982. The Use of Tooth Wear as a Guide to the Age of Domestic Ungulates. In: Wilson, B., Grigson, C. and Payne, S., eds. *Aging and Sexing Animal Bones from Archaeological Sites. (BAR British Series 109)* Oxford: 91–108.

Grantham, B.J. 1992. *Modern Buqata and Ancient Qasrin: The Ethnoarchaeology of Cuisine in the Golan Heights* (M.A. thesis, University of Alabama). Tuscaloosa.

Grantham, B.J. 1996. *A Zooarchaeological Model for the Study of Ethnic Complexity at Sepphoris* (Ph.D. dissertation, Northwestern University). Illinois.

Grigson, C. 1995. Plough and Pasture in the Early Economy of the Southern Levant. In: Levy, T.E., ed. *The Archaeology of Society in the Holy Land*. London: 245–263.

Hongo, H. and Meadow, R.H. 1998. Pig Exploitation at Neolithic Çayönü Tepesi (southern Iran). In: Nelson, S. M., ed. *Ancestors for the Pigs: Pigs in Prehistory* (MASCA Research Papers in Science and Archaeology 15). Philadelphia: 77–98.

Horwitz, L.K. 1989. Diachronic Changes in Rural Husbandry Practices in Bronze Age Settlements from the Refaim Valley, Israel. *Palestine Exploration Quarterly* 121: 44–54.

Horwitz, L.K. 1996. Faunal Remains from Areas A, B, D, H and K. In: Ariel, D.T. and De Groot, A., eds. *Excavations at the City of David 1978–1985 Directed by Y. Shiloh IV* (Qedem Reports 35). Jerusalem: 302–317.

Horwitz, L.K. 1998. Animal Bones from Ḥorbat Rimmon: Hellenistic to Byzantine Periods. *ʿAtiqot* 35: 65–76.

Horwitz, L.K. 2004. Animal Bones. In: Figueras, P., ed. *Ḥorvat Karkur ʿIllit: A Byzantine Cemetery Church in the Northern Negev (Final Report of the Excavations 1989–1995)*. Beer Sheva: 323–348.

Horwitz, L.K. 2006. Mammalian Remains from Areas H, L, P and Q. In: Mazar, A., ed. *Excavations at Tel Beth-Shean 1989–1996, Volume I: From the Late Bronze Age IIB to the Medieval Period*. Jerusalem: 689–710.

Horwitz, L.K. 2008. From Food to Function: Fauna and Bone Tools from Roman–Byzantine Horvat Hazan. In: Bar, S., ed. *In the Hill-Country, and in the Shephelah, and in the Arabah (Joshua 12, 8): Studies and Researches Presented to Adam Zertal in the Thirtieth Anniversary of the Manasseh Hill-Country Survey*. Jerusalem: 236–258.

Horwitz, L.K., Tchernov, E. and Shimon, D. 1990. Subsistence and Environment on Mount Carmel in the Roman–Byzantine and Mediaeval Periods: The Evidence from Kh. Sumaqa. *Israel Exploration Journal* 40: 287–304.

Johnstone, C.J. 2004. *A Biometric Study of Equids in the Roman World* (Ph.D. dissertation, University of York). York.

Lemoine, X., Zeder, M.A., Bishop, K.J. and Rufolo, S.J. 2014. A New System for Computing Dentition-Based Age Profiles in *Sus Scrofa*. *Journal of Archaeological Science* 47: 179–193.

Lyman, R.L. 2008. *Quantitative Paleozoology*. Cambridge.

Lyman, R.L. 1994. *Vertebrate Taphonomy*. Cambridge.

Manor, M., Rabinovich, R. and Horwitz, L.K. 1996. Diachronic Changes in Urban Diet: The Historical Periods at Bet She'an, Israel. *ArchaeoZoologia* VIII: 89–104.

Masseti, M. 2009. Carnivores of Syria. *ZooKeys* 31: 229–252.

Mendelssohn, H. and Yom-Tov, Y. 1999. A Report of Birds and Mammals which have Increased Their Distribution and Abundance in Israel due to Human Activity. *Israel Journal of Zoology* 45: 35–47.

Motro, H. 2004. Equid Skeletons from the Frankish Castle of Vadum Iacob: Archaeozoological Evidence of a Massacre (M.A. thesis, Hebrew University of Jerusalem). Jerusalem.

Payne, S. 1973. Kill-Off Patterns in Sheep and Goats: The Mandibles from Aşvan Kale. *Anatolian Studies* 23: 281–303.

Pines, M., Sapir-Hen, L. and Tal, O. 2017. Consumption and Disposal Practices in the Southern Levant in Late Antiquity: Animal Bones from 'Απολλωνία/Σώζουσα's Hinterland as a Case Study. *Zeitschrift des Deutschen Palästina-Vereins* 133: 186–204.

Rephael, O. and Lernau, O. 1996. Faunal Remains from Bab-el-Hawa: An Iron Age–Byzantine Site in the Golan Heights. *ArchaoZoologia* VIII: 105–118.

Rielly, K. 1993. The Animal Bones from Tell al-Husn (Area XXXIV) and the Abbasid Complex (Area XXIX). In: Walmsley, A.G., Macumber, P.G., Edwards, P.C., Bourke, S.J. and Watson, P.M., eds. The Eleventh and Twelfth Seasons of Excavations at Pella (Tabaqat Fahl) 1989–1990. *Annual of the Department of Antiquities of Jordan* 37: 218–221.

Sade, M. 2007. Faunal Remains. In: Gophna, R., Taxel, I. and Feldstein, A. *Kafr ʿAna: A Rural Settlement in the Lod Valley* (Salvage Excavation Reports 4). Tel Aviv: 103–107.

Sade, M. 2012. The Archaeozoological Finds. In: Fischer, M., ed. *Ḥorvat Meṣad: A Way-Station on the Jaffa-Jerusalem Road* (Monograph Series of the Institute of Archaeology of Tel Aviv University 30). Tel Aviv: 263–272.

Sapir-Hen, L., Pines, M. and Tal, O. 2014. Animal Economy and Social Diversity in Byzantine Apollonia/Sozousa. *Levant* 46: 371–381.

Sasson, A. 2008. *Animal Husbandry in Ancient Israel.* London.

Sasson, A. 2009. Faunal Remains. In: Taxel, I. *Khirbet es-Suyyagh: A Byzantine Monastery in the Judean Shephelah* (Salvage Excavation Reports 9). Tel Aviv: 183–185.

Silver, I.A. 1969. The Aging of Domestic Animals. In: Brothwell, D.R., Higgs, E.S. and Clark, G., eds. *Science in Archaeology: A Survey of Progress and Research.* London: 283–302.

Tal, O. 2009. A Winepress at Apollonia-Arsuf: More Evidence on the Samaritan Presence in Roman–Byzantine Southern Sharon. *Liber Annuus* 59: 319–342.

Tal, O. and Taxel, I. 2012. Socio-Political and Economic Aspects of Refuse Disposal in Late Byzantine and Early Islamic Palestine. In: Matthews, R., Curtis, J., *et al.*, eds. *Proceedings of the 7th International Congress on the Archaeology of the Ancient Near East, 12–16 April 2010, the British Museum and UCL, London 1: Mega-Cities and Mega-Sites, the Archaeology of Consumption and Disposal, Landscape, Transport and Communication.* Wiesbaden: 497–518.

Tal, O. and Taxel, I. 2017. More than Trash Cultic Use of Pottery Lamps Found in Late Antique Dumps: Apollonia (Sozousa) as a Test Case. In: Tal, O. and Weiss, Z., eds. *Expressions of Cult in the Southern Levant in the Greco-Roman Period: Manifestations in Text and Material Culture* (Contextualizing the Sacred 6). Turnhout: 181–193.

Tsahar, E., Izhaki, I., Lev-Yadun, S. and Bar-Oz, G. 2009. Distribution and Extinction of Ungulates during the Holocene of the Southern Levant. *PLoS ONE* 4: e5316.

Wapnish, P. 1984. The Dromedary and Bactrian Camel in Levantine Historical Settings: The Evidence from Tell Jemmeh. In: Clutton-Brock, J. and Grigson, C., eds. *Animals and Archaeology: Early Herders and Their Flocks* (BAR International Series 202). Oxford: 171–200.

Wapnish, P. and Hesse, B. 1979. Appendix D: The Faunal Remains from Byzantine Jemmeh. In: Schaefer, J. *The Ecology of Empires: An Archaeological Approach to the Byzantine Communities of the Negev Desert* (Ph.D. dissertation, University of Arizona). Arizona: 293–306.

Zeder, M.A. 2006. Reconciling Rates of Long Bone Fusion and Tooth Eruption and Wear in Sheep (Ovis) and Goat (Capra). In: Ruscillo, D., ed. *Recent Advances in Aging and Sexing Animal Bones* (Proceedings of the 9th Conference of the International Council of Archaeozoology, Durham, 2002). Oxford: 87–118.

Zeder, M.A. and Lapham, H.A. 2010. Assessing the Reliability of Criteria Used to Identify Postcranial Bones in Sheep, *Ovis*, and Goats, *Capra. Journal of Archaeological Science* 37: 2887–2905.

CHAPTER 21

MOLLUSC REMAINS (AREAS AA–DD)

Oz Rittner and Henk K. Mienis

While parts of Apollonia were excavated in the past (Roll 1999), those excavations were followed more recently when the ruins of the Crusader castle on the sandstone promontory and the adjoining city were renovated. The entire site was declared a National Park and additional areas to the east, which were off limits for a considerable time, became available for survey and excavation.

One of these new projects was carried out during two seasons in 2012 and 2013 when a team led by Oren Tal (Tel Aviv University) excavated, along with other features, a large dump (Area CC) which had been in use during the Late Byzantine period. The molluscs encountered during the excavation of that area are the subject of this report.

MATERIAL AND METHODS

Shells were collected according to size, based on on eyesight and by means of sieving the excavated material. The extracted archaeomalacological material was identified by the authors using the mollusc collection of the Steinhardt Museum of Natural History and Israel National Center for Biodiversity Studies (SMNH). Most of the material was identified immediately. In a few cases, the shells were compared with better preserved material of more recent origin present in the Steinhardt Museum of Natural History collection.

RESULTS

Since the shells were collected from a dump which had been in use during the Byzantine period, the identified material has been catalogued according to the different loci. In this way the shells from 156 different loci have been studied.

For the nomenclature of the marine shells, the names adopted by the World Register of Marine Species (WoRMS) were used; for the freshwater bivalves the nomenclature proposed on the Mussel Project Web Site (MUSSELp) was followed; while for the land snails the names used in the SMNH Mollusc Collection were employed.

The archaeomalacological material belonged to 29 taxa identified at specific level and one taxon at generic level. The studied material is here enumerated in systematic order according to families and within the same family in alphabetical order.

PHYLUM MOLLUSCA, CLASS GASTROPODA

Area	*Locus*	*Description*
FAMILY PATELLIDAE		
Patella caerulea (Linnaeus, 1758)		
AA	10031	One complete shell

Area	*Locus*	*Description*
Patella ulyssiponensis (Gmelin, 1791)		
CC	30061	One damaged shell
Family Cypraeidae		
Cypraea pantherina (Lightfoot, 1786) – Fig. 21.1: 1		
CC	30060	One heavily damaged shell
Erosaria spurca (Linnaeus, 1758)		
AA	118	One complete shell
AA	120	One complete shell
AA	10019	One complete shell
CC	603	One complete shell
CC	607	One complete shell
CC	615	One complete shell
CC	617	One complete shell
CC	623	One complete shell
CC	632	One complete shell
CC	641	One complete shell
CC	643	11 complete shells and one fragment
CC	656	One complete shell
CC	659	One complete shell
CC	30036	Three complete shells
CC	30052	One fragment
CC	30060	Nine complete shells (two with natural holes)
CC	30061	Three complete shells
CC	30063	Four complete shells and three broken shells
CC	30071	One complete and one broken shell
CC	30074	One complete shell
CC	30082	Two complete shells
CC	30108	One complete shell
CC	30118	Seven complete shells
CC	30119	One broken shell
CC	30122	One complete shell
CC	30123	One complete shell
CC	30131	One complete shell, one shell with the dorsum removed and one fragment
CC	30134	One complete shell
CC	30138	One complete shell
CC2	30003	One complete shell
DD2	926	One complete shell
Luria lurida (Linnaeus, 1758)		
CC2	30003	One fragment of a labial lip
Monetaria moneta (Linnaeus, 1758) – Fig. 21.1: 2		
CC	30119	One specimen without the dorsum (removed artificially)
Zonaria pyrum (Gmelin, 1791)		
CC	643	One complete shell
CC	30060	One complete shell with a natural hole
CC	30061	One complete shell
CC	30066	Two complete shells

Area	Locus	Description
CC	30071	Eight complete and two damaged shells
CC	30074	Two complete shells
CC	30119	One complete shell
CC	30131	One complete shell

Family Naticidae

Neverita josephinia Risso, 1826

Area	Locus	Description
CC	30036	One complete shell

Family Cassidae

Semicassis granulata undulata (Gmelin, 1791)

Area	Locus	Description
CC	30061	One complete shell
CC	30100	One fragment of the outer lip with the last whorl
CC	30123	One complete shell. Probably collected alive
DD1	758	One fragment of the lip

Family Ranellidae

Charonia variegata (Lamarck, 1816)

Area	Locus	Description
BB2	163	One lip of the aperture
BB2	164	One broken shell missing the apex and the body whorl
BB	444	One lip of the aperture
CC	652	One fragment of the siphon canal with part of the aperture
CC	30027	One fragment of the aperture and the outer lip

Family Muricidae

Bolinus brandaris (Linnaeus, 1758)

Area	Locus	Description
AA	101	One fragment of a siphonal canal with part of the last whorl. Beach rolled
AA	102	One fragment of a siphonal canal with part of the last whorl. Beach rolled
AA	111	One shell with a missing siphonal canal. Beach rolled
AA	133	One fragment of the last whorl. Beach rolled
AA	138	One shell with a missing siphonal canal. Beach rolled
AA	10003	One half of a shell with a missing siphonal canal. Beach rolled
AA	10004	One fragment of the siphonal canal
AA	10023	One shell with a broken siphonal canal
AA	10029	One fragment of the siphonal canal with part of the first whorls. Beach rolled
AA	10031	Two shells with broken siphonal canals and one fragment
AA	10056	One shell with a broken siphonal canal
AA	10062	One fragment of a siphonal canal
AA	10075	One damaged shell
AA	10077	Two fragments of the last whorl. Beach rolled
AA2	165	One shell with a hole in the last whorl and a missing siphonal canal. Beach rolled
AA2	168	One shell with a broken siphonal canal and lip. Beach rolled
AA2	174	One shell with a missing siphonal canal. Collected alive
AA3	13007	One complete shell
BB2	157	One shell with a broken siphonal canal
BB2	162	One half of a shell. Beach rolled
BB2	164	One shell fragment. Beach rolled
CC	300	One shell with a broken siphonal canal
CC	408	One shell with a broken siphonal canal and a large hole in the last whorl

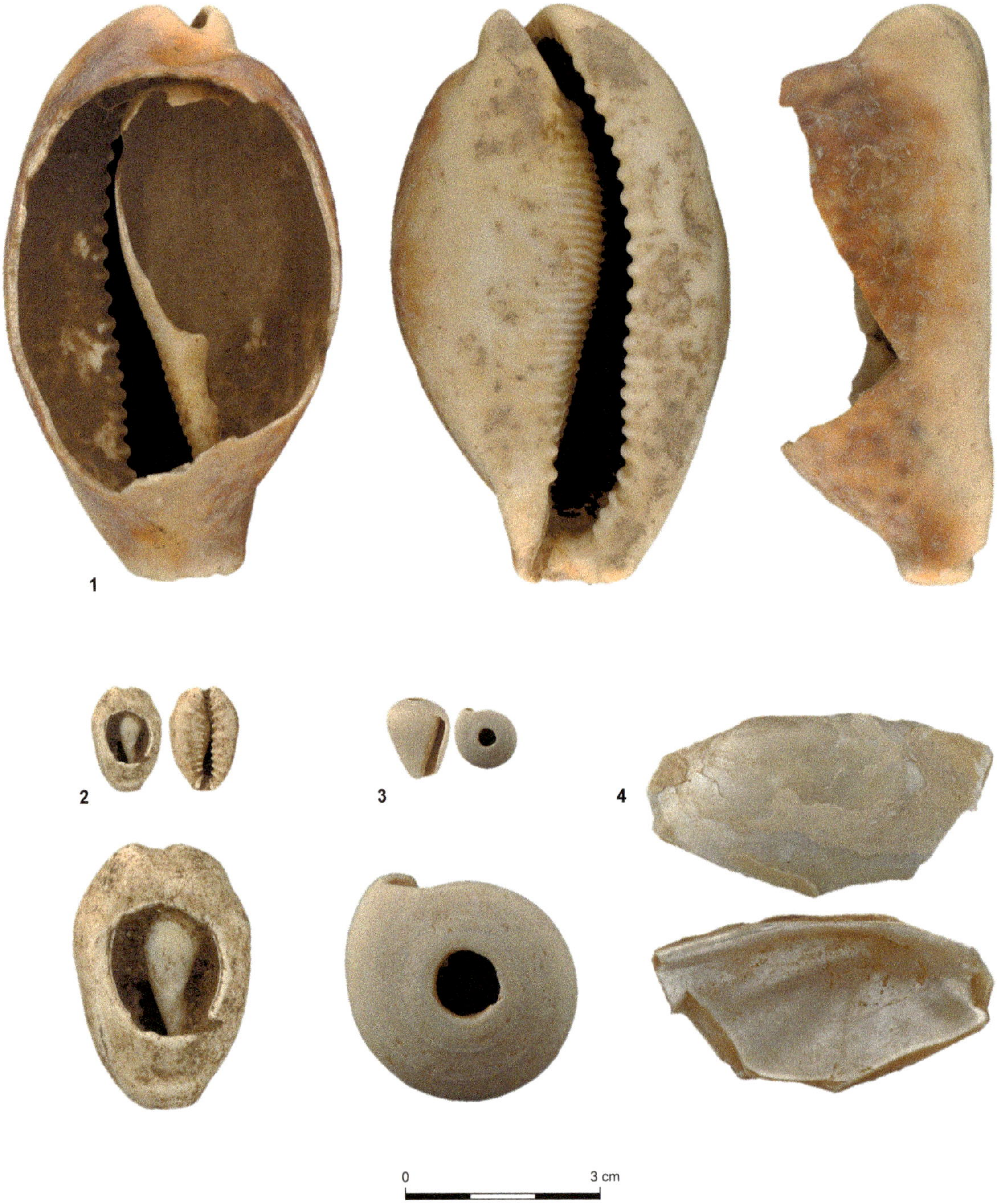

Fig. 21.1: *Cypraea pantherina*: (1) a heavily damaged shell; (2) *Monetaria moneta*: shell bead with the dorsum artificially removed; (3) *Conus mediterraneus*: showing a man-made hole in the apex; (4) *Chambardia rubens arcuta*: a damaged valve with an interior showing a layer of Mother-of-Pearl.

Area	*Locus*	*Description*
CC	617	One specimen missing part of the last whorl
CC	643	Two shells with broken siphonal canals
CC	659	One fragment
CC	30004	One shell with a broken siphonal canal
CC	30015	Two shells with broken siphonal canals_
CC	30037	One fragment of the last whorl
CC	30038	One shell with a broken siphonal canal
CC	30048	One fragment of a siphonal canal. Beach rolled
CC	30060	Three broken shells. Beach rolled
CC	30061	Three shells with broken siphonal canals
CC	30063	One shell with a broken siphonal canal
CC	30065	One broken shell. Beach rolled
CC	30069	One shell with a broken siphonal canal
CC	30071	One broken shell
CC	30074	One shell with a broken siphonal canal
CC	30118	One fragment of a siphonal canal and part of the last whorl and one fragment of a siphonal canal
CC	30119	One fragment of a siphonal canal
DD	40001	One shell fragment
DD1	753	One shell missing the siphona canal. Beach rolled
DD1	779	One broken shell without a siphonal canal and lip and four shell fragments
DD2	927	One fragment of a siphonal canal with part of the adhering last whorl. Beach rolled
Area	877	One shell with a damaged last whorl
Hexaplex trunculus (Linnaeus, 1758)		
AA	101	One complete shell
AA	137	One piece of the siphonal canal and adhering last whorl. Beach rolled
AA	138	One piece of the siphonal canal and adhering last whorl. Beach rolled
AA	10031	One shell fragment
AA	10032	One fragment of the siphonal canal. Beach rolled
AA	10038	One fragment of the first whorls. Beach rolled
AA	11010	One shell with a broken siphonal canal
AA1	252	One small piece of the columella. Beach rolled
AA2	12022	One fragment of the spire. Beach rolled
BB	416	One shell with a damaged apex and a large hole in last whorl. Beach rolled
BB	450	One shell showing three holes caused by a predator. Beach rolled
BB2	162	One fragment of the last whorl. Beach rolled
CC	30015	One broken shell
CC	30036	One shell with a broken siphonal canal
CC	30060	Three shells (two damaged). Beach rolled
CC	30067	One shell with the aperture damaged during the excavation
CC	30071	One complete shell
CC	30074	One complete shell. Beach rolled
CC	30115	One broken shell
CC	30126	One damaged shell. Beach rolled
DD1	750	One part of the last whorl including the siphonal canal. Beach rolled
DD1	752	One fragment of the siphonal canal. Beach rolled
DD1	754	One fragment of the siphonal canal. Beach rolled

Area	*Locus*	*Description*
DD1	777	One fragment of the siphonal canal. Beach rolled
DD1	779	14 shell fragments
DD1	801	One small piece of the columella. Beach rolled
DD2	908	One shell with a hole in the last whorl. Beach rolled
DD3	854	One fragment of the siphonal canal and attached part of the last whorl. Beach rolled

Stramonita haemastoma (Linnaeus, 1767)

AA	114	One shell, the lip is broken and missing. Beach rolled
AA	129	One shell, the lip is broken and missing
AA	10027	One fragment of the last whorl
AA	10031	One broken shell
AA	10034	One broken shell
AA1	207	One part of the last whorl with the siphonal canal. Beach rolled
AA2	12009	One fragment of the last whorl
BB2	162	One broken shell, last whorl missing. Beach rolled
CC	623	One complete shell_
CC	30015	One complete shell_
CC	30036	One damaged shell
CC	30060	Two damaged shells. Beach rolled
CC	30061	One broken shell
CC	30071	One broken shell and two fragments
CC	30105	One complete shell_
DD1	789	One complete shell
DD1	801	One part of the columella and penultimate whorl. Beach rolled
DD2	907	One shell with only part of the last whorl, aperture and siphonal canal. Beach rolled
DD2	909	One fragment missing the last whorl. Beach rolled
DD2	910	One part of the columella and penultimate whorl. Beach rolled

Family Columbellidae

Columbella rustica (Linnaeus, 1758)

AA	10077	One complete shell
BB2	164	One complete shell

Family Nassariidae

Tritia circumcinctus (A. Adams, 1852)

AA	10070	One complete shell

Family Conidae

Conus mediterraneus Hwass, 1792 – Fig. 21.1: 3

AA	10003	One shell with a broken lip
AA	10031	One complete shell with a man-made hole in the apex
CC	649	One shell with a broken lip
CC	30074	One damaged shell
CC	30148	One shell with a broken lip

Family Enidae

Buliminus labrosus labrosus (Olivier, 1804)

CC	30060	Four complete shells (one broken)
CC	30061	Five complete shells

Area	Locus	Description
CC	30081	One complete shell
CC	30082	One complete shell
CC	30118	One complete shell
Family Hygromiidae		
Monacha obstructa (L. Pfeiffer, 1842)		
CC	643	One damaged shell
CC	30061	One complete shell
Monacha syriaca (Ehrenberg, 1831)		
CC	643	One complete shell
CC	30063	Two complete shells
CC	30131	One broken shell
Family Helicidae		
Helix engaddensis engaddensis Bourguignat, 1852		
CC	30060	One shell fragment
CC	30063	One shell with a damaged aperture and one shell with a damaged last whorl
CC	30082	One complete shell
Levantina spiriplana caesareana (Mousson, 1854)		
CC	30052	One complete specimen, three damaged specimens and one shell fragment
CC	30060	One damaged shell
CC	30061	Seven shells (six damaged)
CC	30063	Two shells with damaged outer lips
CC	30071	One complete shell and one fragment
Theba pisana (Müller, 1774)		
CC	30061	Four shells (one damaged)
CC	30063	Three complete shells

Class Bivalvia

Area	Locus	Description
Family Glycymerididae		
Glycymeris nummaria (Linnaeus, 1758) – Fig. 21.2		
AA	101	One valve with a damaged ventral margin
AA	104	One complete valve with remains of mortar and a natural hole and one valve fragment
AA	111	Four valves (one with natural hole), one with a damaged ventral margin and one slightly broken valve with a natural hole
AA	114	Three valves and one fragment
AA	116	Two valves with natural holes (one slightly broken)
AA	118	Three valves with damaged ventral margins (one with a natural hole)
AA	120	One valve with a broken ventral margin
AA	10011	Two fragments
AA	10014	One damaged valve
AA	10018	One complete valve
AA	10031	One complete valve, eight damaged valves (three with a natural hole) and eight fragments
AA	10052	One damaged valve with a natural hole, two broken valves and four fragments
AA	10066	One damaged valve

Fig. 21.2: A typical recent *Glycymeris nummaria* beach.

Area	*Locus*	*Description*
AA	10067	One broken valve and one fragment
AA	10077	One damaged valve and one fragment
AA	10078	One fragment
AA1	202	One slightly broken valve, one valve with a natural hole and four fragments
AA1	207	One complete valve with a small natural hole and four small fragments
AA1	252	One valve with a hole caused by a predator
AA2	12009	One complete and one damaged valve
AA7	205	One complete valve with a natural hole and one fragment
BB	442	Two complete valves, two slightly broken valves and two fragments of valves with natural holes
BB	443	One fragment of a valve
BB	444	Two valves with damaged ventral margins and one unbonal fragment with a natural hole
BB	446	One complete valve with a small natural hole
BB2	162	One complete valve
BB2	164	One complete valve
CC	408	One slightly broken valve
CC	600	One complete valve, two broken valves and four fragments
CC	602	One complete valve and two broken valves
CC	613	Four complete valves, four broken valves and two fragments
CC	615	One broken valve
CC	617	One complete valve and two broken valves (one recently broken probably during the excavation and one with natural hole)
CC	618	One complete valve and two damaged valves

Area	*Locus*	*Description*
CC	619	One complete valve and two broken valves with natural holes
CC	621	One complete valve and two broken valves with natural holes
CC	623	12 complete valves (two with natural holes), four broken valves and two fragments
CC	627	One complete valve, six damaged valves (four with natural holes) and two broken valves
CC	632	One slightly broken valve and one partial valve
CC	641	Six complete valves (two with natural holes) and nine damaged valves (two with natural holes)
CC	642	One damaged valve
CC	643	38 complete valves (14 with natural holes), five valves with damaged ventral margins (three with natural holes), 26 damaged valves (nine with natural holes) and three fragments
CC	656	One broken valve
CC	659	Two complete valves (one with a natural hole) and three valves with broken ventral margins
CC	693	One complete valve with a natural hole
CC	30036	Seven complete valves, six damaged valves (four with natural holes), five broken valves and 13 fragments
CC	30050	Two damaged valves (one with natural hole)
CC	30052	One complete valve with a natural hole, 14 damaged valves (eight with natural holes), one broken valve and one fragment
CC	30056	One complete valve
CC	30060	47 complete valves (27 with natural holes), 104 damaged valves (48 with natural holes) and 24 fragments
CC	30061	22 complete valves (11 with natural holes), 65 damaged valves (29 with natural holes) and nine fragments
CC	30063	56 complete valves (24 with natural holes), 99 damaged valves (53 with natural holes) and 14 fragments
CC	30065	Ten complete valves (two with natural holes), 25 damaged valves (eight with natural holes), 11 broken valves and seven fragments
CC	30066	Two damaged and two broken valves
CC	30067	Two damaged valves
CC	30069	Three damaged valves (one with a natural hole) and one broken valve
CC	30071	44 complete valves (15 with natural holes), 66 damaged valves (40 with natural holes), 40 broken valves and 27 fragments
CC	30073	One damaged valve
CC	30074	37 complete valves (six with natural holes), 56 damaged valves (eight with natural holes), 14 valves with broken ventral margins and 23 fragments
CC	30079	12 complete valves (three with natural holes), 14 damaged valves (two with natural holes) and one fragment
CC	30081	Three complete valves, two valves with a broken ventral margin and two fragments
CC	30082	24 complete valves, 37 damaged valves (13 with natural holes), 25 valves with broken ventral margins, one broken valve and 11 fragments
CC	30089	One complete valve, four valves with broken ventral margins, four damaged valves and one fragment
CC	30100	Seven complete valves, 20 damaged valves and two broken valves
CC	30106	Two complete valves, six valves with broken ventral margins and two broken valves
CC	30114	Five complete valves, six damaged valves (one with a natural hole), three valves with broken ventral margins (one with a natural hole) and three fragments
CC	30118	43 complete valves (17 with natural holes), 36 valves all with broken ventral margins, 18 damaged valves (four with natural holes) and 17 fragments
CC	30119	Three complete valves, 12 valves with broken ventral margins (three with natural holes), four broken valves and three fragments
CC	30122	One damaged valve and one fragment
CC	30123	Four complete specimens (two with natural holes and one with remains of mortar), five broken valves and one fragment
CC	30130	Three complete valves and one fragment
CC	30131	Nine complete valves (five with natural holes), 12 valves with broken ventral margins (five with natural holes), eight damaged valves and one fragment

Area	*Locus*	*Description*
CC	30134	Four complete valves (two with natural holes), five valves with broken ventral margins and four fragments
CC	30135	Three valves with broken ventral margins
CC	30138	One complete and one broken valve
CC	30145	One complete valve
CC	30148	17 complete valves (two with natural holes), 17 damaged valves (six with natural holes), seven valves with broken ventral margins and six fragments
CC	30154	One valve with a broken ventral margin
CC	30161	Seven complete valves and seven damaged valves with natural holes
CC2	31001	One complete valve with a natural hole and two fragments
DD	40001	Three complete valves, four valves with broken ventral margins and one fragment
DD	40002	Two complete valves, four valves with broken ventral margins and one fragment
DD	40005	Two valves with the inner part filled with mortar and two fragments
DD1	751	One complete valve with a natural hole
DD1	779	16 small fragments of valves
DD1	802	50+- fragments of valves covered with mortar and 16 fragments of valves
DD2	900	One valve with a small natural hole
DD2	901	Two complete valves, one with a natural hole
DD2	903	One complete valve
DD2	906	Two valves (one with a natural hole) and one slightly broken valve
DD2	914	One slightly broken valve
DD2	926	One valve with a natural hole
DD2	990	One complete valve and one slightly broken valve
DD2	991	Six complete valves (four with natural holes), partial valve with a natural hole and one fragment of a valve
DD3	857	One valve with a natural hole

Family Iridinidae*

Chambardia rubens arcuta (Cailliaud, 1823) – Fig. 21.1: 4

AA	10031	One small shell fragment
AA1	11052	One valve with a broken ventral margin
BB	442	One broken valve
CC	612	One broken valve
CC	622	One fragment of a valve

Family Spondylidae

Spondylus gaederopus Linnaeus, 1758

AA	112	One valve with a heavily damaged ventral margin
BB	444	One valve with a heavily damaged ventral margin
CC	30036	One broken valve
CC	30060	One damaged valve (broken during excavation)
CC	30061	One damaged valve
CC	30074	One valve
CC	30082	One valve

Family Cardiidae

Acanthocardia tuberculata (Linnaeus, 1758)

BB	442	One broken valve

* Until recently this species was known as *Chambardia rubens arcuata*, an invalid emendation of the original orthography *arcuta*.

Area	*Locus*	*Description*
CC	643	One complete and one broken valve
CC	30060	Four shell fragments
CC	30061	Two complete valves and two fragments
CC	30065	Two shell fragments
CC	30071	One complete valve
CC	30074	Two damaged valves
CC	30082	One complete and one broken valve
CC	30114	One complete valve with a natural hole
CC	30118	Two complete valves and one broken valve
CC	30119	One complete valve
CC	30122	One broken valve
CC	30148	One broken valve with a natural hole and two fragments
CC	30161	One complete valve
Acanthocardia sp.		
CC	30061	One complete heavily abraded valve
Cerastoderma glaucum (Poiret, 1789)		
CC	30063	One complete valve
FAMILY DONACIDAE		
Donax trunculus Linnaeus, 1758		
CC	30060	Two damaged valves
CC	30071	One complete valve
CC	30074	One complete valve
CC	30145	One complete valve
FAMILY VENERIDAE		
Paphia rhomboides (Pennant, 1777)		
CC	30065	One shell fragment

DISCUSSION

COMPOSITION

The studied material from 156 loci from the Byzantine dump at Apollonia-Arsuf consisted of more than 2039 shells or shell fragments (one sample was so numerous in fragments that it has been entered as 50+ fragments). From the ecological point of view, these shells may be classified as follows:

Gastropoda	293
Marine	247
Terrestrial	46
Bivalvia	1746
Marine	1741
Freshwater	5

According to these numbers, the bulk of the material (97.5 %) consisted of marine molluscs, which is quite understandable for a Mediterranean coastal site.

Geographic Origin

From a zoogeographical point of view, the molluscs originated from four different areas:

Apollonia-Arsuf and surroundings: six species of terrestrial snails (46 items):

Buliminus labrosus labrosus	12
Monacha obstructa	2
Monacha syriaca	4
Helix engaddensis engaddensis	4
Levantina spiriplana caesareana	17
Theba pisana	7

Mediterranean Sea (1986 items)

Patella caerulea	1
Patella ulyssiponensis	1
Erosaria spurca	80
Luria lurida	1
Zonaria pyrum	19
Neverita josephinia	1
Semicassis granulata undulata	4
Charonia variegata	5
Bolinus brandaris	59
Hexaplex trunculus	43
Stramonita haemastoma	23
Columbella rustica	2
Tritia circumcinctus	1
Conus mediterraneus	5
Glycymeris nummaria	1698
Spondylus gaederopus	7
Acanthocardia tuberculata	28
Acanthocardia species	1
Cerastoderma glaucum	1
Donax trunculus	5
Paphia rhomboides	1

Red Sea or even further away in the Indian Ocean (2 items):

Monetaria moneta	1
Cypraea pantherina	1

Egypt, River Nile (five items):

Chambardia rubens arcuta	5

These data clearly show that most of the shell material (97.4%) consisted of local Mediterranean species, as would have been expected for this coastal site. Most of the shells are highly abraded specimens and fragments which were washed ashore to the site at the foot of the promontory. Among these shells, *Glycymeris nummaria* was by far the most common: 85.5% of the Mediterranean shells belonged to this species. Like today (Fig. 21.2), during Byzantine times it was probably the most abundant species on the beach, which well-collaborates the results of the age of the *Glycymeris* valves currently washed ashore (Sivan *et al.* 2006).

The fact that *Erosaria spurca*, a local Mediterranean Cowry species, turned out to be the second most abundant species is interesting. It was more common in the dump than any of the three Muricid species which had been exploited intensively at Apollonia-Arsuf for the production of purple dye (Karmon 1999). It is a well-known fact that Cowry shells have been used extensively as shell beads by either removing the dorsum of the shell or by punching one or two holes in the extremities on either side of the shell. In this way shells could be strung or sewn onto a piece of cloth. However, in the case of *Erosaria spurca* from the dump, 71 out of a total of 80, i.e., 78.5%, of the Cowries consisted of complete shells which had not been manipulated.

Two marine species originated from much farther away. *Cypraea pantherina* (Fig. 21.1: 1) is a large Cowry species restricted in its distribution to the Red Sea (Heiman 2002). It is a relatively common species in the Gulf of Aqaba/Elat, Gulf of Suez and in the Red Sea proper. The single shell of this species from the dump is missing its dorsum (roughly broken) and the missing parts were not found among the studied material.

Monetaria moneta (Fig. 21.1: 2) is also a Cowry species that has been found in the Red Sea area but is absent from the Gulf of Aqaba/Elat, instead being found more to the south in the Red Sea proper (Heiman 2002). However, in the Indian Ocean from the coast of East Africa eastwards far into the Pacific Ocean, it is an abundant species. Therefore, the possibility that the single manipulated shell arrived at Apollonia-Arsuf from somewhere in the Indian Ocean cannot be ruled out.

Five of the species whose remains were found in the dump still live among the ruins of Apollonia-Arsuf (Mienis and Rittner 2015). Only *Levantina spiriplana caesareana* has disappeared probably due to radical renovations at the archeological site carried out in the last decade. Although *Monacha obstructa*, *Monacha syriaca*, *Helix engaddensis engaddensis* and *Theba pisana* are typical species for the coastal area, *Buliminus labrosus labrosus* and *Levantina spiriplana caesareana* have been introduced to the site most probably with stones brought for building purposes to Apollonia-Arsuf from limestone quarries somewhere in the hills to the east. Both *Buliminus* and *Levantina* hide in crevices in limestone rocks.

The freshwater mussel *Chambardia rubens arcuta* was brought to the site most likely by ship from the Nile River in Egypt, although recently it has been discovered that it also lived for some time in North Sinai in the so-called Pelusiac Branch of the Nile and the Eastern Canal (Mienis 2015).

This zoogeographic information demonstrates that the people of Apollonia-Arsuf maintained connections with areas such as Egypt, the Red Sea and maybe even the Indian Ocean.

CLIMATE

The geographical distribution of the land snails in Israel is closely related to the climatic characteristics of a certain area, i.e., in most cases the amount of yearly rainfall determines the range of a certain species (Heller 2009). In the case of the six species of land snails found in the dump of Apollonia-Arsuf, all are characteristic of a typical Mediterranean climate, i.e., dry summers and rainy winters. According to this information the climate during the Byzantine period was most likely more or less the same as the climate today.

It is unfortunate that micro molluscs, i.e., specimens with a shell size of less than 5 mm, do not appear in the studied material, especially since those tiny species are more indicative of a certain climate. The subterranean living snails forms an exception because they are far less affected by the climate than most other species. One and the same subterranean species may be encountered in areas characterized by an annual rainfall of 1,200 mm, such as on Mount Hermon, but also in areas with 50 mm or less, such as in the Negev. Such species belonging to the genera *Cecilioides* and *Calaxis* are known from Apollonia-Arsuf (Mienis and Rittner 2015), but were most likely missed in the dump when sieves with too large of mesh size were used.

EXPLOITATION OF THE MOLLUSCS

The nature of the excavated site, being a dump, does not allow the placement of the more unique specimens in the right context. Therefore, these species can only be mentioned along with their already known past usages and together with a logical explanation for their presence in the dump.

ORNAMENTATION

Throughout the history of mankind, shells in the form of shell beads and pendants have been exploited in the making of ornaments. Such beads were not always strung; there are also cases known where they were attached to pieces of cloth as adornments (Mienis 1988).

Among the shells found in the dump, several of them were identified as having been manipulated into beads or pendants. The single shell of *Monetaria moneta* (Fig. 21.1: 2) had its dorsum artificially removed in order to use it as a shell bead.[1] This was common practice in ancient times (Jackson 1916b), and it is still in practice to a much lesser degree today in East Africa (McMillan 1968; Cambridge 1969). The shells of this particular species have not only been used as beads, but also as a currency ('money cowry'), especially in West Africa (Jackson 1916b; Fearer Safer and McLaughlin Gill 1982). Although coins were minted far before the Byzantine period, the use of *Monetaria moneta* and its related species *Monetaria annulus* in the trade market was still much in practice at that time and for a millennium to come. On the African continent where this species played a major role in any kind of trade, the shells were collected from the Eastern part of the continent and then brought to the West and North African areas where this species is absent and, therefore, was in great demand. These shells were also brought to the Mediterranean area from somewhere in the Indian Ocean area, where the species is much more commonly found than in the Red Sea. The value of these shells in Africa started to drop only from the 18th century when ships loaded with 'money cowries' arrived in Africa in order to trade the shells for slaves. In some parts of Africa 'money cowries' were legal tender until the 19th century.

Any cowry shell may have served also as an amulet for luck, especially for fertility (Schilder 1952). The single heavily damaged shell of *Cypraea pantherina* (Fig. 21.1: 1) found at Apollonia might have served as such a fertility amulet before it broke, because that Red Sea species was mentioned in particular for that purpose by Schilder (1923: as *Cypraea vinosa*, a junior synonym of *Cypraea pantherina*).

Among the numerous local cowries of Mediterranean origin, *Erosaria spurca*, *Luria lurida* and *Zonaria pyrum* have shells with natural holes or even their dorsum roughly removed (man-made holes). It is not clear whether they were collected in this state of preservation on the beach by the inhabitants of Apollonia or if the damage was caused during trials to turn these specimens into shell beads.

Among the five shells of *Conus mediterraneus* (Fig. 21.1: 3) recovered from the dump, one specimen shows a man-made hole in the apex of the shell. This is the common method used for centuries in the Levant to turn a cone shell into a shell bead.

Among the numerous valves of *Glycymeris nummaria* found in the dump, there are quite a few which have holes in the umbo of the valve. It is often difficult to judge whether such a hole was made by human manipulation of the valve or caused in a natural way after the death of that bivalve. However, in either instance the valve could have been used as a shell pendant.

"CASSID" LIPS

Among the preserved shells were four specimens of *Semicassis granulata undulata*, a local gastropod species from the Mediterranean Sea often found on the beach in small numbers after winter storms. Two are complete shells; another consists of the fairly heavy outer lip with a small part of the last whorl (body-whorl) still attached to it and one represents a fragment of such a lip. The latter is usually classified as a 'Cassid' lip, a mysterious item found among the shells at numerous archaeological sites whose purpose, maybe as an ornament, is still a riddle (Reese 1989).

1 The removal of the dorsum creates a hole which allows the use of the shell as an ornament because without a hole somewhere in the shell it is impossible to string it or to attach it to a piece of cloth.

SHELL TRUMPETS

Among the material are five shell fragments of *Charonia variegata*, a species which is relatively large in most areas of the Mediterranean but remains relatively small in the Eastern Mediterranean. Therefore, it is often classified under the subspecific name *Charonia variegata seguenzae* (Aradas and Benoit 1871). It is better known by its vernacular name, 'Triton' or 'Trumpet' shell. The genus *Charonia* shows a circum-(sub)tropical distribution and it has been exploited as a shell-trumpet wherever it is found (Jackson 1916a). Åstrom (1990) and Reese (1990) have reviewed finds of such shells from sanctuaries and graves in the Eastern Mediterranean. Since then, other specimens were excavated from different sites in Israel; examples are a fragment from Hellenistic Jerusalem (Mienis 1992), a complete specimen from a Byzantine house in Jerusalem (Mienis 2000), two fragments at Tel Kabri (Mienis 2002) and another large fragment at an Islamic site in Ramla (yet unpublished). In spite of the fact that it is a fairly large species, the extremely large body whorl is relatively thin and that part is often heavily damaged. The finds of the five fragments at Apollonia-Arsuf well-represent such damage. Unfortunately, they lack any signs of modification; therefore, it is impossible to know whether they had been used as shell trumpets.

PURPLE DYE

Three species of Muricid snail, which have been intensively exploited for the production of purple dye, have been recovered from the dump. *Bolinus brandaris* was represented by 59 items, *Hexaplex trunculus* by 43 and *Stramonita haemastoma* by 23. The majority of these 125 items consisted of old beach rolled fragments. It is possible that they were once part of the living snails used for purple dyeing during the Persian and Hellenistic periods at Apollonia as described by Karmon (1999). However, it is rather doubtful that purple dyeing was still carried out even at a very low level during the Byzantine periods at Apollonia/Sozousa.

MOTHER-OF-PEARL

Chambardia rubens arcuta (Cailliaud 1823) (Fig. 21.1: 4) is a fairly large freshwater mussel originating from the River Nile in Egypt. The presence of this species in archaeological sites in Israel is well-documented in numerous papers dealing with finds from sites from the Natufian to well into the Early Islamic period (Reese, Mienis and Woodward 1986; Mienis 2005). The meat of this mussel species is edible, and the beautiful rose-colored Mother-of-Pearl from the interior of the valves has been exploited for a multitude of items in Egypt (Falkner 1981; 1982; Boessneck, Driesch and Ziegler1989). Unfortunately, the five fragments found in the dump do not show any trace of manipulation; therefore, the reason why *Chambardia* had been brought to Apollonia can only be guessed.

FOOD

Land snails at archaeological sites are not only useful for reconstructing past climates, they may also reveal something about food habits in the past. It is, for example, a well-known fact that even today Christians in Israel eat land snails (Bar 1977; Mienis 2014). Larger species like *Helix engaddensis*, as well as all subspecies belonging to the *Levantina spiriplana*-complex and *Theba pisana* are collected in the fields (*Helix* and *Theba*) or among the rocks (*Levantina*) after rainy days when these snails appear in large numbers. Sometimes even relatively small species such as *Xeropicta vestalis joppensis* are collected for food (Mienis 1985a). Most of these species are native to Apollonia-Arsuf and its vicinity. The only exception is *Levantina spiriplana caesareana*, but as has already been explained, that species together with another rock living species, *Buliminus labrosus labrosus,* most probably reached the region of Apollonia with stones quarried in the hills more to the east. Yet the small number of shells of such edible land snails found in the dump rules out almost at once the possibility that they formed the leftovers of snail meals (Mienis 1985b). It is therefore better that they should be classified as components of the local environment which might have been exploited occasionally now and then on a small scale as an additional food source.

Another possibility is that living specimens of *Levantina spiriplana caesareana* were brought intentionally as a food source to Apollonia-Arsuf in order to grow them in gardens, as is often done with species of *Helix*, *Levantina* and subspecies of the *Cornu aspersum*-complex in monasteries all over Israel today; however, this does not explain the presence of other mountainous but non-edible species like *Buliminus labrosus labrosus*, *Paramastus episomus* and *Euchondrus septemdentatus* found among the ruins of Apollonia (Mienis and Rittner 2015).

BUILDING MATERIAL

Some of the valves of *Glycymeris nummaria* found in the dump were filled with a whitish mortar-like substance. This is usually a firm sign that such valves were used as building material. At many archaeological sites not only along the coast but also inland, thick layers of marine shells have been found under floors or in walls. Whole valves or fragments of *Glycymeris nummaria* formed, in many cases, over 90% of fills. The remaining 10% usually consisted of other common species washed ashore along the Mediterranean coast. Such building material has an insulating effect, and so floors and walls treated in this way are far less humid. A mixture of seashells and mortar has also often been used to fill spaces between roughly cut stones. This can still be seen not only at Apollonia, but also at other coastal sites such as Yavneh-Yam more to the south and Tel Dor to the north.

CONCLUSIONS

Archaeomalacological remains, i.e., shells found at archaeological sites, may provide archaeologists with a wealth of information (Mienis 2004). In the case of the shells found in the dump dating from the Byzantine period at Apollonia-Arsuf/Sozousa, they have provided information concerning: trade routes revealed by the zoogeographic origin of the shells; the climate according to the presence of certain terrestrial snails; the possible usage of shells as ornaments in the form of shell beads and pendants, 'Cassid' lips, shell trumpets and Mother-of-Pearl; the use of these species as food; and last but not least, their exploitation as building materials.

The reliability of the information provided by the malacologist to the archaeologist depends heavily on the quality and quantity of the preserved material for further study. The preservation of three shells of edible land snails may provide some information concerning changes in the climate, while the preservation of hundreds of edible land snails may be interpreted as firm evidence that the species in question was indeed exploited as a food source. Although the studied material from the dump provided important data, if shells of species smaller than 5 mm had been collected, the results would have been more reliable.

REFERENCES

Åstrom, P. 1990. Triton Shells in East Mediterranean Cults – Introduction. *Journal of Prehistoric Religion* 3–4: 5–6.

Bar, Z. 1977. Human Consumption of Land Snails in Israel. *Basteria* 41: 43–58.

Boessneck, J., Driesch, A. von den and Ziegler, R. 1989. Die Tierreste von Maadi and Wadi Digla. In: Rizkana, I. and Seeher, J., eds. *Maadi III: The Non-lithic Small Finds and the Structural Remains of the Predynastic Settlement*. Mainz am Rhein: 87–128.

Cambridge, P. 1969. Cowries in Aden and Africa. *The Conchologists' Newsletter* 28: 78–79.

Falkner, G. 1981. Mollusca. In: Martin, G.T., ed. *The Sacred Animal Necropolis at North Saqqâra: The Southern Dependencies of the Main Temple Complex* (Excavations at North Saqqâra Series; Excavation Memoir 50). London: 140–144.

Falkner, G. 1982. Molluskenfunde der Ausgrabungen des Deutschen Archäologischen Instituts Kairo im Satettempel auf Elephantine. In: Boessneck, J. and von den Driesch, A., eds. *Studien an subfossielen Tierknochen aus Ägypten* (Münchner Ägyptologische Studien 40). Munich: 152–172.

Fearer Safer, J. and McLaughlin Gill, F. 1982. *Spirals from the Sea: An Anthropological Look at Shells*. New York.

Heiman, E.L. 2002. *Cowries of East Sinai*. Jerusalem.

Heller, J. 2009. *Land Snails of the Land of Israel: Natural History and a Field Guide*. Sofia and Moscow.

Jackson, J.W. 1916a. Shell Trumpets and Their Distribution in the Old and New World. *Memoirs and Proceedings of the Manchester Literary and Philosophical Society* 60: 1–22.

Jackson, J.W. 1916b. The Use of Shells for the Purposes of Currency. *Memoirs and Proceedings of the Manchester Literary and Philosophical Society* 60: 1–72.

Karmon, N. 1999. Muricid Shells of the Persian and Hellenistic Periods. In: Roll, I. and Tal, O. *Apollonia-Arsuf: Final Report of the Excavations, 1: The Persian and Hellenistic Periods (with Appendices on the Chalcolithic and Iron Age II Remains)* (Tel Aviv University, Monograph Series of the Institute of Archaeology 16). Tel Aviv: 269–280.

McMillan, N. 1968. The Preparation of Cowry-shells for Use as Counters. *The Conchologists' Newsletter* 25: 51.

Mienis, H.K. 1985a. Enkele verdere gegevens betreffende de consumptie van landslakken in Israël. *Correspondentieblad van de Nederlandse Malacologische Vereniging* 225: 63–65.

Mienis, H.K. 1985b. Four Shells – Four Stories. *Trowel and Patish* 2: 2–4.

Mienis, H.K. 1988. The Marine Molluscs. In: Bar-Yosef, O. and Alon, D. Nahal Hemar Cave. *ʿAtiqot* 18: 47–49.

Mienis, H.K. 1992. Molluscs. In: de Groot, A. and Ariel, D.T., eds. *Excavations at the City of David 1978–1985 Directed by Yigal Shiloh III: Stratigraphical, Environmental, and Other Reports* (Qedem 33). Jerusalem: 122–130.

Mienis, H.K. 2000. Molluscs from the Excavation of Horvat Raqit, Carmel. *De Kreukel* 36: 89–90.

Mienis, H.K. 2002. Archaeozoological Remains. II. Molluscs. In: Kempinski, A., Scheftelowitz, N and Oren, R., eds. *Tel Kabri: The 1986–1993 Excavation Seasons* (Tel Aviv University, Monograph Series of the Institute of Archaeology 20). Tel Aviv: 402–408.

Mienis, H.K. 2004. When Shells begin to Talk. Archaeomalacology: An Important Tool for the Archaeologist with Examples from the Excavation of Mallaha, Hula Valley, Israel. In: Öztürk, B. and Salman, A., eds. 1st National Malacology Congress (with International Participation). *Turkish Journal of Aquatic Life* 2: 111–116.

Mienis, H.K. 2005. Nile Mussels in the Kitchen of the Monastery of Martyrius, Judaean Desert. *The Archaeo+Malacology Group Newsletter* 8: 2–3.

Mienis, H.K. 2014. Shells from Area Z. In: Geva, H., ed. *Jewish Quarter Excavations in the Old City of Jerusalem Conducted by Nahman Avigad, 1969–1982. Volume VI: Areas J, N, Z and Other Studies*. Jerusalem: 373–376.

Mienis, H.K. 2015. Freshwater Molluscs of African Origin, Which Inhabited the Pelusiac Branch of the Nile River and the Eastern Canal in North Sinai, Egypt, and the Possible Role of these Ancient Water Bodies in the Settlement of Species of Nilotic Origin in Israel. *Ellipsaria* 17: 23–25.

Mienis, H.K. and Rittner, O. 2015. A Note Concerning the Land Snails of the National Park Apollonia (Tel Arshaf), Israel. *Triton* 31: 27–34.

Reese, D.S. 1989. On Cassid Lips and Helmet Shells. *Bulletin of the American Schools of Oriental Research* 275: 33–39.

Reese, D.S. 1990. Triton Shells in Eastern Mediterranean Cults – Triton Shells from East Mediterranean Sanctuaries and Graves. *Journal of Prehistoric Religion* 3–4: 7–14.

Reese, D.S., Mienis, H.K. and Woodward, F.R. 1986. On the Trade of Shells and Fish from the Nile River. *Bulletin of the American Schools of Oriental Research* 264: 79–84.

Roll, I. 1999. Introduction: History of the Site, Its Research and Excavations. In: Roll, I. and Tal, O. *Apollonia-Arsuf Final Report of the Excavations I: The Persian and Hellenistic Periods (with Appendices on the Chalcolithic and Iron Age II Remains)* (Tel Aviv University, Monograph Series of the Institute of Archaeology 16). Tel Aviv: 1–62.

Schilder, F.A. 1923. *Cypraea vinosa* Gmel. in Geschichte und Urgeschichte. *Archiv für Molluskenkunde* 55: 204–206.

Schilder, M. 1952. Die Kaurischnecke. *Die neue Brehm-Bücherei* 46: 1–48.

Sivan, D., Potasman, M., Almogi-Labin, A., Bar-Yosef Mayer, D.E., Spanier, E. and Boaretto, E. 2006. The *Glycymeris* Query along the Coasts and Shallow Shelf of Israel, Southeast Mediterranean. *Palaeogeography, Palaeoclimatology, Palaeoecology* 233/1–2: 134–148.

SECTION FOUR

REGIONAL STUDIES

CHAPTER 22

APOLLONIA GLASS AND ITS MARKETS: AN ANALYTICAL PERSPECTIVE

Ian C. Freestone

In the 6th–7th centuries CE, the glassmaking furnaces of Apollonia/Sozousa were at the center of a network which supplied glass to workshops across the world. The signature Apollonia product was not a fabricated object, but raw or primary glass, distributed in angular chunks or lumps and melted to be reshaped in secondary workshops in numerous locations, to meet the demands of their own consumers.

A light translucent greenish-blue, Apollonia type glass appears to have been used to manufacture a wide range of vessel forms, as well as sheet glass for windows. However, its composition suggests that it may have been a less workable glass than contemporary glass produced in Egypt, or the Roman glass of the 1st to 3rd centuries CE.

To identify glass originally made in Apollonia, we are dependent upon the analysis of the glass material by the methods of the physical sciences. Recent work on elemental and isotopic compositions emphasizes not only the extent of the markets for Apollonia glass, but also just how much remains to be understood about the industry, its competitors and its duration.

APOLLONIA GLASS IN COMPOSITIONAL CONTEXT

Isotopic evidence, produced mainly by Patrick Degryse and colleagues (Degryse 2014), has shown that throughout the first eight centuries CE, glass making was overwhelmingly based in the eastern Mediterranean. By melting a mixture of Egyptian natron with a quartz-rich sand which had appropriate contents of calcium carbonate (typically around 15% by weight shell or limestone) and low amounts of naturally-occurring iron oxides (responsible for the green-blue color), a weakly colored soda-lime-silica glass could be produced with working temperatures which were readily achieved in the workshops of the period.

Glass from the primary tank furnaces at Apollonia has been analyzed on several occasions for major components (Freestone, Gorin-Rosen and Hughes 2000; Tal, Jackson-Tal and Freestone 2004; Freestone, Jackson-Tal and Tal 2008) and the results indicate it to be a soda-lime-silica glass (Table 22.1) with low amounts of contaminants, such as the oxides of iron, potassium and magnesium and around 3% alumina, Al_2O_3, which is inherited from the glass-making sand. Strontium isotopes indicate that it was made using shell-bearing coastal sand, while its neodymium isotope ratio is an important reference point for glass made from the sands of Levantine coast, which ultimately derive from the Nile (Freestone *et al.* 2003; Freestone, Wolf and Thirlwall 2009; Brems *et al.* 2018).

The need for copious supplies of a sand of just the right composition, as well as for a sustainable source of fuel (it is estimated that a furnace would have been heated to over 1100° C for several weeks; Sode and Kock 2001; Van Beeuman *et al.* 2011) possibly with social and political factors which are not yet clear, appear to have resulted in the movement of primary glass production centers to new locations at several times throughout the first millennium CE. The analysis of raw glass fragments from Apollonia and other glassmaking centers on the coast of the modern State of Israel, such as Bet Eliʿezer (Ḥadera)

TABLE 22.1. MEAN COMPOSITIONS OF GLASS FROM THE SITE OF APOLLONIA (1–3) AND GLASS FROM OTHER SITES IN ISRAEL (4) AND CYPRUS (5) THOUGHT TO HAVE BEEN MADE IN APOLLONIA. METHODS: SEM-EDS (1); EPMA (2, 3, 5); LA-ICPMS (4)

	Freestone, Gorin-Rosen and Hughes. 2000	*Tal, Jackson-Tal and Freestone 2004*	*Freestone, Jackson-Tal and Tal 2008*	*Phelps et al. 2016*	*Ceglia et al. 2015*
SiO_2	70.71	71.97	70.58	71.36	70.34
Al_2O_3	3.06	3.38	3.13	3.16	3.11
Fe_2O_3	0.47	0.46	0.57	0.47	0.47
MgO	0.63	0.63	0.73	0.56	0.65
CaO	8.08	8.29	8.55	8.33	8.65
Na_2O	15.18	13.65	14.63	14.34	15.51
K_2O	0.72	0.52	0.70	0.62	0.61
P_2O_5	0.15	0.05	0.07	0.10	0.09
Cl	0.84	0.84	0.79	0.83	0.88
SO_3	0.30	0.10	0.12	NA	0.12

and Jalame (near Haifa), convincingly demonstrates that each had a characteristic compositional range, which was relatively constant over their particular period of operation. This observation underpins much current work on glass sources and in particular allows the distinction to be made between glass made in Syria-Palestine and glass made in Egypt. At present, it is possible to identify about ten compositional groups, each representing the output of a primary production center in a specified period, many of which may be distinguished on the basis of their TiO_2, Al_2O_3 and SiO_2 contents, as shown in Fig. 22.1. The diagram shows clear differences between glass made from the coastal sands of Syro-Palestine and those of Egypt. However, while most of the Egyptian production centers are well separated in terms of composition and may be distinguished from each other, there is relatively strong overlap between the three known major Palestinian production centers so far recognized.

The Palestinian productions correspond to: (1) Roman glass vessels of the first three to four centuries CE grouped with vessels and production waste from the 4th century production site of Jalame; (2) primary production waste from Apollonia itself, probably 6th to 7th centuries CE and (3) primary production waste from the late 7th to 8th century production site at Bet Eliᶜezer. Distinction between these three groups of products is desirable if the extent of trade in Syro-Palestinian glass at any particular time is to be understood, but discrimination is not always straightforward or unambiguous, due to the overlaps in the compositions of the glass produced in the respective locations. The location of glassmaking in the 5th century is less clear; Jalame production appears to have ceased in the 4th century (Weinberg 1988), so presumably production began in the Apollonia region around this time. However, we have no well-dated archaeological evidence for this, and analysis of well contextualized and dated glass from the 4th to 6th centuries is needed to resolve the issue.

There is a general decline in the soda content of glass over the first millennium CE, as shown in Table 22.2, where it is also seen that Apollonia glass was significantly lower in soda than the earlier productions. It is also noteworthy that, at any particular time, the glass currently believed to have been made in Egypt contains in general about 3% more soda than the glass made in Palestine, consistent with the proximity of the Egyptian furnaces to the natron sources. Easier to melt and work, the Egyptian glass must have been preferred by the artisans who worked the glass into vessels and was probably more expensive to acquire (Freestone *et al.* 2015). The decline in soda content between the "Roman" glass of the 1st–4th centuries and the "Byzantine" glass of the 6th–7th offers one compositional marker to help differentiate the product of Apollonia from that of Jalame and Bet Eliᶜezer.

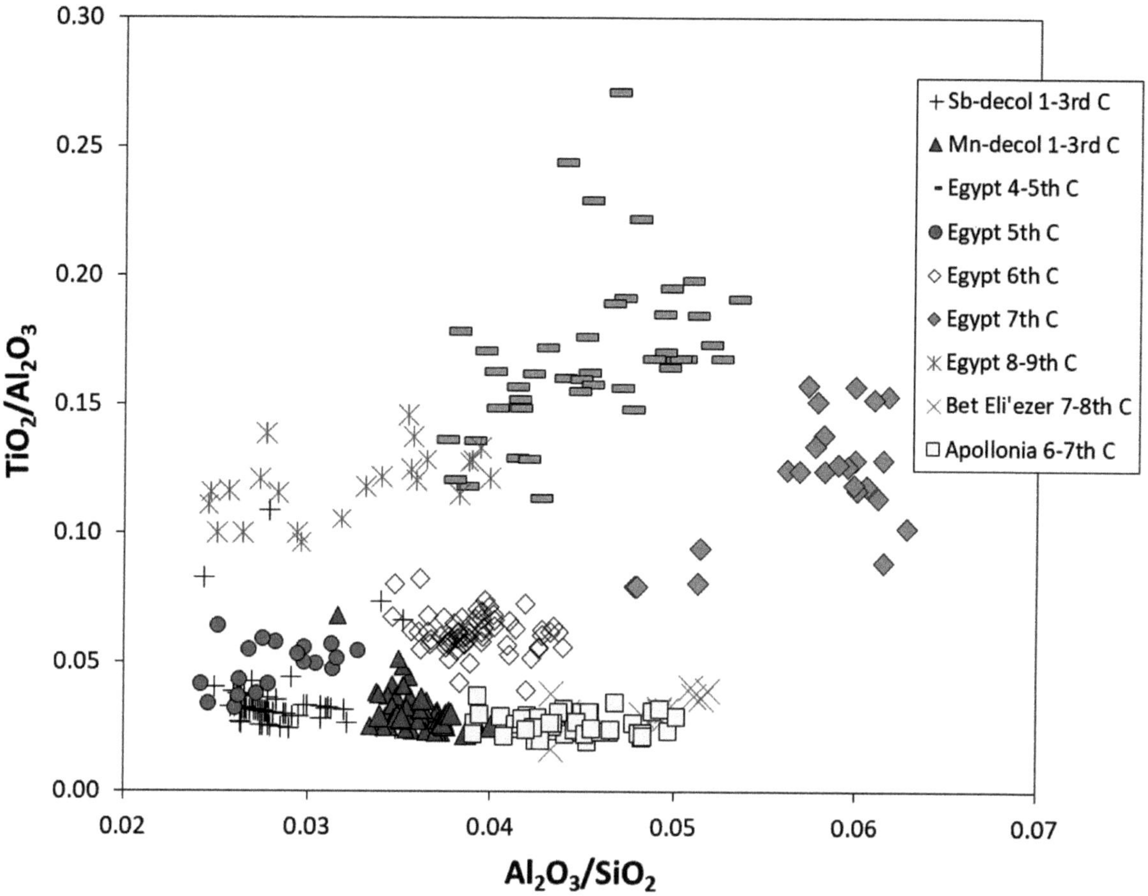

Fig. 22.1: Ratios of titanium oxide, alumina and silica, showing the separation between Egyptian primary glass with higher TiO_2 and Levantine glass. Note the overlap between the various Levantine types: Roman Mn-decolourized, Apollonia and Bet Eliᶜezer. For sources, see Freestone *et al.* (2018: Fig. 8.1) except Apollonia glasses, which in this figure are data of Phelps *et al.* (2016).

TABLE 22.2: MEAN SODA CONTENTS OF NATRON GLASS TYPES BELIEVED TO HAVE BEEN MADE IN EGYPT AND IN PALESTINE OVER THE FIRST MILLENNIUM CE. THE 2ND–3RD CENTURY GLASSES ARE SB-DECOLORIZED (EGYPTIAN) AND MN-DECOLORIZED (LEVANTINE) GLASSES FROM THE ADRIATIC WRECK *IULIA FELIX*

	Weight Percent Na_2O				
	Egyptian Glass		*Levantine Glass*		
Century	*m*	*sd*	*m*	*sd*	*Data source*
1st BCE			17.6	1.1	Jerusalem: Freestone unpublished
2nd–3rd CE	19.8	0.5	16.8	0.8	Iulia Felix: Silvestri 2008; Silvestri, Molin and Salviulo 2008
4th CE			15.7	0.9	Jalame: Brill 1988
5th CE	19.1	1.4			HIMT: Foy *et al.* 2003
6th CE	17.8	1.1			Foy 2.1: Cholakova, Rehren and Freestone 2015
6th–7th CE			14.4	1.2	Apollonia: Freestone, Gorin-Rosen and Hughes 2000; Tal, Jackson-Tal and Freestone 2004; Freestone, Jackson-Tal and Tal 2008
7th CE	17.0	1.3			Egypt I: Ceglia *et al.* 2015
7th–8th CE			12.5	1.5	Bet Eliᶜezer: Freestone, Gorin-Rosen and Hughes 2000; unpubished
8th–9th CE	15.0	0.5			Egypt II: Bimson and Freestone 1985; Freestone *et al.* 2015

Additionally, there is a general increase in alumina with the passage of time and there are changes in the lime content of the glasses; these latter variations appear to be related to variations in sand composition. Expressed as Na_2O/SiO_2 and CaO/Al_2O_3 ratios, the glass of the three Levantine groups is displayed in Fig. 22.2. There are significant overlaps, especially between Apollonia and Jalame. Relating a single piece of glass to its origin would therefore be problematic. However, an assemblage of glass which matches the spread of the Apollonia field can lead to a more confident assignation. There are other helpful indicators of the date of an assemblage. In particular, manganese oxide (MnO) is frequently present in 4th century Jalame glass, and manganese and/or antimony is typically present in Roman glass of the 1st to 3rd centuries. However, manganese and antimony are at background (sand) levels in all primary glass analyzed from the Apollonia furnaces. This is consistent with the findings of Foy *et al.* (2003), who observe that deliberately added manganese is not present in Levantine chunk and green-blue vessel glass after the 5th century. The implication here is that the Apollonia product was not decolourized to produce a truly clear and colorless glass, but exported in the characteristic limpid aqua blue. Using the presence/absence of manganese plus the contents of soda, silica, lime and alumina can give us a useful indication of the occurrence of glass from Apollonia as opposed to glass from other Levantine centers.

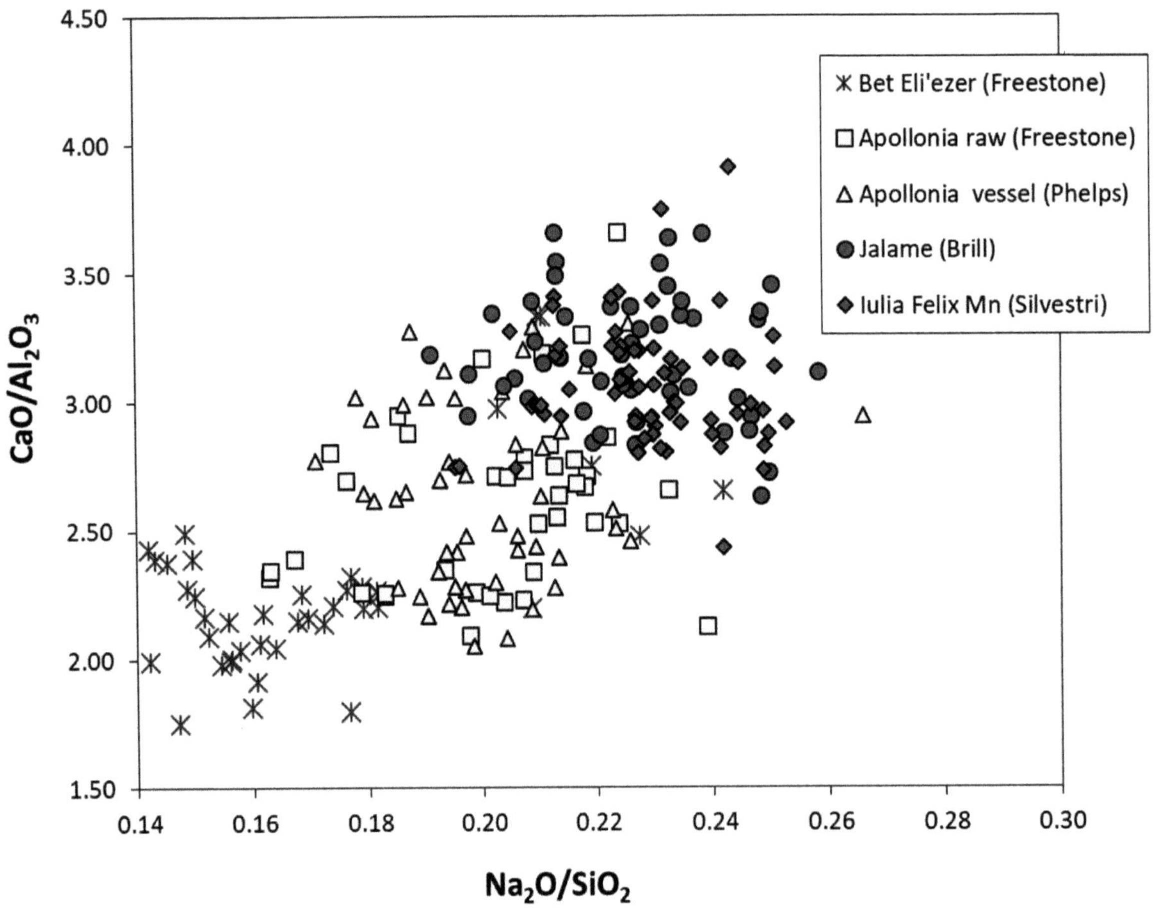

Fig. 22.2: Distinction between glasses produced in Apollonia, glass made in Bet Eliʿezer and Roman Levantine glass of the 1st–3rd centuries CE. Although the populations are relatively distinct, there is significant overlap between the groups.

APOLLONIA GLASS IN SECONDARY PRODUCTION AND CONSUMER CONTEXTS

Apollonia glass has been recognized as the overwhelmingly dominant type in glass vessels excavated in Israel in the 6th–7th century up to the introduction of glass from the Bet Eliʿezer furnaces in the early 8th century by Phelps *et al.* (2016). Similarly, in Jordan, analysis of 6th–7th century glass at sites such as Umm el-Jimal (Al-Bashaireh *et al.* 2016) and Jerash (Barford *et al.* 2018) clearly affiliate the glass to Apollonia production. A number of earlier studies of sites such as the Byzantine glass workshop near Ramla (Tal, Jackson-Tal and Freestone 2008) and sites in Jordan (Rehren *et al.* 2010) assigned the glass to the "Levantine I" group of Freestone, Gorin-Rosen and Hughes (2000). "Levantine I" is an umbrella group which was originally established to include glass from both Jalame and Apollonia. The low soda contents and lack of manganese in the glasses of the assemblages cited is characteristic of Apollonia production.

Elsewhere in the Mediterranean, an intensive study of 6th–7th century glass from Cyprus indicates Apollonia glass as a major component of the assemblages (Ceglia *et al.* 2015, their Levantine I). Further afield, Apollonia glass has been identified for example in 6th–7th century contexts in Carthage (Schibille, Sterrett-Krause and Freestone 2017), and in Visigothic Spain (De Juan Ares *et al.* 2019). "Levantine I" glass composition, which is similar to Apollonia glass, also occurs extensively elsewhere, but the extent to which these assemblages are from the furnaces at Apollonia or from earlier Levantine furnaces, such as those at Jalame, is unclear at present as the distinction between the two sources is blurred. Systematic studies are required to test the possibilities.

APOLLONIA GLASS IN MOSAIC *TESSERAE*

Although it might be anticipated that only the highest quality colorless glass would be used as the base glass for the expensive colored glasses in mosaics, in practice the analysis of *tesserae* from the Roman period (1st–4th centuries) indicates that the craftsmen who made the opaque colours did not exercise a general preference for colorless glass, and the base glasses were frequently a mixture of primary glass from Egypt and the Levant, which had been melted together in recycling processes. Before coloration, these recycled glasses were typically pale blue, similar in intensity to the blue of freshly made Apollonia glass, and it can therefore be assumed that this weak coloration did not significantly interfere with the strong blues, reds, yellows and greens of the *tesserae*. In view of this, it is not surprising that we find strong evidence for the use of Apollonia glass as a base in many opaque *tesserae* of the Byzantine period, particularly given the important role of mosaics in many Byzantine churches (e.g., Neri *et al.* 2017, Fiorentino *et al.* 2018; 2019).

Where the *tessera*-glasses were colored is unclear at present. Neri *et al.* (2017) observe that Levantine glass was used specifically as a base for green and turquoise *tesserae* from Kilise Tepe (Cilicia, Turkey), whereas other colors were based on an Egyptian glass known as Foy 2.1. One possible interpretation of this finding is that different colors were made in different workshops. However, another possibility is that the craftsman chose their base glass very carefully. The Apollonia glass is low in manganese which, if present in glasses melted under the oxidizing conditions needed to color copper-bearing glasses turquoise, will tend to give a pink hue, spoiling the intended color. Therefore, Apollonia glass may have been preferred over Mn-bearing Egyptian glass to produce greens and pale blues for technical reasons.

Apollonia glass appears to have been used as the base for a range of colors. For example, analyses of *tesserae* from Shiqmona, Israel (Freestone, Bimson and Buckton 1990), show compositional features characteristic of Apollonia glass and suggest, for example, that Apollonia glass was sometimes colored purple by the addition of manganese and also was used in some cases as the base glass for gold leaf *tesserae*. However, the impression from a cursory survey of analyses of *tesserae* outside the Levant is that Egyptian glass, especially Foy 2.1, was more common in mosaics than Apollonia glass in the 6th–7th centuries. It is noteworthy that some earlier analyses do not appear to match any of the currently recognized groups and a careful analysis and synthesis of all of the extant data would be very useful. This might include a comparison of the base glasses used for *tesserae* with those of contemporary vessel and window glass use in the same regions, as this would provide some indication of the location of coloration workshops.

REGIONAL COMPETITION AND RECYCLING

As noted above, glass from Apollonia was not the only raw material available to the glassworker. As appears to have been the case throughout the first millennium CE, raw glass was also made on a large scale in Egypt. Egyptian glass is typically distinguished geochemically by its higher contents of elements such as titanium and zirconium, reflecting the characteristics of Egyptian sands. Outside the Levant, Apollonia glass can be found in association with several other identified compositional types which are currently believed to have originated in Egypt: série 3.2 of Foy *et al.* (2003) characteristic of the 5th century; série 2.1 of Foy *et al.* (2003) characteristic of the 6th century; and 7th century Egypt I (Gratuze and Barrandon 1990). Assemblages which include both Levantine (probably Apollonia) and Egyptian glass are widely reported (see below).

Freestone *et al.* (2015) suggested that there was competition between Egyptian and Levantine glassmakers in the 8th–9th centuries, while Freestone *et al.* (2018) suggested that the Egyptian glassmakers of the 4th century went so far as to deliberately color their glass yellow-green, to effectively brand it in opposition to the green-blue glass of the Levant.

Of importance to the understanding of the constraints on the production of Apollonia glass and its use is the differences in the recipe between Egypt and the Levant. As observed in Table 2, over most of the first millennium, Egyptian raw glass typically contained about 3% more soda than the glass made in the Levant and therefore is likely to have been a more fluid and easier to work material, workable over a longer range of temperatures. The closer situation of the Egyptian furnaces to the main sources of natron in the Wadi Natrun and the Delta meant increased accessibility of this key constituent. The controlling factors are likely to have been complex and involved issues such as taxation and local control of the resource as well as transportation costs.

The glassworkers who shaped the artefacts are likely to have preferred Egyptian glass over the Apollonia material because of its workability, and consequent economies in terms of fuel, time, effort and skillset (Freestone *et al.* 2015, 2018). At long distances from the source, where any differences in distribution costs between Egyptian and Levantine glass are likely to have been relatively small, Egyptian glass is therefore likely to have been more profitable to the intermediaries or merchants who sold the glass. Hence in the 6th–7th centuries outside the Levant, the quantity of Egyptian glass, notably Foy 2.1, in any specific assemblage has been reported to be high or sometimes dominant (see, e.g., for Cyprus, Ceglia *et al.* 2015; northern Italy, Maltoni *et al.* 2015; 2016; Danube region, Cholakova, Rehren and Freestone 2015; Spain, De Juan Ares *et al.* 2019). On the other hand, closer to the primary furnaces, in the Levant Apollonia glass is the dominant glass type present, to the virtual exclusion of Egyptian glass (Rehren *et al.* 2010; Al-Bashaireh *et al.* 2016; Phelps *et al.* 2016; Barfod *et al.* 2018). Even so, the proximity to the primary glassmaking furnaces does not seem to have rendered unnecessary the extensive recycling of Apollonia glass, evidence for which is present in a number of assemblages and at present appears especially prominent at sites such as Petra (Rehren *et al.* 2010), Jerash (Barfod *et al.* 2018) and Umm el-Jimal (Al-Bashaireh *et al.* 2016), which are situated further from the coast, hinting perhaps at some locational control.

CONCLUSIONS

Apollonia was a major producer of raw glass in the 6th–7th centuries CE and had a long reach, its products travelling the length of the Mediterranean and beyond. It appears to have been the dominant producer in the Levant in the 6th–7th centuries, but the precise chronology is yet to be determined. During this period, Apollonia glass was in competition with glass made in Egypt, which had better melting and working properties. Even so, Apollonia glass is widespread. The relative distributions of Levantine and Egyptian glasses have the potential to cast some light on the operation of the ancient economy. However, there is a need for many more studies of well contextualized glass with robust chronologies for a better understanding of the shifts in production which occurred along the eastern Mediterranean coast and for improved discrimination between the products of the various Levantine furnaces.

REFERENCES

Al-Bashaireh, K., Al-Mustafa, S., Freestone, I.C. and Al-Housan, A.-Q. 2016. Composition of Byzantine Glasses from Umm el-Jimal, Northeast Jordan: Insights into Glass Origins and Recycling. *Journal of Cultural Heritage* 21: 809–818.

Barfod, G.H., Freestone, I.C., Lichtenberger, A., Raja, R. and Schwarzer, H. 2018. Geochemistry of Byzantine and Early Islamic Glass from Jerash, Jordan: Typology, Recycling, and Provenance. *Geoarchaeology* 33: 623–640.

Bimson, M. and Freestone, I.C. 1985. The Discovery of an Islamic Glass-making Site in Middle Egypt. *Annales du 10e Congres de l'Association Internationale pour l'Histoire du Verre, Madrid-Segovia 23–28 September 1985.* Amsterdam: 237–243.

Brems, D., Freestone, I.C. Gorin-Rosen, Y., Scott, R., Devulder, V., Vanhaecke, F. and Degryse, P. 2018. Characterisation of Byzantine and Early Islamic Primary Tank Furnace Glass. *Journal of Archaeological Science: Reports* 20: 722–735.

Brill, R.H. 1988. Scientific Investigations of the Jalame Glass and Related Finds. In: Weinberg, G.D., ed. *Excavations at Jalame: Site of a Glass Factory in Late Roman Palestine*. Columbia, Miss.: 257–291.

Ceglia, A., Cosyns, P., Nys, K., Terryn, H., Thienpont, H. and Meulebroeck, W. 2015. Late Antique Glass Distribution and Consumption in Cyprus: A Chemical Study. *Journal of Archaeological Science* 61: 213–222.

Cholakova, A., Rehren, T. and Freestone, I.C. 2015. Compositional Identification of 6th c. AD Glass from the Lower Danube. *Journal of Archaeological Science: Reports* 7: 625–632.

Degryse, P. 2014. *Glass Making in the Greco-Roman World: Results of the ARCHGLASS Project*. Leuven.

De Juan Ares, J., Vigil-Escalera Guirado, A., Caceres Gutierrez, Y. and Schibille, N. 2019. Changes in the Supply of Eastern Mediterranean Glasses to Visigothic Spain. *Journal of Archaeological Science* 107: 23–31.

Fiorentino, S., Chinni, T., Cirelli, E., Arletti, R., Conte, S. and Vandini, M. 2018. Considering the Effects of the Byzantine–Islamic Transition: Umayyad Glass Tesserae and Vessels from the *qasr* of Khirbet al-Mafjar (Jericho, Palestine). *Archaeological and Anthropological Sciences* 10: 223–245.

Fiorentino, S., Vandini, M., Chinni, T., Caccia, M., Martini, M. and Galli, A. 2019. Colourants and Opacifiers of Mosaic Glass Tesserae from Khirbet al-Mafjar (Jericho, Palestine): Addressing Technological Issues by a Multi-Analytical Approach and Evaluating the Potentialities of Thermoluminescence and Optically Stimulated Luminescence Dating. *Archaeological and Anthropological Sciences* 11: 337–359.

Foy, D., Picon, M., Vichy, M. and Thirion-Merle, V. 2003. Caractérisation des verres de la fin de l'Antiquité en Méditerranée occidentale: l'émergence de nouveaux courants commerciaux. In: Foy, D. and Nenna, M.-D., eds. *Echanges et commerce du verre dans le monde antique: actes du colloque de l'Association française pour l'archéologie du verre, Aix-en-Provence et Marseille, 7–9 juin 2001*. Montagnac: 41–85.

Freestone, I.C., Bimson, M. and Buckton, D. 1990. Compositional Categories of Byzantine Glass Tesserae. *Annales du 11e Congres de l'Association Internationale pour l'Histoire du Verre, Basel, 29 August – 3 September, 1988.* Amsterdam: 271–280.

Freestone, I.C., Gorin-Rosen, Y. and Hughes, M.J. 2000. Primary Glass from Israel and the Production of Glass in Late Antiquity and the Early Islamic Period. In: *La Route du verre: Ateliers primaires et secondaires du second millénaire av. J.-C. au Moyen Age*. Lyon: 65–83.

Freestone, I.C., Leslie, K.A., Thirlwall, M. and Gorin-Rosen, Y. 2003. Strontium Isotopes in the Investigation of Early Glass Production: Byzantine and Early Islamic Glass from the Near East. *Archaeometry* 45: 19–32.

Freestone, I.C., Jackson-Tal, R.E. and Tal, O. 2008. Raw Glass and the Production of Glass Vessels at Late Byzantine Apollonia-Arsuf, Israel. *Journal of Glass Studies* 50: 67–80.

Freestone, I.C., Jackson-Tal, R.E., Taxel, I. and Tal, O. 2015. Glass Production at an Early Islamic Workshop in Tel Aviv. *Journal of Archaeological Science* 62: 45–54.

Freestone, I.C., Wolf, S. and Thirlwall, M. 2009. Isotopic Composition of Glass from the Levant and South-Eastern Mediterranean Region. In: Degryse, P., Henderson, J. and Hodgins, G., eds. *Isotopes in Vitreous Materials*. Leuven: 31–52.

Freestone, I.C., Degryse, P., Lankton, J., Gratuze, B. and Schneider, J. 2018. HIMT, Glass Composition and Commodity Branding in the Primary Glass Industry. In: Rosenow, D., Phelps, M., Meek, A. and Freestone I.C., eds. *Things That Travelled: Glass in the First Millennium CE*. London: 159–190.

Gratuze, B. and Barrandon, J.N. 1990. Islamic Glass Weights and Stamps – Analysis Using Nuclear Techniques. *Archaeometry* 32: 155–162.

Maltoni, S., Chinni, T., Vandini, M., Cirelli, E., Silvestri, A. and Molin, G. 2015. Archaeological and Archaeometric Study of the Glass Finds from the Ancient Harbour of Classe (Ravenna-Italy): New Evidence. *Heritage Science* 3: 13.

Maltoni, S., Silvestri, A., Marcante, A. and Molin, G. 2016. The Transition from Roman to Late Antique Glass: New Insights from the *Domus of Tito Macro* in Aquileia (Italy). *Journal of Archaeological Science* 73: 1–16.

Neri, E., Jackson, M., O'Hea, M., Gregory, T., Blet-Lemarquand, M. and Schibille, N. 2017. Analyses of Glass Tesserae from Kilise Tepe: New Insights into an Early Byzantine Production Technology. *Journal of Archaeological Science: Reports* 11: 600–612.

Phelps, M., Freestone, I.C., Gorin-Rosen, Y. and Gratuze, B. 2016. Natron Glass Production and Supply in the Late Antique and Early Medieval Near East: The Effect of the Byzantine-Islamic Transition. *Journal of Archaeological Science* 75: 57–71.

Rehren, T., Marii, F., Schibille, N., Stanford, L. and Swann, C. 2010. Glass Supply and Circulation in Early Byzantine Southern Jordan. In: Drauschke, J. and Keller, D., eds. *Glass in Byzantium – Production, Usage, Analyses*. Mainz: 65–81.

Schibille, N., Sterrett-Krause, A. and Freestone, I.C. 2017. Glass Groups, Glass Supply and Recycling in Late Roman Carthage. *Archaeological and Anthropological Sciences* 9: 1223–1241.

Silvestri, A. 2008. The Coloured Glass of Iulia Felix. *Journal of Archaeological Science* 35: 1489–1501.

Silvestri, A., Molin, G., Salviulo, G. 2008. The Colourless Glass of Iulia Felix. *Journal of Archaeological Science* 35: 331–341.

Sode, T. and Kock, J. 2001. Traditional Raw Glass Production in northern India: The Final Stage of an Ancient Technology. *Journal of Glass Studies* 43: 155–169.

Tal, O., Jackson-Tal, R.E. and Freestone, I.C. 2004. New Evidence of the Production of Raw Glass at Late Byzantine Apollonia-Arsuf, Israel. *Journal of Glass Studies* 46: 51–66.

Tal, O., Jackson-Tal, R.E. and Freestone, I.C. 2008. Glass from a Late Byzantine Secondary Workshop at Ramla (South), Israel. *Journal of Glass Studies* 50: 81–95.

Van Beeumen, R., Degryse, P., Eisenga, M. and Muijsenberg, E. 2011. Numerical Modelling of Ancient Primary Glass Furnaces. *Proceedings of the 11th International Seminar on Furnace Design Operation & Process Simulation.* Velké Karlovice, Czech Republic: 141–149.

Weinberg, G.D., ed. 1988. *Excavations at Jalame: Site of a Glass Factory in Late Roman Palestine: Excavations Conducted by a Joint Expedition of the University of Missouri and the Corning Museum of Glass.* Columbia, Miss.

CHAPTER 23

CARPE MOMENTO: IN QUEST OF THE MATERIAL EVIDENCE OF THE BATTLE OF ARSUF (7 SEPTEMBER 1191)[1]

Rafael Y. Lewis

In the fall of 2013 and summer of 2014, a "Battlefield Archaeology" survey was conducted in the fields northeast of Arsuf (medieval Arsur). The main objective of the survey was to find the location of a historical event, dated to 7 September 1191 CE, known as the Battle of Arsuf. Another goal was to understand the historical event in light of archaeological and environmental evidence. Due to the dynamic and ever-changing landscape of the Arsuf hinterland, the archaeological study presented here required looking beyond the boundaries of the conventional archaeological site reconnaissance and basic field-survey and site-detection methods. In this paper, it is argued that the significance of historical events—such as battles, political assassinations and even natural disasters—which are of *short durée* must be drawn from the structural (i.e., *longue durée*) and the circumstantial-cyclical (i.e., *medium durée*) categories. In addition, events can only be fully understood by evaluating their broader perspective, moving from the macro (as represented by the landscape) to the micro (as represented by the specific artifact). In fact, the approach taken by the Annales School has been adopted here and is considered to be a positive avenue to broadening knowledge (Braudel 1980: 6–9, 25–38; 1995: 24–33). This is in contrast to the Positivistic-Historical approach, introduced by the Prussian historian Leopold von Ranke, which attributes great importance to events of revolutionary significance and the roll call of leaders.

The Battle of Arsuf is considered to be one of the key events of the Third Crusade and, consequently, it has been the focus of a good deal of historical research (Oman 1924: 305–319; Smail 1956: 156–165; Gillingham 1999: 188–191; Lyons and Jackson 1982: 337–339; Prawer 1984: 74–77; Roll 2007: 35–38; Nicolle 2005: 55–89; Asbridge 2010: 466–476; Ehrlich 2014; Kedar 2015).[2] Some of these studies considered aspects of geography and topography. But like many other battlefields in the Levant, the Arsuf battlefield was excluded from archaeological study (Lewis 2013: 1–3; Ehrlich 2014: 110–111).[3] Written sources are probably the most important evidence available for a historical account, but related

1 Some of the results presented in this paper were published by the author in 2016 (Lewis 2016: 460–489).

2 The survey was carried out as a post-doctoral research project by the author at Tel Aviv University, Department of Archaeology and Ancient Near Eastern Cultures under the supervision of Prof. Oren Tal. I am indebted to Prof. Tal and the Israel Antiquities Authority (IAA) for supporting this study during the 2013–14 academic year. I would also like to thank Dr. Huake Kenzler for his remarks on the manuscript and to the rest of the Apollonia excavation team from Tel Aviv University and the University of Tübingen for their support during the project and also to Prof. Benjamin Z. Kedar for the elucidating discussion we had on the subject matter.

3 The main primary sources for the battle are the *Itinerarium peregrinorum et gesta regis Ricardi* (chronicles and memorials of the reign of Richard I) and *Ambroise (L'Estoire de la guerre sainte)*, as well as Bahāʾ al-Dīn Ibn Shaddād (al-Nawādir al-Sulṭāniyya), Ibn al-Athīr (al-Kāmil f īʾl-taʾrīkh), Imād al-Dīn al-Isfahānī and Abū Shāma (Kitāb al-rawḍatayn).

environmental and archaeological perspectives might significantly improve the understanding of historical events such as the Battle of Arsuf.[4]

THE BATTLE OF ARSUF

The decisive Frankish defeat at the Battle of Hattin (3–4 July 1187 CE), the capture of the "True Cross" and the fall of Jerusalem all led to the Third Crusade (Prawer 1984: 117–124; Kedar 1992; Herde 2002; Ehrlich 2007; Lewis 2013: 335–373; Kedar 2015: 117). The ultimate goal of the campaign was to reclaim Jerusalem, an objective that was not achieved. After the surrender of Acre to the Crusaders on 12 July 1191 and the departure of Philip II Augustus to France, a decision was made by Richard I to march on Jaffa and to capture its important port; this was done in order to secure constant provisions and possible reinforcements for the planned siege of Jerusalem.[5]

The Battle of Arsuf was the chief open field violent engagement of the Third Crusade (Roll 2007: 36). Important as the Arsuf events are, it should be remembered that this was only a continuation of the monumental siege warfare that had been taking place for years on the plain of Acre, on its shore and in proximity of its walls (Prawer 1984: 63–64, 70–71). The main effect of the three years of fighting near Acre was that both the Crusaders and Muslims (for their own reasons) were seeking a decisive result which would end the long campaign (Ehrlich 2014: 109).

THE MAIN EVENTS DURING THE MARCH ALONG THE COASTAL PLAIN

With their heads set towards Jerusalem (via Jaffa), the Crusader forces started marching along the coastline on 22 August 1191.[6] The men marched close to the seashore, with their right flank protected by the sea. The Crusader fleet followed and (given the fact that the Egyptian fleet had been captured at Acre) provided them protection from this direction and supplementary provisions (Gillingham 1999: 174). The knights were divided into several bodies, each of those groups protected by infantry and archers, keeping the Muslims at a distance from the knights and their horses. In order to assist the infantry men, who suffered the most from the Muslim skirmishers, Richard I divided them into two groups: one group of men marched closer to the enemy while the other group of infantry recuperated to the west at some distance from the Muslims. The Crusaders generally marched southwards, but, as in the days prior to the march, they had to face the enemy inland, depending upon the enemy's position from the north through the east and south (Nicolle 2005: 67).

On 1 September, the Crusader forces left Caesarea and marched for 5 km to Flum Mort (the "Dead River," modern Hadera River). On 3 September the Crusader forces continued the march southwards and by the end of that day, having suffered many losses due to the heat and enemy ballistic fire,[7] they camped at Flum Sale (the "Salty River," modern Alexander River), where they rested for two more days. On 5 September, they marched into the Arsuf forest; though they had anticipated that the Muslims would set the forest on fire while crossing it, their prediction was wrong, and they made their way further to Flum de Rochetaillée (Nahar al-

4 This research focuses on the events that occurred between the river Falik (modern Poleg) and the fields to the east of 12th–13th century Arsur (today the northern part of Nof-Yam, one of the neighborhoods of Herzliyya). The archaeological study focused on the area between Nof-Yam to the south, the Apollonia National Park to the west, the modern coastal road to the east (Road No. 2), and Kibbutz Shefayim to the North.

5 Two semantic notes: Owing to the many different geographical and cultural origins of the Christians participating in this specific campaign, the term "Crusaders" is preferred; the term "Franks" will be used when one is referring to the Latin inhabitants of the Latin Kingdom of Jerusalem and other events from its days. Because of the way Crusader forces were structured with each knight riding under a specific flag, the term "forces" is more appropriate than the word "army."

6 According to Gillingham, Richard I's fighting march was the ultimate demonstration of the way in which to apply this technique (1999: 174).

7 Richard himself was also injured by an arrow.

Falik, modern Poleg River) with almost no casualties. After camping one night by the river[8] on Saturday 7 September, the Crusaders made their way to Arsur (Apollonia-Arsuf, on modern Herzliyya's northwestern town limits), positioned 8 km to the south of their last encampment position (Richards 2007: 390–391 [Ibn al-Athīr]; Richards 2002: 170–174 [Bahāʾ al-Dīn Ibn Shaddād]; Oman 1924: 304–309; Lyons and Jackson 1982: 334–336; Prawer 1984: 72–74; Gillingham 1999: 174–178; Nicolle 2005: 55–66; Roll 2007: 36–37).

According to Bahāʾ al-Dīn Ibn Shaddād: "He (Saladin) rode out and drew up his divisions for battle, with every intention of bringing the enemy to a pitched battle that day" (ed. Richards 2002: 174). It seems that Richard I was aware of this situation and therefore took more care than usual in organizing his men on the march, moving up and down the lines of his men (Ambroise [ed. Hubert and La Monte 1976: 252, Lines 6207–6210]; Gillingham 1999: 176; Nicolle 2005: 67).

The march that day was led by the Templers, behind them came the Bretones and the men of Anjou and then Guy de Lusignan, the former king of Jerusalem, with the Poitevins. The Normans and English marched in the next division, guarding the king's standard; behind them marched the French contingents; the Hospitallers closed the march (Ambroise [ed. Hubert and La Monte 1976: 250–251, Lines 6167–6194]; Stubbs 1864: 260–261; Gillingham 1999: 176; Nicolle 2005: 67).

Saladin's skirmishers attacked the Crusaders from the early morning, but when they were close to Arsuf (in mid-morning, or "at the third hour" according to the *Intinerarium*, i.e., 9:00 a.m.), the Muslims intensified their attack, almost breaking through the Crusader infantry and killing many of their horses. The Hospitallers in the rear were the subject of constant attacks (Bahāʾ al-Dīn Ibn Shaddād [ed. Richards 2002: 174]; Ambroise [ed. Hubert and La Monte 1976: 252–253, Lines 6212–6300]; Stubbs 1864: 262; Nicolle 2005: 74). Several times during that day, the master of the order approached Richard I seeking permission to charge the enemy, but was sent back by the king, telling him to endure and to wait for the trumpets' command. Saladin kept increasing the pressure on the Crusaders' rearguard, throwing into the arena his own personal guard as reinforcement, leaving only a handful of people by his side (Bahāʾ al-Dīn Ibn Shaddād [ed. Richards 2002: 175]; Nicolle 2005: 75). Finally, the Grand Master of the order, Garnier de Naples, and Baldwin Carew, a knight who came with Richard, could not restrain themselves anymore and charged from the rear, crying "Saint Jorge (George)!" (Ambroise, ed. Hubert and La Monte 1976: 258–259, Lines 6420–6433). The two knights were soon followed by the rest of the host. Though a premature charge had been made, Richard seized the moment and supported the Hospitallers' attack and soon thereafter almost all of the knights[9] broke through the infantry line and swept the field from west to east as a great wave of body and steel. As Richard had predicted, the first premature cavalry charge did not throw the Muslims out of balance and it took at least two more attacks. The charging forces held back their horses at the forest's edge and did not press the charge any further, thus avoiding possible Muslim ambush or cutting off the Crusaders' cavalry from their infantry.[10] The series of charges made by the Crusaders pressed Saladin to withdraw, leaving the field with many of his men behind and others wounded. The defeat was such that Saladin found no consolation even from his admirer, Bahāʾ al-Dīn Ibn Shaddād. Saladin's son (al-Afḍal) was among those who stood firm but "was shaken by this day" (Richards 2002: 175–176).

PREVIOUS HISTORICAL RESEARCH

The Battle of Arsuf has attracted the attention of a numerous scholars. Raymond Smail (1956: 163–165) and Tomas Asbridge (2010: 466–476) argued that Saladin urged his men to attack when he saw that the

8 Probably, on a small hill next to Flum de Rochetaillée (Nicolle 2005: 74).

9 The Normans and English (Anglo-Normans) were held in reserve (Gillingham 1999: 178; Nicolle 2005: 78).

10 It is possible that the infantry drew closer to the knights after the first charge (Nicolle 2005: 79). Ibn al-Athīr said that the Crusaders did not realize this was a real rout and not a diversion; had the pursuit been continued, the Muslims would ultimately have been destroyed (Richards 2007: 391).

enemy was nearing Jaffa. Richard I expected this attack and prepared his troops for it. Smail and later Asbridge pointed out that while the Crusaders' victory was considered a decisive one, its aftermath was rather modest. This is because the Muslim forces were still a pending threat which kept the Crusaders from making any attempt to take Jerusalem. Malcolm Cameron Lyons and D.E.P. Jackson (Lyons and Jackson 1982: 338) say that though the Crusaders "had scored an undoubted success, the Muslim rout was, in fact, little more than an undignified and expensive version of their usual tactic" and that the fall of Acre, which had involved a great many of Saladin's elite forces from his naval fleet, was a much more significant event to him than those taking place near Arsuf. The fact that the Crusaders were not able to trap the Muslims, and that they also lost many horses in the battle, would have a great effect on what was yet to come. David Nicolle argues that Richard was not seeking direct confrontation with Saladin (Nicolle 2005: 37–38). Michael Ehrlich suggested that the Battle of Arsuf was inevitable because both Saladin and Richard I were seeking a decisive encounter, motivated by Richard's intention to retake Jerusalem, and that while Saladin lost the campaign, he did actually achieve his goal since Jerusalem was not taken by the Crusaders (Ehrlich 2014). Benjamin Kedar investigated King Richard's battle plan for Arsuf. He argues (very convincingly) that the successful fighting march led by the English king was an outcome of the lessons learned from the mistakes of the Hattin campaign (Kedar 2015: 117), which involved the distance the Crusaders covered during every day of the march down the Coastal Plain; the time designated for recovery after a single day's march; maintenance of a good communication and provision line with his fleet; preventing Saladin's men from surrounding the troops by marching close to the Mediterranean; and finally keeping his men in tight formation undermining Saladin's efforts to divide them into smaller groups as he had successfully done at Hattin (Kedar 2015: 118). Furthermore, Kedar (based on historical, cartographic and geological evidence) presents a reliable reconstruction of the relic Forest of Arsuf and shows the significant role that the Forest of Arsuf played during the later stages of the march from Acre and during the battle itself. Kedar argues that Richard's plan was to bring the Muslims into close combat in the vicinity of the village of Arsuf, where, presumably, the forest was located more to the east of the coastal road, which created an ideal battlefield of approximately 3 × 3 km. The circumstances which led to the premature charge of the rearguard created the situation whereby the battle took place in an area to the north of where Richard intended and which left two thirds of his men at a significant distance from Saladin's main body of men (Kedar 2015: 125–132).

Though there is no doubt that the forest of Arsuf played a significant part in the results of the battle, it is just one of many elements which should be considered. As will be seen, involving environmental and archaeological perspectives can contribute significantly to understanding both Richard's and Saladin's battle plan and to the part that the location of the forest and Arsuf's geographical context played in these events, making it a key point position during the Third Crusade.

THE METHODOLOGICAL CHALLENGE[11]

Joining the premature cavalry charge, Richard I seized the moment and swept the Muslims off the fields of Arsuf. Can an archaeological research project also "seize" such a brief moment in the *longue durée* of human history? Or, in other words, can archaeologists find the material imprint of an event that lasted no more than a few hours, or even minutes, outside the boundaries of a traditional archaeological site and within a vast and ever-changing landscape? Most archaeological studies in the Levant focus on the archaeological site and the landscape is mainly the subject of regional and developmental surveys. When a settlement is taken by an abrupt and violent action, even if it is resettled later, there is a good chance

11 The methodology used during this study was based on that employed in the author's Ph.D. dissertation: *The Archaeology of Conflicts: The Decisive Stage of the Battle of Hattin as a Case Study* (University of Haifa, 2013), under the supervision of Prof. Adrian J. Boas.

that some of the finds related to the specific violent event will be found at a destruction level. On the other hand, archaeological finds which are left in the open field as the result of a conflict occurring outside the boundaries of the conventional archaeological site are much more exposed to the ravages of man-made and environmental forces. The development of archaeological methods and field surveys in the last three decades, such as Archaeology of Conflicts or Battlefield Archaeology, enables archaeologists today to locate and study the material signature of events of limited duration in the landscape (Lewis 2013: 35–42). The only way to fully understand the material aspect of a given event is by making a thorough study of the available environmental and man-made features, those existing both before and after the event, and by examining such features that might have preserved the material signature of a given event through time (Lewis 2013: 70–84 [see n 11]).

THE ARCHAEOLOGICAL SURVEY TECHNIQUE USED

The data presented in this study may be divided into three main categories: (1) environmental evidence; (2) material cultural evidence; and (3) written sources. Since the overall aim has been to try and locate a specific historical event that occurred within a given landscape, the most appropriate archaeological reconnaissance method to use—out of several field survey techniques practiced in our region—is that of Landscape Archaeology. The important difference between this method and the other available field survey methods is that it focuses on the *total* archaeology of a landscape, with the "site" itself (i.e., the settlement—in this case, Apollonia-Arsuf) as only one of its indicative features.[12] Hence, the mosaic of archaeological features which makes up the overall landscape is actually the site and not any one of its specific features. The underlying concept of this "site-less" approach is that in order to understand the meaning of a single find or a feature (e.g., an agricultural terrace; a fence-wall; an arrowhead; a horseshoe; a potsherd; etc.), its contextual emplacement within an environment and the manner in which it relates to other components must first be understood. The ways in which objects are scattered over the landscape must then be examined stratigraphically. It is only with the creation of a map, which theoretically reconstructs the overall landscape on the eve of the battle, that it is then possible to proceed to locate the physical traces of its material imprint. Subsequently, the primary written evidence is then referred to and revisions might ultimately be made based on a comparative study of additional available source materials.

The surveyed area of the battle of Arsuf (as mentioned above) was divided into several main zones according to main topographic features. After an extensive survey and excavation, it was sub-divided into two prime areas (A and B) with the abandoned road that once connected the modern coastal highway to the abandoned Israel Military Industries Ltd. Plant which served as a border between these areas. The different archaeological features (modern features included) were studied in relation to each other and according to their discreet, expanded or focal nature, and then put into related clusters within each zone.

THE METAL DETECTOR SURVEY

The metal detector is the most useful tool to learn about the material signature of a short-term historical event in a survey. However, it is essential that the metal-detecting work is done only during the final stages of the fieldwork, and only after having first completed the landscape survey and its suggested reconstruction. Contrary to the common practice in Battlefield Archaeology, an independent grid was not deemed necessary during the fieldwork at Arsuf and the metal detecting survey was conducted according to the character of the features surveyed.

12 The dispute as to the exact definition of an archaeological "site" is not relevant here simply because in Landscape Archaeology, all man-made features are examined on an equal basis (even modern elements are not excluded from the survey, and these also need to be documented and studied).

The survey was conducted at the point of those clusters or within specific archaeological features which are of major interest for the overall understanding of the landscape (i.e., the metal detector was used at the location of features which had the potential of answering specific questions relating to the study area). The metal detecting survey was used in this research to verify data derived from the landscape archaeology survey. It was used to examine whether there might be a material signature on the battlefield of Arsuf itself and the potential for future, more extensive, research.

THE INFRASTRUCTURE: LONGUE DURÉE ENVIRONMENTAL CONTEXT

In order to be able to reconstruct historical events, environmental conditions such as soil, heat, humidity, radiation, sunlight and moonlight need to be investigated; all have direct influence on military campaigns and on the preservation of finds.[13]

GEOGRAPHIC OVERVIEW

The Battle of Arsuf took place on the Coastal Plain of Israel, in the southern part of the Sharon plain. This region extends between the Yarqon River in the south and the Crocodile River in the north (5 km north of Caesarea). The Sharon Plain is about 15 km in width and extends from the foothills of the Samaria hills to the Mediterranean. Three ridges of hills, which are parallel to each other and formed from *kurkar* (fossilized dune sandstone) rocks, subdivide the Sharon Plain into three valleys (Fig. 23.1). The streams running from the foothills of Samaria to the sea penetrated the three ridges and enabled sand from the sea to come to shore and create dunes; when the streams were blocked, swamps were created. The *kurkar* ridge closest to the coast is characterized by a steep cliff. Some of the larger Hellenistic and Roman settlements in the Sharon Plain, including Caesarea and Apollonia-Arsuf, were built on top of this ridge (Gophna and Ayalon 1998: 8). On its eastern side, the ridge gradually slopes down to the so-called Sharon swale, an elongated valley that extends between the first and second *kurkar* ridges. The traditional and the present coastal road runs along the eastern border of this valley beginning at the foot of the second *kurkar* ridge. The second ridge from the west is formed from a stronger type of *kurkar* rock, serving as an adequate platform for the establishment of settlements throughout the ages. Since it provided a useful foundation for building purposes, it was also used for quarrying building-stones and for hewn burial caves and some agricultural installations (Gophna and Ayalon 1998: 8; Gibson 2003: 8).

The valley to the east of the second ridge is blanketed with alluvial soil. Today, the third *kurkar* ridge is almost completely covered with a red sandy soil and appears to merge with the red sand hills (*ḥamra*) that lie to the east (Gophna and Ayalon 1998: 8; Karmon 1961: 43–46). The Sharon region (especially the eastern valley) is poorly drained and occasionally, in wintertime, water accumulates and swamps are created (Gophna and Ayalon 1998: 8). Due to the bad drainage of the Sharon Plain, it was populated sporadically throughout most eras. Only when a centralized power and/or a strong political entity controlled the Sharon (such as in the Middle Bronze Age, the Roman period or in the present day) and invested in draining the swamps, the area became more hospitable and permanent settlements were founded.[14] Drainage systems had to be maintained and, once neglected, the swamps reappeared once again. Because of the dunes and swamps, the Sharon was unattractive for agriculture and settlement in many periods; subsequently throughout most of human history, the Sharon Plain served mainly as a route through which people traveled (Safrai *et al.* 1990: 249; Ehrlich 2014: 113–114).

13 The road system was also added to this part of the paper because of the strong link between roads and topography (Lewis 2016: 105).

14 There is evidence that in the landscape of Tel Dor, the swamps began to be drained during the Late Persian and Early Hellenistic periods, a process that seems to have been largely accomplished during the 2nd century BCE (Gibson 2003: 8).

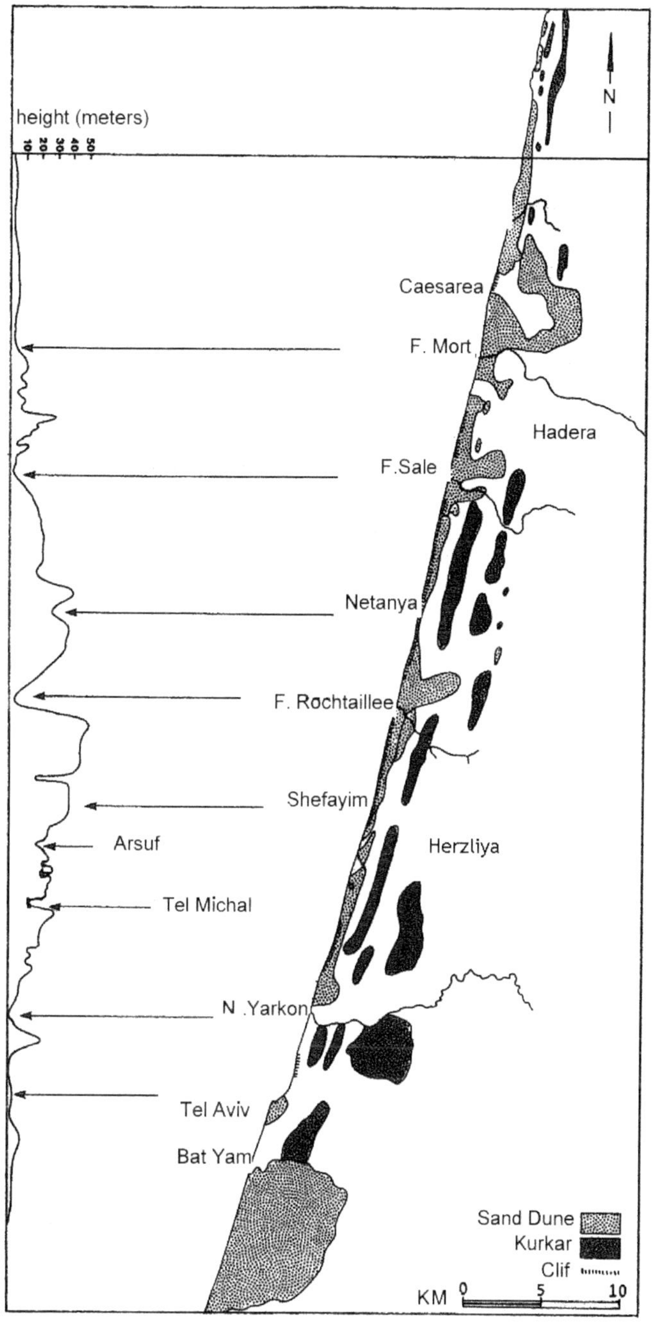

Fig. 23.1: Map of the Sharon Plain. Location of *kurkar* ridges and sand dunes (Gavish and Bakler 1990: Map 2).

Today the Sharon region is one of the most densely populated and cultivated areas in Israel. The battlefield lies in the area of the modern town of Herzliyya, Kibbutz Shefayim, and the villages of Rishpon, Kfar Shmaryahu, Arsuf (the modern one) and the village of Arsuf-Kedem. The survey area borders the abandoned Israel Military Industries Ltd. Plant that stretches along the first *kurkar* ridge on its west. Unfortunately, the activity (some of it destructive) carried out by the plant[15] was not confined to the inner part of its fences, as other activities as well as maneuvers of tractors took place in the fields to

15 The Israel Military Industries Ltd. Plant specialized in the development of explosives and "active armor" for army vehicles such as D9 tractors. Their performance when carrying the armor was tested in areas east of the factory.

its east. To the east, the area of the survey borders the modern coastal highway. This six-lane road that runs from south to north along most of the coastline of Israel is used as a major trunk road.[16]

Communications—Road Systems

Topography usually determines the way in which a network of roads is laid out in the landscape. Generally, there is a strong link between land structure and the location of roads in antiquity (Karmon 1985b: 161; Safrai *et al.* 1990: 253; Gibson 1995: 237–258; Lewis 2013: 269; Lewis 2016: 105). In addition, *continuity* is one of the most important aspects of Landscape Archaeology. In relation to roads, it can be seen that people used the same tracks for thousands of years; the so-called *Via Maris* or the *Coastal Road* are just two evident examples. Because of these two factors (topography and continuity), roads should be classified and understood as part of the structural features of the *longue durée*.

Archaeologists have suggested different ways in which to classify roads (Roll 1996: 153–154; Gibson 1995: 237; Wilkinson 2003: 60, 62, 113, 116). Due to the Landscape Archaeology approach of this research, Shimon Gibson's model for the categorizations of roads has been adopted: international roads (highways); regional roads; and local roads (Gibson 1995: 237).

The main difference between Gibson's approach and that of other researchers is that his classification is free from directly referencing a specific construction technique, period or culture.[17] Gibson regards roads as communication-systems that link different types/levels of settlements and trade centers with other landscape components such as agricultural fields, industrial and agricultural installations, burial complexes, etc. (Gibson 1995: 237; Lewis 2013: 269).

Due to their bad state of preservation, it is hard to reconstruct the ancient road systems in the western part of the Sharon Plain based on the existing archaeological record. Consequently, other sources were relied on, such as the position of ancient urban centers, mid-19th to mid-20th century cartography, and on the earliest aerial photographs, which were taken before the intensive modern development (Roll and Ayalon 1989: 222–223; Roll 1994: 38–40; Safrai *et al.* 1990: 249, 256–258; Wilkinson 2003: 33–37; Lewis 2013: 120–123, 133–138; Lewis 2016: 106–107).

Major Roads

The Traditional International Highway (Fig. 23.2, Road 1)[18]

The *traditional international highway* that crosses through the Sharon was probably the most important road in the vicinity, although its exact course at different periods is still uncertain (Safrai *et al.* 1990: 252; Roll and Ayalon 1989: 223). Shimon Applebaum suggested that the road actually ran along two parallel courses: the eastern one, beneath the western foot of the Samarian hills (beneath the present day Road No. 4) and another course about 3 km to the west, along the eastern valley (Applebaum 1985: 67–68). Others, however, argued that the first route was actually only a series of local roads connecting small villages in Samaria, and that this route had no overall topographic justification (Safrai *et al.* 1990: 252; Roll and Ayalon 1989: 223). In contrast, the western route (which runs by important Early Islamic, Frankish and Mamluk settlements, such as Kefar-Saba, Jaljulia and Nebi Yamin) has no archaeological evidence supporting its existence in antiquity (Roll and Ayalon 1989: 223–224; Safrai *et al.* 1990: 252).

16 The information collected during the survey was studied against the material collected during a previous large-scale salvage excavation project in the area.

17 Israel Roll classified roads into four categories: countryside roads; local roads; main roads; Roman roads (Roll 1996: 153–154); John Wilkinson's classification is formal and posits these classifications: paved roads; paved roads in highlands; cuttings (mountain crossings); linear hollows; rural tracks with boundary walls; stepped tracks; wheel ruts; desert tracks (Wilkinson 2003: 60, 62, 113, 116).

18 This was located outside the boundaries of the survey area.

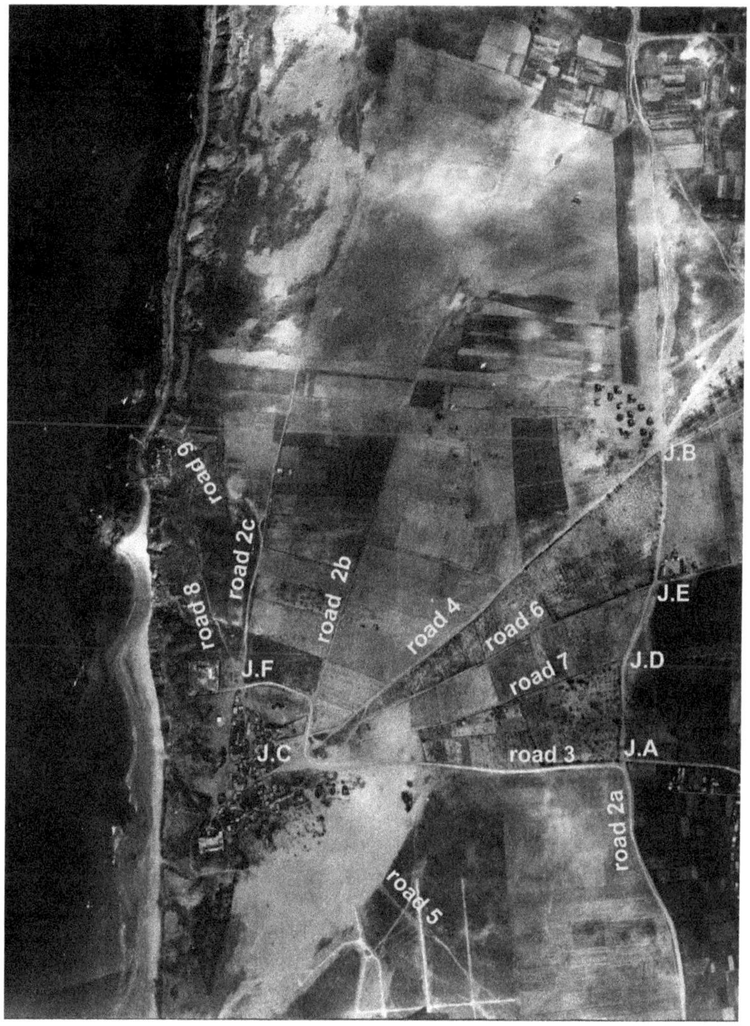

Fig. 23.2: Road and junctions at the vicinity of Apollonia-Arsuf (aerial photograph (dev-12 60196021. 28.1.1946).

Junction	*Roads*	*Coordinates (Israel New Grid)*
A	2a & 3	182830/677245
B	2a & 4	183000/677820
C	3, 4 & 5	182145/677470
D	2a & 7	182870/677410
E	2a & 6	182920/677560
F	2c & 8	182048/677610

The Coastal Highway (Fig. 23.2: Road 2a–c)

Israel Roll and Eitan Ayalon suggested that the coastal highway was first charted in the Roman period along the coast itself, but probably due to the penetration of sand inland, it was moved to the western slope of the second *kurkar* ridge along the western valley where the coastal highway runs at present (Roll and Ayalon 1989: 224–225). The Roman legions headed by Titus marched on this route on their way from Jaffa to Caesarea. The road can be seen on the Peutinger table map alongside Apollonia. Roll and Ayalon pointed out that this road became even more important in the days of the Latin Kingdom of Jerusalem because there were many settlements along the Mediterranean coast. It is reasonable to assume that Richard I marched his troops here on the way to Jaffa (Roll and Ayalon 1989: 225–226).[19] It is almost impossible to pinpoint the actual track in the area of Apollonia-Arsuf, and a cartographic survey shows at least three alternate possibilities that might have been based on the ancient track, if there had been only a single ancient trail (Fig. 23.2, road 2a–c).

Regional Roads

Most of the east–south roads in the region of the Sharon Plain extended to Apollonia-Arsuf. The most important of these was the one that connected Apollonia with Kefar-Saba and Nablus (Fig. 23.2, road 3). The second regional road is the one connecting Apollonia with Sebastia (Fig. 23.2, road 4). The third regional road is the one leading to Lod and Jerusalem via Antipatris (Fig. 23.2, road 5) (Roll and Ayalon 1989: 226).

Local Roads

There are several local roads between Arsuf (al-Haram) and the surrounding landscape. These roads mainly served to connect to higher level roads, fields and industrial and agricultural installations. Good examples for this are the two local roads (Fig. 23.2, roads 6 and 7) which run through the fields between and parallel to regional roads 3 and 4. These two roads might actually mark an alternative track to the two regional roads. Two additional roads are those leading from the village of al-Haram to Arsuf Castle, one that runs along the watershed of the first *kurkar* ridge (Fig. 23.2, road 8), and the other (Fig. 23.2, road 9) that connects the city gate with the coastal road (Fig. 23.2, road 2c).

Road Junctions

There are six main road junctions in close proximity of Apollonia-Arsuf. Junction A connects roads 2 and 3 (Fig. 23.2); junction B connects roads 2 and 4 (Fig. 23.2); junction C at the eastern border of al-Haram connects roads 3, 4, and 5 (Fig. 23.2). Since the three junctions are located so close to each other, it might be argued that they all represent one junction, a focal point of regional and probably international importance.

WEATHER CONDITIONS

Temperature, Radiation and Humidity

Temperature, sun radiation and humidity are elements that can affect the endurance of both men and animals and therefore play significant roles in the way a conflict may develop and culminate as well as on the preservation of conflict-related artifacts. The climate on the Sharon Plain is Mediterranean. August is the hottest month of the year, but the highest temperatures in the Sharon are actually measured during the fall and spring. The temperature between the two main seasons can rise up to 40°C (in the shade). Near the coastline, the number of days in which the temperature is higher than 30°C is relatively low, while inland approximately 50 days per year have higher temperatures than 30°C. The sun radiation in the Sharon is relatively lower than in other regions in Israel due to the fact that there is cloud cover many days throughout the year (165 calories per square cm). However, fog during the daytime is not a common phenomenon in the Sharon; it usually happens only during the second half of the night and disappears soon after sunrise (Jaffe and Fiedel 1990: 99–100). In the summer, high humidity develops due to the level of evaporation of seawater, while the stable air prevents the movement of water molecules into the atmosphere; the humidity measures between 70%–85% during the day and at night can rise up to 95%. In addition, there are 200–240 nights of dew in a year and the majority are in summer time (Jaffe and Fiedel 1990: 100).

19 This in contrast to Karmon (1985a: 58–60), who points to a decline in Frankish settlement along the coast and the rise in the importance of the eastern route catalogued here as Road 1 (Fig. 23.2).

Wind Direction and Velocity

It is clear that wind direction and velocity can have a significant influence on humans, especially on their capabilities of maneuvering and on their sight. These could be of great importance to the outcome of historical events and understanding them.[20]

The winds in the coastal region of the Eastern Mediterranean usually start blowing in the morning, first from the southwest and during the day moving clockwise, reaching the northwest in the afternoon. Usually the winds stop in the evening and start blowing again during the second half of the night. They grow stronger with the winds coming from the highland region (Samaria). This is the general characteristic of winds throughout the year, but especially in summer. During the transition between seasons hot, dry and turbulent eastern winds descend from Mount Carmel and Samaria to the Sharon and can reach speeds of 20 knots (37.04 km per hour) and more, and in winter reach speeds of more than 30 knots (55.56 km per hour) (Jaffe and Fiedel 1990: 100).

Sunlight and Moonlight

Sunlight and moonlight can have a great effect on organisms; therefore, it is surprising that there are hardly any references to such elements in the literature concerning historical events. Time calendars of sunlight and moonlight are of enormous use in modeling military campaigns, and in many cases give significant information about the actual events or limit their time frame. According to the cosmological data from the Tel Aviv University Wise Observatory in Ramon, the sun rose at 5:22 on 6 September 1191 and set at 17:50. This gave the two forces at least 12.28 hours of sunlight. If the battle had not taken place in the fields of Arsuf but closer to Jaffa, the Crusader forces would have had to march nearly 20 km. This would not have been an easy challenge and an almost impossible task to accomplish under fighting conditions.[21] That night, the moon rose 1.27 hours after sunset. Since the night of 5 September 1191 had a full moon, it was most likely a very clear night. In these lunar conditions, the two rivals could theoretically have been fighting continuously through the night. Such a clear night could have made nighttime horse riding possible, but there would have hardly been any cover from arrows with such moonlight.

The march to Jaffa during the Third Crusade shows that the Latin forces preferred to locate their encampments near running-water streams. Hence, it was interesting to learn how much daytime the Crusaders would have had in order to travel from one encampment to the next one during each day. By camping next to Wadi al-Falik the night before the battle, the Crusaders were provided with a good source of water, which also allowed them to camp at a well-protected position that overlooked the land to the north, east and south. This would have been very important on the clear night of 6 September 1191. On the next morning, the moon set only at 06:35, which was 1.12 hours after sunrise (Table 23.1).

Another point that should be taken into consideration is that the Crusader force was marching to the south, but during their march, the Muslim archers were positioned to the east of the Crusaders, which gave the former a clear advantage during the early morning over the Latin forces who faced not just the Muslims, but also the sun. Therefore, the possibility should be considered that the order to continue the march southwards was given to the Crusader forces each morning only after the sun was high enough in the sky to be out of the archers eyes.

---

20 Among the "famous" winds that played a significant role in human history: the wind that played first against and then in favor of the Roman legion during the final stages of the siege of Masada (73 CE) (Josephus, *War* VII, 8, 5 [ed. Thackeray]); the Japanese Kamikaze (divine wind) said to have saved Japan from Mongol invasions of Japan in 1274 and again in 1281 (Turenbull 2010: 32–50, 55–79); the landing of William I on England's coast in 1066; the "Protestant Wind", the storm that prevented Spain from invading England in 1588 (Lindgrén and Neumann 1985).

21 During the march to Tiberius, the Franks covered a distance of about 17 km on the first day.

Table 23.1: Solar and Lunar Activity on the Week of the 1–7 September 1191, Taken from the Wise Observatory, Tel Aviv University

Sunday	*Monday*	*Tuesday*	*Wednesday*	*Thursday*	*Friday*	*Saturday*
1	2	3	4	5	6	7
2156313.5 23:24	2156314.5 23:28	2156315.5 23:32	2156316.5 23:36	2156317.5 23:40	2156318.5 23:44	2156319.5 23:48
SR05:19	SR05:19	SR05:20	SR05:21	SR05:21	SR05:22	SR05:23
SS17:57	SS17:55	SS17:54	SS17:53	SS17:51	SS17:50	SS17:49
MR15:11	MR15:55	MR16:35	MR17:12	MR17:48	MR18:23	MR19:00
MS00:46	MS01:56	MS03:06	MS04:17	MS05:26	MS06:35	MS07:43

Longitude: 34.8500 Latitude: 32.0000 Time Zone: 2.0
SR- Time of sunrise; SS- Time of sunset; MR- Time of moonrise; MS- Time of moonset. Constructed: July 1998, by Eran Ofek, eran@wise.tau.ac.il URL: http://wise-obs.tau.ac.il/~eran/Wise/wise_calen.html

THE LOCATION OF THE ARSUF (SHARON) FOREST

The forest of Arsuf/Arsur was once a very large area of woodland that covered most of the Sharon plain of modern Israel (Waisel and Agami 1990: 118–120; Ehrlich 2014: 113; Kedar 2015: 125–130). According to Claude Conder and Horatio Kitchener: "The country south-west of Mukhalid is an open woodland of oak, the trees attaining a fair size" (Conder and Kitchener 1881: 136). The two identify the wood as the Crusader's forest of Arsur, located between the Salty River (Nahr Iskanderuneh/modern Alexander) and *Rochetaillie* (al-Falik/Poleg) (Conder and Kitchener 1881: 136). The forest may also be seen delineated on the *Survey of Western Palestine* map from 1880 (Conder and Kitchener 1880: Sheet X, scale: one inch to the mile), together with the writing "Oak Forest." The marking of the trees on the map start approximately at the village of Mukhalid; though it is clearthat the marking of trees on the map extends southwards from the al-Falik River and as far south as Kefar Saba on the southeast, and almost as far as al-Haram (Sayiduna [Sidna] Ali) on the southwest (Fig. 23.3). According to Ambroise, the day before the battle, the Crusader forces came out of the forest and camped on open land near Rochetaillie. It could be understood from Ambroise that the Arsuf forest's southern border was on the banks of Rochetaillie/al-Falik (Prawer 1984: 74), but it is clear from the eyewitness cited in Bahāʾ al-Dīn Ibn Shaddād's description of the battle that the three charges made against the Muslims took place near the woods and in that direction (Richards 2002: 175).

Reconstructing the landscape of the southern Sharon Plain on the eve of the battle also deals with the location of the Arsuf forest. The literary sources reporting on the Battle of Arsuf give the approximate western boundary of it. According to Bahāʾ al-Dīn Ibn Shaddād, the Crusader forces charged three times against their enemy. Those cavalry charges were directed (mainly) towards the east because of the danger of being drawn into an ambush (in the forest) and thus the charges were stopped at its edge (Richards 2002: 175). Ibn al-Athīr (ed. Richards 2007: 39) wrote: "[...], close to the Muslims there was a grove of dense trees which the Muslims entered and the Franks suspected that it was a trick, so they withdrew and took the pressure off them." Ambroise (ed. Hubert and La Monte 1976: 261, Lines 6519–6520) claims that the Muslims fled into the woods, climbed trees and hid behind bushes. In contrast, in a letter written by Richard I addressed to the Abbot of Clairvaux (dated to 1 October 1191), the King of England claims that he chased his enemy "for a whole league" (Edbury 1996: 180), over a distance of over 5.5 km. Ambroise also says that the fugitives filled the countryside for a distance of two leagues (about 11 km), and some were chased westwards towards the sea:

> And some gave up their mounts to flee
> As best they could towards the sea,
> And flung them from the cliff tops steep
> Full ten ells down into the deep
> (Ambroise, ed. Hubert and La Monte 1976: 261, Lines 6523–6529).

Yehuda Karmon makes a clear association between the location of the *ḥamra* and the location of the forest. In two maps (dealing with the settlements and roads in the Bronze Age and Iron Age and in the Roman–Byzantine periods), the oak forest extended all the way to the western (first) *kurkar* ridge and even to the Mediterranean coastline (Karmon 1961: 45, 55, Maps No. 1 and 2). In the third map attributed to the Crusader period, Karmon replaces the *ḥamra* with sand dunes. Doing so, he moved the line of the *ḥamra* and therefore the forest about 3 km to the east, placing the western border of the forest at the trough between the second and third *kurkar* ridge (Karmon 1961: 59, Map. No. 3; Kedar 2015: 131 Fig. 7.3). It seems that Karmon based the location of the forest on the testimony of Ambroise (Karmon

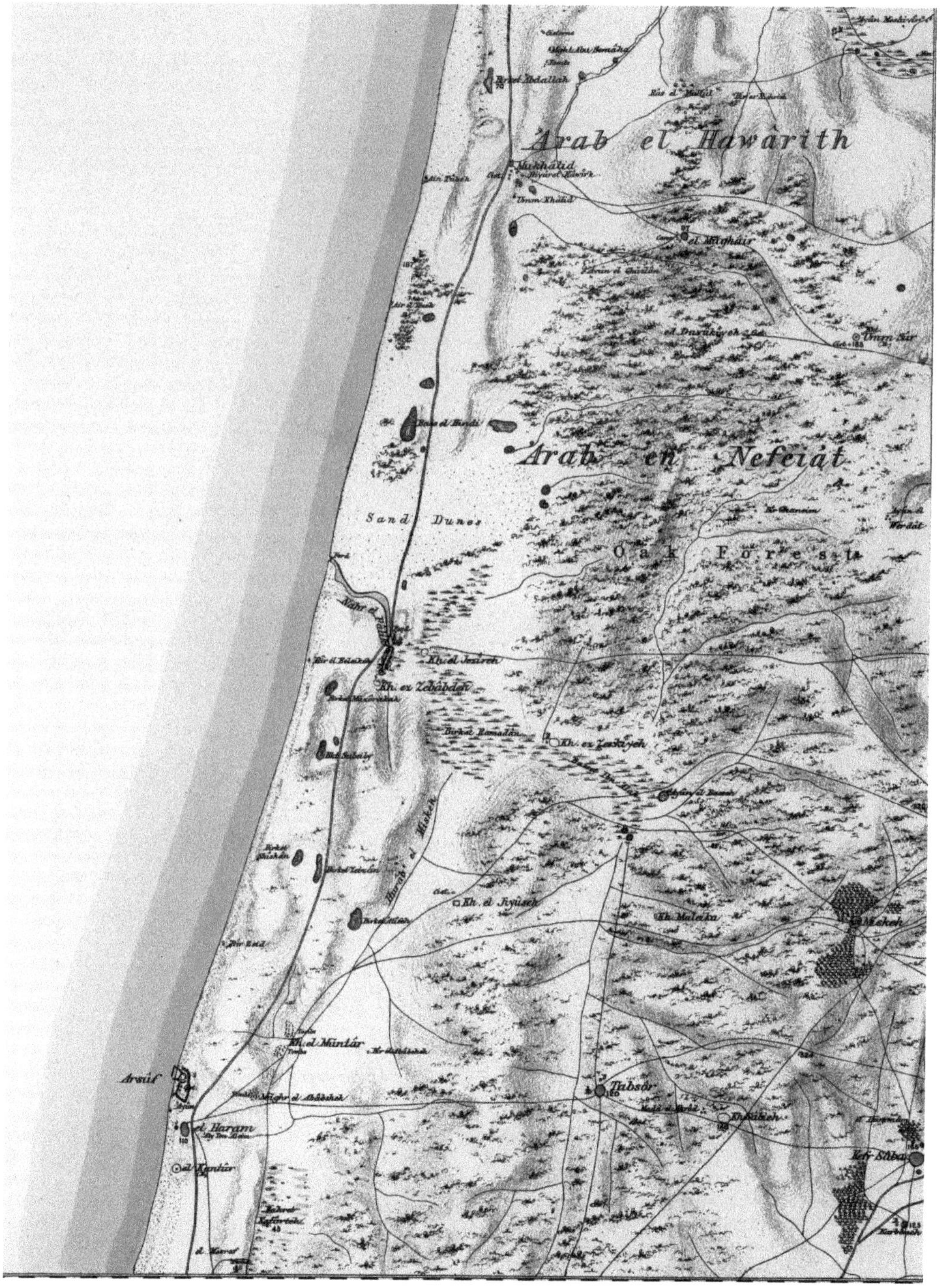

Fig. 23.3: Palestine Exploration Fund (PEF) map of the Arsuf area (Conder and Kitchner 1881).

1961: 58); however, his reading of Ambroise seems to be incorrect. There is no reason to believe that the oak forest was located much further to the west as in Karmon's other two maps. On Jacotin's map (on the southern part of Sheet No. 45 Césarée, scale 1:100,000), the forest extended westwards to the south of al-Haram (Fig. 23.4). Jacotin's map is very important for the understanding of cultivated areas, for estimating the outlines of the forested areas and for the reconstruction of the pre-cadastral Arsuf landscape (Gibson 1995: 52). On an aerial photo (taken by the Bayerische Flieger on December 29th 1918, flight 304; 189, hour 12:00, height 3000 m) there are no remains of a forest or of any significant tree; however, the sand (entering the mainland from the west in areas where there are openings in the first *kurkar* ridge) creates shapes of crescents open to the west (Fig. 23.4). This sand migrating to the land is a well-known phenomenon and might be the result of environmental change and/or human activities; in this case it seems to be the effect of the abandonment of the coaxial field system (see below). In Ashqelon,

a)

b)

Fig. 23.4: (a) Jacotin map with the outline of Arsuf forest, 1799. (b) Aerial photograph of Arsuf (29.12.1918 fl. no. 304) (note the similarity of the forest outline in the Jacotin map and the location of sand dunes seen in the photograph).

for instance, abandonment of the coaxial field system to the south of the ancient site (after 1948) and the construction of an electric power station to the south of the city resulted in massive changes along the shore and with the diffusion of sand inland. In fact, these features created a border of non-sandy land which was very similar to the shape of the western border of the forested area as seen on the Jacotin map.

CULTURAL/CYCLICAL: MEDIUM DURÉE

THE CRUSADER FIGHTING MARCH

The movement of armed troops within a given landscape depended upon their fighting skills and techniques, their numbers, and the limitations imposed by the topography which they traversed (Lewis 2013: 107–109). The "fighting march" was a technique adopted from the Byzantine army (Bennett 2001: 14). It enabled the Crusaders to move their forces from one place to another through a hostile landscape which was dominated by an enemy that usually had supremacy in numbers (Smail 1956: 156–165; Bennett 2001; Lewis 2013: 203–211). Generally, the Crusader forces, when they marched, consisted of a main body of mounted knights encircled by rings or defensive lines of infantry and Turcopoles (mounted archers), which were both used to hold off and counter-attack Muslim skirmishers (Harari 1997: 86–102). While on the march, the Crusader forces were usually divided into three main bodies of horsemen, with the Hospitallers or the Templers knights positioned at the rearguard or vanguard, and the king and his men at the center. The number of defensive lines of foot soldiers encircling the mounted troops depended on the way the main body was arranged, according to topography on the one hand and according to the position of the enemy on the other. When the order to charge was given, the horses and riders would break through the lines of defense that opened for them.

The efficiency of the charge was thus dependent on the amount of the destruction inflicted upon the enemy. The more horses linked together, the more destructive the results. When the horses moved in a column, they were much more vulnerable to an enemy's attack and their charge was thus less efficient. During the fighting march, the troops were limited to the pace of the foot soldiers, but this tactic allowed the Crusaders to move through the landscape without being dependent on roads or on outside provisions (Smail 1956: 304–305; Bennett 1989; Bennett 2001; Lewis 2013: 200–211).[22]

However, there are a few points that need to be added to previous studies on this fighting technique. First, concerning the description provided by Ambroise of the light and swift Muslim cavalry, it is not certain that the Muslim cavalry was more lightly armed than the Crusaders. It seems that the mobility of the Muslim forces was not necessarily related to their cavalry being more lightly equipped than the Crusaders, but had more to do with their tactics and the way in which they understood the landscape and moved through it in relation to manpower and their objectives (Harari 1997: 114–115; Lewis 2013: 210–211). It also seems that Richard I was, by then, well acquainted with eastern fighting techniques, to the extent that he employed them himself at a later time in the campaign while camped at *Beit Nuba* (*Bethnoble*), where he used Turcopoles in his attack on the Muslim caravan (Ambroise, ed. Kahneman 2005: 387, Lines 10405–10410).

During the march, Richard I divided the infantry in order to let some of them rest, providing himself with an additional line of defense and enlarging the distance from the enemy's arrows to his unprotected horses. The fact that some of his men could rest probably helped Richard I to keep his men in close formation (which comes across as the most important element in the deployment of his fighting march technique), not being dragged back by those not keeping up with the rest and breaking up into small groups which could easily be wiped out by the Muslims.

22 The years between the First and Third Crusade provide many examples in which these tactics were deployed successfully (or unsuccessfully) by the opponents; these have been discussed more than once in past research (Smail 1956: 157–164; Bennett 2001; Prawer 1984: 55–56; France 2000: 60–62; Lewis 2013: 204–207).

It should also be taken into account that Guy de Lusignan, former king of the Latin Kingdom of Jerusalem, was riding with Richard I throughout all of the fighting march from Acre to Arsuf. David Nicolle has raised the possibility that he was in tactical control of Richard's central division (Nicolle 2005: 67). Guy may be held responsible for the catastrophic results of the fighting march to Tiberias during the Hattin campaign. But it should not be forgotten that by the time of the reclaiming of Acre, Guy was probably the most experienced leader to be found anywhere, having led his men many times through different terrains using the fighting march technique (Lewis 2013: 206–207). Guy was likely a great asset to Richard I during his march to Jaffa, and perhaps had a significant part in the success of the march.

The Coaxial Landscape of Arsuf

In the last hundred years, due to modern developmental activities in relation to the movement of sand dunes, the landscape of Arsuf (including areas protected by the antiquities law) went through a significant change. A series of aerial photographs taken in 1918 and in the mid-1940s reveal an entirely different landscape from the one visible today. In two aerial photos dated 28 January 1946, three different kinds of field systems, typical of different periods, can be traced. The most recent field system is represented mostly by Jewish settlements such as Herzliyya and Rishpon and especially the fields between them. These fields are large rectangular shapes (Fig. 23.2); second are the rectangular but more oblong *Musha* fields, typical of the late Ottoman period, such as near the Arab village of al-Haram (Fig. 23.2). The third field system, which predates the other two and which had a major influence on the layout of the entire landscape, is the coaxial field system (Dauphin 1986; Fleming 1987; Frankel *et al.* 2001: 113–114).

The main characteristic of the coaxial field system is that all of the different features that comprise it were organized in relation to a (usually) dominant man-made feature of a discrete nature, such as a boundary wall or a road. This feature served as the backbone of the entire system. Another characteristic is in the asymmetric appearance of the system caused by the irregularity in the size and shape of plots. An additional characteristic of coaxial field systems is that unlike many other field systems, coaxial systems are "terrain-oblivious"; hence, they will run along axial features across hills, streams, and valleys, and in the case of Arsuf they even "ignore" the second *kurkar* ridge to the east of the city (Fleming 1987; Williamson 1987: 429–430).

This type of field system has been found in a number of environments and in association with a variety of soil types. Coaxial fields were laid on clayish, rocky, alluvial, basaltic and sandy terrains. The fact that such systems were spread out also on poor agricultural land has influenced their survival to this day. This was because at times when only prime land was cultivated, the low quality land was either left untouched or used for grazing purposes only. The idea behind coaxial systems is that it was a means through which strong centralized powers could maximize their control over the land by subdividing every available plot. This is soon reflected in better and improved tax collecting. In relation to battlefields, the different features of such a field system can manipulate the movement of people through the landscape directing movement through specific paths and junctions.

In Israel, coaxial field systems have been found in the Upper and Lower Galilee, in the area of Nablus (Shechem), Modiʿin and Ashqelon. Previous research suggests dating this cultural phenomenon to the Late Roman period or, more specifically, to the time of the Severan Emperors (from the late 2nd to the mid-3rd century CE; see Lewis 2013: 306–317). It transpires that at Arsuf, just as in other regions in Israel, Late Roman landscaping is evident in the main settlements and in the construction of paved roads. Apparently, the Romans reshaped the entire hinterland, and this system prevailed until the mid-20th century when modern development began reshaping the traditional landscape once again.

THE HISTORICAL EVENT: SHORT DURÉE

CONCLUSIONS

The following are conclusions based on the study presented above and the author's field work. It will deal with the following aspects: The Implication of Land Structure on the Movement of Troops in the Sharon Plain; Location of the Encampment on the Evening of the Battle; Location of the Arsuf Battlefield (7 September 1191); Location of the Arsuf Battlefield (19 September 1918) and with the Battle of Arsuf (7 September 1191) in the Setting of the Arsuf Landscape.

THE IMPLICATION OF LAND STRUCTURE ON THE MOVEMENT OF TROOPS IN THE SHARON PLAIN

The Crusaders marched to Arsuf, but where exactly did the march take place? Was it on the coast itself, on one of the *kurkar* ridges, or perhaps in the valleys between them? To answer, the following needs to be considered: during his march southwards, Richard I was accompanied with a fleet that supplied him with provisions. Although some of the vessels accompanying the troops were able to anchor near the shore, they could only do so when there was no danger of hitting a reef. Richard's land troops had to stay either in eye contact with the fleet, or at least be able to send and receive signals from the fleet. Therefore, the Crusaders had to march relatively close to the beach, as described in the Regis Ricardi (Stubbs 1864: 261). Another aspect to be considered about where the troops marched was that if and when the ships landed near the shore, they needed to be protected by the land troops. It was very difficult to sail parallel to the Crusader's line-of-march. Thus, coordinating the next meeting point of the land march and the fleet by a river or a well-known settlement would help in case of lack of eye contact between the land force and the fleet. The waterfront at Arsuf may have been the only port where a vessel might anchor between Caesarea and Jaffa (Roll and Ayalon 1989: 230). Hence, it is highly likely that the Crusaders would have tried to camp next to the town, despite the fact that it was in Muslim hands.

The width of the 12th century coastline between the sea and the first *kurkar* ridge is not known; as wide as the coast may have been, from Wadi al-Falik to Arsuf the coast is characterized by the western cliffs of the first ridge, and any force marching along the coastline itself would have been dominated from the cliffs. Lyons and Jackson claimed that Saladin did not defeat the Crusaders at Arsuf because, unlike Hattin, he did not use the superior numbers that he had in his favor which would have allowed him to surround the Crusaders (Lyons and Jackson 1982: 337; based on Ambroise, ed. Hubert and La Monte 1976: 251, Lines 6195–6200). Tactically, had the Crusaders marched further inland and not along the western valley, the Muslims would have had enough space to deploy their fighting technique and might have used the prevailing topographical conditions to split the Crusader-line-of-march into smaller groups and to cut these off from the fleet. Therefore, the conclusion is drawn that the Crusaders' line-of-march could only have been in the westernmost valley between the first and second *kurkar* ridges and on the eastern slopes of the first ridge.

As mentioned above, when the Crusaders entered the forest of Arsuf they were worried that the Muslims would set it on fire (Ambroise, ed. Hubert and La Monte 1976: 248, Lines 6095–6100). Through most of the Crusader march to the south, the wind was blowing at their backs—i.e., the wind direction moved the dust away from them, giving them an advantage in ballistic range. The wind direction can also provide another explanation as to why Saladin preferred attacking the rearguard throughout most of the march. Positioning his troops to the east or to the southeast of the marching Crusaders would put his archers in an inferior position. In contrast, if the account given by the Regis Ricardi of clouds of dust covering both the Crusaders and Muslims is true (probably just a metaphor or dramatization; see Stubbs 1864: 271), it is likely that in the early hours of 7 September the wind was not blowing hard or in a clear direction and did not provide an advantage to either of the two rivals.

The Location of the Encampment on the Evening of the Battle

Marching along the coast, the Crusaders crossed (and encamped next to) several streams flowing from the eastern highlands to the Mediterranean. It is evident from both the accounts of the Third Crusade and from the way in which the encampments were established–as studied at *Safoire* by the author–that the Crusaders preferred camping next to running water, and in different groups along one of the river banks (Lewis 2013: 337–346). On the eve of the battle, the Crusader forces encamped next to Wadi al-Falik. Early in the Middle Bronze Age and later in the Roman period, a cut was made in the *kurkar* ridge in order to allow the water to flow to the west, and as a result, drain the swamp (Ehrlich 2014: 113–114). Even if the swamps of Wadi al-Falik were not dry, as Kedar (2015: 119) has suggested, it was not a serious obstacle for the Crusaders. It is likely that after over two weeks of marching along the Mediterranean the Crusaders were very familiar with crossing water streams such as Wadi al-Falik. If the stream was too deep, they could simply cross it close to its connection with the sea without making a long detour (Fig. 23.5). As can be seen on a German military map from 1918, which was based on the *Survey of Western Palestine* map (from 1880, but with additions), where the main road runs along the coast, it crosses a stream close to the connection with the sea where the water depth is low (Reichsamt für Landesaufnahme 1918: Map No. 50. Tūl Kerm, scale 1:50.000; Kedar 2015: 131, Fig. 7.3).

It could be that, owing to the full moon that night, some of the troops preferred to camp at more secure locations, such as the hill to the south, known as Tel ʿAshir, located just north of the current Wingate Sports Institute (Barkan 2010).

The road system is crucial for the understanding of the battle; Smail (1956: 304–305) argued that the Crusaders were not dependent on roads when applying the fighting march technique. Smail's analysis would infer that the study of road-systems is not relevant for the study of any other Frankish military affair that involved this tactic. However, a separation should be made here between the physical road (the surface one walks or rides on) and the general meaning of the term *road*. Even if not physically traveled by the Crusaders, it is evident from the road-system map that there were at least four land roads in the sub-region. One of these was international, and three were regional roads leading to and from Apollonia-Arsuf. This, in fact, makes the town one of the best networked settlements in the southern Sharon Plain, and the crossroad to its east plays a significant role in the understanding of the Battle of Arsuf. This is because crossroads are points for decision-making; if one wants to influence the decision of an opponent, then a road junction would be the right place to do this. The road junction near Arsuf must be regarded as a regional focal point. Connecting a large number of different levels of roads, it was the most important junction between Caesarea and Jaffa. It is evident that this focal point attracted a lot of human activity, including that of human conflict (Gichon 1990: 289–315).[23]

Location of the Arsuf Battlefield (7 September 1191)

The metal detecting survey, which was carried out in a very limited area and which did not suffer severely from modern development activities, revealed a handful of artifacts that could be related to the conflict of September 1191 (Figs. 23.6–23.7, 23.9). The artifacts were found mainly in a shallow ground depression that measured 35 × 80 m. It appears that only an intensive future program of research, using highly sensitive equipment beneath the dunes, might unravel the material imprint of this battle.[24]

23 For structural reasons, Arsuf remained an important junction even after it was taken by the Mamluk army in late April 1265 (Tal and Roll 2011), while the settlement itself had no apparent significance.

24 Future research may be impossible to conduct due to the rate of modern development in the area and the fact that many of the fields that remain to be explored in Arsuf, and at other battle sites in modern Israel, have not been officially declared as "archaeological sites"; therefore, they are not protected by the Israeli antiquities law and are more vulnerable to future development (Lewis 2013: 383–384).

Fig. 23.5: View northwest from Tel ʿAshir, the shallow stream of the Poleg stream (Flum de Rochetaillée / Wadi al-Falik), where it enters the Mediterranean today (photo by H. Kenzler).

There are several reasons to believe that the medieval metal artifacts located during this study are related to the event of 7 September. Firstly, their late 12th–early 13th century dates (Fig. 23.9) indicate this, but also their relative location in the landscape and the description of the written evidence. The finds might have found their way to the various locations during some other event (or events) and not during the battle of Arsuf. Such an occurrence of the relocation of a find is probably mostly related to the "violin key horseshow nail" (Fig. 23.9: 3),[25] a type of find highly expected along the course of a frequently traveled road such as the one to the northeast of Arsuf. Other finds, such as the two arrowheads (Fig. 23.9: 1–2), the iron plate—which looks like a fragment of a great helm (Fig. 23.9: 5)—and the horse fitting (Fig. 23.9: 4), are very likely to be the result of a violent conflict which had elements of both long range ballistic shooting and close combat.[26] These should therefore should be associated more comfortably with the Battle of Arsuf or, more specifically, to the eastern line of the Christian troops. These finds can actually be used in order to locate the western border of the relic oak forest. Taking into account that the three charges made by the Crusader forces were (mainly) targeted towards the east, measuring the range of an arrow and the distance of an effective cavalry charge would point to the approximate distance of the western border of the Arsuf forest.[27] If Karmon (1961: 59, Map. No. 3) misinterpreted the written sources which he used for his Crusader period map of the landscape, the western border of the Arsuf forest might have been much more to the west, as suggested in the other two maps published by Karmon d (1961: 45, 55, Maps No. 1 and 2).

25 A "violin key horseshoe nail" is a type of horseshoe nail of western European origin; it can be found at Frankish sites in the Latin kingdom of Jerusalem and at countless sites in France and England dating to the same period (Fig. 23.9: 3).

26 Different kinds of warfare leave a variety of of material imprints. Unlike long range ballistic fighting (pre-gunpowder), when targets were hit and later stripped of their armor or clothing which left behind the arrowheads, in close combat it is very likely that part of the armor and clothing would be ripped during combat.

27 It is not known whether the three charges continued to cover a great distance, or if the Crusader cavalry withdrew to the back (reassembled under the flag) and recharged on the same field repeatedly. If the charges were not continual, it would mean that the distance between the marching Crusader column to the forest edge should be brought even more to the west.

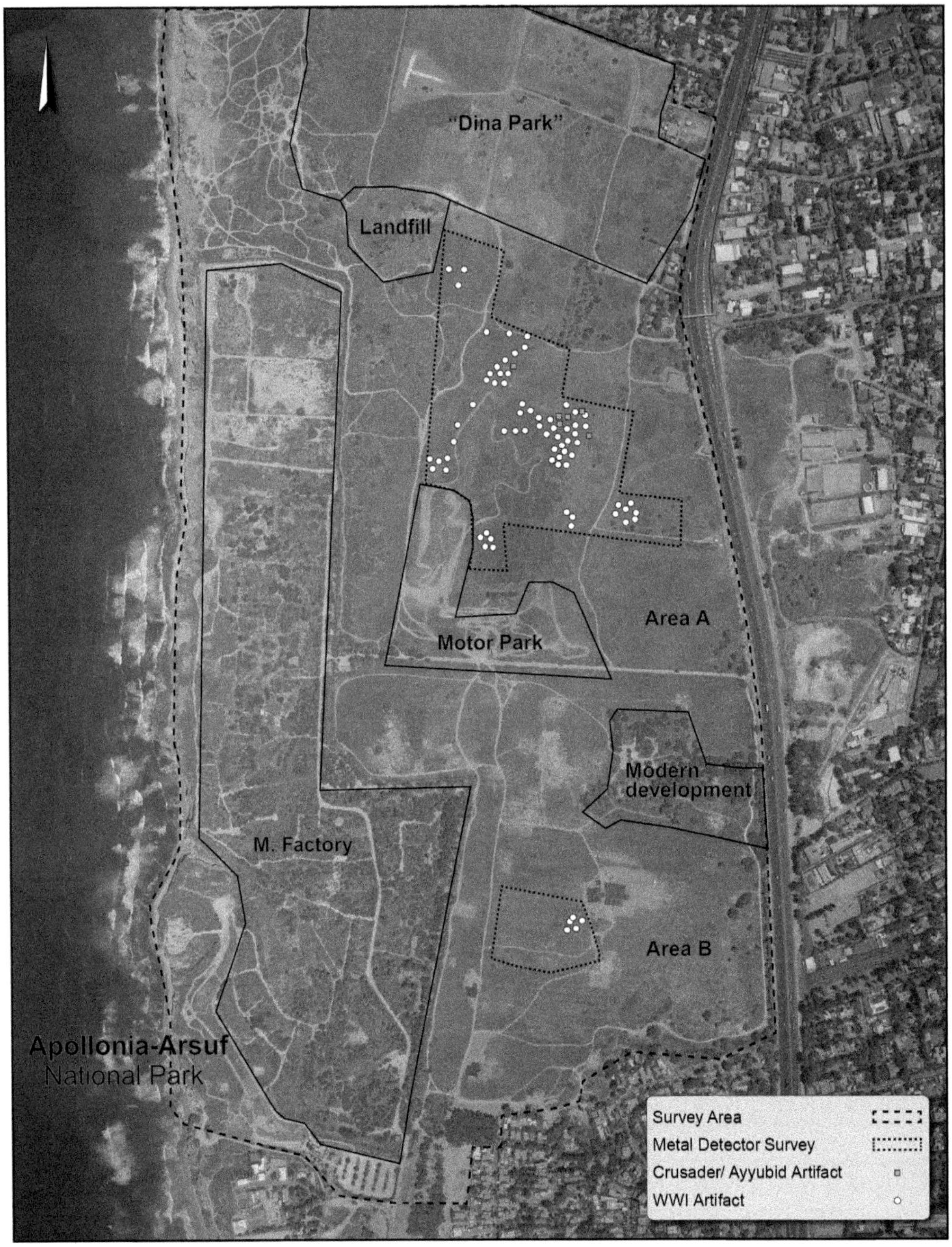

Fig. 23.6: Area of archaeological survey and location of artifacts (note the salvage operations in Area BB undertaken by the IAA and TAU).

Location of the Arsuf Battlefield (19 September 1918)

It is a common phenomenon in the Levant that historical events such as battles from different periods are fought on the same fields (Lewis 2013: 43). In that respect, it is interesting to point to the fact that this also works for the battlefield of Arsuf (Fig. 23.8). Unlike the very modest number of medieval remains found in the area surveyed, what has survived is a very strong material signature of another conflict occurring 727 years later, during the Great War (Fig. 23.6).

Shortly after the troops commanded by Field Marshal E.H.H. Allenby had crossed the River Auja (Yarkon) during the battle of Jaffa, on 23 December 1917, they advanced 8 km along the coastline to

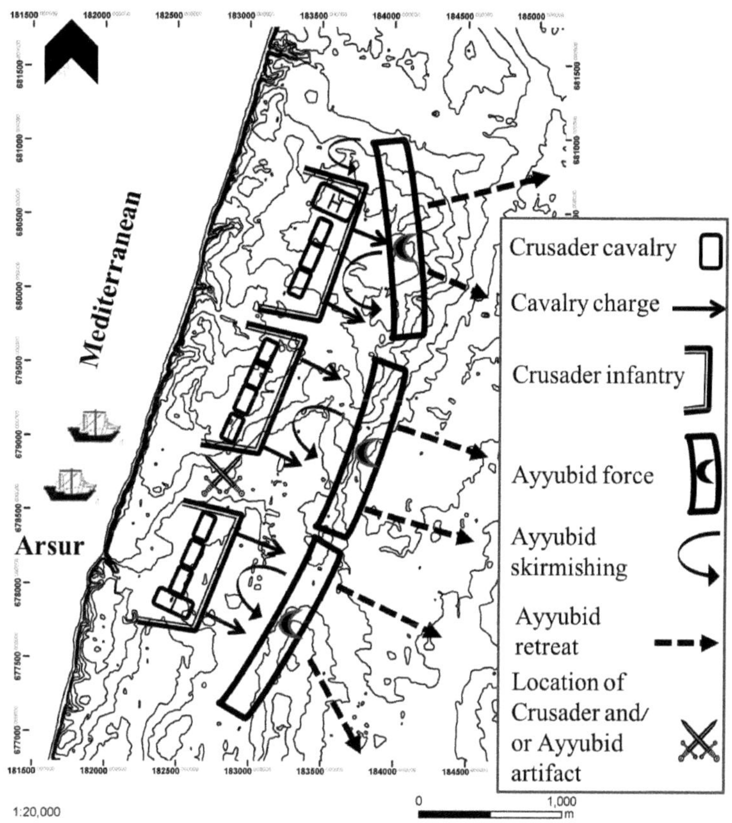

Fig. 23.7: Arsuf, September 7th, 1191, battle plan with location of Crusader and/or Ayyubid artifacts.

Arsuf, capturing key Ottoman Turkish positions and establishing them as their front. Arsuf/Apollonia served as the frontline for the British forces from December 1917 to 19 September 1918. In the area surveyed (Fig. 23.6), the metal detector revealed fragments of shells and bullets. In one of his letters addressed to Clive Wigram (Assistant Private Secretary and Equerry to the King), Allenby wrote:

> My Staff calculated for me that by the middle of September (1918) my troops would be reorganized and sufficiently trained to undertake a decisive attack, with reasonable chance of succeeding (Hughes 2004: 196).[28]

These finds are most likely the material evidence for the Battle of Sharon/Samaria/the Great Offensive that was fought between 19–25 September 1918 and ended later with the great Ottoman defeat in the Jezreel valley (Gichon 1990: 304; Bruce 2002: 166–168; Hughes 2004: 116–120; Grainger 2006: 234–235).

Alternative explanations are that the finds could be the remains of either the intensive training undertaken by the Egyptian Expeditionary Force prior to its offensive move or of the exchange of fire during those long months (December 1917 to September 1918) when Arsuf was at the northwestern tip of the front.

The Battle of Arsuf (7 September 1191) in the Setting of the Arsuf Landscape

Bahāʾ al-Dīn Ibn Shaddād describes how Saladin and his brother were constantly supervising their men along the lines. Saladin was accompanied by only two "spear mounts" (Richards 2002: 175). The Crusader leaders acted in a similar way and, for example, on the day of the battle, Count Henry de Champagne was

28 Allenby explains that his main motivation of choosing 4:30 on 19 September to be the day was: "-the moon being just short of the full; with a short period of darkness between moonset and sunrise-" (Hughes 2004: 196). With the moon at their backs, his men could use the late hours of the night to storm enemy lines and to advance north quickly.

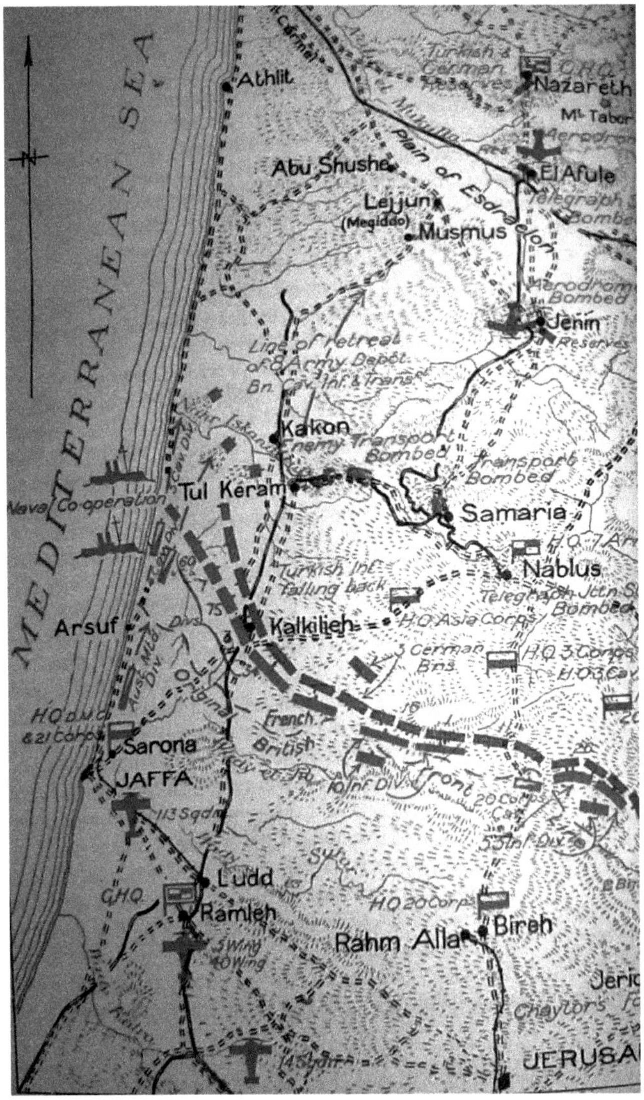

Fig. 23.8: Commencement of battle at the western part of the front, at zero hour 19.9.1918 (Gullett 1941: Map 38).

put in charge of the troops marching close to the mountains, constantly riding up and down the frontline (Ambroise, ed. Hubert and La Monte 1976: 251, Lines 6190–6194).

The rings of defense provided by the foot soldiers during the fighting march supplied the commanders with (literally) a shield that served to keep them safe and put them in a situation that enabled them to make clear decisions. This isolation of the commander from direct danger could also sometimes detach him from his surroundings, thus preventing him from reading the military situation correctly. Richard I exhibits one of the rare cases of a man who, due to his maneuverability, could look at the field from a wide perspective of the landscape even during a fighting march, and especially regarding the location of his troops and the position of the enemy. Gillingham claims that:

> The only difference between the battle of Arsuf and the fighting of the last two and a half weeks was that, by committing his main force to the attack, Saladin would be giving Richard a chance to deliver one of the famous Frankish charges. If he could seize the moment, victory would be his (Gillingham 1999: 176).

The battlefield was in Richard's control mostly because he looked at the field from a wide perspective, the result of his personal maneuverability in the landscape, responding in an *ad hoc* way

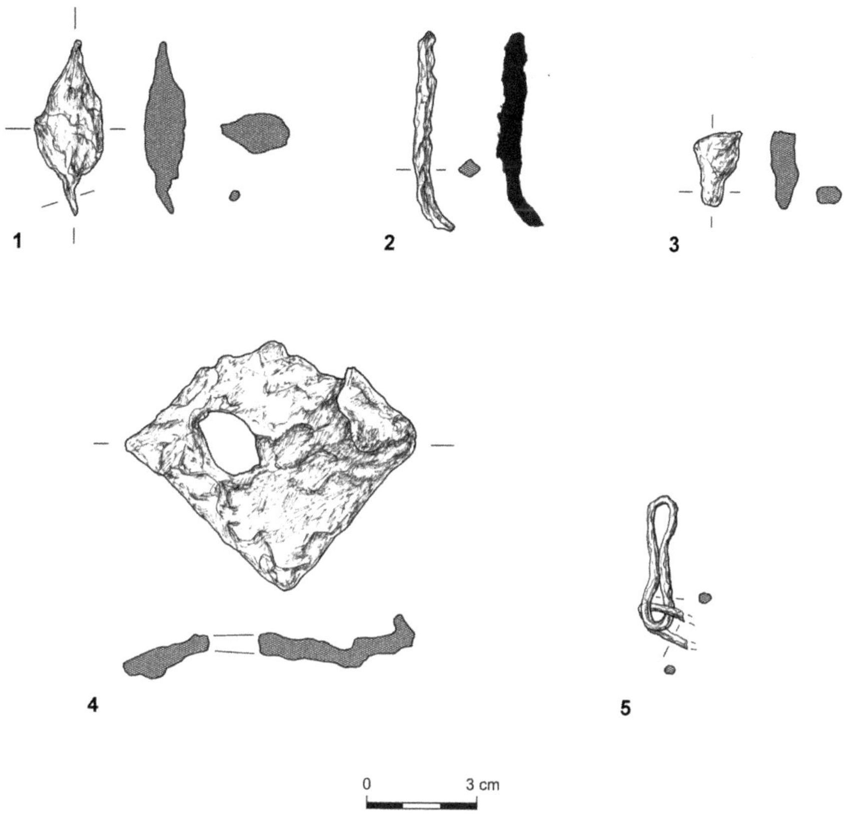

Fig. 23.9: Selected Finds from the Survey

No.	*Basket No.*			*Date*
1	B. 17	Arrowhead. Iron. Elliptic section	Davidson 1952: Pl. 92.1559; Khamis 1996: 219, Fig. XVIII.1.6; Grey 2000: 135, Fig. 11.3.47; Raphael 2008: 264, Fig.4; Lewis 2013: 461, Pl. 28.1	12–14 c. CE
2	B. 4	Arrowhead. Iron. Rhomboid section (badly corroded after extracted from site).	Dean 1927: 37, Fig. 53; Davidson 1952: Pl. 91.1529, 1530; Dar 1994: 358–359, Fig. 20.14–15; Getzov 2000: 99, Fig. 29.2; Serdon 2005: 122, ty. L; Raphael 2008: 263, Fig. 2; Barbé 2010: 348, Fig. 112.3; Lewis 2013: 447, Pl. 14.3	12–14 c. CE
3	B. 18	Horseshoe nail. Iron. "Violin key"	Green 1966: 307, Fig.1; Maccari-Poisson 1993: 147, Fig. 105; Demians d'Archimbaud 1980: IV, Pl. 417.79; Boas 1999: 164, Fig. 6.2.8; Getzov 2000: 100, Fig. 30.13; Clark 2011b: 86–87, Fig. 64, 66, 67, 80, 82–85; Lewis 2013: 456, Pl. 23.1–12	12–13 c. CE
4	B. 33	Plate (part of "Great helm"?). Iron.	Dean 1927: 37, Fig. 53a	13 c. CE
5	B. 100	Horse harness fittings (part of curb bit?). Iron.	Clark 2011a: 53, Figs. 38–39	13 c. CE

to any vulnerability in the Frankish battle tactics, and thus he was able to seize the moment (*Carpe Momento*) when an opportunity arose.

As mentioned earlier, Smail and Asbridge have separately argued that Saladin urged his men to attack when he saw that his enemy was nearing Jaffa. Ehrlich recently argued convincingly that both Saladin and Richard were seeking a pitched battle. Ehrlich is also justified in arguing that: "Arsur was the most suitable combat area in the coastal plain..." (Ehrlich 2014: 117).[29] The historical, physiographical, environmental and archaeological evidence presented above strengthens the possibility that it was in the interest of both rivals to bring this conflict to a decisive end. Although, as a result of this study, it is evident that the Arsuf battlefield was smaller than what had been previously suggested, the event happened in a nearly perfect place for a cavalry charge.[30] At the same time, it can be argued that it was also in the interest of Saladin to attack at Arsuf. It seems that Saladin was (perhaps) not aware, or at least not completely convinced, that the Crusader preliminary target was Jaffa and not Jerusalem. The "Arsuf junction" presented a dilemma: one can either go south along the coast to Jaffa or proceed to the east to Jerusalem. As seen above, Arsuf represented in the past one of the most important road junctions in the Sharon. The same road junction played a crucial role in two historical conflicts (the Third Crusade and in the Great War) with 727 years separating the two battles. Arsuf was the first place encountered in the march down the coast from where the Crusaders could actually leave the coastal road and then go east to Jerusalem. Marching to Jerusalem through the broad Lydda (Lod) plain could suit their battle tactics in the best way. Saladin probably remembered very clearly the event occurring on that same plain on 25 November 1177, later known as the Battle of Montgisard, during which his army suffered a major loss at the hands of the Franks led by Baldwin IV, during which Saladin had almost been killed (Ehrlich 2013). Saladin undoubtedly took a greater risk by attacking the Crusaders at Arsuf; a decisive loss on his side might have sent the Crusader army straight on to Jerusalem. Since Ehrlich, and Kedar more recently, argued convincingly that it was Richard's plan to attack at Arsuf, this makes the risk that Saladin took even greater. As mentioned earlier, the Muslim defeat at Arsuf might have not been more than a moral blow; the capture of Acre was much more significant.

Saladin took the risk and attacked with all his might. He lost the battle, but the events at Arsuf contributed significantly to the overall strategy of Saladin. Hence, from his point of view, it was the attack on the Crusaders at Arsuf that influenced their decision to march south to Jaffa and not to Jerusalem. The indecision of the Crusaders gave Saladin and his men the opportunity to skirmish the Crusaders for yet another year, exhausting them both physically and mentally. This was a strategy that eventually worked in the Muslims' favor.

REFERENCES

Applebaum, S. 1985. The Hellenistic, Roman and Byzantine Periods. In: Porat, Y., Dar, S. and Applebaum, S. *The History and Archaeology of Emek-Hefer*. Tel Aviv: 60–71 (Hebrew).

Asbridge, T. 2010. *The Crusades: The War for the Holy Land.* London.

Barbé, H. 2010. *Le château de Safed et son territoire a l'epoque des croisades* (Ph.D. dissertation, Hebrew University of Jerusalem). Jerusalem.

Barkan, D. 2010. Tel ʿAshir. *Ḥadashot Arkheologiyot—Excavations and Surveys in Israel* 122. http://www.hadashot-esi.org.il/Report_Detail_Eng.aspx?id=1326&mag_id=117.

29 The Yarkon River (River Auja) is the main land obstacle on the Coastal Plain and could provide Saladin an excellent point to attack, though it is evident that the Crusaders had no problem crossing water obstacles.

30 Pushing the cavalry charge a bit more towards the south, to the Arsuf junction itself, might have resulted in a more decisive victory for the Crusaders.

Bennett, M. 1989. La Règle du Temple as a Military Manual or How to Deliver a Cavalry Charge. In: Harper-Bill, C., Holdsworth, C.J. and Nelson, J.L., eds. *Studies in Medieval History for R. Allen Brown*. Wolfeboro: 7–19.

Bennett, M. 2001. The Crusaders' 'Fighting March' Revisited. *War in History* 8: 1–18.

Boas, A.J. 1999. *Crusader Archaeology: The Material Culture of the Latin East*. London.

Braudel, F. 1980. *On History*. Matthews, S., trans. Chicago.

Braudel, F. 1993. *A History of Civilizations*. Mayne, R., trans. London.

Bruce, A. 2002. *The Last Crusade: The Palestine Campaign in the First World War*. London.

Clark, J. 2011a. Harness Fittings. In: Clark, J., ed. *The Medieval Horse and Its Equipment c.1150–c.1450*. London: 43–74.

Clark, J. 2011b. Horseshoes. In: Clark, J., ed. *The Medieval Horse and its Equipment c.1150–c.1450*. London: 75–123.

Conder, C.R. and Kitchener, H.H. 1880. *Map of Western Palestine in 26 Sheets*; Sheet Number X. London.

Conder, C.R. and Kitchener, H.H. 1881. *The Survey of Western Palestine, Memoirs of the Topography, Orography, Hydrography, and Archaeology I: Galilee*. London.

Dar, S. 1994. *The History of Hermon: Settlements and Temples of the Itureans*. Tel Aviv (Hebrew).

Dauphin, C.M. 1986. Golan Survey 1985. *Israel Exploration Journal* 36: 273–275.

Davidson, G.R. 1952. *Corinth: Results of Excavations Conducted by The American School of Classical Studies at Athens. Volume XII: The Minor Objects*. Princeton.

Dean, B. 1927. *The Exploration of a Crusader Fortress (Montfort) in Palestine: A Report of Exploration Made by the Museum 1926* (Part II of The Bulletin of The Metropolitan Museum of Art). New York.

Demians d'Archimbaud, G. 1980. *Rougiers, village médiéval de Provence. Approches archéologiques d'une société rurale méditerranéenne* (Ph.D. dissertation, University of Paris I, 1978). Lille.

Edbury, P.W. 1996. *The Conquest of Jerusalem and the Third Crusade: Sources in Translation* (Crusades Text in Translation 1). Aldershot.

Ehrlich, M. 2007. The Battle of Hattin: A Chronicle of a Defeat Foretold? *Journal of Medieval Military History* 5: 16–32.

Ehrlich, M. 2013. Saint Catherine's Day Miracle – The Battle of Montgisard. *Journal of Medieval Military History* 11: 95–106.

Ehrlich, M. 2014. The Battle of Arsur: A Short-Lived Victory. *Journal of Medieval Military History* 12: 109–118.

Fleming, A. 1987. Coaxial Field Systems: Some Questions of Time and Space. *Antiquity* 61 (231): 188–202.

France, J. 1999. *Western Warfare in the Age of the Crusades 1000–1300*. New York.

France, J. 2000. Crusading Warfare and its Adaptation to Eastern Conditions in the Twelfth Century. *Mediterranean Historical Review* 15: 49–66.

France, J. 2009. The Revival of Latin Christendom and the Crusades in the East. In: Bennett, M., ed. *The Medieval World at War*. London: 85–111.

Frankel, R., Getzov, N., Aviam, M. and Degani, A. 2001. *Settlement Dynamics and Regional Diversity in Ancient Upper Galilee: Archaeological Survey of Upper Galilee* (IAA Reports 14). Jerusalem.

Gavish, E. and Bakler, N. 1990. The Sharon Costal Strip – Geomorphlogical and Sedimentological Factors and Processes. In: Grossman, D., Degani, A. and Shmueli, A., eds. *Hasharon Between Yarkon and Karmel*. Tel Aviv: 61–82 (Hebrew).

Getzov, N. 2000. An Excavation at Ḥorbat Bet Zeneta. *ʿAtiqot* 39: 75–106.

Gibson, S. 1995. *Landscape Archaeology and Ancient Agricultural Field Systems in Palestine* (Ph.D. dissertation, University College London). London.

Gibson, S. 2003. From Wildscape to Landscape: Landscape Archaeology in the Southern Levant – Methods and Practice. In: Maeir, A.M., Dar, S. and Safrai, Z., eds. *The Rural Landscape of Ancient Israel* (BAR International Series 1121). Oxford: 1–25.

Gichon, M. 1990. The Sharon from a Military-Geographic Perspective. In: Grossman, D., Degani, A. and Shmueli, A., eds. *Hasharon Between Yarkon and Karmel*. Tel Aviv: 289–315 (Hebrew).

Gillingham, J. 1999. *Richard I*. New Haven.

Goodall, I.H. 1990. Horseshoes. In: Biddle, M., ed. *Artifacts from Medieval Winchester, Part II: Object and Economy in Medieval Winchester*. Oxford: 1054–1067.

Gophna, R. and Ayalon, E. 1998. *Archaeological Survey of Israel: Map of Herzliyya (69)*. Jerusalem.

Grainger, J.D. 2006. *The Battle for Palestine 1917*. Woodbridge.

Green, C. 1966. The Purpose of the Early Horseshoe. *Antiquity* 40: 305–308.

Grey, A. 2000. The Metalwork. In Harper, R.P. and Pringle, D., eds. *Belmont Castle: The Excavation of a Crusader Stronghold in the Kingdom of Jerusalem*. Oxford and New York: 131–137.

Gullett, H.S. 1941. *The Australian Imperial Force in Sinai and Palestine: 1914–1918 (11th edition)*. Sydney.

Harari, Y.N. 1997. The Military Role of the Frankish Turcopoles: A Reassessment. *Mediterranean Historical Review* 12: 75–116.

Herde, P. 1966. Die Kämpfe bei den Hörnern von Ḥiṭṭīn und der Untergang des Kreuzritterheeres (3. und 4. Juli 1187). Eine Historisch-Topographische Untersuchung. *Romische Quartal Schrift fur christliche Altertumskunde und Kirchengeschichte* 61: 1–50.

Herde, P. 2002. Die Kämpfe bei den Hörnern von Ḥiṭṭīn und der Untergang des Kreuzritterheeres (3. und 4. Juli 1187). Eine Historisch-Topographische Untersuchung. In: Herde, P., ed. *Studien zur Papst- und Reichsgeschichte, zur Geschichte des Mittelmeerraumes und zum kanonischen Recht im Mittelate.* Stuttgart: 97–153.

Hubert, M.J. and La Monte, J.L., eds. 1976. *Ambroise. The Crusade of Richard Lion-Heart*. New York.

Hughes, M. 2004. *Allenby in Palestine: The Middle East Correspondence of Field Marshal Viscount Allenby June 1917–October 1919*. Gloucestershire.

Jacotin, P.M. 1826. *Carte topographique de l'Egypte et de plusieurs parties des pays limitrophes. Flle. 45, Césarée.* 1:100,000. Paris.

Jaffe, S. and Fledel, H. 1990. The Climate of the Sharon. In: Grossman, D., Degani, A. and Shmueli, A., eds. *Hasharon Between Yarkon and Karmel*. Tel Aviv: 99–102 (Hebrew).

Kahneman, I., ed. 2005. [Ambroise]. *The History of the Holy War: History in Verse of the Third Crusade*. Jerusalem (Hebrew).

Karmon, Y. 1961. Geographical Influences on the Historical Routes in the Sharon Plain. *Palestine Exploration Quarterly* 93: 43–60.

Karmon, Y. 1985a. The Physiography of the Sharon and Its Influence on Urban Development. In: Biger, G. and Schiller, E., eds. *Selected Articles in the Geography of Israel* (Ariel 40–41). Jerusalem: 11–133 (Hebrew).

Karmon, Y. 1985b. Geographical Influences on the Historical Road Systems in the Sharon. In: Biger, G. and Schiller, E., eds. *Selected Articles in the Geography of Israel* (Ariel 40–41). Jerusalem: 161–170 (Hebrew).

Kedar, B.Z. 1992. The Battle of Hattin Revisited. In: Kedar, B.Z., ed. *The Horns of Hattin*. Jerusalem: 190–207.

Kedar, B.Z. 2015. King Richard's Plan for the Battle of Arsūf/Arsur, 1191. In: Halfond, G.I., ed. *The Medieval Way of War: Studies in Medieval Military History in Honor of Bernard Bachrach*. New York: 117–132.

Kershon, R. 1982. Defense on the Turks – A Study on the Eradication of the Gall Oak Forests in the Lower Sharon. *Layaran* 32 (1–4): 50–53 (Hebrew).

Khamis, E. 1996. The Metal Objects. In: Ben-Tor, A., Avissar, M. and Portugali, Y. *Yoqneʿam I: The Late Periods* (Qedem Reports 3). Jerusalem: 218–235.

Lewis, R.Y. 2013. *Archaeology of Conflicts: The Decisive Stage of the Battle of Hattin as a Case Study* (Ph.D. dissertation, University of Haifa). Haifa (Hebrew, with English Abstract).

Lewis, R.Y. 2015. Crusader Battlefields: Environmental and Archaeological Perspectives. In: Boas, A.J., ed. *The Crusader World*. Oxon and New York: 460–489.

Lewis, R.Y. 2016. Wiser Than the One Who Walks In It: How to Identify a Dirt Road? In: Shafer-Elliot, C., ed. *Five Minutes Archaeology of the Southern Levant*. Sheffield: 105–108.

Lindgrén, S. and Neuman, J. 1985. Great Historical Events that were Significantly Affected by the Weather: 7, "Protestant Wind" – "Popish Wind": The Revolution of 1688 in England. *Bulletin of American Meteorological Society* 68: 634–644.

Lyons, M.C. and Jackson, D.E.P. 1982. *Saladin: The Politics of The Holy War*. Cambridge.

Maccari-Poisson, B. 1993. Les objects et leurs function: Métaux, os et pierre. Pipionnier, F., ed. *Le Château d'Essertines, Loire* (Document d'archéologie en Rhone-Alpes). Lyon: 139–159.

Massé, H., ed. 1972. *Imād al-Dīn al-Isfahānī: Conquéte de la Syrie et de la Palestine par Saladin*. Paris.
Nicolle, D.C. 1993. *Hattin 1187, Saladin's Greatest Victory*. London.
Nicolle, D.C. 2005. *The Third Crusade 1191: Richard the Lionheart, Saladin and the struggle for Jerusalem*. Oxford.
Oman, C. 1924. *A History of the Art of War in the Middle Ages*. London.
Prawer, J. 1984. *A History of the Latin Kingdom of Jerusalem 2: The Crusades and the Second Kingdom*. Jerusalem (Hebrew).
Raphael, K. 2008. A Thousand Arrowheads from the Crusader Fortress at Vadum Iacob. In: Bar, S., ed. *In the Hill-Country and in the Shephelah, and in the Arabah (Joshua 12, 8): Studies and Researches Presented to Adam Zertal in the Thirtieth Anniversary of the Manasseh Hill-Country Survey*. Jerusalem: 259–269.
Reichsamt für Landesaufnahme 1918. *Karte von Palästina: Map of Tül Kerm 1:50,000*. Berlin.
Richards, D.S., ed. 2002. *The Rare and Excellent History of Saladin or al-Nawādir al-Sulṭāniyya wa'l-Maḥāsin al-Yūsufiyya by Bahā' al-Dīn Ibn Shaddād* (Crusade Text in Translation 7). Aldershot.
Richards, D.S., ed. 2007. *The Chronicle of Ibn al-Athīr for the Crusading Period from al-Kāmil fī'l-ta'rīkh. Part 2: The Years 541–589/1146–1193: The Age of Nur al-Din and Saladin* (Crusade Texts in Translation 15). Aldershot.
Roll, I. 1994. Survey of Roman Roads in Lower Galilee. *Excavations and Surveys in Israel* 14: 38–40 (Hebrew).
Roll, I. 1996. The Road Types in Israel during the Roman–Byzantine Period. *Ariel* 119–120: 151–156 (Hebrew).
Roll, I. 2007. The Encounter of Crusaders and Muslims at Apollonia-Arsuf as Reflected in the Archaeological Finds and Historical Sources. In: Roll, I., Tal, O. and Winter, M., eds. *The Encounter of Crusaders and Muslims in Palestine*. Tel Aviv: 9–104 (Hebrew, with English Abstract).
Roll, I. and Ayalon, E. 1989. *Apollonia and Southern Sharon: Model of Coastal City and Its Hinterland*. Tel Aviv (Hebrew, with English Abstract).
Rosen, J. 2000. Crusader-Period Horseshoes from Ḥorbat Bet Zeneta. *ʿAtiqot* 39: 107–108.
Safrai, Z., Grossman, D., Frenkel, J. and Rainey, A.F. 1990. The Roads of the Sharon. In: Grossman, D., Degani, A. and Shmueli, A., eds. *Hasharon Between Yarkon and Karmel*. Tel Aviv: 249–262 (Hebrew).
Serdon, V. 2005. *Armes du diable: Arcs arbalètes au Moyen Âge*. Rennees.
Smail, R.C. 1956. *Crusading Warfare (1097–1193)*. Cambridge.
Stubbs, W. 1864. *Chronicles and Memorials of the Reign of Richard I. 1: Chronicles and Memorials of Great Britain and Ireland during the Middle Ages*. London.
Tal, O. and Roll, I. 2011. Arsur: The Site, Settlement and Crusader Castle, and the Material Manifestation of Their Destruction. In: Tal, O., ed. *The Last Supper at Apollonia: The Final Days of the Crusader Castle in Herzliya*. Tel Aviv: [8]–[51].
Tatcher, A. 2009. Miscellaneous Finds From Strata 5–1. In: Getzov, N., Avshalom-Gorni, D., Gorin-Rosen, Y., Stern, E.J., Syon, D. and Tatcher, A. *Ḥorbat Uẓa: The 1991 Excavations II: The Late Periods* (IAA Reports 42). Jerusalem: 182–187.
Thackeray, H.St.J., ed. 1928. *Jewish War, Books V–VII*, Vol. 3 (LCL 210). Cambridge, MA.
Turenbull, S. 2010. *The Mongol Invasions of Japan, 1274 and 1281 (Campaign)*. Oxford.
Upton-Ward, J.M., trans. 1992. *The Rule of the Templars: The French Text of the Rule of the Order of the Knights Templar*. Woodbridge.
Wilkinson, T.J. 2003. *Archaeological Landscapes of the Near East*. Tucson.
Williamson, T. 1987. Early Co-axial Field Systems on the East Anglian Boulder Clays. *Proceedings of the Prehistoric Society* 53: 419–431.
Winters, H.A. 2001. *Battling the Elements: Weather and Terrain in the Conduct of War*. Baltimore.
Waisel, Y. and Agami, M. 1990. The Vegetation of the Sharon Plain. In: Grossman, D., Degani, A. and Shmueli, A., eds. *Hasharon Between Yarkon and Karmel*. Tel Aviv: 109–122 (Hebrew).

SECTION FIVE

SUMMARY AND CONCLUSIONS

CHAPTER 24

THE SITE AND ITS IMMEDIATE HINTERLAND IN LATE BYZANTINE TIMES

Oren Tal

BYZANTINE APOLLONIA/SOZOUSA

Located on the Mediterranean coast of Israel some 17 km north of Jaffa (ancient Joppa, south of Tel Aviv) and 34 km south of Caesarea, the site of Apollonia-Arsuf has been excavated almost continuously during the last 40 years. Once a modest coastal settlement, Apollonia-Arsuf became the urban center of the southern Sharon Plain (at least its coastal strip) as early as the Persian period through the Crusader period. It is mentioned in a series of classical sources from the Roman period (Flavius Josephus, ed. Marcus, *Jewish Antiquities* 13.395; Pliny the Elder, ed. Mayhoff, *Natural History* 5.69; Ptolemy, ed. Müller, *Geography* 5.15.2), which mostly relate to Judea's coastal towns.

In written sources from the Byzantine period, it is recorded twice in the anonymous *Cosmography of Ravenna* (ed. Schnetz 1940: 2.14.2 and 5.7.2; see also *Itineraria Romana*, ed. Schnetz, 1940: II, 25, 90 and 133) in a list of urban centers of *Iudaea-Palaestina*, where it appears after Caesarea and before Joppa, and again between Joppa and Caesarea in a long list of the coastal cities of Sinai and Palestine.[1] Apollonia also appears in the detailed list of twenty-five cities of that name compiled by Stephanus Byzantius under number 13 "near Joppa" (ed. Meineke 1849: 106).[2] On the other hand, Apollonia does not appear in early ecclesiastical lists. Two 19th-century scholars, Stark and Clermont-Ganneau, assumed that the reason for its absence derived from the fact that Apollonia's name had been changed to Sozousa—a common change for cities named after Apollo Sōter in Byzantine times (Stark 1852: 452, No. 5; Clermont-Ganneau 1896: 337–339). Later texts and critical editions of texts, which recount the Persian-Sassanian capture of Jerusalem, record the death of the patriarch Modestus in a town named Sozos: Sozousa in Georgian texts and Arsuf in Arabic texts (ed. Garitte 1960: 55; 1953: 38, 70; 1974: 131). Official documents of the synod of Ephesus held in 449 CE indicate that in the mid-5th century, Sozousa was a town in the Byzantine province of *Palaestina Prima* and that its Christian community was headed by a bishop. Bishops of Sozousa appear again in the records of two 6th-century ecclesiastical meetings (*Acta Conciliorum Oecomenicorum*; ed. Schwartz 1940: 80, 188; ed. Straub 1971: No. 1, 221). They may have served in the church with an inscribed mosaic floor that was uncovered in Apollonia in 1962 and 1976 (Birnbaum and Ovadiah 1990; Roll 1999: 31, 45).

1 The *Cosmography of Ravenna* was compiled soon after 700 CE from earlier sources that go back to Early Byzantine or even Roman times (see ed. Schnetz 1942; Dilke 1985: 174–176).

2 It is worth noting that in Stephanus Byzantius's text the name *Sozousa* (ed. Meineke 1849: No. 1, 596) is mentioned (see below), probably because Stephanus used sources from different periods: one from Roman times when listing *Apollonia*, and a second from Byzantine times when mentioning *Sozousa*. For Apollonia, see also ed. Billerbeck 2006: 228–229.

The importance of Sozousa in Late Byzantine Palestine (6th–7th centuries CE in archaeological terms) seems to have been enhanced by the large and affluent Samaritan community that resided in the town until the Islamic conquest, as is evident from the archaeological finds (Sections 1 and 2, above; see also Tal 2015).[3] Arsuf is also mentioned in connection with the Sassanian military campaign in the Holy Land (ed. Garitte 1960: 4, 42; 1974: 75, 104; see also Peeters 1923–1924: 13; Schick 1995: 20–25). As there is no evidence of destruction, it may be assumed that the town surrendered peacefully to its Persian-Sassanian conquerors (Schick 1995: 250; for the archaeological evidence cf. Tal and Taxel 2012: 499–501; Tal and Bijovsky 2017; and below). The *Acta Anastasii Persae* relate that the escort conveying the relics of the Christian martyr Anastasius the Persian from Caesarea to Jerusalem in 631—soon after the Persians evacuated Palestine—marched via Sozousa. This indicates that the name Sozousa continued to be used for Apollonia-Arsuf until the Islamic conquest (ed. Flusin 1992: 1: 105; 2: 339).

BYZANTINE OCCUPATION REMAINS

Extensive excavations at Apollonia-Arsuf over the last 27 seasons (1977–2018) have uncovered numerous architectural remains from the Byzantine period. The site extended over an unwalled area of some 28 hectares—the largest area in its history of occupation. Among the architectural remains are a church (Birnbaum and Ovadiah 1990), possibly a Samaritan synagogue (Tal 2015) and industrial quarters with winepresses (Chapter 10; Tal 2009), oil presses, plastered pools, and raw glass furnaces (Chapters 9, 10; Tal, Jackson-Tal and Freestone 2004; Freestone, Jackson-Tal and Tal 2008; see also Roll 1999: 7–10). Excavations at the site's Byzantine-period agricultural and industrial hinterland on the eastern outskirts revealed several additional architectural remains—winepresses, field towers, tombs (mostly of earlier periods) and other installations—as the area was used mainly for growing crops. Refuse pits in the area were utilized for the disposal of waste from the settlement, and their contents served as fertilizer to enrich the soil in the nearby fields (above Chapters 1–6).

There is every reason to believe that the medieval walled town of Arsuf occupied the core site of the Byzantine town of Sozousa. Deposition of coin finds (as well as hoards) are helpful when reconstructing site formation in the transition between the Roman and Byzantine periods and the Byzantine and Early Islamic periods. The geographical distribution of Byzantine coins in excavated areas inside and outside the medieval walled town is very useful in this respect (Fig. 1.2). While areas of excavations inside the walled town show a continuity in the use of Roman and Byzantine coins (e.g., Areas E and R) or alternatively, show predominance for Byzantine and later coins (e.g., Areas T, U and W), those areas located outside the walled town offer a different picture.[4]

The coins unearthed in both Area M (located on the south outside the walled medieval town) and Area O (located on the north outside the walled medieval town), suggest a 4th-century CE expansion of the site. Most coins found in the Byzantine hoard recovered from Area M (above Chapter 18) are dated to the second half of the 4th century CE,[5] while the remainder are dated to the 5th, 6th and early 7th centuries CE.[6]

3 It should be emphasized, however, that Abū L-Fatḥ reports Samaritan synagogues in villages between Zaytā (north of Ṭūl Karem) and Arsuf, but only a Dosithean (not Samaritan) "meeting place" in Arsuf in the early 9th century, long after the Islamic conquest (cf. Levy-Rubin 2002: 69–70).

4 During 27 seasons of excavations (since 1977) approximately 1,250 coins were recovered from the site. To these, approximately 900 coins may be added from excavations carried out in 2012–2013 just to the east of the Apollonia National Park (above Chapter 18).

5 Excavations in Area M yielded 42 coins altogether. The 11 4th CE coins in the hoard are the earliest coin finds discovered in the area.

6 Of the 36 identifiable coins found in Area M, only one postdates the recorded Persian-Sasanian occupation of 614 CE—a coin that was minted in Alexandria and is attributed to the later years of Heraclius (632–641 CE).

Among the 15 identifiable coins (out of a total of 34) from Area O, the earliest coin is a 3rd century CE type, followed by two 4th century CE types.[7]

While Area K (in the east) and Area N (in the southeast) yielded few coins, the recently excavated Area CC in the site's immediate eastern hinterland lends support to this reconstruction. Large-scale excavations in this area yielded over 800 bronze (and one gold) coins. Over 260 identifiable coins were read from Area CC, and the majority of the coins (over 95%) are dated to within the 4th–6th centuries CE, suggesting that use of the area by the site's inhabitants occurred sometime during these centuries. Other recovered finds from all these areas, such as fragments of pottery and glass vessels, support the chronological evidence, namely occupation from the 4th century CE.

As to the transition from the Byzantine and Early Islamic periods, it may be noted that there is ample evidence for a reduction in the size of Sozousa in the 7th century, as evidenced from all excavation areas outside the medieval fortification line—Areas M, O, K and N, as well as Area CC. Excavations in these areas, located within the assumed limits of the Byzantine period town (or right outside them), included large Late Byzantine period refuse pits (centralized town dumps, especially in Areas M, N and CC), providing evidence for the limits of the Late Byzantine town, whose area can be estimated at 28 hectares (as stated above).

Pottery, glass and coins found in these dumps suggest that although no evidence of visible destruction by Persian-Sasanian conquerors in 614 CE is attested in Sozousa, many of its inhabitants abandoned the site (or found themselves victims of the invasion). This can be deduced from the fact that very few of the coins discovered in these areas postdate this event, and none of the pottery and glass finds can contradict a date of abandonment in the early 7th century CE.

BYZANTINE IMMEDIATE HINTERLAND

Before elaborating on the immediate hinterland of the site, it should be borne in mind that the site periphery was surveyed and excavated quite often due to development works in one of modern Israel's intensively developed regions—the central Coastal Plain. Earlier surveys were largely assembled in the Map of Herzliyya which was published in the framework of the Archaeological Survey of Israel (Gophna and Ayalon 1998: 13*).[8] Based on this publication, it is known that the Byzantine settlement flourished during the Byzantine period at some 40 sites (including the mother settlement of Apollonia/Sozousa and some necropoleis; see Tal 1995; Agmon 2017), which were documented by means of surveys and excavations in the less than 10 km^2 survey map of Herzliyya in which Apollonia/Sozousa forms the northwesternmost site. These sites were distributed throughout the map area—on the coast, on the *kurkar* (fossilized dune sandstone) ridges, in the area of drained marshland and on the *ḥamra* (red loam) hillocks.[9] These site remains are comprised of winepresses, oil presses, potter's kilns and raw glass furnaces which attests to the economy of the population. The intensity of the Byzantine settlement at the time probably necessitated deforestation and preparation of land tracts for agricultural cultivation, including the marshlands that are known in the region. Indeed, the "Herzliyya Marsh" was drained in an impressive quarrying and construction operation, consisting of a 200 m long tunnel that drained the water to the sea (Gophna and Ayalon 1998: Site 37).

7 The 3rd century CE type is a coin dated to the reign of Gallienus (260–268 CE; Chapter 18: No. 15), while the two 4th century types are coins dated to 305–311, 364–378 CE respectively (Chapter 18: Nos. 18, 60). The remainder are almost exclusively dated to the 6th century CE. Three tentatively postdate 614 CE based on stylistic considerations: two coins that may be assigned to 624/5 CE and 630–641 CE respectively (Chapter 18: Nos. 350–352), and another, as in Area M, assigned to the later years of Heraclius (630–641 CE; Chapter 18: No. 353).

8 See online version in: http://survey.antiquities.org.il/index_Eng.html#/MapSurvey/21.

9 For the geology of the region, see Gophna and Ayalon 1998: 8*–9*; and, more specifically, Tal 1999.

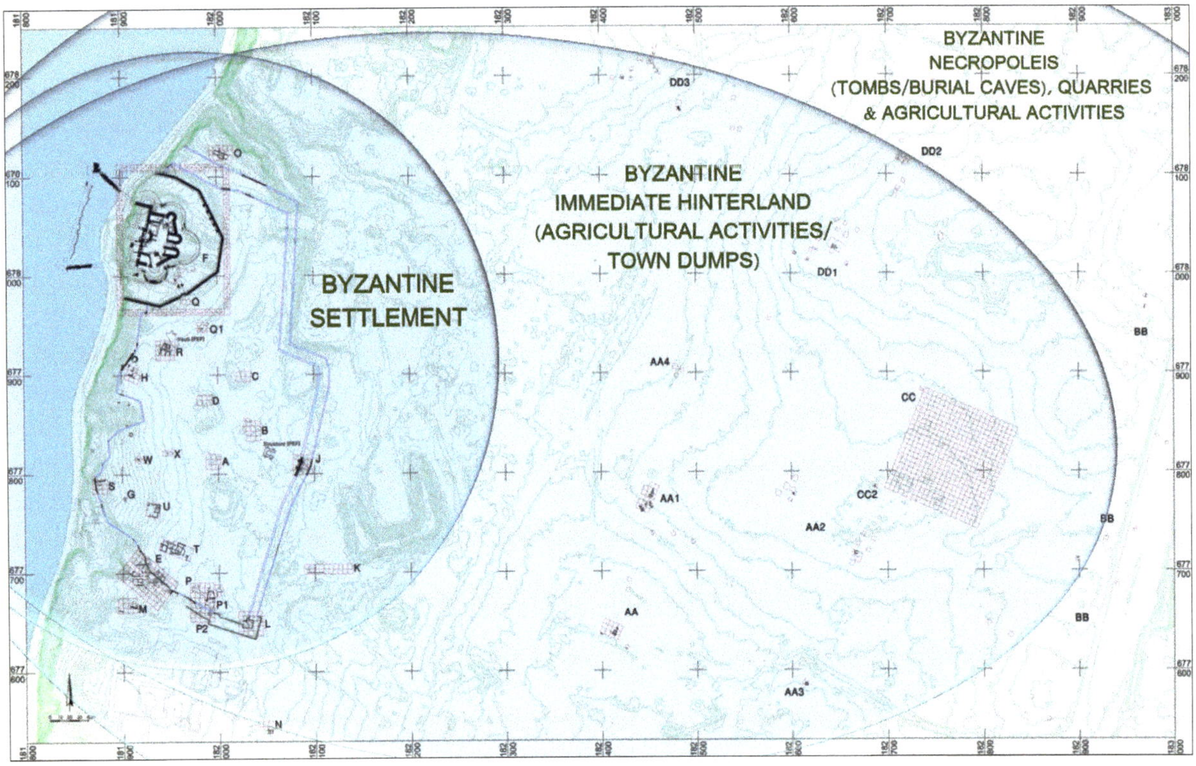

Fig. 24.1: Apollonia-Arsuf, general site plan divided by functional "belts."

The large scale excavations at the Byzantine site, especially in its immediate hinterland, enabled a higher resolution of its physical division into functional "belts" (Fig. 24.1):

1. The Byzantine inhabited settlement, adjacent to the seacoast;
2. The Byzantine immediate hinterland, where agricultural activities in the form of field towers and winepresses were uncovered and disposal activities of human and industrial waste were unearthed in the form of town dumps, on the edges of the inhabited eastern, northern and southern settlement;
3. The Byzantine period necropoleis to the east (tombs and burial caves) where agricultural and other activities (such as quarrying building materials; Tal 1996) also took place (cf. Gophna and Ayalon 1998).

This suggested functional division is based on the results of many excavations by either Tel Aviv University or the Israel Antiquities Authority in the course of the last four decades. The fact that Byzantine period activity was the most dominant at the site and its hinterland throughout its history encourages investigation into the physical division far beyond its inhabited perimeters.

Elsewhere we have discussed the rural nature of the area to the south of Apollonia-Arsuf on both sides of the Yarqon estuary (Tal and Taxel 2010; 2015). We tried to show that the rural area between Joppa and Apollonia-Arsuf (i.e., the central Coastal Plain or southern Sharon) was heavily occupied by Samaritans (and to a lesser extent Christians) during the Late Roman and Byzantine periods. This process probably started sometime after the Second Jewish Revolt and, as the archaeological evidence indicates, accelerated during the 3rd and 4th centuries CE, at a time when quite a few Jewish settlements that had been abandoned in either the late 1st or early 2nd century CE were re-occupied by Samaritans in the forms of villages and farms. There were also several Samaritan settlements that had not been previously occupied by Jews. All these Samaritan settlements continued to exist well into the Early Islamic period (Roll and Ayalon 1989: 137–183, 231). The local settlement pattern, as reflected in the better-known excavated and/or surveyed sites in this region, is composed of small- to medium-sized villages and farms. Many of these settlements existed in their "Byzantine" form until the 8th century CE, when a gradual decrease in their size and population led to near total abandonment in centuries to follow. This change can be related to the increased insecurity and sharp deterioration in the economic conditions of the Samaritans (as well as of the rest of the *dhimmīs* [non-Muslims]). This process started with the ʿAbbasid period, in the second half of the 8th century, by means of persecution by the contemporary caliphs and their governors, resulting in local revolts and disasters. Furthermore, at that time, the Muslim authorities prohibited the drinking of wine, which certainly caused a major economic decline in many settlements where viticulture was a main source of livelihood. Consequently, the number of rural Samaritan settlements was substantially reduced, and most of the Samaritans were either concentrated in towns and cities or settled in villages in the mountainous region of Samaria (see, in this respect, Levy-Rubin 2002: 29–31; Schur 2002).[10] The evidence from the winepress complex discovered in Apollonia-Arsuf (esp. in Areas AA1 and O; Chapters 3, 10) shows that a somewhat similar process occurred approximately two centuries earlier. The effects of the persecutions of the Samaritans by Justinian are not totally clear in the archaeological record. However, it is possible that the Samaritan viticulture industry was abandoned in the town of Sozousa from this date on and was now concentrated in the rural Samaritan settlements of the region.

Another aspect of the economic life of Byzantine Sozousa relates to the production of raw glass. While evaluating the evidence at hand, it has been suggested in the past that it seems likely that the Church, as the center of political and social power in Late Byzantine Sozousa, may have played an important role in the production and circulation of the raw glass produced at the site. There is, however, no direct evidence for such an involvement except for pieces of information on the economic involvement of the Church (as an administrative body) in the daily life of the Byzantine world (Jones 1964: 830–834, and esp. 894–910). Private entrepreneurship seems less likely given the massive scale of production at the site.

The impact of this production at the site is apparent in the following periods of its occupation (and even in the later phases of the Byzantine occupation). Raw glass refuse is used as building material in the Early Islamic and the Crusader period building remains at the site—with the Crusader castle (Area F) being the most significant building project that used raw glass refuse in its construction.

REFERENCES

Agmon, Y. 2017. Kefar Shemaryahu. *Ḥadashot Arkheologiyot—Excavations and Surveys in Israel* 129. http://www.hadashot-esi.org.il/Report_Detail_Eng.aspx?id=25349&mag_id=125.

Billerbeck, M., ed. 2006. *Stephani Byzantii Ethnica* 1. Berlin.

Birnbaum, R. and Ovadiah, A. 1990. A Greek Inscription from the Early Byzantine Church at Apollonia. *Israel Exploration Journal* 40: 182–191.

Clermont-Ganneau, C. 1896. *Archaeological Researches in Palestine during the Years 1873–1874,* 2. London.

Dilke, O.A.W. 1985. *Greek and Roman Maps (Aspects of Greek and Roman Life)*. London.

Flusin, B., ed. 1992. *Saint Anastase le Perse et l'histoire de la Palestine au début du VIIe siècle:* 1 and 2. Paris.

Freestone, I.C., Jackson-Tal, R.E. and Tal, O. 2008. Raw Glass and the Production of Glass Vessels at Late Byzantine Apollonia-Arsuf, Israel. *Journal of Glass Studies* 50: 67–80.

Garitte, G., ed. 1953. *Expugnationis Hierosolymae A.D. 614* (Corpus Scriptorum Christianorum Orientaium 341, Scriptores Arabici 27). Louvain.

Garitte, G., ed. 1960. *La prise de Jérusalem par les Perses en 614* (Corpus Scriptorum Christianorum Orientaium 203, Scriptores Iberici 12). Louvain.

10 The chronicle of Abū l-Fatḥ (dated to 1355 CE, but referring to the early 7th to early 10th centuries) mentions many Samaritan villages, most of which are identified with places in the northern and central Samaria hills, though a few others—at least some of which were also Samaritan settlements—are yet unidentified (Levy-Rubin 2002: 183–186, Geographical Appendix).

Garitte, G., ed. 1974. *Expugnationis Hierosolymae A.D. 614* (Corpus Scriptorum Christianorum Orientaium 348, Scriptores Arabici 29). Louvain.

Gophna, R. and Ayalon, E. 1998. *Archaeological Survey of Israel: Map of Herzliyya (69)*. Jerusalem.

Jones, A.H.M. 1964. *The Later Roman Empire 284–602: A Social, Economic, and Administrative Survey* 1–2. Oxford.

Levy-Rubin, M. 2002. *The* Continuatio *of the Samaritan Chronicle of Abū L-Fatḥ Al-Sāmirī Al-Danafī* (Studies in Late Antiquity and Early Islam 10). Princeton.

Marcus, R., ed. 1943. *Jewish Antiquities, Books XII–XIII*, Vol. 5 (LCL 365). Cambridge, MA.

Mayhoff, C., ed. 1906. *Plini Secundi Naturalis Historiae* 1. Leipzig.

Meineke, A., ed. 1849. *Stephani Byzantii Ethnicorum quae supersunt.* Berlin.

Müller, C., ed. 1901. *Claudii Ptolemaei Geographia* 2 (revised ed. by C.T. Fischer). Paris.

Peeters, P. 1923–1924. La prise de Jérusalem par les Perses. *Mélanges de l'Université Saint Joseph de Beyrouth* 9: 1–42.

Roll, I. 1999. Introduction: History of the Site, Its Research and Excavations. In: Roll, I. and Tal, O. *Apollonia-Arsuf: Final Report of the Excavations, Volume 1: The Persian and Hellenistic Periods (with Appendices on the Chalcolithic and Iron Age II Remains).* (Monograph Series of the Institute of Archaeology 16). Tel Aviv: 1–62.

Roll, I. and Ayalon, E. 1989. *Apollonia and Southern Sharon: Model of a Coastal City and Its Hinterland.* Tel Aviv (Hebrew).

Schick, R. 1995. *The Christian Communities of Palestine from Byzantine to Islamic Rule: A Historical and Archaeological Study*. Princeton.

Schnetz, L., ed. 1940. *Cosmography of Ravenna. Itineraria Romana 2: Ravennatis anonymi cosmographia et Guidonis geographica.* Leipzig.

Schnetz, J. 1942. Untersuchungen über die Quellen der Cosmographie des anonymen Geographen von Ravenna. In: *Sitzungsberichte der Bayerischen Akademie der Wissenschaften, Philosophisch-Historische Abteilung* 6: 1–87.

Schur, N. 2002. Persecutions of Samaritans by the Abbasids and the Disappearance of the Samaritan Rural Population. In: Stern, E. and Eshel, H., eds. *The Samaritans*. Jerusalem: 587–590 (Hebrew).

Schwartz, E., ed. 1940. *Acta Conciliorum Oecomenicorum* 3. Berlin.

Stark, K.B. 1852. *Gaza und die philistäische Küste*. Jena.

Straub, J., ed. 1971. *Acta Conciliorum Oecomenicorum* 4. Berlin.

Tal, O. 1995. Roman–Byzantine Cemeteries and Tombs around Apollonia. *Tel Aviv* 22: 107–120.

Tal, O. 1996. A Salvage Excavation at Herzliya Beth. *Tel Aviv* 23: 235–243.

Tal, O. 1999. The Natural Environment. In: Roll, I. and Tal, O. *Apollonia-Arsuf: Final Report of the Excavations, Volume 1: The Persian and Hellenistic Periods (with Appendices on the Chalcolithic and Iron Age II Remains).* (Monograph Series of the Institute of Archaeology 16). Tel Aviv: 76–82.

Tal, O. 2009. A Winepress at Apollonia-Arsuf: More Evidence on the Samaritan Presence in Roman–Byzantine Southern Sharon. *Liber Annuus* 59: 319–342.

Tal, O. 2015. A Bilingual Greek-Samaritan Inscription from Apollonia-Arsuf/Sozousa: Yet More Evidence of the Use of εἷς θεὸς μόνος Formula Inscriptions among the Samaritans. *Zeitschrift für Papyrologie und Epigraphik* 194: 169–175.

Tal, O. and Bijovsky, G. 2017. A Hoard of Fourth–Fifth Century CE Copper Coins from Sozousa. *Israel Numismatic Research* 12: 147–158.

Tal, O., Jackson-Tal, R.E. and Freestone, I.C. 2004. New Evidence of the Production of Raw Glass at Late Byzantine Apollonia-Arsuf, Israel. *Journal of Glass Studies* 46: 51–66.

Tal, O. and Taxel, I. 2010. A Reappraisal of the Archaeological Findings at Tel Ḥashash: On the Archaeology of the Yarqon Estuary from Classical Times to Late Antiquity. *Palestine Exploration Quarterly* 142: 95–126.

Tal, O. and Taxel, I. 2012. Socio-Political and Economic Aspects of Refuse Disposal in Late Byzantine and Early Islamic Palestine. In: Matthews, R., Curtis, J., eds. *Proceedings of the 7th International Congress on the Archaeology of the Ancient Near East, 12th–16th April 2010, the British Museum and UCL, London 1: Mega-cities and Mega-sites: The Archaeology of Consumption and Disposal, Landscape, Transport and Communication.* Wiesbaden: 497–518.

Tal, O. and Taxel, I. 2015. *Samaritan Cemeteries and Tombs in the Central Coastal Plain: Archaeology and History of the Samaritan Settlement outside Samaria (ca. 300–700 CE)* (Ägypten und Altes Testament 82). Münster.

LIST OF LOCI

Tamar Harpak, Oren Tal and Hagi Yohanan

Areas AA–DD

Area	*Locus*	*Old Reference*	*Square*	*Height (Opened)*	*Height (Closed)*	*Associated Loci/ Features*	*Description*	*Permit No.*
AA	100	General		18.65			Surface	A-6549/12
AA	101	F202	K5	18.51	17.3	133	Surface	A-6549/12
AA	102	F203	G6	18.65	17.14	112	Surface	A-6549/12
AA	103	F40		18.33	18.33	120	Surface	A-6549/12
AA	104	F201	E4	18.65	17.47	111	Surface	A-6549/12
AA	105	F204	E6	17.72	17.29	110	Surface	A-6549/12
AA	106	F39	F8	20	17.81	115	Surface	A-6549/12
AA	107	F38		17.72	17.44	116	Surface	A-6549/12
AA	108	F37		17.87	17.64	118	Surface	A-6549/12
AA	109	F41	E8	20	18.08	114	Surface	A-6549/12
AA	110	F204	E6	18.91	17.74	105, 138	Fill	A-6549/12
AA	111	F201	E4	17.47	17.15	104, 117, 131	Fill	A-6549/12
AA	112	F203	G6	17.14	16.92	102, 124	Fill	A-6549/12
AA	113	F204	E6	17.61	17.29	105, 119	Collapse	A-6549/12
AA	114	F41	E8	18.08	16	109, 370	Fill	A-6549/12
AA	115	F39	F8	17.81	16.99	106, 129	Fill	A-6549/12
AA	116	F38		17.44	17.18	107, 126	Fill	A-6549/12
AA	117	F201	E4	17.17	16.03	111, 104	Fill	A-6549/12
AA	118	F37		17.64	17.12	108, 128	Fill	A-6549/12
AA	119	F204	E6	17.29	16.45	113	Fill	A-6549/12
AA	120	F40		18.13	16.94	103, 130	Surface	A-6549/12
AA	121	F203	G6	17.06	16.03	123	Fill	A-6549/12
AA	122	F203	G6	17.06	16.03	123	Fill	A-6549/12
AA	123	F203	G6	17.06	16.03	121, 122, 374	wall	A-6549/12
AA	124	F203	G6	17.39	16.93	112	Fill	A-6549/12
AA	125	F202	K5	17.16	17	135	Fallen stones	A-6549/12
AA	126	F203	G6	17.58	17.18	116, 132	Fallen stones	A-6549/12
AA	127	F201	E4	17.96	17.05	140	Installation	A-6549/12
AA	128	F37		17.12	16.82	128	Fill	A-6549/12
AA	129	F39	F8	16.99	16.49	115, 136	Fill	A-6549/12
AA	130	F40		18.03	17.64	120, 157	Fill	A-6549/12
AA	131	F201	E4	17.15	16.92	145	Fill	A-6549/12
AA	132	F38		17.18	16.87	126	Fill	A-6549/12

Area	*Locus*	*Old Reference*	*Square*	*Height (Opened)*	*Height (Closed)*	*Associated Loci/ Features*	*Description*	*Permit No.*
AA	133	F202	K5	16.93	16.57	101, 142, 143	Fill	A-6549/12
AA	134	F203	G6	17.18	16.37	123	Fill	A-6549/12
AA	135	F203	G6	17	16.42	125	Fill	A-6549/12
AA	136	F39	F8	16.49	16.06	129	Fill	A-6549/12
AA	137	F41	E8	16.99	16.21	109, 370	Fill	A-6549/12
AA	138	F204	E6	16.45	15.93	119	Fill	A-6549/12
AA	139	F203	G6	16.78	16.32		Wall	A-6549/12
AA	140	F201	E4	17.05	16.8		Fill	A-6549/12
AA	141	F40		16.94	16.78	103	Surface	A-6549/12
AA	142	F202	K5	16.57	16.68	133, 143	Section/Fill	A-6549/12
AA	143	F202	K5	16.57	16.44	142	Installation	A-6549/12
AA	144	F202	K5	16.93	16.5	133	Fallen stones	A-6549/12
AA	145	F201	E4				Removal of fallen stones	A-6549/12
AA	146	F201	E4	17.18	16.79	111	Fill	A-6549/12
AA	147	F203	G6	16.42	16.25	135, 123	Fill	A-6549/12
AA	148	F201	E4	17.02	16.77	127	Wall	A-6549/12
AA	149	F201	E4	16.93	16.7	127	Wall	A-6549/12
AA	150	F201	E4	17.96	17.14	127, 154	Removal of fallen stones	A-6549/12
AA	151	F203	G6	16.35	16.25	139, 125	Pebbles floor	A-6549/12
AA	152	F201	E4	17.7	17.14	127	Fill	A-6549/12
AA	153	F203	G6	16.25		151	Fill	A-6549/12
AA	154	F201	E4	17.14	16.95	153	Fill	A-6549/12
AA	155	F201	E4	17.5	16.71	127	Wall	A-6549/12
AA	156	F201	E4	16.79	16.48	155	Section	A-6549/12
AA	157	F40		16.61		130, 158	Fill	A-6549/12
AA	158	F40		16.75	16.61	157	Fill	A-6549/12
AA	159	F40					Removal of fallen stones	A-6549/12
AA	370	F41	E8	16.21	15.73	137	Fill	A-6549/12
AA	371	F203	G6	16.3	15.8	153	Fill	A-6549/12
AA	372	F40		18.03	17.1	130, 372	Section	A-6549/12
AA	373	F40		17.64	17.1	372	Fill	A-6549/12
AA	374	F203		16.5	16	123	Wall	A-6549/12
AA	375	F205	H6	16.4	16		Fill/Collapse	A-6549/12
AA	10000		General				Surface	A-6825/13
AA	10001		F7	18.2	18.1		Surface	A-6825/13
AA	10002		G7	18.2	17.76	10035	Surface	A-6825/13
AA	10003		F6	18.2	18.15	10011	Surface	A-6825/13
AA	10004		G6	18.2	18.06	10016	Surface	A-6825/13
AA	10005		G5	18.2	18.06	10017	Surface	A-6825/13
AA	10006		E6	18.2	18.04	10013	Surface	A-6825/13
AA	10007		F5	18.2	18.11	10019	Surface	A-6825/13

Area	*Locus*	*Old Reference*	*Square*	*Height (Opened)*	*Height (Closed)*	*Associated Loci/ Features*	*Description*	*Permit No.*
AA	10008		E7	18.27	18.08	10012	Surface	A-6825/13
AA	10009		E5	18.25	18.11	10020	Surface	A-6825/13
AA	10010		D6	18.27	18.1		Surface	A-6825/13
AA	10011		F6	17.56	17.31	10003	Fill	A-6825/13
AA	10012		E7	18.08	17.76	10008	Fill	A-6825/13
AA	10013		E6	18.04	17.7	10006	Fill	A-6825/13
AA	10014		E6	18.04	17.68	10006	Fill	A-6825/13
AA	10015		E7	17.94	17.71	10012	Fill	A-6825/13
AA	10016		G6	18.06	17.5	10004	Fill	A-6825/13
AA	10017		G5	17.13	16.98	10005	Fill	A-6825/13
AA	10018		G6	17.54	16.92	10016	Fill	A-6825/13
AA	10019		F5	17.32	17.05	10007	Surface	A-6825/13
AA	10020		E5	17.64	17.33	10009	Surface	A-6825/13
AA	10021		E4	17.55	16.76	10035	Surface	A-6825/13
AA	10022		G4	17.82	16.65		Surface	A-6825/13
AA	10023		F4	17.25	16.88	10036	Surface	A-6825/13
AA	10024		E6	17.78	17.4		Surface	A-6825/13
AA	10025		E7	17.71	17.63	10008	Surface	A-6825/13
AA	10026		G5	16.98	16.63	10005	Fill	A-6825/13
AA	10027		G6	16.92	16.36	10026	Fill	A-6825/13
AA	10028		H6	16.58	17.19	10050	Surface	A-6825/13
AA	10029		H5	17.35	16.73	10042	Surface	A-6825/13
AA	10030		H4	17.52	16.77		Surface	A-6825/13
AA	10031		H4	17.52	16.77		Surface	A-6825/13
AA	10032		K4	17.43	16.95	10052	Fill	A-6825/13
AA	10033		E5	17.33	16.75	10020	Fill	A-6825/13
AA	10034		F5	17.05	16.59	10019	Fill	A-6825/13
AA	10035		F6	17.71	16.42	10003	Surface	A-6825/13
AA	10036		E4	16.76	16.37	10021, 10037	Fill	A-6825/13
AA	10037		F4	16.88	16.36	10023	Fill	A-6825/13
AA	10038		E4	17.5	16.42	10043	Fill	A-6825/13
AA	10039		G5	16.63	15.9	10026	Fill	A-6825/13
AA	10040		G5	17.07	16.7	10026	Fill	A-6825/13
AA	10041		F-5/6	17.6	17.03	10019	Fill	A-6825/13
AA	10042		G5	17.07	16.14	10026	Wall	A-6825/13
AA	10043		H5	16.73	16.41	10029, 10043	Fill	A-6825/13
AA	10044		E4	16.76	16.44	10037,	Fill	A-6825/13
AA	10045		E4	16.29	16.29	10037	Fill	A-6825/13
AA	10046		G5	15.9	15.8	10041	Fill	A-6825/13
AA	10047		F6	17.42	16.92	10040	Fill	A-6825/13
AA	10048		G5/6	18.06	16.63	10039	Fill	A-6825/13
AA	10049		E4	17.16	19.09	155	Fill	A-6825/13
AA	10050		G7	16.9	16.35	10055	Surface	A-6825/13

Area	Locus	Old Reference	Square	Height (Opened)	Height (Closed)	Associated Loci/ Features	Description	Permit No.
AA	10051		H6	17.19	16.95	10028	Fill	A-6825/13
AA	10052		K4	16.95	16.59	10031	Fill	A-6825/13
AA	10053		F6	16.92	16.55	10046	Fill	A-6825/13
AA	10054		H6	17.19	16.73	10050	Fill	A-6825/13
AA	10055		G7	16.35	15.9	10049, 10002	Fill	A-6825/13
AA	10056		G5	17.19	16.84	123	Fallen stones	A-6825/13
AA	10057		G5	17	16.7	139	Fallen stones	A-6825/13
AA	10058		G5	16.97	16.71	123	Fallen stones	A-6825/13
AA	10059		G5	17.13	16.92	123, 139	Fallen stones	A-6825/13
AA	10060		H6	16.73	16.42	10050	Fill	A-6825/13
AA	10061		G5	16.5	15.97	139	Fill	A-6825/13
AA	10062		H5/6	16.68	16.68	10029	Fill	A-6825/13
AA	10063		H5/6	6.331	16.33	10029	Fill	A-6825/13
AA	10064		H5	16.33	16.33	10042	Fill	A-6825/13
AA	10065		G5	16.01	16.01	139	Fill	A-6825/13
AA	10066		H5	16.25	16.25	10064	Fill	A-6825/13
AA	10067		K4	16.23	16.23	10052	Fill	A-6825/13
AA	10068		G-H5/6	17.09	16.62		Fill	A-6825/13
AA	10069		G-H5/6	16.62	16.02	139	Fill	A-6825/13
AA	10070		K4	16.59	16.18	10052, 10090	Fill	A-6825/13
AA	10071		H5/6	16.77	16.42	10075	Fallen stones	A-6825/13
AA	10072		G-H5/6	16.96	16	10041, 139	Wall	A-6825/13
AA	10073		G6	16.35	16.14	10071	Fill	A-6825/13
AA	10074		G6	16.35	16.14	139	Wall	A-6825/13
AA	10075		H5Q6	16.77	16.42	10066	Fallen stones	A-6825/13
AA	10076		G-H/6	17.09	16.27	10072	Fill	A-6825/13
AA	10077		H5/6	16.42	15.93	10075	Fill	A-6825/13
AA	10078		G6	16.82	16.1	10051	Fill	A-6825/13
AA	10079		H5/6	16.96	16	10077	Fill	A-6825/13
AA	10080		H6	16.42	16.1	10075	Fill	A-6825/13
AA	10081		G5	17.1	16.98		Wall	A-6825/13
AA	10082		H6	16.05	15.92		Wall	A-6825/13
AA	10083		H5	17.01	16.95	10072	Fill	A-6825/13
AA	10084		G5	17.2	16.96	10041, 139	Fill	A-6825/13
AA	10085		G5	16.35	16.16	10041	Fill	A-6825/13
AA	10086		G6	16.35	16.16	10032	Wall	A-6825/13
AA	10087		H5	16.62	15.99	10041	Fill	A-6825/13
AA	10088		HG/6	17.19	15.8		Fill	A-6825/13
AA	10089		E4				Threshold	A-6825/13
AA	10090		K4	16.23	15.9	10052	Wall	A-6825/13
AA	10091	F206/ F203	G-H5/6				Field tower	A-6825/13
AA1	201	General					Surface	A-6549/12
AA1	202	34		19.57	19.42		Surface	A-6549/12

Area	*Locus*	*Old Reference*	*Square*	*Height (Opened)*	*Height (Closed)*	*Associated Loci/ Features*	*Description*	*Permit No.*
AA1	203	35		20.36	19.52	232, 238	Surface	A-6549/12
AA1	204	36		20.4	19.19	220	Surface	A-6549/12
AA1	205	87	E4	20.36	19.91	250	Surface	A-6549/12
AA1	206	88	E5	20.58	20.41	209	Surface	A-6549/12
AA1	207	89	E6	20.76	20.4	224, 225	Surface	A-6549/12
AA1	208	90	E7	21.3	21.05		Surface	A-6549/12
AA1	209	88	E4	20.38	20.28	206, 211, 212-3	Floor	A-6549/12
AA1	210	34		19.42	19.26		Wall	A-6549/12
AA1	211	88	E4	20.44	19.9	209	Fallen stones	A-6549/12
AA1	212	88	E5	20.41	19.39	209	Fill	A-6549/12
AA1	213	88	E5	20.38	19.8	209	Fill	A-6549/12
AA1	214	90	E8	21.05	20.16	208	Winepress vat (circular)	A-6549/12
AA1	215	90	D7/E7	20.96	19.8	208	Winepress vat (square-shaped)	A-6549/12
AA1	216	90	D7/E7	20.96	19.8	215	Fill	A-6549/12
AA1	217	34		19.42	18.89	210	Fill	A-6549/12
AA1	218	34		19.42	18.2	210	Fill	A-6549/12
AA1	219	34		19.42	19	210	Fill	A-6549/12
AA1	220	36		19.19	19.07	204	Fill	A-6549/12
AA1	221	36		19.19	19.07	220	Section/Fill	A-6549/12
AA1	222	90	E7	20.99	19.84	208	Winepress vat (square-shaped)	A-6549/12
AA1	223	90	E7	20.99	19.84	222	Fill	A-6549/12
AA1	224	89	E5	20.4	19.88	226	Installation	A-6549/12
AA1	225	89	E6	20.4	20.07	207	Fill	A-6549/12
AA1	226	89	E6	20.59	19.59	224	Fill	A-6549/12
AA1	227	90+	E8	21.15	20.86	214	Fill	A-6549/12
AA1	228	88	E4	20.74	20.44	209	Wall	A-6549/12
AA1	229	90	E7	20.94	19.57	222	Fill	A-6549/12
AA1	230	89/90	E6/E7	21	20.26		Fill	A-6549/12
AA1	231	90	E7	20.3	20.26	215, 222	Fill	A-6549/12
AA1	232	35		19.52	19.02	203, 239	Fill	A-6549/12
AA1	233	89	E6	20.46	20.13	234	Fallen stones	A-6549/12
AA1	234	89	E6	20.47	20.13	235	Installation	A-6549/12
AA1	235	89	E6	20.02	19.88	224	Fill	A-6549/12
AA1	236	90	E7	20.19	19.84	222	Fill	A-6549/12
AA1	237	89	E6	20.47	20.13	234	Fill	A-6549/12
AA1	238	35		19.02	18.83	202, 239	Fill	A-6549/12
AA1	239	35		18.83	18.77		Fill	A-6549/12
AA1	240	90	E7	19.84	19.84	222	Mosaic floor	A-6549/12
AA1	241	89	E6	20.13	20.13	234	Mosaic floor	A-6549/12
AA1	242	89	E6	19.88	19.88	224	Plaster floor	A-6549/12
AA1	243	87	E4	19.91	19.49	205, 250	Fill	A-6549/12

Area	*Locus*	*Old Reference*	*Square*	*Height (Opened)*	*Height (Closed)*	*Associated Loci/ Features*	*Description*	*Permit No.*
AA1	244	89	E6	20.13	19.97	234	Fill	A-6549/12
AA1	245	90	E3	20.89	20.75		Fallen stones	A-6549/12
AA1	246	90	E7	19.84	19.39	222	Fill	A-6549/12
AA1	247	90	E7	20.89	20.75		Installation	A-6549/12
AA1	248	90	E7	20.75	20.76	247	Mosaic floor	A-6549/12
AA1	249	87/88	E4/E5	20.58	19.82		Fill	A-6549/12
AA1	250	87	E4	19.82	19.75	205, 243	Pebbles stones	A-6549/12
AA1	251	89	E6	20.44	20.35	225	Pebbles stones	A-6549/12
AA1	252	85		20.57	19.66	267	Surface	A-6549/12
AA1	253	86	E6	20.57	19.77	265	Surface	A-6549/12
AA1	254	90+	E8	21.1	20.3	214	Fill	A-6549/12
AA1	255	88	E5	20.24	19.8		Fill	A-6549/12
AA1	256	89	E6	20.35	20.19		Installation	A-6549/12
AA1	257	88	E5	20.24	20.06	209	Fill	A-6549/12
AA1	258	90	E7	20.75	20.65	227	Fill	A-6549/12
AA1	259	90+	E8	20.65	20.16	214	Fill	A-6549/12
AA1	260	90+	E8	20.16	20.16	214	Mosaic floor	A-6549/12
AA1	261	90	D7/E7	19.8	19.8	215	Mosaic floor	A-6549/12
AA1	262	90+	E8	19.8	19.67	214	Fill	A-6549/12
AA1	263	90+	E8	19.62	19.62	214	Mosaic floor	A-6549/12
AA1	264	90	D7/E7	19.8	19.6	215	Fill	A-6549/12
AA1	265	86		20.07	19.72	253, 266	Fill	A-6549/12
AA1	266	86		19.72	19.67	265	Fill	A-6549/12
AA1	267	85		19.6	19.49	262	Fill	A-6549/12
AA1	268	34		19.42	18.9		Fill	A-6549/12
AA1	11000		E9	21.39	21.032	11013	Surface	A-6825/13
AA1	11001		D9	21.29	20.77	11011	Surface	A-6825/13
AA1	11002		C8	21.1	20.73	11008	Surface	A-6825/13
AA1	11003		C7	20.97	20.54	11005	Surface	A-6825/13
AA1	11004		E8	21.36	21.14	11006	Fill	A-6825/13
AA1	11005		C7	20.7	20.08	11003	Fill	A-6825/13
AA1	11006		E8	21.14	20.98	11004	Fill	A-6825/13
AA1	11007		E9	21.17	20.25	11000	Fill	A-6825/13
AA1	11008		C8	20.73	20.46	11012	Fill	A-6825/13
AA1	11009		D8	21.34	20.83	11020	Surface	A-6825/13
AA1	11010		D7	20.99	20.26	11028	Surface	A-6825/13
AA1	11011		D9	20.77	20.51	11016	Fill	A-6825/13
AA1	11012		C8	20.46	20.15	11008	Fill	A-6825/13
AA1	11013		E9	21.03	20.36	11000	Fill	A-6825/13
AA1	11014		C7	20.54	19.4	11003	Fill	A-6825/13
AA1	11015		E8	20.95	20.76	11017	Fill	A-6825/13
AA1	11016		D9	20.51	19.99	11011	Fill	A-6825/13
AA1	11017		E8	20.76	20.23	11006	Fill	A-6825/13

Area	*Locus*	*Old Reference*	*Square*	*Height (Opened)*	*Height (Closed)*	*Associated Loci/ Features*	*Description*	*Permit No.*
AA1	11018		D6	20.76	20.49	11035	Surface	A-6825/13
AA1	11019		D5	20.69	20.37	11034	Surface	A-6825/13
AA1	11020		D8	20.83	20.33	11009	Fill	A-6825/13
AA1	11021		E8	21.09	20.32	11026	Installation	A-6825/13
AA1	11022		D8-E8	20.98	20.44	11024	Winepress vat (circular)	A-6825/13
AA1	11023		E5	20.65	20.34		Fill	A-6825/13
AA1	11024		D8	20.89	20.6	11019	Fill	A-6825/13
AA1	11025		D4	20.62	20.4	11032	Surface	A-6825/13
AA1	11026		D8	20.85	20.52	11022	Fill	A-6825/13
AA1	11027		D6/7	20.59	20.31		Fill	A-6825/13
AA1	11028		D7	20.66	20.24	11010	Fill	A-6825/13
AA1	11029		D8/E8	20.52	20.52		Mosaic floor	A-6825/13
AA1	11030		D8/E8	20.6	20.6		Mosaic floor	A-6825/13
AA1	11031		D4	20.46	19.97	11025	Fill	A-6825/13
AA1	11032		D4	20.46	20.32	11025	Fill	A-6825/13
AA1	11033		E5	20.34	20.65	255, 257	Fill	A-6825/13
AA1	11034		D5	20.37	20.22	11019	Fill	A-6825/13
AA1	11035		D6	20.49	20.26	11018	Fill	A-6825/13
AA1	11036		D6-7	20.68	20.32		Fill	A-6825/13
AA1	11037		D5	20.22	20.18	215	Fill	A-6825/13
AA1	11038		D4	19.97	19.97	11032	Mosaic floor	A-6825/13
AA1	11039		D5	20.22	20.21	11057	Fill	A-6825/13
AA1	11040		D6	20.26	19.78	11035	Fill	A-6825/13
AA1	11041	88	D5/E5	20.34	20.14		Fill	A-6825/13
AA1	11042		D4	20.08	19.8	11072	Pebbles stones	A-6825/13
AA1	11043		C5	20.72	20.6	11054	Surface	A-6825/13
AA1	11044		D4	20.08	19	11047	Fill	A-6825/13
AA1	11045		D4	20.4	19.6	11025	Fill	A-6825/13
AA1	11046		C4	20.37	20.26	11052	Surface	A-6825/13
AA1	11047		D5	20.01	19.74	11037	Fill	A-6825/13
AA1	11048		D4	19.97	19.87	11045	Fill	A-6825/13
AA1	11049		D5	20.37	20.09	11039	Fill	A-6825/13
AA1	11050		D5	20	19.74	11019	Fill	A-6825/13
AA1	11051	88	E5	20.77	20.7	206, 11056	Surface	A-6825/13
AA1	11052		C4	20.26	20	11046	Fill	A-6825/13
AA1	11053		D4	19.97	19.97	11048	Fill	A-6825/13
AA1	11054		C5	20.6	20.36	11043	Fill	A-6825/13
AA1	11055		D4	19.97	19.7		Fill	A-6825/13
AA1	11056	88	E5	20.7	20.44	11051	Fill	A-6825/13
AA1	11057		D4/5	20.63	20.37		Fill	A-6825/13
AA1	11058		C4	20.31	20.11	11052	Fallen stones	A-6825/13
AA1	11059		D4/5	20.37	20.1	11032	Fill	A-6825/13

Area	*Locus*	*Old Reference*	*Square*	*Height (Opened)*	*Height (Closed)*	*Associated Loci/ Features*	*Description*	*Permit No.*
AA1	11060		C4	20.31	20.11	11058	Removal of fallen stones	A-6825/13
AA1	11061		D4/5	20.41	20.32	11032	Fill	A-6825/13
AA1	11062		D4/5	20.1	14.7	11037	Fill	A-6825/13
AA1	11063		D4/5	20.32	20.1	11037	Fill	A-6825/13
AA1	T11064		D5	20.08	19.95	11040	Grave/Fill	A-6825/13
AA1	11065		C5	20.36	19.98	11054	Fill	A-6825/13
AA1	11066	88	E5/F5	20.43	19.9	11067	Installation	A-6825/13
AA1	11067	88	E5	20.43	19.9	11066	Fill	A-6825/13
AA1	11068	88	E5	20.54	14.7	11066	Fill	A-6825/13
AA1	11069		C4/D4	20.58	19.91		Fill	A-6825/13
AA1	11070		D6	20.26	20.16	11040	Fill	A-6825/13
AA1	11071		D5/6	20.69	20.26		Fill	A-6825/13
AA1	11072		D3	20.27	20.2	11042	Fill	A-6825/13
AA1	11073		C4	20.34	19.84	11046	Fill	A-6825/13
AA1	11074		C5	19.98	19.74	11065	Fill	A-6825/13
AA1	11075	88	E5	20.48	19.8	11066	Fill	A-6825/13
AA1	11076	88	E5/F5	20.46	20.1		wall	A-6825/13
AA1	11077	88	E5	20.47	20.43	11066	Fill	A-6825/13
AA1	11078		D3	20.2	20.08	11042	Fill	A-6825/13
AA1	11079		D3	20.2	20.08	11078	Fill	A-6825/13
AA1	11080							A-6825/13
AA2	160	A2		24.21			Surface	A-6549/12
AA2	161	F31		23.49	23.37	183, 359	Surface	A-6549/12
AA2	162	F32		23.53	23.33	181, 188	Surface	A-6549/12
AA2	163	F33		23.6	23.36	190, 191	Surface	A-6549/12
AA2	164	F30		23.9	23.44	180	Surface	A-6549/12
AA2	165	F96		23.82	23.17		Fill	A-6549/12
AA2	166	F29		23.8	23.64	175	Surface	A-6549/12
AA2	167	F28		24.45	23.62	170	Fill	A-6549/12
AA2	168	F27		24.56	23.68	172	Fill	A-6549/12
AA2	169	F28		24.29	23.69	187	Scattered stones/ Fill	A-6549/12
AA2	170	F28		24.34	24.29	167	Fill	A-6549/12
AA2	171	F91		23.17		173	Human bones	A-6549/12
AA2	172	F27		24.38	24.14	174	Fallen stones	A-6549/12
AA2	173	F91		23.82	23.71	171	Section	A-6549/12
AA2	174	F27		24.14	24.12	172	Fill	A-6549/12
AA2	175	F29		23.64	23.29	176	Limestone	A-6549/12
AA2	176	F29		23.2	23	166	Fill	A-6549/12
AA2	177	F91		23.71	23.55	178, 179	Wall	A-6549/12
AA2	178	F91		23.71	23.17		Fill	A-6549/12
AA2	179	F91		23.71	23.33		Fill	A-6549/12
AA2	180	F30		23.44	23.16	164	Fill	A-6549/12

Area	*Locus*	*Old Reference*	*Square*	*Height (Opened)*	*Height (Closed)*	*Associated Loci/ Features*	*Description*	*Permit No.*
AA2	181	F32		23.39	22.33	162	Fill	A-6549/12
AA2	182	F27		24.12	23.51	364	Fill	A-6549/12
AA2	183	F31		23.37	22.72	161	Fill	A-6549/12
AA2	184	F91		23.22	23.06	185	Wall	A-6549/12
AA2	185	F91		23.22	22.92	184	Wall	A-6549/12
AA2	186	F27		24.56	23.68	168	Fill	A-6549/12
AA2	187	F28		23.92	23.84	169	Refuse pit	A-6549/12
AA2	188	F32		23.84	22.85	162	Fill	A-6549/12
AA2	189	F32		22.81	22.58	181	Limestone	A-6549/12
AA2	190	E33		23.36	23.08	358	Fill	A-6549/12
AA2	191	F33		23.36	22.49	355	Fill	A-6549/12
AA2	192	F30		23.18	23.04	180	Fill	A-6549/12
AA2	193	F91		23.82	23.33	196	Fill	A-6549/12
AA2	194	F91		23.38	23.15		Wall	A-6549/12
AA2	195	F91		23.09	22.85	194, 188, 177	Fill	A-6549/12
AA2	196	F91		22.85	22.75	193	Sand	A-6549/12
AA2	197	F91		24.21	23.17		Fill	A-6549/12
AA2	198	F30		23.16	22.57	192	Fill	A-6549/12
AA2	199	F30		22.98	22.74	198	Fill	A-6549/12
AA2	355	F33		22.56	22.45		Limestone sand	A-6549/12
AA2	356	F32		22.99	22.66	188	Limestone sand	A-6549/12
AA2	357	F30		22.57	22.44		Limestone sand	A-6549/12
AA2	357	F33		23.08	23.12	199	Limestone sand	A-6549/12
AA2	358	F33		22.99	22.75		Limestone sand	A-6549/12
AA2	359	F31		22.99	22.73	161	Fill	A-6549/12
AA2	360	F31		22.75	22.3	359	Limestone sand	A-6549/12
AA2	361	F33		23.73	23.58	355, 358	Pebbles floor	A-6549/12
AA2	362	F32		23.18	22.74		Fill	A-6549/12
AA2	363	F30		23.02	22.88	192	Fill	A-6549/12
AA2	364	F27		24.12	23.68	182	Scattered stones/ Fill	A-6549/12
AA2	365	F31		22.73			Grave	A-6549/12
AA2	12000		A2	24.12			Surface	A-6825/13
AA2	12001		C3			Cancelled	Surface	A-6825/13
AA2	12002		C4	23.78		12014	Surface	A-6825/13
AA2	12003		C5				Surface	A-6825/13
AA2	12004		C6	24.11	23.83	12009	Surface	A-6825/13
AA2	12005		D3			Cancelled	Surface	A-6825/13
AA2	12006		D4			Cancelled	Surface	A-6825/13
AA2	12007		D5	23.88	23.57	12010	Surface	A-6825/13
AA2	12008		D6			Cancelled	Surface	A-6825/13
AA2	12009		C6	23.83	23.21	12004	Fill	A-6825/13
AA2	12010		D5	23.57	23.06	12007	Fill	A-6825/13
AA2	12011		C6	23.78	23.18		Fill	A-6825/13

Area	*Locus*	*Old Reference*	*Square*	*Height (Opened)*	*Height (Closed)*	*Associated Loci/ Features*	*Description*	*Permit No.*
AA2	12012	C6	C6	23.21	23.1	12009	Fill	A-6825/13
AA2	12013		C5/6	23.86	23.1		Fill	A-6825/13
AA2	12014		C4	23.42	23.19	12002	Fill	A-6825/13
AA2	12015		C5	23.48	23.23	12017	Fill	A-6825/13
AA2	T12016		E9	23.02	22.69	12018	Grave (empty)	A-6825/13
AA2	T12017		C5	23.23	23.11	12015	Grave	A-6825/13
AA2	T12018		E9	22.69	22.57	12020	Grave	A-6825/13
AA2	12019		General				Fill	A-6825/13
AA2	12020		E9	22.69	22.57	12018	Fill	A-6825/13
AA2	12021		C5	23.23	23.11	12017	Fill	A-6825/13
AA2	12022		C5	23.54	23.21	10023	Fill	A-6825/13
AA2	12023		C5	23.52	23.18	10022	Fill	A-6825/13
AA2	12024		C5	23.52	23.18		Wall	A-6825/13
AA2	12025		C5	23.54	23.4	12024	Fill	A-6825/13
AA2	12026		C5	23.57	23.4	12010	Fill	A-6825/13
AA2	12027		C5	23.11	23.08	12017	Fill	A-6825/13
AA2	12028		C5	23.11	22.96	12024	Fill	A-6825/13
AA2	12029		C5/D5	23.48	22.98		Fill	A-6825/13
AA2	12030		C5	23.09	22.96	185	Fill	A-6825/13
AA2	12031		C5/6	23.71	23.45	177	Fallen stone	A-6825/13
AA2	12032		C5/6	23.75	23.47	12033	Wall	A-6825/13
AA2	12033		C5/6	23.75	23.47	12032	Fill	A-6825/13
AA2	12034		C6	23.08	22.93	177	Fill	A-6825/13
AA2	12035		C5				Wall	A-6825/13
AA2	12036		C5				Field tower	A-6825/13
AA3	13000		B2	18.37	18	13003	Surface	A-6825/13
AA3	T13001		B2-C2	18.35	18	440	Built tomb	A-6825/13
AA3	13002		C2	18.3	17.66	13000	Fill	A-6825/13
AA3	13003		B2	18.57	18.35	13000	Fill	A-6825/13
AA3	13004		B2	18	17.33	13003	Fill	A-6825/13
AA3	13005		B2	18	17.73	13002		A-6825/13
AA3	13006		B2	18.25	12.73	13002	Fill	A-6825/13
AA3	13007		B2	18.75	17.73	13000	Fill	A-6825/13
AA3	13008		B2-C2	18.65	18.25		Fill	A-6825/13
AA3	13009		B2-C2	18.23	17.66	13003	Fill	A-6825/13
AA3	13010						Installation	A-6825/14
AA3	13011		B2	18.45	17.95	13010	Fill	A-6825/15
AA3	13012		B2-C2	18.4	17.95	13011	Collapse	A-6825/16
AA3/BB	402	45		23.86	23.36	409	Fill	A-6549/12
AA3/BB	403	46		24.33	23.79	410	Fill	A-6549/12
AA3/BB	404	44		25.71	24.72	405	Fill	A-6549/12
AA3/BB	405	44		24.72	24.5	404	Fill	A-6549/12
AA3/BB	406	47		26.63	25.33		Fill	A-6549/12

Area	*Locus*	*Old Reference*	*Square*	*Height (Opened)*	*Height (Closed)*	*Associated Loci/ Features*	*Description*	*Permit No.*
AA3/BB	407	50		29.3	28.18	432	Fill	A-6549/12
AA3/BB	408	42		18.43	18.31	400	Fill	A-6549/12
AA3/BB	409	45		23.36	23.19	402	Fill	A-6549/12
AA3/BB	410	46		23.79	23.59	403	Fill	A-6549/12
AA3/BB	411	47		25.33	24.86		Fill	A-6549/12
AA3/BB	412	47		25.33	24.84		Fill	A-6549/12
AA3/BB	413	49		30.47	29.37	419	Fill	A-6549/12
AA3/BB	414	48		29.78	28.66		Fill	A-6549/12
AA3/BB	415	43		19.62	16.97	401	Fill	A-6549/12
AA3/BB	416	92		28.81	27.87	423	Fill	A-6549/12
AA3/BB	417	52		29.19	28.54	420	Fill	A-6549/12
AA3/BB	418	51		28.55	27.65	424	Fill	A-6549/12
AA3/BB	419	49		29.21	29.05	413	Pebbles	A-6549/12
AA3/BB	420	42		18.31	18.22	426	Pottery layer	A-6549/12
AA3/BB	422	49		29.05	28.72	419	Fill	A-6549/12
AA3/BB	423	92		27.87	27.5	416	Fill	A-6549/12
AA3/BB	424	51		27.68	27.37	427	Pebbles	A-6549/12
AA3/BB	425	52		27.74	27.54	429	Stone layer	A-6549/12
AA3/BB	426	42		18.05	18.03		Stone layer	A-6549/12
AA3/BB	427	51		27.86	27.37	424	Plaster floor	A-6549/12
AA3/BB	428	92		28	27.84	425	Fill	A-6549/12
AA3/BB	429	52		27.74	27.54	416	Refuse pit	A-6549/12
AA3/BB	430	42		18.03	18	426	Stone foundation	A-6549/12
AA3/BB	431	49		29.21	29.05	422	Fallen stones	A-6549/12
AA3/BB	432	50		28.91	28.68	407	Stone layer	A-6549/12
AA3/BB	433	42		18	17.62	440	Fill	A-6549/12
AA3/BB	434	42		18.22	17.15	440	Fill	A-6549/12
AA3/BB	435	42		18	17.95	430	Foundation	A-6549/12
AA3/BB	436	42		18	17.62	440	Fill	A-6549/12
AA3/BB	437	42		18.06	18	440	Plaster floor	A-6549/12
AA3/BB	438	42		18.05	18	437	Plaster floor	A-6549/12
AA3/BB	439	42		18.22	18.07		Cancelled	A-6549/12
AA3/BB	440	42		18.35	17.95		Installation	A-6549/12
AA3/BB	441	42		17.15	16.79	434	Fill	A-6549/12
AA3/BB	441	53		29.51	29	447	Fill	A-6549/12
AA3/BB	442	54		27.49	27	444	Fill	A-6549/12
AA3/BB	443	55		27.09	26.01	443	Fill	A-6549/12
AA3/BB	444	54		27	26.4	442	Fill	A-6549/12
AA3/BB	445	54		25.91	25.83	442	Fill	A-6549/12
AA3/BB	446	54		26.4	26.37	445	Stone layer	A-6549/12
AA3/BB	447	53		29	27.58	441	Fill	A-6549/12
AA3/BB	448	55		25.82	25.7	449	Fill	A-6549/12
AA3/BB	449	55		26.01	25.82	450	Stone layer	A-6549/12

Area	*Locus*	*Old Reference*	*Square*	*Height (Opened)*	*Height (Closed)*	*Associated Loci/ Features*	*Description*	*Permit No.*
AA3/BB	450	55		25.82	25.71	449	Fill	A-6549/12
AA3/BB	451	53		28.06	27.65	447	Stone layer	A-6549/12
CC	600	78	E13	25.61	25.31	613	Surface	A-6549/12
CC	601	77	F11	25.33	25.02	614, 620	Surface	A-6549/12
CC	602	76	G11	25.33	24.77	619	Surface	A-6549/12
CC	603	72	E10	25.44	25.06	609	Surface	A-6549/12
CC	604	73	F10	25.44	24.91	616, 621	Surface	A-6549/12
CC	605	74	G10	25.35	25	617	Surface	A-6549/12
CC	606	75	H10	25.28	24.77	618, 632	Surface	A-6549/12
CC	607	81	E7	25.49	25.09	627, 659	Surface	A-6549/12
CC	608	80	E6	25.49	25.48	626, 630	Surface	A-6549/12
CC	609	79	F5	25.34	25.14	603	Surface	A-6549/12
CC	610	82		24.22	24.16	611	Surface	A-6549/12
CC	611	82		24.16	23.71	612, 629	Wall	A-6549/12
CC	612	82		24.16	23.77	611	Fill	A-6549/12
CC	613	78	E13	25.31	24.77	600	Fill	A-6549/12
CC	614	77	F11	25.02	24.68	601	Fill	A-6549/12
CC	615	72	E10	25.06	24.77	609	Fill	A-6549/12
CC	616	73	F10	24.91	24.59	604	Fill	A-6549/12
CC	617	74	G10	25	24.33	605	Fill	A-6549/12
CC	618	75	H10	24.77	24.32	606	Fill	A-6549/12
CC	619	76	G11	24.77	24.3	602	Fill	A-6549/12
CC	620	77	F11	24.68	24.57	601	Fill	A-6549/12
CC	621	73	F10	24.91	24.59	604	Fill	A-6549/12
CC	622	77	F11	24.57	24.46	614, 622	Pottery layer (refuse dump)	A-6549/12
CC	623	72	E10	24.71	24.45	633	Pottery layer (refuse dump)	A-6549/12
CC	624	78	E13	24.77	24.39	613	Fill	A-6549/12
CC	625	81	E7	25.09	24.85	642	Pottery layer (refuse dump)	A-6549/12
CC	626	80	E6	25.18	24.66	608	Fill	A-6549/12
CC	627	79	F5	25.14	24.48	637	Pottery layer (refuse dump)	A-6549/12
CC	628	77	F11	24.45	23.52	622	Fill	A-6549/12
CC	629	82		24.16	23.76	611	Fill	A-6549/12
CC	630	80	E6	24.66	23.82	608	Fill	A-6549/12
CC	631	78	E13	24.39	24.02	624	Fill	A-6549/12
CC	632	75	H10	24.31	23.78	606	Fill	A-6549/12
CC	633	72	E10	24.45	24.21	623	Fill	A-6549/12
CC	634	78	E13	25.31	24.39	631	Fill	A-6549/12
CC	635	80	E6	25.49	24.38	626, 630	Fill	A-6549/12
CC	636	83		24.08	23.33	638	Surface	A-6549/12
CC	637	79	F5	25.14	24.5		Fill	A-6549/12
CC	638	83		23.33	22.78	636	Fill	A-6549/12

Area	*Locus*	*Old Reference*	*Square*	*Height (Opened)*	*Height (Closed)*	*Associated Loci/ Features*	*Description*	*Permit No.*
CC	639	73	F10	24.59	24.59	616, 621	Pottery layer (refuse dump)	A-6549/12
CC	640	83		22.78	22.42	638	Fill	A-6549/12
CC	641	72	E10	24.31	24.44	623	Pottery layer (refuse dump)	A-6549/12
CC	642	81	E7	25.12	24.91		Fill	A-6549/12
CC	643	79	F5	25.01	24.5	627	Pottery layer (refuse dump)	A-6549/12
CC	644	101		23	22.66	653	Surface	A-6549/12
CC	645	99		23.06	22.49	651	Surface	A-6549/12
CC	646	96		24.76	24.5	650	Surface	A-6549/12
CC	647	24		24.71	24.24	652	Surface	A-6549/12
CC	648	100		23.94	23.6	658	Surface	A-6549/12
CC	649	99		23.06	21.78	651	Surface	A-6549/12
CC	650	96		24.5	24.09	646	Fill	A-6549/12
CC	651	99		23.49	21.91	645, 649	Fill	A-6549/12
CC	652	24		24.24	23.39	647	Fill	A-6549/12
CC	653	101		22.66	22.14	656	Fill	A-6549/12
CC	654	100		23.6	23.44	658	Fill	A-6549/12
CC	655	24		24.09	23.51	652	Fill	A-6549/12
CC	656	101		22.9	22.55	653	Fill	A-6549/12
CC	657	96		24.09	23.55	650	Fill	A-6549/12
CC	658	100		23.44	22.85	654, 648	Fill	A-6549/12
CC	659		E7	24.91	24.7	625	Pottery layer (refuse dump)	A-6549/12
CC	30000		D3	25.14	24.55	30014	Surface	A-6825/13
CC	30001		D4	25.14	24.7		Surface	A-6825/13
CC	30002		E3	25.12	24.22	30025	Surface	A-6825/13
CC	30003		F3	25.14	24.62	30021	Surface	A-6825/13
CC	30004		F4	25.14	25.02	30013	Surface	A-6825/13
CC	30005		G3	25.11	24.47		Surface	A-6825/13
CC	30006		G4	25.11	24.69	30038	Pottery layer (refuse dump)	A-6825/13
CC	30007		H3	25.11	24.32	30043	Surface	A-6825/13
CC	30008		I3	25.11	24.31	30045	Surface	A-6825/13
CC	30009		I4	25.12	23.49		Surface	A-6825/13
CC	30010		I5	25.12	24.39	30016	Surface	A-6825/13
CC	30011		H5	25.12	24.85	30042	Surface	A-6825/13
CC	30012		E4	25.14	24.96	30023	Surface	A-6825/13
CC	30013		F4	25.02	24.56	30004	Fill	A-6825/13
CC	30014		D3	24.55	24.37	30000	Fill	A-6825/13
CC	30015		F5	24.98	24.31	30012	Pottery layer (refuse dump)	A-6825/13
CC	30016		I5	24.72	24.28	30010	Pottery layer (refuse dump)	A-6825/13

Area	*Locus*	*Old Reference*	*Square*	*Height (Opened)*	*Height (Closed)*	*Associated Loci/ Features*	*Description*	*Permit No.*
CC	30017		D3	24.37	24.15	30014	Fill	A-6825/13
CC	30018		E4	24.65	24.51	30012	pottery layer (refuse dump)	A-6825/13
CC	30019		E4	24.99	24.57	30012, 30018	Fill	A-6825/13
CC	30020		E5	25.24	25.1	30036	Surface	A-6825/13
CC	30021		F3	24.46	24.06	30003	Fill	A-6825/13
CC	30022		F3	24.13	24.02	30021	Fill	A-6825/13
CC	30023		F4	24.96	24.56	30012	Fill	A-6825/13
CC	30024		I5	24.28	24.03	30016	Fill	A-6825/13
CC	30025		E3	24.23	24.06	30002	Fill	A-6825/13
CC	30026		H4	24.9	24.71	30044	Surface	A-6825/13
CC	30027		B5	25.18	24.99	30037	Surface	A-6825/13
CC	30028		G6	25.2	24.61	30063	Surface	A-6825/13
CC	30029		G7	25.24	24.85	30069	Surface	A-6825/13
CC	30030		F6	25.46	24.99	30060	Surface	A-6825/13
CC	30031		F7	25.39	25.22	30061	Surface	A-6825/13
CC	30032		H6	25.27	24.82	30052	Surface	A-6825/13
CC	30033		H7	24.94	24.85	30065	Surface	A-6825/13
CC	30034		I6	24.79	24.39	30066	Surface	A-6825/13
CC	30035		I7	25.04	24.47	30067	Surface	A-6825/13
CC	30036		E5	25.19	24.78	30020	Fill	A-6825/13
CC	30037		G5	25.14	24.49	30027	Pottery layer (refuse dump)	A-6825/13
CC	30038		G4	24.77	24.6	30006	Pottery layer (refuse dump)	A-6825/13
CC	30039		F5	24.31	24/20	30015	Fill	A-6825/13
CC	30040		D6	25.41	25.26		Surface	A-6825/13
CC	30041		D7	25.41	25.2		Surface	A-6825/13
CC	30042		H5	24.78	24.57	30011	Pottery layer (refuse dump)	A-6825/13
CC	30043		H3	24.32	24.16	30007	Fill	A-6825/13
CC	30044		H4	24.71	24.1	30026	Pottery layer (refuse dump)	A-6825/13
CC	30045		I3	24.29	23.48	30008	Fill	A-6825/13
CC	30046		D5	26.22	24.98	30069	Surface	A-6825/13
CC	30047		I8	25.12	24.58	30068	Surface	A-6825/13
CC	30048		E8	25.36	24.74	30070	Surface	A-6825/13
CC	30049		F5	24.98	24.31	30039, 30015	Fill	A-6825/13
CC	30050		F8	25.22	24.95		Surface	A-6825/13
CC	30051		H5	25.23	24.9		Fill	A-6825/13
CC	30052		H6	24.82	23.71	30032	Pottery layer (refuse dump)	A-6825/13
CC	30053		D8	25.36	24.87		Surface	A-6825/13
CC	30054		G8	25.35	25.09	30089	Surface	A-6825/13
CC	30055		E9	25.4	24.89	30082	Surface	A-6825/13

Area	*Locus*	*Old Reference*	*Square*	*Height (Opened)*	*Height (Closed)*	*Associated Loci/ Features*	*Description*	*Permit No.*
CC	30056		D9	25.45	24.73	30146	Surface	A-6825/13
CC	30057		F9	25.35	25.11	30087	Surface	A-6825/13
CC	30058		H8	25.07	24.15	30083	Surface	A-6825/13
CC	30059		H9	25.01	24.83	30088	Surface	A-6825/13
CC	30060		F6	25.11	23.06	30030	Pottery layer (refuse dump)	A-6825/13
CC	30061		F7	25.13	23.8	30031	Pottery layer (refuse dump)	A-6825/13
CC	30062		E5	24.78	24.2	30036	Fill	A-6825/13
CC	30063		G6	25.12	23.91	30028	Pottery layer (refuse dump)	A-6825/13
CC	30064		G7	24.85	24.75	30029	Fill	A-6825/13
CC	30065		H7	24.84	24.31	30033	Pottery layer (refuse dump)	A-6825/13
CC	30066		I6	24.58	23.46	30034	Fill	A-6825/13
CC	30067		I7	24.51	24.26	30035	Fill	A-6825/13
CC	30068		I8	25.88	23.65	30017	Fill	A-6825/13
CC	30069		D5	24.98	24.5	30046	Fill	A-6825/13
CC	30070		E8	25.01	24.8	30048	Pottery layer (refuse dump)	A-6825/13
CC	30071		G7	24.75	23.8	30069	Pottery layer (refuse dump)	A-6825/13
CC	30072		G5	24.49	24.23	30037	Fill	A-6825/13
CC	30073		H6	24.35	24.31	30052	Pottery layer (refuse dump)	A-6825/13
CC	30074		F8	24.95	24.35	30050	Pottery layer (refuse dump)	A-6825/13
CC	30075		H7	24.34	24.13	30065	Fill	A-6825/13
CC	30076		H11	25.14	24.95	30129	Surface	A-6825/13
CC	30077		H12	25.3	25.12		Surface	A-6825/13
CC	30078		I10	25.22	24.91		Surface	A-6825/13
CC	30079		I11	25.21	24.91	30125	Surface	A-6825/13
CC	30080		I12	25.28	24.85		Surface	A-6825/13
CC	30081		E8	24.99	24.43		Pottery layer (refuse dump)	A-6825/13
CC	30082		E9	25.02	24.77	30055	Pottery layer (refuse dump)	A-6825/13
CC	30083		H8	24.8	24.38	30058	Fill	A-6825/13
CC	30084		I7	24.24	24.17	30062	Fill	A-6825/13
CC	30085		F7	24.41	24.22	30061	Fill	A-6825/13
CC	30086		I8	24.36	24.2	30068	Fill	A-6825/13
CC	30087		F9	25.14	24.73	30057	Fill	A-6825/13
CC	30088		H9	25.03	24.25	30059	Fill	A-6825/13
CC	30089		G8	25.17	24.61	30054	Fill	A-6825/13
CC	30100		E7	24.93	24.75		Pottery layer (refuse dump)	A-6825/13

Area	*Locus*	*Old Reference*	*Square*	*Height (Opened)*	*Height (Closed)*	*Associated Loci/ Features*	*Description*	*Permit No.*
CC	30101		G6	24.29	24.28	30063	Fill	A-6825/13
CC	30102		G7	24.38	24.18	30071	Fill	A-6825/13
CC	30103		F6	24.38	24.25	30060	Fill	A-6825/13
CC	30104		I9	25.19	24.97	30132	Surface	A-6825/13
CC	30105		G12	25.39	25.06		Surface	A-6825/13
CC	30106		E11	25.6	25.32	30148	Surface	A-6825/13
CC	30107		F12	25.44	25.18		Surface	A-6825/13
CC	30108		E9	24.77	24.53	30082	Fill	A-6825/13
CC	30109		H8	24.38	24.3	30083	Fill	A-6825/13
CC	30110		H8	24.3	24.04	30109	Fill	A-6825/13
CC	30111		H9	24.25	24.08	30088	Fill	A-6825/13
CC	30112		E7	24.45	24.35	30100	Fill	A-6825/13
CC	30114		E8	24.8	24.63	30081	Fill	A-6825/13
CC	30115		D11	25.51	25.18	30136	Surface	A-6825/13
CC	30116		I6	24.84	24.37	30122	Fill	A-6825/13
CC	30117		I7	25	24.4	30124	Fill	A-6825/13
CC	30118		F9	24.73	24.43	30087	Pottery layer (refuse dump)	A-6825/13
CC	30119		I10	24.91	24.29	30078	Fill	A-6825/13
CC	30120		I12	24.85	24.18	30080	Fill	A-6825/13
CC	30121		H12	25.12	24.37	30077	Fill	A-6825/13
CC	30122		J6	24.45	24.38	30116	Pottery layer (refuse dump)	A-6825/13
CC	30123						Cancelled	A-6825/13
CC	30124		J7	24.49	24.31	30117	Pottery layer (refuse dump)	A-6825/13
CC	30125		I11	24.91	24.28	30079	Fill	A-6825/13
CC	30126		E12	25.63	25.44		Surface	A-6825/13
CC	30127		D12	25.45	25.36	30143	Surface	A-6825/13
CC	30128		D10	25.49	25.35	30151	Surface	A-6825/13
CC	30129		H11	24.95	24.6	30079	Fill	A-6825/13
CC	30130		G12	25.06	24.45	30105	Fill	A-6825/13
CC	30131		G8	24.61	24.3	30089	Pottery layer (refuse dump)	A-6825/13
CC	30132		I9	24.97	24.22	30104	Fill	A-6825/13
CC	30133		G9	25.25	25.14		Surface	A-6825/13
CC	30134		E11	25.32	24.75	30106	Fill	A-6825/13
CC	30135		F12	25.18	24.57	30107	Fill	A-6825/13
CC	30136		D11	25.18	24.7	30115	Fill	A-6825/13
CC	30137		D13	25.57	25.07		Surface	A-6825/13
CC	30138		F13	25.58	25.48		Surface	A-6825/13
CC	30139		E12	25.44	24.71	30126	Fill	A-6825/13
CC	30140		H13	25.34	25.25		Surface	A-6825/13
CC	30141		I13	25.35	25.25		Surface	A-6825/13

Area	*Locus*	*Old Reference*	*Square*	*Height (Opened)*	*Height (Closed)*	*Associated Loci/ Features*	*Description*	*Permit No.*
CC	30142		D12	25.3	25.02	30127	Fill/wall	A-6825/13
CC	30143		D12	25.3	24.83	30127	Fill	A-6825/13
CC	30144		I10	24.29	24.2	30119	Fill	A-6825/13
CC	30145		G9	25.14	24.58	30133	Fill	A-6825/13
CC	30146		D9	24.89	24.59	30056	Fill	A-6825/13
CC	30147		E9	24.53	24.44	30108	Fill	A-6825/13
CC	30148		E11	24.75	24.53	30134	Pottery layer (refuse dump)	A-6825/13
CC	30149		C12	25.4	24.9		Surface	A-6825/13
CC	30150		C13	25.4	25		Surface	A-6825/13
CC	30151		D10	24.6	24.6	30128	Fill	A-6825/13
CC	30152		F9	24.43	24.35	30118	Fill	A-6825/13
CC	30153		G8	24.3	24.2	30131	Fill	A-6825/13
CC	30154		G13	25.31	25.22		Surface	A-6825/13
CC	30155		E11	24.53	24.47	30148	Fill	A-6825/13
CC	30157		C12	25.4	24.78	30149	Fill	A-6825/13
CC	30158		C12/D12	25.45	25.23		Fill (baulk)	A-6825/13
CC	30159		D12/13	25.45	25.09		Fill (baulk)	A-6825/13
CC	30160		G9	24.58	24.35	30145	Pottery layer (refuse dump)	A-6825/13
CC	30161		E12	24.71	24.57	30139	Pottery layer (refuse dump)	A-6825/13
CC	30162		E8	24.47	24.37	30081	Fill	A-6825/13
CC	30163		I9	24.22	24.12	30132	Fill	A-6825/13
CC	30164		D12/13	25.09	24.6	30159	Fill	A-6825/13
CC2	31000		General			31002, 31003	Fill	A-6825/13
CC2	31001		D3	22.3	21.8	611	Fill	A-6825/13
CC2	31002		D4	22.26	21.08	611	Fill	A-6825/13
CC2	31003		D4	21.83	21.83	611	Fill	A-6825/13
CC2	31004		D4/5	22.2	21.08	611	Fill	A-6825/13
DD1	750	F13		23.83	23.49	765	Surface	A-6549/12
DD1	751	F19		23.24	22.57	755	Surface	A-6549/12
DD1	752	F22		22.1	21.24		Surface	A-6549/12
DD1	753	F14		25.02	23.6	778	Surface	A-6549/12
DD1	754	F19		22.85	22.33	769	Fill	A-6549/12
DD1	755	F16		27.07	26.94	751	Installation	A-6549/12
DD1	756	F98		27.2	26.83	760	Surface	A-6549/12
DD1	757	F14		24.49	24.43		Fill	A-6549/12
DD1	758	F13		23.21	22.6		Fill	A-6549/12
DD1	759	F21		27.43	26.58	776	Surface	A-6549/12
DD1	760	F17		26.69	25.56	756	Fill	A-6549/12
DD1	761	F18		26.12	25.47	781	Fill	A-6549/12
DD1	762	E93		27.22	26.98	768	Surface	A-6549/12
DD1	763	F15		25.34	24.94	779	Fill	A-6549/12

Area	*Locus*	*Old Reference*	*Square*	*Height (Opened)*	*Height (Closed)*	*Associated Loci/ Features*	*Description*	*Permit No.*
DD1	764	F13		22.58	22.51		Fill	A-6549/12
DD1	765	F13		22.51	22.06	750	Fill	A-6549/12
DD1	766	F16		27.4	25.92	769	wall	A-6549/12
DD1	767	F98		27.19	25.93		Fill	A-6549/12
DD1	768	F93		26.92	26.33	762	Fill	A-6549/12
DD1	769	F16		27.07	26.88	754	Winepress vat (square-shaped)	A-6549/12
DD1	770	F16		27.16	23.61	769	Fill	A-6549/12
DD1	771	F16		27.29	26.56	769	wall	A-6549/12
DD1	772	F10		27.18	25.89	769	wall	A-6549/12
DD1	773	F16		27.49	25.84	769	wall	A-6549/12
DD1	774	F16		27.27	26.3	769	Fill	A-6549/12
DD1	775	F16		27.39	26.74	769	Fill	A-6549/12
DD1	776	F21		26.58	26.37	759	Fill	A-6549/12
DD1	777	F16		26.92	26.85	770	Fill	A-6549/12
DD1	778	F14		25.16	24.5		Stone table	A-6549/12
DD1	779	F15		24.87	24.6	763	Fill	A-6549/12
DD1	780	F15		24.72	24.64	779	Fill	A-6549/12
DD1	781	F18		26.04	25.92	761	Stone table	A-6549/12
DD1	782	F14		25.21	25.16	778	Stone table	A-6549/12
DD1	783	F14		24.98	24.82	782	Stone table	A-6549/12
DD1	784	F16		27.46	27.07	769	Winepress treading floor	A-6549/12
DD1	785	F16		26.75	25.55	769	Winepress vat (square-shaped)	A-6549/12
DD1	786	F16		27.43	26.96	785	Wall	A-6549/12
DD1	787						Cancelled	A-6549/12
DD1	788	16N		27.84	27.36	800	Surface	A-6549/12
DD1	789	16S		27.85	26.95	804	Surface	A-6549/12
DD1	790	16W		27.68	26.92		Surface	A-6549/12
DD1	791	16E		28.16	27.38	794, 795	Surface	A-6549/12
DD1	792	16NE		27.83	27.56	793	Fill	A-6549/12
DD1	793	16NE		28.16	27.26	792	Fill	A-6549/12
DD1	794	16E		27.41	27.03	795	Wall	A-6549/12
DD1	795	16E		27.53	27.06	794	Wall	A-6549/12
DD1	796	16E		27.19	26.92	705	Fill	A-6549/12
DD1	797	16E		27.69	27.24	795	Fill	A-6549/12
DD1	798	16		27.18	26.96	766	Fill	A-6549/12
DD1	799	13S		27.6	27.46	784	Fill	A-6549/12
DD1	800	16N		27.47	27.21	788	Fill	A-6549/12
DD1	801	143		25.89	25.23	809	Surface	A-6549/12
DD1	802	16		27.39	26.95	784	Pebbles floor - removal	A-6549/12
DD1	803	16		27.21	26.95	784	Fallen stones	A-6549/12

Area	*Locus*	*Old Reference*	*Square*	*Height (Opened)*	*Height (Closed)*	*Associated Loci/ Features*	*Description*	*Permit No.*
DD1	804	16S		26.95	27,10	789	Fill	A-6549/12
DD1	805	16		27.39	27.5	784	Fill	A-6549/12
DD1	806	14S		23.8	24.98		Fill	A-6549/12
DD1	807	16E		27.53	27.1	794	Fill	A-6549/12
DD1	808	14S		26.5	25.66		Fill	A-6549/12
DD1	809	24S		25.66	25.5	801, 810	Refuse pit	A-6549/12
DD1	810	14S		25.24	25.2	809	Jar	A-6549/12
DD1	40000		General				Surface	A-6825/13
DD1	40001		C3	27.35	26.9	40007	Surface	A-6825/13
DD1	40002		C6	27.25	26.85	40005, 40006	Surface	A-6825/13
DD1	40003		D9	27.3	26.3		Surface	A-6825/13
DD1	40004		E9	27.3	26.3		Surface	A-6825/13
DD1	40005		C6	26.9	26.85	40002	Hearth	A-6825/13
DD1	40006		C6	26.85	26.55	40002	Fill	A-6825/13
DD1	40007		C3	27.2	26.9	40001	Installation	A-6825/13
DD1	40008		C3	26.9	26.63	40001	Fill	A-6825/13
DD1	40009		C6	26.9	29.85	40002	Ash layer	A-6825/13
DD2	900	65		25.3	24.88	910, 914	Surface	A-6549/12
DD2	901	59		25.83	25.18	915	Surface	A-6549/12
DD2	902	60		25.97	25.27		Surface	A-6549/12
DD2	903	61		26.04	25.45	920	Surface	A-6549/12
DD2	904	62		26.28	25.39	918	Surface	A-6549/12
DD2	905	63		26.52	25.5		Surface	A-6549/12
DD2	906	64		26.22	25.52		Surface	A-6549/12
DD2	907	57		29.83	28.83		Surface	A-6549/12
DD2	908	12		27.52	26.7		Surface	A-6549/12
DD2	909	68		24.7	23.47		Surface	A-6549/12
DD2	910	65		25.28	24.98	900	Fill	A-6549/12
DD2	911	65		24.98	24.89	910	Fill	A-6549/12
DD2	912	69		25.09	24.39	917, 924	Surface	A-6549/12
DD2	913	67		24.65	23.72	919	Surface	A-6549/12
DD2	914	65		24.89	24.22	900	Fill	A-6549/12
DD2	915	58		27.96	27.73	901	Fill	A-6549/12
DD2	916	58		28.79	27.96		Surface	A-6549/12
DD2	917	69		24.39	23.47	912	Fill	A-6549/12
DD2	T918	62		26.04	25.61	904	Burial jar	A-6549/12
DD2	919	67		23.72	23.06	913	Fill	A-6549/12
DD2	T920	61		25.77	25.43	903, 931	Burial jar	A-6549/12
DD2	921	61		26.03	25.66	918	Fill	A-6549/12
DD2	922	67		23.72	23.21	919	Fill	A-6549/12
DD2	923	69		23.47	22.08	912	Installation	A-6549/12
DD2	924	69		24.39	23.55	912	Fill	A-6549/12
DD2	925	66		23.83	22.74		Surface	A-6549/12

Area	*Locus*	*Old Reference*	*Square*	*Height (Opened)*	*Height (Closed)*	*Associated Loci/ Features*	*Description*	*Permit No.*
DD2	926	59/60		25.9	25.5	901	Fill	A-6549/12
DD2	T927	61		26.7	26.53	933	Burial jar	A-6549/12
DD2	928	61		26.47	26.24	932	Fill	A-6549/12
DD2	T929	62		26.58	26.21	932	Burial jar	A-6549/12
DD2	930	12		27.18	25.18		Fill	A-6549/12
DD2	931	12N		25.77	25.38	920	Ash layer - burnt olives	A-6549/12
DD2	932	12N		27.28	25.9	928, 929	Fill	A-6549/12
DD2	933	12N		27.64	26.48	927	Fill	A-6549/12
DD2	990	70		23.48	23.28	991, 992	Surface	A-6549/12
DD2	991	70		23.28	23.01	990	Refuse pit	A-6549/12
DD2	992	70		23.01	22.8	990	Fill	A-6549/12
DD2	993	70		22.8	22.55	992	Fill	A-6549/12
DD2	994	70		23.01	22.6	991	Fill	A-6549/12
DD2	995	70		23.01	22.3	991	Refuse pit	A-6549/12
DD2	996	70		22.3	22.05	997	Fill	A-6549/12
DD2	997	70		22.05	21.9	996	Fill	A-6549/12
DD3	851	10		21.5	20.11	866	Fill	A-6549/12
DD3	852	11		21.84	19.9	868	Fill	A-6549/12
DD3	853	94		24.14	23.51	865	Fill	A-6549/12
DD3	854	1		27.41	25.62	864	Fill	A-6549/12
DD3	855	9		22.81	22.12	867	Fill	A-6549/12
DD3	856	6		26.55	25.68	872	Fill	A-6549/12
DD3	857	2		27.11	26	870	Fill	A-6549/12
DD3	858	5		26.2	25.46	863	Fill	A-6549/12
DD3	859	4		27.81	26.11		Fill	A-6549/12
DD3	860	3		27.31	26.38		Fill	A-6549/12
DD3	861	3		26.38	26.12		Stone cover	A-6549/12
DD3	862	6		25.88	25.68	856	Grave	A-6549/12
DD3	863	5		25.64	25.47	858	Grave	A-6549/12
DD3	864	1		25.62	25.01	854	Fill	A-6549/12
DD3	865	94		24.01	23.51	873	Plaster with stone	A-6549/12
DD3	866	10		21.04	20.11	851	Fill	A-6549/12
DD3	867	9		22.12	22	855	Fill	A-6549/12
DD3	868	11		19.9	18.87	852	Fill	A-6549/12
DD3	869	3		26.24	25.92		Stone cover	A-6549/12
DD3	870	2		26.67	26.12	857	Fill	A-6549/12
DD3	871	2		26.06	25.67	870	Stone cover	A-6549/12
DD3	872	6		26.6	25.77	856	Fill	A-6549/12
DD3	873	94		23.75	21.5	865	Winepress vat (circular)	A-6549/12
DD3	874	10		2021	2011	866	Sandstone	A-6549/12
DD3	875	11		20.18	19.87	868	Sandstone	A-6549/12

Area	*Locus*	*Old Reference*	*Square*	*Height (Opened)*	*Height (Closed)*	*Associated Loci/ Features*	*Description*	*Permit No.*
DD3	876	4		26.22	26.18		Sandstone pavement	A-6549/12
DD3	877	94N		24.6	23.92	882	Fill	A-6549/12
DD3	878	1E		26.78	26.64	880	Fill	A-6549/12
DD3	879	3E		28.32	35.47	883	Fill	A-6549/12
DD3	880	1E		26.71	25.85	878	Grave	A-6549/12
DD3	881	6N		25.85	25.42		Fill	A-6549/12
DD3	882	94N		24.04	23.98	877	Fill	A-6549/12
DD3	883	3EWN		28.31	25.57	879	Fill	A-6549/12
DD3	41000			26.8		41006	Surface	A-6825/13
DD3	T41001			26.8	25.7	871, 41007	Grave	A-6825/13
DD3	T41002			26.7	26.2	41008	Grave	A-6825/13
DD3	T41003			26.7	25.9	869, 41009	Grave	A-6825/13
DD3	T41004			26.7	26.3	41010	Grave	A-6825/13
DD3	T41005			26.8	26	880, 41001	Grave	A-6825/13
DD3	41006			26.6	25.7	41002	Fill	A-6825/13
DD3	41007			26,50	26.2	41003	Fill	A-6825/13
DD3	41008			26.52	26.3	41004	Fill	A-6825/13
DD3	41009			26.8	26	41005	Fill	A-6825/13
DD3	41010			26.2	25.9	41007	Fill	A-6825/13
DD3	41011						Cancelled	A-6825/13
DD3	41012			26.5	26.2		Fill	A-6825/13
DD3	41013						Cancelled	A-6825/13
DD3	41014					41015	Cancelled	A-6825/13
DD3	41015			26.8	25.7	42003	Fill	A-6825/13
DD3	T42000			26.9	25.7	862, 42004	Grave	A-6825/13
DD3	T42001			27.1	26.3	863	Grave	A-6825/13
DD3	42002			27		42000	Surface	A-6825/13
DD3	42003			26.8	25.7	42001	Fill	A-6825/13
DD3	42004			27	26.3	42001	Fill	A-6825/13

Areas M, N, and O

Area	*Locus*	*Square*	*Height (Opened)*	*Height (Closed)*	*Associated Loci / Features*	*Description*	*License No.*
M	7000	F2	30.75	30.65	7007, 7008,	Surface	G-59/2006
M	7001	E2	30.71	30.68	7005, 7006	Surface	G-59/2006
M	7002	F3	28.6	27.65	7013	Surface	G-59/2006
M	7003	E3	28.06	27.75	7011	Surface	G-59/2006
M	7004	G3	31.72	31.37		Wall w-e	G-59/2006
M	7005	E2	30.68	30.46	7001	Fill = 7008	G-59/2006
M	7006	E2	30.65	30.96	7001, 7010	Ash center = 7007 in the pit	G-59/2006
M	7007	F2	30.65	30.45	7000	Ash center = 7006 in the pit	G-59/2006

Area	*Locus*	*Square*	*Height (Opened)*	*Height (Closed)*	*Associated Loci / Features*	*Description*	*License No.*
M	7008	F2	30.55	30.45	7000	Fill = 7005	G-59/2006
M	7009	E/F-2	30.96	27.4		Installation (pit)	G-59/2006
M	7010	E/F-2	30.96	30.23	7006	Fill	G-59/2006
M	7011	F2	27.75	27.04	7003, 7014	Fill	G-59/2006
M	7012	E2	30.23	29.6		Fill	G-59/2006
M	7013	F3	27.65	27.27	7002, 7015	Sand	G-59/2006
M	7014	F3	27.04	26.26	7011	Sand	G-59/2006
M	7015	F3	27.27	26.76	7013	Section in L7013	G-59/2006
M	7016	G3	27.96	27.79		Fill	G-59/2006
M	7017	G3	27.96	27.38	7022	Fill	G-59/2006
M	7018	F2				Sand	G-59/2006
M	7019	E2	27.4	26.87		Pit within I7009	G-59/2006
M	7020	G3	28.19	27.96	7016	Surface	G-59/2006
M	7021	D2	27.22	27.21		Surface	G-59/2006
M	7022	G3	27.25	27.13	7017	Fill	G-59/2006
M	7023	F2	26.49	26.3		Light fill (in pit)	G-59/2006
M	7024	E2	26.46	26.38	7012	Fill = 7023	G-59/2006
M	7025	F2	26.6	26.5	7008	Ash center	G-59/2006
M	7026	F2	29.9	29.6	7008	Fill (new pit)	G-59/2006
M	7027	D2	27.21	26.79	7021	Fill	G-59/2006
M	7028	F1	29.9	29.6	7012	Surface	G-59/2006
M	7029	F1	30.45	29.6	7008	Fill = 7009	G-59/2006
M	7030	F2	30.96	30.55	7008	Pit within 7009	G-59/2006
M	7031	F1	27.21	26.79	7021, 7032, 7033	Fill = 7030	G-59/2006
M	7032	D2	26.7	26.55	7027, 7033	Assemblage of pottery	G-59/2006
M	7033	D2	26.79	29.71	7027	Fill	G-59/2006
M	7034	E2	26.62	30.2	7010, 7019, 7046	Fill	G-59/2006
M	7035	E2	26.62	30.24	7012, 7046	Fill	G-59/2006
M	7036	E2	29.6	28.9	7034	Ash center	G-59/2006
M	7037	F2	29.89	29.13	7034	Fill with pieces of plaster	G-59/2006
M	7038	E1	27.3	26.57	7040	Surface	G-59/2006
M	7039	D2	26.5	26.46	7033	Fill	G-59/2006
M	7040	E1	29.3	30.2	7038, 7042	Fill	G-59/2006
M	7041	F1	29.6	28.9	7031	Fill	G-59/2006
M	7042	E1	28.9	28.2	7040	Ash center	G-59/2006
M	7043	F1	28.9	28.7	7041	Fill	G-59/2006
M	7044	F1	28.2	27.8	7040	Fill	G-59/2006
M	7045	F2	30.04	30.2	7033, 7047	Fill	G-59/2006
M	7046	E2	27.8	27.4	7034, 7035	Fill	G-59/2006
M	7047	D2	29.71	30.37	7033	Fill	G-59/2006
M	7048	D2	31.2	30.84	7059, W7055	Surface	G-59/2006
M	7049	F-1/2	29.6	29.5	7029	Ash layer	G-59/2006

Area	*Locus*	*Square*	*Height (Opened)*	*Height (Closed)*	*Associated Loci / Features*	*Description*	*License No.*
M	7050	D-1/2	30.84	29.99	7048, 7060	Ash layer	G-59/2006
M	7051		30.22			Wall w-e	G-59/2006
M	7052	F1	28.9	27.9	7041	Pit under 7041	G-59/2006
M	7053	E2	27.4	27.2	7046	Fill	G-59/2006
M	7054	F2	30.12	29.67		Retaining wall	G-59/2006
M	7055	D2	29.99	29.55		Wall in I7047	G-59/2006
M	7056	F2	28.9	27.9		Fill	G-59/2006
M	7057	D2	30.37	29.99	7048, 7060		G-59/2006
M	7058	D2	30.37	29.99		Wall n-s	G-59/2006
M	7059	D2	30.37	29.78	7048	Fill	G-59/2006
M	7060	D2	29.99	29.63	7050, 7057	Fill	G-59/2006
M	7061	F1	27.9	25.99		Fill	G-59/2006
M	7062					Cancelled	G-59/2006
M	7063	F2	30.45	30.15		Wall e-w	G-59/2006
M	7064					Cancelled	G-59/2006
M	7065					Cancelled	G-59/2006
M	7066					Cancelled	G-59/2006
M	7067					Cancelled	G-59/2006
M	7068					Cancelled	G-59/2006
M	7069					Cancelled	G-59/2006
M	7070	D2	29.92	29.66	7059, 7072	Fill	G-56/2009
M	7071	D2	30.11	29.86	7047	Fill	G-56/2009
M	7072	D2	29.66	29.34	7070	Sand/beach-rock	G-56/2009
N	5000	General	31.53	31.3		Surface	G-28/2002
N	5001	A2	31.3	31.2		Fill	G-28/2002
N	5002	A2	31.35	31.19		Fill	G-28/2002
N	5003	A1	31.65	31.53		Fill	G-28/2002
N	5004	A1	31.3	30.98		Fill	G-28/2002
N	5005	A2	31.4	31.17		Raw glass furnace fill	G-28/2002
N	F5006	A2	31.17	31.17		Raw glass furnace remains	G-28/2002
N	5007	A2	31.27	31.1		Wall	G-28/2002
N	5008	A1	31.2	30.98		Wall	G-28/2002
N	5009	A2	31.14	30.98		Wall	G-28/2002
N	5010	A2	31.25	31.15		Wall	G-28/2002
N	5011	A2	31.2	31.07		Wall	G-28/2002
N	5012	A2	31.2	31.07		Fill west to the furnace	G-28/2002
N1	5015	General	31.72	31.4		Fill	A-7911/2017
N1	5016	C5	31.4	31.35		Fill	A-7911/2017
N1	5017	C6	31.35	31.3		Furnace	A-7911/2017
N1	F5018	D6	31.3	31.3		Stone floor	A-7911/2017
N1	5019	D6	31.3	31.2		Fill	A-7911/2017
O	8000					Surface	G-56/2009

Area	*Locus*	*Square*	*Height (Opened)*	*Height (Closed)*	*Associated Loci / Features*	*Description*	*License No.*
O	8001	C6	30.32	29.72		Fill	G-56/2009
O	8002	C4W	30.82	30.63		Fill	G-56/2009
O	8003	C4E	30.77	30.62		Fill	G-56/2009
O	8004	B5	31.11	30.71		Fill	G-56/2009
O	8005	C5	30.27	29.98	8012	Wall e-w	G-56/2009
O	F8006	C5	29.97	29.97	8012	winepress treading floor	G-56/2009
O	F8007		29.51	29.51	8001	Plaster floor	G-56/2009
O	8008	C6	30.06	29.34	8008	Fill	G-56/2009
O	8009	C6	30.93	30.2	8227	Fill	G-56/2009
O	8010	C6	30.06	29.71		Wall e-w	G-56/2009
O	I8011	C6	30.11	30		Raw glass furnace remains	G-56/2009
O	8012	C5	29.97	29.6		Fill	G-56/2009
O	8013	C4W	30.63	30.33	8002	Fill	G-56/2009
O	8014	C4W	30.62	30.42	8003, 8016	Fill	G-56/2009
O	8015	B5	30.71	29.95	8029	Fill	G-56/2009
O	8016	C4	30.42	30.2	8014	Raw glass furnace remains	G-56/2009
O	8017	B5	30.58	30.23	8015	Raw glass furnace remains	G-56/2009
O	8018	B5	30.58	30.23	8011	Raw glass furnace remains	G-56/2009
O	8019	C4W	30.33	29.97	8013, 8025	Fill	G-56/2009
O	8020	B4	30.87	29.91	8024	Fill	G-56/2009
O	8021	C4E	30.19	29.88		Fill	G-56/2009
O	8022	C6	29.68	29.51	8007	Fill	G-56/2009
O	F8023	C4	30.37	29.98	8021, 8025	Earth floor	G-56/2009
O	8024	B4	29.96	29.9	8020, 8030, 8031	Fill	G-56/2009
O	8025	C4W	29.98	29.67	8021	Fill	G-56/2009
O	8026	B5	30.23	29.81	8015, 8055	Fill	G-56/2009
O	8027	B6	30.2	29.85	8009	Fill	G-56/2009
O	8028	C4W	29.95	29.67	8015	Fill	G-56/2009
O	8029	C4W	29.95			Wall	G-56/2009
O	8030	B4	29.69		8024	Wall	G-56/2009
O	8031	B4	29.69	28.85	8024	Fill	G-56/2009
O	8032	B4	29.69	29.37	8024	Fill	G-56/2009
O	8033	C6	30.19	29.49		Wall	G-56/2009
O	8034	B6	29.85	29.63	8048	Fill	G-56/2009
O	8035	B5	30.15	29.88	8054	Fill	G-56/2009
O	8036	C4E	29.43			Pit	G-56/2009
O	F8037	B6	30.02	30.02		Mosaic floor	G-56/2009
O	8038	C4E				Wall	G-56/2009
O	8039	C4E	29.86			Wall	G-56/2009
O	8040	C4E	29.96			Wall	G-56/2009
O	8041	C4W	29.31	28.99		Wall	G-56/2009
O	F8042	C4W	29.15	29.15		Floor	G-56/2009

Area	*Locus*	*Square*	*Height (Opened)*	*Height (Closed)*	*Associated Loci / Features*	*Description*	*License No.*
O	8043	C4W	29.15	29.15		Fill	G-56/2009
O	8044	C4E	29.78	29.5		Fill	G-56/2009
O	F8045	C3/B3	29.15	29.15		Stone floor	G-56/2009
O	8046	C3	29.15	28.69		Fill	G-56/2009
O	8047	C6	30.42	29.78		Fill	G-56/2009
O	8048	B6	29.63	29.23		Fill	G-56/2009
O	8049	B3	30.63		8052, 8053	Fill	G-56/2009
O	8050	C4-5	31.08	30.28		Fill	G-56/2009
O	8051	C6	30.06			Fill	G-56/2009
O	8052	B3	29.68	28.82		Fill	G-56/2009
O	8053	B3	28.69	27.69		Fill	G-56/2009
O	F8054	B5	29.88	29.88	8035	Mosaic floor (around winepress circular vat)	G-56/2009
O	8055	B5	29.88	29.8	8026	Fill	G-56/2009
O	8056	B5-6	30.56	30.42		Fill	G-56/2009
O	8057	C3	29.22	38.69		Fill	G-56/2009
O	8058	B/C-6	30.05	29.7		Fill	G-56/2009
O	8059	C4W-E	28.82	28.65		Fill	G-56/2009
O	F8060	B5	29.71	29.71		Mosaic floor	G-56/2009
O	8061	B5	29.71	27.32		Winepress vat (circular)	G-56/2009
O	8062	B5	29.71	29.15		Winepress vat (intermediary)	G-56/2009
O	8063	B5	30.72	29.6		Fill	G-56/2009
O	8064	B6-C4	29.8	29.71	8051, 8034	Fill	G-56/2009
O	8065	C6-B6	29.23		8048	Fill	G-56/2009
O	F8066	C6	29.45	29.45		Plaster floor	G-56/2009
O	F8067	C6	29.71	29.71		Plaster floor	G-56/2009
O	8068	C6				Fill	G-56/2009
O	8069	B6	29.72/ 29.69	29.46		Wall e-w	G-56/2009
O	8070	B5	29.7	29.54	F8075	Fill	G-56/2009
O	8071	B/C-6	29.64	29.23		Fill	G-56/2009
O	8072	C-4/5	29.88	29.71		Wall n-s	G-56/2009
O	8073	B6		29.35	8065	Fill	G-56/2009
O	8074	B5	29.91	29.71		Wall e-w	G-56/2009
O	F8075	B5	29.54	29.54		Mosaic floor	G-56/2009
O	8076	B6	29.46	29.46	8070	Fill	G-56/2009
O	8077	B6	29.46	29.26		Fill	G-56/2009
O	8078		29.39	28.63		Wall	G-56/2009
O	F8079	B3	29.15	29.15		Floor	G-56/2009
O	8080					General no of winepress	G-56/2009

LIST OF WALLS

AREAS AA–DD

Wall No.	Old Reference	Height (Opened)	Height (Closed)	Axis	Thickness	Length	Courses (No.)	Loci Above	Abutting / Combined	Area	Description	Permit No.
W123	F203	17.06	16.3	E-W	0.6	2		112		AA	Foundation courses	A-6549/12
W139	F203	16.78	16.32	N-S	0.4	4.4	4		W10041	AA		A-6549/12
W148	F201	17.02	16.77	N-S	0.26	0.94	4		W149	AA		A-6549/12
W149	F201	16.93	16.7	E-W	0.3	1.2	1		W148, 155	AA	Part of I127	A-6549/12
W155	F201	17.5	16.71	N-S	0.5	1	5		W149	AA		A-6549/12
W374	F203	16.5	16	SE-NW	0.5	1				AA		A-6549/12
W10041	G5	17:07	16:14	E-W	0.6	2.3	3	10026	W139	AA		A-6825/13
W10072/1	G-H5/6	16.87	16.35	N-S	0.55	3.7	5		W10041	AA	Parallel to 174	A-6825/13
W10072/2	G-H5/6	16.35	16	N-S	0.55	2.1	1	10083		AA	Earlier to 10072	A-6825/13
W10074	G6	16.35	16.04	N-S	0.5	2.1		W139		AA	Earlier then 139	A-6825/13
W10082	H6	16.05	15.92	E-W	0.5	1.9	1	10065		AA	Approaches to 10074	A-6825/13
W10086	G6	16.35	16.16	E-W	0.5	0.9	1	10061		AA		A-6825/13
W10088	G5			N-S	0.5	1.6	1	10017		AA		A-6825/13
W10090	K4	16.23	15.9	E-W	0.5	0.9	1			AA		A-6825/13
W210	34	19.43	19.19	N-S	0.62	2.2	1	201		AA1		A-6549/12
W228	98	20.44	20.24	E-W	0.34	1.5	1	206		AA1	Around floor 209	A-6549/12
W11076	E5	20.46	20.2	E-W	0.5	2	1			AA1		A-6825/13
W177	F91	23.3	22.7	E-W	0.7	2.5	3		W185, W194	AA2		A-6549/12
W185	F91	23.22	22.92	N-S	0.7	1.6	2		W177, W194	AA2		A-6549/12
W194	F91	23.2	22.9	E-W	0.6	2.1	2		W177, W185	AA2		A-6549/12
W12024	F91	22.9	22.7	E-W			1	177		AA2		A-6825/13
W12032	F91	22.7	22.6	E-W			1	194		AA2		A-6825/13
W12307	F91									AA2	Cancelled	A-6825/13
W611	82	24.16	23.76	N-S	0.6	2.3	2	610		CC	Pier on west	A-6549/12
W30142	D12	25.3	25.02	N-S	0.4	1.4	1	30127		CC	With threshold	A-6825/13

Wall No.	*Old Reference*	*Height (Opened)*	*Height (Closed)*	*Axis*	*Thickness*	*Length*	*Courses (No.)*	*Loci Above*	*Abutting / Combined*	*Area*	*Description*	*Permit No.*
W776	F-16	24.7	25.92	N-S	0.5	2		754	W771W772, W773	DD1	West wall	A-6549/12
W771	F-16	27.43	26.56	E-W	0.6	4.6	1	754	F769, W766	DD1	Makes corner with 766	A-6549/12
W772	F-16	27.12	25.89	E-W	0.6	1.8	1	754	F769, F785, W766	DD1	Central wall connect to 766	A-6549/12
W773	F-16	27.49	25.84	E-W	0.5	1.6	1	770	F785, W766	DD1	Makes corner with 766	A-6549/12
W786	F-16	27.43	26.96	N-S	0.55	1.8	1	754	W772, W773, F785	DD1	East of 785	A-6549/12
W794	16E	27.41	27.03	N-S	0.4	0.8	1			DD1		A-6549/12
W795	16E	27.53	27.06	E-W	0.4	0.8	1			DD1		A-6549/12

Areas M, N and O

Wall No.	Square	Height (Opened)	Height (Closed)	Axis	Thickness	Length	Courses (No.)	Loci Above	Abutting / Combined	Area	Description	License No.
W7004	G3	31.72	31.37	W-E	0.6	4.46	2	7020	7002	M	Wall	G-59/2006
W7051	E2	30.22		W-E						M	Wall	G-59/2006
W7054	F2	30.12	29.67	W-E						M	Retaining wall	G-59/2006
W7055	D2	29.99	29.55	W-E	0.45	0.92	2	7033	W7058	M	Wall in I7047	G-59/2006
W7058	D2	30.37	29.99	N-S	0.6	2.15	3	7048	W7005	M	Wall	G-59/2006
W7063	F2	30.45	30.15	W-E								G-59/2006
W5007	N5	31.27	31.1	E-W	0.25	6.5			F5006	N	Wall	G-28/2002
W5008	N5	31.2	30.98	N-S		2.8				N	Wall	G-28/2002
W5009	N5	31.14	30.98	N-S						N	Wall	G-28/2002
W5010	N5	31.25	31.15	E-W	0.22	6.1			F5006	N	Wall	G-28/2002
W5011	N5	31.2	31.07	N-S	0.3	3				N	Wall	G-28/2002
W8005	C5	30.27	29.98	W-E	0.4	4.5		8012	W8072, W8033,W8074,F8060	O	Wall	G-56/2009
W8010	C6	30.06	29.71	E-W	0.4	4			F8067	O	Wall	G-56/2009
W8029	C4W	29.95		E-W	0.5	3.5		8028, 8041	W8039, W8042, F8045	O	Wall	G-56/2009
W8030	B4	29.69		E-W	0.4	6.5		8024	W8072,8031, 8032	O	Wall	G-56/2009
W8033	C6	30.19	29.49	N-S	0.5	6		8027	W8005, W8074, W8072, F8060	O	Wall	G-56/2009
W8039	C4E	29.86		N-S	0.5	2.5		8025	W8029	O	Wall	G-56/2009
W8040	C4E	29.96		N-S	0.4	2		8025	W8005	O	Wall	G-56/2009
W8042	C3	29.25		N-S	0.5	1		8046	W8029	O	Wall	G-56/2009
W8069	B6	29.72/ 29.69	29.46	E-W	0.5	3.5			W8077	O	Wall	G-56/2009
W8072	C-4/5	29.55		N-S	0.5	5		8015, 8026	F8060, W8005,W8074,W8033	O	Wall	G-56/2009
W8074	B5	29.91	29.71	E-W	0.5	4		8015 ,8026	W8033, F8060	O	Wall	G-56/2009
W8077	B6	29.49	29.26	E-W	0.5	2		W8069	F8035	O	Wall	G-56/2009
W8078		29.39	28.63							O	Wall	G-56/2009